Thriving in Crisis

THE SHENG YEN SERIES IN CHINESE BUDDHIST STUDIES

THE SHENG YEN SERIES IN CHINESE BUDDHIST STUDIES

Edited by Daniel B. Stevenson and Jimmy Yu

Funded jointly by the Sheng Yen Education Foundation and the Chung Hua Institute of Buddhist Studies in Taiwan, the Sheng Yen Series in Chinese Buddhist Studies is dedicated to the interdisciplinary study of Chinese language resources that bear on the history of Buddhism in premodern and modern China. Through the publication of pioneering scholarship on Chinese Buddhist thought, practice, social life, and institutional life in China—including interactions with indigenous traditions of religion in China, as well as Buddhist developments in South, East, and Inner/Central Asia—the series aspires to bring new and groundbreaking perspectives to one of the most historically enduring and influential traditions of Buddhism, past and present.

Michael J. Walsh, *Sacred Economies: Buddhist Business and Religiosity in Medieval China*

Koichi Shinohara, *Spells, Images, and Maṇḍalas: Tracing the Evolution of Esoteric Buddhist Rituals*

Beverley Foulks McGuire, *Living Karma: The Religious Practices of Ouyi Zhixu (1599–1655)*

Paul Copp, *The Body Incantatory: Spells and the Ritual Imagination in Medieval Chinese Buddhism*

N. Harry Rothschild, *Emperor Wu Zhao and Her Pantheon of Devis, Divinities, and Dynastic Mothers*

Erik J. Hammerstrom, *The Science of Chinese Buddhism: Early Twentieth-Century Engagements*

Jiang Wu and Lucille Chia, editors, *Spreading Buddha's Word in East Asia: The Formation and Transformation of the Chinese Buddhist Canon*

Jan Kiely and J. Brooks Jessup, editors, *Recovering Buddhism in Modern China*

Geoffrey C. Goble, *Chinese Esoteric Buddhism: Amoghavajra, the Ruling Elite, and the Emergence of a Tradition*

Thriving in Crisis

Buddhism and Political Disruption

in China, 1522–1620

Dewei Zhang

Columbia University Press

New York

Columbia University Press
Publishers Since 1893
New York   Chichester, West Sussex
cup.columbia.edu

Library of Congress Cataloging-in-Publication Data
Names: Zhang, Dewei, author.
Title: Thriving in crisis : Buddhism and political disruption in China, 1522–1620 /
Dewei Zhang.
Description: New York : Columbia University Press, 2020. | Series: The Sheng Yen series
in Chinese Buddhist studies | Includes bibliographical references and index.
Identifiers: LCCN 2019047186 (print) | LCCN 2019047187 (ebook) |
ISBN 9780231197007 (cloth) | ISBN 9780231551939 (ebook)
Subjects: LCSH: Buddhism—China—History—960-1644. |
Buddhism and politics—China—History.
Classification: LCC BQ645 .Z43 2020 (print) | LCC BQ645 (ebook) |
DDC 294.30951/09031—dc23
LC record available at https://lccn.loc.gov/2019047186
LC ebook record available at https://lccn.loc.gov/2019047187

Cover image: Detail from *Painting of Elegant Gathering* 雅集圖 by
Chen Hongshou 陳洪綬. Courtesy of the Shanghai Museum
Cover design: Chang Jae Lee

To my grandfather Liu Yichang 劉益長 *(1908–1996)*

Contents

Illustrations

Tables

Preface

The sixteenth day of the first month of 1565 was an ordinary day for most people in China, but a sad one for the monks of the Great Baoen monastery 大報恩寺 in Nanjing. Its abbot, Xilin Yongning 西林永寧 (1483–1565), died that day at the age of eighty-two. Having served as the abbot of this monastery for thirty-four years and concurrently as a top monastic official in the Nanjing Central Buddhist Registry (*senglu si* 僧錄司) for twenty-five years, Yongning was highly esteemed not only by the Baoensi community but also by the entire Buddhist world in the Jiangnan region. The Baoensi monks also felt disturbed by Yongning's prediction that their monastery would decline. To their surprise, his solution to the bad situation was to entrust them to a young monk eventually known as Hanshan Deqing 憨山德清 (1546–1623). It took the Baoensi monks little time to realize that their leader's prophecy was not empty talk. The first major challenge facing the monastery was ironically generated by Yongning himself—or, to be more precise, by his funeral, which was estimated to cost three hundred taels of silver. Yongning left behind only about thirty taels, so the difference had to be met by a loan at a very high interest rate. When the funeral was over, the Baoensi monks began to worry about the debt. A meeting was convened, but no good idea was put forth. Finally, Deqing suggested selling Yongning's belongings and part of the monastery's land holdings. This was accepted, and the debt was taken care of. One year later, much more severe challenges emerged as a fire, caused by lightning, destroyed the main body of the monastery. Allowing such a degree of damage to an imperially sponsored monastery constituted a heavy offense. As many as fifteen superintendent monks were hence thrown into prison and were rumored to face the death sentence. Baoensi monks started to flee in panic, but Deqing did not. He instead occupied himself with taking care of his imprisoned colleagues and attempting to overcome the crisis. Shortly after Emperor Jiajing (r. 1522–1566) died, the indicted monks were set free with relatively minor punishments. Subsequently, spurred by the dilapidated state of the monastery, Deqing and a fellow monk named Xuelang Hong'en 雪浪洪恩 (1545–1607) vowed to rebuild it at any cost. At the turn of the Wanli era (1573–1620), despite Hong'en's opposition, Deqing set off to North China in search of the Dharma and support for the monastery. In time, he spent most of his life outside the Jiangnan region where the Great Baoen monastery was located, and even became the mentor to the reigning emperor's mother. In 1589, as a way of expressing respect to him, a copy of the Buddhist canon, a rare imperial gift, was bestowed from the inner court to the Great Baoen monastery and further enhanced its reputation and appeal.

In contrast, Hong'en chose to stay on and remained very active in the Jiangnan region. Finally, with support from local society, he managed to reconstruct the Baoen stupa, a landmark of the monastery. The efforts of these two friends represented two ways of restoring the Great Baoen monastery—drawing resources from the inner court and from local society, respectively—but neither of them was successful in completely fulfilling their vow. Eventually, the monastery was fully rebuilt in 1699, early in the Qing dynasty (1644–1911), with government money.

The preceding narrative, derived mainly from Deqing's autobiography, includes many puzzling points. Built by the Yongle emperor (r. 1403–1424) in memory of his mother, the Great Baoen monastery was one of the biggest monasteries owning a great amount of imperially bestowed land. Why did it become so financially strapped in the last years of the Jiajing era that it could not even afford its abbot's funeral? Was it a common practice to sell monastic property? How did this affect the *saṃgha* in the long run? Was it fair for those arrested monks to face the threat of the death sentence? If not, how did they come to face such heavy charges? Turning to Deqing's departure from the Jiangnan region, why did it happen at the turn of the Wanli era? Why did he head for North China rather than stay in Jiangnan to seek local or regional support? Deqing and Hong'en would both become influential masters, but how and to what extent did their different choices affect their growth as religious leaders? As for the restoration of the monastery, which was the most decisive of all the forces involved in the process: eminent monks, the *saṃgha*, the inner court, the local society, or the government? More intriguingly, to what extent was this not a story about a single monastery but the experience of the contemporary *saṃgha* as a whole? These questions concern the entire history of Chinese Buddhism in late imperial China, but many of them have not been adequately answered by previous scholars. Providing answers to these problems was the initial motivating force that engaged me in this study.

I would like to first express particular thanks to my thesis adviser, Professor Jinhua Chen, at the University of British Columba (UBC), who has given me sufficient freedom to shape my academic style but never forgotten to remind me of those most important issues. His support continues as generous as ever even after I have graduated. Without his constant support and encouragement, it would have been impossible for me to complete this study of Buddhist revival. I also offer my deep gratitude to the other two committee members at UBC. Professor Timothy Brook has set a formidable academic standard for me with his careful and insightful review of my ideas, just as Philip Kuhn did for him at Harvard University many years ago. He even generously shared his research notes with me. Professor Leo Shin has warmed my life at UBC with his patience and shining smile but has at the same time insisted on training me step-by-step in the strictest way. When I started reworking the dissertation into the book manuscript, I was very fortunate to work at McMaster University as a postdoctoral fellow. It is Professor James Benn, my supervisor there, who has since sailed me through the challenging process. I deeply appreciate him for his patience and wisdom.

I am also deeply indebted to the feedback, support, criticism, and encouragement I have received over the years of struggling through various stages of research and writing. When I started writing my UBC dissertation, Professor Chen Yunü 陳玉女 at National Cheng Kung University in Taiwan sent me her articles and books, including her unpublished dissertation, from which I have drawn much inspiration. In 2010–2011, when I spent one year at Kyoto University revising the dissertation, Professor Funayama Tōru 船山徹 directed me to make good use of relevant materials preserved in Japan. Professor Chün-fang Yü at Columbia University has given me detailed and insightful suggestions, both as an external examiner of the dissertation and as a reviewer of the book manuscript. Of particular importance was her reminder that I should keep a balance between different opinions and methodologies. Moreover, Professors Daniel Stevenson at the University of Kansas, Jimmy Yu at Florida State University, Zhu Honglin 朱鴻林 (Chu Hung-lam) at the Hong Kong Polytechnic University, Gong Jun 龔隽 at Sun Yat-sen University, Kimura Kiyotaka 木村清孝 and Ochiai Toshinori 落合俊典 at the International College of Postgraduate Buddhist Studies (ICPBS), Marcus Bingenheimer at Temple University, Paul Crowe at Simon Fraser University, Daniel Overmyer, Francesca Harlow, and Josephine Chiu-Duke at UBC have all contributed to my research in different ways. Four anonymous readers for Columbia University Press reviewed my manuscript. Thanks to their advice and assistance, I have corrected some errors and inaccuracies, and I take responsibility for those that remain.

While writing the original dissertation, I received major support from Bukkyō Dendō Kyōkai 仏教伝道協会 (Society for the Promotion of Buddhism). It allowed me to study in Japan for one year, which has proved a significant experience in my academic life. I would also like to acknowledge the help of the Social Sciences and Humanities Research Council of Canada, for it was during the term of my postdoctoral research under its sponsorship that I finished the first revision of the manuscript. The Grant for Book-Length Monographs on Chinese Buddhism by Dharma Drum Mountain in Taiwan sponsored the publication of this book, which I appreciate very much.

I thank my friends, particularly Chi Limei 池麗梅, Tim Sedo, Eric Greene, Robban Toleno, Jeff Horowitz, Kang Hao 康昊, and Dai Lianbin 戴聯斌 for their reading of and comments on the dissertation and the manuscript. I also wish to express my gratitude for the support given me by the faculty, staff, and librarians at UBC, Kyoto University, the ICPBS, McMaster University, University of Macau, Sun Yat-sen University, and Jinan University in Guangzhou. The Department of Philosophy at Sun Yat-sen University and my family friend Zhao Dong-mei 趙冬玫 provided me, respectively, with an office to work in and a house to live in while I suffered hard times, for which I am deeply grateful. I am indebted also to Lowell Frye and Wendy Lochner, both of whom as editors have guided me through the editing process of Columbia University Press.

Special and deepest thanks are owed to my wife, Zhao Lingyun 趙淩雲, and my parents, who have all supported me without reservation throughout my years of education and research. Without their indulgence, I would not have arrived at this point, let alone complete this study. I dedicate this book to my grandfather Liu Yichang 劉益長 (1908–1996). His wisdom has kept me warm deep in my heart and encouraged me to keep moving even in the hardest times.

An African proverb says that it takes a whole village to educate a child. This casts a light on the pathway of my growth and, in a broader sense, reveals the secret in the development of human civilization. After having benefited so much from others, it is my turn to do something good for society.

Abbreviations and Conventions

FCZ Jinling fancha zhi 金陵梵剎志
HJAS Harvard Journal of Asiatic Studies
HSMY Hanshan dashi mengyou ji 憨山大師夢遊集
HZD Huangshan zhi dingben 黃山志定本
JAS Journal of Asian Studies
JXZ Mingban Jiaxing dazangjing 明版嘉興大藏經
KXT Kuaixuetang ji 快雪堂集
MKCY Mizang Kai chanshi yigao 密藏開禪師遺稿
RXJW Rixia jiuwen kao 日下舊聞攷
SKHB Beijing tushuguan cang zhongguo lidai shike taben huibian 北京圖書館
　　藏中國歷代石刻拓本彙編
T Taishō shinshu Daizōkyō 大正新修大藏經
WLYH Wanli yehuo bian 萬曆野獲編
X Shinsan dai Nihon zoku zōkyō 新纂大日本續藏經
YHD Yuan Hongdao ji jianjiao 袁宏道集箋校

CONVENTIONS

1. I have tried to be as lexically precise as possible in translating from the Chinese, but I have also kept an eye on Chinese and English usage. Chinese words are transliterated in the pinyin system. In translating official titles, I generally follow Charles Hucker, *A Dictionary of Official Titles in Imperial China*. The titles of primary sources are translated into English at their first appearance in the main text.

2. For a monk like Hanshan Deqing, Hanshan is his literary name (*hao*), while Deqing is his Dharma name. As a rule, this book refers to a monk by his Dharma name after citing his full name at first appearance and uses his literary name only occasionally.

3. Full citations from the three Buddhist canons cited in this book include title, fascicle number, the abbreviation of the canon, volume number, text number, page, register (a, b, or c), and line number. For example, *Hanshan laoren mengyou ji* 憨山老人夢遊集 30, in *X*, vol. 73, no. 1456, 680a6–8.

4. For convenience, the lunar calendar is used for the month and day while the Western calendar for the year. For rare events considered significant in this study, I also give the Western dates in parentheses. The tool used to covert the dates is the online one provided by Academia Sinica Computing Center (http://sinocal.sinica.edu.tw/).

5. The degree was a significant indicator of political, social, and cultural status. In addition to the years of birth and death, I thus provide, when applicable, the highest degree a scholar-official obtained in the civil service examination (e.g., *jinshi*) and when. In Ming and Qing China, the chance for scholar-officials who obtained the *jinshi* degree in the same year to create a close network was much higher than for those who did not.

Chronology

1537	Huo Tao 霍韜 destroys about one hundred and forty nunneries in Nanjing and forces about five hundred nuns to return to secular life
	Shixingsi 實性寺 in Shaoxing 紹興 is destroyed
1541	Jiajing survives an attempted assassination
1550	Eunuchs rebuild Jietansi 戒壇寺 in Beijing, with a Daoist statue included in it
	Eunuchs gradually turn Huguosi 護國寺 into their ancestral temple
1554	Puhuisi 普惠寺 in Jiaxing 嘉興 is destroyed
1565	Xilin Yongning 西林永寧 dies; Hanshan Deqing 憨山德清 is tasked with saving the dilapidated Great Baoen monastery
1566	The ordination platforms in Beijing and Hangzhou are closed and not reopened until fifty years later
1567	Miaofeng Fudeng 妙峰福登 visits Putuo Island and later meets Deqing in Nanjing
1572	Deqing arrives in Beijing, where he meets Fudeng again. The following year they go to Mount Wutai and live there for the following ten years
1573	Emperor Wanli ascends the throne at the age of ten. In the following decade, the court is controlled by senior Grand Secretary Zhang Juzheng 張居正, Empress Dowager Cisheng 慈聖, and the eunuch Feng Bao 馮保
	Cisheng and eunuchs come to patronize Puansi 普安寺
	Feng Bao renovates Huguosi
1573~1582	With major support from the inner court, leading monasteries in Beijing are (re)built and allegedly become more magnificent than those in Nanjing
1574	Shixingsi is restored
1576	Puhuisi is restored by Lu Guangzu 陸光祖
1581–1582	A Dharma assembly is held at Mount Wutai, leaving a profound impact on Deqing's life and career
1582	Zhang Juzheng dies; Zhu Changluo 朱常洛 is born; Feng Bao is exiled
	Deqing visits Beijing from Shanxi and lives nearby in search of support from the inner court
1583	Zhang Juzheng's house is confiscated
	Deqing is forced to head for Mount Lao 嶗山 in Shandong
1584	Fudeng visits Beijing in response to Cisheng's call, while Deqing declines, isolating himself from the world
	Mizang Daokai 密藏道開 and Zibo Zhenke 紫柏真可 set up contact with Cisheng through eunuchs

1585	Li Zhi 李贄 shaves off his hair and resigns from office. Yuan Hongdao 袁宏道 visits Li several times in the following few years
1586	Lady Zheng 鄭 gives birth to Zhu Changxun 朱常洵, Wanli's third son, which starts the succession issue at Wanli court
1586–1587	Cisheng bestows fifteen sets of the Buddhist canon, which encourages Deqing as their recipient to leave his isolation at Mount Lao
1587	Feng Mengzhen 馮夢楨 retreats to Hangzhou after being demoted from the post of Hanlin bachelor in Beijing and starts a close connection with Zhenke and Daokai
1589	Cisheng distributes more than twenty sets of the Buddhist canon for the benefit of Zhu Changluo, Wanli's first son and the future crown prince
	Lady Zheng dispatches eunuchs to Mount Tai requiring the abbot of Sanyang abbey 三陽觀 to pray for Zhu Changxun
	Deqing returns to the Great Baoen monastery; Cisheng agrees to help restore the monastery
	Zhenke and Daokai initiate the huge project of carving the Jiaxing canon
1590	Wanli claims that the crown prince will be officially established in two years
	Deqing is sued by the Daoist Geng Yilan 耿義蘭 for robbing the grounds of a Daoist abbey to construct Haiyinsi 海印寺, but he easily wins the case
1590–1592	Lady Zheng prays in the Daoist Dongyue temple 東嶽廟 in Beijing on behalf of her son Zhu Changxun, hinting in public that he is the crown prince
	Around 1590, patrons of Dongyue temple soar in number
1592	Wanli breaks the promise to announce the crown prince, and the succession issue continues
	The anxious Empress Wang 王 carves the *Guanyin lingke* 觀音靈課
	Deqing meets Zhenke in Beijing and is reminded of emerging dangers
	Tanzhesi 潭柘寺 is renovated and expanded on a large scale under the charge of the eunuch Xu Zhengguang 徐正光, whom Cisheng trusts
1592–1594	Deqing frequently visits Beijing and prays at Cishousi 慈壽寺 for the sake of Zhu Changluo
1594	Lady Zheng dispatches eunuchs to Sanyang abbey on Mount Tai to pray for Zhu Changxun, who is called *taizi* 太子 (crown prince) again

1595	Deqing is exiled to Guangdong; the eunuch Zhang Ben 張本 is sentenced to death
	Wanli is absent from the ceremony celebrating Cisheng's birthday
	Yuan Hongdao takes up the post of magistrate of Suzhou
1596	Lady Zheng prays in Sanyang abbey again for her son
1597	Yuan Hongdao resigns his office but takes up another post in Beijing the next year
1598	The first "evil pamphlet" (*yaoshu* 妖書) event breaks out
	The Putao Association 葡萄社 is convened; Yuan Hongdao composes the *Xifang helun* 西方合論 sometime later
1598–1600	Wanli bestows the Buddhist (and Daoist) canon on a large scale
1598–1605	Yuan Hongdao changes his outlook substantially after witnessing a series of deaths
1600	Wanli shows favor to the Daoist Geng Yilan, who had charged Deqing without basis
1601	Zhu Changluo is established as the crown prince but threats to him persist
	Zhenke visits Beijing; eunuchs rush out to welcome him, but his disciples and friends all warn him of imminent danger
1602	The Putao Association disbands; its major members include several of Zhu Changluo's tutors
	Li Zhi dies in prison
	Wanli recovers from an acute illness, which becomes the chance for him to improve his relationship with his mother
1603	The second evil pamphlet event takes place
1603–1604	Zhenke dies behind bars. Wuqiong Zhenfa 無窮真法, from Mount Emei, dies mysteriously, and Wuyan Zhengdao 無言正道, from Shaolinsi 少林寺, is thrown into prison. Jieshan Furu 戒山傅如 is arrested and taken to Beijing from Hangzhou
1606	Around this year, the so-called Donglin faction 東林黨 arises
1608	Yuan Hongdao returns to Beijing; he is disappointed with the state of Buddhism there but fulfills his official responsibility effectively
	Feng Mengzhen dies
1610	Pumen Weian 普門惟安 visits Beijing to elicit support for Ciguangsi 慈光寺
	Yuan Hongdao dies
1611	Factionalism at the Wanli court intensifies
1612	Fudeng dies. Ciguangsi receives imperial favor from both Cisheng and Wanli

1614	Cisheng dies; Ye Xianggao 葉向高 resigns his office
1615	Yunqi Zhuhong 雲棲袾宏 dies
1617	Zhencheng dies
1620	Wanli dies; Zhu Changluo dies
1623	Deqing dies
1625	Weian dies
1666–1670	Ciguangsi is finally expanded with support from local merchants
1680s	The revival of Chan Buddhism ceases, and the gentry's patronage of Buddhism declines
1699	The Great Baoen monastery is rebuilt with government money Chongfusi 崇福寺 and Tanzhesi both thrive with royal patronage during the early Qing

Thriving in Crisis

Introduction

This is a systematic study of the late-Ming Buddhist renewal primarily from the religiopolitical perspective, with equal weight placed on the historical process of the renewal and on the elements, structures, dynamics, and mechanisms behind its evolution. Across the three dimensions of time, space, and society, the bulk of this study explores how the Buddhist movement took place at different social levels in different regions over the one hundred years of the Jiajing-Wanli era (1522–1620). The more theoretical portion of it seeks to understand how, why, and to what extent this revival evolved as a reaction and adjustment of Buddhism to the contemporary religiopolitical environment by bringing the history into dialogue with the relevant intellectual, regional, economic, and cultural background. It is more about the people, institutions, and events that were closely related to the religious movement than it is about doctrinal developments and intellectual history, which are dealt with only incidentally here.

In what follows I briefly discuss three questions: How do we understand the late-Ming Buddhist renewal? Why should this revival be approached from the religiopolitical perspective? And, how have I designed this study and why?

THE LATE-MING BUDDHIST RENEWAL

The late-Ming Buddhist renewal was not as self-evident a religious movement as we may imagine; only around the 1980s was it defined as such following a major paradigm shift in methodology in the study of Chinese Buddhism.

Modern research on Chinese Buddhism was long dominated by two paradigms that unfairly discriminate against Ming Buddhism. Buddhism is a highly sophisticated ethical, philosophical, and metaphysical system that has experienced transformations and changes while maintaining fundamental continuity. But more than just ideas, Buddhism is a religion that, according to the neutral description of Joachim Wach, is expressed by humankind in three forms: theoretical (thinking, speaking), practical (doing, acting), and social (fellowship, community). It is the fitting together of these expressions that forms a complex and unique religious tradition that represents a universe of meaning.[1] Buddhism has become rooted in Chinese society so deeply that everywhere we look we see Buddhist beliefs and practices intertwined with the cultural, social, political, and economic activities that make up Chinese life. In light of its various dimensions, Chinese Buddhism should not be viewed and evaluated from a single perspective. Modern research on Chinese Buddhism, however, was long dominated by two paradigms that, by nature, have a bias against the religion in late-imperial China. The first paradigm is what we may call Sui-Tang centrism, which, deriving from Japanese scholars of Chinese Buddhism, stresses the theoretical originality and doctrinal "pureness" of Buddhism from that period. These Japanese scholars, living mostly during the Meiji and Taishō eras of the late nineteenth and early twentieth centuries, believed that Buddhism during Sui-Tang (581–907) China embodied its highest achievement in East Asia. Retrospectively, the standards they established were closely linked with ideological and nationalist causes, enabling them to assert that Chinese Buddhism became inferior after the Tang and it was Japanese Buddhism that inherited the glory.[2] As Japan's influence rose quickly in the world starting in the early twentieth century, this view has since fundamentally shaped the theoretical framework and conceptual models for the study of Chinese Buddhism. The second paradigm was the so-called Protestant tendency that developed among Western scholars beginning in the late nineteenth century. It describes Chinese and East Asian Buddhism more as a philosophy than as a religion and understands it more on the basis of what Buddhists say they do than of what they actually do. This tendency was incredibly misleading and perplexing to people observing Buddhism as practiced in East Asia, leading them to ridicule elements in it for not being scientific, rational, and egalitarian.[3] These two paradigms shared contempt for the practical and social dimensions of Buddhism, and their convergence caused a disparaging of late-imperial Buddhism as degenerate and morally reprehensible.[4] Ming Buddhism was not an exception. Although Chen Yuan 陳垣 had already published his seminal work in the 1940s,[5] it received only intermittent and superficial attention from scholars.

Only around the 1980s did a major change occur in the study of Ming Buddhism. The glory of Sui-Tang Buddhism was effectively challenged as a legendary reconstruction by monks and literati of later generations, especially those in the Song.[6] Sui-Tang centralism has since collapsed, although its influence still lingers.[7] Furthermore, reflection on Protestant Buddhism has also called more attention to Buddhist practices in real life.[8] A conceptual shift hence followed, from which new modes of understanding and new priorities have evolved to allow late-imperial Chinese Buddhism to be revealed in its own light. Chün-fang Yü's monograph on Yunqi Zhuhong 雲棲袾宏 (1535–1615), published in 1981 as one of the earliest English-language studies on post-Tang Buddhism, embodies the paradigm shift. It challenges previous scholarship by redefining the late Ming as a period during which Buddhism experienced a major renewal, and during which the popularization and synthesis characteristic of the period were not stigmatized but served as a foundation for further exploration.[9] Before long, this redefinition of late-Ming Buddhism was corroborated by and obtained a fuller appreciation from other scholars, among whom Timothy Brook's monograph on Jiangnan gentry and Buddhism, completed in 1984 as a Ph.D. dissertation and published in 1993, created a most influential mode, approaching the field from a sociological perspective.

But it is challenging to conceptualize "the late-Ming Buddhist renewal" that is premised on the "decline-renewal" pattern even in a relatively precise way. Buddhist accounts during the late-Ming period indeed include such Chinese equivalents of the term "renewal" or "revival" as *fuzheng* 復振, *fuxing* 復興, *zhongxing* 中興, *dazheng* 大振, *chongzheng* 重振, *zaizheng* 再振, and *youzheng* 又振, but instead of describing the state of Buddhism in general, on most if not all occasions they were used in a rhetorical way to glorify the progress a certain master had made on individual Buddhist temples or lineages. More important, unlike the case of Northern Song Tiantai circles,[10] these Buddhist statements failed to turn the normative use of those terms among monastic and lay Buddhists into an entrenched historical trope.[11] Two hundred years later, when leading clerics and laypeople sought to reform Buddhism during the late Qing and early Republican period, it seems that they reached a consensus that late-Ming Buddhism had been reinvigorated to such a degree that it deserved to serve as a model for themselves. Master Taixu 太虛 (1890–1947), a most influential Buddhist reformist, for example, claimed that "during the late-Ming period, the philosophical discourse of Confucianism thrived greatly; so did Buddhism. . . . Such prosperity of the Dharma [i.e., Buddhism] was unseen since the Tang dynasty [618–907]. When Master Lingfeng Ouyi [Ouyi Zhixu 蕅益智旭 (1599–1655)] appeared, [he], especially, was a rising star in younger generations" (晚明之世, 儒者講學大盛, 佛

教亦時興起 . . . 法運之盛, 唐以來所未曾有也. 逮靈峰蕅益師, 尤在後起.).[12] Ouyi Zhixu was the youngest of the "four great masters of late-Ming China." Nonetheless, none of the Buddhist accounts discussed late-Ming Buddhism in detail. In the 1970s, Araki Kengo noted that there was a revival of Buddhism in the late-Ming, but,[13] without further elaboration, he mentioned it simply as a phenomenon, and the late-Ming Buddhist renewal was not developed as a concept by Chün-fang Yü until the paradigm shift that took place around the 1980s. In 1987, when the scholar-monk Shengyan 聖嚴 (1930–2009) published his study on late-Ming Buddhism, he also claimed that "it would not be wrong to view the late Ming as a period when Chinese Buddhism revived."[14] Despite these precedents, what the Buddhist renewal means is far from unequivocal. When pressed to answer, scholars have tended to name such things as the emergence of prominent masters, institutional reforms within the *saṃgha*, increased patronage of local gentry in Jiangnan, new adherents in vast numbers, loosened restrictions on Buddhism, or widespread circulation of Buddhist texts. All these, however, were not the renewal itself but merely relevant phenomena or outcomes of it. To compound things further, in recent years scholars of modern Chinese Buddhism have tended to believe that the decline-renewal pattern was partly a discourse strategy of contemporary reformists. For them, the acclaim given to late-Ming Buddhism by reformists like Master Taixu was largely out of a desire to justify their criticism of contemporary Buddhism. Under the strong influence of so-called Japanese New Buddhism (Shin Bukkyō 新仏教), they labeled Chinese Buddhism after the early Ming as "funerary Buddhism" (死人佛教) for its practice of allegedly excessive funeral rituals.[15] Against this background, the need to conceptualize the Ming Buddhist renewal has become more pressing.

Jiang Wu was the first to respond to the need at length. He devoted one chapter to the discussion, asserting that "the cycle of revival and decline, rather than being gauged by the intensity of Buddhist activities, should be rephrased as expansion beyond and retreat behind the boundary set by the society."[16] This distrust of the intensity of Buddhist activities as a reliable indicator has much to do with his conviction that the routine forms of Buddhist practice were maintained within the *saṃgha* even during the quiet period of Buddhist decline, which in turn follows Holmes Welch's classic study on the Chinese *saṃgha* at the turn of the twentieth century.[17] More important, understanding the cycle of revival and decline in this way is related directly to his understanding of the dynamics and mechanism behind the cycle. According to Wu, Buddhism had invisible boundaries imposed upon it by society. It would obtain a greater development once it broke through them, but such an expansion was inevitably temporary because the resistance Buddhism sparked from society would finally push it back across those boundaries.[18] Apparently this way of thinking was stimulated by Timothy Brook, who studied late-Ming Buddhism by stressing active patronage of Buddhism by local gentry in Jiangnan in the context of a state-society division, and who even extended the discussion through applying this methodology to the late Southern Song and late Qing dynasties.[19] Jiang Wu made admirable efforts to establish a theoretical gauge for understanding the state of Buddhism in society and the dynamics enabling a change of its status, but it would seem that expansion beyond or retreat behind the boundary is more a result that requires explanation than a cause that can determine the development of Buddhism. Thus, the causal relationship he attempted to establish between the boundaries society set for Buddhism and the rise and fall of the latter is at best plausible,[20] and more exploration is needed.

Following Wu's line of inquiry, this study attempts to conceptualize the Buddhist renewal in a relatively clear way. It understands the renewal as a strong, phenomenal, and large-scale resurgence of enthusiasm with monastic Buddhism that involves all walks of society and that projects itself, to varying degrees, in the spiritual, intellectual, and material forms within the *saṃgha* and beyond. It sees three basic modes in the state of Buddhism—declining, stable, and flourishing—with each corresponding to a range of fluctuation of Buddhist activities. Both decline and flourishing are a deviation from stability, though in opposite directions, while a renewal refers to an outstandingly visible return of religious enthusiasm after experiencing a period of decline. Both the intensity and the quality of Buddhist activities are crucial to distinguish these states, but unlike the Sui-Tang centralism and its overemphasis on doctrinal creativity, these activities are defined in a much broader sense, including all the theoretical, practical, and social forms. This was the case with late-Ming China, where huge numbers of people engaged in Buddhism in all three aspects. Although the results may not live up to some people's expectations in theoretical creativity and sophistication, the progress Buddhism made in the practical and social dimensions indeed restored its vitality to some degree, as is well supported by the fruitful research on Buddhist practices in the past decade. By contrast, the decline of Buddhism is understood as a state in which there is a strong and large-scale retreat from enthusiasm for Buddhism among the elites, making them, en masse, reluctant to engage in and make active contributions to the religion.

Implicitly but significantly, understanding the state of Buddhism in this way is inextricably related to social stratification. Hierarchies do exist among Buddhist adherents, wherein elite participants tend to be valued more highly in society than ordinary ones and are thus more influential than the latter. Sociologically, the distinction between elites and nonelites often has to do with discourse and is considered intimately related with power. In recent decades scholars have given more careful examination of the elite as a concept in the context of late-imperial China.[21] Based on these discussions but used in a broader sense, the term "elites" in this study refers loosely to those groups whose members, with the necessary resources and means in hand, exercised dominance in one or more significant aspects of society in a relatively reliable and continuous way. Manifesting themselves as eminent monks within the *saṃgha* or as figures like emperors, inner-court elites—high-ranking court women and eunuchs—scholar-officials, and merchants in the secular world, the elites made a large impact on the development of Buddhism, though not always positively. Crucially, more often than not the elites were vastly different from the ordinary people in understanding and practicing Buddhism,[22] and their large-scale return to monastic Buddhism is a precondition for a religious movement to be called a renewal. Nonetheless, although their retreat from Buddhist activities signifies a decline, it does necessarily follow that the ordinary adherents would leave as well. This understanding helps explain the seemingly inexplicable phenomenon cited by Jiang Wu that the routine practices were maintained even in the so-called period of decline.[23]

Returning to the present study of late-Ming Buddhist renewal, instead of discussing the entire spectrum of Buddhism, it deals with only some parts of it, and two points deserve further clarification at the outset. First, this study concentrates only on monastic Buddhism. Full of stratifications, Buddhism as an institutional religion can be further divided into monastic and folk Buddhism.[24] Folk Buddhism, also called popular Buddhism by many people in hopes of stressing that it has been practiced not only by commoners but also by all people in society, "may be understood as a persistent, complex, and syncretic dimension of the Buddhist tradition characterized by beliefs and practices dominated by magical intent and fashioned with the purpose of helping people cope with the uncertainties and exigencies of life."[25] In contrast, monastic Buddhism has its institutions and clergy, and it is usually state sponsored, perceived as mainstream (and thus believed to be rooted in fundamental Buddhist doctrines), and practiced by people who allegedly understand the essence of Buddhism. In late-Ming China when monastic Buddhism was experiencing a major reinvigoration, folk Buddhism thrived as well, but with a different pacing, following different logics, and going in different directions.[26] These distinctions between the two, although made by scholars rather than existing in reality in such a clear-cut way, are still a convenient tool for analysis. When the present study discusses the state of Buddhism, we are thus dealing with monastic Buddhism, leaving folk Buddhism to other scholars for separate handling.[27] Second, although monastic Buddhism did have a huge following among the ordinary social classes, this study focuses only on elite participants and likewise leaves ordinary followers aside for separate handling. As discussed in the preceding, not only were these elites vastly different from the ordinary in understanding and practicing Buddhism but also their large-scale return to monastic Buddhism constituted a precondition for the emergence of a Buddhist renewal. With such a focus on elite participants, it is hoped this study will reduce the confusion that would otherwise be caused by handling them together with ordinary followers.

BUDDHISM, STATE, AND POLITICS IN CHINA

This study takes as a starting point the question of how the late-Ming Buddhist renewal became possible after a stagnant period of more than one hundred years,[28] and it approaches the reinvigoration from both religious and nonreligious perspectives to look for the required dynamics and momentum.

What makes Buddhism a religion undergirds this study, even if it is not often the focus of attention. As a religion that has a set of distinctive beliefs and rituals, Buddhism not only helps people define their ultimate concerns and meet their soteriological needs—such as whether life has meaning, where to find that meaning, and how to fulfill their destined responsibilities—but also promotes their actual well-being in such ways as warding off suffering. This is where the attractiveness of Buddhism essentially comes from, serving as a rationale for people to draw close to and follow its path. Current studies on late-Ming Buddhist masters, especially on Yunqi Zhuhong by Chün-fang Yü and Jennifer Eichman, demonstrate this point very well. Religious motivations worked everywhere in the renewal, which by definition had a large-scale upsurge of enthusiasm for Buddhism. In particular, scholars have argued that "feelings of vulnerability to physical, societal, and personal risks are a key factor driving religiosity."[29] So existentialist anxiety and social vulnerability often mutually reinforce in an age of sociopolitical disruption, which was the case with the mid- and late-Ming period. Against this background, this study frequently asks such questions as to whom Buddhism was directed, what concerns it addressed, and how it fit their motives in confronting, controlling, or even escaping the exigencies of life.

Despite the significance of religious motivations, however, the most telling factors and elements discussed in this study are the extramural ones, with the stress on the context in which Buddhism existed and interacted with other elements.

Insofar as its doctrines and practices remain stable, changes in the extent to which Buddhism strikes a chord with people is essentially decided by how much it resonates with their nonreligious needs. Although scholars tend to agree that few ideas and practices appearing in late-Ming Buddhism were new, the Buddhist renewal did produce prolific writings and did involve huge numbers of people. This unexpected leap toward enthusiasm for Buddhism thus suggests that external factors—beyond religious motivations—made a large-scale contribution to the renewal and should be considered alongside religious factors. This study thus raises the following questions: How and to what degree was Buddhism chosen when responding to chilling realities? What affected people's stance toward Buddhism? Since Buddhism remained marginal and under constant surveillance, how did it respond to extramural changes, and how effective was the response? How did the newly emerged need for Buddhism exert force on it, and in which directions did this force push or pull? How did the results affect its fate in the long run? The attempts to answer these questions constitute the main body of this study.

The study of Buddhism of the late Ming (and of the early Qing, which is frequently discussed with it) has achieved great progress since the 1980s, but a lacuna in the field is clear as well. So far, the field has been approached primarily from two perspectives. The intellectual-history perspective was pioneered by Araki Kengo in the 1960s and has since been carried on primarily by Japanese scholars and those under their influence.[30] Cutting across the boundaries between Confucianism and Buddhism, these scholars take the new developments in Buddhism as part of a significant intellectual redirection initiated by the Wang Yangming school of neo-Confucianism. They stress the influence that scholar-officials simultaneously received from Confucianism and Buddhism and look closely at how their response affected the growth of Buddhism. The sociological approach in this field derived its direct intellectual provenance from Chün-fang Yü's study on Zhuhong[31] and from Timothy Brook's monograph examining gentry patronage of Buddhism in Jiangnan against the background of the state-society division; these model studies provide a methodological framework worthy of emulation.[32] In recent years, this approach has been broadened both to include such groups as eunuchs and women and to encompass more types of Buddhist practices. We might note, among others, studies on pilgrimage by Chün-fang Yü and Susan Naquin; on Buddhist sacred sites by Marcus Bingenheimer; on the religious life of eminent monks by Beverley McGuire; on male elite Buddhist fellowship in Jiangnan by Jennifer Eichman; and on bodily practice, especially self-inflicted violence, by Jimmy Yu.[33] Despite these achievements, however, late-Ming Buddhism is apparently short of studies from other views, among which the lack of systematic and effective political study has affected our understanding of the field in a profound but negative way.

The study of Chinese Buddhism has been heavily informed by political approaches because its development has been deeply involved with politics. Buddhism entered China around the first century largely as a consequence of its quick spread, which was initiated in the first place under the political aegis of the legendary King Aśoka (ca. 304–232 BCE), and has since become a shaping force of Chinese society. But unlike Christianity in Europe, Buddhism in China was never a state structure in its own right. Its growth was inextricably intertwined with politics, and their relationship was essentially determined by their strength in relation to each other. During the medieval period, China's political system underwent major changes, and, after a protracted process, the secular power enhanced its ability to monitor and interfere with Buddhist affairs. Keeping abreast of the process, Buddhism in China transformed into Chinese Buddhism, and its influence over Chinese politics expanded consistently as well. In other words, relations between Buddhism and the state were often symbiotic at the time. During the Sui and early Tang period, Buddhism nearly became a state ideology in the effort to unify China after a long-term political division, and it was used to religiously legitimize kingship in general and repeated usurpations in particular. Historically, it was during this period that Buddhism reached a peak both in theoretical creativity and in sociopolitical influence. Well matched in strength, both the state and Buddhist institutions could undertake major initiatives and spark a strong response from the other side. It was an age when they both were eager to protect and expand what they perceived as their own interests. This complexity and richness in the *saṃgha*-state relationship has provoked strong scholarly interest, leading to many political approaches in this field of historical inquiry.[34] What has proved strikingly attractive is that the relationship can be and has been investigated from both sides.

The political perspective is even more important for the study of late-imperial Buddhism. The mid-Tang dynasty saw a turning point in the *saṃgha*-state relationship, with the state taking prominence. Challenges to Buddhism came from at home and abroad. In India, Buddhism declined around the eleventh century. In China, the aristocrats (*shizu* 士族) had bolstered the influence of Buddhism socially and financially in the early medieval period, but their gradual bowing out from history during the Tang changed the playing field forever. Buddhism would no longer have a close ally of the same type. As for the state, political centralization increased over time and, despite some setbacks, had reached a peak by the Ming. Meanwhile, neo-Confucianism, which had an entrenched conflict with Buddhism, came to dominate as state ideology. Gradually, faith in Chinese

Buddhism became confined mostly to private life and its significance in the political world waned. The state took the lead in the relationship, leaving Buddhism in a subordinate position.[35] Consequently, it is hard to understand the development of Buddhism without taking politics into consideration, although the opposite does not necessarily hold true.[36]

When it comes to approaching late-Ming Buddhism from a political viewpoint, however, we are challenged to study it in a more imaginative and innovative way. The state-society division that is currently dominating the field as a framework for analysis was preconditioned by major political disruptions. According to Timothy Brook, there was a consistent tension between "the localist turn" (in Peter Bol's term) and "state activism" (in Brook's own term) during political and cultural turmoil.[37] Of the striking congruence between the prominence of the localist turn and the occurrence of the late-Ming Buddhist renewal, Brook has convincingly argued that it had a great deal to do with the local gentry's seeking for autonomy in a fight against the state by drawing close to Buddhism and turning it into a kind of public sphere. Also, he relates the decline of gentry patronage of Buddhism after the 1680s to the expansion of state activism, arguing that the latter redirected gentry activism and funds from Buddhist institutions toward infrastructural projects favorable to state concerns. In this way, Brook has implied that the evolution of the renewal was contingent on contemporary politics, which was later followed by Jiang Wu in his research on Chan revitalization in seventeenth-century China.[38] In reality, however, so far the political study of late-Ming Buddhism has been insufficient and fragmentary: after Chen Yuan's excellent study on how Buddhism developed under strong political influence during the Ming-Qing transitional period, there was a disruption of forty years, and only in the 1980s was the approach picked up again. Scholars such as Chen Yunü 陳玉女, Jiang Canteng 江燦騰, and Du Changshun 杜常順 are among those who took an interest in the field. Taking research of medieval Buddhism as their model, however, they have generally confined themselves to the imperial court and leading monks, without much reflection on the methodologies they employ.[39] In fact, for late-imperial China there is a huge number of historical materials available, such as collected works, biographies of eminent monks, historical literature, miscellaneous notes (biji 筆記), letters, diaries, local and monastic gazetteers, and epitaphs and inscriptions. This unprecedented accessibility to materials, in kind and in quantity, enables us to raise new questions and to answer them in a more concrete and tangible way, thereby making it possible to have a more nuanced and systematic understanding of how late-Ming Buddhism evolved under the influence of politics.

GOALS, APPROACHES, METHODOLOGY,
AND KEY CONCEPTS

This study of the late-Ming Buddhist renewal has two main goals. The first is to examine how it developed and evolved simultaneously in the three dimensions of time, region, and society. The second is to explore the dynamics and mechanism behind the process by combining religious and sociopolitical structural factors and the initiative of the people involved. In the course of pursuing these goals, I take special interest in exploring how politics was translated into positive or negative impacts on Buddhism—in what ways and through what channels—and thus in what sense and to what degree it shaped its evolution.

Considerable effort is made in this study to visualize the development of the renewal through tracing and evaluating its unfolding in a straightforwardly material way. The lengthy and often uphill process of building up religious passion in the revival manifested itself ubiquitously in theoretical, practical, and social forms. Some results were discernible but hard to measure, such as resurgent appreciation of the Buddha's holiness, a passion for his teachings and the *saṃgha*, and a desire to live in the Buddhist way. But the enthusiasm also projected itself in a material way. This enables us to trace the evolution of the renewal on a more concrete basis, just as we observe the unseen wind through the marks it leaves in sand. This study looks at, among other material and behavioral markers, changes in temple-building activity and in the activity of eminent monks. Arguably the most important human and material assets, temples and eminent monks could and did respond sensitively to changes within the *saṃgha* and beyond. In this way, we can expect to chart the development of the renewal in a visible and measurable way, a challenging task for any study of a religious movement that involves a huge number of people and lasts a long time.

Specifically, the evolution of the renewal is examined here in the three dimensions of time, region, and society, about which this study offers novel perspectives and understandings when compared with current scholarship. The Buddhist renewal lasted as long as one hundred years, so instead of discussing it ambiguously as a whole, this study distinguishes its developmental stages with suitable units of time.[40] Moreover, it takes into consideration periods beyond the renewal itself, so as to reveal the structural factors underlying it. In regard to region, this study seeks to understand how Buddhism in areas like Beijing, Nanjing, and Jiangnan took on regional characteristics and, instead of compartmentalizing those areas, works hard to discover the holistic picture of Buddhism that emerges through understanding how regional factors interacted on a higher level. The social dimension is much more complicated. The focus of this study is not on events per se but on the participants who shaped the religious movement, considering that late-imperial Chinese Buddhist institutions, no longer able to rival the state, had little chance to stage dramatic events with political significance. Aside from eminent monks, a traditional subject of study, and the Jiangnan-based local gentry who became the foci of interest after Brook's successful research, this study extensively examines such elite participants as emperors, court women, and eunuchs. Of significance, they are viewed here both as the subject affected by politics and as the agent through whom politics realized its effects on Buddhism. And their activities relevant to the renewal are understood as a dialectical dialogue between individual initiative and their roles as members of the system of dominance, thereby being inevitably conditioned by the sociopolitical institutions. Furthermore, not being "atomized," these elites are understood as embedded in networks. Present here is a special interest in understanding how changes in the outside world were translated into an impetus that moved these participants closer to Buddhism.

In methodology, this study has drawn its most important inspiration from the French Annales school.[41] Following the school's emphasis on placing a study within a relatively long period, this research, instead of starting in the early Wanli era (1572–1620) when the religious movement emerged, begins by looking deeply into the Jiajing era (1521–1567). Through examining the roots of what would eventually grow into a full-scale renewal, the hope is to create a much more coherent picture and time frame of the overall revitalization. Moreover, in echoing the emphasis of the Annales school on structural factors, this study examines the early Ming, when state ideologies were set up and Buddhist polices designed. Consequently, it approaches the renewal from three perspectives of about fifty, one hundred, and two hundred years. Regionally, instead of ambiguously dealing with China as a whole, this study focuses on North China (as a specific region; defined in chapter 3) and the Jiangnan region, two major Buddhist centers at the time, by examining first their respective developments and then their interactions on the national level. I explore a number of case studies to avoid studying history without people, and I then blend them with quantitative analysis, primarily in the last chapter, to combine macroscopic narrative and microscopic historical analysis. This study draws on insights from other disciplines as well. As a study that foregrounds the key role of politics in a religious movement, it naturally draws from political science. With its analysis of the complexities of the spread and reception of Buddhism, it also borrows from communication studies to trace the agents, networks, and media on which the expansion of the renewal depended.

Two concepts from communication studies, though not dealt with expressly, prove particularly useful. One is "opinion leaders," who, held in high esteem, interpret and communicate their messages to a primary group. The other is "agenda setting," which points to the tremendous influence that opinion leaders exert on audiences with their choice of what stories to value and how much prominence and space to give them.[42]

Under strong influence from these theories, explicitly or implicitly, two key concepts other than Buddhism provide an overall framework for this book: history and politics. I explain them briefly in the way they affect the design of this study.

History involves the interplay and interaction of diverse elements and forces. Though one is tempted to try to uncover the causal relationships between them, at times we cannot even name all the constituent parts working behind the scenes. Thus, seeking to understand the strong relevance among different factors including politics is a more practical choice.[43] Furthermore, accidental events can constitute a crucial juncture on some occasions, highlighting the role of individual initiative, but history is not purely a string of accidental events. Occasionality and contingency are likely most noticeable in a short period, but viewing things in a broader context and in the *longue durée*, we often, if not always, find out that a structural factor is underlying history and deciding the final outcomes. This study uses three temporal frames to investigate the history of the late-Ming Buddhist renewal in order to detect both the general tendencies visible over the long term and fluctuations visible in the short term—that is, the influence of both structural factors and individual initiative, respectively.

Politics is understood here as a process during which decisions are made and imposed, thereby involving competition, negotiation, compromise, and cooperation between social groups with different or even contradictory interests. Politics exerts influence universally, but what it actually means is vastly different for different social groups and different regions, depending largely on their relative positions in the power structure. In particular, in the historical context of Ming China, this study handles constitutional politics and normal politics separately, bringing into sharper focus their inherent conflicts, which frequently had the elites trapped. Constitution is of course a modern concept, but in premodern China there was something with a similar function and status, usually in the form of "royal ancestral instructions" (*zuzong jiafa* 祖宗家法 or *zuxun* 祖訓). A constitution legalizes the overarching political structure as well as the regulations and ideology that support the operation of normal politics and tends to be stable, while normal politics is characterized by the arts of compromise and changing priorities that respond to the realities of the time. The tension between the two, when building up to a critical level, will skew the political system and its operation and lead to an overall crisis. What makes a locality more or less susceptible—for better and for worse—to politics? No simple answers exist, because diverse local agendas play a vital role.

ORGANIZATION

This book consists of eight chapters arranged in three parts, plus an introduction and a conclusion. Chapter 1 sets up the surroundings for the late-Ming Buddhist renewal by examining the establishment of the Buddhist and political institutions and their interplay throughout the dynasty. The institutionalization and legalization of Buddhism in the early Ming imposed structural restrictions on its development by limiting its role in the sociopolitical and intellectual life. But as serious political and ideological crises erupted and kept widening in the Jiajing-Wanli period, a pressing need was created for Buddhism as an alternative value system to Confucianism, thus giving it a chance to rebound.

Chapters 2 through 5 investigate how the elites in the secular world, including emperors, court women, eunuchs, and scholar-officials, contributed to the evolution of Buddhism. The influence of these actors had distinct social, regional, and temporal features. Their relationships with Buddhism are understood in connection with their distinctive backgrounds and their dynamic interplay with one another.

The focus of chapters 2 and 3 is on top political figures who played an unparalleled role in setting the direction for Buddhism to develop. Jiajing's suppression of Buddhism is examined in chapter 2 as the preparatory stage of the renewal. The suppression evolved as a result of the interplay between the emperor's personal religious preferences, contemporary politics, and established policies. It deepened the crisis facing Buddhism, but the limitation in Jiajing's control over the situation also allowed an initial recovery of Buddhism in Beijing. Chapter 3 moves to Emperor Wanli 萬曆 (r. 1573–1620) and his mother, Empress Dowager Cisheng 慈聖 (1545–1614). As a significant player in the early-Wanli political arena, Cisheng's timely appearance provided a most needed and powerful traction for the development of Buddhism. As her tension with Wanli escalated over the establishment of the crown prince, however, her abilities to patronize Buddhism were seriously hampered by the Wanli emperor, who represented the institutional force that affected Buddhism. The shock waves were sent out throughout the Buddhist world.

The next two chapters examine eunuchs and scholar-officials, who, according largely to their own interests and agendas, could affect Buddhism in Beijing and Jiangnan, respectively, in distinct ways. Chapter 4 examines Ming eunuchs well known for their generous support of Buddhism in Beijing and nearby regions. During the first two decades of the Wanli era, armed with their unique institutional advantages, eunuchs served financially as Cisheng's major ally and contributed greatly to Beijing's rise as a Buddhist center. Afterward, highly sensitive to the changes borne on the political winds, they quickly shunned Buddhism amid the growing tension between Wanli and Cisheng. Finally, a case study of Huguosi 護國寺 is presented to illustrate how eunuchs channeled their suppressed voices by translating their resources into support to a temple. Chapter 5 turns to scholar-officials, who, trapped in the inherent tension between their multiple identities, kept adjusting their distance from Buddhism. Growing active in local society, especially in Jiangnan, they were a serious threat to Buddhism in the Jiajing era, but their connections with Buddhism were reforged in the Wanli era. Feng Mengzhen 馮夢禎 (1548–1608, *jinshi* 1577) and Yuan Hongdao 袁宏道 (1568–1610, *jinshi* 1591) are examined as case studies to reveal how scholar-officials came to embrace Buddhism and find themselves in a confusing space between Confucianism and Buddhism. Scholar-officials might have dreamed of achieving autonomy in their patronage of Buddhism, but my examination of the collapse of the Putao Association 葡萄社 shows how this illusion was shattered under political and ideological pressures at the turn of the seventeenth century.

Chapters 6 and 7 shift the focus from the external world to the *saṃgha* itself to see how and to what extent the *saṃgha* shaped the renewal. These chapters examine eminent monks and Buddhist institutions separately, assuming that they acted not only passively in response to external factors but also positively out of an initiative to reinvigorate Buddhism.

Chapter 6 examines the endeavor of leading Buddhist masters, the most valuable and most mobile assets of the *saṃgha*, to revitalize Buddhism, as well as the price they paid for their efforts. Hanshan Deqing 憨山德清 (1546–1623), Zibo Zhenke 紫柏真可 (1543–1604), and Miaofeng Fudeng 妙峰福登 (1540–1612), all closely tied to the inner court and with local society, chose distinct strategies for their religious undertakings. In particular, it turned out that the ways they chose to handle politics made a tremendous impact on their personal lives as well as on the Buddhist renewal as a whole. Chapter 7 explores how temples experienced ups and downs by attracting various powers and interacting with them. Five temples are chosen, and their respective histories are examined in relation to the cooperation and competition of the participating forces, particularly those between the imperial court and local society. The results reveal that, despite their efforts, few temples during the period could control their own fates, reflecting a general loss of autonomy for the *saṃgha*.

Finally, chapter 8 examines the unfolding of the Buddhist renewal as a whole, under the influence of internal and external forces. Based on quantitative analysis of the mobility of eminent monks and fluctuations in temple-building activities, this chapter first paints a multilayered picture of the Buddhist renewal based on evolutions in the dimensions of time, geography, and society. Next it reveals how the evolution of the renewal was relevant to politics, highlighting Beijing's loss of its leading role in the Buddhist world when the larger regional context is brought into view. Finally, it identifies for the first time an age, shortly after the turn of the seventeenth century, when confidence in the future of Buddhism was at a low ebb.

The conclusion briefly reviews the whole story of the Buddhist renewal, highlights how profoundly its evolution was affected by politics, and ends with an evaluation of its strengths and weaknesses in a broader context.

I

Setting the Stage

The occurrence of the late-Ming Buddhist renewal was not predetermined but path dependent. It adapted and evolved primarily in response to multifarious changes in the contemporary world, and yet it also strongly reflected the legacy of past centuries. This chapter sets the stage for the renewal by examining the interrelated religious and secular surroundings in which Buddhism existed and drew resources. It seeks to detect structural factors,[1] in the early-Ming politico-religious context, that would contribute to the evolution of late-Ming Buddhism two hundred years later. In particular, it scrutinizes how a serious political and ideological crisis in the mid and late Ming, deriving from the structural weakness of the power hierarchy, worked behind the process leading to the religious renewal.

REGULATING BUDDHISM AS A PART OF STATE BUILDING

Buddhism obtained a legal position in ideologically Confucianized Ming China at the cost of being regulated by restrictive policies and measures, and the process can be seen as largely part of an ongoing project of state building. First designed by Zhu Yuanzhang 朱元璋, the founding Hongwu emperor (r. 1368–1398), and then modified by his son the Yongle emperor (r. 1403–1424), these policies and regulations redefined the role of Buddhism according to the interests of the state. They set the official tone of the Ming state in handling Buddhist matters and remained relatively consistent throughout the dynasty. Despite controversies over how well they were enforced, it is beyond question that they greatly impacted the development of Buddhism through working as a functional factor and shaping the religious surroundings.

"Useful" Buddhism in Confucianized Ming China

Buddhist adherents though they may have been in their private lives, the early-Ming emperors formulated their policies related to Buddhism in accordance with the needs of the state rather than with their personal religious faith. Hongwu had been a monk in his early years, but he established as state ideology neo-Confucianism, which had entrenched conflicts with Buddhism. He indeed left a position for Buddhism in his empire but, notably, justified the decision by emphasizing its role of supporting governance in an implicit way (*anzhu wang-gang* 暗助王綱 or *yinxu wangdu* 陰翊王度).[2] This utilitarian stance determined the ways in which Hongwu treated Buddhism and had a profound impact on the development of Buddhism throughout the dynasty. Among other factors deserving particular attention is that Hongwu reclassified the *saṃgha* by amplifying the differences between various Buddhist traditions and showing a preference of one over the others.

In 1391, the emperor classified Buddhism into the three categories of Chan 禪, *jiang* 講 (doctrinal schools), and *jiao* 教 (esoteric Buddhism).[3] State classification of Buddhism was not without precedents, but two points make Hongwu's case exceptional. First, Hongwu replaced the conventional *lü* 律 (Vinaya) school with the *jiao*, which, although it had a history going back to mid-Tang China, was newly defined with a specialized task of providing ritual services especially at funerals.[4] This replacement functioned to rob Buddhism of a fair amount of institutional autonomy because the Buddhist community would have been poorly equipped to combat the state's legal codes had it no longer understood its own legal code.[5] Second, he treated the three categories of Buddhism not equally but with distinctly different measures. He declared,

> I have observed that Buddhism and Daoism each have two sorts of clerics. Buddhism has Chan and *jiao* [esoteric rituals], while Daoism has Zhengyi [Orthodox Unity] and Quanzhen [Complete Perfection]. Both Chan Buddhism and Quanzhen Daoism focus on self-cultivation and the maintenance of one's original nature, thereby benefiting only [the practitioners] themselves. Both *jiao*

Buddhism and Zhengyi Daoism specialize in saving [the masses] and are aimed expressly at filial sons and kind parents. They improve human relations and keep social customs simple. How great they are!

朕觀釋道之教各有二等徒, 僧有禪有教, 道有正一有全真. 禪與全真, 務以修身養性, 獨為自己而已; 教與正一, 專以超脫, 特為孝子慈親之設, 益人倫, 厚風俗, 其功大矣哉![6]

Among the Buddhist traditions Hongwu's predilection was for *jiao* Buddhism, which he believed was most efficient in encouraging people to act morally and fulfill their Confucian duties. This choice constituted a sharp contrast with the scholar-official's penchant for Chan Buddhism, reflecting less the emperor's personal preference than his effort to redefine Buddhism according to his agenda as a ruler.[7]

Hongwu forcefully advanced his agenda by singling out *jiao* Buddhism to receive lavish state patronage, which eventually suppressed scholar-officials' discourse control of Buddhism and fundamentally altered the course of Buddhism. Hongwu confined Chan and *jiang* monks to their temples, allowing them to contact the outer world only through a monk referred to as *zhenji daoren* 砧基道人 (the man of the Way in charge of monastic landholdings),[8] but he gave the *jiao* monks permission to move freely. More important, he granted the *jiao* monks the privilege of offering paid Buddhist services to ordinary people, with the other two categories excluded from so doing. This lucrative monopoly on funeral services was truly a gift that kept on giving—the more services they offered, the more income they guaranteed. Positively, this arrangement encouraged Buddhist monks to delve still deeper to meet the needs of the masses, especially the need for funeral rites in a country that was increasingly Confucianized, thereby facilitating a further infiltration of Buddhism in China. Negatively, *jiao* Buddhism was quickly recast as a strikingly lucrative tradition, with true devotion discarded in favor of funerary ritual. As the *jiao* monks outnumbered those of the other two groups, a permanent change occurred in the composition of the clergy.[9] Since performing rituals meant little more than following formulaic rules, the *jiao* monks were the least refined among the clergy and often criticized as lazy and corrupt. Thus, the greater their percentage of the whole institution was, the less attractive and respectable Buddhism became to the elites. Such an estrangement from the elites forced Buddhism to depend more on nonelite supporters, which stimulated a further need for *jiao* Buddhism and worsened the imbalance between the three categories of Buddhism.

Regulating Buddhism Through Policies

Working from this pragmatic view, Hongwu spent dozens of years in designing policies to regulate Buddhism. His policies and measures varied greatly with what he perceived at a given time as necessary for the benefit of the state, and they covered a wide range, from the scale of Buddhist institutions, the quantity and quality of clerics, and their relationship with society to the practices conducted within the *saṃgha*.

Hongwu was supportive of Buddhism in the early years of his reign. This stance might have had something to do with his short experience as a monk in a temple before joining the late-Yuan rebellion that eventually pushed him onto the throne.[10] In 1368, he set up the Bureau of Buddhist Patriarchs (*shanshi yuan* 善世院) to administer the *saṃgha* and granted its director the high rank of 2b.[11] He summoned a good number of eminent monks to the imperial capital, with whom he discussed Buddhist teachings. He held the Dharma assembly (*fahui* 法會) annually in the first five years of his reign, and he even knelt before Buddha statues. In 1372, he ordered the compilation of a new version of the Buddhist canon, which would not be finished until 1401.[12] In the same year, he had officials count Buddhist and Daoist monks all over the country and gave them ordination certificates (*dudie* 度牒) without charge. He allowed monks to travel everywhere to preach Buddhist teachings and even sent some eminent monks to other countries as envoys.

Hongwu imposed restrictions on Buddhism as well, which seems to have been primarily for administrative purposes. In 1372, he had a registration booklet called the *Zhouzhi ce* 周知冊 (Register known everywhere) circulated all over the country in an attempt to detect fake monks. One year later, alarmed by the soaring number of Buddhist and Daoist monks, which had jumped to ninety-six thousand from fifty-seven thousand in a single year, he set limits on their number by ordering that novice monks (*xingtong* 行童) be denied full ordination until they had passed required exams and that women under forty be prohibited from becoming nuns. In 1377, aiming at standardizing Buddhist teachings, he stipulated that all monks study the *Heart Sutra*, the *Diamond Sutra*, and the *Laṅkāvatāra sūtra* as annotated by Zongle 宗泐 (1327?–1407).

A radical change in the emperor's stance occurred around 1381, and after that his major efforts were aimed at placing Buddhism under strict control. He did this partly through active intervention, by law or by force, in the personnel management within the *saṃgha* and beyond. In the sixth month of that year, Hongwu instituted the Central Buddhist Registry (*senglu si* 僧錄司) in place of the

Bureau of Buddhist Patriarchs. This department was responsible for registering and supervising monks, organizing the qualification exams for the ordination certificate, and recommending candidates for vacant abbacies.[13] Ten months later the registry system was ordered to be established over the entire empire and would persist throughout the dynasty. Compared with the Bureau of Buddhist Patriarchs, the Central Buddhist Registry had the advantage of enforcing its orders at the local level. But one man's gain is another's loss. As the system was universally established in every province, prefecture, subprefecture, and county, the running of the *saṃgha* was intervened in by the state and its independence seriously weakened. According to the new regulations, for example, Buddhist monastic officials were be assigned by the Ministry of Rites, and the abbacy of important temples could not be appointed without permission from this ministry.[14] Viewed in this light, it is not accidental that the rank of the head of the Central Buddhist Registry was lowered to 6a from the 2a of that of the Bureau of Buddhist Patriarchs. In 1384,[15] Hongwu finally delineated the procedure for becoming a monk: nobody was allowed to be tonsured privately. To obtain the ordination certificate, applicants first had to meet age limits and then take an exam that was held every four years. The state rather than the *saṃgha* itself was in the position to decide the results. What's more, in 1391 a total of sixty-four monks were sentenced to death on the charge of plotting to revolt through conniving with northern barbarians (*tonglu* 通虜). Very likely these monks were implicated in the Hu Weiyong 胡惟庸 (d. 1380) case, which, as I discuss later, was invented by the emperor as part of a large-scale purge of anyone he conceived as dangerous. All but one monk was executed, and a book titled *Qingjiao lu* 清教錄 (A record of purifying the [Buddhist] teaching) recording the alleged misconduct and the names of the criminals was compiled and circulated. This massive killing sent a serious warning to the *saṃgha* and required absolute obedience to the monarch's authority.[16]

With the undeclared intention to reduce the number of Buddhist temples, Hongwu took a more radical step of amalgamating them. In the sixth month of 1391, he decreed that no matter how many temples they had before, each prefecture, subprefecture, and county was allowed to keep only one large temple.[17] The following month, as a more practical alternative he instead ordered both newly founded chapels (*anyuan* 菴院) and old temples without imperially bestowed name tablets (*ming'e* 名額) to be abolished. The monks of the abolished temples, if more than thirty in number, were required to live together to form a large public monastery (*conglin* 叢林)[18] or else to be incorporated into other temples.[19]

Hongwu also sought to minimize if not cut off the links of the *saṃgha* with society, from which they drew their resources. In 1386, he demanded that temples with land-tax obligations assign a *zhenji daoren* as the only person responsible for communicating with the secular world on behalf of the temple.[20] In the seventh month of 1391, on the pretext that monks were still intermingling with the masses, he ordered that all monks live together in the temples according to their classifications.[21] An even stricter order was issued three years later banning monks from associating with officials and from traveling to towns and villages to collect donations.[22] Together these orders confined monks to temples, and the isolation from the secular world—particularly from the well-educated scholar-officials—contributed greatly to the intellectually and socially drained state of Buddhism. I return to this issue in the following.

Having no intention to abolish Buddhism, the emperor did not totally revoke support to it. In Nanjing, for example, he designated five state-sponsored monasteries, which, along with three other major monasteries, were granted nearly five hundred *qing* 頃 (8,235 acres) of land and enjoyed the exemption of the land tax and corvée labor.[23] He prohibited monks from selling monastic land, ordering the confiscation of any such property if sold to the laity.[24] He forbade officials to confiscate amalgamated temples, leaving them to the affected monks. He even made an exception for Chan and *jiang* monks, who were prohibited from leaving their registered temples without official approval, insofar as they planned to seek instruction elsewhere.[25]

These policies crafted by Hongwu underwent minor modifications during the Yongle reign (1402–1424), and the majority of them were reaffirmed and incorporated into the Ming Code, which persisted throughout the dynasty.[26] The Yongle emperor expanded the Buddhist registry system further to the frontier regions. More important, he repeatedly imposed restrictions on the numbers of monks and temples. In the eleventh month of 1402, when he had just ascended the throne, for instance, Yongle reaffirmed the order of amalgamating temples.[27] In 1417, he issued an order prohibiting monks and nuns from building new chapels.[28] The following year, he changed the interval between ordinations for monks from three to five years. In the same year he also issued the following edict:

Henceforth, the maximum number of people allowed to become Buddhist and Daoist monks is forty in a single prefecture, thirty in a single subprefecture, and twenty in a single county. Only those aged between fourteen and twenty who have obtained permission from their parents are allowed to apply to the authority. Only if their neighbors have attested that there is nothing wrong are they allowed to enter a temple. After receiving instruction from a master for five years, [they] may go to the Central Buddhist/Daoist Registry to take the exam should they be versed in various scriptures. Only when they prove indeed to be good at scriptures will they be given a Dharma name and the ordination certificate.

今後為僧道者, 府不過四十人, 州不過三十人, 縣不過二十人. 限年十四以上二十以
下, 父母皆允, 方許陳告有司. 鄰里保勘無礙, 然後得投寺觀, 從師受業者五年後,
諸經習熟, 然後赴僧錄、道錄司攷試. 果諳經典, 始立法名, 給與度牒.[29]

Apparently, Yongle carried on his father's policy of setting limits to the amount and quality of monks in the empire.

In particular, Yongle had a discriminatory policy against nuns. In 1420, at the time of suppressing a rebellion, the emperor ordered all Buddhist and Daoist nuns in Beijing and Shandong to be sent to the capital lest the female leader of the rebels pretend to be a nun in order to escape. This action was expanded in vain to the entire empire several months later. Nonetheless, Yongle ordered all nuns to return to secular life and prohibited women from becoming nuns in future. This single act would later be cited to support a bias against nuns.[30]

Downward Spiral of Buddhism

The making of the early-Ming legislation and its implementation in subsequent times joined to shape the legacy that mid- and late-Ming Buddhism inherited, but it is a problem as to the evaluation of their actual impact on the development of Buddhism. Ming polices concerning Buddhism were initially studied in the 1920s.[31] But only in the 1990s did Timothy Brook argue convincingly that these policies had nearly added up to suppression, causing a separation between the *saṃgha* and society.[32] As for patronage arrangements that occasionally took place between the throne and the *saṃgha*, he points out that they were not a matter of state policy.[33] By contrast, most scholars have tended to recount what the early-Ming emperors did to Buddhism and list the prescriptive regulations. In fact, the complexity of this issue requires novelty and originality in approach. On top of what the emperors did to Buddhism, similar weight should be placed on what they did not do and the enforcement of relevant policies and measures in local society and their actual effects.

Let us first consider some basic estimates regarding the results brought about by the enforcing of these laws and policies before examining their consequences. Generally, the early-Ming regulations were more ambitious and enforced with far greater energy when compared with those enacted in former regimes, but the degrees to which they were successful varied considerably.

Following previous practice, Hongwu extended legal recognition only to certain numbers of Buddhist institutions. From this point until the Wanli era, those measures intended to reduce the numbers and the scale of Buddhist temples were carried out with considerable success. This can be seen from two perspectives. First, temples were amalgamated as required, and it seemed that the closer an area was to Nanjing, the early-Ming capital, the better the guidelines were adhered to.[34] For instance, in Suzhou prefecture, as many as 308 temples and chapels were amalgamated and fifty-seven *conglin* were preserved.[35] In Songjiang 松江 prefecture, 154 chapels and temples were amalgamated and thirty large public monasteries were preserved.[36] In Hangzhou prefecture, which was comparatively far from Nanjing, 284 chapels and temples were absorbed and 158 large public monasteries were left.[37] In northern China, which was even farther from the imperial capital, only five small temples were recorded as amalgamated in Daming 大名 prefecture during the Hongwu era,[38] and no evidence shows that these policies were ever enforced in Baoding 保定, Zhending 真定, and Taiyuan 太原 prefectures.[39] These results reveal regional differences in enforcing central-government orders in the early Ming,[40] although they may reflect the quality of the available resources as well.[41] Furthermore, although some newly built temples were legitimized by obtaining a name tablet from an emperor,[42] the strategy of reducing new temples worked pretty well before the Wanli era. For instance, ninety-two temples in Huzhou 湖州 prefecture and 115 temples in Hangzhou were built, rebuilt, or renovated in the Hongwu era, but the figures in these two prefectures dropped to nine and eight, respectively, in the Yongle era. Suzhou prefecture was somewhat different in that the number dropped only slightly, from sixty-three to fifty-seven.[43] Surely the devastating wars in the Yuan-Ming transition created a pressing need for temple repairs during the Hongwu era, but the vast differences between the Hongwu and Yongle eras still reveals an effective cut in the number of temples following the enforcement of the policies. As a result, with the significant exception of Beijing, the new imperial capital after the 1420s (dealt with separately in this study), temple building slowed significantly in most other regions.

In contrast, the effort to limit the number of monks was less successful. Monks in the empire would have been fewer than ten thousand had Hongwu's regulations been followed strictly. But as many as twenty-five thousand ordination certificates were issued in the Chenghua era (1465–1487) alone.[44] Scholars disagree about the consequences of the practice, but many believe that it brought about a far-reaching change to the *saṃgha*. In the early Ming, the certificate was free, but a candidate monk was required to meet set requirements, such as age limit and passing of the exams. In 1451, however, it was announced that a novice monk could obtain the certificate as long as he delivered five *dan* 石 of rice to Sichuan for military use.[45] This marked the start of the selling of ordination certificates (*yudie*

鬻牒) in the Ming dynasty.[46] As this notorious practice became a convenient recourse for the government to collect money for urgent causes, money became the standard in deciding the qualifications for a monk.[47] Thus both the state and the *saṃgha* found their ability to maintain the quality and quantity of the clergy seriously weakened, although how the results actually affected the development of Buddhism remains controversial.[48]

Economically, the Ming state brought an abrupt end to the prosperity the *saṃgha* had enjoyed in the preceding dynasty. With a status much higher than that of Daoism and Confucianism, Buddhism thrived in the Yuan dynasty to such an extent that some scholars believe that this was the religion's most fortunate time.[49] Buddhist monasteries lost some of their assets in the late-Song wars, but with government assistance, they not only recovered their losses but also obtained the chance to gain new assets.[50] The amount of land owned by some monasteries, consisting of paddy and dry fields, hills, ponds, and forest, was stunning. For example, the Great Chengtian Husheng monastery 大承天護聖寺 had more than 162,000 *qing* (2,668,140 acres) of land. The paddy and dry fields belonging to the Great Huguo Renwang monastery 大護國仁王寺 amounted to 108,000 *qing* (1,778,760 acres). Xuanzhongsi 玄中寺 had more than forty branch temples, and its monks boasted that they had scores of thousands of *mu* of lands in northern China. In total, it is estimated that monastic lands in the Yuan amounted to no less than 300,000 *qing* (4,941,000 acres).[51] Among them more than half came from the emperors: the official history records that as much as 167,980 *qing* (2,766,631 acres) of land was bestowed to Buddhist monasteries in this dynasty.[52] Things changed radically in the Ming dynasty, however, and the monastic economy hence shrank drastically. The *saṃgha* lost great amounts of property in the late-Yuan wars, but, to its disappointment, the Ming government showed little interest in helping it to recover the losses.[53] Moreover, the Ming emperors granted the *saṃgha* new lands only begrudgingly. To my knowledge, the largest patch of land bestowed to a monastery throughout the dynasty was that to Great Gongde monastery 大功德寺 in Beijing, the amount of which was only slightly more than 400 *qing* (6,588 acres).[54] And the second largest was about 250 *qing* (4,118 acres), given to Jiangshansi 蔣山寺, a Nanjing monastery later renamed Linggusi 靈谷寺.[55] The percentage of monastic lands in the total amount of farmland thus dropped. Besides, although imperially bestowed land enjoyed the exemption of both land tax and corvée labor, most of the monastic land was liable for the land tax.[56]

Following the line of Brook's argument, I would say that these Ming policies and measures carried on the efforts of preceding dynasties to weaken the autonomy of the *saṃgha* but reached a higher level. The efforts of the early-Ming emperors to reorganize the *saṃgha* placed Buddhism under stricter control of the state and, whether intended or not, seriously weakened the independence of the *saṃgha* institutionally, socially, economically, and intellectually.

Most strikingly, Buddhism completely lost its institutional autonomy after being restructured by a state known for its active intervention. While in India the *saṃgha* was reportedly an autonomous organization that organized itself according to the precepts, in China it faced sustained pressure from the state, which sought its submission by preventing it from forming a hierarchical system with its own central authority. With the establishment of the monastic officials system, which can be traced back to the Northern Wei (386–534), and of the state-sanctioned regulations regarding the selection of qualified monks, which can be traced back to the Kaiyuan era (713–741), the state forcefully intervened in the autonomy of the *saṃgha* and sparked strong opposition from the latter.[57] By the early Ming, the establishment of the Central Buddhist Registry had become significant both symbolically and in practice: As the administration of the *saṃgha* was absorbed into the everyday operation of the bureaucracy, the state further strengthened its exercise of authority by having the *saṃgha* embedded still deeper in the existing system while the institutional autonomy of the *saṃgha* was further weakened. The enforcement of temple amalgamation had similar consequences as every temple was forced to find a place within an intricate hierarchical network.

Equally important, the economic independence of the *saṃgha* was seriously compromised beginning in the early Ming for multiple reasons, whose consequences were further exacerbated by other policies. Clearly the Ming state was reluctant to act for the benefit of Buddhism. Viewed over a longer time frame, this was continuing a practice of weakening the economic privilege of Buddhism, which can be traced back at least to the mid-Tang dynasty. Shortly after Buddhism entered China, the way of living of Chinese monks changed vastly from begging to depending on the temple with which they were affiliated, and this in turn required a healthy monastic economy. The *saṃgha* obtained incomes from clients in exchange for its religious services and received contributions from its generous adherents, but it was the incomes gained from such sources as land assets, houses, mills, shops, and forest that constituted a much more reliable economic basis for its activities.[58] In particular, "land was always the key factor in determining a monastery's status as a viable social entity. Thousands of small Buddhist temples and monasteries dotted the landscape of the medieval Chinese social world, and those that existed over centuries most likely were bound to their land accumulation practices."[59] China's monastic economy thrived most during the medieval period, owing largely to land and house donations to the *saṃgha* by the aristocracy (*shizu* 士族) and the royal family.[60] Beginning in the mid-Tang, the amount of imperially bestowed land dwindled while the levying of land taxes on monastic landholdings gradually became a common practice by the state. The Five Dynasties (907–960) and the Song (960–1276) period were a transitional period, during which the flourishing of the monastic economy was generally limited to southern China.[61] In light of this, the unwillingness of the Ming state to strengthen the Buddhist economy was consistent with the long-standing practice that was only temporarily interrupted during the Yuan.

Notably, the negative consequences these policies caused were only amplified through interacting with one another. Simply put, as the monastic economy was crippled while the monk population kept growing, the *saṃgha* found it increasingly difficult to maintain a healthy state, and the situation was further exacerbated by the need to squeeze more monks into fewer temples.[62] A rapid downward spiral in the monastic economy followed. On the one hand, evidence shows that there were increasing numbers of cases in which resident monks stole or sold temple property, or in which monks abandoned their temples to avoid paying taxes. On the other hand, such a desperate situation gave rise to a pressing need to seek resources from the secular world, which, paradoxically, made the *saṃgha* likely to yield to the latter and become its prey. Also, a fall was precipitated in the quality of clerics because, against this backdrop, a "bad money driving out good" mechanism started working and made *jiao* Buddhism still more attractive for ordination.[63] But the widespread presence of these less-qualified monks devalued Buddhism in the eyes of the elites. Consequently, it is not that surprising to see that after the Yongle era Buddhism lost momentum, institutionally, financially, socially, and intellectually.

THE COMEBACK OF BUDDHISM IN A TROUBLED PERIOD

After thriving during the early Ming, Buddhism appears to have fallen into a stagnant state during the ensuing one hundred years. The situation would have persisted had nothing important happened to provide it with new traction. But the Buddhist church itself, already in a downward spiral, cannot be the answer. Thus, we now turn to external circumstances to see how an important sociopolitical disruption that occurred in mid- and late-Ming China provided new opportunities for Buddhism to adapt and grow.

A Structurally Flawed Political Framework

Ming China restructured its political system and concluded a tendency to concentrate political power in the hands of the ruler. Hongwu commanded power to an unprecedented level. He first weakened the power of his ministers through waves of cruel purges that claimed the lives of some of his foremost assistants.[64] Afterward, he spent decades restructuring the political system, the central part of which was abolishing the post of chief minister (*zaixiang* 宰相) to prevent power from being concentrated in a single department and establishing the censorial system to keep court officials under close surveillance. In this way, emperors could control officials more conveniently but were less likely to be challenged by them.[65] Hongwu enshrined his political legacy in the *Huang Ming zuxun* 皇明祖訓 (The ancestral instructions of the august Ming) and granted it "constitutional" status by prohibiting his descendants from making any changes to it.[66] This reformed power system was never followed in a strict sense, but the structural problems inherent in it nonetheless built up over time and finally became unsolvable. For the purpose of this study, I limit discussion to the three major political forces on the central government level—the emperor, the grand secretary (*daxueshi* 大學士), and the eunuchs. Not only did their interplay provide the backdrop against which the late-Ming Buddhist revival occurred but also, more directly, with enormous resources in their hands these external elites had a remarkable impact on its evolution.

The most important change to the restructured political system was the rise of both the Grand Secretariat (*neige* 內閣) and eunuchs to share the emperor's supreme power but, notably, without any legal foundation. After abolishing the position of chief minister, Hongwu and his successors quickly set up the Grand Secretariat, consisting of three or four grand secretaries as their private assistants to handle the strenuous administrative task. Beginning in the early fifteenth century, however, the Grand Secretariat had its power expanded to such a degree that it became the de facto head of the bureaucracy.[67] A similar story happened with the eunuchs. Hongwu took pains to rein in the eunuchs' influence, depriving them as a group of any political role in the empire.[68] Only a few years after Hongwu's death, however, his son, Emperor Yongle, started relaxing the restrictions on eunuchs. What was worse, with the introduction of the so-called *piaoni* 票擬 (draft comments) and *pihong* 批紅 (imperial rescripts in vermilion ink) as a regular procedure of administration,[69] the eunuchs became an inevitable bridge between the emperor and the grand secretary and, in the absence of well-defined oversight from both sides, obtained opportunities to

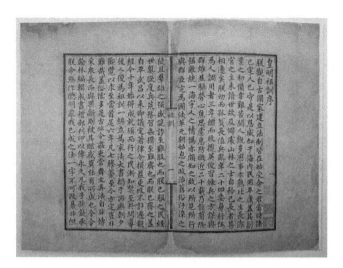

FIGURE 1.1 *Huang Ming zuxun* 皇明祖訓, printed by the Hongwu court

Courtesy of the National Library of China, Beijing

manipulate if not to assert control over state affairs. Eventually, the eunuchs rose to be a major player in the political arena, and the Directorate of Ceremonial (*sili jian* 司禮監) became a corridor of power believed to be parallel and comparable to the Grand Secretariat.

Such a remolding of the political system against its initially intended purposes made it structurally prone to crises, becoming a major source of structural tension plaguing the Ming court. On the part of the emperors, seeking absolute authority pushed them to the opposite side of other members of the imperial household and their ministers, who would take the *Ancestral Instructions* and Confucianism as a handy lever to balance their authority. With regard to the grand secretaries, their status was tricky. A scholar once commented that "the power held in the hands of the grand secretaries was so enormous that they looked like the chief minister in the Han and Tang dynasties; the only difference is that they lacked the title of the chief minister" (閣權之重儼然漢、唐宰輔, 特不居丞相名耳).[70] The term *yanran* here is revealing: although functioning like the chief minister, the grand secretary never had the latter's legal status. As far as eunuchs are concerned, they were still less justifiable in their influence than the grand secretary. But in cases when conflicts between the emperor and the grand secretary escalated, they would obtain better opportunities to expand their influence by cooperating with either of them—they sided with the emperor on most occasions—and thus become a decisive force in politics.

Political Crisis During the Mid and Late Ming

Although Hongwu's original design of the political system existed largely nominally, the inherent tension among the three major political forces mounted up over time and finally broke out in the early Jiajing period.[71] From then until the end of the dynasty, political uncertainty dominated the court and society. Over the course of time, some major political events, examined in following chapters, punctuated the trajectory of Buddhism.

Emperor Jiajing ascended the throne in 1521 after the Zhengde emperor died young without a son or brother. Jiajing was Zhengde's cousin, but he refused to continue Zhengde's line of succession nominally and instead insisted on establishing his own. A clash thus occurred between the emperor and top officials, bringing about a series of events collectively called the Great Rites Controversy (*dali yi* 大禮議).[72] Jiajing relentlessly punished a number of officials opposing his attempts and even killed a few. Eventually, he not only fulfilled his initial wish but also reconfirmed with court officials that an absolute obedience to the emperor was a matter of their professional ethics.[73] Meanwhile, his aggressiveness also intensified his clashes with court officials and poisoned his relationships with them.[74] History repeated itself before long. Emperor Wanli, Jiajing's grandson, was only ten years old when he succeeded to the throne in 1572. In the following decade, a triangle of power consisting of Empress Dowager Cisheng 慈聖 (1545–1614), Wanli's birth mother, Zhang Juzheng 張居正 (1525–1582), then the senior grand secretary, and Feng Bao 馮保 (d. 1583), who headed the eunuchs, guaranteed the smooth operation of the government. These three brought the last golden age to the empire through a series of reforms, but the power structure collapsed abruptly following Zhang's untimely death in the sixth month of 1582. A few months later, convinced that Zhang had made an "unconstitutional" intrusion on his power, Wanli took revenge by placing dozens of Zhang's family members under house arrest.[75] Afterward, Wanli held on to his supreme power watchfully, no longer allowing anybody, including his mother, to share it.

Despite their greed for power, both Jiajing and Wanli were notorious for being remiss in their administrative responsibilities, especially in the second half of their respective reigns. In 1541, Jiajing narrowly survived an attempted assassination carried out by a court girl.[76] During the subsequent twenty-five years, he retreated to Xiyuan 西苑 (West Park), an enclosed palace, and occupied himself with Daoist rituals in the pursuit of longevity.[77] He continued to control state affairs through the proxy of the grand secretary, Yan Song 嚴嵩 (1480–1565), for nearly twenty years. Wanli was bothered primarily by the "succession issue" (*guoben zhizheng* 國本之爭), which haunted the court in various forms for three decades.[78]

Wanli intended to install Zhu Changxun 朱常洵 (1586–1641), his third son by a favorite courtesan, rather than Zhu Changluo 朱常洛 (r. 1620), his first son, as the crown prince. According to the *Ancestral Instructions*,[79] Zhu Changluo had the prior right of succeeding to the throne, and, probably more important, his status obtained firm support from Cisheng and the majority of court officials. Daring not to announce the replacement, Wanli vented his anger by handling state affairs in a most damaging way.[80] Consequently, distrust quickly intensified between the emperor, the inner-court elites, and the courtiers.

Major political problems were hence triggered surrounding the grand secretaries, who were in an awkward situation. On the one hand, once they had helped emperors to stabilize their rule, the grand secretaries would always feel the heavy hand of their rulers and shrank quickly in power and influence.[81] On the other hand, they were increasingly the target of constant attack. As censors became more aggressive and influential,[82] tensions escalated, and officialdom was sundered by distrust and the imperial court bitterly split. Eventually, starting in 1593, purely political conflicts evolved into political confrontations and led to divisive factionalism at court. The so-called Donglin faction (*Donglin dang* 東林黨), consisting primarily of upright and staunch scholar-officials, first took shape, and other factions soon appeared in response. Before long, factionalism ran rife at court,[83] with most important officials involved. This constant strife, coupled with the emperor's absence, brought about grave consequences symbolically and in practice.

Taking advantage of the emperors' dysfunction and the prevalence of court factionalism, eunuchs considerably enhanced their influence in political life. The mid- and late-Ming emperors effectively controlled the eunuchs and forced their submissiveness.[84] Thus the eunuchs tended to side with emperors whenever a choice was necessary. But their relationship with court officials was another story. In the second half of the Jiajing period when the emperor retreated to Xiyuan, for example, they had much leeway to do what they wanted and were in a better position to negotiate with court officials. This tendency intensified in the Longqing and the early Wanli eras, when eunuchs were even able to manipulate the selection of the grand secretary and, through cooperation or counteraction, affected their career life tremendously.[85]

A Shaken State Ideology and the Comeback of Buddhism

The repercussions of the political crisis during the mid and late Ming reverberated far beyond the operation of the political system. On the one hand, its desperate cruelty and ubiquity created the religious need to take refuge from the chaos. On the other hand, the ever-worsening situation weakened the ability of the state to control society and, probably more important, shook state ideology, confusing behavior norms. Many of the elites took Buddhism as an alternative to Confucianism, and the chance for Buddhism to reenter people's lives and thus thrive became practically possible.

Let us focus only on the ideological crisis that entailed new opportunities for Buddhism among the elites. Confucianism had a strong this-worldly orientation, stressing the individual's moral cultivation and responsibility for the state and society, asserting that "[people] should be the first to worry about state affairs, while the last to enjoy themselves" (先天下之憂而憂, 後天下之樂而樂).[86] As the Ming ideology, the Cheng-Zhu school of neo-Confucianism profoundly shaped the mind-set of Chinese people, dictating to them—especially to scholar-officials—how to live. Since this school was in constant competition for influence with Buddhism, even if the elites were at times attracted to Buddhism, they nonetheless placed Confucianism above Buddhism and confined Buddhism to their private lives lest it hinder their public careers. But the state ideology did not function unproblematically. In times when elites found it increasingly hard to fulfill their intended roles, when the state was no longer considered the default place to realize their dreams, and when the risk of a flare-up was very real in their conflicts with the emperor, the supporting ideology would get shaken and a confusion of behavior norms surface.

This was the case with mid- and late-Ming China when the sinister political reality repeatedly dampened the elites' conventional enthusiasm for public service. A role adjustment occurred among scholar-officials in political and social life. A growing number of officials chose to resign or delay taking up their duties.[87] More profoundly, an identity crisis attended these elites following such alterations in role and status. One example demonstrates this point clearly. Shortly after Ye Xianggao 葉向高 (1559–1629, *jinshi* 1583) left office as senior grand secretary in 1613, he confided to a close friend that

since I resigned and returned home, in retrospect, I found everything [as illusory] as flowers in the sky or the moon [reflected] in water. . . . Mr. Lijiu said that many people have been misled by [the conviction] that they, although in seclusion, should be concerned with matters at court. He is certainly correct in this respect.

自罷政歸來, 回視一切如空花水月 … 李九老嘗言 "江湖而懷廟廊之憂, 此語誤了多少人," 殊甚有見.[88]

Mr. Lijiu refers to Li Tingji 李廷機 (1542–1616, *jinshi* 1583), a resigned senior grand secretary. It may be not surprising that Li and Ye would have had such feelings if we knew more about their career trajectories.[89] Nonetheless, given that they were both appointed to the highest civil position, their doubts as to long-entrenched Confucian duty reveals that, on a deeper level, there was a serious identity crisis that was shaking state ideology.

The impact of the ideological crisis was amplified as it happened to correspond with intellectual and socioeconomic changes of the time. Beginning in the early sixteenth century, China experienced an economic boom that provided local elites, especially Jiangnan gentry, with the economic foundation to act fairly independently of the state. Meanwhile, intellectually, the rapid popularity that the Wang Yangming school of neo-Confucianism enjoyed at the cost of the Cheng-Zhu school during the Wanli era decisively opened Confucian scholars to influence from Buddhism.[90] In contrast with Zhu Xi, who stressed following the "objective" principles (*li* 理), Wang Yangming insisted on establishing independent subjectivity by giving supremacy to the mind (*xin* 心). This shift of focus from principles to the mind not only allowed people to emancipate themselves from outside authority, including the emperor and the state, but also functioned as a bridge between Confucianism and Buddhism, especially Chan. This intellectual emancipation manifested itself in the spiritual and daily life of the elites.

Against this background, Buddhism came back onstage and embarked on a path that would lead to its renewal. Since the regulating function of the official ideology had grown shaky, a structural dissolution in the once-stable milieu followed, and people were forced into a process of "role bargaining" to define their roles in a new system. But to rebuild behavioral norms and recover balance in their mental and spiritual worlds required the support from an alternative system of meaning. This gave Buddhism, which had never completely vanished from the horizon despite official restrictions on its influence, a chance to be invoked as a favorable option.[91] This did not mean a total abandonment of Confucian responsibility or a Confucianized Buddhism; instead, as I describe in chapter 5, it tended to mix Confucianism and Buddhism. As a result, a number of elites not only let the tangible political world slip out of their view but also acted as patrons much closer to Buddhism in a fight against the state for more autonomy. This reclamation of its influence among the elites enabled Buddhism to obtain new momentum. The religion's prospects brightened. And now we are ready to examine more concretely how its growth would accelerate toward a Buddhist renewal.

Buddhism in the Ming was institutionalized and legalized by the state on the assumption that it was useful in maintaining good governance and social order. The basic mode of the state-*saṃgha* relationship was thus determined. On the part of the state, control and political exploitation lay at the core of its treatment of Buddhism. On the part of Buddhism, absorbed as a constituent part into a system designed to support the state and society, its development had been highly relevant to major changes of other parts of the system, especially politics, for better or for worse. This top-level design shaped the religiopolitical background for the development of Ming Buddhism and would function as the structural factor behind the late-Ming Buddhist renewal.

Historically, with the enforcement of the policies and measures aimed to weaken the independence of Buddhism, the *saṃgha* was effectively isolated from society, the practice of *jiao* Buddhism was greatly encouraged at the expense of Chan and *jiang* Buddhism, and a rapid downward spiral in the monastic economy occurred beginning in the early Ming under the dual pressure of the rising population of monks and the falling numbers of temples. All this gravely impaired the health of Buddhism institutionally, economically, and intellectually. As a result, after a brief flourishing that reflected the glory left by Yuan Buddhism, Ming Buddhism lost much of its vitality and fell into a stagnant state starting in the early fifteenth century. A vicious circle was hidden in this situation: the more anemic the *saṃgha* was, the more desperately it called for support from the extramural world, and the weaker it was, the more easily it was preyed upon by the latter.

A decisive chance did not surface for Buddhism to change course until the mid-Ming period when drastic changes took place in the political world. Hongwu thoroughly restructured the political framework of the empire, but as the grand secretary and the eunuchs rose unexpectedly within the power structure, the formation of a tripod of power caused a structural problem in the political system. Tensions between the three major political forces built up over time and finally broke out during the Jiajing and Wanli period. All players involved were bruised, the separation between the state and society widened, and state ideology was shaken. This sociopolitical disruption proved beneficial for Buddhism. Concretely, certain events, which I discuss later, had an impact on the development of Buddhism. On a more abstract level, to some extent the sociopolitical disruptions actually promised a better prospect for Buddhism. First, the restrictions the state had imposed on Buddhism loosened. Probably of greater significance, however, as political disillusionment grew, serious challenges arose against Confucianism as the destabilizing state ideology and resulting identity crisis among scholar-officials provoked calls for an alternative value system. In this context,

Buddhism was invited back into private and public life and asked to play a more important role.

With this picture in mind, we are now ready to see how the elites within the *saṃgha* and beyond, including emperors, inner-court women, eunuchs, scholar-officials, and monks brought about and shaped the Buddhist renewal through their actions and interactions. Their activities are understood primarily in connection with contemporary politics, as well as with their unique backgrounds and agendas, which were so significant for the growth of Buddhism.

2

Emperor Jiajing (r. 1522–1566)

A Four-Decade Persecutor

S tanding at the top of the political hierarchy, Ming emperors had
unrivaled authority within the realm to affect Buddhism, for better
or worse. But it is not easy to understand the motivations behind
their handling of the religion and to evaluate their actual influence for a couple
of reasons. They were individuals like all of us but they were also sole sovereigns
with supreme power—these emperors had distinctly different but closely interrelated roles to play. They exerted influence either directly as the highest political leaders, with the assistance of state ideology and the bureaucracy system, to
enforce their orders, or implicitly as influential "opinion leaders" by creating a particular politico-religious environment to encourage their subjects to emulate
them. Furthermore, although the emperors had established roles to play and
behavioral norms to follow, they could also act quite freely because of their personal preferences or interactions with others. All these factors add to the complexity of understanding the parts they played in the development of Buddhism.

The next two chapters are devoted to these top political players, with frequent
asides to explore their personal histories and motivations, to see how they combined to shape the late-Ming Buddhist renewal in certain ways. I begin in this
chapter examining the Jiajing era as the preparatory stage of the renewal. Buddhism was in clear decline when Jiajing came to the throne in 1521,[1] but it
rebounded significantly soon after the emperor died four decades later. A most
puzzling part in this reversal story was that Jiajing, infatuated with Daoism,[2] had
a growing antipathy toward Buddhism and imposed strict restrictions on Buddhism throughout his reign. How could this dramatic reversal have happened?
From where did Buddhism obtain its momentum? What role did Jiajing play in
the process? To answer these questions requires us to examine how the emperor

treated Buddhism and keep alert to those subtle but meaningful changes in it. This is not an easy task. Unlike his Daoist association, which has sparked strong scholarly interest, little attention has been given to Jiajing's relationship with Buddhism, let alone a comprehensive and in-depth study.[3]

This chapter examines Jiajing's persecution of Buddhism on two levels, which, it is hoped, will help in solving the puzzle. It chronicles critically Jiajing's dealings with Buddhism, with particular attention to the link between its changes and those in the political and religious worlds. It also discloses how a repressive politico-religious environment in terms of Buddhism, under Jiajing's influence, immediate or not, was shaped at different levels. This result further deteriorated the milieu where Buddhism existed and, as discussed in subsequent chapters, deepened the crisis that drained the resources available to the religion.

PUTTING BUDDHISM UNDER ATTACK

Jiajing remained hostile to Buddhism over the forty-five years of his reign and consistently put it under attack, but the measures he took to handle Buddhism were complicated and sometimes subtle, showing a clear correlation with contemporary political changes and his personal piety. This connection was especially evident in the first half of his rule when he, as an emperor ascending the throne unusually from the position of a local prince dwelling far from the imperial capital, traversed a long path before reclaiming supreme authority: he first managed to stabilize the court from its shaky foundation and then retrieved power from the hands of the grand secretary.

"How far this could really be from the final years of the Zhengde reign"

In the first few years of his reign, Jiajing was cautious in handling religious affairs, with a clear attempt to shape himself as a Confucian emperor. He imposed a ban on Buddhism and Daoism. In the fourth month of 1521 when declaring his enthronement, for example, Jiajing dismissed all Buddhist and Daoist monastic officials on the charge that they had illegally achieved promotion through Zhengde's personal favor.[4] He also approved in the same year a memorial suggesting that anyone building Buddhist or Daoist temples privately or ordaining

Buddhist or Daoist monks without official permission should be punished, and that the temples involved should be dismantled and their property confiscated.[5] Shortly after, he ordered the dismantling of Baoansi 保安寺 and the removal of Buddhist statues in the Great Nengren monastery 大能仁寺. These acts were intended to show his determination to observe the *Ancestral Instructions* and not tolerate heterodoxy. Given that Jiajing was a new emperor struggling to establish his authority in a totally strange environment, we can expect that this standard stance would minimize possible criticism and help him to win support from the courtiers.

Nevertheless, Jiajing did not completely hide his fondness for Daoism, for which he received criticism. In the fourth month of 1523, Yang Tinghe 楊廷和 (1459–1529, *jinshi* 1478), the senior grand secretary, submitted a memorial warning the emperor not to conduct *zhaijiao* 齋醮 (Daoist services) in the inner court.[6] Yang took aim at eunuchs, claiming they were testing the young emperor with Daoism after having corrupted politics in previous reigns.[7] Thus, the head of the eunuchs should be punished for leading the emperor astray, and the rest should be banished. For the emperor himself, Yang's suggestion was to stop all Daoist services and to take as his top priority "respecting Heaven, imitating the imperial ancestors, cultivating virtue, and protecting one's body" (敬天法祖, 修德保身).[8] In the same vein, a censor compared the emperor's former restrictions on Buddhism and Daoism with his recent belief in Daoism, warning him "how far this could really be from the final years of the Zhengde reign. We secretly worry about Your Majesty" (此其去正德末年復能幾何? 臣等竊爲陛下憂之).[9] In Yang's eyes, the eunuchs neither observed the ancestral regulations nor paid respect to public opinion; instead, they encouraged the performance of Daoist services with the wrong claim that it would prevent calamities and attain blessings. Jiajing was positive in response, expressing appreciation for these admonishments.

His positive attitudes toward officials' warnings during the period, however, were more likely for political causes than out of religious faith. At the time, Jiajing was relying heavily on Yang Tinghe to stabilize the court. Additionally, the censor's rhetoric might have spoken to Jiajing's secret desire to break with the preceding reign and differentiate himself from the notoriousness of the Zhengde emperor. On the other hand, Jiajing's interest in Daoism was not incidental. Jiajing was born in Anlu 安陸 (present-day Zhongxiang 鍾祥, Hubei province), a region where people had maintained for centuries strong enthusiasm for Daoism, particularly the Zhengyi school (formerly the Way of Celestial Masters [*tianshi dao* 天師道]), strongly associated with performing Daoist rituals. Jiajing's father, influenced deeply by the local convention, gave himself the title of *chunyi daoren* 純一道人 (Man of the Way of purity and concentration) and frequently prayed in the Daoist manner in his palaces. Raised in and exposed to such a local and family milieu of Zhengyi Daoism before his arriving in Beijing at the age of fifteen, Jiajing developed a strong devotion to the Zhengyi school, particularly with its theories and practices in search of longevity.[10] So, unsurprisingly, Jiajing's interest in Daoism did not cease. In 1524, he ordered the recompilation of the Daoist canon, which had been newly compiled from 1422 to 1455. In the same year he also summoned Shao Yuanjie 邵元節 (1459–1539), a Daoist expert at performing the Daoist *zhaijiao*, from Jiangxi to Beijing. Before long, convinced by Shao's theories and practices that this master was exactly the person he was searching for, the emperor invited him to reside in the capital, where he would grant him unprecedented favors in the following fifteen years.[11]

"I fear that some people might deride me for partiality"

Following his success in expunging Yang Tinghe's influence from the court around the year 1527, Jiajing greatly enhanced his authority and became assertive in political life. Correspondingly, though still restrained in political life, in the religious realm he started initial discriminatory measures against the Buddhist faith.

In the eighth month of 1527 as his birthday was approaching, the emperor curtailed conventional religious services that were held every year praying for the emperor's longevity. He justified the decision as follows:

> If a ruler desires to live longer, he cannot achieve it through *zhaijiao*. [Instead], he will surely get it if [he] can pay respect to Heaven and stay cautious as to what would hurt his body and impair his life. From now on, on the birthday of an emperor, it is not allowed to hold vegetarian feasts at the three inner-court scripture workshops [*nei jingchang* 內經廠] and the two monasteries outside the palace. As the saying goes, there will be a measure of benefit for every measure saved. Only the offerings in the Chaotian abbey should be preserved so as to model on the sacrifice of spring praying [for the harvest] and that of the autumn repaying [of the gods for their favors]. [In this way,] we can demonstrate [our] intention to glorify the [Confucian] orthodoxy.

> 夫人君欲壽, 非事齋醮能致.果能敬天, 凡戕身伐命事, 一切致謹, 必得長生. 今將內三經廠, 外二寺, 凡遇景命初度, 一應齋事, 悉行禁止. 所謂省一分有一分益. 止存朝天宮一醮, 以仿春祈秋報, 庶見崇正之意.[12]

The inner-court scripture workshops were in charge of the making and circulation of the Buddhist canon (both in Chinese and in Tibetan) and the Daoist canon, respectively.[13] The two monasteries outside the palace may refer to the Great Xinglong monastery 大興隆寺 and the Great Longfu monastery 大隆福寺, two gigantic Buddhist institutions outside the Forbidden City.[14] The Chaotian abbey included several thousand dwellings and was the location of the Daoist registry (daolu si 道錄司).[15] This Daoist temple was originally built in Nanjing. With the moving of the imperial capital from Nanjing to Beijing, a new Chaotian abbey was constructed in Beijing in 1433 and renovated in 1481.

Jiajing's arguments here exhibit a strong Confucian tone that might have met the expectations of his court officials, but another account of the event reveals a different story. According to the new account, Jiajing continued after the preceding citation, "I have wanted to say this for a long time, but I [keep silent] for fear that people might deride me for partiality. I am now telling you [my ministers] about this so as to express my intention to glorify the orthodoxy" (朕此意欲言已久, 恐人譏朕偏向, 特於卿等言之, 庶見崇正之意).[16] The importance of this vivid detail lies in the fact that it demonstrates Jiajing's effort to find a balance between public opinion and his religious preference. He was consciously tailoring himself to match the Confucian expectations people held for an emperor. But no matter how hesitant he was, he did not abandon Daoism. The term "partiality" also suggests that he was comparing Buddhism with Daoism. In this sense, Jiajing's choice of a Daoist temple in this situation also reveals his gradual independence from the influence of court officials.

Such a vacillation typical of a transitional period manifested itself in other events as well. Four months later, the emperor gave full support to a memorial requiring that strict restrictions be placed on Buddhism. In the memorial, Huo Tao 霍韜 (1487–1540, jinshi 1514) asked the emperor to reaffirm twelve established regulations, at least three of which were aimed at Buddhism: (1) drawing up the Zhouzhi ce and circulating it throughout the empire, (2) prohibiting anyone from abandoning their household without official permission, and (3) forbidding any temples from possessing lands of more than sixty mu, with the excess redistributed to commoners.[17] The emperor told Minister of Rites Fang Xianfu 方獻夫 (1485–1544, jinshi 1505),

Huo Tao is surely correct when he recently said that "the flourishing of Buddhism and Daoism is [a sign] of the decline of kingly rule." Now, I order officials to check Buddhist and Daoist monks who have no ordination certifications. From now on, it is not allowed to ordain [monks] and to build Buddhist and Daoist temples privately. Violators will be punished without exception.

昨霍韜言"僧道盛者, 王政之衰也," 所言良是. 今天下[18]僧道無[19] 度牒者, 其令有
司盡為查革. 自今不許開度及私創寺觀, 犯者罪無赦.[20]

It is unmistakable in this account that Buddhist and Daoist nuns were all subject to restrictions. Nonetheless, Daoist nuns were exempted in another account
recording the event, with Buddhist nuns being the only object of prohibition.[21]
This exclusion betrays Jiajing's real intent. In fact, when the decree was reissued
sixteen years later, it comes as no surprise that Buddhist nuns were singled out to
be banned, with Daoist nuns not even mentioned.[22]

By the year 1530, in collaboration with his ministers, Jiajing further deprived
Buddhism of its prestige by targeting Yao Guangxiao 姚廣孝 (1335–1418), a
respected monk and politician of the early Ming. When Emperor Yongle was still
prince of Yan, Yao was not only the first to encourage him to revolt but also made
a great contribution to Yongle's final success in claiming supreme power. Yao was
hence ranked first among all of Yongle's assistants and served as the foremost politician in the Yongle court, but he remained a monk until his death. In his memory, as the highest honor available to any official in imperial China, Yao's statue
was brought into the imperial ancestral temple to receive sacrifices.[23] In the eighth
month of 1530, however, Minister of Rites Li Shi 李時 (1471–1538, *jinshi* 1502),
Grand Secretary Zhang Cong, and other officials submitted a joint memorial
requiring the removal of Yao's statue. Although acknowledging Yao's great service to the Yongle emperor, they insisted that he had obtained sufficient reward
and suggested that his statue be moved to the Great Longxing monastery to accept
the Spring and Autumn sacrifices by the chamberlain for ceremonials (*taichang*
太常). In this way, they concluded that "it would make orderly and solemn the
rites of sacrifice in the imperial ancestral temple and at the same time satisfy the
need for the state to requite the meritorious" (庶宗廟血食之禮秩然有嚴, 而朝廷
報功之意兼盡無遺矣). The Great Longxing monastery was an important Beijing temple where Yao Guangxiao had once taken up residence and where the
Central Buddhist Registry was held. Jiajing approved of this suggestion, ordering the statue to be removed after reporting to the imperial ancestors.[24]

Apparently, this act was intended to debase Buddhism, and an interesting point
hidden in this story was that Jiajing himself facilitated the enforcement of this
plan. Censor Liao Daonan 廖道南 (d. 1547, *jinshi* 1521), who had sided with the
emperor in the Great Rites Controversy, was probably the first to propose the
removal of Yao's statue. In a decree Jiajing first cites Liao's suggestion and then says,

Given that Guangxiao has long shared the sacrifice for his accomplishments that
had been established in the age of my imperial ancestors, probably it should not

change abruptly. But Guangxiao was a Buddhist monk. [If he] is allowed to enjoy the sacrifice with other distinguished ministers on the side of Emperor Dezu and Emperor Taizu,[25] [I] am afraid that it is not reasonable. Although officials of rites say that [we should] observe the established regulations with awe, this is not the [right] way of respecting ancestors.

夫廣孝在我皇祖時建功立事, 配享已久, 或不當遽更. 但廣孝系釋氏之徒, 使同諸功臣並食于德祖太祖之側, 恐猶未安. 禮官雖曰遵畏成典, 實非敬崇祖宗之道.[26]

Such a change was politically sensitive, but in this decree the emperor showed his dexterity in handling complex situations. He turned toward Confucianism by highlighting Yao Guangxiao's status as a Buddhist monk, which made it much easier to enlist support from court officials. Finally, Buddhism was sacrificed in the name of Confucianism.

The 1530 event had political significance as it was also a test of officials' attitudes toward the emperor. Given that Jiajing was then rather active in Daoist affairs, it is highly unlikely that his ministers did not know that in doing so the emperor intended to check Buddhism. Most officials chose to cooperate with the ruler, but one censor was an exception. In a memorial presented the following month, the censor Gao Jin 高金 (dates unknown, *jinshi* 1526) first praised the emperor for canceling the sharing sacrifice of Yao Guangxiao, saying that people saw this action as a sign of the emperor's reverence for the orthodox and repulsion for the heterodox. Then he turned to the *zhenren* 真人 ("genuine person"; i.e., Daoist) Shao Yuanjie, charging that he was falsely favored by the emperor and detrimental to the government. Finally, he presented several ways to punish Shao and promised that in this way "heterodoxy would be expelled and orthodoxy glorified" (異端斥而正道崇). Probably to the censor's surprise, however, the emperor ordered the imperial bodyguard (*jinyiwei* 錦衣衛) to arrest him and investigate who was instigating him behind the scenes. The emperor further ordered the Ministry of Rites to deliberate this matter. In response, Li Shi replied, "The cancellation of Yao's sharing sacrifice in the imperial ancestral temple is to rectify the Sacrificial Corpus, while the use of Yuanjie is to pray for blessings and to exorcise evils. Since they are two different things, [how to deal with them] is at the discretion of Your Majesty" (撤配享者所以正祀典, 而用元節者所以為祈禳. 事既不同, 惟上裁之).[27] Given that the emperor's partiality for Daoism over Buddhism in this event was palpable, Li Shi's buck passing betrayed his cowardice in face of pressure from the ruler. The censor was victimized, and the emperor gained a complete victory. From then on, the emperor no longer veiled his religious preference. Two years later, these ministers even participated in the Daoist service with the emperor.[28]

"Converting Buddhist Monks to Orthodoxy"

As Jiajing obtained a more comfortable position in both his political and religious life after 1530, he began to suppress Buddhism more vehemently. In 1535, the Great Xinglong monastery was destroyed by fire. This monastery, originally called Qingshousi 慶壽寺, was the biggest Beijing monastery and where Yao Guangxiao had lived for years. When learning of this accident, a censor submitted a memorial:

> When Your Majesty ascended the throne, [you] ordered [officials] to destroy Buddhist monasteries inside the capital and outside, to eliminate [unqualified] monks and nuns, and to ask all officials under Heaven to persuade Buddhist monks to return to secular life. [You] are going to get rid of Buddhism gradually so as to bring the world back to the prosperity of the Three Dynasties. This is the mind of Heaven, which has been confirmed by the calamity of the Great Xinglong monastery. That Your Majesty expels Buddhism is in much agreement with the mind of Heaven. [Thus,] Heaven will assist you [with this undertaking] in secret, and Your Majesty will accomplish it without hindrance.

> 皇上禦極, 命京師內外並毀寺宇, 汰尼僧, 申勑天下臣工勸諭僧人還俗, 將漸除之, 以挽回天下於三代之隆. 此天之心也, 即今大興隆寺之災可驗. 陛下之排斥佛教, 深契天心, 天固默相, 陛下順成之耳.[29]

This censor audaciously tailored the memorial to cater to the emperor. In fact, Daoism, which was simply not mentioned in this memorial, had been the target of attack by Jiajing in the early years. This exclusion avoided embarrassing the emperor by exposing discontinuities in his stance. Furthermore, eradicating Buddhism was only something the censor invented to please the emperor. Jiajing's purpose in the former edict was to put Daoism and Buddhism, especially Tibetan Buddhism, under control. Finally, this censor justified the emperor's banishment of Buddhism in the name of Heaven and predicted its success.

The ways in which this censor suggested Buddhism be curbed are aggressive, straightforward, but somewhat naive. First, the Ministry of Rites should reiterate the prohibition against Buddhism and make it known to everybody. Second, Buddhist statues in all temples should be destroyed by water or fire. In this way, the censor asserted, Buddhist monks would scatter automatically because they had nothing to rely on, and that Buddhism would completely disappear in the empire in the following decades. The emperor was not as simpleminded as the censor. He only said that the Great Xinglong monastery would never be rebuilt. Since the Buddhist registry and Yao Guangxiao's spirit tablet had been housed in the monastery before the fire, the Ministry of Rites requested that they both be moved to the Great Longshan monastery and that monks originally affiliated with the monastery be dispersed to other temples. The emperor readily approved the ministry's advice.[30]

By the year 1537, it had become evident that the emperor was suppressing Buddhism in two directions. Positively, he demanded the implementation of decrees regarding converting Buddhist monks to orthodoxy (*huazheng* 化正). Monks were encouraged to return to secular life. Negatively, he forbade the renovation of Buddhist temples in an attempt to let them decay naturally over time. He also prohibited children from being sent into temples and ordained privately; otherwise their parents and neighbors should be punished as accomplices.[31] Obviously, with the command of absolute power at court, Jiajing no longer veiled his attack on Buddhism. In 1543, two more edicts were issued to impose further restrictions on Buddhism.

From a retrospective analysis, it was in the second decade of his reign that Jiajing treated Buddhism in the harshest ways, and the reasons for it may be as much political as religious. First, Jiajing had seriously weakened potential protest against his religious life as he had removed prominent high-ranking officials who dared to defy his orders. Second, after being restrained in the early years of his reign, Jiajing's interest in Daoism became much more intense after 1536.[32] That Buddhism competed and clashed with Daoism was not a new story. As Daoist priests enjoyed a rapid rise in the Jiajing court, it is no coincidence that Buddhism suffered crueler persecutions.

Closing the Ordination Platform

The biggest turning point in Jiajing's religious life came in 1542 in the wake of an assassination attempt from which he narrowly escaped. Shocked, the emperor attributed his survival to the favor of the gods and ordered Daoists to perform rituals at Chaotian abbey for seven days to express his gratitude. More than forty white cranes allegedly flew across the sky during the rituals, which was praised by the courtiers as an auspicious sign of the emperor's merits.[33] After that, Jiajing moved to the secluded Xiyuan, where he occupied himself practicing Daoist rituals for longevity, but he maintained a hold on the court through the proxy of the grand secretary Yan Song 嚴嵩 (1480–1567, *jinshi* 1505). This absence from routine administration alleviated the pressure imposed on Buddhism and, as I describe in chapters 4 and 5, allowed the suppressed enthusiasm for Buddhism to build up.

During this period of more than twenty years, Jiajing tended to forget Buddhism as long as it kept out of social and political trouble, but the restrictions on the religion were still in place, and certain events punctuated the relatively quiet history of Buddhism. In 1546, a censor noticed that monks at Tianningsi 天寧寺 in Beijing were active. He requested the emperor punish the leaders, including a Dharma master called Tong 通, on the charge that they had consumed large amounts of donations and caused social unrest. He also suggested prohibiting gatherings of more than one hundred participants at the preaching of Buddhist teachings. The emperor sanctioned the memorial and arrested the leading monks as proposed. Interestingly, he also targeted patrons by ordering the Ministry of Rites to restrict them.[34] In the remaining years of the Jiajing era, we see that both the *saṃgha* and its patrons were careful to restrain their activities to avoid government interference.

A move with far-reaching consequences was Jiajing's closing of the ordination platform (*jietan* 戒壇). In the ninth month of 1566, upon Jiajing's order, the Guangshan ordination platform 廣善戒壇 at Tianningsi was closed and monks and nuns were no longer allowed to appear there, whether for preaching the Buddhist teachings or receiving the precepts. Ward-inspecting censors (*xuncheng yushi* 巡城禦史) were required to check Buddhist temples inside Beijing and beyond and arrest anyone remaining at the ordination platform and repatriate the monks there to their hometowns.[35] Also, they were ordered to register both the Buddhist temples and monks under their jurisdictions, checking them frequently. An abbot would be punished if a monk belonging to his temple was found to disappear, and the same for anyone claiming to have received the precepts but committing adultery and other unlawful affairs.[36]

This prohibition had as much to do with popular religion as with Buddhism itself, reflecting Jiajing's consistent antipathy toward Buddhism. Early that year, news came that some followers of the White Lotus teaching (*bailian jiao* 白蓮教) had pillaged the Guangshan ordination platform.[37] In response, a censor presented a memorial decrying that "vicious people and bandits have been on the same path since ancient times" (自來妖盜爲一途). He cited several recent rebellions before arriving at the conclusion that they were all instigated by heterodox teachings. Thus, he suggested imposing a ban on itinerant monks lest they delude the masses, which was strongly endorsed by the Ministry of War. Jiajing responded by closing off the Guangshan ordination platform, targeting Buddhism rather than the White Lotus movement.[38] Viewed in a broader context, this was just another case in which Buddhism was implicated with popular religion. The White Lotus teaching was thriving in northern China, but, as Ter Haar aptly points out, "White Lotus" was actually a label that officials could conveniently apply to any folk religion that they conceived as rebellious and thus deserved to be suppressed.[39]

Buddhism had made immense efforts to distinguish itself from the suspicious White Lotus teaching, and the ordination platform was key to maintaining the health of the *saṃgha*. This action by the emperor thus demonstrates at best his indifference to the interests of Buddhism or, at worst, a twist of the knife to punish the religion.

No matter what the reason was, this closure was a far-reaching blow to Buddhism. After Jiajing's death efforts would be repeatedly made to reopen the ordination platform, but they all aroused opposition, and consequently the ban would not be lifted until 1613.[40] During the next fifty years or so, the absence of the ordination platform exacerbated slack discipline within the *saṃgha*.[41] Hanyue Fazang 漢月 法藏 (1573–1635), a famous Linji Chan monk, witnessed the changes and commented around 1624 about how hard Buddhism had been hit by the measure:

Since [the ordination platform] was banned, respectable old masters hid themselves all their lives and declined to preach [the precepts]. From the Wanli era onward, younger generations, who did not receive the precepts, have not observed the rituals performed at the [ordination] platform and the conferment of the precepts. [They all] think that individuals should not confer the precepts privately, and that it is necessary to wait for the state to lift the ban. They have thus shelved the Vinaya texts and focused on the learning of expressing one's feelings. [This] has led younger generations to study lovable and charming stuff and infringe on the precepts publicly. Since [they] do not understand their minds, they even slander the seeking of Buddhist instruction and turn to incorrect teachings. With the wide spread of heretical teachings, authentic Chan Buddhism has become extinct. Since [wrong teachings] have circulated for a long time, vagabonds, who do not belong to the four categories of people, considered that there were no precepts to restrain those leaving their households. [They] thus took the tonsure to cover up their bad activities. Once [they] were no longer endured by the secular world, [they] immediately shaved off their hair by themselves and rushed into the *saṃgha*. For a variety of bad behaviors, because of the lack of those who know the genuine teachings to preside over [the *saṃgha*] and deliver instruction, they simply cannot be gotten rid of. As laypeople have become accustomed to these excesses and willfulness, they no longer view it as unusual even when they watch [monks] eating meat, drinking wine, and committing adultery and no longer criticize them. [These acts] fall beyond the control of secular law, while nobody advocates the application of the Vinaya. If one indeed advocated the [Vinaya], he would be considered to have violated the ban and thus suffer criticism. Secretly, I [Fa]zang am worried that unpredictable things may happen in the future, violating both the Vinaya and the law of the state.

自禁以後, 老師宿德, 終其身焉卷懷不講. 萬曆以來, 後進知識自不受戒, 不見壇
儀授法, 通謂戒不應自授, 須候國家開禁, 遂置律藏於無用之地, 但習展胸臆, 俾
後生晚學, 沿襲輕華, 公行犯戒, 既不知心地, 甚至謗及參禪, 返非正法. 肆行邪
說, 禪宗正法卻滅. 循流既久, 致令四民之外無賴之徒, 以出家無戒防制, 遂以剃
頭為藏垢容惡之府, 稍不為世法所容者, 便自行剃落, 闖入法門. 種種不肖, 既無
真法住持教誡, 則無從驅擯. 浮濫既習, 使白衣見其葷酒淫汙, 亦不為奇特, 無復
譏謙. 官法收攝不到, 佛法無人舉揚, 設或舉揚, 翻以為犯禁而排之 藏窕抱杞憂,
恐將來或有不測, 使佛法與國法兩蔽.[42]

This shocking depravity was part of the negative legacy Jiajing left to Buddhism. In order to bring Buddhism back onto the right track, some leading monks in the Wanli era would thus advocate restoring the precepts.[43]

FORMING A REPRESSIVE ENVIRONMENT
FOR BUDDHISM

As the highest political leader, Jiajing could shape the general surroundings and thus significantly impact Buddhism, but the results are hard to evaluate precisely. For one thing, once conflicts arose between his multiple identities, Jiajing frequently made compromises in order to accommodate competing interests and thus distorted his intended purposes toward Buddhism. For another, people differed vastly in their willingness and capability when obeying Jiajing (as a ruler) or imitating him (as a moral model) and, to compound things further, their own agendas were still at work behind the scenes. I examine two cases to illustrate the depth and complexity of Jiajing's influence in eventually creating a repressive environment, usually not single-handedly but in collaboration with others.

Extended Influence: The Case of Nanjing

Down to local society, where magistrates acted upon their more-or-less accurate idea of official policies and the emperor's orders, Jiajing's anti-Buddhism rhetoric was generally effective in forming an environment unfriendly or even hostile to Buddhism. A case in point was Nanjing, a major Buddhist center in the Jiangnan region for centuries. Although Buddhism in the city recovered some vitality in the early Ming because of Hongwu's assistance, it lost steam again after the

Yongle era, just as happened in other places. The situation became even worse after 1536 when Huo Tao became the minister of rites in Nanjing. Huo felt it necessary to make Nanjing a model city in prohibiting privately built nunneries and forcing nuns to resume secular life. He said,

It has come to my attention that we formerly received an edict that requires Buddhist monks to be transformed to orthodoxy and return to secular life.... [But] officials in charge have never enforced the order, leaving nunneries and chapels untouched as before.... Copper statues in every nunnery should be collected and sent to the Ministry of Works, where they are to be melted for reuse elsewhere, and the numbers of them should be reported to the ministry for future monitoring. As for the utensils used to worship the Buddha and the property donated by diverse families, they are allowed to be distributed among the nuns equally. The [records concerning] the grounds of the nunneries and their lands should all be reported to the ministry, which will call in people to purchase them and give the money to the nuns so as to support their lives after returning to secular life. Nuns under the age of fifty are all required to marry. For those above fifty, if reluctant to marry, they are to be returned to their relatives to live together with them. If people hide nuns and purposely fail to report nunneries, all people of the locality will be arrested and interrogated. The nuns will be allowed to return home within one month. As for the property and the money gained from [the selling of] the grounds [of their nunneries] and monastic lands, they can go to the ministry to take its share.

查先年奉旨, 僧徒化正還俗 . . . 所司全不奉行, 至今庵院如故. . . . 各庵銅像, 該城收送工部銷毀, 以備鑄別用, 具數呈部查考, 其供佛物器, 及各家前後捨施財物, 盡聽尼僧各自均分. 庵院地基田土, 盡數報部, 召人承賣, 取價均給尼僧還俗, 以資養贍. 各尼年五十以下俱令出嫁, 五十以上不願嫁者, 著親屬領回, 相依居住. 敢有容匿尼僧, 漏報庵院, 先將地方人等拿問. 尼僧聽令一月內歸還本家. 該得財物地基田土價銀, 聽赴部告領.[44]

The edict here refers to the one issued by Jiajing in the 1527 campaign. Ten years after its issuing, Huo Tao was not satisfied with the enforcement in a city as significant as Nanjing. With careful arrangements clearly intended to minimize resistance from locals, Huo resolved to carry out the edict. Finally, he identified sixty-eight privately built nunneries, seventy-one nunneries built in the guise of shrines or family temples, and nearly five hundred nuns—two hundred and ten of them under the age of fifty. He closed all the nunneries, with some repurposed as temporary residences for officials or as community schools (*shexue* 社學).

Following Huo's large-scale closing of nunneries, another campaign was advanced in Nanjing two years later. Zhan Ruoshui 湛若水 (1466–1560, *jinshi* 1505), the Nanjing minster of the war, ordered the dismantling of Buddhist temples in the first public announcement he issued:

> Buddhist and Daoist clerics, male and female, eat food without cultivating fields, wear clothes without feeding silkworms, and enjoy leisure without working hard. They are indeed great parasites. [We] have frequently received imperial edicts requiring us to close and dismantle Buddhist temples and return [monks] to secular life. This is because [the emperor] takes pity on them for their not belonging to the four categories of common people, which is harmful to the principles of the universe. . . . [I] have found that there are still many Buddhist temples and nunneries without imperially bestowed name tablets in every district. Is this not because [military] officials of the Warden's Office [*bingma si* 兵馬司] and [civil] officials of the counties fail to fulfill their duties? From now on, officials of the Warden's Office are allowed to report on [existing nunneries] in succession so that they will be closed and dismantled. . . . If these officials continue to disobey orders as before, they will be recorded as incompetent in office.

> 夫僧尼道士, 不耕而食, 不蠶而衣, 不役而逸, 誠為大蠹. 屢奉欽依禁革, 拆毀寺院, 化之還俗, 所以哀矜其不得為人世之四民, 抑且有傷化理也. . . . 訪得各城無敕額庵寺, 尚多隱匿者, 非兵馬及該縣官吏不用命之咎乎? 自今以後, 許兵馬官一一陸續報呈, 以憑拆毀. . . . 兵馬等官有仍前不用命, 即記以為不職.[45]

Unlike Huo Tao, who limited his attack to nunneries, Zhan Ruoshui expanded the target to include all Buddhist temples without imperially bestowed name tablets. Santa chapel 三塔庵, a branch temple of the state-sponsored Tianjiesi 天界寺, was such a case. Privately built in 1397, this chapel had three halls, about twenty rooms, and thirty-nine *mu* of land. In 1519, the chapel sold the land to build fifteen chambers for cremation. In 1538 Huo Tao prohibited the monks there from cremating the dead, but the order was simply ignored. One year later, Zhan Ruoshui arrested the monk in command. He sold its building materials after having dismantled the chapel, confiscated the money for public use, and changed the grounds to a public graveyard for the poor.[46]

Both the high relevance between the ruler's stance and local officials' actions and those officials' flexibility in handling Buddhism deserve attention. The ruler's stance clearly played an exemplary role among local officials for acting against Buddhism. In light of that, it is not coincidental that the two moves by Huo Tao and Zhan Ruoshui, respectively, both occurred in the second decade when the emperor was harshest to Buddhism. Despite similarities in their actions, interestingly, officials could be driven by totally different motives. In the case of Zhan Ruoshui's complying to tighten restrictions on Buddhism, unlike the emperor, who was engrossed in Daoism, Zhan seems to have been driven primarily by an emergent movement seeking to enforce Confucian agendas in local society.[47] Zhan distinguished himself from the emperor by including Daoist clerics in his attacks, but he was not reluctant to follow the emperor to suppress Buddhism. In another case, Xu Shi 徐杖 (1519–1581, *jinshi* 1547), very likely a staunch Confucian who was the military governor of Zhejiang,[48] closed the Wanshou ordination platform 萬壽戒壇 at Zhaoqingsi 昭慶寺 following Jiajing's closure of the Guangshan ordination platform. The Wanshou ordination platform, located in Hangzhou, was a major destination for southern monks to receive the precepts, but Xu Shi did not mind striking another blow to Buddhism by closing it. On the other hand, the flexibility of the local bureaucracy in handling Buddhism liberally or with restraint catches our attention. In Huo Tao's aforementioned case, it may be an exaggeration to say that local officials never enforced the edict, as Huo Tao claimed, but the freedom they enjoyed is still unambiguous. In fact, with his citation of a decree initially issued by the Yongle emperor, Huo Tao himself attested to the freedom: given that the edict remained a dead letter for most of the time after the early fifteenth century, Huo Tao's choosing to bring it back to life reflects more his own agenda than a real necessity.

Returning to the situation in Nanjing, as a result of their iron fists, Huo and Zhan gave a major hit to Buddhism in the city. A later Buddhist account bemoaned that no Buddhist temples in the city had survived the destruction.[49] This sorry state of Nanjing Buddhism would become even worse by the final years of the reign. This constituted the background against which the Great Baoen monastery encountered so many difficulties following Xilin Yongning's funeral. In a broader view, Nanjing was not an exception. Since Jiajing's unambiguous antipathy toward Buddhism endured nearly half a century, it is not surprising that Buddhism suffered in this repressive environment.

Limits on Imperial Influence: The Case of
Huanggu Baomingsi 皇姑保明寺

But there was always a limit for Jiajing as an emperor to exert his influence. This was even the case with the inner court, which was within his direct reach. Thus, no matter how repressive and hostile it was, the environment for Buddhism was still porous, at least for the moment. The ups and downs of a nunnery called Huanggu Baomingsi illustrate this point well.

As part of the first wave of attack against Buddhism, Baomingsi was struck in the twelfth month of 1527 when Fang Xianfu submitted a memorial that accused Buddhist nuns of being harmful to social morals. Originally built in the early Tianshun era (1457–1464), Baomingsi was reportedly associated with the capture of Emperor Ying (r. 1435–1449, 1457–1464) by Mongolian troops in 1449. Since then, it carried a strong imperial flavor and enjoyed patronage from court women. By the time when Jiajing ascended the throne, the nunnery had become the base for female Buddhist adherents in the inner court. Thus it was targeted in Fang's memorial. Confucian values were cited in making the accusation, which was in line with the ongoing Confucianism-colored Great Rites Controversy, which involved both Jiajing and Fang Xianfu.[50] Moreover, Jiajing went against Buddhist nuns because of both their religious faith and their gender. Disagreeing with Fang's advice to preserve Baomingsi to accommodate the affected old nuns, he radically insisted that all the nunneries be destroyed on a clear basis: "Nuns are different from Buddhist and Daoist monks in that they are more harmful to morals. This is also the case with nunneries when compared to Buddhist and Daoist temples" (尼僧與僧道不同, 風俗之壞者甚之, 而尼僧寺與僧寺道觀又不同).[51] Gender discrimination was apparently at work behind the scenes, reflecting a growing difficulty encountering female clerics in an increasingly Confucianized country. Nonetheless, despite the various motives, as scholars have convincingly argued this move against Baomingsi was essentially politically driven in an attempt to weaken if not purge the influence left by the preceding Zhengde court.[52]

But Jiajing did not obtain an outright victory and his goal was compromised. To the emperor's chagrin, it turned out that the nunnery was strongly backed by court women, including his mother, Empress Dowager Zhangsheng 章聖 (d. 1538). He tried to persuade his mother and sister to renounce their fervent devotion to Buddhism but failed. Thus, the filial piety stressed by Confucianism became a hindrance to his goal, leaving the emperor in a dilemma.[53] Under their pressure, Jiajing finally revoked the order to dismantle Baomingsi. He complained to his ministers that the nunnery was really detrimental to good governance. Compromise was the strategy characteristic of Jiajing's actions during this period, and this time it was filial piety in his way. But this setback was not a major failure, for Jiajing nonetheless left significant marks on the nunnery. After escaping the destruction attempt, Baomingsi was clearly reshaped by taking on a more Daoist flavor. For example, Daoist elements came to dominate in the *baojuan* 寶卷 (precious volumes) compiled in the nunnery after that event.[54] Images of Daoist deities were erected close to Buddhist statues to receive worship, and Buddhist nuns residing there were described to have dressed like Daoist nuns, with their hair not shaved off.[55]

The nunnery continued to receive limited support in the remaining years of the Jiajing era, revealing how the generally repressive surroundings were still porous and thus instrumental for Buddhism to survive. Jiajing agreed to preserve Baomingsi until the homeless nuns had died on the condition that no new members would be allowed to be taken in. Afterward, however, this order was simply ignored and support for the nunnery continued. In 1533, for example, a copper bell originally made in 1462 was recast and donated to Baomingsi. Twenty names were engraved on the bell as patrons, with Empress Dowager Zhaosheng 昭聖 (1471–1541), Empress Dowager Zhangsheng, Jiajing's older sister Princess of Yongchun 永淳 (d. 1540), and his wet nurse appearing on the top part. Empress Dowager Zhaosheng's two brothers and their wives also appeared. Short though it is, this name list discloses the immense support the nunnery enjoyed from members of the imperial household and the strong potential of court women in patronizing Buddhism. It is also worth noting that only eight eunuchs were

FIGURE 2.1 A bronze bell for Baomingsi 保明寺, sponsored by Jiajing court women in 1533

Courtesy of Luo Fei

present on the occasion.[56] Given that Ming eunuchs were most generous in supporting Buddhism, it is unusual that they participated in the project collectively sponsored by the most influential court women in only such a negligible degree. Unmistakably, this highly restrained participation suggests that a repressive atmosphere indeed existed within the inner court and effectively limited the resources Buddhism could obtain. On the other hand, given that they were all important eunuchs, their presence also betrays suppressed enthusiasm among the eunuchs for Buddhism, an issue to which I return subsequently.

This was not the only case in which Jiajing restrained suppression of Buddhism; in some cases, Jiajing had to intervene when anti-Buddhist zeal among local officials became so unrestrained as to cause major trouble. As an extension of the 1527 campaign against nuns, for example, six hundred nunneries were reportedly closed in Beijing,[57] to which the emperor signaled his consent with silence. But at the same time he arrested Xu Yiming 徐一鳴 (*jinshi* 1517), the deputy provincial education commissioner (*tixue fushi* 提學副使) in Jiangxi, on the charge of destroying temples and expelling monks under his jurisdiction. For this seemingly contradictory decision, Jiajing explained that it was because Xu had caused a disturbance.[58] Apparently, in the areas beyond the Forbidden City's walls, the emperor had to rein in radical local bureaucrats lest they make trouble by following his religious preference.

That some room was still left for Buddhism to survive during this era can be understood at two levels. Regardless of his personal religious faith, Jiajing as ruler generally acted without violating the "constitutional" *Ancestral Injunctions* and, except for closing the ordination platform, did not change established policies related to Buddhism. In this sense, the early-Ming utilitarian justification of Buddhism provided some protection to the religion. For example, no monks or nuns were killed when several hundred nunneries and temples were closed in Beijing and Nanjing, respectively, a sharp contrast with what happened in the suppression by Emperor Tang Wuzong (r. 840–846) in 845 or that by Zhou Shizong (r. 954–959) in 955.[59] In fact, Jiajing enforced his orders in only a relatively lenient way. He was wise enough to know when to give in, as demonstrated in the case of Baomingsi. Also, it was probably because he believed that the seriously crippled Buddhism no longer warranted violent attack. Although afflicted by a serious financial crisis,[60] for example, he and his ministers did not take as a major concern the monastic economy, which they cited at times only as conventional rhetoric or as an excuse for embezzling monastic property. Obviously, the monastic economy had been weakened by Hongwu's design. On a personal level, despite his engrossment with Daoism, Jiajing was not subject to the control of any religion. Though counterintuitive, this was beneficial to Buddhism. Daoist monks certainly had a hand in Jiajing's suppression of Buddhism, but they were much less aggressive when compared with their counterparts in former persecutions of Buddhism. A good example is the Daoist Tao Zhongwen 陶仲文 (1475–1560), who enjoyed Jiajing's unabated favor for two decades but who nevertheless acted carefully.[61] This caution cannot be completely explained away by citing Tao's personal character; it also reflects the restriction the emperor imposed on Zhengyi Daoism. This control of Daoism, intended or not, helped to prevent Buddhism from further damage. In fact, the rare peace that Buddhism had was in the second half of the reign, when Daoism took absolute predominance over Buddhism at court.

Jiajing's anti-Buddhist stance was unmistakable and consistent, but the severity varied greatly with the extent to which he controlled the court and in relation to the contemporary sociopolitical climate. During the first two decades when he was active in political life, although Jiajing aptly adjusted his stance to Daoism and Buddhism, a general tendency was clear: he was increasingly harsh on Buddhism. The toughest point came around the year 1540, which was followed by a reversal in the wake of his retreat to Xiyuan. After that, his repressive policy remained effective, but the emperor himself scarcely attacked Buddhism so long as it kept out of trouble.

Jiajing's harshness toward Buddhism reflected his religious preference as an individual, but as an emperor he did not alter the established position of the state, with the important exception of closing the ordination platform. Religious piety, political calculation, and perceived cultural and moral ideals all worked behind his antipathy toward Buddhism. Notably, on some occasions his target was not Buddhism in general but particular groups like nuns.

Both as an emperor commanding his subjects to observe his orders and as a role model inviting others to follow voluntarily, Jiajing had a profound effect on the Buddhism of his age. In the inner court, he was successful in holding back enthusiasm for Buddhism among the courtly elites. In local society outside the capital, the effect of his antipathy toward Buddhism was often amplified when local officials, as demonstrated by the Jiangxi and Nanjing cases, modeled themselves on him while maintaining their own agendas. This situation persisted for nearly fifty years and thus fostered an environment generally hostile to Buddhism. Nevertheless, chances still existed for Buddhism to survive as numerous compromises were made to accommodate competing interests. In particular, the repressive milieu Jiajing created became somewhat slack when his life was approaching its end, leaving room for court women and eunuchs to support Buddhism in a modest but determined way. Politics clearly worked as an overarching factor orchestrating a variety of variables and drove things forward as intended.

Viewed in a broader context, Jiajing's anti-Buddhist rhetoric and actions continued the post-Tang practice by the state of weakening if not humiliating Buddhism. How did the sweeping atmosphere Jiajing helped to shape affect the way others handled Buddhism? How did they in turn shape the development of Buddhism collectively? What legacy did the Jiajing era leave to Buddhism in ensuing times? These questions are taken up in the ensuing chapters.

3

Empress Dowager Cisheng (1545–1614)

A Great Patron

Jiajing's smothering repression of Buddhism stopped only in the Longqing reign (1567–1572), which removed taboos on Buddhism.[1] In the following Wanli era when Buddhism experienced a major renewal, the emperor, deeply mired in protracted and divisive court strife, frequently confronted Empress Dowager Cisheng, who happened to be a most devout and generous patron of Buddhism. Thus, this chapter examines how Wanli and Cisheng shaped the growth of Buddhism, though frequently in opposing directions. These two figures were supposed to follow the regulations established according to their roles, with Wanli as emperor representing the institutional restriction to Cisheng as a court woman. A consistent and extensive effort made throughout this chapter is to explore how Cisheng, a woman totally confined to the inner court, could be so powerful and effective a force in opposition to the reigning emperor. Thus, it may be helpful to keep in mind that Cisheng is examined here not only as an individual woman but also as a coordinator who attracted many people around her to form a fluid network. These people varied greatly with time in composition, including eunuchs, court women, scholar-officials, members of the imperial household, and eminent monks. Although never constituting the opposition party in the modern sense of the term, they acted in concert on many occasions, and the influence of the ally extended beyond the political to the religious field.

This chapter first examines the inner-court chaos that caused great fluctuations in the Wanli-Cisheng relationship and the involvement of Buddhism and Daoism in the process. Then it traces Cisheng's patronage of Buddhism over time and across regions, highlighting its connection with court strife. The last section explores the roles and limitations of Cisheng and Wanli, respectively, in the shaping of the politico-religious environment.

COURT STRIFE AND THE INVOLVEMENT OF RELIGIONS

Cisheng is described in her official biography of the *Mingshi* 明史 as a devout Buddhist who, with support from her emperor son, spent enormous amounts of money in building Buddhist temples within and outside Beijing. Her enthusiasm even foiled Zhang Juzheng's attempt to curb her expenditures on Buddhism. But this biography sheds only little light on the tremendous influence she exerted in the political and religious realms at the time, let alone her impact on the Buddhist renewal.[2] In this section, I attempt to raise and answer some basic questions, including the ways in which Cisheng obtained her influence and the response it triggered from others, especially Wanli.

Untypical but Nonetheless a Court Woman: The Life of Cisheng

Cisheng was born in a commoner family in Huo 漷 county, a suburb of Beijing where her ancestors as soldiers had moved from Shanxi province during the Yongle era. Her father was a bricklayer, while nothing is known about her mother. Despite her background, clearly Cisheng received a good education, which very likely contributed to her success in the inner court.[3] A drastic change came after Cisheng was taken into the court of the Prince of Yu 裕, the crown prince and future Longqing emperor. Cisheng was selected only as a court lady in the first place, but unlike most of her fellows, who had to endure a boring life there, she fortunately obtained the opportunity to give birth to the Prince of Yu's first son in 1563, when she was eighteen. Four years later, following the ascendance of the prince to the throne as the Longqing emperor, Cisheng was promoted to honored consort. Cisheng enjoyed Longqing's favor, as evidenced by the birth of two more children in the following few years, but she nonetheless kept on good terms with Empress Chen 陳 (d. 1596), Longqing's formal wife, who had no child but could become Cisheng's major rival in the competition for Longqing's attention. This handling reflected Cisheng's wisdom to maximize her interests through cooperation with others, even rivals, a feature that characterized her life.

With remarkable wisdom, Cisheng contributed greatly to the flourishing of the early Wanli era. Wanli was simply too young when he succeeded to the throne at age ten, which created the possibility that the situation at court could fall into chaos. In reality, however, this period of ten years proved to be the last golden age of the dynasty. Cisheng's strategy was simple: cooperate closely with Zhang Juzheng 張居正 (1525–1582, *jinshi* 1547) and the eunuch Feng Bao 馮保 (d. 1583), with state affairs entrusted to them without reservation. In return for her trust, Zhang Juzheng and Feng Bao served her, Wanli, and the state with full loyalty and stabilized the shaky situation. Their alliance continued smoothly until Zhang Juzheng's death in 1582 thus representing an ideal collaboration of the three major political forces in the Ming.

Notably, very resolute and rational in educating young Wanli, Cisheng formed a basic mode of the mother-son relationship from the very start. On the one hand, by working with Zhang Juzheng and other officials, she created the best possible environment for the young emperor to grow. On the other hand, she was quite strict with him. For example, following Zhang Juzheng's suggestion, before Wanli's marriage she resided in the same palace with the emperor so as to oversee him at all times. She always woke him up in early morning, even in the cold of winter. An extreme case occurred in 1580. One night this young emperor got drunk and asked a eunuch to sing a song. When the eunuch declined, Wanli threatened to kill him but, finally, in jest only cut his hair instead. Cisheng was enraged the next day after receiving a report of the event. She had Wanli kneel and began to scold him. She even summoned Zhang Juzheng and other top officials to the palace, hinting that she was considering replacing Wanli with his younger brother as ruler. This shocked everyone, including Wanli himself. Finally, the event was settled only after the emperor issued an edict expressing regret for his misdeed and drove the eunuchs he favored out of the court.[4] This edict was actually prepared by Zhang Juzheng, and its scathing and humble words allegedly soured the relationship between Wanli and his chief minister and his mother.[5] Nonetheless, it appears that this way of education indeed helped to form a mother-son relationship in favor of Cisheng: Wanli became a son well known for filial piety, and Cisheng established herself as a mother Wanli found very hard to defy directly throughout her life.

Meanwhile, Cisheng carefully avoided abusing power to challenge the established system. Even in the early years when she was most influential, Cisheng consciously refrained from interfering with state affairs too much. On two occasions, for instance, out of her belief in Buddhist nonkilling she requested Zhang Juzheng to put off or temporarily cancel capital punishment, but she gave up immediately when the latter said that the exemptions would go against the law.[6]

Another instance concerns a corruption case in which her father and brother were both convicted. Upon learning of the news, Cisheng did not intervene in the affair on behalf of the two men but instead sent them a box containing the tool used by a bricklayer. This was an embarrassing gift intending to remind them of their base origins. Such caution also applied to her relationship with the adult Wanli. Once Wanli started to rule the country independently after Zhang Juzheng's death, Cisheng remained restrained in her treatment of this emperor son.

Cisheng's caution in exerting power was not only a personal choice; on a deeper level, it had a great deal to do with the institutionalized restrictions that the Ming political structure imposed on court women. In order to preclude political trouble caused by women as seen in previous dynasties, strict surveillance was placed on them by Ming emperors throughout the dynasty. Unsurprisingly Hongwu set the basic tone in dealing with women around him, warning his descendants that "if [court women] receive excessive favor, [they] will be proud and overstep their positions, thereby disordering the proper relationship between superior and inferior. Few dynasties can pass without disaster if their governance is in the hands of court women" (恩寵或過, 則驕恣犯分, 上下失序. 歷代宮闈, 政由內出, 鮮不為禍).[7] He prohibited court women from receiving requests from court officials lest they connive.[8] He also forbade them from burning incense in Buddhist and Daoist temples, performing exorcism, and praying to the stars, probably because all these activities could be used for illegal purposes. For the empress, who functioned as the head of the court women, he placed a rigorous check on her power by stipulating that her influence not extend beyond the inner court.[9] These regulations were all aimed at excluding the empresses and court concubines from state affairs and remained in effect throughout the Ming.[10] In Cisheng's case, too, boundaries were imposed around her political and religious life. Cisheng did break the restrictions at times, but she had to act within set boundaries, which were represented first by Zhang Juzheng and later by her emperor son.

Cisheng lost the privilege she had enjoyed in the first decade in the wake of Wanli's independent rule, and, under the circumstances, she had to find another way to maintain influence. Capable, wise, resolute but sensitive and restrained—these descriptive terms disclose the multiple and sometimes contradictory layers in Cisheng's character. Although never a court woman as ambitious as Empress Wu (r. 690–705) to build her own reign, Cisheng was reluctant to totally give up influence, so she aptly turned her attention from the political to the religious realm. A particularly revealing case is her self-promotion as a bodhisattva called Nine-Lotus Bodhisattva (*jiulian pusa* 九蓮菩薩). In the seventh month of 1586, some red lotus flowers with multiple layers (*chongtai* 重台) were found blossoming in the Cining palace 慈寧宮, where Cisheng was living. Owing to their rare shape and structure, this kind of lotus flower was traditionally seen as a rare auspicious sign in China. Top officials were invited into the palace to view the flowers and composed poems in memory of their presence. A painting titled *Ruilian dashi xiang* 瑞蓮大士像 (Portrait of propitious lotus and Guanyin [i.e., Avalokiteśvara]) was finished the following year and engraved on a stela in Cishousi 慈壽寺, Cisheng's private temple. Two years later, the painting was slightly modified and renamed *Nine-Lotus Bodhisattva*, which, by Cisheng's order, was printed and circulated widely. Interestingly, the painting hints that Cisheng was Guanyin as it was allegedly drawn by replacing the original Guanyin portrait by Wu Daozi 吳道子 (ca. 680–759) with Cisheng's. Probably from then on Cisheng was called Nine-Lotus Bodhisattva.[11] Like most women at the time, Cisheng had strong faith in the bodhisattva Guanyin, whose embroidered portrait she hung up in a palace to venerate. How could a woman as devoted as Cisheng dare to call herself a bodhisattva? After examining Cisheng's Guanyin-related activities, Chün-fang Yü rightly points out that they can all be "seen as interconnected parts of a grand plan. Religious faith and the desire for self-aggrandizement were probably intricately entwined within their motives."[12] In retrospect, however, this self-aggrandizement would not limit itself to the religious realm; in the following succession-issue difficulties it would, at least partly, lead to Cisheng's confrontation with Wanli.

Political Involvement of Buddhism and Daoism

Three women other than Cisheng played a crucial part in Wanli's life and thus in the succession issue. The first was Wanli's empress, surnamed Wang 王, who married him in the second month of 1578. Cautious and smart, Empress Wang (1564–1620) won Cisheng's favor. But she did not obtain the emperor's love and, more important, she did not give birth to a boy, who would have the indisputable right of succeeding to the throne.[13] Lady Wang 王 (1565–1611) was another girl brought into the inner court by the 1578 wedding. Originally a court lady serving Cisheng in the Cining palace, she entered Wanli's life only by accident: One day when the emperor came to the palace, he was suddenly attracted to the girl and thus had an affair with her. Such occurrences were not uncommon for an emperor, but it became a problem when Lady Wang was later found to be pregnant. Wanli's response was to deny the affair when asked by his mother, but the deceit was revealed because of an eye witness.[14] In the eighth month of 1582, Lady Wang gave birth to Zhu Changluo 朱常洛 (r. 1620), Wanli's first son.

Unfortunately for the lady, however, she never obtained Wanli's love, and the connection with the emperor proved a nightmare rather than a blessing.[15] Wanli first declined to treat her in the due manner and then abandoned her to an isolated palace, where even her son was not easily allowed to visit her. In 1611, she died lonely at the age of forty-six.[16] The third woman was Lady Zheng 鄭 (1565–1630), Wanli's favorite. Beautiful, smart, and well educated, Zheng quickly defeated her rivals in the inner court and rose to be a courtesan (妃) in 1582.[17] But she failed in a competition to give birth to Wanli's first son. Two of the three boys she produced lived, among whom Zhu Changxun 朱常洵 (1586–1641) was the oldest.[18] Although Zhu Changxun was only Wanli's third son and three years younger than Zhu Changluo, with his birth Wanli immediately granted Lady Zheng the title of imperial honored consort (*huang guifei* 皇貴妃). Given that the title was inferior in rank only to empress, unambiguously this granting signified Wanli's unusual favor toward Lady Zheng. It sparked wide suspicion that the emperor was planning to replace the empress and establish Zhu Changxun as the crown prince, thereby marking the start of the succession issue. Zheng maintained Wanli's favor throughout his life, although her family were infamous for their misdeeds. A story says that before a Daoist god she had the emperor write down a promise that Zhu Changxun would succeed to the throne.[19] Although this cannot be substantiated by other sources, with the emperor's indulgence Lady Zheng seemed to believe that the replacement was not a long-term pipe dream but a fast-approaching reality. During a period as long as three decades, she acted recklessly and caused a series of critical political crises, in which other court women were also implicated.[20]

The protracted succession issue was punctuated by certain events that, with the involvement of different religious traditions on behalf of different forces, marked the different phases of the ever-changing religious surroundings within the inner court. The first important but oft-ignored period was that between 1590 and 1594. In the first month of 1590, under pressure of his mother and his courtiers, Wanli claimed that he would settle the succession issue in two years. He painted the plan as nonpartisan by claiming that it would reasonably balance reality and what was required by the *Ancestral Instructions*. But in doing so he was actually risking his credentials as the arrangement would soon be put to the test. For the present purposes, it is worth noting that this announcement also stirred the women in the inner court to action and that, as tensions escalated, they all turned to gods for supernatural assistance.

Bold and aggressive, Lady Zheng showed little hesitation in confessing to gods, especially Daoist gods, that in the battle she aimed at replacement, a goal she and the emperor had to deny at court. At her request, Wang Xijue 王錫爵 (1534–1614,

jinshi 1562), the senior grand secretary, composed an inscription that was erected, in the third month of 1592, before the Dongyue temple 東嶽廟 in Beijing. One paragraph of it reads as follows:

> Imperial Honored Lady Zheng and the crown prince who is third in seniority among his brothers, together with royal family members, eunuchs, and others, make hats, clothing, belts, incense, paper money, paper horses, palaces, corridors for the emperor and empress [of Mount Tai], and pay due respect to [other] deities according to their status. This grand ceremony [of prayer] has now been accomplished after the three years from *gengyin* [1590] to *renshen* [1592].

> 皇貴妃鄭氏暨皇三太子集諸宮眷、中官等制帝后冠服、束帶、香幣、紙馬及宮殿
> 廊廡, 神祇咸致禮有差. 自庚寅迄壬辰, 曆三載, 盛典告成.[21]

Several points in the inscription and the stela demand attention. First, it is incredible to see the term *huang san taizi*, literally "the crown prince, third in seniority among his brothers." Only two months before the stela was erected, Wanli had harshly punished some censors and officials who pressured him into settling the succession issue as promised and declined to announce anybody as the crown prince. In such an extremely politically sensitive time, it is hard to believe that a politician as experienced as Wang Xijue could use the term in public. A reasonable surmise is that the term was inserted by Lady Zheng herself when engraving the inscription in stone. The second point concerns the temple itself. It is true that the Dongyue temple involved enjoyed popularity in the capital region and had a huge following,[22] but very likely Lady Zheng's choice of the temple as the place for praying had much to do with the term *dongyue*, "Eastern Marchmount." *Dongyue* refers to Mount Tai, the sacred mountain that had strong political implications in imperial China and received constant offerings from the court.[23] Mount Tai was also closely linked to the crown prince because of its location in eastern China. The east was conceived in traditional China as the direction of the crown prince, and so the latter was called *donggong* 東宮 (eastern palace). The last point concerns a eunuch highlighted in the first line on the back of this stela for his contribution to the project. The fact that this eunuch occupied a high post in the Qianqing palace 乾清宮, where Wanli lived, probably suggests that the emperor was aware of or even acquiesced in the contents of the stela.

This stela, with those worrying points, was not an exception in publicizing Zheng's replacement attempt. Three other stelae have been discovered in recent years, and they record three Daoist sacrifices (*jiao* 醮) at the Sanyang abbey 三陽觀, a Daoist temple on Mount Tai, commissioned by Lady Zheng for Zhu

Changxun.[24] Notably, these religious services were conducted over a period as long as seven years, respectively in the tenth month of 1589, first month of 1594, and ninth month of 1596.[25] The last two stelae are similar in contents except for the eunuch involved. But if compared with the earlier 1589 stela, two changes in them stand out. First, the term *huangzi* 皇子 (prince) used in 1589, which undoubtedly referred to Zhu Changxun, was replaced by *taizi* 太子 (crown prince). Given that the nomination of the crown prince would not be announced by Wanli until the year 1601 and Lady Zheng's deep-seated animosity toward Zhu Changluo, the term *taizi* here must refer to Zhu Changxun. Second, eunuchs from the Qianqing palace got involved in all three events. Their presence was ordered by Lady Zheng in 1589 but, judging from the use of the term *mingzhi* 明旨 (imperial decree),[26] by Emperor Wanli himself in 1594 and 1596. More important, the two eunuchs present in the 1594 stela appeared in the stela of the Dongyue temple as well. Thus, it is not without cause that the term *huang san taizi* appeared in the Dongyue temple stela. Together, these four stelae form clear evidence that Wanli, despite his repeated denial in public, was surely with Lady Zheng when the latter sought the replacement on behalf of her son during the period.

In the face of the seemingly insurmountable threat from Lady Zheng (and Wanli), Empress Wang and Lady Wang (and Zhu Changluo) similarly turned to gods, not Daoist but Buddhist, for survival. Poor though she was in health, Empress Wang died only a few months earlier than Wanli. During the period of more than four decades, as the barrier in the way for Lady Zheng to become empress, she was thus in constant danger. Had she been replaced by Lady Zheng for any reason, Zhu Changxun would have become the crown prince and thus resolved the succession issue legally and naturally. In 1590, for example, the danger facing Empress Wang was already noted by Wang Xijue in a memorial to Wanli: "A rumor has it in the outer court that the empress is sick. This cannot be confirmed or denied. Those with dark personalities have even surmised [the intention] of Your Majesty in an extremely disgraceful way, which causes pain in my heart" (外間宣傳中宮有疾, 嫌疑之間, 甚而以小人極曖昧之心窺皇上, 臣竊痛之).[27] Threatened and without a trustworthy force to rely on, Empress Wang was found to turn to supernatural powers for assistance. In the first month of 1592, she sponsored the printing of the *Guanyin lingke* 觀音靈課 (Efficacious divinations by praying to Guanyin) and revealed her fears in the votive text:[28]

> I, the empress of the Great Ming, frequently recite the *Guanyin lingke* after fasting, bathing, and burning incense . . . [and] the response is usually efficacious. [So I] ordered its carving and printed one hundred copies for distribution. . . .

[I] wish the inner court to be pure and propitious and the whole empire to be peaceful.

大明中宮皇后, 每齋沐焚香, 捧誦《觀音靈課》 . . . 屢屢感應. 遂命鋟梓, 印施百卷 . . . 願宮闈清吉, 海宇萬安.[29]

This sponsorship occurred at a sensitive time. As the deadline the emperor had promised for solving the succession issue was approaching, Empress Wang must have felt upset, fearing that she would be removed from the position or even physically eliminated. At such a dangerous and worrying moment, she turned to divinations and Guanyin, then the most popular Buddhist bodhisattva among women, for relief.

Just as Wanli stood behind Lady Zheng, Cisheng stood by Empress Wang, Lady Wang, and Zhu Changluo as a more reliable support to get them through the crisis. Cisheng was careful and consistent in protecting the two women, frequently through frustrating Lady Zheng's ambitions.[30] For example, Wanli once requested Cisheng to grant Lady Zheng a set of utensils available only to an empress. This was a test that violated the regulations. Cisheng did not turn down the request, but she cleverly degraded the utensils and gave them to other court women as well the next day. Yanfasi 衍法寺, where Empress Wang printed the *Guanyin lingke*, also saw cooperation between the empress and Cisheng in a renovation project taking place from 1591 to 1594.[31] Cisheng's backing of Lady Wang is unmistakable as well. From a stela erected in 1595 we know that Cilongsi 慈隆寺, built by Lady Wang, received its name tablet from Cisheng. This stela is hard to read because of long-term exposure to weathering, but the term *huang zhangzi* 皇長子 (first son of the emperor) appears many times.[32] Apparently, Lady Wang built the temple for the sake of her son and received endorsement from Cisheng. On another occasion, Lady Wang's name appeared together with that of the Princess of Ruian 瑞安, Cisheng's only daughter, at the Dongyue temple. Lady Wang was unable to afford the same sumptuous expenses as Lady Zheng, but she was doing exactly what her rival did.[33]

Cisheng's protection of the weak helped maintain a fragile balance with Wanli, which paradoxically postponed the solution of the succession issue. Although restrained from intervening in politics, Cisheng refused to yield to Wanli in the succession issue that surfaced in the wake of the birth of Zhu Changxun. Aside from the "constitutional" support from the *Ancestral Instructions of the Ming*, Cisheng benefited also from a tradition in the Ming court: despite their political significance, such things as establishing the empress and the crown prince were seen as the family affair of the royal household and thus under the jurisdiction of the empress dowager. As discussed in the Nine-Lotus Bodhisattva case, Cisheng desired to retrieve lost influence in a certain way. In this light, her firm stance in the succession issue was at best meant to maintain the established rule and at worst to create leverage to counter Wanli's challenge. No matter what the reason was, over the course of fighting against the emperor, a loose group took shape surrounding Cisheng and shared an interest in supporting Zhu Changluo (and thus the two women). This group consisted of high-ranking officials, eminent monks, ordinary scholar-officials, and even some eunuchs. In its gradual unfolding, what happened to them would have a tremendous impact on the fate of Buddhism at the time.

Cisheng's head-on confrontation with Wanli over the succession issue soured their relationship and cost her a high price in a most visible way during the decade from 1595 to 1604. In the second month of 1594, Wanli finally allowed Zhu Changluo to receive formal education after a failed scrambling to explain the delay of several years. This halted the crisis starting in 1590,[34] but for Wanli it was a setback that forced him to break a significant promise to his favorite woman. Wanli launched a counterattack before long and exacted from Cisheng a high price for her narrow victory the following decade. In the spring of 1595, Wanli arrested Hanshan Deqing 憨山德清 (1546–1623), the eminent monk Cisheng had taken as her master just a few months earlier and finally exiled him to southern China (I return to this story in chapter 6). At the end of that year Wanli did not attend the annual ceremony celebrating Cisheng's birth, which was his only absence from the event in his mother's life. In the following year, Zhang Cheng 張誠 (fl. 1596), a leading eunuch who was highly respected even by court officials, was demoted and exiled to Nanjing. It is worth noting that the charge against Zhang was that his younger brother was related by marriage to the Earl of Wuqing (*Wuqing bo* 武清伯), Cisheng's brother and thus Wanli's maternal uncle.[35] In 1600 the emperor even granted the Daoist Geng Yilan 耿義蘭 (1509–1606) the title *fujiao zhenren* 扶教真人 (authentic person protecting the teaching) and a copy of the Daoist canon. This was a provocative act toward Cisheng, considering that Geng was the very person who had triggered Deqing's arrest and exile. Sometime before 1601, Cisheng fell seriously ill. The Princess of Rongchang 榮昌 (1582–1647) built a temple to thank the gods after her recovery,[36] but to my knowledge Wanli did nothing for her.

The impasse seems to have continued until 1604. In the tenth month of 1601, in a decisive move Wanli announced Zhu Changluo as the crown prince, thereby paving the path to a reconciliation with his mother. Four months later, Wanli fell ill, and the situation was so acute that he left a last will before losing consciousness. Although mysteriously he recovered the next day, this event provided the emperor with a rare chance to see his real relationship with these women, discovering that it was not Lady Zheng but his mother and Lady Wang who were really concerned about him.[37] Shortly thereafter, Wanli granted the Earl of Wuqing some gifts, signaling an initial thaw in the mother-son relationship.[38] In 1604 Wanli ordered the building of two temples for Cisheng's health,[39] which marked the end of the antagonism with his mother that had lasted more than ten years.

Notably, during this period when the emperor often faced political failure, Wanli changed the battlefield to religion (especially Buddhism) and obtained support from state ideology. Cisheng was immune to direct attack. She greatly benefited from her status as the empress dowager and from the mother-son mode she had established, but this was not the case with Buddhism, which she most favored, and for the loose group surrounding her. Powerful and patient enough, Wanli would hunt them down sooner or later. Interestingly, the emperor who failed in the succession issue largely because of the *Ancestral Instructions* turned to the same source of authority to claim the right for himself when persecuting Buddhism. Consequently, what was impacted by the deteriorated mother-son relationship was not limited to Cisheng herself but spilled over to those related to her. I deal with these events in greater detail in the following chapters.

Afterward, the mother-son relationship remained warm until Cisheng's death in 1614. During this period, Cisheng appeared in public life again, but with a much lower frequency than she had in the first decade. She was even cursed by Lady Zheng, who stooped to black magic while not accepting the failure in the succession issue.[40] And finally, before her death Cisheng managed to force Zhu Changxun out to Henan, where, as a local prince, he was no longer allowed to return to the capital without the emperor's permission.[41] Wanli continued to indulge Lady Zheng but no longer had any interest in changing the crown prince. Thus the mother-son relationship stayed relatively stable. Wanli built several temples for Cisheng's health and supported, in collaboration with Cisheng, Buddhist temples and monks on some occasions.

CISHENG, THE GREATEST PATRON OF BUDDHISM

Records about Cisheng's religious life are generally fragmentary and sometimes even inconsistent, which is understandable given that she was a woman closely confined to the inner court. She had a complex relationship with the bodhisattva Guanyin. Despite Cisheng's boldly shaping herself as the Nine-Lotus Bodhisattva, she (and Wanli) continued to support Putuo Island during the three decades beginning in 1586 and thus helped to refresh the status of the island as the Chinese Mount Potalaka.[42] She had links with Chan masters as well. She read Buddhist sutras, especially the *Lengyan jing* 楞嚴經,[43] but her interest in Buddhism was clearly more in practice than in its abstract theories. She chanted sutras in her palace morning and afternoon. Despite the dominance of Buddhism in Cisheng's religious life, it is also worth noting that she was open to folk religions and Daoism as well, which may well reflect the reality of the contemporary religious world. Although most active in the Wanli era, Cisheng's turning to the supernatural world can be traced back to the preceding Longqing era.[44] She once donated to Baomingsi, the aforementioned nunnery, which had become the base for a sect called Xi dasheng jiao 西大乘教 (western Mahayana sect). This sect, though very likely a kind of Buddhism in Cisheng's eyes, is categorized as a folk religion by modern scholars.[45] What is now called folk religion was actually an integral part of Cisheng's religious life. This is not surprising considering that folk religion had been spreading rapidly in northern China, where Cisheng was raised and grew up, since the middle sixteenth century.[46] Daoism appeared in Cisheng's religious life as well. She was not a Daoist follower, but she tended to resort to Daoism when health problems came up in her or her family members.[47] In order to cure her eye diseases, for example, she turned more to Daoism than Buddhism beginning in 1584.

Nonetheless, Cisheng projected her enthusiasm for Buddhism in a material way, providing us with convenient methods for understanding relatively easily her influence on Buddhism. Based on all fragmentary material I have collected regarding her Buddhist activities, I group them into three fields for the convenience of analysis: financial support of Buddhist temples, distribution of the Buddhist canon, and direct links with monks. Wanli's activities are discussed as well when applicable.

Before engaging in a deeper discussion, let me first explain a few of categories used here and elsewhere throughout this study. By "North China," I refer to the region consisting of Shuntian 順天 and Baoding 保定 prefectures in Beizhili 北直隸 (Northern Metropolitan Region) and Taiyuan 太原 prefecture in Shanxi province.[48] I also single out Beijing in this region as a separate category for comparison. By "Jiangnan" I mean the region consisting of Yingtian 應天, Zhenjiang 鎮江, Changzhou 常州, Suzhou 蘇州, and Songjiang 松江 prefectures in Nanzhili 南直隸 (Southern Metropolitan Region), and Huzhou 湖州, Jiaxing 嘉興, Hangzhou, Shaoxing 紹興, and Ningbo 寧波 prefectures in Zhejiang province.[49] These two regions, each consisting of several prefectures with geographical proximities, are chosen primarily because of their central importance in the world of late-Ming Buddhism. The decision I have made about the scale of these regions and their component parts is somewhat subjective, but it should not be seen as a barrier to achieving my main goal here, which is detecting spatiotemporal changes both within each region and in their relative weights in the Buddhist world. In terms of time, the forty-two years Cisheng spent in the Wanli era are separated into four phases. These stages are roughly equal in length—about ten years. Of importance, since it happened that they were punctuated by major changes in the political world, each corresponds to a significant up or down in the mother-son relationship. To be specific, Cisheng was most influential during the first phase by cooperating with Zhang Juzheng and Feng Bao. In the second stage, her political influence waned substantially, and the mother-son relationship kept worsening over the succession issue. During the following ten years starting in 1595, the relationship remained frozen most of the time and recovered a little only in the last two years following the establishment of the crown prince. In the final phase, Cisheng maintained a warm relationship with Wanli until her death. Dividing the phases in this way, there is the benefit of discovering possible links between the religious life within the inner court and the ever-changing world outside.

Financially, Cisheng patronized at least forty-nine Buddhist temples throughout her life, assisting them with (re)building or renovating projects, erecting Buddha statues, or, in a few cases, purchasing monastic lands. Table 3.1 discloses the spatiotemporal features of her patronage in this respect.

The table shows the distribution of Cisheng's patronage and its fluctuation over time and across space. Geographically, 53 percent of her resources were used in Beijing and 67 percent in North China. In contrast, only 10 percent was invested in the Jiangnan region, which, as shown in chapter 8, was the only region comparable to North China in term of its weight in the contemporary Buddhist world. It is also worth noting that after Wanli 22 (1594) the temples that Cisheng supported in southern China—mainly in Jiangnan and Sichuan—outnumber those in North China, by a ratio of roughly two to one. She did not support any temples in some provinces, like Fujian, Guangdong, and Guizhou. During the first decade, Cisheng's interest was completely in North China, while in the second decade, although Beijing and North China remained the focus of her attention, her patronage began extending southward to Central China and the Jiangnan region. These two phases, put together, account for 71 percent of the monasteries receiving her financial support. After that, a drastic decline in funding occurred.[50] The number of temples Cisheng sponsored in the next ten years dropped by 71 percent from the preceding eleven years, and then there was a slight recovery in the final ten years of her life. Not coincidentally, none of Cisheng's projects during this period was carried out as quickly as before, and some were not completed at all.[51]

Wanli patronized Buddhist temples as well, but in a manner far less extensive and intensive than that of his mother. He supported more than ten Buddhist

TABLE 3.1 The spatiotemporal distribution of Cisheng's
monastery projects

Place			Time (Wanli)				
			1–10	11–22	23–32	33–42	Total
Beizhili	Non–North China						
	North China	Non-Beijing	2	1			3
		Beijing	10	11	2	3	26
Shanxi	North China		2	2			4
	Non–North China						
Henan				2			2
Shandong				2			2
Zhejiang	Non-Jiangnan						
	Jiangnan			1		1	2
South Zhili	Jiangnan				1	2	3
	Non-Jiangnan				1		1
Huguang					1		1
Jiangxi				2			2
Sichuan					1	2	3
Total			14	21	6	8	49

temples, exclusive of those sponsored in his name during the first decade. His independent patronage was first recorded in Wanli 25 (1597) but became more regular only after Wanli 30 (1602). Geographically, he had nearly equal interest in temples in Beijing and those in Jiangnan. Three of the six cases in which Wanli patronized Beijing temples occurred after 1602, for the benefit of his mother, reflecting an improvement in their relationship.

Intellectually, Cisheng and Wanli greatly sped up circulation of the Buddhist canon within the empire. At least four editions of the Buddhist canon were carved and circulated in the Ming dynasty,[52] and the northern canon (Ming beizang 明 北藏), the sequel of which was compiled and carved under Cisheng's direction,[53] is the best in quality. This canon was used exclusively by the imperial family as a gift to temples and monks they favored. Thus, the bestowal of this canon carried a strong imperial flavor, signifying a great honor and an asset for the recipients.

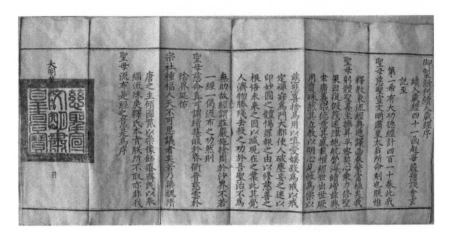

FIGURE 3.1 Wanli's preface in a bestowed Buddhist canon, with Cisheng's seal included

Courtesy of Darui Long

Table 3.2 provides a survey of the bestowed copies of the northern canon during the Wanli period.[54]

Some points in this table deserve further discussion. First, the distribution was highly uneven in time, with four waves of bestowal appearing in Wanli 14–15, 17, 27–28, and 42. More concretely, twelve copies were sent out in the first decade, and the number rose to thirty-three in the next twelve years. In the decade after Wanli 22 (1594), the bestowal of the canon increased slightly, and then dropped by 57 percent in the fourth decade. During the five years between Cisheng's and Wanli's deaths, only three copies were issued. Wanli 14–15 and 27–28 were the two periods seeing the highest numbers of distributed copies, but some years, from Wanli 23 (1595) to Wanli 26 (1598), for instance, saw no canon sent out at all. Geographically, North China received thirty-nine copies while the Jiangnan region obtained thirty-three, together taking up 64 percent of all granted canons. Furthermore, if not considering the fourteen copies whose bestowal years cannot be identified, we can see that in the first twenty-two years North China received 66 percent, while Jiangnan received 29 percent of the given canons. After that, Jiangnan outweighed North China with a ratio of 38 percent to 26 percent. In particular, Beijing's change in these two phases is conspicuous: this city obtained twenty-four copies and was ranked first among all recipient cities, but its percentage in the whole country dropped from 40 in the first half to 8 in the second.

So far, scholars have tended to assume that these canons were all sent out by Cisheng, at most in the name of Wanli, but this assumption is open to question.

TABLE 3.2 The spatiotemporal distribution of the northern canon in the Wanli era

Place		1–10	11–22 — 11–13	14–15	16–22	23–32 — 27	28	29–32	33–42	43–48	Unclear	Total
Beizhili	Non–North China							1		2		3
	North China Non-Beijing — Beijing	9	2	6	1		1	3			2	24
Shanxi	North China	2		3		3	2		2			12
	Non–North China										3	3
Shaanxi				1							1	2
Liaodong			1									1
Henan				1								1
Shandong				1		1		1				3
Zhejiang	Non-Jiangnan			1			1				1	3
	Jiangnan			2		2	2		4		1	11
Nanzhili	Jiangnan	1		4	3	3	1	3	5		2	22
	Non-Jiangnan					1	1		1		1	4

(continued)

TABLE 3.2 The spatiotemporal distribution of the northern canon in the Wanli era *(continued)*

Place	Time (Wanli)										
		11–22			23–32						
	1–10	11–13	14–15	16–22	27	28	29–32	33–42	43–48	Unclear	Total
Fujian				1	1	1			1		4
Huguang			1	1						1	3
Jiangxi		1	1		1		1	1		1	6
Guangdong										1	1
Guangxi							1				1
Sichuan			1		1			1			3
Yunnan			1	1			1				3
Guizhou							1	1			2
Subtotal		4	22	7	13	9	13				
		33			35						
Total	12	33			35			15	3	14	112

The bestowed canons each had the protection edict (*huchi* 護敕), which was required to be carved on a stone stela and erected in the patronized temple. If issued in the same period, these edicts are identical in contents except for the time of bestowal, the name of the receiving temple, and its abbot. I have identified three types of edicts, each revealing the distinctive background for a particular wave of bestowals. Based on these edicts, we know that when fifteen copies of the canon were granted around the year 1586, they were given out following Cisheng's orders,[55] and we know that it was Cisheng who had printed and distributed more than twenty copies at her own expense three years later in 1589.[56] But later, in 1599 and 1600, Wanli himself became the major force behind a wave of bestowals.[57]

The bestowals were as much religious as political, and the shift from Cisheng to Wanli as the driving force in the distribution of Buddhist canons has a strong political implication. Wanli proclaimed in the 1584 edict, "The Buddhist teachings have all been included in the canon. It is beneficial to protect the state and to assist the people by using [the canon] to transform and guide good people and to enlighten the deluded" (佛氏之教, 具在經典.用以化導善類, 覺悟群迷, 于護國佑民, 不為無助).[58] He justified the bestowals in the utilitarian way that Hongwu had also used to accommodate Buddhism in a Confucian-oriented empire. In the 1589 edict, Cisheng said, "May the emperor and the crown prince rule the world under Heaven forever, the ministers be loyal, and children be filial" (祝皇帝皇儲而永禦萬邦, 願臣忠子孝).[59] These wishes were suitable for Cisheng's status as Wanli's mother and the head of the inner court, but she mentioned also the crown prince, who, judging from her consistent stance, must have referred to Zhu Changluo. As such, she actually had implicated Buddhism in the succession issue. Compared with the first two, the 1599 edict has the strongest political flavor. Wanli declared therein:

> With sincerity, I print the Buddhist canon and bestow it on temples in the capital and famous mountains all over the country for worshipping. . . . [I wish] it should make me healthy and peaceful, as well as keep the inner court stable and in order. [I] repent for [my] previous misdeeds and pray for longevity and never-ending blessings. [I wish that] the people should be tranquil, the country be safe, and the world under Heaven be peaceful. [In this way], [people] in the four seas and eight directions will all be converted to the good teaching of compassion [i.e., Buddhism], and I will be able to rule the state in the way of nonaction.

> 朕發誠心, 印造佛《大藏經》, 頒賜在京及天下名山寺院供奉 . . . 保安眇躬康泰, 宮壺肅清, 懺已往愆尤, 祈無疆壽福, 民安國泰, 天下太平. 俾四海八方, 同歸仁慈善教, 朕成恭已無為之治道焉.[60]

The emperor himself represents a key mention in this edict. His top concern was to keep the inner court stable and in order. Given that Wanli was still mired in the succession issue, this edict may reveal how troubled and weary he felt about the strife at court. Interestingly, he expressed regret for his misdeeds as well. Wanli was anything but a fool. He acknowledged mistakes but showed no intention of making changes. Instead, he wished to continue ruling in the so-call way of non-action, which was clearly a Daoist-style euphemism for his lazy administration. According to table 3.2, at least twenty-two copies were bestowed by the emperor in these two years, behind which was likely a practical and urgent need caused by the ongoing wars against Japan in Korea.[61] In fact, at the same time Wanli also sponsored the printing and spread of the Daoist canon, which carried the same "protection edict." Wanli did have a deteriorated relationship with Buddhism during the period, but during such risky times he was desperate for supernatural support, no matter which religion could provide it.

Finally, let us turn to human resources and look at the relationship that Cisheng and Wanli enjoyed with monks. They appointed eminent monks as abbots, honored them with titles and the purple robe, helped them to build or repair temples, and invited them from all over the country to the capital to expound Buddhist teachings.[62] Although Wanli's cases are too few to be analyzed, Cisheng was very active in this regard, for better or for worse.

Table 3.3 reveals some important points regarding Cisheng's links with monks: (1) Two-thirds of the monks who had links to Cisheng were eminent monks. Despite controversies over eminent monk as a category, such a high percentage nonetheless implies her enormous influence on monastic elites. (2) It was in North China, especially Beijing, that most of the connections were established, revealing the fact that Cisheng helped to attract those monks to the capital where she spent her entire life. (3) As time passed, there are signs that Cisheng expanded her networks beyond the capital: of all the places where she was in contact with monks, for example, the percentage from North China dropped from 61 to 50 before and after 1594 (Wanli 22). Interestingly, although the Jiangnan region was the only comparable competitor of North China, it did not gain much from the latter's losses. In fact, during the two phases, Jiangnan's percentage in the entire country slightly decreased from 14 to 13. (4) The post-1594 period deserves particular attention for two reasons. First, five monks suffered persecution. Second, the number of monks once linked with Cisheng dropped significantly when compared with the first half of the era: by 57 percent, from fourteen to six in Beijing, or by 43 percent, from twenty-eight to sixteen in the entire empire.

TABLE 3.3 Cisheng's connection with monks

Place			Time (Wanli) 1–22	23–42	The victimized*	Total
Beizhili	Non–North China					
	North China	Non-Beijing				
		Beijing	14 (11)†	4 (2)	2 (2)	20 (15)
Shanxi	North China		3 (2)	2 (1)		5 (3)
	Non–North China					
Henan			1		1	2
Shandong						
Zhejiang	Non-Jiangnan		1 (1)			1 (1)
	Jiangnan		3 (2)			3 (2)
Nanzhili	Jiangnan		1 (1)	2		3 (1)
	Non-Jiangnan			1 (1)		1 (1)
Fujian			1			1
Huguang			1 (1)	1 (1)		2 (2)
Jiangxi					1	1
Sichuan			2 (2)		1 (1)	3 (3)
Yunnan			1 (1)			1 (1)
Guizhou				1		1
Total			28 (21)	11 (5)	5 (3)	44 (29)

* The monks falling into the category of victimized refers to those who suffered persecution in one way or another.
† The parenthetical numbers are those of the eminent monks whose biographies are taken from the five *Biographies of Eminent Monks* (*Gaoseng zhuan* 高僧傳) of the Ming. For more information on these biographies, see chap. 8, n. 3.

Taking all three fields into account, we can describe Cisheng's activities related to Buddhism as follows: (1) Cisheng's patronage of Buddhism was most active in the first two decades, which was followed by a drastic fall, from roughly 1595 (Wanli 23) to 1602 (Wanli 30). Finally, it gained new momentum in her remaining life but only to a relatively moderate degree. Notably, this curve matches closely the ups and downs in the mother-son relationship. (2) Geographically, Cisheng's patronage was concentrated in Beijing but, as time passed, the circle expanded beyond North China to other regions. (3) Changes in the manner of patronage between the first and second half deserve attention. Cisheng was active in supporting temples financially in the first two decades and bestowed the Buddhist canon in large quantities during the period from 1586 to 1594. It was also during this period that she had the greatest number of contacts with monks. After that, she maintained this contact, although on a decreased scale, but reduced patronage sharply in temple construction and canon distribution, both of which were costly.[63] These changes may reflect a drop in the resources Cisheng could mobilize or command.

The strong relevance implied by the parallel between the changes in Cisheng's patronage of Buddhism and those in the mother-son relationship brings light to the role that Wanli (and court politics) played in shaping the religious milieu in which Buddhism existed and developed. Unlike Jiajing, who was hostile to Buddhism, Wanli held a neutral if not positive attitude toward the religion. Without seeking to play a role in the Buddhist world on his own initiative, Wanli had some positive but simple connections with Buddhism: he helped spread the Buddhist canon, but he established no meaningful connection with any monks. But that was merely one side of the relationship. The involvement of Buddhism in the succession issue can be traced back at least to 1589, the same year when Lady Zheng commissioned the first Daoist service at the Sanyang abbey on Mount Tai. That year, on Cisheng's orders, Hanshan Deqing was busy praying for the crown prince at Cishousi. Also in the year when Cisheng bestowed the seventeen copies of the Buddhist canon at her own cost, she made it clear that it was done largely for the interest of the crown prince.[64] All this sent an unambiguous message to the emperor that the Buddhist *saṃgha* was standing by his mother in support of Zhu Changluo. The mother-son tension over the succession issue escalated over time, and when the relationship reached its lowest point around 1595, Wanli took Buddhism as the target of attack so as not to defy his mother directly. After that, both the discontinuity in Cisheng's lavish patronage of Buddhism and the five cases of persecuting monks followed. In this sense, Wanli arose as an insurmountable force to shape the contemporary Buddhist world, especially in the second half of his reign, but primarily in a negative way.

CISHENG, A MIXED BLESSING

Cisheng's patronage had the potential to alter the contours of Buddhist institutions both because it brought a striking amassing of material resources to favored temples and monks and because, as politico-social capital rarely seen in local society, it could attract more inputs from other social groups. But statistics cannot tell vivid stories about how the influence unfolded step-by-step. Let us first take a close look at Cisheng's religious activities, especially in the early years when she was most active. Cisheng indeed concentrated huge amounts of resources in the capital region and helped to attract many capable monks to the city from all over the country. But as a court woman lacking institutional support, how could she do that so successfully? In addition, what implications did Cisheng's multifarious activities have for the growth of Buddhism, which had suffered a long-term decline and even persecution? I argue that they provided the initial traction for a new start in the early years and continued to function as an important powerhouse in the ensuing period. I test this argument in the following and examine why and how they could work as such.

Making Beijing the Buddhist Center

Cisheng showed a remarkable willingness and ability to secure support for Buddhism from the very start of the Wanli reign. A particularly illustrative case relates to Baomingsi. In the tenth month of 1572, four months after Wanli succeeded to the throne, Cisheng sponsored the casting of a copper bell for the nunnery. This bell, still extant, is engraved with the names of as many as seventeen hundred patrons. Apart from Cisheng herself, it includes names of court women, influential officials, powerful eunuchs like Feng Bao, and large numbers of ordinary people.[65] Notable is that only twenty names were mentioned when the bell for the same nunnery was cast in 1533 under the sponsorship of Empress Dowager Zhangsheng, Jiajing's mother. Such a sharp difference in both the number and the status of the sponsors is stunning. It not only reflects a recent surge in repressed enthusiasm for Buddhism among the inner-court elites but also demonstrates Cisheng's marvelous ability to mobilize resources for the benefit of Buddhism.

This kind of concerted action among the inner-court elites was characteristic of the Buddhist projects in which Cisheng engaged during the early-Wanli years, among which Cisheng's cooperation with eunuchs deserves particular attention.

After having spent more than twenty years in northern China beginning in the Longqing period, Hanshan Deqing was familiar with what happened within the *saṃgha* in Beijing. He composed an account of Cisheng's initial involvement in Buddhism, behind which was a clear cooperation between Cisheng, the eunuchs, and monks.

> Only in the *renshen* year of the Longqing era [1572] did the late emperor start to glorify Buddhism. [He] held a ritual for good fortune at Puansi. The master was responsible for performing the ceremonies and instigated responses [as expected from Heaven] with his sincerity. [Thus he] received immense imperial favor, with vegetarian food and gifts all coming from the inner court. In the first year of our reigning emperor, the Holy Mother of the two palaces commissioned the Buddhist ceremony on a grand scale for the benefit of the country. When holding religious rituals, they chose the master's temple in most cases.

> 隆慶壬申, 先帝始崇佛道, 就普安建吉祥道場. 師主壇筵, 精誠感格, 恩渥頒隆, 齋饋盡從中出. 今上元年, 兩宮聖母為社稷祈福, 大作佛事, 凡建立齋壇, 多就師所.[66]

"The master" here was Gufeng Juechun 古風覺淳 (1511–1581). The two empress dowagers referred to Cisheng and Rensheng 仁聖 (d. 1596), Emperor Longqing's empress. The implication of choosing Puansi cannot be understood without referring to the larger context. Puansi was originally built in the early Ming. When it was repaired in 1561, the project was sponsored by a group of eunuchs who, though limited in number, included all the most powerful figures.[67] It was Xu Jie 徐階 (1503–1583, *jinshi* 1523), the senior grand secretary, who composed the piece commemorating the event. Apparently, the temple enjoyed great support from both the inner and outer courts, which was rarely seen in the Jiajing era. As for Juechun, he was a native of Baoding prefecture, Beizhili, and resided in Puansi for almost twenty years during the Jiajing era. Having formerly studied under Baozang Zicheng 寶藏自成 (1472–1560) at Guangjisi 廣濟寺 in Beijing,[68] Juechun was versed in Buddhist doctrines and had discussed the Tiantai and Huayan teachings with Dharma masters like Yijiang Zhenfeng 一江真灃 (fl. 1560) and Daqian Changrun 大千常潤 (1514–1585). Although later not regarded as an eminent monk, he managed to secure support from eunuchs, who invited him to be the abbot of Puansi after the 1561 project. After Jiajing's death a few years later, it seems that his close relationship with the eunuchs (and thus the inner court) continued, which explains why Longqing chose Puansi as the site at which to perform the rituals. For Cisheng's part, interestingly, she first sponsored the monastery at her own cost. This act served as a gesture to the eunuchs for their cooperation, to which she as a newly installed empress dowager unsurprisingly received an active response. In this way, Puansi became an important place (but of course not the only one) where Cisheng forged a network linking herself with the eunuchs and the monk Juechun, whom they backed. Thus, it is natural that Cisheng (and Rensheng, in this case) chose Puansi to conduct the ceremonies. This connection was further confirmed again a few years later when Juechun's disciple was chosen as Wanli's "substitute monk" (*tiseng* 替僧).[69]

In 1578, in a significant move Cisheng invited Juechun to be the abbot of Cishousi, the temple central to her religious life. This temple, having four halls and about one hundred rooms, was originally the mansion of an influential eunuch. In 1576, with support from the emperor, powerful eunuchs, and other inner-court members, it was turned into a temple intended for prayers for Cisheng's longevity. Cisheng from then on took Cishousi as her private temple, lavishing money on it and frequently holding Buddhist services there. Inviting Juechun to Cishousi was a successful strategy, enabling Cisheng to shift her main attention from Puansi to her own temple while maintaining a close relationship with the eunuchs through the monk. Afterward, with Cishousi as a unique stage, Cisheng indeed maintained a connection with the eunuchs, eminent monks, and even scholar-officials that was at times quite close. Deqing observed the temple's central role in Cisheng's religious life:

> By the time of our Holy Mother, [she] has surpassed [the people of] previous ages in terms of preaching and spreading the Three Jewels. Buddhist temples thus are scattered everywhere like stars and chess pieces; [among them] this temple is the only place adored by all people. Endless Dharma treasure flows out of it, while all virtues flow into it. This temple is the hinge of the Dharma gate and a temporary rest place for "good men." The person heading it holds the cardinal principle of the Great Teaching [i.e., Buddhism] and acts as the model [for people] within the four seas, which is definitely not an insignificant task.

> 至我聖母, 弘通三寶, 超越前代. 琳宮紺宇, 棋布星分. 獨此寺為天下大觀, 無盡法藏, 從此而出; 一切功德, 從此而入. 為法門之樞紐, 知識之蘧蘆. 當其任者, 持大教之綱維, 為四海之觀望, 殊非細事.[70]

Deqing was insightful when he highlighted the importance of Cishousi for the empress dowager's religious life, but his stress on the challenge facing the abbotship needs explanation.

Choosing the abbot for Cishousi was not an easy task because the position was multifunctional in advancing Cisheng's interests. Juechun not only served as its

FIGURE 3.2 Yong'an Wanshou pagoda 永安萬壽塔 at Cishousi 慈壽寺

Photo by Thomas Child (1841–1898)

abbot until his death in 1581 but also passed the position on to his disciple and thence to his "Dharma grandson." These three monks, judging from available material, were at most mediocre in quality and spiritual achievements. This monastery was actually not short of the presence of high-quality monks, including Hanshan Deqing and Zibo Zhenke 紫柏真可 (1543–1604), who had a close connection with Cisheng. Not denying the possibility of accidental reasons, this choice of abbot may well reflect the grim but practical aspect of Cisheng's Buddhist undertakings. For a woman confined to the inner court physically and legally, Cishousi was not merely a temple; it was also the center of a network where Cisheng contacted the outside world in an otherwise illegal or unavailable way. Among all the attributes expected of the abbot, the most important one was not his spiritual achievements but his ability to bridge differing forces on Cisheng's behalf. This role could not be accomplished without the confidence of all the participating forces, a privilege that Juechun and his Dharma descendants had owing largely to their close relationship with the eunuchs that monks like Deqing and Zhenke, who came from Jiangnan, did not possess.

This close cooperation between Cisheng, the eunuchs, and other elites proved effective and powerful, leaving before long a significant impact on the religious landscape. Their lavish patronage, concentrated on Beijing, led to the building or renovation of eight large monasteries in the first six years of the Wanli era, for example.[71] Shen Defu 沈德符 (1578–1642), a famous and largely reliable observer of late-Ming society, reported,

There is a monastery named Haihui south of the capital. . . . It was rebuilt in Wanli 2 [1574] and looks magnificent. In the same year, Cheng'ensi was also constructed at the southwest corner with more splendor. . . . The one outside the city [of Beijing] is called Cishousi. Eight *li* away from the Fucheng gate,[72] its construction was sponsored by Empress Dowager Cisheng. . . . This project started in Wanli 4 [1576] and was finished two years later. A stupa named Yong'an stands directly behind the mountain gate. Beautiful, splendid, and tidy . . . it cost a large amount of money. Cisheng's donation was followed by assistance from other members of the royal family; hence it could be completed so rapidly. . . . By the third month of Wanli 5 [1577], our reigning emperor began to build Wanshousi for himself seven *li* outside the Xizhi gate. . . . Compared with Cishousi, it is even grander. . . . It occupies more than four *qing* [sixty-six acres] of fields and moreover was completed within one year. At that time, Feng Bao, the powerful eunuch who was leading the Directorate of Ceremonial, oversaw the project. He first assisted it with ten thousand taels of [his own] silver, and then, from the Prince of Lu, princesses, and honored consorts to the eunuchs, everyone donated to it. Its luxuriousness is more than several times that of the three biggest monasteries in Jinling [i.e., Nanjing] in color and decoration. In terms of the prosperity of Buddhist monasteries, it is almost comparable to those recorded in the *Luoyang qielan ji*.[73] When I visited Wanshousi again, it happened that the monks there were praying for blessings on the emperor's behalf. Almost one thousand people were chanting Buddhist sutras, and they sounded like the roar of the sea. Among them was the leading monk, who was under twenty years old and looked as beautiful as a pretty woman. All monasteries mentioned above were supported by the emperor and the empress dowager with their surplus. As for gathering labor and collecting construction material, they were all attended to by the powerful eunuchs and generally had nothing to do with civil officials. [Thus], ordinary people could hardly feel to have been bothered by those labor-consuming projects. . . . Previously, Empress Dowager Rensheng also gave out her surplus money to build Renshousi at a place several *li* south of the city.

今京師城南有海會寺者, . . . 今上萬曆二年重修, 已稱鉅麗. 本年又於城之西南隅鼎建承恩寺, 其壯偉又有加焉. . . . 其在城外者曰慈壽寺, 去阜成門八里, 則聖母慈聖皇太后所建 . . . 始於萬曆四年, 凡二歲告成, 入山門即有窣堵坡高入雲表, 名永安塔 . . . 所費甚多. 蓋慈聖既捐帑, 各邸俱助之, 因得速就如此. . . . 至五年之

三月, 今上又自建萬壽寺於西直門外七里.... 視慈壽寺又加麗焉.... 凡占地四頃
有奇, 亦浹歲即成. 時司禮故大璫馮保領其事, 先助萬金. 潞邸及諸公主諸妃嬪,
以至各中貴, 無不捐資. 其藻繪丹艧, 視金陵三大剎不啻倍蓰. 蓋塔廟之極盛, 幾
同《洛陽伽藍記》所載矣. 予再遊萬壽時, 正值寺衲為主上祝釐, 其梵唄者幾千
人, 聲如海潮音. 內主僧年未二十, 美如倩婦.... 以上諸剎, 俱帝后出供奉之羨,
鳩工聚材, 一以大璫蕆之, 有司例不與聞, 民間若不知有大役.... 先是, 萬曆二年,
仁聖太后亦出羨金, 建仁壽寺於城南數里.[74]

Apparently, the patronage from the inner court provided Beijing Buddhism with
fresh momentum. In a material way that was concrete and visible, this concentrated presence of royal patronage sent an unequivocal message of safety and hope
to the Buddhist world. How encouraging it must have been for the *saṃgha* that
had just experienced Jiajing's suppression!

This paragraph reveals as much of Cisheng's strength as of her weakness. It
must have been stunning for her contemporaries to see how quickly Cisheng had
made such huge changes. Subsequent to one after another of those spectacular
projects' being completed, they would have firmly established Cisheng's image as
a most generous and influential patron of Buddhism in the eyes of contemporary
people, within the *saṃgha* and beyond. On the other hand, clearly all the projects allegedly led by Cisheng were a collective effort by inner-court elites, including the young reigning emperor, princes, princesses, eunuchs, and court women.
In other words, her success was contingent upon the cooperation of others. How
could Cisheng coordinate such cooperation on so large a scale? Much of the
answer lies in the freedom and influence she enjoyed during the first decade, a
condition that also implies inherent limits and fragility in her ability to mobilize resources.

Aside from Beijing, Mount Wutai in Shanxi province was also a significant
place attracting much of Cisheng's attention and thus woven into her religious
enterprise during the early Wanli era. It was reported that

[Cisheng] performed Buddhist services on a large scale to pray for posthumous
blessings for the deceased emperor and to protect the reigning emperor. Among
all the famous mountains, she started with Mount Wutai. [She] invited twelve
eminent monks, with Chan master Erhu at Fenglinsi as their leader. The
master . . . was native to Taiyuan, Shanxi. . . . The Holy Mother built Fenglinsi
for him to reside in. After the completion of the temple, considering that Mount
Wutai is one thousand *li* away from the capital and that the mountain itself is
several hundred *li* deep, [she] ordered a reception temple to be built by the
Fangshun bridge of Mancheng county, Baoding subprefecture, and named it
Dacixuanwen. . . . The master is admired within the *saṃgha*, and his reputation

reaches the inner court. . . . People like the eunuch Mr. Xu and others all respect him deeply.

為資先帝, 保聖躬, 大作佛事. 天下名山, 自五臺始. 延高僧十二員, 以鳳林寺二虎禪師為首座. 師 . . . 山西太原人 . . . 聖母為建鳳林寺以居之 寺完, 以臺山去京千里, 山深數百里, 仍就保定府滿城縣方順橋邊, 置接待寺一所, 額名大慈宣文 . . . 師道重方外, 名達內庭 . . . 若供奉徐公 . . . 輩, 皆深重師.[75]

Chan master Erhu refers to Zhuoan Chetian 卓庵徹天 (d. 1577),[76] and Fenglinsi was located in a quiet valley five miles away from the city of Taihuai 臺懷, Shanxi. The eunuch surnamed Xu was Xu Zhengguang 徐正光 (b. 1550), a native of Baoding county, from which Juechun came as well. Cisheng had multiple reasons to establish a close connection with Mount Wutai,[77] a major Buddhist center in northern China acknowledged as the bodhisattva Mañjuśrī's abode since the early eighth century. Given the transportation technology available at the time, Mount Wutai was within an ideal distance from Beijing, enabling Cisheng to project influence to it conveniently without necessarily getting the monks there involved in the political troubles that frequently plagued Beijing.[78] Also, it happened that two local princes in the region shared Cisheng's enthusiasm for Buddhism.[79] Xu Zhengguang played a key role in making Mount Wutai and nearby areas inseparable from Beijing in Cisheng's early religious enterprises, through a network linking Cisheng, the eunuchs, and Buddhist masters.

> [He] built Mingyinsi outside the Chongwen gate of the capital, to which he donated a copy of the Buddhist canon and invited the monk Yongqing as its abbot. He rebuilt Longquansi at the Jiulu ridge at Mount Wutai, Shanxi province. . . . Also [he] rebuilt Fengxiangsi north of Quyang county, Zhending [prefecture]. . . . He has silently assisted the Holy Mother in fulfilling her favor to famous mountains and major monasteries within the realm and publicizes her teachings.
>
> 於都城崇文門外, 建明因寺一區, 印施佛大藏經一部, 延沙門永慶為住持. 於山西五臺舊路嶺, 重修龍泉寺 . . . 又於真定曲陽縣北, 重修鳳祥寺一所 . . . 域內名山大刹, 凡聖母功德所被者, 靡不默助皇猷, 敷揚慈化.[80]

Longquansi and Mingyinsi, though located in the Wutai region and Beijing, respectively, were fraternal temples.[81] Yongqing was Yangya Yongqing 仰崖永慶 (fl. 1590), who was active in the Beijing Buddhist world.[82] Via the network established between temples, it became possible for Cisheng to link herself with monastic and secular elites, inside and outside the capital.

Extended but Structurally Unstable Influence

The inner-court patronage of Buddhism that was led by Cisheng in the early Wanli era was consequential symbolically and in practice. It was of national significance—that is, important to regions other than Beijing as well. On the one hand, with the rapid and extraordinary concentration of material resources, Beijing became a magnet that attracted monks from all directions in search of resources or instruction, thereby playing the role of the educational center that produced new blood by facilitating their maturity and spreading their influence. As shown in table 3.3, most of the links with her were set up in northern China, especially in Beijing, which is understandable given the religious context at the time. During the first decade, the monks known to reside in the temples under Cisheng's patronage were mostly local—that is, from North China. But as time passed, a noticeable shift occurred in the origins of the monks Cisheng entrusted and supported, and evidence shows that those increasingly present were eminent monks, who were from other regions, especially the Jiangnan region and Sichuan. This shift had many implications given that behind local monks were the eunuchs, while behind eminent monks were scholar-officials. The presence of these eminent monks would help to magnify her influence within the *saṃgha*, but what about the eunuchs and the monks they supported?

In parallel with these monks' moving northward, the inner-court influence went southward. The bestowal of the Buddhist canon deserves particular attention in this regard. After arriving at its destination, the canon was symbolic of imperial favor and often sparked strong interest in the favored temple from local society, thereby helping improve its situation. Furthermore, it was a common practice that once bestowed, a canon was always escorted by a few eminent monks to its destination.[83] The presence of these monks, after covering a long distance, facilitated the communication between Buddhist communities in different places. For example, the abovementioned Yangya Yongqing was active primarily in Beijing and Mount Wutai, but, by Cisheng's order, he once sent a copy of the canon to Guoqingsi 國清寺 at Mount Tiantai 天臺 in Zhejiang and another to Huanglongsi 黃龍寺 at Mount Lu 盧山 in Jiangxi. On the way to and back from Guoqingsi, he had interactions with monks in Hangzhou, and the canon itself was visited to pay respects by literati as famous as Feng Mengzhen 馮夢禎 (1548–1605, *jinshi* 1577)—to whom I return in chapter 6.[84] Given that the *saṃgha* in Jiangnan had not yet recovered, the signal and incentive sent by their presence should not be underestimated. In another instance, Ben'an 本安 (dates unknown) delivered a copy of the Buddhist canon to Mount Jizu 雞足 in Yunnan in 1589. Finally, although his fellow monks returned as planned, Ben'an decided to remain at Huayansi 華嚴寺 on the mountain and would stay there until his death. His action proved to have greatly helped the rise of the mountain, located in a frontier area, as a new Buddhist sacred site.[85]

The patronage was by no means a one-way relationship that benefited only Buddhism, however; it was of great assistance to Cisheng as well by enabling her to link with a world that was otherwise inaccessible and to form a network centered on her that worked to extend her influence. The three categories of Cisheng's activities related to Buddhism, although separated from one another primarily for the purpose of analysis, are nonetheless useful in constructing a basic mode in her extension of influence. When patronizing a temple by commissioning it to conduct Buddhist services or bestowing it with the Buddhist canon, Cisheng projected her influence beyond the inner court to local society, where the favored temples were actually turned into a nexus linking her and other groups, especially eminent monks and scholar-officials sympathetic toward Buddhism. As this large-scale patronage and support were conducted wave after wave all over the country, a virtual circle gradually took shape surrounding Cisheng among the huge following she attracted within the saṃgha and beyond. The boundaries of the circle tended to be loose and fluid, but, as time passed, the dominant position that the eunuchs had enjoyed during the first decade gradually weakened as the weight of eminent monks and scholar-officials increased significantly. In the case of Yangya Yongqing, who was trusted and relied upon by Cisheng, for example, he hosted quite a few celebrities while serving as the abbot of Longhuasi 龍華寺, including monks like Hanshan Deqing and Zibo Zhenke and scholar-officials like Feng Mengzhen and Dong Qichang 董其昌 (1555–1536, *jinshi* 1589). In fact, Hanshan Deqing and Zibo Zhenke were also found active at Cishousi and Longquansi, and their closeness with Cisheng can be discerned from some events that took place in 1592. Zhenke arrived at Tanzhesi 潭柘寺 from Mount Wutai on the fifteenth day of the fourth month. Although the temple was in secluded mountains about thirty miles west of Beijing, Cisheng soon dispatched two eunuchs to bring vegetarian food to him. Nearly one month later, on the thirteenth day of the next month, Zhenke discovered at Yunjusi 雲居寺 some Buddha relics that were originally buried by Emperor Sui Wendi (r. 581–604). On the first day of the sixth month, about half a month later, Cisheng had already taken these relics in the inner court to worship.[86] This network established surrounding Cisheng could compensate, at least partly, for the institutional support she did not have. With its assistance, Cisheng could exert influence in an unofficial but still potent way, which actually evaded established restrictions on a court woman.

Unlike what some members may have imagined, however, the status of being the mother of the reigning emperor was never safe enough to guarantee the circle for two reasons. First, the definition of Buddhism as heterodoxy remained throughout the Ming, never being justified even in the first decade. Second, Cisheng's influence in the politico-religious realm had an inherent fragility from the very start and was thus unstable, depending on certain exceptional but onetime advantages she enjoyed, such as the fact that Wanli was underage when ascending the throne, Zhang Juzheng's connivance as a political ally, and Wanli's filial piety. Her backing of Buddhism did not proceed without resistance. For example, in the fourth month of 1574, Cisheng donated three thousand taels of silver intending to build a temple at Zhuozhou 涿州, her birthplace, but it drew criticism from officials, who complained that Buddhism was heterodoxy and that Cisheng had recently built several temples.[87] More important, despite her lavishing patronage on Buddhism, Cisheng had to limit her Buddhist belief to the private sphere and avoid changing relevant policies. A case in point is the Wanshou and Guangshan ordination platforms, which were officially closed before Jiajing's death. When the Longqing emperor fell ill a few years later, eunuchs requested, under the pretext of wishing to pray for him, that the two platforms be reopened. Although approved by the emperor, this suggestion was strongly opposed by a censor, who claimed that ordaining monks at the platform would mix men and women, invite adultery, and harm public morals.[88] As Longqing died soon after, the closing of the two ordination platforms was reaffirmed when Wanli announced his enthronement.[89] In the second month of 1579, Cisheng decided to take steps on behalf of the saṃgha. She told Zhang Juzheng, "Previously when His Majesty had the measles, [I] promised monks that they could perform rituals at the ordination platform to ordain monks. Since the emperor has been healed, [I] should fulfill the pledge" (前因皇上出疹, 曾許僧人于戒壇設法度眾.今聖躬萬安, 宜酬還此願). Measles was surely a serious threat to children in premodern China, and the chance for a child to survive was basically in the hands of fate. Not being convinced, Zhang emphasized that the strict ban that Jiajing had imposed on the ordination platform was to preclude the congregation of monks and the threat of disrupting traditional morality and social order. Citing the fact that a monk had been arrested in the preceding year because of a disturbance he caused by gathering monks, Zhang asked, "How could we start it once again?" Eventually, Cisheng gave up, accepting Zhang's advice to express gratitude to the gods in the imperial ancestral temple for Wanli's recovery.[90] She would not try the same thing again for the rest of her life, probably because she recognized that the policy change was something beyond her reach as a court woman.[91]

In this context, although the existence of the Cisheng-led network helped her to magnify her influence, it also brought about the danger of extending the impact on Buddhism to local society through this network, whereas her influence might otherwise have been confined to the inner court. The problem was that although the network was originally established because of a shared interest in Buddhism, the circle could coordinate and mobilize, to varying degrees, its members to action in political affairs, which they did. As the mother-son tension escalated over the succession issue, some members were implicated in court strife, and a link with Cisheng was no longer a pure blessing because they became targeted in the emperor's counterattack. After 1594, five monks, as shown in table 3.3, suffered persecution owing largely to their connection with Cisheng. I return to these cases in greater detail in chapters 6 and 8. Also, during this period we see a significant drop in Cisheng's support of Buddhism, which reveals the fragility inherent in her patronage. As for how these limitations and her shift in priorities were realized, an answer should be sought not only in the prescriptive regulations but also in the historical context. I explore these problems and their implications for the growth of Buddhism in the following chapters.

In similarly significant but quite different ways, Cisheng and Wanli both shaped the evolution of late-Ming Buddhism, by their direct contribution or by shaping the contemporary politico-religious environment. Given the scope of her contribution, Cisheng was arguably the most generous and influential supporter of Buddhism throughout the Ming. During the early Wanli era, with her timely presence after Jiajing's hostility and her extraordinary success in mobilizing resources, Cisheng made it possible for Buddhism to change course. In particular, she provided the initial momentum to help North China, particularly Beijing, attract a number of established or promising monks from all over the country. Meanwhile, as the temple-based flow of people and resources facilitated communication between different areas, her influence was projected well beyond the capital. In light of that fact, Cisheng's activities and the rise of Beijing had a national significance in the Buddhist world. I return to this issue in chapter 8.

Wanli was not generally hostile toward Buddhism, nor did he alter the stance of the state to Buddhism. But he represented the institutional force that could restrain Cisheng. Cisheng and Wanli took turns leading their relationship and their roles in shaping the religious environment. Cisheng secured great support and patronage from the inner and outer court for Buddhism during the first two decades when she could influence Wanli effectively, but her capability in this regard was unstable and contingent on the political climate, especially her relationship with Wanli. Wanli started turning the tables on Cisheng in the wake of the collapse of the triangle of power. As the mother-son tension over the succession issue eventually evolved into a head-on confrontation, the emperor took punitive measures against Buddhism during a period of ten years or so. Eventually, he weakened her influence to such a degree that she was not able even to protect a few of Buddhist masters she most respected. As I discuss in chapters 5, 6, and 8, Wanli's persecutions changed the landscape of Buddhism significantly and, just like Cisheng's activities in the early years, had an empire-wide significance in the Buddhist world as well.

The timing, extent, and nature of Cisheng's and Wanli's involvement with Buddhism matched changes both in the political climate and in their relationship, revealing how strongly their actions were conditioned by contemporary normal politics, especially court strife, and the underlying structural factor discussed in chapter 1. Wanli and Cisheng were not only subject to the impact of politics like anyone else but also themselves represented politics on many occasions. Cisheng managed to garner large support and patronage for Buddhism during the first two decades owing to certain onetime advantages but then suffered severe restrictions because of a constant exposure to two vulnerabilities: her status as a court woman and Buddhism as heterodoxy. Consequently, she lost the cooperation with Wanli and court elites she had had in the first two decades and could no longer afford such costly projects with the limited resources at her command. To compound things, although Buddhism was officially defined as heterodoxy, Cisheng was in a politically correct stance while fighting against the reigning emperor on the succession issue. Wanli was at times tolerant because of the pressure from the *Ancestral Instructions*, but he attacked Buddhism and Cisheng's allies at other times by citing different entries of the same "constitution" imposing restrictions on Buddhism as heterodoxy.

The nature of the Cisheng-linked network, a double-edged sword, deserves particular attention. Positively, the network coordinated many people siding with Cisheng into a community, and their shared interest in Buddhist doctrine or practice provided strong momentum for the evolution of Buddhism. For Cisheng's part, the network made it possible for her to extend her influence within the *saṃgha* and beyond, even without institutional support. In unfavorable situations, however, the network risked magnifying the harm to Buddhism that might otherwise have been confined to the inner court.

As part of an endeavor to better comprehend how and to what extent Cisheng and Wanli actually affected the ongoing Buddhist renewal, this chapter seems to raise more questions than it has solved. The heart of the problem is that their effects cannot be determined with reference only to them; we have to consider the agency of other historical actors who had a role in accepting Cisheng's and Wanli's policies and practices. For example, how could the ups and downs of the mother-son relationship be so powerful in affecting the evolution of Buddhism? Once the mother-son tension had eased after 1602, why could Cisheng not regain the influence she had had in previous years? Regarding the five cases of persecution, conventional Buddhist historiographers tend to describe the emperor as the only "bad guy" behind the scenes, but was this true? If not, how did other forces join in the process? How did the tragedies affect the life of the monks involved? What signal did these persecutions send out to the *saṃgha*? When did the *saṃgha* get the message and how did it respond? In particular, to what extent did Cisheng's politically orthodox stance affect the attitude of those close to her and thus influence Buddhism? Did a link with Cisheng enhance the chances of a monk's becoming "eminent"? If yes, how? It is not easy to tackle these questions. My attempts to answer them constitute the major body of this study on the emergence and actual evolution of the Buddhist renewal.

4

The Eunuchs

Organized but Not Always Reliable

N o matter how powerful and influential they were, Jiajing, Wanli, and Cisheng were only a tiny part of the agents through which politics exerted influence on Buddhism, and what they really affected was only part of the entire Buddhist world.[1] To better understand the full spectrum of the political impact on Buddhism and the complicated mechanism working behind it, I now turn to other elite groups active in the vast outside world, especially in local society. These elites functioned in two ways. Through "role modeling" or as part of the institutional system, they acted as proxies through which imperial family members actualized their influence, thereby linking the isolated inner court with local society. At the same time, they acted at their discretion, not necessarily in line with the imperial family, and could thus strengthen or compromise the latter's influence on Buddhism. This was because, although overshadowed by the emperors and the state, benefiting from their identity as other than political elites, they could draw resources from other sources as social, economic, and cultural elites. Eventually, with their actions, intra- actions within their circles, and interactions with other social groups, these elite groups contributed greatly to the shaping of the extramural environment, especially the politico-religious context where Buddhism existed and evolved.

The ensuing two chapters bring a sharper focus to the eunuchs and scholar-officials, respectively, the chief force affecting Buddhism in Beijing and Jiangnan. At the core they ask some basic questions: Why did these groups change their attitude toward Buddhism over time? How were they able to do so? Why did they adopt differing stances regarding Buddhism though living in the same politico-religious milieu? What factors affected their stances? In what context and in what way could they adjust their behavior and through what mechanisms? In order to tackle these questions, as with my examination of these top political figures, I approach these groups from both structural and contextual perspectives. Structurally, the parameter for their behavior related to Buddhism was set by the policies and ideology established in the early Ming, which, although somewhat attenuated in the mid and late Ming, would still sometimes trigger an attack when violated. Additionally, a cultural psyche unique to a group and the region where they had long lived would also affect as structural factors their stance concerning Buddhism. Contextually, the interests and agendas of these groups were fluid to some degree while responding to real-life pressure, especially to political pressure, and were frequently in tension because of their distinctive backgrounds. With these variables combined with general modes of action in mind, it is possible to explain their handling of Buddhism in a fuller way.

This chapter is devoted to Ming eunuchs as the major social force affecting Buddhism in Beijing and nearby regions. It begins with an investigation into the motivations for the eunuchs to back Buddhism and the organizational advantages they had to do so. Then it proceeds to trace fluctuations in their relationship with Buddhist institutions over one hundred years, highlighting why and how they constantly adjusted the distance to Buddhism according to the changing political winds. The last section concerns Huguosi 護國寺, a rare case from which we can closely observe how the eunuchs translated their privilege into continuous support to a temple and, of more importance, detect their long-suppressed voice.

THE EUNUCHS IN ACTION

An upsurge emerged among Ming eunuchs to patronize Beijing Buddhism. It was observed that

> from the Liao and Jin dynasties to the Great Yuan dynasty, the capital [i.e., Beijing] did not pass through a single year without building Buddhist monasteries. By the Ming, no chief eunuchs went without building Buddhist temples. [As a result,] Buddhist temples [in this area] are twice as thriving as the Jianzhang [palace], which had tens of thousands of doors.[2] By the middle of the Chenghua era [1465–1487], inside the capital and beyond, there were 639 Buddhist temples bearing imperially bestowed name tablets.

> 都城自遼金以後, 至於大元, 靡歲不建招提. 明則大璫無人不建佛寺, 梵宮之盛, 倍於建章萬戶千門. 成化中, 京城內外勅賜寺觀至六百三十九所.[3]

Another account confirms that all Beijing temples that had been built by this time during the Ming had been supported by eunuchs,[4] and the trend continued until the end of the Zhengde era. Why did these eunuchs lavish excessive support on Beijing Buddhist institutions? Part of the answer may lie in a confession by a contemporary eunuch: "Eunuchs have the deepest belief in [the law of] cause and effect [i.e., the karmic retribution], and a great number of them are fond of Buddhism" (中官最信因果, 好佛者眾).[5] But religious faith alone cannot explain all. How could and did Ming eunuchs mobilize resources? How did they choose which temple would receive sponsorship and adjust if necessary?[6] All these questions invite a deeper investigation.

Spatial Distribution of the Forces of Patronage of Buddhism

Many ways were available to Ming figures for involvement in Buddhist affairs. Those in Beijing, for example, could recommend monastic officials, request a name tablet, or arrange for an exemption of the land tax and corvée for their favored temples. Those outside the capital could financially support Buddhist projects individually or in groups. For other high-profile figures, money was not necessarily the only form of donation—a piece of writing or a drawing could work as well if not better. Among the multiple ways of enacting patronage, sponsoring temple-building projects had the advantage of making visible invested resources like money, time, and human labor. Tracing them as a tangible indicator can thus aid in visualizing the fluctuations in patrons' relationships with Buddhism. This approach suffers the weakness of overlooking the differences in the scale of the investments, but it is nonetheless useful in revealing trends when the collected data is big enough.

Although all existed in the same politico-religious context, the chief force affecting Buddhism varied greatly by region, especially in Beijing and North China and the Jiangnan region. In Beijing, 296 Buddhist temples and chapels are recorded to have been built, rebuilt, or renovated during the Jiajing-Wanli period, among which the major patrons of 166 projects are known to us.[7] Table 4.1 shows the contributions of different social groups to these projects.

"Local people" in the table is a loosely defined category consisting of ordinary local residents, villagers who often organized under something like the "incense associations" (xianghui 香會), and imperial bodyguards (jinyiwei 錦衣衛) and other low-ranking military officials. Most of these people were poorly educated and had only limited incomes. The eunuchs are listed here as a separate category for comparison. The table indicates that the eunuchs were the largest group

TABLE 4.1 Social and temporal analysis of patrons in the Beijing area

Time		Eunuchs	Imperial member	Local people	Monks	Scholar-officials	Total
				Groups			
Jiajing	1–22	12	2	4	2		
	23–45	26	1	3	3		
	Unclear[†]	7		3	3		
*Subtotal**		45 (68)	3 (5)	10 (15)	8 (12)		66 (100)
Longqing*		3 (25)	3 (25)	2 (17)	4 (33)		12 (100)
Wanli	1–22	25	17	7	4	2	
	23–48	10	6	1	11	2	
	Unclear[†]	5					
*Subtotal**		40 (44)	23 (26)	8 (9)	15 (17)	4 (4)	90 (100)
Total*		88 (52)	29 (17)	20 (12)	27 (16)	4 (2)	168 (100)

* Amounts consist of the count of a category and its percentage value.
† "Unclear" includes those who cannot be categorized on the basis of current information.

patronizing temple-building projects in both the Jiajing and Wanli eras. Together with members of the royal household, they supported nearly three-quarters of the building projects.[8] In contrast, local people, monks, and scholar-officials together accounted for about one-quarter. Recent research has also confirmed this principal role that the eunuchs played in patronage. Susan Naquin observes that "local families seem to have been overshadowed by the much richer and more powerful society associated with the imperial court,"[9] and that "eunuch initiative was especially important during the first half of the [Ming] dynasty, but even as the number of new temples gradually decreased, eunuchs continued to play a vital role as patrons."[10] Similarly, Chen Yunü has argued that Ming eunuchs were decisive in the rise and fall of Buddhism in Beijing.[11]

Compared with Beijing, the social composition of patrons in the Jiangnan region and their contributions to Buddhism were totally different. Let us take a close look at Suzhou and Nanjing, two regions typical of Jiangnan in terms of Buddhism. According to the gazetteer of Suzhou prefecture published in 1693, 129 construction projects took place during the Jiajing-Wanli period, among which the major patrons of eight-one cases were identifiable.

TABLE 4.2 Social and temporal analysis of patrons
in Suzhou prefecture

Time		Group				Total
		Imperial member	Local people	Monks	Local officials	
Jiajing	1–22			4		
	23–45			5		
	Unclear[†]		3	5		
Subtotal*			3 (18)	14 (82)		17 (100)
Longqing*			1 (25)	3 (75)		4 (100)
Wanli	1–22	1	8	15		
	23–48		10	22	2	
	Unclear[†]		4	8		
Subtotal*		1 (2)	22 (37)	35 (58)	2 (3)	60 (100)
Total*		1 (1)	26 (32)	52 (64)	2 (3)	81 (100)

Source: Suzhou fuzhi 蘇州府志 (1693; repr., Taipei: Dongfang wenhua gongying she, 1970).

In table 4.2, scholar-officials are included under "local people" rather than dealt with as a separate category as in table 4.1, because, unlike in Beijing, they took the leading role in most cases and made major contributions that the gazetteer authors listed under the category of "Local People." This regional difference in the role of scholar-officials is clarified in chapter 7. Table 4.2 shows that the projects carried out in Suzhou during the Wanli period expanded to more than three times the number of the Jiajing period. As far as the social origins of the patrons is concerned, we see that the eunuchs totally disappeared, and the imperial family members' contribution is negligible, while "local people" contributed toward one in three of the projects. Monks in this area appear to have been much more active than their counterparts in Beijing given that they led nearly two-thirds of the projects. But notably, their share kept falling during this period while that of locals increased over the same time. These two tendencies toward opposite outcomes may reflect the fact that local society was increasingly mobilized to support Buddhism, the significance of which I turn to later. Local officials appear in connection with only two cases, but the timing of their appearance in the second half of the Wanli era is symbolically important, given that they represented a certain degree of public support of Buddhism from local authorities.

A similar picture can be drawn for the building of Nanjing temples. According to He Xiaorong, during the mid-Ming the temple building in the city of Nanjing was attributed mainly to monks and less so to officials and eunuchs, meaning that the *saṃgha* had to rely on itself rather than on secular support. In the late Ming, temple building in Nanjing won new momentum and, as with Suzhou, scholar-officials outweighed monks, and the two groups together constituted the major driving force.[12] From the time of the Xuande emperor (r. 1426–1435) to that of Chenghua (r. 1465–1487), temples, though most privately founded, tended to seek state recognition by requesting a bestowed name tablet, but from then until the Wanli era (probably with the exception of the Zhengde era) the practice decreased significantly and only few desired to do so after that until the Wanli era, implying either a relaxation of the control of the state over the *saṃgha* or increased tension between the *saṃgha* and the state.[13] In spite of differences in the extent to which scholar-officials were active in relation to monks, He's research has confirmed some points elicited from the Suzhou case: "Local people" contributed little to temple-building projects during the Jiajing period, but they rose to be the chief force in the Wanli era. Given that Suzhou and Nanjing were fairly representative of Jiangnan cities in terms of Buddhism, this increased enthusiasm for Buddhism among "local people" may well reflect the general trend in the region.

In the matter of patronizing Buddhism, the two tables reveal not only how different these social groups could be in the same region but also how different the same group could be in different regions. Let us put aside discussing their leading role in a region for the moment and first look at why they could not act in another region. The distance between Beijing and Jiangnan explains the limited role that the eunuchs and royal family members played in Jiangnan, but it is surprising to see that the large number of scholar-officials resident in Beijing had the lowest participation in Buddhism there. Beneath this vastly unbalanced regional distribution, discussed in chapters 6 and 7, which profoundly affected the evolution of late-Ming Buddhism, were some structural factors at work.

In studying the attitude of the Hebei gentry toward Buddhism, Timothy Brook points out that there were vast regional differences between these figures and their counterparts in Jiangnan.

From the editorial comments that compilers inserted into their gazetteers, it is clear that the Hebei gentry liked to complain about the power and influence of religious communities and institutions in their local societies. Their complaint is of a piece with the northern gentry's reputation as a dourly Confucian lot who were unsympathetic to the cultural and political enthusiasms of their southern counterparts. The southern taste for abbatial friendships and monastic patronage so strong among the gentry in the Yangzi River valley was not something most of them shared, except during the heady days of the late Ming. A distrust of such cultural indiscretion dovetailed with their grumpy attitude toward the richly non-Confucian world humming around them, a world in which popular religious practices went on out of their sight and made them anxiously dream of restoring a staunchly Confucian dominion of rites and deference. That dominion may never have existed, but appealing to it was a way of putting themselves between the people and the state, and giving themselves the illusion of having a more secure place in the order of things.[14]

This observation related to the long-entrenched cultural psyche that the northern gentry were more Confucian-oriented and less sympathetic to Buddhism is insightful, and it is applicable to native scholar-officials in Beijing, which was adjacent to Hebei.

The double identity unique to Beijing, both as the imperial capital and as a locality, may have further discouraged scholar-officials from engaging in the Buddhist affairs in the city. First, Beijing had at least one million inhabitants by the 1550s, and of those originally from outside Beijing were a number of successful merchants and scholar-officials. But the handling of local matters there was characterized by the involvement of the court and frequent disruptions caused by activities of the imperial family, both of which clearly or potentially discouraged these immigrants from participation. Susan Naquin, for example, has noted that the government there was even reluctant to share with local elites the responsibility for the distribution of charity. Such a low degree of participation prevented these elites from acting as a group and from forming a clear and solid consciousness of community, which their counterparts managed in the Jiangnan region. Second, active participation in local affairs was a significant and effective way for the elite to amass cultural capital, but in Beijing "the state guarded its organizational authority, earned cultural capital itself, and strengthened political rather than social bonds of obligation and gratitude."[15] Third, in a region as politically sensitive as Beijing, scholar-officials there had a natural tendency to hide their religious preference so as to avoid possible criticism from their rivals. Consequently, any possible enthusiasm among these outsiders for Buddhism was suppressed, diminishing the investment they might otherwise have been inclined to make in Buddhist institutions.[16] In particular, although in their hometowns many of these scholar-officials were known to be patrons of Buddhism, in Beijing they engaged in Buddhist building projects so rarely that I have located only four cases,[17] although they did on occasion write pieces for temples.

Why Did the Eunuchs Patronize Buddhism?

The pivotal importance of the eunuchs for Beijing's temple building during the Jiajing-Wanli period raises some questions, including their motivations and the way in which they mobilized resources. Before addressing these questions in the context of mid- and late-Ming China, let us take a more general look at their modes of behavior, with particular attention to their motivations and organizations.

The eunuchs had long gravitated to Buddhism before the founding of the Ming, and among other reasons the physical element deserves particular attention. Castration not only changed the eunuch's physical form but also created a serious cultural and social stigma in traditional China because the removed part was so closely linked with the identity of being a man and being a son.[18] In studying the veneration centered on the Famensi 法門寺 relic at the Tang court, Eugene Wang has aptly pointed out that

> at the deepest psychological level, eunuchs were probably the social group in medieval China, next to women, who were most sensitive to the issue of body. Their castrated body condemned them to carry a perpetual stigma. The Buddhist view of the individual's body as ephemeral, abominable, and a barricade to enlightenment must have carried a welcome message. The appeal to the eunuchs of the idea of the Dharma Body or True Body, which transcends individual bodies, is self-evident.[19]

Jinhua Chen has also noted the natural sympathy between eunuchs and Buddhist monks derived from their shared physical "mutilation."[20] In addition to passive solace, Buddhism also provided eunuchs with a more positive solution to their mutilated body. In a story, for example, one eunuch in the Northern Qi (550–577) felt ashamed of his body for being mutilated. Inspired by the self-immolation of a prince, he submitted a memorial to the emperor requesting to practice Buddhism in mountains, which was approved. In the mountains, the eunuch recited the *Huayan jing* day and night, made obeisance to the Three Treasures, and repented for his sins. Finally, he declined to eat but only drank water and became very faint after the passage of twenty-one days. "Suddenly, his hair was completely regenerated, and his male body was recovered" (忽感髮鬢盡生, 復丈夫相).[21] In this story, once repeated by figures as authoritative as Fazang 法藏 (643–712), the third patriarch of the Huayan school, Buddhism was clearly associated with the physical repair of eunuchs' castrated bodies.

Faced with multiple, intersecting layers of discrimination as a result of their identity, eunuchs in imperial China would also find especially attractive the promise in Buddhism of salvation without distinction, and the Buddhist clergy at times consciously worked to affirm that promise. A relevant case, though not so early, can be seen in Cisheng's bestowing of a scroll painting to the eunuch Jiang Dayin 姜大隱 (d. 1590 or later). In a piece Deqing wrote in memory of that event, he says,

> I once read [a story from] the *Biographies of Qingliang Mountain*. When Wuzhu entered the Jingang (Skt. *vajra*) cave and talked to Mañjuśrī, he saw a multitude of bodhisattvas descending from the sky. [Wuzhu] thus asked, "From where are these dragons and elephants coming?" Mañjuśrī replied, "They are tens of thousands of my adherents in this cave. They are returning [home] after having accomplished their missions of benefiting the sentient beings." [Wuzhu] asked again, "Why are they not known by people in the world?" Mañjuśrī responded, "They may manifest as emperors, empresses, imperial courtesans, and empress dowagers, or as officials, laypeople, eunuchs, wealthy householders, monks, and nuns. [They] change in accordance with the group they belong to, and these changes are endless. [So,] how could you discuss them according to the trace they leave?" . . . You should take [this scroll] as proof of your benefiting sentient beings. When [you] return to the [Jingang] cave in the future, [I] believe that Mañjuśrī will deem it as evidence matching [your mission].

> 余嘗讀《清涼傳》, 至無著入金剛窟, 與文殊茶話間, 見諸大士自雲中冉冉而下. 因問, "此眾龍象何自而來?" 殊曰: "此吾窟中一萬眷屬, 各於十方世界利生, 緣畢而歸也." 又問: "世何不知?" 殊曰: "或現帝、后、妃女、國太母身, 或現宰官、居士、黃門、長者、比丘、僧尼。隨類皆入, 化化無窮, 安可以迹較之耶?" . . . 公當持此以為利生之券. 他日歸來窟中, 想文殊見之必合符驗也.[22]

Qingliang refers to Mount Wutai, and Wuzhu to Chan master Wuzhu Wenxi 無著文喜 (821–900), whose miraculous meeting with Mañjuśrī was a fabulous story recorded in the *Guang Qingliang zhuan* 廣清涼傳. The story tells that Master Wuzhu once saw several high-ranking officials entering the cave. When inquiring about who they were, he was informed that "they are [among] ten thousand bodhisattvas who have propagated the Buddhist teachings everywhere in place of Mañjuśrī, and who are now returning to the cave after resigning the office they have served for a long time" (是一萬菩薩, [代?]帝揚化諸處. 任官歲久職滿, 却歸此窟).[23] In the original version of the story these bodhisattvas were only ambiguously mentioned to be officials in the secular world, but, in sharp contrast, Deqing added a list detailing the statuses and posts they had once held, with eunuchs included. Deqing did nothing wrong when viewed from the basic

Buddhist tenet of eliminating distinction. But in this way, with the authority borrowed from the established text, Deqing's reinterpretation gave eunuchs an unmistakable promise that they would become bodhisattvas, no different from groups as honorable as emperors and empress dowagers. Eunuchs would readily receive this promising prospect and display their enthusiasm for Buddhism accordingly.

During the Ming, as the serving staff in the inner court, eunuchs took charge of Buddhist affairs there as part of their responsibilities. They ran the inner scripture workshops, where the Chinese and Tibetan Buddhist canons were printed for bestowal. Scores of them were trained to conduct Buddhist services on such occasions as the emperor's birthday, the new year festival, and the fifteenth of the seventh lunar month.[24] They were also placed in state-sponsored temples, like the Great Huguo Longshan monastery 大護國隆善寺, Dongyue temple 東嶽廟, Shefansi 捨飯寺, and Lazhusi 蠟燭寺.[25] In some cases, by order or the request of members of the royal house, eunuchs also served as their personal agents to assist in Buddhism-related activities.

But a much more powerful motivation that drove Ming eunuchs to support Buddhism was the multiple functions Buddhism could serve for their personal interests, both in life and posthumously.[26] Evidence abounds about the intimate relationship between eunuchs and monks. Many eunuchs took shelter in temples before entering the inner court, and at the same time some monks gained eunuchs' assistance when leaving the household. In some extreme cases, eunuchs even became monks, or vice versa. With regard to their huge expenditures on temple-building projects, one critic revealed that eunuchs were motivated by "nothing more than [receiving] worship [at Buddhist temples] after their deaths and [garnering] the field of merit at present" (不過自為身後香火供, 眼前福田之計).[27] These points are echoed in another source:

> [Since you eunuchs] have already enjoyed wealth and honor,
> what you worry about is nothing in life but that after death.
> [Your] high grave and great well are comparable to those of princes and
>   dukes,
> and then [you] intend to leave fame in history by making use of
>   Buddhist temples.
> Mountains as high as nine *ren*[28] are removed so that they look as flat as
>   a mat,
> and halls and pavilions [built on them] are towering, standing in
>   beautiful forests, and reflecting [the shadow of] clouds and
>   the sun.

> After having requested the emperor to bestow the name tablets [on the temple],
>
> [you] further request the protection edict for the monks [there].

人間富貴爾所有, 不慮生前慮生後.
高墳大井擬王侯, 假藉佛宮垂不朽.
鑿山九仞平如席, 殿閣翠飛照雲日.
已請至尊親賜額, 更為諸僧求護救.[29]

Obviously, these projects were not only religious; the eunuchs also used the patronage of Buddhist institutions to their advantage.

While alive, eunuchs, especially high-ranking ones, could expect to enjoy a comfortable time and even obtain material benefits in the temples they sponsored. Eunuchs followed a standard process when sponsoring a temple, first looking for a reliable monk to take up the abbacy and then securing the imperially sanctioned name tablet for the temple.[30] In this way, the temple was legalized, and the abbot was officially recognized. But at the same time the legal procedure made the temple practically private, meaning that since then the temple became the eunuch's personal estate and the abbot the agent running the temple on his behalf. Thus, it was reported that many high-ranking eunuchs treated the temples they sponsored as a resort. They not only frequently visited them for breaks but also used them for meeting court officials, which would otherwise have been under close surveillance, if not totally prohibited. In addition, economic causes worked behind the scenes. As part of justifying a patronized temple, eunuchs usually arranged for a "protection edict" for it. This edict not only helped to protect the temple from intervention or encroachment by local authorities or powerful families but also always came with an exemption of monastic lands from corvée and surplus tax. This privilege strongly tempted eunuchs to maximize monastic landholdings, many of which were occupied illegally. With a temple built on them, the occupation could be conveniently legalized by the accompanying protection edict. In an investigation conducted in 1530, for example, 419 imperial estates (皇莊) and monastic lands, amounting to 44,125 *qing*, were found in six prefectures in the capital region.[31] Although no further information is available, very likely monastic lands made up a sizable proportion.

After their death, eunuchs could depend on the patronized temples for posthumous benefits, which proved particularly important for this group, who lacked children or other institutional support to rely on. Many temples were found in the early Qing to be built close to the Beijing city wall, and they were actually eunuchs' graveyards where the abbots were tasked with praying for the eunuchs' posthumous blessings and maintaining their graves.[32] The life of Ming eunuchs, especially the working of their relationships with monks, can be illustrated by a memoir left by Xin Xiuming 信修明 (d. 1950 or later), who once served as the abbot of Huguosi 護國寺, one of the two Beijing temples used exclusively for old eunuchs since the Ming. According to the memoir, eunuchs had two choices when turning old. One was to become a Buddhist or Daoist monk, and the other was to join a *yihui* 義會 (charitable association). Eunuchs with religious beliefs preferred the former, having their names registered in a temple as monks so as to collect money and resources for their retired life, while the rest tended to gather in the form of *yihui* to support temples. In order to join a *yihui*, a eunuch had to pay twenty taels of silver as the membership fee after submitting a reference letter from an existing member. Three years later, he was allowed to reside and take meals in the temple. More important, the temple would take care of his funeral when he died and, after that, offer sacrifices to him on such days as the Spring Festival and Qingming Festival.[33] The *yihui* addressed the eunuchs' major concerns after they turned old and died and thus persisted among eunuchs until the fall of the Qing.[34]

A Group Organized to Support Buddhism

Ming eunuchs showed a clear tendency to back temple projects in a joint and communal way, which was heavily based on the existing organizations among them and accompanying ethics. In 1538, for example, Gao Zhong 高忠 (1496–1564), then a eunuch in the Directorate of Palace Eunuchs (*neiguan jian* 內官監), gathered his fellow eunuchs to set up a *yihui*. They purchased a graveyard from the Chen and Fan families in Daxing county, Beijing, at two hundred seventy taels of silver. Then they built on the land a chapel called Donglin 東林, where they arranged for a monk to manage it. Three years later, they bought eighty-seven and half *mu* of land for the temple.[35] It is worth noting that a society like the *yihui* among eunuchs was an organized gathering according to the established system rather than a random and casual one. Ming eunuchs were each affiliated with one of twenty-four yamens 衙門 (bureaus).[36] As time passed, a natural feeling of belonging grew within each yamen. A practice constructive in establishing a consciousness of membership was that eunuchs from the same yamen worshipped their guardian gods in a fixed temple—seventeen of them can still be identified[37]— and temples like Guangjisi 廣濟寺 and Shoumingsi 壽明寺 were backed by the same yamen generation after generation. Thus, it would be natural to discover that eunuchs in the same yamen were acting together when sponsoring temple projects.

A more active and powerful mechanism that worked to lead eunuchs into collective activities was a pseudofamily relationship among them. After being taken into the inner court, a novice eunuch would be immediately assigned to a powerful eunuch as a *mingxia* 名下 (subordinate) and thus linked to the existing network.[38] Interestingly, this network was structured much in imitation of the lineage system of ordinary people. A resource says,

> The *benguan* [superintendent] was similar to the grand examiner in the metropolitan examination, the old uncle of *zhaoguan* [looking after] to the assistant examiner, *tongguan* to the pupils of the same master. As for the relationship of the *benguan* with his *mingxia* and that of the *zhaoguan* with his *zhizi* [nephews], they were like that of a grand examiner with his pupils or that of father and son.

> 本管者是甲科之大主考, 照管老叔者視房考, 同官者視同門. 本管之於名下, 照管之於姪子, 猶座師之視門生, 亦若父子焉.[39]

As in the lineage system, the vertical link between a *benguan* and his *mingxia* was much stronger than the horizontal one between *tongguan*s. Compared with colleagues who were assigned in the same yamen only randomly, eunuchs organized in such a pseudofamilial way were much closer to one another, making it possible to form a faction centered on an influential *benguan*. More often than not, members of the same faction acted in concert with one another, and there was a high degree of uniformity in their activities, sacred or secular. For example, they could organize a *nianfo hui* 念佛會 (Society for reciting the Buddha's name) on a striking scale.[40] In 1581 when Qianfosi 千佛寺 was rebuilt, as many as 652 eunuchs gathered to recite the Buddha's name.[41]

Weak though the strength of most eunuchs was, their separate strength could be maximized once orchestrated on the basis of the existing system. This was true once it was used in the religious field. In order to start an initiative like building a temple or purchasing a graveyard, a common practice was that a *benguan* first proposed the plan, which was usually justified by an argument for the public interest of the faction, and then sought coordination from his *mingxia* or *tongguan*, often in the form of the *yihui*. In addition, cooperation that crossed the boundaries between different yamens was also possible, for eunuchs belonging to one faction could be assigned to other yamens.

FIGURE 4.1 A *yihui* 義會 stela recording land assets, erected by eunuchs in 1548

Courtesy of Luo Fei

Aside from mobilization from inside through their interactions, eunuchs also drew resources from local society owing to a new status we may call semilocal elites in the capital region.[42] The numbers of eunuchs were limited in the early Ming, with most coming from captives or felons, but the population of this group increased steadily through the dynasty. Starting in the Jingtai era (1450–1456), lured by the privileges eunuchs enjoyed, some ordinary men castrated themselves in anticipation of becoming a eunuch.[43] Although illegal and prohibited repeatedly by the government, this practice still tempted more and more aspirants as the chance always existed for some to succeed.[44] By the Chenghua era, more than ten thousand eunuchs, one hundred times those in the Hongwu era, were reported to be working in the inner court.[45] The numbers continued to soar as more self-castrated men appeared after the Jiajing era, and by the Wanli era, it was said that eunuchs, plus those serving them as servants, artisans, chefs, and laborers, numbered no fewer than several hundred thousand.[46] Not only did the share of eunuchs legally chosen from the capital area and neighboring regions increase steadily but also the majority of the illegally self-castrated also originated from these areas. Consequently, the portion of eunuchs coming from Beijing and nearby areas escalated, whose effects were amplified by the large scale of eunuchs. Alongside their status as inner-court elites, Ming eunuchs took up a new identity of local elites because of their deep rootedness in the local society of the imperial capital and surrounding areas.

This unusual status had the potential to enhance the eunuchs' capability to support temple-building projects. The reason was simple: no longer purely strangers coming from the inner court, on the stage provided by these projects eunuchs gained more opportunities to cooperate with a variety of local forces, which benefited one another. In 1493 when a eunuch was in charge of a project in the Beijing suburbs, for example, he led a project of renovating a temple there, with other patrons, including the imperial bodyguard, local officials, and local residents.[47] In another case, two eunuchs who were superintending a mausoleum project in Changping 昌平 county for the Wanli emperor helped renovate four temples there and one more in a neighboring county.[48] Conversely, there were also cases in which local residents lent a hand to temple projects that eunuchs had initiated. In 1492, the eunuch Liu Yuanmou 劉原謀 (dates unknown), together with the An (安) family and other local residents, constructed Longquansi 龍泉寺 ninety li outside Beijing.[49] In 1504, when eunuchs were short of money in rebuilding the Guanwang temple 關王廟, they received much money and support from officials, local gentry, and commoners.[50] In 1527, the eunuch Wang Xiang 王祥 (dates unknown) rebuilt Hufasi 護法寺 in Shuntian prefecture through working with descendants of a retired official. Other patrons in the project included Wang Xiang's *mingxia*, his fellow eunuchs in the same yamen, imperial bodyguards, and common villagers.[51]

The ability of Ming eunuchs to weave a network that crossed the boundaries of social class, gender, and financial status was a double-edged sword, granting them a remarkable potential to impact the Beijing *saṃgha* positively or negatively. As a large group, the eunuchs, even if only partly organized, would be able to mobilize massive amounts of resources to back Buddhism. But the fragility inherent in the pseudofamilial relationship was evident and inevitable. Once an influential *benguan* died or lost power, it usually meant the end of the groups (and thus the *yihui*) built around him. Thus those temples under their sponsorship sought patronage as widely as possible to neutralize possible dangers generated by reliance on a single faction, but the fluctuation of different forces among the eunuchs left clear marks on their fortunes. In this sense, Chen Yunü has rightly pointed out that the division and combination of factions in the twenty-four yamens was the decisive factor in the rise and fall of Ming Buddhist institutions in Beijing.[52] A more fundamental change came following the fall of the Ming: the highest population of eunuchs was only about three thousand in the ensuing Qing dynasty, although the organizations persisted.[53] This issue cannot be discussed here in detail, but it is no coincidence that throughout the dynasty only thirty-one Buddhist temples are recorded to have been built in Beijing.[54] After the eunuch population dropped, the shortage of resources accordingly was not nearly filled by other sources.[55]

THE EUNUCHS AND BUDDHISM IN THE MID AND LATE MING

Although Ming eunuchs were generally supportive of Buddhism, their handling of Buddhism during the mid and late Ming cannot be really understood without connection with the highly volatile political world. As a group whose power and influence were essentially dependent on the emperor's favor, Ming eunuchs proved most sensitive to changes in the political climate. They adjusted their stances swiftly in alignment with the emperors so as to protect if not maximize their own interests. Since there were drastic changes in the ways the sovereigns dealt with Buddhist affairs during the Jiajing-Wanli period, the priority eunuchs gave to the rulers' preferences over their own made their relationship with Buddhism complex.

The Eunuchs and Buddhism in the Jiajing Era

Although the eunuchs had attracted harsh criticism for their lavish patronage of Beijing temples, such a close link was substantially compromised during the first half of the Jiajing period. Shortly after his ascending the throne, Jiajing replaced key eunuch officials in the twelve directorates (*jian* 監) with eunuchs he had brought to Beijing from Hubei.[56] Staying with those long-trusted eunuchs in a completely strange environment made the young emperor feel more comfortable, but the replacement constituted a major challenge for Buddhism to fix the relationship with the eunuch leaders coming from a distinct religious environment thousands of miles away. This was no easy task. More important, as Jiajing's hostility toward Buddhism grew, eunuchs had little choice but to abide by it, regardless of their personal faith. This resulted in a low participation of the group in Buddhist temple projects and thus a drop in building completions. According to table 4.1, eunuchs engaged in seven cases in the first six years of the Jiajing era, and then the number drifted lower, with only five during the fifteen years from 1528 to 1543. This drastic drop in patronage is in line with the escalating pressure on Buddhism at court.

During the second half of the Jiajing era, although the ban on Buddhism was still in place, signs of recovery surfaced in the relationship between the eunuchs and Buddhism. There was little politics could do to change the psychological, social, and economic causes that pushed the eunuchs toward Buddhism. More important, the politico-religious environment during the period started changing in a direction beneficial to reinstall the conventional relationship between the eunuchs and Buddhism. For one thing, Jiajing's retreat to the secluded Xiyuan helped to relieve the eunuchs from his heavy hand, allowing them to look after their own interests, including their religious faith. Second, the eunuchs had secured a more comfortable position in court politics through the nearly two-decade collaboration that Yan Song sought to maintain his position as the senior grand secretary. Thus this period saw a gradual and covert recovery of the eunuchs' patronage of Buddhism. It is worth noting that these figures in the most powerful positions, although originally coming from Hubei, started to take a leading role in these activities, and that the closer the emperor approached to death the stronger the eunuchs' support of the Buddhist community. Eventually, as shown in table 4.1, the eunuchs' patronage of Buddhist institutions doubled in the latter half on the basis of the former.

This freedom should not be exaggerated, however, and the eunuchs still had to be cautious and restrained in backing Buddhism, because the emperor, though physically absent from court, kept relentless control of them.[57] There was a noticeable unwillingness for the eunuchs to publicize their contributions to the *saṃgha*, which they would have done eagerly if in favorable surroundings, or they tended to downplay them. Consider the case of Jietansi 戒壇寺 west of the capital. Founded in the Tang dynasty with the name Huiju 慧聚, this temple had some eminent monks as its abbots and built an ordination platform in the Liao dynasty (907–1125). It had become a temple of importance in northern China by the end of the Yuan dynasty. During the Ming, eunuchs sponsored its renovation at least three times. The first was carried out from 1434 to 1440 by Wang Zhen 王振 (d. 1449), the most powerful eunuch of the age. This renovation also brought the temple a new name, Wanshou 萬壽—literally, "wishing the ruler a long life."[58] Nearly forty years later, the hall housing the ordination platform was repaired and, owing to the eunuchs' efforts, an edict was issued in 1480 announcing that its abbot had been promoted to the right Buddhist rectifier (*jueyi* 覺義) of the Central Buddhist Registry. After an interval of seventy years, the eunuch Ma Yu 馬玉 (dates unknown) and his fellows started rebuilding this temple again in 1550. Ma Yu, a native of Shuntian prefecture in Beijing, served in the Directorate of the Imperial Studs (*Yuma jian* 御馬監) and was then in his seventies. They rebuilt almost all major buildings of the temple, including the main hall, five smaller halls, and three pavilions. Interestingly, for the first time in the history of the temple a statue of Zhenwu 真武 (Perfected Warrior) was also installed in a hall for worship. Zhenwu rose to be the foremost Daoist god in the Ming dynasty primarily for his alleged contribution to Emperor Yongle's victory over his nephew, Emperor Jianwen.[59] Installing this Daoist god in such an important Buddhist temple was unusual, revealing a secret desire of these eunuchs to increase the survival chances of Jietansi in the unfavorable circumstances.[60] I described in chapter 2 similar strategies used by Baomingsi. Similarly, a stela was erected six years (1556) after the completion of this project, but the names of the twenty-six eunuch patrons were not revealed until 1565 when another stela was put up.[61] The delay of six years to erect the first stela, the interval of nine years between the two stelae, and the differences in their contents are all revealing. They suggest that the eunuchs started engaging in Buddhist activities again in the second half of the era on occasions unnoticed by the emperor, and that the eunuchs became even bolder near the time of the emperor's death. Twenty-six is indeed not a big number, but the eunuchs included in the list were all central figures with power. The small number may show a relatively low level of the eunuchs' participation in the Buddhist program, but the high ranks of these figures suggest the promising potential of the temple. Unmistakably, this reflects the characteristic of a transition period that was still overshadowed by the absent emperor.

The Eunuchs, Cisheng, and Buddhism in the Early Wanli Era

The eunuchs' enthusiasm for temple-building projects mounted in the Longqing era. Longqing was a mediocre and short-lived emperor who showed little discrimination or preference in religion. Xu Jie, the senior grand secretary during the Jiajing-Longqing transition period, drove Daoism away from the court by taking advantage of Jiajing's death. A member of the Wang Yangming school, Xu Jie lent no support to Buddhism, nor did he continue to put it under harsh restrictions. But the rest of the grand secretaries all endorsed Buddhism: Zhao Zhenji 趙貞吉 (1508–1576, *jinshi* 1535) and Chen Yiqin 陳以勤 (1511–1586, *jinshi* 1541) were both Buddhists, and Gao Gong 高拱 (1513–1578, *jinshi* 1541) even composed the piece for Jietansi in 1556 in praise of the eunuch Ma Yu's rebuilding of it. Under these conditions, the relationship between the eunuchs and Buddhism continued to improve.

During the first half of the Wanli era, the eunuchs constituted a major part of the pro-Buddhism circle centered on Cisheng, who was then active in the political realm and on good terms with her emperor son. The eunuchs frequently participated in the projects Cisheng initiated to patronize Buddhism on her behalf, and in some cases they stayed in the temple for several years organizing and supervising the projects.[62] They did so not merely because of the requirements of duty; many of them were Buddhist adherents, and it was thus in their interest to cooperate with Cisheng to form a pro-Buddhist circle around her, which attracted more eunuchs to the religion. A good example is Zhang Wen 張穩 (1552–1610?), a eunuch in the Cining palace where Cisheng resided. Zhang believed in the Pure Land and led an association that focused on reciting the Buddha's name.[63] Jiang Dayin, another attending eunuch in the Cining palace, was given a scroll painting inscribed by Cisheng in praise of his outstanding service related to Buddhism.[64] Cisheng sometimes lent support to the eunuchs in other ways. When the eunuch Wang and his fellows built Cihuisi 慈慧寺, Cisheng handwrote the name tablet for the temple.[65] She did the same thing again when another eunuch finished building Baoensi 報恩寺 in Beijing.[66]

More specifically, in the first decade, instead of on their own initiative, the eunuchs flocked in stunning numbers to support Cisheng-led temple projects, most of them in the capital region, and thus guaranteed their success. Following Wanli's ascendancy to the throne, Cisheng wasted no time to launch waves of Buddhist patronage. Notably, the projects she led all featured large-scale mobilization among the inner-court elites, especially the eunuchs. While taking charge of the Wanshousi project, for example, Feng Bao 馮保 (d. 1583) donated ten thousand taels of silver, which may have been out of his own pocket or simply a collective contribution of all the eunuchs.[67] On another occasion, one thousand four hundred eunuchs appeared on a 1581 stela, with almost all important directors of eunuchs included.[68] Clearly these eunuchs were mobilized mainly on the organizational basis discussed in the preceding. This huge number constituted a sharp contrast with the 1565 stela erected at Jietansi with only twenty-six names. Where did such a huge number of eunuch backers come from? Perhaps in the 1565 case the number was purposely cut down in an attempt to circumvent political trouble. More likely, we see here an explosion of the once-suppressed enthusiasm of inner-court elites that was backed by organized eunuchs in a favorable political climate. Cisheng was a court woman in the Ming court, a status determining that the resources under her command must have been limited. Thus, the presence of these organized and large-scale eunuchs was not only a supplement to but a major avenue of economic resources for Cisheng to defray the huge expenditures of these projects. In this sense, through working with Cisheng, the eunuchs joined as a crucial force to shape a religious environment most favorable for Beijing Buddhism during the early Wanli era.

During the second decade the eunuchs increasingly engaged in Buddhist affairs outside the capital, and the results not only extended Cisheng's influence beyond the capital but also helped to establish a realm-wide network linking Cisheng with scholar-officials and eminent monks, especially those in Jiangnan. Under orders from Cisheng (and at times Wanli), the eunuchs left their traces all over the country. They held vegetarian feasts for monks in areas like Mount Pan 盤山 close to Beijing, Mount Wutai in Shanxi, Putuo Island in Zhejiang, and Mount Jizu in Yunnan province. They carried hundreds of cassocks and the purple robe (*ziyi* 紫衣) and granted them to eminent monks to acknowledge their achievements.[69] For example, when Su'an Zhenjie 素庵真節 (1519–1593) was lecturing on the chapter on the Jeweled Stupa (*baota pin* 寶塔品) of *The Lotus Sutra* at Qixiasi 棲霞寺 in Nanjing in the early Wanli era, a eunuch reportedly witnessed that a real precious pagoda appeared in the air before his seat and, thrilled, granted him a cassock in Cisheng's name.[70] The key role eunuchs played in distributing inner-court resources enabled them to impact the fate of a temple or a monk. The eunuch Xu Zhengguang 徐正光 (b. 1550), for example, brought Zibo Zhenke 紫柏真可 (1543–1604) to Cisheng's attention, which not only expanded Cisheng's influence to Jiangnan but also benefited Zhenke by promoting his reputation in the Buddhist world. More important, their presence in local Buddhist society bridged the inner court and local Buddhist institutions, especially those in Jiangnan, which would otherwise never have interacted. A network, though somewhat loose, was woven as a consequence. A particularly illustrating case concerns Sun Long 孫隆 (1530?–1609), a eunuch who was long resident in Jiangnan. In 1590, Sun brought to Lingyinsi 靈隱寺 in Hangzhou a scroll of the bodhisattva Guanyin—very likely the Nine-Lotus Guanyin—conferred by Cisheng.[71] Ten years later, he arranged for three copies of the Buddhist canon to be bestowed to Hangzhou and Suzhou. Notorious though Sun was for stirring up large-scale disturbances, his channeling of imperial resources to the Jiangnan *saṃgha*, which was much appreciated by local elites,[72] nevertheless brought him a temple while he was alive.

The Eunuchs, Wanli, Buddhism, and Daoism in the Late Wanli Era

But the eunuchs were not a reliable force that Cisheng (and thus Buddhist institutions) could always depend on; as the mother-son tension escalated in the third decade, the eunuchs significantly reduced their involvement with Buddhism lest it be viewed as binding them to Cisheng. The money-consuming nature of Cisheng-led ventures exposed the eunuchs involved to the threat of being charged with embezzling construction funds. This was a real risk even in the early Wanli reign. When Feng Bao, Cisheng's chief ally, was arrested in late 1582, it was said that more than one million taels of silver were discovered at his home. Little is known about how the reported wealth was amassed, but Feng was charged by his political rivals with embezzlement while supervising temple-construction projects, to which we know he donated at least ten thousand taels of silver on one occasion. As the mother-son tension escalated and Buddhism became caught up in court strife, patronizing Buddhism in the inner court was no longer a simple choice of religious faith but gradually perceived as siding with Cisheng against Wanli. As a group depending on the emperor's favor for their influence, the eunuchs were highly sensitive to any political changes and would do anything to avoid offending the reigning ruler. Unsurprisingly, therefore, it can be expected that the eunuchs would change course, sooner or later. It appeared that the turning point came in the wake of a death sentence in 1595. Zhang Ben 張本 (d. 1602 or later) was a eunuch heavily relied upon by Cisheng in fulfilling her Buddhism commissions. In 1581, he appeared at Mount Wutai by Cisheng's orders to pray for the birth of the crown prince.[73] Shortly thereafter, Zhang Ben followed Cisheng's command and brought Buddhist statues and a copy of the Buddhist canon to Miaofeng Fudeng 妙峰福登 (1640–1612), another leading monk, at Yongningsi 永寧寺 on Mount Luya 蘆芽, Shanxi.[74] In the campaign in which Cisheng distributed fifteen copies of the Buddhist canon starting in 1586, Zhang Ben was seen to deliver one to Deqing, who was then at Haiyinsi 海印寺 of Shandong province. Afterward, he continued serving Cisheng, leaving his mark at Buddhist sites all over the empire, such as Qixiasi 棲霞寺 in Nanjing, Huguo caoansi 護國草庵

寺 on Mount Emei, Ayuwangsi 阿育王寺 in Ningbo 寧波, and Baotuosi 寶陀寺 on Putuo Island.[75] All of a sudden, in 1595 Zhang Ben was arrested, thrown into prison, and then sentenced to death.[76] The charge levied against the eunuch was that he had invented Cisheng's order to grant Deqing the Buddhist canon, but he was clearly a victim of court strife given that all this occurred amid the highest tension between mother and son.[77] This death sentence was a stark lesson to others, warning the eunuchs that loyalty to Cisheng and involvement in Buddhist affairs could be a life-or-death matter. Under such critical conditions, as shown in table 4.1 the eunuchs' patronage of Buddhist projects during the latter half of the Wanli era dropped by 60 percent compared with the first half, reflecting their response to the changing political world by shifting or at least hiding their fondness for Buddhism. With their departure, we see a drop in Cisheng's patronage of Buddhism.

At the same time a surge occurred among the eunuchs to support Daoism, clearly with the resources previously used for the Buddhist cause.[78] Neither Buddhism nor Daoism won particular favor from Wanli in his early years. But as the court was growing divided by the succession issue starting in 1590, it seemed that Daoism gradually became Wanli's preference. This may reflect not so much his real enthusiasm as his desire to distinguish himself from Cisheng. As previously discussed, Lady Zheng 鄭 (1565–1630) repeatedly invoked Daoist gods for support, and it was in the Daoist Dongyue temple that Wanli allegedly promised Lady Zheng to replace Zhu Changluo with Zhu Changxun as his successor.[79] Regarding Wanli's preference for Daoism, Deqing commented that it was because the emperor was infuriated by the predominance of Buddhism at court. Despite his mishandling of some events cited as evidence, Deqing rightly caught the increased tension between the two religions along the line between the mother and the son.[80] As for the eunuchs, Wanli's inclination toward Daoism turned into pressure on them and eventually caused a U-turn in their stance toward Buddhism in favor of Daoism. But to be clear, this rapid redirection had little to do with whether a sharp change actually occurred in their faith. Besides, on occasions beyond Wanli's attention, the eunuchs could still support Buddhism on a relatively smaller scale but, notably, those with whom they cooperated were no longer Cisheng but local people, which suggests that they functioned more as local elites than as court elites.

Consider the case of Dongyue temple 東嶽廟 in Chaoyang 朝陽 district, Beijing. This temple was built in 1319 and remained the largest Daoist temple belonging to the Zhengyi school in northern China. The name Dongyue (Eastern Marchmount) refers to Mount Tai in Shandong province, and the principal god worshipped at the temple, *dongyue dadi* 東嶽大帝 (Great Emperor of the

Eastern Marchmount), was long believed by Chinese people to be the god in charge of human life and death. The *dongyue* cult fluctuated over time, but it did not gain much popularity prior to the first decade of the Wanli era, nor did it secure much support from the eunuchs. For example, on a stela erected in 1570 commemorating a renovation of the god's statue, the eunuchs made up only about 10 percent of the more than two hundred patrons.[81] In a renovation project carried out six years later, although it was backed by Cisheng and Wanli, the names of the eunuchs carved on it dropped to five.[82] This negligible number formed a sharp contrast with the names in thousands carved on the stelae for Buddhist projects Cisheng sponsored at the time. Starting in 1582, however, there was a decided increase in both the frequency of new projects and the numbers of patrons related to the Dongyue temple. A 1585 stela lists more than four hundred patrons, with some eunuchs as leaders.[83] Five years later, two more stelae were erected at this temple, one bearing the names of fifty eunuchs plus about three hundred commoners and the other more than one thousand.[84] This striking increase in the number of patrons in so short a period is quite unusual. Given that the eunuchs appearing in the Buddhist projects, including those sponsored by Cisheng, kept decreasing in number after 1582,[85] and that court strife became fiercer around 1592, it may be safe to say that this result was partly an expansion of the combat in the secular world to the supernatural one.

We should pause here to consider the "incense communities" (*xianghui* 香會) frequently seen at the Dongyue temple. First, the term indicates that the eunuchs tended to rely on a certain kind of association to organize themselves, whether it be a Buddhist or a Daoist occasion. Second, a close look at these "incense communities" reveals that, although often led by eunuchs, they had large numbers of noneunuch members consisting of court courtesans, imperial military officials, and ordinary people, particularly women. This composition of membership reconfirms the status of Ming eunuchs as semilocal elites, which helped them embed in the network linking all social groups in Beijing and thus enhanced the vitality and flexibility of the "incense associations."[86]

HUGUOSI 護國寺: A VOICE FOR UNDERREPRESENTED EUNUCHS

Timothy Brook has skillfully argued that monastic patronage in late-Ming China was a means for local gentry in Jiangnan to claim autonomy from the state. This was generally not the case with the eunuchs in Beijing. Even in the Cisheng-led

Buddhist projects where they functioned as the main contributing force, the role of the eunuchs was overshadowed by the empress dowager, and their contribution was never fully acknowledged, a result reflecting their marginal and subordinate place in the hierarchy of power. Nonetheless, as significant political players, the eunuchs wanted to express their honor and dream, and the suppressed voice was indeed heard in the special case of Huguosi. Located in western Beijing, Huguosi became a eunuchs' ancestral temple in the sixteenth century and thereafter enjoyed their support for as long as four centuries, until the end of the Qing dynasty (1644–1911). More than twenty stelae erected in front of the temple tell the rich and complex history of the temple. A scrutiny of them furnishes us with details about how the eunuchs organized themselves to back Buddhist institutions and how structural and contingent factors worked behind the volatile relationship between the eunuchs and Beijing temples.

The eunuch Gangtie 鋼鐵 worshipped at Huguosi for more than four hundred years was a mysterious or legendary figure. Though widely acclaimed by the eunuchs for his great achievements, information about Gangtie was vague at best and conflicting at worst. Gangtie's name did not appear until 1495. Since then, five stelae in front of the temple claim that he followed Hongwu to fight everywhere, while others say that his contribution was made over the course of assisting Emperor Yongle to triumph over Emperor Jianwen militarily. Even in the Ming the authenticity of these records had already become a focus of debate, and critics pointed out that they could not be confirmed by official histories or other reliable sources.[87] So far scholars have reached a consensus that Gangtie was more a legendary figure than a historical person. Liang Shaojie, for example, points out that Gangtie was very likely invented by drawing on the model of the eunuch Wang Yan 王彥 (1372?–1445) active in the Yongle era.[88] Zhao Shiyu, after having examined all the stelae available, has discovered that Gangtie's image was shaped and built up with more details as time passed.[89] No matter who Gangtie was, it is uncontroversial that the eunuchs perceived him as a representative and a paragon for them as a group.

It took generations for the eunuchs to build Huguosi and set up the narrative template to recount its stories. A temple called Lingfusi 靈福寺, built in the Yuan, was first related to Gangtie's grave in 1442 when the eunuch Li De 李德 (d. 1448 or later) renovated a graveyard that had halls, shrines, ornamental arches (*pailou* 牌樓), and stone gates. Fifty years later, in 1490, another eunuch, Huang Zhu 黃珠 (dates unknown), came to repair the temple and the grave. Not long afterward, owing to the effort of Tan Chang 覃昌 (1433–1493), the head of the Directorate of Ceremonial, Emperor Hongzhi ordered that Gangtie be officially worshipped every year at the Qingming Festival, a conventional day when Chinese people visit their family tombs.[90] This marked a decisive step in the process of institutionalizing the Gangtie cult. Since that time, a shrine seems to have been built exclusively for the eunuch. In 1527, a Buddhist temple was built within the tomb site, probably on the foundation of Lingfusi. This temple was the start of Huguosi. But only three years later, Zhang Zuo 張佐 (d. 1542 or later), the head of the Directorate of Ceremonial, claimed in a visit to the grave that such a Buddhist temple was not suitable for the deceased and the loyal spirits.[91] He thus removed the temple and built for Gangtie a shrine instead. A major change occurred in 1550 when Mai Fu 麥福 (d. 1553) and Gao Zhong 高忠 (1496–1564),[92] the two most powerful eunuchs in the Directorate of Ceremonial and Palace Eunuchs (*neiguan jian* 內官監), respectively, came to the shrine and (re)built nine rooms and one stone gate for it. In addition, they purchased a patch of land to construct Huguosi. It is said that "they considered that Mr. Gang had made contributions to the country. For fears that his shrine would later be damaged by farmers and woodcutters [i.e., ordinary people], [they] invited monks with great virtues and competence to run [the temple]. [Monks] would pass on generation by generation, thereby making it possible to maintain the sacrifice rituals [in the shrine]" (公等念剛公有功於國, 恐後為耕樵所廢, 延訪行能之僧守之 相傳崇奉, 香火庶得經久).[93] These arrangements finalized the network involving Huguosi, which went in the following way: the eunuchs first supported the temple with property and land assets and then requested the monks depending on it to take care of the shrine and the grave site, which would later become a cemetery for eunuchs.

The two major twists in the process reflected not so much changes in the eunuchs' religious belief as their timely responses to the contemporary political winds. Both Zhang Zuo and Mai Fu started serving Jiajing when the latter was still a local prince,[94] and thus they must have been well aware of Jiajing's religious preferences. But Zhang Zuo's visit to Gangtie's grave occurred in the early Jiajing era, when the emperor was growing active in suppressing Buddhism, and the timing largely explains why Zhang replaced Buddhist Huguosi with a shrine—a Confucian building. Unlike with him, Mai Fu's and Gao Zhong's patronage of Huguosi came in the latter half of the Jiajing era, when Jiajing's retreat to the isolated Xiyuan made it possible for the eunuchs to renew their patronage of Buddhism in a cautious but resolute manner. Huguosi benefited from this tendency. In another case related to Dahuisi 大慧寺, it was also Mai Fu, in command of the Eastern Depot, who protected the Buddhist temple by building not a Confucian shrine but two Daoist abbacies.[95] These cases demonstrate the eunuchs' efforts to strike a balance between contemporary politics and their religious faith. In other words, careful though they were, they would also resist political intervention into their religious life when possible.

Not unlike other eunuch-led Buddhist projects, the history of Huguosi was also closely related to organized associations—in this case the Heishanhui 黑山 會. This name frequently appears on stelae, but its reference is somewhat confusing and could have initially been a place-name.[96] Nonetheless, as time passed there was a clear tendency to understand the *hui* in the term as a "society." When Huang Zhu repaired the grave, for example, the funding came from his own donations and those of his fellow eunuchs in the same yamen. But when Mai Fu and Gao Zhong carried out the renovation, those to whom they "appealed for donations" were members of associations (約會諸公).[97] On the back of a stela erected in the same year has twenty-four names, including "Zhang Wuben and other members of a *yihui*" (義會張務本等). The different interpretations of the term *hui* might have reflected the historical development of the site: it was first regarded as the location of Gangtie's grave, which attracted some eunuchs for burial there after their deaths in anticipation of meeting (i.e., *hui*) their hero in the afterlife.[98] Eventually, a cemetery for eunuchs came into being, Huguosi became a temple exclusively attending old eunuchs, and some *yihui* were established in support of the temple so as to ensure that Gangtie's shrine and the deceased eunuchs buried there could be treated properly.

The activities centered on Huguosi as an ancestral temple provided the eunuchs with a unique opportunity to build their collective identity and image. Though a significant political force in practice, Ming eunuchs as a group still had few opportunities to give voice in public, and their reputation grew worse beginning the mid-fifteenth century. Against this background, it is worth noting that the Directorate of Ceremonial directly led most of the projects related to Huguosi and the shrine throughout the Ming. In 1573, the head of the Directorate of Ceremonial, Feng Bao, renovated Huguosi and the shrine. He also donated 211 *mu* of land and one garden to the temple-shrine complex. In 1591, Zhang Cheng 張誠 (d. 1596 or later), the head of the Directorate of Ceremonial, renovated the buildings and purchased more than 60 *mu* of land nearby for the temple and the shrine. The pattern of purchasing monastic lands and repairing buildings was repeated again sixteen years later: the head of the Directorate of Ceremonial, Chen Ju 陳矩 (d. 1608), built rooms and purchased lands for the temple.[99] The presence of the Directorate of Ceremonial, the highest of all eunuch yamens, was practically instrumental in eliciting support from high-ranking court officials— usually in the form of composing inscriptions. But more important, this directorate was then acting to build the identity of eunuchs as a well-organized group and shape their collective image. The key words appearing in these stela inscriptions are *zhong* 忠 (loyalty), *huguo* 護國 (protecting the state), and *huamin* 化民 (cultivating the common people).[100] Instead of viewing them simply as hypocritical, the choice of these terms reflected the strategy of the leading eunuchs to (re) shape their collective image in the hostile context by highlighting their support of and abiding by the values deeply entrenched in Chinese society.

Also, the leaders of the eunuchs found a special stage at this temple for themselves to build their individual images. Although a closed circle open only to eunuchs, Huguosi was a semipublic sphere considering that these eunuchs had considerable influence in both the inner court and local society. This temple offered leading eunuchs a special stage otherwise inaccessible to them to express their grievances and pride as individuals. Most eunuchs present in the stelae were those with good reputations. For example, Tan Chang won respect from his contemporaries in the Chenghua era.[101] Zhang Zuo, Mai Fu, and Huang Jing were all described in the official history as submissive.[102] As for Feng Bao, despite his occasional abuse of power, he contributed greatly to the golden decade of the early Wanli era. Chen Ju was even more outstanding as his performance in the succession issue won him a rare praise of "impartiality, kindness, and having good understanding of important matters" (平恕識大體).[103] A pertinent case concerns Feng Bao. In 1573, Feng Bao erected a stela that includes the richest details about Gangtie's life. Interestingly, for the first time it claimed that Gangtie helped Yongle to discover Yao Guangxiao, the aid key to the success of Yongle's usurpation. With this addition, Zhao Shiyu points out that Feng Bao was hinting at his own achievements, particularly his "discovery" of Zhang Juzheng.

A brief survey of what happened to Huguosi later in the Qing, though beyond the scope of this study, may help to reveal the dynamics behind its survival and development in a new age. As the eunuchs' power was significantly curbed in the Qing, Huguosi no longer had the lavish support it had enjoyed from the eunuchs, but almost at the same time it started drawing local resources very actively, thereby transforming itself from an organization exclusively for the eunuchs into a place where the eunuchs met locals. The eunuchs' cooperation with local residents continued to increase beginning in the early Qing. A stela erected in 1701 shows that, aside from eunuchs, its patrons included the magistrate of Fangshan 房山 county and laypeople in nearby villages.[104] Later, when a society called *Gangzu shenghui* 剛祖聖會 (holy association for Patriarch Gang) took shape, although still led by eunuchs, it had local residents and even shop owners as its members.[105] With this coalition, a collection of generally underrepresented, low social-capital individuals had become increasingly networked and motivated. A temple fair called *Heishan shenghui* 黑山聖會 (holy fair at Heishan) also developed around

Huguosi and Gangtie's legend. All these widened the basis on which Huguosi could rely, allowing it to survive or even thrive after the eunuchs' patronage dwindled substantially.

Ming eunuchs as a group were a significant but unreliable force for the development of Buddhism. They were drawn to Buddhism for a variety of reasons, including economic and social reasons worthy of more attention. Benefiting from the large scale of their population, organizational advantages that allowed them to mobilize resources from within, and their dual identity as both court elites and semilocal elites, the eunuchs as a group were able to command considerable resources. Thus, their decisions about how to use the resources had a great impact. Nonetheless, because of their subordinate and often illegal role in the political hierarchy, they were not in a position to define and defend their interests and agendas in a relatively independent way. They had to remain sensitive to changes in the political climate, especially the emperors' stances on religious issues, and they had to swiftly adjust their distance from religion, and hence the resources they invested in Buddhism, accordingly. As a result, the eunuchs were a significant but not always reliable force that Buddhist institutions could depend on. This volatility had the great potential to impact the *saṃgha* under their sponsorship, positively or negatively.

Over the Jiajing-Wanli period of nearly one hundred years, as demonstrated by their participation in the Buddhist temple projects, there was an N-shaped relationship between the eunuchs and Buddhism. The eunuchs kept away from the *saṃgha* amid the ruler's increasing hostility to Buddhism in the first half of the Jiajing era, but they took a turn by moving steadily closer to it in the second half when the pressure became somewhat relaxed. This upward tendency in their relationship continued in the Longqing era and reached a peak in the first two decades of the Wanli era, manifesting itself in cooperation with Cisheng on Cisheng-led Buddhist projects. Their support essentially decided the scale of Cisheng's patronage of Buddhism and thus had considerable impact on the *saṃgha* in the capital region within their direct reach, and at a few significant Buddhist sites beyond the capital that were closely linked to the royal family. Given that the resulting quick rise of Beijing in the Buddhist world was the most important event in the early state of the renewal, the significance of their huge support goes far beyond regional boundaries. Nonetheless, the eunuchs wasted little time changing course again—turning to Daoism at the cost of Buddhism—as the tension between mother and son escalated. Their rush to the Dongyue temple starting in 1590 was such a case, and table 4.1 shows that their participation in Buddhist projects decreased by about 60 percent during the second two decades of the era. Thus, unsurprisingly we have seen that Cisheng's patronage of Buddhism dropped at the same time.

The eunuchs' proximity to the political power center subjected them to direct influence from rulers while enabling them to react in a subtle and timely way. This two-edged nature of their status as court elites made their activities seemingly self-contradictory and at odds with the current at times. Their cautious but determined involvement in Buddhist affairs during the second half of the Jiajing era, including the case of Huguosi, supports this point.

Notably, alongside their traditional status as court elites, Ming eunuchs obtained a new identity as semilocal elites in Beijing. This role, arguably unique to the dynasty, was derived both from their origins and their large scale. It prompted the eunuchs to serve as a bridge linking the inner court and Beijing's local society, thereby enhancing the support they could mobilize on behalf of Buddhism. In a broader view, the extension of the eunuch-led *yihui* to include commoner supporters, as demonstrated by the survival of Huguosi in the Qing, would later help to cushion shocks that the Beijing *saṃgha* felt in the wake of the eunuchs' departure as a major backing force, as well as those from other significant sociopolitical changes.

5

Scholar-Officials

Struggling for the Right Position

As with the eunuchs in Beijing, scholar-officials were crucial to the growth of Buddhism in regions outside the capital, especially in Jiangnan, over the Jiajing-Wanli period. But these scholar-officials differed greatly from the eunuchs in their way of handling Buddhism. This comes as no surprise given that they were distinctly different in educational background, personal preferences, sources of power and influence, ways of organizing themselves, and the resources they commanded. This chapter hence historicizes how scholar-officials dealt with Buddhism to reveal their influence in the ongoing Buddhist renewal.

This chapter begins with a survey of scholar-officials' shifting attitudes toward Buddhism chronologically. It pays careful attention to the motives and logic that structurally affected their decision making in the volatile politico-religious environment, thereby exposing much of the oft-ignored hard or even dark side that beset the relationship. Then it turns to exploring how Buddhism was embedded in scholar-officials' lives and thought to function during the Wanli period. Based on the two case studies of Feng Mengzhen 馮夢楨 (1548–1608, *jinshi* 1577) and Yuan Hongdao 袁宏道 (1568–1610, *jinshi* 1592), it scrutinizes how typical scholar-officials came to embrace Buddhist ideas, what they expected of Buddhist institutions and individuals, and what Buddhism actually meant to them not only in their intellectual and spiritual world but also in the context of everyday life. Finally, it examines the rise and fall of the Putao Association 葡萄社, a literati Buddhist association in Beijing, to see how their seeking autonomy in Buddhism broke out as an illusion largely because of the crossfire triggered by the political, ideological, and intellectual divisive lines.

DRASTICALLY CHANGING TREATMENTS OF BUDDHISM

So far, most attention has been given to the cozy side in the relationship between scholar-officials and Buddhism, which, based primarily on accounts by those sympathetic to the religion, has the hidden agenda of justifying or glorifying their association with Buddhism. But the hard or even dark side that as a structural factor beset the relationship requires more attention to reveal the complexity. Based on this understanding, I now survey scholar-officials' handling of Buddhism over a span of one hundred years.

Dual Identities of Scholar-Officials and Buddhism

Scholar-officials' relationship with Buddhism had multiple dimensions, some of which have received much exposure while others, especially the uneasy or even antagonistic side, have not. It would be useful here to go back a few steps to first highlight some of the features of Ming scholar-officials, especially their dual identity, which is captured in the English translation of the term *shi dafu* 士大夫, "scholar-official." Redundant though it may at first appear, this effort will situate us in a better position to apprehend the institutional factors affecting their stance toward Buddhism.

Scholar-officials must be understood in relation to Confucianism, in which they were trained and defined, and to the state, which monopolized the right to grant them their status and its accompanying advantages. Scholar-officials emerged as a major sociopolitical force following the gradual bowing out of the medieval aristocracy after the middle of the Tang dynasty. Once they passed the civil-service examination based on the Confucian classics, they were qualified to receive an official post, which was directly associated with the distribution of desirable status, prestige, and financial wealth. Thus, for scholar-officials Confucianism was a source of not only ideas and ideals but also immense material interest, and the exam system became a powerful tool for the state to regulate its relationship with these sociopolitical elites. As political centralism advanced in late-imperial China, the degree of their reliance on—or the loss of their independence to—the state increased.[1]

On the other hand, scholar-officials attempted to claim a certain degree of autonomy from the state on two fronts. As Peter Bol has convincingly argued, far from an ideological justification for a stagnating and autocratic state, as conventional wisdom has suggested, neo-Confucianism emerged and evolved as a constructive, even radical response to dramatically changing times.[2] Against this background, scholar-officials, with their mastery of the Confucian classics, reserved for themselves the role of chosen agent of the unchallengeable but inexpressible Way. Thus they obtained a lever against emperors who were supposed to obey the Mandate of Heaven. Even after neo-Confucianism was established as the state ideology beginning in the Yuan, behind the political ethics they advocated—a ruler should perform his duties as a ruler and a minister perform his as a minister—was the implication that "a minister does not necessarily serve as a minister if a ruler fails to fulfill his own duties." In other words, scholar-officials prioritized achieving the Way (*dao* 道) over serving secular power.[3] This sparked suspicion from the emperor, who tended to require their absolute obedience.

Related to their dual identity, with one foot in the imperial court and the other in local society, scholar-officials had another front at which to compete against the state for influence. Beginning in the Southern Song, scholar-officials aspiring to maximize their interests tended to invest more time and resources in local society, where they, as local elites, could obtain and maintain influence in a comparatively easy and reliable way.[4] This reorientation from the central government to local society was, in large part, because, as the number of examination candidates greatly increased while the quota of official posts remained nearly unaltered, the exam system proved increasingly unreliable as a way to success. The situation became even worse in the Ming.[5] On the part of the state, unable to extend its influence deep into local society because of technical limits and notions about how to govern, it left local society in the hands of local elites. Ideally this cooperation could have two winners, with the state keeping things in order while scholar-officials advanced their interests. But since there was a hidden possibility of a centrifugal effect once scholar-officials took root in local society, the state would act to check the tendency if it believed that they had passed the threshold into utter autonomy.

Nevertheless, this separation between scholar-officials and the state should not be exaggerated. Politically, unlike medieval Europe, late-imperial China's characteristic of increased centralism provided the motive and the capability to prevent a complete confrontation between the state and society. In the worst situations, replacing an old dynasty with a new one would function as the easing mechanism to lessen escalated tension and start a new cycle. Culturally, the concept of *tianxia* 天下 (under Heaven) has occupied a place of pride from the early stages of Chinese history, making it a kind of shared mission among Chinese people to avoid a total confrontation between the state and society. Not only a

Confucian value, this is also part of the bodhisattva spirit emphasized by Chinese Buddhism, though in a twisted way.[6] Likewise, scholar-officials cherished the notion of *tianxia shi* 天下士 (scholars devoting themselves to advancing the interests of all people) as the highest ideal, stressing a commitment to the world beyond one's own interests. During a major sociopolitical crisis, therefore, leaving the world behind was not really an option for most of them.[7]

As far as their handling of Buddhism is concerned, despite their official stance scholar-officials could embrace Buddhism in a mutually beneficial way. For Buddhism, their active engagement was clearly an asset. In particular, in late-imperial China they came to stand at the center of the textual formulation and dissemination of Buddhist teachings and new doctrinal developments. For scholar-officials, Buddhism meant aesthetic appreciation, intellectual pleasure, and social capital, much more than what it meant to the eunuchs. Most important, it was a value system that provided a template other than Confucianism to make sense of the world and decide how to experience it. In peaceful times, the conviction that "the ordinary mind is the way" (平常心是道) as advocated by Chan Buddhism worked in two seemingly contradictory ways.[8] It led them to be content with life as it was while appreciating the world aesthetically on the one hand and justified whatever natural and practical desires they had as human beings on the other. In her study of the Tang literatus Bai Juyi 白居易 (772–846), Jinhua Jia has aptly named this nuanced and enjoyable balance the "medium-degree hermitage" (*zhongyin* 中隐).[9] In crisis, when life and property became so fragile, both the rule of karmic retribution and the hope of entering the blissful Pure Land after death were attractive to scholar-officials. Notably, despite its promotion of nonattachment, Chan Buddhism could also be a source of courage in fulfilling their sociopolitical responsibilities.

But embracing Buddhist ideas brought about a schism in the lives of scholar-officials, both as individuals and as a group. Individually, since Confucianism determined the purpose scholar-officials were trained for and provided the access to practical interest they aspired to, few scholar-officials would abandon Confucianism completely in favor of Buddhism.[10] Even in the so-called three-teachings-in-one strategy, the tension between these conflicting traditions stubbornly persisted in the resulting hierarchical system. In major crises scholar-officials fond of Buddhism would find their lives full of self-contradictory efforts, trapped in their sociopolitical responsibility while seeking personal comfort and accomplishment. As a group, many of them insisted that Buddhism was a risky heterodoxy and embracing the religion was a grave betrayal of the Confucian commitment. Thus, scholar-officials were divided and fiery exchanges among them flared up time after time.

Indifference or Encroachment: The Jiajing Period

Neither scholar-officials nor Buddhist institutions were able to define their relationship from the very start of the Ming; with the enforcement of Hongwu's policies aimed to delink them, scholar-officials became increasingly irrelevant to Buddhist affairs. The negative impact of this unconcern was amplified in its association with other restrictions on Buddhist institutions. Wu Kuan 吳寬 (1435–1504, *jinshi* 1472), for example, observed a financial bankruptcy taking place in the *saṃgha* in Jiangnan.

> By our [Ming] dynasty, it became a law for the first time that [people] were not allowed to build [Buddhist temples] without permission. Moreover, Hongwu even issued an order of amalgamation because he disliked the confusion of [current] temples. How could [people] dare to construct more? Buddhist temples fell into decay again in the past more than one hundred years, but few have the ability to repair [themselves]. This is because in previous dynasties Buddhist temples had many fertile lands without limitation, but now they have all been confiscated. [Moreover, these lands] do not enjoy exemption from the land tax, and [their quotas] are roughly the same as the [land] of common people. [As a result], monks cannot afford even their clothes and food, so how could they have the spare time to repair [temples]?

> 至國朝始著於律,不得擅有興建,況洪武初厭其煩襟,且有歸併之令,尚何敢於興建乎? 百餘年來, 寺復就弊, 而能修葺者少. 蓋前代寺多腴田, 略無限制, 今則悉入於官. 凡賦稅之徵, 無可蠲免, 大率與農民相等. 則人人謀衣食之不贍, 何暇於修葺乎?[11]

Clearly, the state was the dominant force that regulated the *saṃgha* and resulted in the sagging monastic economy. Nothing was mentioned about scholar-officials' role in the process, which may not be surprising given the unconcern characteristic of the period.

During the first half of the Jiajing era, scholars-officials stood still farther away from Buddhism. While serving as local bureaucrats, they followed the emperor's order to restrict Buddhist institutions and at times added extra measures either to cater to the ruler or to serve their own agendas. Some temples were changed into schools or government offices.[12] In the Nanjing case examined in chapter 2, several hundred Buddhist temples and chapels were destroyed.[13] While active as local elites, not unlike the eunuchs in Beijing scholar-officials in Jiangnan tended to minimize, if not cease altogether, their support for Buddhism. In Suzhou, for example, as table 4.2 shows, only in three cases did local people contribute to Buddhist construction projects during the entire Jiajing era.

Unlike the eunuchs, who did not actively seek encroachment on the *saṃgha* for their own interests, some scholar-officials were a serious threat to Buddhism in an age when Buddhism had lost protection from the state while local lineages became increasingly aggressive. Monastic lands in the Ming fell into two categories, with the imperially bestowed exempt from the burden of paying the land tax, while the remainder was not. But even for the taxable lands, the tax applied to them was that for civilian land (*mintian* 民田) rather than that for public land (*gongtian* 公田), which was much higher. Thus, the tax took up only a small portion of the rent they expected to collect, and the surplus was purposely left to the Buddhist community to support its operations. This privilege, however, turned into an invitation for violation during the Jiajing era. On the part of scholar-officials, the higher they were in rank, the more exemption they enjoyed from land taxes and corvée, and the easier it was for them to conceal all or part of their taxable lands.[14] Meanwhile, as their lineages became increasingly powerful after 1536 because of a radical reform that allowed common people to establish their own ancestral temples, scholar-officials obtained new aid in enhancing their influence in local society.[15] Working together, these factors encouraged scholar-officials to encroach on monastic assets. In 1527, for example, powerful families were charged for occupying many monastic lands.[16] In 1535, Fang Xianfu and Huo Tao, the two who took radical measures to destroy nunneries in Beijing and Nanjing, respectively, were impeached for seizing monastic lands in their native districts. In 1537, when local officials in Fujian suggested confiscating the land assets of abandoned temples, a concern arose that powerful families could take advantage of it to encroach on the *saṃgha*. Against this background, some monks submitted monastic assets to powerful lineages in exchange for protection of their personal interests.[17]

The situation became even worse during the second half of the era, when officials dealt with Buddhist monasteries more relentlessly. On the one hand, most scholar-officials remained indifferent to Buddhism, leaving some important temples in a situation such that they were unable to provide enough food for resident monks.[18] Susanna Thornton has noted that in Hangzhou, for example, "until the 1570s, without obvious support from any emperor, Buddhist monasteries at the local level were shunned by the elite, starved of investment, and taxed almost to extinction."[19] On the other hand, incursion into monastic assets became even more aggressive when officials struggled to collect money in whatever way they could in a worsening fiscal situation:[20] Jiajing still lavished funds on Daoism,[21] but military expenses soared following defensive wars against intrusions by Mongolians in northern China and by Japanese pirates in coastal regions. An illuminating case was Fuzhou 福州 and Quanzhou 泉州 in Fujian province. Fujian allegedly had the largest acreage of monastic lands in China, while the largest acreage within Fujian was in Quanzhou.[22] This may not be an exaggeration, as evidenced by the fact that by the early sixteenth century they still amounted to 20 percent of the total farmland in several counties there. But things changed significantly during the Jiajing era. In Quanzhou, although the ratio of civilian lands to monastic lands was one to six in the middle of the Southern Song, a large amount of land was sold by the government to defray military expenses in the Jiajing era. Kaiyuansi 開元寺, the most renowned temple in Quanzhou, for example, was forced to sell 23,621 *mu*, 86 percent of its total farmland, retaining only 2,684 *mu*.[23] In addition, considerable surtaxes were relentlessly imposed on monastic lands during this period. Yongjue Yuanxian 永覺元賢 (1587–1657), the abbot of Gushansi 鼓山寺 in Fuzhou, attested that during the Jiajing period not only did people donate little to the monastery but also half its estates were seized. Furthermore, he complained that local officials drew 60 to 80 percent of the monastery's income for military use in the wars against Japanese pirates and asked for even more after the wars were over. Under this pressure, "how could monks not become destitute and escape from the temple?" Yuanxian asks indignantly.[24]

Parallel to their heavy-handed treatment of Buddhism as official representatives, scholar-officials could be very aggressive in snatching monastic lands and assets in an environment unfavorable to Buddhist monasteries. For example, Sheng'ensi 聖恩寺, a famous Suzhou temple, lost half its grounds, where a villa was first built by a provincial student and then occupied by a powerful lineage. The temple took the grounds back only in 1592 because of Empress Dowager Cisheng's 慈聖 (1645–1614) intervention.[25] Another case illustrates the fragility of the *saṃgha* in the face of the encroachment. Chen Huan 陳寰 (1477–1539, *jinshi* 1511), a native of Changshu 常熟, was the chancellor of the National University (*guozijian jijiu* 國子監祭酒) and a believer in geomancy (*kanyu* 堪輿). While looking for a grave site for his mother, Chen found most propitious the grounds of Weimosi 維摩寺 located on a hill close to the city of Changshu.[26] He offered to purchase the temple at a high price but was declined. Then one day he ordered several hundred of his servants to rush into the temple, and they moved the entire structure to the foot of the hill. Enraged, an old monk of the temple led followers, including his disciple Fangxian 方顯 (dates unknown) to Beijing to file a suit against Chen. It happened that the official investigating the case was Chen's acquaintance. Conniving with a ward-inspecting censor, he beat the old monk to death and forced his disciples to sign a contract selling the temple to Chen.

On their way back home, one of the disciples died mysteriously, believed to have been poisoned. Furious, Fangxian and the deceased monk's nephew returned to Beijing and filed another charge against Chen. This time the case was assigned to a touring censorial inspector (*xun'an yushi* 巡按禦史), who in turn asked the prefect of Changshu to take care of it. The prefect flogged the two men each with forty blows of the stick and sentenced them to be exiled. Eventually, the truth was revealed when a surveillance commissioner summoned the two men, who were found to be unable to move. The penalties imposed on Fangxian and his fellows were reduced, Chen's servants were flogged with forty blows, and the temple was returned to the monks. But, surprisingly, Chen Huan was not punished at all. Probably the reality was too grim and hopeless. Feng Mengzhen, who narrated this story, finally turned to karmic retribution and added an unsubstantiated end to the story: the following year Chen Huan suddenly caught a terrible illness, and in trance he said that a monk was beating him. He cried out for forgiveness all day and night but died shortly afterward, and so did his wife.[27] Money, arrogance, plots, violence, and the abuse of public power through a network linking scholar-officials were all involved in this case. Buddhist institutions were unmistakably preyed upon by the local powerful, but, deprived of legal and institutional protection, the only defense available to them was the law of karmic retribution, which was not necessarily always practical.

Reaccommodation but Without Fundamental Changes: The Wanli Period

Following the coming together of such favorable factors as the intellectual reorientation of the elites, Cisheng's timely staging as a significant patron, the widening state-society division, and economic prosperity, the Wanli period saw a remarkable reaccommodation by scholar-officials to Buddhism. This intimacy, described as similar to "a lid to a box," has received much attention from scholars like Timothy Brook and Araki Kengo. But due attention should also be given to the harsher side of the equation, which persisted in the relationship, to counter the somewhat one-sided emphasis.

During the Wanli era evidence is ample about how active the literati were in protecting and patronizing Buddhism, including preventing further robbing of monastic assets by the powerful, recovering lost resources, and arranging part or full tax exemption for monastic lands. For example, the grounds of Yuanfengsi 元封寺 in Fengyang 鳳陽 were occupied by a powerful family. One official adjudicated that the land should be returned to the temple, but another declined to make a decision when the accused made a countercharge. Learning of that, Lu Guangzu 陸光祖 (1521–1597, *jinshi* 1547) asked Feng Mengzhen to step in, and the latter then turned to an official for assistance.[28] It is unclear from available materials if their efforts were effective. In another case taking place in 1590, Lu Guangzu wrote a letter to a local official on behalf of Longyousi 龍遊寺 and made an exemption for part of its land tax.[29]

Despite their new enthusiasm, scholar-officials' backing of Buddhist institutions was not always reliable, especially in situations when financial support was involved. In 1589, for example, Xu Yan 徐琰 (dates unknown) invited Chan master Tianji 天際 (d. 1599), who had won a reputation by burning one finger to worship the Buddha, to be the abbot of Huqiusi 虎丘寺 in Suzhou. Once serving in the Court of Imperial Squad (太僕寺), Xu called for donations for the temple of two taels of silver and five *dan* 石 of rice each month. His appeal received a positive response from his friends, including the Yu 于 family in Jintan 金壇 and the He 賀 family in Danyang 丹陽. Thus, in the first few years the temple was financially sustainable and able to support dozens of monks living with Tianji. But this typical story of cooperation between scholar-officials and Buddhist monks did not last long. In 1595, Tianji fled to Nanjing. This seemingly sudden flight was actually triggered by the failure of the two families to donate as promised for the past two years. Feng Mengzhen wrote a letter on Tianji's behalf asking the two families to keep their promise. It is unclear whether the letter worked, but four years later when Feng visited the temple again, he found that the sick Tianji had stopped eating but was worried about donations. Feng wrote another letter and, twenty days later, rice from the Yu family finally arrived in response. Relieved somewhat, Tianji died four days later.[30] The scholar-officials involved in this case, including the two families, Xu Yan, and Feng Mengzhen, belonged to a small but close network that, centered on Zibo Zhenke 紫柏真可 (1543–1604), was carving the Jiaxing canon.[31] And the importance of Huqiusi for them lies, in part, in the fact that it was where Zhenke had become a monk. The membership of the group explains Feng's willingness to write the letters and the positive responses he received. Since support from even such a close group was unreliable, it seems reasonable to wonder what could happen to other temples without these advantages. In fact, this unreliability was no exception, as the following chapter demonstrates.

The preying on monastic assets by powerful families continued, though to a much lesser degree, and the government was too weak, if not reluctant, to stop them. Nostalgic about what he perceived as Hongwu's protection of the interests of the *saṃgha*, Zhanran Yuancheng 湛然圓澄 (1581–1626), a leading Chan master, complained that at the time "the authorities would not fix the problem when monastic lands were occupied by a powerful family, nor would they protect the monks when the latter were insulted by laypeople" (田產為勢豪所佔, 而官府不之究. 僧為俗人所辱, 而官府不之護).[32] Similarly, as late as 1607, Ye Xianggao 葉 向高 (1559–1627, *jinshi* 1583), the grand secretary, lamented that

> in recent years . . . local officials have looked down on Buddhist monks and refused to treat them as equally as common people. Taking advantage of that, local powerful families treated [the *saṃgha*] as if it were their inherited asset, raising its assigned land-tax quota but reducing its land rents. Such encroachments and embezzlement have taken place every day without interruption, and before long [the *saṃgha*] will no longer have any land.

> 近世 ... 守土之吏, 復賤棄緇流不得與齊民齒. 閭右之豪, 因以為利, 若故業然. 加 賦減租, 日侵月削, 浸淫不止, 且至無田.[33]

The two shared a concern that local lineages' encroachment on monastic assets, which was indulged by local authorities, would seriously harm the *saṃgha*. This concern was not without foundation. While in office in Nanjing, Ye had already witnessed the loss of part of the imperially bestowed lands of state-sponsored monasteries to the hands of powerful families. Borrowing the founding emperor's authority, he and fellow officials stepped up pressure on these families to return the lands. Finally, the latter yielded but with the condition of reducing about one-third of the land rent given to the temples. Unfair though the condition was, both Ye and the affected temples accepted the results with clear satisfaction. In this case, the stepping in of government officials proved that Buddhism indeed had a somewhat improved sociopolitical environment during the Wanli period, but the compromised results revealed its weakness in the face of the aggressiveness of powerful local lineages. Since even the state-sponsored monasteries were not immune to encroachment, it is not hard to imagine that other temples with lesser protection were more vulnerable.

EMBRACING BUDDHISM: TWO CASES

For the close relationship between scholar-officials and Buddhist institutions during the Wanli period, more research is needed to see how scholar-officials came to embrace Buddhism and the way in which Buddhist ideas and individuals functioned as a powerful force to shape their life and thought. This section scrutinizes the two cases of Feng Mengzhen and Yuan Hongdao, two typical and influential literati who were well known for their deep connection with and great contribution to Buddhism. Feng and Yuan belonged to the same network of literati, although it seems that there was no direct connection between them. Both prolific writers, they have left huge amounts of material in diverse forms, including essays, poems, letters, and even diaries.[34] These materials provide a window through which we can see how Buddhism penetrated into their lives, and how their multiple identities—as Confucian scholar-officials and as Buddhists—and the inherent conflicts affected their experiences in, and response to, the world. Also, it should be kept in mind that the parts of their lives examined here are associated mainly with Jiangnan and Beijing, respectively, the two regions key to the Buddhist renewal.

Feng Mengzhen: Forsaking the World That Forsook Him

In his early life, Feng Mengzhen had a promising political career and lacked any serious interest in Buddhism. Born to a poor merchant family, Feng came first in the metropolitan examination in 1577. This was a great success for any scholar-official seeking a degree. Then he was assigned as a Hanlin Bachelor (*shujishi* 庶吉士). Reserved for new *jinshi* of outstanding literary talent, the post of Hanlin Bachelor was seen by contemporaries as a shortcut to the Grand Secretariat beginning in the mid-fifteenth century.[35] With such rosy prospects, Feng enjoyed the life at court, composing poems and studying Daoism with such friends as Tu Long 屠隆 (1545–1605, *jinshi* 1577) and Shen Maoxue 沈懋學 (1539–1582, *jinshi* 1577). But before long, in the autumn of that year, Zou Yuanbiao 鄒元標 (1551–1624, *jinshi* 1577) was exiled in a move to oppose Zhang Juzheng 張居正 (1525–1582, *jinshi* 1547), who exempted himself from mourning observance for his father. Infuriated by the event, Feng fell seriously sick and left the court soon after.

Over the following few years Feng repeatedly moved between Beijing and his native district, and in this chaotic time Buddhism crept into his life. Feng resided at home for three years, during which period he spent time studying with Luo Rufang 羅汝芳 (1515–1588; *jinshi* 1553), a respected scholar of the Wang Yangming school. In 1580, he returned to Beijing. Two years later, he met Bianrong Zhenyuan 遍融真圓 (1506–1584), the leading Huayan and Chan master of the period, and Hanshan Deqing 憨山德清 (1546–1623), then still a new star. No details about their conversations are available. These meetings may not be as accidental as they appear, considering that at the time Beijing, owing largely to Cisheng's efforts, was a rising attraction in the Buddhist world that brought elite monks from every corner. But in the same year, Feng had to return home once again because of his father's death. Over the next three years of mourning Feng started studying Buddhism with Zhenke, and since then maintained a very close relationship with the master.[36]

In 1586 Feng returned to the capital, where a heavy blow awaited that would change his life completely. In the following year, he was suddenly demoted on a charge of being fickle (*fuzao* 浮躁). Aware that it was revenge for his refusal to give the top rank in an exam to a certain person as requested by a grand secretary, Feng took the radical move of quitting and retreated to Hangzhou. Over the subsequent years, his life in the city impressed people there so deeply that they believed he was "as free as an immortal." His diary and letters to friends, however, reveal that he was actually experiencing a difficult time. He was frequently ill, which nearly claimed his life on one occasion.[37] His hair turned white in his forties, about which he worried very much. His economic situation was so uncertain that he repeatedly complained in many letters how difficult it was to sustain his family. Reputation and wealth usually came with the winning of a degree, but Feng jeopardized both with his resignation. To complicate matters further, Hangzhou was then suffering a series of natural disasters, including flooding and drought, that caused many deaths. Thus Feng was forced to make a modest living by tutoring students in preparation for the civil service exam. Also, he accepted several small gifts of silver from friends and wrote to thank them.[38] In hindsight, it might be true that Feng was better off than ordinary people, but maintaining a decent life was always a burden to him.

It was during this period of retreat that Buddhism became deeply embedded in Feng's everyday life. Following his withdrawal from the imperial court, Feng was very active in Jiangnan and played a leading role among scholar-officials there. From his diaries, we find that almost every day he had activities related to Buddhism, including visiting monks and temples, reading sutras, assisting in recovering lost monastic assets, and discussing Buddhist teachings with friends. Also, his diaries disclose a hidden link between living in this way and a general disappointment in his life. Feng sought comfort in Buddhist ideas, especially Chan thought, in order to resist the distress caused by his demotion. His poor health drove him closer to Buddhist ideas as well because, as he often claimed, it repeatedly reminded him how impermanent life and reputation in fact were. In 1587, when he was only forty, for example, he lamented that he was already old because his hair was white and he was missing teeth. He asked, "How could I long remain attached to the burning house [i.e., the secular world] at the cost of the great matter of thousands lives and ten thousand kalpas?" (豈能久戀火宅, 擔閣千生萬劫大事乎?).[39] "The great matter" here refers to that of life and death, a typical Buddhist notion that reminds us of impermanence. Feng's concern about the fragility of life was further reinforced by his friends' tragic experiences. Learning of the death of a friend who had entered the Hanlin Academy with him at the same time, Feng lamented for days and concluded in a letter to another friend,

> People really should enjoy life while they can. We are now recalling the cheerful time shared at the Hanlin Academy fifteen or sixteen years ago. How could we regain it? Later on, it would be impossible [for us] not to miss today's life.

人生真宜行樂. 即今追想十五六年前同館歡聚時光景, 那可復得? 他時後日, 又未免再想今日光景耳.[40]

"Enjoying life" was established as the prime goal, but it may be less a positive individualism in the modern sense of the term than a passive (and hidden) response to the loss of his political life and to the formidable pressure of everyday living. The measures Feng took to accomplish the goal varied over time, and during this phase of his life he had recourse to Buddhism.

Feng benefited a great deal from Mizang Daokai 密藏道開 (dates unknown), Zibo Zhenke's most capable disciple and Feng's most important mentor in his spiritual life. Daokai had a remarkable ability of attracting scholar-officials to establish a network surrounding his master. Feng respected Daokai and Zhenke very much and appreciated the strict way in which they disciplined him. A typical pattern of their correspondence is that Feng first confessed to Daokai about his wrongdoings and then received stern directions from the latter about how to fix them.[41] For the Jiaxing canon project with far-reaching importance that was initiated by Zhenke and Daokai, Feng took part in it as a major patron from the very start while still in Beijing. Without Daokai's strict drilling, it would be hard to imagine that Feng would later be eulogized by Zhenke as one of the two chief protectors of Buddhism (hufa 護法) at the time.

The aforementioned network functioned not only in Feng's religious life; it also had an impact on Feng's secular life by linking him with a broader circle consisting of eminent monks and scholar-officials.[42] In 1593, after spending several years of a hermitlike life in Hangzhou, Feng was appointed to be the assistant subprefect (pan 判) of Guangde 廣德 (present-day Guangde, Anhui). Although the details are unclear, this arrangement seems to have been made by Lu Guangzu and Feng's friends at the Hanlin Academy.[43] When serving as the minister of personnel Lu Guangzu was well known for promoting capable officials to suitable positions, but in his private life Lu was one of the few most important patrons of Buddhism who maintained close connections with Daokai and Zhenke.[44] Guangde was in the vicinity of the Jiangnan region, about two hundred miles northwest of Hangzhou. When Feng was still hesitant to take the post, a letter from Daokai came to tell him that this action was urged by Lu Guangzu and that Feng would not stay long outside the capital. Daokai insisted that this was the right time for Feng to emerge again.[45] Thus, Feng finally set off to Guangde and, several months later, was indeed promoted to chancellor of the Nanjing National University. Given that personnel matters were among the most secret for the government, Daokai's successful prediction in this case may not be proof of his unusual insight but of his manipulation, at least partly, of the government operation through a network comprising elite monks and literati.

This time Feng stayed in office for four years and performed fairly well, but at the same time he found himself stuck in a painful dilemma. Instead of fulfilling his political ambitions or Confucian mission, Feng admitted at the very beginning that he accepted the chance primarily for the practical consideration of easing his financial burden. In other words, his commitment as a scholar-official to Confucianism and the state had already faded. While in office, he thus behaved with additional caution to avoid trouble,[46] sometimes at the cost of his spiritual life as an individual. For example, Mounts Niushou 牛首 and Qixia 棲霞 were two famous Buddhist sites that Feng could see from his office, but he allowed the restrictions that accompanied his status to withhold the impulse to visit them in a period of at least half a year.[47] Nonetheless, Feng had to face the deep trouble that embroiled the empire. No longer focusing only on his life, Feng frequently discussed contemporary politics with friends in letters. He was worried that Japanese pirates, who had recently defeated the Korean army, would cause major trouble in China's coastal region. He feared that rebellions would arise because natural disasters had left no way for common people to live. He felt upset at the emperor's reluctance to appoint officials necessary for maintaining the operation of the government.[48] All these issues suggest that he was still thinking in the way typical of Confucian intellectuals. But he felt incapable to make any meaningful difference to these problems by himself, which caused him additional distress.

Feng finally resigned his office in clear disappointment. Feng had repeatedly told his friends that he would leave office at some point.[49] Once impeached by a censor in 1596, almost immediately he submitted a memorial requesting permission to retire. The charge was unjust—primarily because Feng, who held a sinecure but had a good reputation, was perceived as an obstacle by those eager for promotion—and it would not have been hard to clear his name, but Feng chose to leave without argument.[50] In explaining this decision to a friend, he claimed straightforwardly that "I am not good at being an official, nor am I fond of holding office" (故不善仕, 亦不樂仕也).[51]

Feng's dislike of being an official, which was not typical for scholar-officials, had strong political implications in the context of late-Ming China and instantiated how a turn to Buddhist affiliations from Confucian ties occurred. Apart from his own adversity, Feng also learned repeated lessons about the nature of political reality from other people. When Ding Yuanjian 丁元薦 (1563–1628, *jinshi* 1586) was impeached, he felt that it was unjust. When Yu Yuli 于玉立 (*jinshi* 1583) was arrested and almost died in prison, he lamented how dangerous the court was. When Luo Yuren 雒于仁 (*jinshi* 1583) submitted a memorial criticizing the emperor's enthrallment with wine, women, money, and arrogance, Feng's sweat ran down his back. When Mao Kuai 懋檜 (1554–1624, *jinshi* 1580) confronted the emperor and some ministers, he felt relieved to know he was only demoted.[52] Feng repeatedly told friends about how disappointed he felt with the contemporary political, social, and economic situation but that he was still hesitant to leave office.[53] It was the "timely" impeachment that encouraged him to make the final decision. He told a friend, "I belong to the green mountains. Now my affinity with the world has come to an end. Junping forsook the world, and the world forsook Junping, too" (不佞弟青山之人, 分與世絕, 君平棄世, 世亦棄君平).[54] "Junping" refers to Yan Zun 嚴遵 (d. 10), a hermit in the Han dynasty who enjoyed a peaceful life in Chengdu after refusing to be an official.[55] With these lines Feng actually announced a separation from the political world, from which he started to seek autonomy.

In the eighth month of 1597, Feng composed four poems for his fiftieth birthday. The first two are on conventional topics, lamenting the rapid passing of time and expressing his desire to return home to enjoy books, nature, beautiful women, and friends. In the last two, notably, he clearly points out that politics is too dangerous. Thus "the sage shakes the clothes [i.e., returns home to live in seclusion] before getting old" (所以賢達人, 未老先拂衣).[56] The fourth tells much about how he resolved to leave office and how enjoyable the new life was.

> Shaking out clothes [I] leave the secular world,
> and always gather with friends of practicing meditation.
> [I] take pains to compose poems for new scenery,
> and my problems are resolved after opening books.
> How could I not long for the seals [of officials]?
> Moral greatness should not be weakened and contaminated.
> How could I not consider for my children and grandchildren?
> [My] purity is enough to leave to them.
> [After] I have exhausted all strategies that could benefit the people,
> Why am I despised for following the Way?

[I] hold a brush pen and write down this piece,
to express my personal desire.

拂衣謝塵氛, 靜侶時相追. 披索詠新賞, 開帙渙所疑. 豈不戀圭組? 天爵無
磷淄. 豈不念子孫, 清白自可詒. 觀民計已極, 從道安足嗤? 申毫著斯文, 聊
以適吾私.[57]

"[After] I have exhausted all strategies that could benefit the people, why am I despised for following the Way?" The Way here is not Confucian but Buddhist. Unabashedly Feng cites his inability as a Confucian official to justify his devotion to Buddhism as an individual choice and thus exposes the causal relationship between the two conflicting ways of life.

As the political world withdrew from his view, Feng started a life in which he "donated his whole life to *prajñā*" (i.e., devoted himself to Buddhism [自今全身已施般若]), as he told Daokai. Although without money to back Buddhist institutions financially,[58] he had enthusiasm, knowledge, and a high reputation to support it in other ways. Feng spent much time in editing the Jiaxing canon. He wrote many pieces to solicit backing for the *saṃgha*, such as building halls or temples, holding vegetarian feasts for monks, purchasing monastic lands, or simply explicating Buddhist doctrine. He also made considerable contribution to the resurrection of the Tiantai school.[59] Notably, once again a large network of literati emerged in the wake of Feng's efforts in this regard. Partly because of his outstanding success in the metropolitan examination and partly because of his taking up as chancellor of the National University, a post that was not politically significant but highly respected in society, Feng was held in high esteem among scholar-officials. This status helped Feng to create and maintain a wide network, along which he extended influence both in Beijing and Jiangnan. For friends who were not Buddhists, Feng tried to convince them on the basis of, it should be noted, the inclemency of politics.[60] For those who shared an interest in Buddhism, he exchanged correspondence in which they discussed their experiences. For instance, he wrote to support Huang Hui 黃輝 (1559–1621, *jinshi* 1589) by praising Huang's immediate resignation after being impeached. He wrote to Dong Qichang 董其昌 (1555–1536, *jinshi* 1589), asking Dong to detect and aid potential Buddhist believers at the Hanlin Academy.[61] In 1597, he even requested an official to assign a certain person as magistrate of Yuhang 余杭 county because the latter as a Buddhist could better protect Buddhism.[62] There were also occasions on which his influence resolved problems even without his direct intervention.[63]

But in the final years Feng Mengzhen lived in a highly controversial manner, which probably suggests both a serious spiritual crisis that he suffered and the limits of Buddhism in the life of scholar-officials. Feng repeatedly vowed to Zhenke and Daokai that he would retreat in order to live a life of seclusion after being done with such secular matters as his children's marriages, but the day never came. His hesitation comes as no surprise given that Feng, like many other scholar-officials, was influenced by Chan Buddhism, especially the Hongzhou school of Chan, in a way that made him believe that spiritual reward could be guaranteed without necessarily sacrificing his secular pleasures.[64] But Daokai disappeared mysteriously around 1597 and then, six years later, in 1603, Zhenke died in a Beijing prison (I return to these two events in greater detail in chapter 6).[65] Feng's reactions to them were bitterly criticized as too indifferent and less than expected.[66] This criticism is not entirely fair,[67] but the absence of those parts we might reasonably anticipate seeing from his writings and diaries indeed says much. Feng was not the type of person who was tough enough to handle hard times in life positively, which Zhenke had rightly predicted.[68] Thus the closer he was to the two masters, the stronger the impact he felt from the two tragedies. Feng may have believed that he could find a safe haven in Buddhism after escaping from the vicious political arena, but the disasters that befell the two masters made the illusion vanish in the starkest way and politics proved to be everywhere. Something must have given way. Very likely a serious spiritual crisis followed, but no evidence exists, which may not be that surprising considering that one-third of the dairies were expunged and that Feng had a motive to maintain his image. What is unmistakably clear is that, after Zhenke's death, Feng lived in a very different or even dissipated way. Beautiful women, delicious food, fine singers, and geomancy dominated his writings and life, while Buddhist ideas and practices almost completely disappeared. Probably the only exception was his presence in the Association for Releasing Life (*fangsheng hui* 放生會) organized by Yunqi Zhuhong 雲棲袾宏 (1535–1615).[69] This "uncontrolled" state reveals Buddhism's limits in regulating the actual life of scholar-officials like Feng. Nevertheless, the way that Feng faced death was reportedly in a typically Buddhist mode. No matter how different he might look, this gesture may suggest that deep in his heart Feng remained a Buddhist until his last breath.

Yuan Hongdao: Riding a Two-Headed Horse

Yuan Hongdao has considerably shaped our impression of the scholar-officials' world of late-Ming China, but his life was actually a compelling drama whose complexity still eludes us. Well known for engagement in Chan, he was at the same time praised by a Buddhist master as important as Ouyi Zhixu as the rein-carnation of Su Shi 蘇軾 (1037–1101, *jinshi* 1057), the long-cherished literati ideal, for his great contribution to Pure Land Buddhism. Let us start with a letter that Yuan wrote to his younger brother, Yuan Zhongdao 袁中道 (1575–1630, *jinshi* 1616), and other friends in the third month of 1595:

> I have taken up the post as the magistrate of Wu county [i.e., Suzhou]. Since Wu county has this magistrate, the Five Lakes [i.e., Lake Tai] have had their master, the Dongting [hill] its ruler, wine its host, tea its bosom friend,[70] and the stone where Master [Dao]sheng [355–434] preached the Buddhist teaching its monk. But I fear that [the task of] a grain collector of five hundred *li* will come to bother me. Taking office will restrict the official, and [I] cannot tell what will happen later.

> 弟已令吳中矣! 吳中得若令也, 五湖有長, 洞庭有君, 酒有主人, 茶有知己, 生公說 法石有長老. 但恐五百里糧長, 來唐突人耳. 吏道縛人, 未知向後景狀如何?[71]

This letter has all the elements that were significant in Yuan's life except beauti-ful women: traveling, wine, literary societies, Buddhism, tea, and a career as a gov-ernment official. At this point, Yuan was worried about the accompanying trou-ble of his being an official, but he still looked to the future with positive anticipation. This optimism was well warranted, considering that he had obtained the *jinshi* degree three years before at the age of twenty-four and that Wu county was such an attractive place for its well-known affluence, concentration of liter-ary talents, and gorgeous scenery.

Despite the hunch that taking public service would conflict with him as a man of letters, it appeared that Yuan underestimated the seriousness of his situ-ation. It took little time for him to go to the opposite side. In the third month of 1596, one year after writing this letter, Yuan submitted a request to resign his office, claiming that he wanted to tend to his grandmother, who was then seri-ously ill. His superior turned a deaf ear to the appeal, so he further claimed that he himself had a serious illness that could not be cured unless he left his posi-tion. He went so far as to request a friend help him obtain permission from the Ministry of Personnel. Finally, he sent his family out of the city and informed his superior that he would leave in any case. As one of the greatest literary writ-ers, Yuan repeatedly and graphically portrayed his pain and fears about being an official. A letter to his friend reads,

> Being an official entails suffering; being a magistrate causes the most suffer-ing of all. If you're magistrate of Wu county, then the suffering is multiplied a

millionfold, worse than the labors of ox or horse. Why? Because superiors visit you like gathering clouds, travelers stop by like drops of rain, papers and documents pile up like mountains, and taxes in cash or grain [must be handled] like an ocean. Even if you work and write morning and night, you still can't keep up with all this! Misery, misery!

人生作吏甚苦, 而作令為尤苦, 若作吳令則苦萬萬倍, 直牛馬不若矣. 何也？上官如雲, 過客如雨, 簿書如山, 錢穀如海, 朝夕趨承檢點, 尚恐不及. 苦哉! 苦哉![72]

Yuan was clearly being facetious in his letter, which paradoxically increased its literary value. In reality, he was well versed in the administration of local government and quick at settling lawsuits.[73] His service of two years there even brought him the reputation of being the best Suzhou magistrate of the past two hundred years.[74] At times, Yuan was proud of his talents in administration as well. In a letter to his friend Tang Xianzu 湯顯祖 (1550–1616, *jinshi* 1583), magistrate of Suichang 遂昌 (present-day Suichang, Zhejiang), he said that being a magistrate was not that difficult, claiming that although Suzhou was well known for being hard to administer, he had put it in order with ease. In a letter to his uncle, he even boasted that there was little benefit except "no hustle" (*bumang* 不忙) when acting as magistrate.[75] The insistence on leaving office by one so obviously competent and promising thus demands explanation.

To understand Yuan's desire to resign we need to go back to the influence he received from both Buddhism and the Wang Yangming school of Confucianism. While still in his post, Yuan once listed five sorts of genuine happiness that he was seeking: satisfying bodily desires like eating and drinking, enjoying sensual pleasures with beautiful women, reading and writing with friends, idly roaming everywhere, and begging after exhausting all his money.[76] Interestingly, begging was included in the list but scholar-officials' conventional ideals, including learning Confucian teachings or serving the state as an upright official, were not. This preference reveals the clear influence left by so-called patriarchal Chan Buddhism (*zushi chan* 祖師禪), whose teachings regarding "letting it be" (隨緣任運) and "ordinary minds as the Way" (平常心是道) had long been cherished by scholar-officials to justify their natural and practical desires as humans. In particular, Yuan's influence came primarily from the layman Pang Yun 龐蘊 (d. 808).[77] Following the logic of such teachers, distinctions between things should be transcended and overlooked. So why bother to consider the difference between mendicancy and Confucian duties? Another significant source of influence was Li Zhi 李贄 (1527–1602), the most iconoclastic philosopher in late-Ming China.[78] Yuan paid his first visit to Li Zhi in 1588, during which he was so impressed by

Li's attitude toward life and his insight into history and society that, in each of the following few years, he always spared some time to spend with him. This association affected Yuan on multiple levels, encouraging him to explore Buddhist teachings and helping to shape the way he responded to the world. Li Zhi had resigned from the post of prefect of Yaoan 姚安, Yunnan, in 1580. Inspired by him, Yuan "felt it really loathsome to wear a hat of black gauze [i.e., serve as an official]" (覺烏紗可厭之甚).[79]

The combined influence of the two traditions apparently weakened Yuan's willingness to endure hardship associated with being an official. Nobody could administer a prefecture like Suzhou without effort. Yuan found out that "although Suzhou is indeed flourishing,[80] being its magistrate is suffering. . . . What the magistrate has to face is grain collectors wearing ragged clothes, cunning people speaking clever words, and prisoners all covered by lice" (金閶自繁華, 令自苦耳 . . . 令所對者, 鶉衣百結之糧長, 簧口利舌之刁民, 及蟣虱滿身之囚徒耳). In a letter written to Tang Xianzu in the autumn of 1595, he regarded those at leisure as the most admirable in the world. By comparison, he complained that

> once I enter Wu county, [I] am like a bird in a cage whose wings are all glued and cannot move. This [career] makes me depressed and sad, causing me to fall into this malignant illness. Roughly speaking, my illness has derived from depression, which in turn comes from being an official. Failing being discharged from this post, I have no way to cure the illness.
>
> 一入吳縣, 如鳥之在籠, 羽翼皆膠, 動轉不得, 以致鬱極傷心, 致此惡病. 大抵病因於抑, 抑因於官; 官不去, 病必不痊.

At this point he regretted not only having taken the post but also having taken the civil service examination and obtained the *jinshi* degree.[81] Yuan was reluctant to undertake public service at the cost of enjoyment, asserting that "after being born into the world, a man just hates not to enjoy himself as early as possible. How can [he] be tied up as an official and allow his ambitions [as vast as] ten thousand miles to wither?" (男兒生世間, 行樂苦不早. 如何囚一官, 萬里枯懷抱?) What was his great ambition? Was it possible to realize his ambition without the advantages deriving from an official post? Enthralled by the idea of resignation, Yuan may not even have considered these problems. Thus, we can reasonably expect that he would pay a price for his ignorance.

Yuan sent seven requests to resign, claiming that it was a matter of life or death.[82] Once the resignation was approved in the first month of 1597, Yuan quickly recovered from his so-called illness.[83] Excited, he felt like a fish released into a river or a tired bird returning to the mountain. His first destination was Hangzhou, where he met with high-profile literati like Tao Wangling 陶望齡 (1562–1609, *jinshi* 1589) and Yu Changru 虞長孺 (1553–1621, *jinshi* 1583). They drank wine and composed poems together and then spent two months in Kuaiji 會稽 and at Mount Tianmu 天目. His next trip was to Mount Huang, where he met Pan Zhiheng 潘之恒 (1556–1621). Shortly after returning to Hangzhou, he set out on another trip to Nanjing and Yangzhou. Evidently Yuan enjoyed this sort of life very much.

But life was not always that rosy; before long the reliance of Yuan as a scholar-official on the state for necessary resources made him submit to reality once again. Only one year after his announcement of renouncing the world, Yuan took up the post of instructor (*jiaoshou* 教授) in Shuntian 順天 prefecture, Beijing. He complained about the high cost of living in the imperial capital, but he fulfilled his responsibilities with ease and was generally satisfied with life there. Sometimes he felt confused about his own actions. In a letter written around the year 1599 Yuan said,

> When serving as the magistrate [of Wu county], I was not content and fell sick from depression. Finally, I quit because of the illness. After my resignation, once again I was not able to live the life of a resigned person. I indulged in nature, traveled around the Wuyue area, and forgot to return home after the passage of one year. When my wits were at an end and money was used up, I found no way to feed my family and had to endure the hardship of travel in search of an education post. [Since] my goals have become increasingly lower and the strategies more inadvisable, [I] don't really understand why I hated to be an official in the first place.

> 僕作知縣, 不安知縣份, 至鬱而疾, 疾而去而後已. 既求退, 復不安求退份, 放浪山水, 周遊吳越, 竟歲忘歸. 及計窮橐盡, 無策可以糊口, 則又奔走風塵, 求教學先生. 其趣彌卑, 其策彌下, 不知當時厭官何意?[84]

The contradiction behind his choices was not so much about changes in his thought as about a simple fact: for scholar-officials, taking up an official post was not only a requirement for them to fulfill their Confucian commitments but also the best means of making a living. In this way, the centrifugal tendency among scholar-officials was effectively reined in by the state through controlling the distribution of resources.

During this period, the first major turn occurred in Yuan's Buddhist thought, from playing with profound doctrines to stressing a lived practice that manifested in real life.[85] The Putao Association in Beijing was a loosely organized affiliation of friends, most of them high-profile scholar-officials. From 1598 to 1600, a shared goal formed among its members to seek a balance between wondrous awakening (*miaowu* 妙悟) and the practice of Buddhist cultivation (*xiuxing* 修行).[86] Yuan recognized that

> awakening and practices of cultivation are like two wheels of a carriage. Previously, [Li Zhi] overemphasized the realization of the truth but completely ignored practice and observance [of the precept]. [I came to realize that his] abandonment of norms of human relations, violation of the guidelines [of conduct], and overindulgence in his habits were an incurable illness.

> 以為悟修猶兩轂也. 向者所見, 偏重悟理, 而盡廢修持. 遺棄倫物, 倜背繩墨, 從放習氣, 亦是膏肓之病.[87]

Thus, despite the strong influence he received from Li Zhi in his early life, Yuan felt that Li Zhi's thought was "still short of stability and practicality" (尚欠穩實). In 1600, in a letter to Li Zhi, Yuan asserted that the precepts were the foundation of Buddhism and that Pure Land Buddhism was the best medicine for benefiting the people. He moved further to criticize people who played with concepts like "nature" and "mind," charging them with deceiving others using unfounded opinions.[88] Implicit in this criticism was a challenge to the "wild Chan" (*kuangchan* 狂禪) represented by Li Zhi.

Much of the credit for this shift should be given to Yunqi Zhuhong, whom Yuan, as an enthusiastic follower, praised on many occasions. Zhuhong, the master with greatest influence within the late-Ming *saṃgha*, attracted a huge number of literati around him. Deeply dissatisfied with the superficiality and corruption of Chan Buddhism at the time, Zhuhong advocated unifying Chan and Pure Land Buddhism. Yuan visited Zhuhong in 1597 while traveling with Tao Wangling in Hangzhou. This meeting planted the seed for his later shift.[89] Shortly after, he extolled that Zhuhong "stressed only the recital of the Buddha's name, which was particularly direct and simple. The six characters [i.e., 南無阿彌陀佛] were able to take in all of Heaven and earth. Why would [people] close their eyes and follow [other] wild interpretations?" (至於單提念佛一門, 則尤為直捷簡要, 六個字中, 旋天轉地, 何勞捏目更趨狂解?).[90]

Notably, little to do with theoretical issues this shift in emphasis between the two traditions was more like a test regarding the effectiveness in handling the demands of everyday life in general and death in particular. From 1598 to 1605 Yuan encountered a series of deaths, most of them untimely, among his family and friends. When his son Kaimei 開美 died young in 1598, Yuan said that he would take the death merely as an ordinary departure of the boy.[91] Despite his composure on the surface, inside he was in agony. In reality, Yuan had lost five children in the previous ten years.[92] One year later, Yuan admitted that he had been terrified by a string of deaths.[93] Probably what most crushed Yuan was the death of his older brother, Yuan Zongdao 袁宗道 (1560–1600, *jinshi* 1586), in the eighth month of 1600. Yuan was especially close to his brother, and the loss of this brother, who was only eight years older than Yuan, made him keenly aware of the fragility of life. Three years later, Yuan wrote in a letter to a friend, "In the past ten years, our friends have become as scarce as stars at dawn. The poplar trees on Boxiu's [i.e., Yuan Zongdao's] grave [have grown up enough] to serve as pillars, how can I not feel disheartened?" (屈指十年之間, 故交落落, 有若晨星. 伯修墓上, 白楊幾堪作柱, 百念哪得不灰冷也?).[94] These deaths repeatedly and painfully warned Yuan of life's impermanence,[95] and "wild Chan" appeared not to be as reliable as Pure Land Buddhism in assisting him to survive these hard times. Changes in his choice thus followed.

In the wake of this shift, Yuan contributed to Buddhism intellectually with a masterpiece titled the *Xifang helun* 西方合論 (A composite discourse on the West [i.e. Pure Land]) completed in 1599. First integrating different schools of Pure Land Buddhism up to his time and then taking them as the foundation to absorb Chan, this book was highly praised. Ouyi Zhixu, for example, believed that every character in it flowed from genuine awakening, without a single one being groundless.[96]

> While young, Yuan Zhonglang [i.e., Hongdao] was so intellectually sharp that he sat and broke the tongues [i.e., defeated] of Chan masters at the time. People who did not really understand him saw him as only another scholar with sharp wisdom. [Yuan] later entered the Dharma realm, devoted himself to the blissful world [of Pure Land Buddhism], and composed the *Xifang helun* of ten fascicles. Each character of it derived from real awakening, definitely none of them is copied from other places or invented by Yuan himself. Although still on the way of comprehending the most profound meaning of the Tiantai school, he had mastered Chan Buddhism completely and run through the [Huayan] thoughts advocated by Fangshan [i.e., Li Tongxuan 李通玄 (635–730)] and Qingliang [i.e., Chengguan 澄觀 (738–839)] with nothing left. Given that it is not easy even for respected and experienced monks to completely master the Buddha's teachings, some people may wonder why [Yuan] as a man who won his *jinshi* degree while young and failed to discard the five desires could accomplish this. They fail to realize that this is not accidental but results from multiple previous lives. Alas!

I heard that the three Yuan brothers were the reincarnation of the three Shu brothers in the Song. Suppose Zhonglang was really Dongpo [i.e., Shu Shi 蘇軾], its mastery of Buddhism had advanced greatly.

袁中郎少年穎悟, 坐斷一時禪宿舌頭, 不知者以為慧業文人也. 後復入法界, 歸心極樂, 述而《西方合論》十卷, 字字從真實悟門流出, 絕無一字蹈襲, 又無一字杜撰. 雖台宗堂奧尚未詣極, 而透徹禪機, 融貫方山、清涼教理無餘矣. 或疑佛祖宗教, 名衲老宿未易遍通, 何少年科第, 五欲未除, 乃克臻此? 不知多生熏習, 非偶然也. 使聞三袁是宋三蘇後身. 噫! 中郎果是東坡, 佛法乃大進矣.⁹⁷

This masterpiece, in some sense, mirrored the progress scholar-officials had made after the Northern Song when Shu Shi lived. In the long term, Yuan's superiority over respected and experienced monks is meaningful as it implied the potential for scholar-officials to obtain a kind of autonomy from the monks. If the clergy no longer lived up to the expectations of them in intellectual and spiritual aspects, it would become possible for scholar-officials as laypeople to take the lead in advancing Buddhism.

Yuan's colorful life during this period ended abruptly when Yuan Zongdao died in 1600. He returned home to Hubei to manage the funeral and would not return to Beijing until six years later. From 1606 to 1610, Yuan resided in Beijing for the third time and reached the climax in his career, demonstrating once again great organizational and administrative talents. For example, he managed to punish crafty clerks in the Ministry of Personnel and set as a rule that they all must be investigated at the end of one year.⁹⁸ He also showed great dexterity and tactical acumen in 1609 when supervising the civil examination in Shanxi. This exam was acclaimed as the best in the entire empire that year, but it was Yuan who as the chief examiner saved half the successful candidates from those originally weeded out by other examiners.⁹⁹ Consequently, he was promoted three times to vice-director of the Bureau of Evaluations (*kaogong yuanwai lang* 考功員外郎) in the Ministry of Personnel in two years.

Surprisingly, during this last phase of his life Yuan took up conventional Confucian responsibilities, showing unprecedented concern for society and the state, both suffering difficulties, and making serious efforts to save them. In a letter written in 1597 when he was traveling around Jiangnan, Yuan declared that "there are three things under Heaven that could disappoint us most, among which the collapse of a country and the ruining of a family are excluded" (弟嘗謂天下有大敗興事三, 而破國亡家不與焉). But as the sociopolitical crisis deepened, he found "it unendurable to record current affairs, and [I] always felt horrified when writing them down" (時事不堪書, 下筆每驚悸). In 1607, Yuan confessed to Huang Hui that although personally he could live a happy life in Beijing, he would be extremely angry every day after reading the court bulletin (*dibao* 邸報). "The situation has become so bad! How can this [downward tendency] be stopped?" (時事如此, 將何底止?), he asked. This was an amazing return to the scholar-official's traditional concern and role. Like Feng Mengzhen, Yuan was obviously trying to maintain his small patch by recourse to Buddhism when the world was raging outside. But unlike Feng, Yuan eventually challenged himself to take up the duty he had previously declined, in hopes of making some difference to the miserable world. In 1606, he told a friend that

> in a recent letter, Tao Shikui said that he has little intention to take office. I said that we Confucians advocate establishing ourselves and benefiting others, and Chan Buddhism advocates saving all sentient beings. The circulation of this slightly warm air is what is relied on in the universe. Letting the air cool without interference, I believe, is not the case even with Buddhism. Were Shu Yuju [i.e., Shu Shi] and Bai Xiangshan [i.e., Bai Juyi] not Buddhist adherents? Reading their works now, [we can sense] how eager they were to save the world.

> 陶石簣近字, 道其宦情灰冷. 弟曰"吾儒說立達, 禪宗說度一切, 皆賴些子暖氣流行宇宙間. 若直憑冷將去, 恐釋氏亦無此公案." 蘇玉局、白香山非彼法中人乎? 今讀二公集, 其一副愛世心腸, 何等緊切![100]

Yuan drew inspiration from both Confucianism and Buddhism. The mention of "Chan Buddhism" here actually refers to the greater idea of the bodhisattva's path of saving all sentient beings. The eagerness to save the world that Yuan read from Shu and Bai is significant. While the state was in major crisis, no matter how unattached they may have looked, scholar-officials would find it simply impossible to totally put aside their Confucian responsibilities.

Compared with the early phases of his life, Buddhist teachings joined to shape Yuan's mentality and way of life from two new perspectives. For one thing, a fresh stress on practicality led him to prioritizing action over thinking. Yuan told a friend, for instance, "Recently I have behaved [in a way] very like that of the bluntest people. No matter how trivial a matter may be, I am determined to resolve it as best as I can" (弟近日頗學下下根行. 一切煩碎等事, 力可能者, 斷斷行之).[101] Second, Yuan drew from Chan Buddhism the courage of taking responsibility in hard times (*danqi* 膽氣). Yuan's criticism of "wild Chan" was to correct what he perceived as wrong rather than totally to abandon Chan Buddhism, which explains why he advocated unifying Chan and Pure Land. In the context of the late years of the Ming, Yuan's stress on the taking responsibility was not an exception to the current.[102]

It is revealing that Yuan, after a painful struggle of many years, eventually drew his eagerness to save the world from Bai Juyi's and Su Dongpo's writings. It carries little significance as to whether this interpretation is correct, but with his readings Yuan proved that in the deepest he remained a Confucian intellectual in the traditional (but maybe not "pure") sense of the term. Looking back at his life, Yuan recognized that "[I] have been riding a horse with two heads, and that is why [I] feel extra suffering!" (一身騎兩頭馬, 此其所以益苦也!). Yuan's suffering derived, in part, from the Wang Yangming school, whose influence he received from Li Zhi. This school carries an inherent tension. It highlights the superiority of subjectivity that requires emancipation from all burdens on the one hand but never forgets taking up the duties for the state and society—the hallmark revealing its Confucianism pedigree—on the other. In his early years, when Yuan refused to accept the price for fulfilling his duties, he was eager to resign. But after a struggle of a decade, Yuan renewed his stance on the world by acknowledging that his personal freedom did not have a natural primacy over sociopolitical responsibilities. He criticized those who despised acts of saving people and benefiting the world, and instead claimed that these matters would help them to become sages and obtain enlightenment. Nonetheless, at the same time he also confessed to a friend honestly,

> I surely should join government service now. That I am still hesitant is because I am lazy rather than that I do not like riches and honor. . . . With regard to [the choice between] advance and retreat, ancient people acted mostly following the natural development of things. . . . Those who stay at court but miss [the life] in the mountains and those who live in the mountains but miss the court, though seemingly distinct, are the same in terms of being entangled and vulgar.

> 弟此時實當出, 所以遲回者, 實迂懶之故, 非真不愛富貴也. . . . 古人進退, 多是水到渠成 . . . 居朝市而念山林, 與居山林而念朝市者, 兩等心腸, 一般牽纏, 一般俗氣也.[103]

Yuan was not the only scholar-official stuck in the tension between personal preferences and state interests, but, not as lucky as many of them, including Bai Juyi and Shu Shi, he lived in a crisis-stricken society. Timothy Brook has pointed out that "to enter public service in the sixteenth and seventeenth centuries was to face severe stress, if not to court outright disaster. . . . Increasingly, it seemed, only the extremes were available: devoted involvement (*jinshi*) to the point of self-destruction or complete withdrawal (*chushi*) in the style of the Buddhist hermit-monk. This extreme polarity did not allow the gentry to choose a combination of both."[104] Yuan was trying to fight against destiny, but unfortunately there was not much time left for him. In the ninth month of 1610, Yuan died at the age of forty-two. As with the death of Yuan's older brother, wine and sex contributed greatly to this untimely fatality. But it was a great regret given that Yuan had allegedly kept eating vegetarian and reduced attachment to sensual desires. This death is symbolically important, disclosing how a talent rarely produced by the positive and bright side of the age was finally killed by its evil and dark side. Two days later, Yuan's second son was born.

ILLUSION OF AUTONOMY: THE FALL OF THE PUTAO ASSOCIATION

Scholar-officials not only acted as separate individuals but also organized themselves through a variety of associations (*she* 社 or *hui* 會). Although much looser when compared with those of the eunuchs, these organizations nonetheless enhanced their embrace of Buddhism. As demonstrated by Feng Mengzhen and Yuan Hongdao, scholar-officials were not born Buddhists; instead, well prepared to deal with practical affairs and serve the state, their turn toward Buddhism denied, at least partly, their roles and responsibilities as scholar-officials. This defeat for Confucianism and the state in a competition with Buddhist ideals would become bitter following the organized involvement in Buddhism among scholar-officials. From the middle of the Ming until the end of the dynasty, the degree to which scholar-officials participated in social, political, and literary associations steadily increased. Of note, many of these associations had Buddhist ideas and practices as an indispensable part of their activities, suggesting a relaxation in the ability of the state to control society. But counterattacks still took place and complicated the situation. Questions thus arise. In late-Ming China, how did the state respond to this "betrayal" of state ideology? How did the expected crossfire between enthusiastic Buddhists and stubborn Confucians affect the solidarity of scholar-officials as a group? How did the life of Buddhist scholar-officials and the evolution of Buddhist ideas and institutions change accordingly?

The Putao Association was such a literati association. After returning to Beijing in 1606, Yuan frequented Chongguosi 崇國寺 and lamented that "eight years have passed swiftly since the Putao Association [started]. Those few [who were active] in this enjoyable place have scattered to the corners of the world like clouds driven by a sea wind. Some even have transformed into other beings [i.e., died]" (葡萄社光景便已八年. 歡場數人, 如雲逐海風, 倏爾天末, 亦有化爲異物者).[105] His deep sentiments were not without reason: both Chongguosi and the Putao Association were central to his Beijing life from 1598 to 1602.

The Putao Association, founded by the Yuan brothers in a vineyard at Chongguosi, was in some sense the culmination of the literati gathering in Beijing during the Wanli period. As a loosely formed group, the association is usually believed to have started in the spring of 1598 when Yuan Hongdao arrived in Beijing. This association had its predecessors. In the winter of 1588, Yuan Zongdao and Dong Qichang organized a society at Longhuasi 龍華寺 to discuss Chan Buddhism, in which Deqing as a star monk appeared at least once. Six years later, the two leaders organized a similar gathering, with Yuan Hongdao included.[106] The next year, at least seven participants, including the Yuan brothers and Tang Xianzu, held another meeting. During this period from 1588 to 1595, according to research by He Qingmei, their meetings attracted nearly twenty participants, and some preexisting networks could be discovered among them: most of them were men who had won the *jinshi* or *juren* degree in the same year (*tongnian* 同年), colleagues working in the same official department, or persons coming from the same home district. Furthermore, these associations were gatherings of superstars: fourteen among the eighteen identified held the *jinshi* degree, with eight serving as officials at the Hanlin Academy. More specifically, the Yuan brothers were renowned for their literary talent, Dong Qichang for painting and calligraphy, and Tang Xianzu for drama writing. These gatherings prepared for the formation of the Putao Association, with many of their participants active in that association.

The Putao Association was a relatively close-knit organization where the participants could claim a kind of autonomy by behaving as they pleased. The association organized scores of gatherings. Aside from the three Yuan brothers, there were at least thirty-five recorded participants, with eight functioning as its major members.[107] In a gathering, "one of the members took turns to prepare vegetarian food. Once arriving, people flocked together to talk. Some walked along the water, some read Buddhist sutras, some gathered to discuss recent news, some sat quietly on meditation divans, and still others composed poems. [They] would not return home until sunset" (輪一人具伊蒲之食. 至則聚譚, 或游水邊, 或覽貝葉, 或數人相聚問近日所見, 或靜坐禪榻上, 或作詩, 至日暮始歸).[108]

Yuan Zongdao once described their activities in vivid detail.

> [In] the vineyard of several *mu*, thick branches are green and dangling.
> [We] take the vine as pennants, leaves as canopy,

tendrils as precious nets, and fruits as a jade necklace.

Cicadas take turns to make sound, which, although noisy, is better than
secular music.

When sitting long facing spring, people still feel that their clothes are
thin even if they have worn extra layers.

Four or five friends come together and break their confusion [easily] in a
smile.

Arranging rope beds [hammocks] along the bank, [we explore]
the profound meaning of Chan Buddhism and make fun of one
another.

[We] fry sunflower and cook it with dew, as well as pick up tea and
choose water to make it.

[Water] drops from stone stairs with a ringing note, and the bronze pot
sounds loudly.

[We] play finger-guessing games in two groups and stretch hands to
throw dice.

A wineglass appears too small when forfeit wine has amassed, so we take
bowl in place of cup.

Hottest summer days are spent here, and ten thousand volumes are kept
on high shelves.

數畝葡萄林, 濃條青若若.
以藤為幡幢, 以葉為帷幕.
以蔓為寶網, 以實為瓔珞.
蜩蟬遞代響, 雖聒勝俗樂.
對泉坐良久, 客衣增尚薄.
同來四五朋, 一笑破纏繳.
依岸排繩床, 禪玄入詼謔.
煎葵帶露烹, 摘茶揀水瀹.
石砌滴琤琤, 銅鐺鳴霍霍.
拇陳分兩曹, 奮爪相攫搏.
觥小罰已深, 取缽代杯杓.
三伏此中消, 萬卷束高閣.[109]

In the gatherings, the participants were engaged in literary and Buddhist activities as well as wine drinking, and it seemed that they tended to accentuate their
otherness as an attractive asset within the seemingly exclusive milieu. Compared with the gatherings organized by the eunuchs, these were smaller and less
devotional. It was amazing to have such a peaceful and friendly place when the

FIGURE 5.1 *Painting of Elegant Gathering* 雅集圖 by Chen Hongshou 陳洪綬

Reprinted with permission from the Shanghai Museum

outside world was raging. Yuan Hongdao enjoyed life there so much that he felt at home whenever he arrived at the vineyard.[110]

But the Putao Association could not always be an Eden immune to secular life; before long it ended abruptly under the pressures of the intellectual and political worlds. The association had its best time around the year 1599, with at least nine gatherings held at the vineyard from spring to autumn. These gatherings enhanced the association's reputation, but, in a place as politically sensitive as Beijing, the increased attention it drew eventually proved not a blessing but a curse. Shen Defu has a brief account of what happened to the Putao Association in connection with the broader context:

Shen Siming [i.e., Shen Yiguan 沈一貫 (1531–1615, *jinshi* 1568)] was then in power. Learned of the popularity [of the Putao Association], he really detested it, especially Huang [Hui]. In the *xinchou* year [1601], Master Zibo entered the capital. Since men of repute in Jiangnan had been long holding alms bowls and pots [for him] [i.e., holding him in high esteem], powerful eunuchs in the inner court hurried to attend on him as if participating in the Dharma assembly at Vulture Peak. Moreover, some people approached him [only] in hopes of gaining reputation. [All of this] resulted in the regret that Taiqiu's [i.e., Chen Shi 陳寔 (104–187)] circle of friends and

acquaintances was too large,[111] and the pure atmosphere of the association [led by] Yuan and Tao vanished. Thus, Huang Shenxuan [i.e., Huang Hui] was most discontented with [Zibo]. [Shen] Siming originally intended to use Zibo to squeeze Huang out, but he shelved the plan after recognizing that they were in conflict. As for Huang, he discovered that the surroundings had changed, which was added to by the impeachment memorials against him. Thus, he resigned office by taking illness as an excuse. By the time, Yufan [i.e., Yuan Zongdao] had died, Zhonglang [i.e., Yuang Hongdao] left and Shikui [i.e., Tao Wangling] left [the capital] to supervise the civil service examination. The association therefore dissolved.

時沈四明柄政, 聞而憎之, 其憎黃尤切. 至辛丑, 紫柏師入都, 江左名公既久持瓶鉢, 一時中禁大鐺趨之, 如真赴靈山佛會. 又遊客輩附景希光, 不免太丘道廣之恨, 非複袁、陶淨社景象, 以故黃慎軒最心非之. 初, 四明欲借紫柏擠黃, 既知其不合, 意稍解. 而黃亦覺物情漸異, 又白簡暗抨之, 引疾歸. 時玉幡先亡, 中郎亦去, 石簣以典試出, 其社遂散.[112]

"Master Zibo" is a reference to Zhenke, and Huang Hui was one of Yuan's best friends and a leading figure in the Putao Association. Some points in this paragraph need further explication.

What made Huang Hui sense "the surroundings had changed" was a string of organized attacks against Buddhism that were instigated for ideological, political, and religious reasons. In the intercalary second month of 1602, Zhang Wenda 張問達 (d. 1625, *jinshi* 1583) submitted a memorial impeaching Li Zhi for deluding the world and cheating the common people with unorthodox doctrines. At the end of the memorial, Zhang fired without warning at Huang Hui and Tao Wangling: "Recently, some gentry and scholar-officials memorize dharanis, recite the Buddha's name, and serve monks with reverence. By holding rosaries in their hands, they believe that they are following the Vinaya precepts; by hanging marvelous images [i.e., Buddha images] in the room, they think that they have converted to Buddhism. They defy the teachings of Confucius while being engrossed in Chan Buddhism" (近來縉紳士大夫, 亦有捧咒念佛, 奉僧膜拜, 手持數珠, 以為律戒; 室懸妙像, 以為皈依; 不遵孔子家法, 而溺意禪教者).[113] A few days later, the minister of rites, Feng Qi 馮琦 (1558–1604, *jinshi* 1577), sent another memorial delivering a similar charge.[114] In response, Wanli took express aim at Huang Hui, saying that "immortality [i.e., Daoism] and Buddhism, distinct [from Confucianism], are suitable to practice alone in mountains and forests. Those fond of them are allowed to resign office and leave. They should not mislead people by advocating Confucianism simultaneously" (仙佛原是異術, 宜在山林獨修. 有好尚者, 任解官自便去, 勿以儒術並進, 以惑人心). On the same day, Censor Kang Piyang 康丕揚 (d. 1632, *jinshi* 1592) also sent a memorial to the emperor proposing that Zhenke be arrested and his followers be expelled from Beijing. Li Zhi, Zhenke, and Huang Hui were then the major protagonists of Buddhism in Beijing. With their being impeached separately in three memorials within ten days, the attacks echoed one another and created tremendous pressure on officials fond of or sympathetic to Buddhism.

These attacks resulted from a deep rift among scholar-officials that had surfaced as a major wave of reaction on the part of conservative Confucians to the surging support for Buddhism. Aware of great changes in the political, social, and intellectual realms, Tao Wangling had pointed out a year earlier that "people here [i.e., in the capital] are increasingly viewing attacks against Chan and the expelling of Buddhist monks as emblematic of heroic conduct and integrity of character. Although our names have not yet been listed in the impeachment memorials, we are actually being expelled. A few like-minded of us have decided to leave hand in hand" (此間諸人, 日以攻禪逐僧爲風力名行. 吾輩雖不挂名彈章, 實在逐中矣. 一二同志皆相約携手而去).[115] Notably, Huang Hui was one of those who had decided to leave.[116] In a letter written later, Tao Wangling uncovered the ideological antagonism in the attacks: "Previously [we] had a learning society here . . . that brought together many talented people. But it was criticized as unorthodox by others and sparked deep hatred and envy. What's unexpected is that the disaster would have begun with Mr. Zhuo[wu] [i.e., Li Zhi]!" (此間舊有學會 . . . 頗稱濟濟! 而旁觀者指目爲异學, 深見忌嫉. 然不虞此禍乃發于卓老也!).[117]

Tao showed keen insight into the rift among scholar-officials, but it may not be that unexpected that Li Zhi fell victim to the divide. Li Zhi was a leading figure of the radical Wang Yangming school that frequently led scholar-officials to Buddhism. As the school expanded at a stunning pace, strong resistance was provoked among scholar-officials and caused a divide that was shocking in its depth, rancor, and intractability. In 1600, Li Zhi was ostracized from Huanggang 黃岡, Hubei, in a move launched by Feng Yingjing 馮應京 (1555–1606, *jinshi* 1592). Li Zhi then moved to Beijing, only to find that Zhang Wenda's charge was waiting for him. Zhang impeached Li as "misguiding people's minds" (惑亂人心) with his unorthodox behavior—shaving his hair off to become an unordained monk despite his earlier career as an official—and thought, which was in wide circulation. At the core of the charge was the ideological concern that Li's mingling of Confucianism and Buddhism had caused identity confusion or even a crisis among scholar-officials that weakened the foundation of the state. Clearly convinced, the Wanli emperor ordered that Li Zhi be arrested and his books be destroyed. On the fifteenth day of the third month of 1602 the imprisoned and desperate Li Zhi committed suicide. As the most influential iconoclastic figure to appear during the early Wanli period, when state control had grown relatively lax, Li's death reflected a backlash aimed to counter that tendency. Feng's criticism of Huang Hui can be understood in the same light. Although Feng thought highly of Huang,[118] he endeavored to hold the latter accountable because "it will be a grave problem for the state if scholar-officials do not concentrate their attention on government affairs" (士大夫精神不在政事, 國家之大患也).[119] More broadly, this intellectual and political groundswell of resistance culminated in the formation of the so-called Donglin faction, which reportedly embodied the moral commitment of scholar-officials.[120] It is no coincidence that Feng Qi, Zhang Wenda, and Feng Yingjing were later listed either as Donglin members or sympathizers.

But why did both Wanli and Shen Yiguan detest the popularity of the Putao Association in the first place? Why was Huang Hui chosen as the point of attack? This leads us to both the succession issue and court factionalism.

The Putao Association emerged in the capital only as an exception in a special period, and its fate was ideologically doomed from the very start. While in power, Zhang Juzheng ordered the destruction of academies (*shuyuan* 書院)—a place where scholar-officials regularly gathered to conduct philosophical discourse.

Aimed at controlling scholar-officials' thought, this move was taken out of ideological concern and partly contributed to the death of He Xinyin 何心隱 (1517–1579), a famous iconoclastic thinker.[121] But the ban on the academies loosened following state recognition of the Wang Yangming school as useful learning two years after Zhang's death,[122] laying the groundwork for the emergence of the Putao Association. Nonetheless, the existence of such a society could not last long. In fact, Beijing was an exception in terms of philosophical discourse (*jiangxue* 講學) and association organizing (*jieshe* 結社): there were more than sixteen hundred academies identified in the dynasty, among which only one was in Beijing; there were more than six hundred literary societies that appeared in this dynasty, among which only ten or so were in Beijing.[123] Such a grossly disproportionate situation exemplifies the strong intention of the government to control public discourse in the politically sensitive region and its remarkable success.[124]

The targeting of Huang Hui seemed to be a religious solution by both the emperor and the senior grand secretary to the political crises.[125] By early 1602, despite the announcement of Zhu Changluo 朱常洛 (r. 1620) as the crown prince, the succession issue lingered and the emperor's relationship with Cisheng remained frozen. Strikingly, the Putao Association had five of Zhu Changluo's nine instructors as its main members,[126] and in the sinister situation certain special feelings seem to have developed between the prince and his instructors. Yuan Zongdao was such an instructor, who would cry secretly at home when hearing rumors about Zhu Changluo.[127] He resisted repeated impulses to resign only because "in such a risky and uncertain time, I find it very hard to shake my clothes to leave [i.e., quit office]!" (當此危疑之際而拂衣去, 吾不忍也!). Unlike Yuan's passivity, Huang Hui as an instructor took active steps to protect Zhu Changluo. In the tenth month of 1600, upon learning that Lady Wang 王 (1565–1611), Zhu Changluo's mother, had almost died because of Wanli's cosseting of Lady Zheng 鄭 (1565–1630), Huang drafted a memorial and requested Wang Dewan 王德完 (1554–1621, *jinshi* 1586), a censor from Huang's province, to submit it. The memorial exasperated the emperor, who threw Wang Dewan into the imperial prison and revoked his qualification as an official, but the move did help to save Lady Wang and stabilize Zhu Changluo's status as the successor.[128] Thus the Putao Association was not merely a literary society but also a sort of headquarters for court officials backing Zhu Changluo. The closer the association was to Zhu Changluo, the farther it was from Wanli. This helps explain why Wanli drove Huang out of the court.

Shen Yiguan's assault on Huang derived from the threat he perceived from the latter. Shen had gone a long way before his becoming the senior grand secretary in the eleventh month of 1601, but then Huang appeared to be a potential challenger following the establishment of Zhu Changluo as the crown prince one month before. This threat could be real. In addition to the general belief in the Ming that the post of instructor to the crown prince was a shortcut to the Grand Secretariat, the aforementioned special feeling between Zhu Changluo and his instructors was an asset to Huang. Moreover, more than an ideological problem, the great popularity that Huang enjoyed among scholar-officials, partly through the Putao Association, was a political one for Shen because it could be translated into political influence once the time was right.[129] Three months later, when Wanli left his last will during an acute illness, this sense of crisis might have deepened, reminding Shen once again of the fragility of his power. In light of that, it may not be accidental that the attack on Huang Hui was launched only one month after Wanli's illness—on the twenty-third of the intercalary second month.

Aware that "the surroundings had changed," Huang Hui wasted no time in resigning his office, which followed the dissolution of the Putao Association. These events exemplify the actual situation in which Buddhism existed at the time, revealing the structural weakness inherent in its lack of institutional support. Timothy Brook has rightly pointed out that "independence from the state was not the theme that late-Ming patrons and apologists struck when they defined the relationship between Buddhism and the state, as their commitment to Confucianism required them to do from time to time. They preferred to picture an interdependent relationship, drawing on the language of earlier edicts of patronage to do so."[130] But as so starkly revealed by Wanli's comments on Feng's memorial, Buddhism was tolerated only as heterodox and was always susceptible to attack for ideological, political, or religious reasons. The red line was always there; although usually less visible, it was available to be invoked in any situation perceived as necessary.

The message sent by the collapse of the Putao Association under ideological and political pressure resonated far more at Chongguosi, at which it was probably aimed. Yuan Hongdao was quick to understand Huang's resignation as an alarming warning of approaching danger,[131] but he could not help but visit Chongguosi again after his return to Beijing several years later. What he found was that "the railings of the well had half collapsed. Only half the grape vines remained, while old trees had almost all been cut down. The old monks formerly in red robes [had passed away] and only [left their portraits] hanging lonely in the Image Hall, with all covered in dust, while a couple of previous novice monks had gotten old and nearly could not recognize Mr. Liu[132] [i.e., Yuan Hongdao himself]" (井牀半落, 葡桃枝僅存其半, 老榦略已伐盡. 向來紅衫老僧寂寞影堂中, 塵灰滿面. 而一二沙彌皆已老, 幾不識劉郎).[133] This description of the scene reflected Yuan's loneliness. Yuan wrote to Huang Hui complaining that there were no friends in

Beijing with whom to discuss Buddhism.[134] In 1598, when Yuan had just arrived in Beijing, a letter he wrote to friends in Suzhou reads, "[I] have many friends in the capital and have learned a great deal [here]. [This place] is not as good as southern China in terms of the pleasure derived from enjoying mountains and water, but it is ten times better in terms of friends with whom one can discuss issues regarding life and death" (京師朋友多, 聞見多. 雖山水之樂, 不及南中, 而性命中朋友, 則十分倍之矣).[135] Things had changed significantly in the past ten years. Yuan attested to the turning point in Beijing Buddhism around the year 1602, an issue to which I return in the last chapter.

Scholar-officials' relationship with Buddhism could fluctuate considerably depending on the time, region, and their roles and was thus not as cozy as we tend to believe. A radical shift in their dominant stance toward Buddhism occurred from the Jiajing to the following Wanli eras, moving generally from indifference to menace to accommodation. More specifically, while in office and under pressure to conform politically, they tended to perform more conservatively in politically charged Beijing than in other regions. As local elites, they were more independent in deciding how to handle Buddhism; this was especially true in Jiangnan, where they could advance their own interests more freely regardless of the government's stance. Compared with the eunuchs, scholar-officials were clearly distinguished by the extent to which they could adjust their stance toward religion and the time frames in which they were able to act. These differences had significant effects on the contour of the late-Ming Buddhist renewal, an issue I address in the last chapter.

Individual scholar-officials could come to embrace Buddhist ideas both for existential concerns in their own lives and owing to influences from the external world. The major intellectual reorientation, characterized by the Wang Yangming school, led them to Buddhism as a template other than Confucianism to experience, sense, and interpret the world. As the tension between the state and society deepened, their patronage and support of Buddhism was both a way of harvesting social capital and of staking a claim for cultural and political autonomy. It should be noted that even in the often hostile sociopolitical world, they made efforts to act upon Buddhist ideals, in a more existentialist sense, in everyday life, especially at critical moments like illness, death, and hard times in their careers, as in the cases of Feng Mengzhen and Yuan Hongdao. The results were an interpretive scaffolding for them to evaluate the credibility of Buddhism and its various schools. Practicality usually took priority, and frequent adjustments thus followed. The focus of Yuan, for example, kept shifting, first from "wild Chan" to Pure Land and then to an emphasis on both.

Structurally, given that scholar-officials relied on the state for status and that Buddhism was officially labeled as heterodox, scholar-officials were deprived of the right to decide their relationship to Buddhism. Instead, politics played a key role in deciding where their relationship could go. Contextually, Jiajing's anti-Buddhism policy contributed greatly to scholar-officials' indifference to or even encroachment on Buddhism, while Cisheng's appearance in the political arena rekindled enthusiasm in the early Wanli years. As the politico-social situation deteriorated, they were further pushed to Buddhism—either to express growing discontent or to claim autonomy from the gloomiest reality—but their turning to "heterodox" Buddhism sparked an ideological backlash aimed at bringing them back. The rise and fall of the Putao Association was significant symbolically and in practice, reflecting stark differences among scholar-officials that mirrored intense confrontations found among the broader public. With the involvement of court strife, the clash spun out of control and its fatal result would redirect the evolution of Buddhism, an issue I take up later.

The rekindled enthusiasm among scholar-officials signaled the approach of the Buddhist revival and provided it with new traction, but because the stand that scholar-officials took toward Buddhism had conditions, these entailed important implications for the evolution of the renewal. There was a virtuous circle of mutual reinforcement. Scholar-officials received guidance from Buddhist masters like Zhenke, Daokai, and Zhuhong in their religious life, and then they contributed to Buddhism in multiple ways. Feng Mengzhen and Yuan Hongdao, for example, enhanced its intellectual vitality with works like the *Xifang helun*. They helped to establish a sound monastic economy. And socially, through their networks and roles, they enhanced the visibility of Buddhism by bringing it to the attention of more people. These efforts provided tremendous momentum that pushed Buddhism toward a dynamic renewal. Still, not always a reliable ally, scholar-officials could withdraw their support of Buddhism. As captured by the metaphor of the two-headed horse, Buddhism never took full control in defining its relationship with scholar-officials. What could happen to Buddhism if scholar-officials, who served as significant intellectual, social, and economic resources, returned en masse to Confucianism and to the state at the cost of Buddhism? I discuss this issue in the conclusion.

6

Eminent Monks

Engaged in, or Entangled with the World?

The secular elites I have examined so far together shaped the evolution of Buddhism both as the affective and affected factors, but by no means could they alone push Buddhism toward a revival. Instead, a favored interaction between these external forces and the intrinsic dynamics of the *saṃgha* was required for the emergence of a Buddhist renewal. In this light, this and the following chapter turn to the *saṃgha* itself to see how its interaction with the secular world, through certain mechanisms, impacted the growth of Buddhism, positively or negatively. To demonstrate the process concretely, I examine eminent monks and Buddhist institutions, respectively. The assumption is that they did not respond to extramural influences only passively; they also had their own agendas to follow and strove to reinvigorate Buddhism by accumulating momentum from within.

This chapter is devoted to eminent monks, the human resources most important and most mobile, by examining the three monks Hanshan Deqing 憨山德清 (1546–1623), Miaofeng Fudeng 妙峰福登 (1540–1612), and Zibo Zhenke 紫柏真可 (1543–1604), all close friends within the same network. They each vowed to complete a major Buddhist project. That all three made such a vow is not coincidental but reflected the mission to revitalize Buddhism that characterized eminent monks of the time. Their efforts were indeed full of passion and energy, driven by a charisma that derived from their religious cultivation and spiritual achievements. Despite this common starting point, however, they achieved different degrees of success in fulfilling their vows and their experiences punctuated key moments in the Buddhist renewal. While religious factors are important, they are not enough to explain the discrepancies in the achievements of these three monks. In fact, although all were intimately linked with the inner court and local society, these masters were distinguished from one another in background, character, and strategies for success. This chapter thus has a special interest in exploring how they became what they were, especially the way in which politics affected their life experiences and shaped their images in history. To that end, it examines what challenges elite monks encountered within the *samgha* and beyond, what strategies they chose, what consequences their efforts brought about in their lives and the development of the Buddhist establishment as a whole, and, eventually, the strength and weakness of the ongoing revitalization.

HANSHAN DEQING: ENTERING THE DHARMA REALM BECAUSE OF THE EMPEROR'S LAW

Controversial though it is as to how to define eminent monks, it is even harder to understand how a monk became eminent. Generally, greater achievements and influence helped to distinguish eminent monks from ordinary monks. During a period as turbulent as the late Ming, in addition to accomplishments in theory, practice, and interaction with other groups, the capability to diagnose paramount challenges facing the *samgha* and resolving them reasonably mattered. But it is naive to believe that such achievements could naturally be translated into influence, let alone the status of eminent monk. Were eminent monks only those recognized for their distinctive valor and achievements? Who had the right, and by what standards, to decide who constituted an eminent monk? What happened to those glorified in life but neglected in death? Puzzles like these loom behind any study of eminent monks.

Active in the Buddhist and secular worlds alike, Hanshan Deqing stood out as a central master who greatly shaped the Buddhist revival. His voluminous works, especially his autobiography annotated by his disciple,[1] make it relatively convenient, though misleading at times, to study his life and thought.[2] Instead of making a comprehensive study, I focus on two interrelated events—his efforts to restore the Great Baoen monastery 大報恩寺 and his exile in 1595—as they are the key to understanding his life and religious undertakings. Among others, I highlight strategies that Deqing used to establish and boost his reputation as well as the connection between his spiritual achievements and contemporary politics.

Efforts to Restore the Great Baoen Monastery

Deqing forced his way into the political arena around the year 1582 while living at Mount Wutai. Deqing and Miaofeng Fudeng began to reside at Mount Wutai, where they occupied themselves primarily with Chan meditation, in 1574. Three years later, Deqing decided to copy the *Huayan jing* with his blood to improve his spiritual achievements and to invoke blessings for his parents.[3] Similarly, Fudeng made his own copy of a sutra in blood. Then, in 1580, they came up with a plan to commemorate the completion of the two copies by holding the Undiscriminating Great Assembly (*wuzhe fahui* 無遮法會, Skt. *pañcavarṣika*).[4] In the fall of the following year when the Dharma assembly was about to start, however, it happened that Empress Dowager Cisheng 慈聖 (1545–1614) sent several eunuch envoys to pray for supernatural assistance at Mount Wutai. This prayer was intended to facilitate the birth of Wanli's first son, who would become the crown prince. Deqing then suggested incorporating their planned Dharma assembly in the prayer service, arguing that this would increase the chance for the prayer to succeed. This proposal, according to Deqing, was objected to by both Fudeng and the envoy eunuchs, but it was finally carried out because of his insistence. In retrospect, this occasion started Deqing's formal involvement in politics that would haunt his remaining life.[5]

A monk as knowledgeable as Deqing surely understood that any matters, once associated with the crown prince, would be politically sensitive. He defended his forceful involvement in the arena by arguing that monks should take the greater responsibility toward the state. This argument gave Deqing moral privilege over other participants, but it reveals little about his motivations unless we relate his action to a broader politico-religious context.

There was a mission that Deqing struggled to fulfill throughout his life. He once confessed that "originally determined to restore my home monastery [*bensi* 本寺], which had been ruined by fire, I thus cultivated myself to wait for the right conditions. Some opportunities came up during the eight years I resided at Mount Wutai. Thus, I lived as a recluse by the Eastern Sea lest I miss the chance if living too far away. This was my real intention" (始予為本寺回祿, 志在興複, 故修行以待緣. 然居臺山八年, 頗有機會, 恐遠失時, 故隱居東海, 此本心也).[6] The *bensi* here refers to the Great Baoen monastery in Nanjing, with which Deqing had been affiliated since the age of twelve. Originally built in the Three Kingdoms period (220–280), this monastery was assigned as one of the three "great imperially sponsored monasteries" (*dasi* 大寺) in the early Ming. But its glory waned

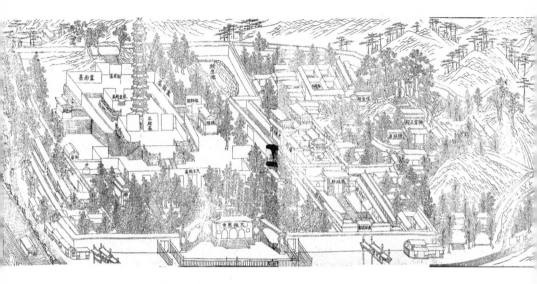

FIGURE 6.1 The Great Baoen monastery 大報恩寺 in Ming Nanjing

Reprinted from the *Jinling fancha zhi* 金陵梵刹志
Courtesy of He Xiaorong

rapidly in the wake of the relocation of the imperial capital from Nanjing to Beijing in the 1420s. The situation was exacerbated during the Jiajing era, as evidenced by the fact when Xilin Yongning 西林永寧 (1483–1565) died in 1565, the monastery found it hard to pay the roughly three hundred taels of silver for his funeral (I began the book with this story). Two years later, a fire caused by lightning burned up three-fourths of its buildings, resulting in the arrest of many monks under the charge of damaging an imperially built monastery. "Eastern Sea" refers to Mount Lao 嶗山, where Deqing lived from 1583 to 1594. In these few sentences, Deqing revealed the underlying logic behind key events in his early life: they were all driven by his mission.

By the end of the Jiajing period the Great Baoen monastery was desperately struggling for survival, and it was at this time that Deqing was tasked to restore it. In 1557 Deqing entered the monastery and was soon selected by Xilin Yongning, the far-sighted monk, to train as the heir. Witnessing the monastery's scrabbling for survival, Deqing had since taken as his mission the salvaging of the sinking ship.[7] But the monastery's decline was just part of the general failure of Buddhist institutions in Jiangnan. On top of that, Jiangnan was then a region very unfavorable to Buddhist communities, and this was true especially for Nanjing, for reasons discussed in chapter 2. Despite their hard efforts, therefore, Deqing and his fellow monks had little to do other than earning minor incomes through lecturing and selling the monastery's lands. Fully aware of the challenges, Deqing vowed with his peer and friend Xuelang Hong'en 雪浪洪恩 (1545–1607), another eminent monk who would later take up the abbotship of the monastery, saying that "for this great cause, it is hard to accomplish unless [we] have great merit [*fude* 福德, Skt. *puṇya*] and wisdom. You and I should work at full strength to cultivate ourselves and wait for the opportunity to come" (此大事因緣, 非具大福德智慧者, 未易也. 爾我當拌命修行, 養以待時可也).[8] This solemn and moving oath exemplifies initiatives within the *saṃgha*, but it also reveals an unmistakable challenge facing the *saṃgha*: lacking institutional support from the state, its fate was expected to hinge on the personal efforts of individual monks. It turned out that this mission was a lifelong one, and Deqing's relevant efforts constituted the overall framework within which we should understand his life prior to the age of fifty.[9] By the time he held the Dharma assembly, Cisheng's extensive patronage of Buddhism, backed by the eunuchs, had lasted for ten years, thereby sending a stable and unequivocal message to the *saṃgha* that the inner court was a safe place to secure considerable support. Deqing, alongside other promising monks, received that message loud and clear. In light of that, his force in connection with the imperial prayer represented a conscious attempt of the Jiangnan *saṃgha* to take advantage of the resource represented by the inner court.

Deqing's activities in the following year confirmed this secret desire to approach the inner court, especially Cisheng. Shortly after the assembly, sometime in 1582, he left Mount Wutai for Zhangshi cliff 障石巖 in Zhending 真定 (present-day Zhengding 正定 in Hebei).[10] The next spring he further moved to the Western Mountains 西山 in Beijing, where a eunuch built a temple for him. That Deqing changed his residence twice within one year after the Dharma assembly, each time moving closer to the capital, is revealing. The 1582 entry in his autobiography reads, "In the eighth month of this year, the crown prince [i.e., Zhu Changluo] was born. I went to the Zhongfeng temple in western Beijing once again" (是年八月, 皇太子生. 予復之京西中峰寺). Not juxtaposed as casually as may appear, the two events had a causal relationship—Deqing was encouraged to move to Beijing by the birth of Zhu Changluo. In doing so, he appeared to have a secret hope of capitalizing in the inner court on his contribution to the prayer.

Before long, however, in the fourth month of 1583 Deqing suddenly left Beijing for Mount Lao, a peripheral coastal area in Shandong. For this action Fuzheng explained that it is because the Undiscriminating Great Assembly was too successful and [Deqing's] fame deriving from the successful prayer for the crown prince was too high. [Moreover], news about his offense to the eunuchs pervaded the inner court, which was even more severe and dangerous.

以當日無遮道場太盛, 為宮闈祈嗣得嗣之名太著, 忤內使之言, 有聞於內, 其事更大, 其名更不可居.[11]

But this explanation simply cannot be true, considering that Deqing had little intention to keep away from the inner court in the first place. In reality, this retreat to a place several hundred miles away from Beijing had much to do with an unexpectedly rapid change in the political climate. When he moved to the capital, what Deqing failed to recognize was that the power triangle had collapsed following the unexpected death of Zhang Juzheng 張居正 (1525–1582, *jinshi* 1547) in the sixth month of 1582, and a thorough reorientation of power was under way. By the end of the year, signaled by the sudden exile of Feng Bao 馮保 (d. 1583) to Nanjing, where he died shortly afterward in prison, it became evident that Wanli had started venting his pent-up anger toward the old system. The situation got even worse by the fourth month of the next year when Zhang Juzheng's hometown house in Jiangling 江陵, Hubei, was confiscated and a couple of his family members starved to death.[12] Cisheng had been in alliance with Feng and Zhang for ten years, but she kept surprisingly silent in the face of these attacks. Whatever the reason was, apparently she was trying to adapt herself to the "new-faced" son with greater caution. These political changes upset Deqing's plan. Living in a cave close to the capital, through eunuchs and court officials, Deqing was watching what was happening at court. And it would not take too long for him to recognize that Cisheng's patronage of Buddhism had already become restricted, at least in the short term. Moreover, the turbulence at the time increased the danger of Deqing's being attacked by the eunuchs he had offended at Mount Wutai. In light of this changed situation, it may thus be no coincidence that Deqing left the capital, then a hotbed of trouble, at the same time Zhang Juzheng's house was confiscated. His destination was Mount Lao, a place bearing religious significance for him. But this was also a choice of splitting the difference, as the place was within a reasonable distance from Beijing lest he "miss the chance if living too far away."

This retreat meant a huge setback for Deqing's plan to approach the inner court, leaving him in a clear limbo for the following few years. Deqing had resided at Mount Wutai for nearly ten years, but that was a deliberate decision intended to advance himself spiritually while waiting for an appropriate opportunity.

To his chagrin, because of bad timing his first major effort in the direction of making a bridge to Cisheng was so easily frustrated by court politics. At Mount Lao, he first lived in a desolate temple, where nobody visited him in the first year. In the following year, Deqing received an invitation from Cisheng to Beijing for his contribution to the prayer ceremony. Unlike Fudeng, who accepted the invitation, Deqing declined the summons. Moreover, after receiving three thousand taels of silver with which Cisheng proposed building a temple for him as an alternative, Deqing performed another noteworthy act by distributing the money, in Cisheng's name, to people in need. In retrospect, the once-escalating tensions at court following the power reshuffle had by then relaxed so that Cisheng could resume support for Buddhism. But very likely Deqing did not exhibit great shrewdness in his response to her offering, probably because of the isolation and its blunting of his sensitivity. More important, restoring the Baoen monastery required an estimated one hundred thousand taels of silver, a huge amount of money at which most people would balk. Deqing was in desperate need of support, but what he required was much more than an "average" monk was supposed to ask—the three thousand taels seem to have been the price Cisheng would offer for him at the time. Thus, Deqing had to await another opportunity to convince them of his greater value.[13]

The following few years at Mount Lao, unfortunately, proved to be dark times for Deqing. In a letter to his disciple Deqing recalled,

[I] hid myself in deep Mount Lao, which, unreachable by human beings, is the realm of gods and ghosts.... [We] cut down trees and bushes, lay down upon wild grass fields, confronted great waves, and crossed over dangerous places. It is impossible to recount all the difficulties and hardships we underwent.... [I] thought that I would die of old age as a recluse and never again appear in the world.

藏修於牢山深處, 人跡所不能至, 神鬼之鄉也 ... 披荊榛, 臥草莽, 犯風濤, 涉險阻, 艱難辛苦, 不可殫述 ... 余亦將謂老死丘壑, 無復人世矣.[14]

The sentence "I would die of old age as a recluse and never again appear in the world" reveals Deqing's loneliness and desperation, considering especially his confession in the same letter that he had never been the reclusive type. Indeed, he explicitly expressed his desperation in a letter to Fudeng, lamenting that "aware that my body is filthy and turbid [in substance] ... I am content to throw [myself] with all its risks to the remotest corner of mountains and seas.... Alas, my life is over. There is no doubt that I will wither like the grass and trees" (然某

自知形器穢濁 . . . 故甘心拌命，擲此山海窮鄉. . . . 嗟乎，某此生已矣，竟同草木
枯槁無疑).[15] Deqing was then forty-two years old but still confined to the isolated periphery, which may explain why he felt so desperate in response to his fate.

But hope had come before Deqing recognized it. Cisheng initiated the first
wave of canon bestowal in 1586, with four copies first delivered to four temples.
Clearly the selection of the four monasteries (and thus their head monks) carried
a special flavor of imperial favor. Thanks to Fudeng's arrangements, one copy
was bestowed on Deqing,[16] who was still confused as to what had happened.
Shortly, Deqing visited Beijing to express appreciation for the imperial favor.
Pleased, Cisheng ordered court women to make donations for Deqing to build a
temple, which she named Haiyin 海印 (Reflection by the Sea). A direct tie
between Deqing and Cisheng was finally established after several tests.

This direct line of communication to Cisheng, which would later grow even
closer, benefited Deqing in multiple regards and greatly facilitated his rise from a
promising monk to a master with national influence. On the one hand, Deqing,
who had been exhausted for a long time, was finally able to settle down to
advance his spiritual achievements.[17] He built a lecture hall to formally expound
the Dharma the next year. On the other hand, after being placed on the right
track, Deqing was rocketing toward success on the imperial stage. Starting in
1589, he spent much more time in Beijing than before, and his frequent visits to
Cishousi 慈壽寺—Cisheng's private temple—bespoke his close ties with the
empress dowager. In 1592, Deqing was granted the purple robe, a symbolic gift of
imperial favor. Also he wrote an essay in memory of three relics that were first discovered by Zhenke at Yunjusi 雲居寺 and then presented to Cisheng for veneration.
Sometime between the eleventh month of 1594 and the second month of the next
year, Deqing's success in the secular world reached its peak: Cisheng became his
disciple and asked Wanli to pay homage to his portrait hung in a palace.[18]

Back to his mission, Deqing's strategies seem to have worked well. In 1589, Cisheng bestowed one set of the Buddhist canon to the Baoen monastery in praise
of Deqing's service, despite that one copy had been sent there three years earlier.
Deqing escorted the canon back to the monastery, which he had never forgotten
in the past two decades. Upon his return to Beijing, Deqing reported to Cisheng
many miracles that had allegedly occurred in the process, with which Cisheng
was very satisfied. Then, Deqing requested her to restore the monastery by saving expenditures on food in the palace. According to him, if she could save a hundred taels of silver a day, it would take only three years to defray the costs. Cisheng accepted the suggestion, ordering that the saving start from the end of that
year.[19] Encouraged by the promising prospect of fulfilling his mission, Deqing
engaged more actively in the religious and political world.

Exile to Leizhou: Being Disciplined by the Son of Heaven

A disaster came after good fortune, as Deqing lamented decades later over a major adversity that followed the peak of his success in the secular world and that had since altered his life completely. In the second month of 1595, Deqing was suddenly arrested and taken back to the capital from Mount Lao. Eight months later, he was exiled to Leizhou 雷州 in Guangdong province, once again a peripheral coastal location but in southern China. He recalled the experience many years later, saying that "[I] riled the emperor, whose rage was [as scary as] a thunderclap in the daytime that makes everybody cover their ears. During the two hundred and more days from being arrested to be released [from prison], I experienced sufferings that cannot be described" (上幹聖怒, 如白日雷霆, 聞者掩耳. 自被逮以至出離二百餘日, 備歷苦事, 不可言).[20]

Current explanations for the arrest tend to suggest that Deqing was a passive victim or scapegoat of court strife. Deqing himself believed that strife among the eunuchs led to his disaster,[21] while Qian Qianyi 錢謙益 (1582–1664, *jinshi* 1610) viewed court officials as the major force pushing the event forward, claiming that their plan was to eventually implicate Cisheng and thus place her donations to Buddhist causes under investigation.[22] Unlike them, Fuzheng unmistakably related this disaster to court strife over the succession issue, which invites more explanation.

> In the *yiwei* year, the crown prince was fourteen years old, but his status as the heir was not established yet, leaving the court in much controversy. The Holy Mother, who backed Taichang, insisted on establishing the eldest son [of the Wanli emperor], while the emperor, who backed the Prince of Fu, preferred the noble one. Nine-tenths of the eunuchs sided with Courtesan Zheng 鄭 (1565–1631), and they were echoed by the powerful officials of the outer court. All these nearly shook the state's foundations.... Upright people [sticking to the principles]... were no more than a few.... People were worried about Patriarch Han because he, as someone who had [vowed to be] aloof from worldly affairs, intervened in the grand affair related to the throne by praying for the begetting of the crown prince at Mount Wutai and [attempting to] protect him at Cishousi.... Villains inside and outside the court who secretly observed the emperor's tendency thus launched attacks on the monk [i.e., Deqing] by ordering a servant at the Eastern Depot to impersonate a Daoist priest and [to issue a charge] related to an unfounded matter. The matter of first cutting off branches and then removing the trunk [i.e., gradual progress] finally

evolved into a serious problem, but it had nothing to do with Daoist priests at Mount Lao. From the fact that the Daoist priest's charge was groundless, [we] know that [the antagonism] in the inner court had become [irreconcilable] like water and fire.... Moreover, [Patriarch Han's] request of the Holy Mother to save money by cutting back one hundred taels of silver a day on food for three years was considerably disadvantageous to the eunuchs, thereby tending to create resentment. Additionally, since the Empress Dowager is prohibited by the *Ancestral Instructions* from intervening in court politics, it is no wonder that people in the inner and outer courts would take advantage of the event to frame [her].

乙未之年, 皇太子生十四歲矣, 而儲位未定, 廷議紛然. 聖母意在泰昌, 議主立長. 皇上意在福王, 議主立貴. 內廷近侍, 左袒鄭貴妃者什九, 外廷權貴因之附和, 幾搖國本.... 而挺持 ... 者, 不過數人.... 識者謂, 臺山祈嗣, 慈壽保嗣, 以出世人幹係國祚大事, 甚為憨祖危之... 內外奸人, 窺伺皇上一時喜怒, 遂令東廠役假扮道士, 影響借釁, 以傾和尚. 披枝去本之勢, 此日真成燎原, 卻與牢山道士全沒交涉. 惟道士沒影響, 知宮庭大水火矣.... 且當日請聖母日減膳饈百兩、三年儲積之說, 大不便於內官, 隙既易生. 況祖制, 母后不得幹與朝政, 宜一時中外之藉端排構也.[23]

"Taichang" refers to Zhu Changluo 朱常洛 (r. 1620) and "Prince of Fu" to Zhu Changxun 朱常洵 (1586–1641). This paragraph casts some light on Deqing's involvement in the succession issue, including his prayer services in Cishousi on behalf of Zhu Changluo. According to Fuzheng, what led to Deqing's disaster were both political and economic factors. First, his siding with Cisheng in the succession issue put him in opposition to the emperor, which result was in turn used by evil eunuchs to oppose him. Second, Deqing's request for Cisheng to save on food hurt the eunuchs' interests. Third, Cisheng's activities were deemed as being in defiance of the established rules. All these made Deqing a victim of court strife.

The Daoist priest involved was Geng Yilan 耿義蘭 (1509–1606), a Shandong native who had won a *jinshi* degree in the Jiajing era. Geng became a Daoist priest at the Taiqing abbey 太清宮 at Mount Lao and then received further Daoist instructions at the Baiyun abbey 白雲觀, the largest Daoist temple in the capital. Located on an excellent site facing the sea, the Taiqing abbey had become so dilapidated that only a few Daoist priests were residing there by the early Wanli era. Deqing thus bought its grounds in 1586 to build Haiyinsi. But this acquisition of property created envy among Daoist priests, who in 1589 accused him of stealing the grounds. Geng Yilan as the head plaintiff was whipped by local officials and sentenced to exile for four years. Deqing's connection with Cisheng may have proved to be an asset in the case, but it did not restrain Daoists from continuing to pursue the issue. In the second month of 1595, with assistance from the head of the Baiyun abbey, who had a close tie with Lady Zheng 鄭 (1565–1630), Geng Yilan submitted a charge against Deqing directly to the emperor. The egregious crimes with which Deqing was charged in the complaint included colluding with eunuchs like Feng Bao 馮保 (d. 1583) and Zhang Ben 張本 (dates unknown), pretending to be a royal family member, issuing fake edicts, occupying the property of Daoist abbeys, beating people to death, and secretly hoarding provisions for a revolt. In a rage, Wanli condemned the governor and investigating officials for "conniving with the evil monk to harm the Way and bring disaster to the common people" (黨援妖僧, 害道殃民).[24] and ordered the Ministry of Punishment to investigate all officials involved.

As shown by the use of the term "evil monk," which betrays Wanli's strong loathing of Deqing, politics left a clear mark on this case and declared the end of Cisheng's generous support to Buddhism over the first two decades. Deqing would have been executed had Geng's charges been validated, and his exile after eight months of investigation proves that most if not all the accusations were unsubstantiated. Nonetheless, Deqing was exiled and Haiyinsi destroyed, while Geng left without any consequences despite his claim that he "would accept being beheaded if any of my words are unfounded!" (若臣半字虛誑, 自甘梟首!). What's more, five years later, the emperor granted Geng the title *fujiao zhenren* 扶教真人 (authentic man protecting the teaching). The Taiqing abbey was restored on the foundations of Haiyinsi, with an accompanying bestowal of a copy of the Daoist canon and one hundred twenty *mu* of land.[25] All these show that Deqing was surely a victim caught up in the head-on confrontation between Cisheng and Wanli. Given the status of Deqing as Cisheng's master, in the broader view his arrest marked in a most graphic way the end of a period during which Cisheng could patronize Buddhism generously and freely. A close link with her was no longer a blessing but a curse. This change, discussed in the final chapter, marked a significant point in the development of late-Ming Buddhism.

But Deqing was not purely a scapegoat; instead he was actually paying a high price for the strategy he chose. The dangers did not come unnoticed. Deqing acknowledged many years later that Zhenke had "told me about the clandestine and subtle situation before my disaster took shape" (當予禍之未形也, 備告之以隱微).[26] Very likely, Deqing received the warning in the summer of 1592 while staying with Zhenke at Yunjusi.[27] By the time the political situation had become so bad that Zhenke had decided to relocate the Jiaxing canon 嘉興藏 project away from Mount Wutai to Jiangnan. Deqing returned to Shandong after that meeting and visited Beijing again in the tenth month of 1594 to celebrate Cisheng's birthday, to which Fuzheng commented,

[Master Han] would not have entered the capital to celebrate [the birthday] and stayed there if not for the restoration of [the Great Baoen] monastery; he would not have caught criticism and gotten into trouble if not for going back and forth between [Shandong and] Beijing and staying there during the three years.

非為修寺, 不入賀留京. 非三年往來留京, 不涉議犯患也.[28]

Apparently, Zhenke's warning did not prevent Deqing from playing with the fire of politics. This is not to say that Deqing was blind to contemporary politics; more likely it was because he found nowhere except Cisheng to rely on for the Baoen project and believed that the empress dowager could guarantee his safety in any eventuality. To his chagrin, these strategies failed after the mother-son relationship reached its lowest point.

Politics did not bring only disaster to Deqing; it was also beneficial in educating the master in some unexpected but profound ways. Deqing was later praised by the Chongzheng emperor (r. 1628–1644) as "being disciplined [*qianchui* 鉗錘] by the Son of Heaven," which remains true to some degree. Being exiled could be educational, and Deqing indeed turned it into a rare chance to improve his spiritual achievements. A case in point is the *Lengjia biji* 楞伽筆記 (A commentary note to the *Laṅkāvatāra sūtra*). Deqing started working on the commentary only twenty days after arriving in Leizhou for fear that he would not live long in such a blazingly hot place.[29] In early 1599, he printed the *Lengjia biji* and circulated it among fellow monks and patrons, implying a kind of defiance to political persecution. More important, the completion of this book marked a major spiritual advancement. In a letter to Fudeng, Deqing explained in detail how his progress was directly related to his exile:

Thus, [I] knew of making progress in Buddhist practice immediately when we met thirty years ago. In the [past] twenty years, I have constantly worked hard to clean up dung, and the earnest ideal of [making progress] has never been far away from my eyebrows [i.e., never put aside]. Regretfully, my ingrained habit was so deep that I was not able to clean karma instantly from current conduct [*xianye* 現業] and flowing consciousness [*liushi* 流識]. . . . When I luckily took Dharmas [i.e., objective phenomena] as the condition for the experiential reality of sentient beings and knew of [something regarding] repaying the Buddha's favor, I immediately took the network of illusion as a means of conducting Buddhist affairs. My mind of assuming [responsibility] was as [earnest] as holding nine tripods, whereas the illness of attachment to the Dharma increased by seven times over the course. I thought that I would fulfill my commission and keep up with former sages, but in reality it is not wise but crazy and foolish. Fortunately, I understood at heart that this act was not correct and that it was just like crossing a river in a dream [i.e., not genuine]. It happened that the Holy Ruler favored me with diamond fire, which pierced through accumulated ignorance and easily broke the root of feeling [accumulated] in past kalpas. Looking back from this point, what happened in the past was all like things occurring in a dream. Thus, I feel lucky and take [the experience] as a most pleasant thing in my life.... In spare time when carrying weapons [like a soldier] is not needed, I only face the *Laṅkāvatāra sūtra* to explore the Buddha's mind seal. I have come to realize that previously I had fallen into the sphere of light and shadow [i.e., illusion], without obtaining the power of authentic insight [*zhijian* 知見, Skt. *jñāna-darśana*]. [From this experience I have learned] that there is more than one expedient way for Buddhas and gods to cultivate sentient beings that have an affinity to Buddhism, and, whether positive or negative, their only purpose is to introduce them to the grand gate of pure liberation. Both the accumulated fires [of hell] and the hill of knives are nothing but the place to attain the truth of nirvana.

故自緣會三十年前, 即知有向上事. 二十年中, 常勤除糞. 此一念苦切之心, 未嘗去於眉睫. 但恨積習深厚, 不能頓淨現業流識... 及幸以法為緣, 知報佛恩, 即以幻網為佛事. 其荷負之心, 實持九鼎. 而法執之病, 益增七重. 將謂不負所生, 敢追先哲, 此實狂愚, 非謂慧也. 幸亦心知非正, 如夢渡河. 念蒙聖主隆恩, 惠以金剛燄, 爍破重昏, 使歷劫情根, 一揮頓裂. 回視昔遊, 皆同夢事. 是故不慧以此慶快平生.... 荷戈之暇, 惟對楞伽究佛祖心印. 始知從前皆墮光影門頭, 非真知見力. 是知諸佛神力調伏有緣眾生, 非止一種方便. 若逆若順, 無非令入清涼大解脫門; 火聚刀山, 無非究竟寂滅道場地.[30]

His mention that he "took the network of illusion as a means of conducting Buddhist affairs" embodies the Mahayana spirit of not forsaking the secular world, but it risks Buddhists' being entangled with the affairs they perceive as illusory and empty. Deqing stuck to the restoration project because of both his loyalty to Xilin Yongning and his mission aimed at revitalizing Buddhism. But this insistence was an attachment to the Dharma that is not necessarily praiseworthy. Fortunately, not only did the unexpected exile directly expose Deqing to negative consequences but also life in exile forcefully emancipated him from the attachment. He later encapsulated this experience of transformation as "entering the Dharma realm because of the king's law" (因王法而入佛法).[31] Cognizant of that, at the end of the letter Deqing thus assured Fudeng that "from now on, it might be safe to say that I will not disappoint my own expectations as well as those of my masters and friends" (而今而後, 或可謂不負已靈, 亦可謂不負師友矣).

Deqing's self-confidence during his exile leads us to his continuous progress in spiritual transformation through repeated self-denial. Deqing acknowledged that while a youth, though versed in Buddhist teachings, he was attached to the world of voice and forms without entering the gate of Buddhism.[32] After spending twenty years at Mount Wutai and Mount Lao, Deqing, together with Zhenke, planned to visit Nanhuasi 南華寺, the sacred place where Huineng's 慧能 (636–713) mummy was housed, to "plumb the origins of Chan" (疏禪源). That was an act symbolic of their determination to revitalize Chan Buddhism, but the plan was ruined by his exile. More important, the great hardship entailed by his exile made Deqing recognize that he nonetheless "had fallen into the sphere of light and shadow without obtaining the power of authentic insight." Only after being forced to directly face existential matters, especially repeated threats of death, was Deqing able to explore "the mind seal of the Buddha." This progressive process of transformation exemplified Deqing's theory of "keeping cultivation after awakening." Also the completion of the *Lengjia biji* reveals the mutually beneficial relationship that Chan Buddhism advocates between knowledge and practice—achieving awakening by means of Buddhist teachings while eliciting Buddhist teachings from awakening.[33]

In addition, the political factors benefited Deqing by constituting a framework, though probably only implicitly, in which his life and religious career were reevaluated and elevated. Serving as Cisheng's master made Deqing arguably the monk second only to Yao Guangxiao 姚廣孝 (1335–1418) in terms of proximity to the political center throughout the Ming. Symbolically and in practice, the presence of this figure held unparalleled significance for Buddhist institutions, which had just suffered Jiajing's persecution. Thus his sudden arrest and exile sent shock waves throughout the *saṃgha* and sparked a shared sentiment of trauma. Zhenke, for example, recited *The Lotus Sutra* one hundred times for Deqing's sake upon learning of his exile[34] and never ceased to work to save him while he lived. Without denying their friendship, behind these efforts was an attempt to advance the interests of Buddhism as a whole. Aware of the sentiments within Buddhist society, Deqing recalled emotionally in a letter to a Vinaya master,

> When I was punished [by the emperor], the *saṃgha* was so shocked that gods and ghosts all cried in panic. Stopping eating food and drinking water only, you made repeated efforts to save me and felt regret that you could not take the punishment for me.... This was what people who cared for the Dharma gate could share joy and sorrow means. [In doing so, you] were concerned only about the Dharma.

憶下劣被罪之秋, 法門震蕩, 神鬼驚泣. 座下辟穀飲水, 再四周旋, 恨不得以身代之.... 是所謂關心法門, 有同體之休戚者. 是以法為懷.[35]

Clearly, Deqing became a representative of the *saṃgha*, and the attack against him was taken as one against Buddhist clergy in general.

In the secular world, politics worked to encourage scholar-officials to express solidarity with Deqing.[36] At the sight of Deqing's visit to pay respects as required, for example, the regional commander (*zongbing* 總兵), surnamed Wang, descended the stairs and released the ropes binding him, saying that "you, Master, are a lofty person wandering beyond the world. Not to mention that you suffered this unexpected disaster only because of praying for the sake of the court. We all respect and admire you deeply. How can we treat you in a normal manner?" (公物外高人. 況為朝廷祈福, 致此奇禍, 何罪之有? 吾輩正中心感重, 豈可以尋常世法相遇?).[37] The term *wubei* (we all) is important, indicating that there was a group of people who believed that Deqing sacrificed himself for the sake of the state. An example that illustrates this is related to a supreme commander (*zongdu* 總督). Deqing found it extremely hard to call out his own name in public, but, because of the commander's insistence, he was forced to perform this embarrassing act every day for an entire year. He believed that this was because the commander, as a military official, knew nothing about treating Buddhist masters with grace. But one day the official invited him for a vegetarian feast and explained, "It is not because I cannot lend convenience to you. Recognizing that you are very proud of yourself, I have attempted to improve your spiritual cultivation a little bit [in this way]" (非我不能假借公. 知公有傲骨, 聊以相成也). This impressed Deqing deeply. In a region beyond the imperial capital, clearly scholar-officials received Deqing more freely, without considering the emperor's stance.[38]

Behind the wide support given to Deqing was a credibility contest between Cisheng and Wanli, with Cisheng winning it. By 1595 the emperor's misadministration had drawn strong indignation from all walks of society, while Cisheng was widely believed to be the last rein on his conduct. This background made it possible to interpret Deqing's siding with Cisheng in a different light, shifting his image from the woman's private master to a hero challenging the emperor in the interests of the greater public. Deqing received great notice after his arrest, but the key to the case was Cisheng's credibility against Wanli's rather than the unjust nature of the case or Deqing's achievements. A loose alliance formed among those with a shared stance against Wanli, and that was also the case in Guangdong, a politically peripheral region where supervision was relatively relaxed when compared with Beijing. While in northern China, though appreciated by some scholar-officials, Deqing concentrated his attention only on the inner court and his links with others was limited. As this mode of activity could not continue in the wake of his exile, Deqing engaged more in worldly affairs and connected more closely with others, especially scholar-officials, who tended to view him as a fighter against a ruler whose actions caused them concern. With the alliance's efforts to glorify him and spread his influence within and beyond the *saṃgha*, Deqing came to seem the eminent monk he now appears to us.[39]

Deqing was not merely a passive victim of politics; at times he enjoyed playing politics as a rhetorical strategy, but the effectiveness of his actions is questionable. In a gathering in 1605, Zhang Wei 張位 (1538–1605, *jinshi* 1568), a former grand secretary, told the guests, "You all know Master Han[shan] is a great good friend [in the Dharma], but you don't know that he has contributed greatly to the state in a secret manner" (人皆知憨師爲大善知識耳, 不知大有社稷陰功也). All being shocked, everybody was eager to know what had happened, which Zhang explained in detail. The way Deqing recounted this story is impressive, making us believe that he was enjoying or even boasting about Zhang's testimony. In fact, a clear infatuation with politics did not fade throughout Deqing's life. One contemporary observed that "Deqing is tending to discuss with the gentry about contemporary events, which has attracted even more followers" (乃謦咳間, 多趨縉紳談時局, 以是信向者愈繁).[40] In this way, Deqing capitalized on his experiences, especially those related to the inner court. This strategy helped reshape his image, but it failed him in fulfilling his major goals, including his initial vow to restore Baoensi and his later reforms at Nanhuasi 南華寺.[41] In 1614, when Cisheng died, Deqing cried bitterly: "Alas! You, O patron [Skt. *dānapati*], have passed away. The vow related to my home monastery will not be fulfilled. Should [I] wait to complete it until the next life?" (悲哉，檀越往矣！本寺之願已矣，豈待再來耶?).[42] His sadness is understandable, but his conviction that Cisheng was the only force he could rely on deserves more exploration, to which I turn in the conclusion.

ZIBO ZHENKE: ENTRAPPED BY POLITICS UNTO DEATH

Zhenke as a leading master had much in common with Deqing, including their spending much time in northern China, especially in Beijing, and their passion for reinvigorating Buddhism. Zhenke maintained a close friendship with Deqing, but their plan to cooperate in such major Buddhist projects as carving the Jiaxing canon and revitalizing Chan Buddhism failed. Eventually, despite Deqing's warning, Zhenke sent himself to Beijing and died in prison there.

Carving the Jiaxing Canon

In 1589, Zhenke and Daokai initiated the project of carving the Jiaxing canon, to be the biggest edition of the canon ever produced in premodern East Asia. In the early stages, they devoted much of their time and energy to the project, with Zhenke as the spiritual leader who laid down the principles while Daokai served as the de facto leader who steered the project.[43] The process, however, was full of accidents, and the time spent on the carving was protracted from an estimated ten years to more than one hundred fifty years.[44] Among other aspects what was particularly important was the abandonment in 1592 of the early carving site at Mount Wutai in favor of Mount Jing 徑山. This relocation from northern China to Jiangnan, which was more than one thousand miles away, profoundly affected the fate of the canon.[45]

Unlike the Baoensi project, in which Deqing was driven largely by personal loyalty, from the very beginning Zhenke consciously viewed the making of a new canon as part of his efforts to salvage Buddhism. After Jiajing's anti-Buddhist persecution lasting nearly half a century, an urgent need to create a new Buddhist canon was felt within the *saṃgha* and beyond in the early Wanli period. Yuan Huang 袁黄 (1533–1606, *jinshi* 1586) was probably the first to raise the proposal, believing that the deteriorated situation would be improved if people had more opportunities to access Buddhist texts. Also, Yuan suggested replacing the concertina binding (*fanjia* 梵筴), the conventional form in which the canon had been made, with the thread-binding form (*fangce* 方冊). He argued that in this way "[the scriptures] would be easily spread everywhere and ready to read by people. [Consequently,] people would tell what is right from what is not, making the orthodox Dharma greatly flourish" (使處處流通, 人人誦習, 孰邪孰正, 人自能辯之, 而正法將大振矣).[46] Viewed in the context of the Wanli era, this may be one of the earliest occasions in which scholar-officials projected their recovered enthusiasm for Buddhism in an intellectual way. But, paradoxically, its utilitarian tendency sparked strong suspicion that it would render the Buddhist scripture less respected.[47] Zhenke stepped in to solve the debate.[48] Like Yuan, Zhenke highlighted the effectiveness of this change in spreading Buddhism. He argued that

> although the sutras in the concertina form are respectable, what benefits can you expect to obtain from respecting them if people do not understand their meaning? Even if [we admit that] the sutras in their thread-binding form are less reputable, they will be circulated widely because they are cheap and easier to produce. [If so, shall we not expect that] one or two among millions of persons

will understand their meaning? . . . Even for those who despise sutras with the binding form, [they] will [first] fall into hell experiencing great suffering and [then] return to the root after experiencing it. Once returning to the root, [they] will understand the reasons for their falling to hell and [thus] correct their mistakes. Once correcting their mistakes, they will change [their attitude toward the sutras] from contempt to respect.

使梵筴雖尊重, 而不解其意, 則尊之何益? 使方冊雖不尊重, 以價輕易造, 流之必溥. 千普萬普之中, 豈無一二人解其義趣者乎? . . . 縱使輕賤方冊之輩, 先墮地獄, 受大極苦, 苦則反本, 反本即知墜地獄之因, 知因則改過, 改過則易輕賤為尊重.⁴⁹

Obviously, Zhenke took widespread circulation of the Buddhist sutras as a means of revitalizing Buddhist practice. In retrospect, his turning the carving project into a mission of more than making a new canon was far-reaching, predicting the eventual fate of the project from the very start.

The fund-raising, a major problem for a large-scale project of this kind, exemplified the dilemma. The expenditures for the project were estimated up to thirty thousand taels of silver. Daokai found the task of collecting the funds so daunting that he vowed that "if anybody donates thirty thousand taels of silver to carve this set of woodblocks, I, Daokai, vow to offer him with my head, eyes, brain, and marrow. Henceforth, [Dao]kai's efforts would not cease before the completion of the carving of the woodblocks" (若有人舍三萬金刻此藏板者, 道開發願以頭目腦髓供養是人. 自今而後, 藏板不完, 開心不死).⁵⁰ Daokai's concern over the financial challenge is understandable given that institutional support for Buddhism had been further weakened since the early Ming. Worse than that, neither Zhenke nor Daokai himself established a Dharma lineage on which they could rely. But, surprisingly, Zhenke turned down Cisheng's offer to sponsor the project exclusively, insisting that the merit of creating such a new canon be maximized by allowing as many people as possible to support it.⁵¹ Behind this decision was his desire to mobilize the masses for the cause of Buddhism rather than simply creating a new canon. Daokai finally split the difference and, in 1586, made a plan to look for forty chief donors (*changyuan* 唱緣), each responsible for one hundred taels of silver a year. Meanwhile, forty extra contributors were prepared to fill any vacancies the chief donors might leave.⁵² Compared with Zhenke's lack of focus in mobilization, this way of fund-raising was more selective and combined flexibility and strength by dividing the daunting task into smaller and manageable parts.⁵³

In light of that, choosing Mount Wutai as the carving site concerned the strategy and the resources they desired to mobilize for the project. Daokai visited

Mount Wutai twice in 1585 and 1586 but prioritized no sites in northern China.[54] To explain this sharp change, a story says that he chose Mount Wutai, Laosheng 牢盛, Lingyan 靈岩, and Shuangjing 雙径 as the candidate sites, with priority given to Mount Lingyan. Hesitant, he turned to supernatural forces. Witnessed by statues of the Buddha, he cast lots three times, and Mount Wutai won out each time. "Now [we] have no choice but to observe the order of the Tathāgata" (今則有不得不遵如來敕命矣), Daokai concluded. It happened that Master Wubian 無邊 (d. 1588), the head of the Miaode chapel 妙德庵 located at the heart of Mount Wutai, passed the chapel to Daokai.[55] Mount Wutai was thus chosen as the site.[56] Without denying this mysterious story, we should first ask why Daokai had narrowed his choices down to the four places, three of which were in northern China.

None of the candidate locations was ideal for the project, which reflects the restrictive conditions under which the leaders of the project had to work. Laosheng refers to Mount Lao, where Deqing lived at Haiyinsi. Historically, it was Daoism rather than Buddhism that had a dominant influence in the area. Things became even more complicated starting in the mid-sixteenth century owing to the rampancy of popular religion, especially the Luo teachings 羅教, which caused much social and political trouble.[57] For Deqing's part, as mentioned, after being trapped in the mountains for three years, his hope to restore Baoensi was reignited by the canon bestowal. Although fully aware of the significance of the project, understandably he could not spare it much time and energy. Mount Lingyan refers to Lingyansi 靈巖寺 at Mount Lingyan, Shandong. One of the Four Famous Monasteries (四大名寺) in Tang China, it was a place where Zhenke had once held the abbacy. But the monastery had fallen into disrepair by that time, and Zhenke's relationship with it was superficial at most.[58] In addition, according to a warning by a monk, the region was not fitting to carry out a religious project requiring a large-scale mobilization of followers. The situation at Mount Wutai was more complicated. On top of its status as China's most important Buddhist sacred site, this mountain was perfectly suitable for making the canon, which represents the Dharma treasure, as it was believed to be the abode of the bodhisattva Mañjuśrī, the guardian of wisdom.[59] The problem was that neither Daokai nor Zhenke had a meaningful connection with the region. Very likely, their hopes lay in Miaofeng Fudeng, who, from his early years, maintained a strong connection with local societies in southern Shanxi, especially the Prince of Shanyin 山陰王 (1558–1603) in Puzhou 蒲州.

Taking as candidates the three places with which they had no real connection may reflect the optimism characteristic of the Buddhist establishment in northern China during the early Wanli period. Of note, all three places were in the fan-shaped region surrounding Beijing, and all those involved were aligned with

Cisheng, who, as discussed in chapter 3, had extended her influence to Mount Wutai. Daokai was by no means unfamiliar with Cisheng.[60] In fact, that the preparation for the project clearly speeded up after 1586 was likely encouraged by the first wave of Cisheng's canon bestowal. In addition to patronage from the inner court, Daokai was clearly optimistic about the support expected from northern China. He once detailed his plan as follows:

> As for the canon-carving project, the conditions in northern China are slightly better [than those in the south]. The chance is eight or nine out of ten that the scheduled event [i.e., the carving project] will be carried out in northern China. Once carved, the [Buddhist scriptures] will be transported to southern China for circulation. [My] plan is to have forty persons serving as the chief donation collectors [*yuanshou* 緣首]. Throughout the project, they each support it with one hundred taels of silver every year. About twenty of these people will be sought from the Yan, Zhao, Qi, and Lu regions. Ten are expected to come from Jiangnan, such as the Yu family in Jintan, the He family in Danyang, and others in places like Wujiang and Songjiang. As for the remaining ten, they should be sought in the two places of Huizhou and Puzhou.

> 刻經因緣, 大都北方緣差勝. 期場十有八九定在北方, 擬刻成則移就南方以流通之. 計得四十人為緣首, 每人歲助百金, 與刻工相終始. 燕、趙、齊、魯大約有二十人. 江南如金壇之于、丹陽之賀, 吳江、松江諸處擬求十人, 外十人則求之徽州、蒲州二處.[61]

This letter was written around the year 1586. Notably, the Yan, Zhao, Qi, and Lu regions were all in northern China, as was Puzhou in Shanxi. This disproportionate reliance on northern China appears unreasonable given that it was far less wealthy than southern China and that Zhenke was deeply rooted in Jiangnan rather than in northern China, but it was consistent with the common optimism for northern China Buddhism at the time. Finally, not only did they choose Mount Wutai but also, very likely encouraged by the prospect of securing support from both the inner court and local society, Daokai also declared that the project would be completed within ten years.[62]

Viewed in this light, relocating the working site from Mount Wutai to Lengyansi 楞嚴寺 in Jiaxing 嘉興 signifies a major setback to the original plan and reveals a significant gap between the ideal and reality. While at Mount Wutai, the project progressed smoothly, and up to 20 percent of the canon was completed.[63] Despite this success, however, the carving site was suddenly moved to Jiangnan. In explaining the decision, Daokai mentioned that "the adherents coming from Jiangnan have been pretty determined [to support it], while those in the north are rarely responsive [to the appeal]" (江南善信頗發肯心, 而北地則罕有應之者).[64] This geographically unbalanced distribution of the donors is substantiated by the existing colophons. During the three years from 1590 to 1592, for example, only twenty-nine fascicles were carved under the sponsorship of eunuchs, greatly disproportionate to the enormous influence they then had on Buddhism in northern China. Similarly, although Daokai had high expectations of the Prince of Shanyin and local elites in Puzhou, their donations were negligible. Why were people in northern China so unresponsive to Daokai's appeals? What had happened in the four years that caused the significant gap between Daokai's assessment and reality? These questions lead us to the strategies used to mobilize resources and the actual responsiveness of various forces, especially the previously examined elite groups. Fortunately, Daokai's works disclose some features of the social networks along which the project was carried out.

First of all, little trace can be found of Daokai's connection with local society in Shanxi,[65] which limited the ability to enlist local support for the project. The Prince of Shanyin offers a good example. Although the prince carved about twenty Buddhist texts on his own initiative, Daokai failed to get him involved in the project. Similarly, the project failed to mobilize support from the *saṃgha* in the north. Xiantongsi 显通寺, the chief temple on Mount Wutai, is a case in point. Daokai once considered making Xiantongsi, a public monastery open to all monks in theory, the carving site but, largely because of the lack of a meaningful relationship with it, he failed to secure it as a stronghold on this sacred mountain.[66] This failure to obtain support from the *saṃgha* is revealing. In late-Ming China, when most public monasteries were run as hereditary temples (*zisun miao* 子孫廟), very likely Zhenke and Daokai were perceived as somewhat aggressive by the monks on Wutai and thus represented more threat than assistance. As a result, few monks would sacrifice their personal interests for the carving project, no matter how beneficial it was to the greater Buddhist community. This hard situation may explain why Daokai accepted Miaode chapel as the carving site so quickly, although it was not his best choice on the mountain.

The contributions from Cisheng and the inner-court elites were highly anticipated, but the organizers' efforts to keep the project independent and Daokai's bitter criticism of the eunuchs substantially compromised this hope. Zhenke maintained a relative balance between Cisheng, Wanli, and the eunuchs. But Daokai was extremely critical or even contemptuous of the eunuchs, although he was able to extend his influence to the inner court.[67] He once warned that "once you get involved with them [i.e., the eunuchs], you will thus lose the chance to improve your learning" (一與此輩從事, 即無能進修己業矣).[68] On another occasion, he told Xu Yan 徐琰 (dates unknown) that "it is not necessary that the

canon-carving project rely on him. There is no need to humble yourself too much"
(刻藏因緣, 未必就賴渠力, 足下亦不必過為委曲). The "him" here was very likely a
powerful eunuch. It seems that this eunuch, together with his fellows, attempted
to take part in the carving project, but finally they may have left the project, by force
or voluntarily.[69] Given that the tension between Cisheng and Wanli was growing
stronger during these few years, probably the eunuchs started dodging Buddhist
projects. Equally important, Daokai's harsh attitude toward the eunuchs, which
was derived partly from his determination to protect the project from being
usurped by them, dampened the eunuchs' enthusiasm. As previously discussed, to
Cisheng the eunuchs were significant for two reasons: they were the foremost supporting force for her religious enterprises and the major avenue for her to link with
the *saṃgha* outside the inner court to decide the use of her resources. Without
their full involvement, Cisheng's participation in the project was correspondingly
greatly weakened. No matter what the reason was, the lack of a support network in
northern China to mobilize and coordinate resources brought grave consequences to the project led by the Jiangnan monks.

Scholar-officials, especially those of high rank, were the force on which Zhenke
and Daokai relied for intellectual and material support, but proved unusually
unstable in the context of late-Ming China. The project formally started with a
ceremonial act in early 1587, during which Daokai made a vow in a Beijing temple. Notably, the nine people joining him in the ritual were all scholar-officials,
including Lu Guangzu 陸光祖 (1521–1597, *jinshi* 1547) and Wang Shizhen 王士貞
(1526–1590, *jinshi* 1547), who were very influential in the empire. Generally, Daokai stressed the need to draw officials in power into the project,[70] which reflects as
much Daokai's personal preference as his intention to avoid political trouble. In
explaining his plan to enlist forty major donors, Daokai commented that "if the
plan is implemented, [we] can eventually shun undesirable things and the collection of funds carried out by separate monks. And the Dharma gate will thus be
free from any worries" (此計行, 而應避之緣及僧家分募之緣可竟謝之, 而法門
終無他慮矣).[71] A close link with the eunuchs was probably what Daokai wanted
to avoid. In addition to their unwelcome intervention in the project, the eunuchs
were socially incompatible with scholar-officials, who tended to despise them.
As for Daokai's unwillingness to let monks go around to raise funds, it was simply because gathering people on a large scale was then politically sensitive. Unfortunately, because of the notorious dysfunction of the Wanli court, scholar-officials
were abnormally unstable, and many of them, capable and respected, resigned
from office. Fu Guangzai 傅光宅 (1547–1604, *jinshi* 1577) was a chief donor, but
when he sought retirement from office, Daokai suggested that he cease his
patronage to free his two assistant donors lest they no longer be willing to
donate.[72] This was not the only discontinued patronage. In 1599, Wang Kentang

王肯堂 (1549–1613, *jinshi* 1589) lamented that the major force that Daokai desired to depend on had collapsed:

> Shortly after [the vow], the forty people [i.e., the chief donors] gradually went against the [current of] the time. Half of them have died and half remain alive, but none continues to serve as officials at court.... Thirteen years have passed since [the start of the project in] the *wuzi* year [1588], but what has been completed is less than half the entire canon.

> 無何, 四十人者漸與時迕, 存殁半, 而登朝食祿者無一焉.... 自戊子迄今, 十三年矣, 而於全藏不能以半.[73]

　　Politics had a direct part in disrupting the project. In the letter bidding farewell to Wang Daoxing 王道行 (*jinshi* 1550), the provincial administration commissioner (*buzheng shi* 布政使) of Shanxi, Daokai pointed out that Mount Wutai had recently experienced "many pernicious obstructions" (近多魔障) and urged Wang to protect Buddhism there.[74] What Daokai was referring to was probably the so-called Wutai case, in which the *saṃgha* was involved in an investigation by the government of a serious destruction of forests at Mount Wutai. In the end, not only did the carving site's conflict with the locals escalate because of Daokai's insistence that merchants and ordinary people rather than the monks take the responsibility for harming forests but also the supply of wood for the project was threatened.[75] Meanwhile, an even greater threat seems to have loomed at court. In the spring of 1592, Lu Guangzu paid a sudden visit to Mount Wutai.[76] He had just resigned from the Ministry of Personnel and, as one of the earliest and most determined patrons, went to the carving site to say farewell. Lu was the strongest and most reliable aid Zhenke could obtain at court, and his departure from office left the canon project vulnerable to attack. This was not only a surmise. The project, because of its privately sponsored origin, was always shaky in legitimacy and invited lingering suspicion at court.[77] Thus, trouble repeatedly followed the project.[78] Around the year 1592, very likely shortly after Lu's resignation, the project drew a new attack from a censor.[79] Although the attack was soon frustrated, it sent an alarming message. Against this background, the carving ceased in the summer of that year, and the site was finally relocated in the fall, which can be taken as a sensitive response to chilly reality.

　　Neither Zhenke nor Daokai lived to see the completion of the project, a result they might have anticipated as the price for loyalty to their mission. Before moving the site, a letter between the master and disciple reveals the principle they shared:

With regard to the canon-carving project, [what I can do] is to devote myself to it until death. Whether or not it will be carried out smoothly and completed successfully all depends on destiny. How can I predict the results? Whenever in danger and difficulties, I always recall what you told me in Tanzhisi: "The Dharma gate is of most importance, to which the canon carving is only second. The canon carving should be done only according to the conditions, and the Dharma gate must not be broken." This is surely the rule worthy of being followed.

至於刻藏公案, 亦但鞠躬盡瘁, 死而後已. 成敗利鈍, 悉付因緣, 豈能逆睹? 苟當緩急危難之際, 每想及老師潭柘塔院"法門為重, 刻經次之. 刻經但隨緣, 法門不可壞"之語, 良足以為軌持矣.[80]

With the priority given to the principles of the Dharma gate over the canon production, Zhenke and Daokai held a respectable stance as courageous Buddhists. But the price proved unexpectedly high: physically and mentally exhausted, Daokai suddenly disappeared one day. After that, Zhenke entrusted the project to his other followers in Jiangnan, the base he had established with Daokai's aid. In the end, the carving project was not completed until nearly two hundred years after Zhenke's death, and this protracted process exemplifies the difficulties facing late-imperial Buddhism.

Death in Prison: The Stage of an Eminent Monk

Finally, Zhenke lost his life in a Beijing prison. On the first day of the twelfth month of Wanli 31 (January 1, 1604), he was arrested at Tanzhesi 潭柘寺, west of Beijing, and thrown into a prison of the imperial bodyguard. Tortured for two weeks, he was then sentenced to execution after the assizes (jiao jianhou 絞監候).[81] "Since the secular world has become as such, what is the point [for me] to keep living?" (世法如此, 久住何為?), Zhenke lamented over the hopeless situation.[82] He died voluntarily two days later.

Zhenke had been in Beijing for three years before his arrest, and his lingering there amid increased tensions may well reflect his habit of staking success on the inner court.[83] It was in a time when Cisheng's relationship with Wanli had reached its lowest point that Zhenke visited Beijing despite strong opposition from his followers. In early 1602, the alarm sounded again when Zhenke was included for impeachment with Li Zhi 李贄 (1527–1602) by the censor Kang Piyang 康丕揚

(d. 1632, *jinshi* 1592), although the emperor tabled the request to arrest him. In the fall of 1603, the situation became so bad that even Deqing, then in Guangzhou thousands of miles away, joined the growing chorus of Zhenke's key allies to persuade him to leave Beijing. Not as unexpected as Deqing's case, Zhenke was fully aware of the impending danger but chose his destiny regardless.[84] In explaining why, he told Feng Mengzhen 馮夢楨 (1543–1608, *jinshi* 1577) that he was challenging himself to confront the dangers as a means of his spiritual cultivation.[85] More important, Zhenke believed that he was risking himself for a greater cause:

> My friends and acquaintances have all advised me to leave the North [i.e., Beijing]. Without denying their good intentions, they do not truly understand who I am and have tried to convince me mostly by citing advantages and disadvantages [of staying in the capital]. I have well understood the advantages and disadvantages for a long time, but such a calculation really is not what I care about. I have been determined to push my way forward in this calculating world. If I am so fortunate as to survive, it will not be too late for me to consider living a determined life.

> 然舊識皆勸我早離北, 雖是好心爲我, 實未知我, 大都爲我者率以利害規我. 若利害, 我照之久矣, 實非我志也. 我志在利害中橫衝直撞一兩番, 果幸熟肉不臭, 徐再撐立奚晚?[86]

During this visit to Beijing, Zhenke had goals he perceived as significant to fulfill, including seeking support for the Jiaxing canon project.[87] His pride and courage in fighting for the sake of Buddhism prevented him from making a decision always in a way of picking the more certain path to victory with less risk. This determination to stay in dangerous Beijing was like a gut check that distinguished him from ordinary monks, but turning a factual judgment into a one of values made it virtually impossible for any further discussion, at which Feng had nothing to do but lament.[88] In retrospect, this lingering constituted a sharp contrast with the decisive retreat of the Jiaxing canon project, but whether Zhenke needed to take the risk is questionable.

The worrying dangers arose from court strife and factionalism that finally ignited Zhenke's case. In the tenth month of 1599, the emperor announced Zhu Changluo as the crown prince, but this did not really resolve the succession issue because Lady Zheng was still widely believed to be plotting a replacement. Against this background, on the eleventh day of the eleventh month of 1603, a leaflet, later known as the evil pamphlet (*yaoshu* 妖書), was found scattered in Beijing streets. It claimed that it was under pressure that Wanli had established Zhu

Changluo as the crown prince and a replacement would soon occur. This leaflet set off a massive political bomb at court. The Grand Secretariat was also taken by surprise, but for an additional reason. At the time the Grand Secretariat consisted of Shen Yiguan (1531–1615), Zhu Geng 朱賡 (1535–1608, *jinshi* 1568), and Shen Li 沈鯉 (1531–1615, *jinshi* 1565), with Shen Yiguan 沈一貫 (1531–1615, *jinshi* 1568) as the senior. The evil pamphlet listed all but Shen Li as participants in the replacement plot, which made Shen Yiguan believe that it was designed by Shen Li to implicate him in the dangerous succession issue. As the conflict between the two Shens escalated, Shen Yiguan had Shen Li's house searched and his student Guo Zhengyu 郭正域 (1554–1612, *jinshi* 1583), vice-minister of rites, arrested.[89] Guo's arrest exposed his correspondence with Shen Lingyu 沈令譽 (dates unknown), a physician and lobbyist who had extensive connections with court officials. It happened that Shen Lingyu was Zhenke's follower, and his involvement in turn implicated Zhenke. Thus, Shen Yiguan moved further to arrest Zhenke and Shen Lingyu on the charge that they had composed the pamphlet, with the intention of forcing them to frame Guo and Shen Li as having designed the politically sensitive event. Viewed in the broader context, such an exposure to fierce attack came at a time when Zhenke had lost the emperor's favor. Unlike Deqing, who totally sided with Cisheng, Zhenke kept a relatively balanced stance between the mother and the son. Wanli could turn a deaf ear to Kang Piyang's attempt to implicate Zhenke in Li Zhi's case, but this time he was enraged because Zhenke had stepped over the line, including engaging in lobbying for the purpose of manipulating the promotion of court officials and criticizing the emperor as unfilial.[90] Infuriating the emperor meant the loss of his protection, leaving Zhenke vulnerable to attack. As court factionalism got involved, the situation finally spun out of control.

Taking a few steps back, this persecution was not an isolated event but part of the ideological and intellectual wave that, as discussed in chapter 5, had resulted in Li Zhi's death and the collapse of the Putao Association.[91] During the sudden arrest of Zhenke, "spies and police were everywhere in the capital. [They] made arrests based simply on rumors and speculation and implicated many people" (緝校交錯都下, 以風影捕繫, 所株連甚衆). As a result, "many people were arrested in the following few days, making everybody in the capital feel endangered" (數日間, 銀鐺旁午, 都城人人自危).[92] This panic also resulted in an escalation of attacks on Buddhists, and it had a far-reaching impact, eventually turning Beijing into a terrifying place for Buddhists. The last chapter shows how this drastic change affected Buddhism in Beijing in particular and in China as a whole.

Unexpectedly, it turned out that this political persecution that claimed Zhenke's life also promoted his image and benefited his religious enterprise even after his death. Wu Zhongyan 吳中彥 (dates unknown), a student of the imperial college (*jiansheng* 監生) who was in prison, witnessed Zhenke's last days. Wu admitted his incapability of understanding Zhenke's profound teachings, but he found Zhenke's deeds both persuasive and educative. Based on proof he perceived as concrete and reliable, Wu asserted that "if [a person of Zhenke's kind] is not the great man of cultivation . . . then we cannot trust any of the sages and men of virtue from ancient times to the present" (如是而曰非大修行人 . . . 則凡古之聖賢, 皆不足信也).[93] This testimony was applicable to most people, especially scholar-officials, and it is important to understand why it was made.

First of all, Zhenke helped to protect significant officials by refusing to frame them. In the first investigation, the interrogator, who sided with Shen Yiguan, asked Zhenke, "Why don't you, an eminent monk, just cultivate yourself deep in mountains? Why have you come to the imperial capital and interfered with official business by associating with scholar-officials?" (你是箇高僧, 如何不在深山修行? 緣何來京城中結交士夫, 干預公事?). The same questions were repeated the following day. Pursuing these questions seemingly irrelevant to the evil pamphlet on which Zhenke was charged was to set a trap—the wide connections Zhenke maintained violated the Ming rules established to separate Buddhist monks from society, especially scholar-officials. But much to the relief of Shen Yiguan's political rivals, including Guo Zhengyu, who likely had evicted Zhenke from Nanjing a few years earlier,[94] Zhenke finally foiled the interrogator's sinister attempt at framing. This was not a minor matter. Decades later, Qian Qianyi 錢謙益 (1582–1664, *jinshi* 1610) still lamented with pain, "Happy with implication, evil people attempted to use the Great Master [i.e., Zhenke] as a net to abolish good scholar-officials opposing them and finally dared as far as to kill the arhat" (奸邪小人, 快心鈎黨. 欲借大師為一網, 斬艾賢士大夫之異己者, 遂不憚殺阿羅漢).[95] Evidently, Zhenke was viewed as a heroic victim in the fight of good scholar-officials against evil ones. Given that most of those saved were from Jiangnan or closely linked with Jiangnan, Zhenke's chivalrous deed elevated his reputation to a new level, especially among Jiangnan scholar-officials.

No less important, Zhenke turned his death into a kind of performance that was quick, free, and self-controlled. It is said that he decided when to leave this world. On the last day, Zhenke first cleaned his mouth with ginger soup at the crack of dawn and then, having chanted the Buddha's name, left his cell to sit in an open court of the prison. Fellow prisoners came out to find that he had closed his eyes without a word and thus believed that he had died. Learning of that, a censor surnamed Cao 曹 (dates unknown), in the same prison, rushed to see the master and shouted from afar, "It's good that you have left." All of a sudden Zhenke opened his eyes and looked at Cao, smiled, crossed his legs with his hands, and then passed away. In this way, Zhenke claimed ultimate autonomy despite being physically confined to a prison.[96] Even more amazingly, Zhenke's body proved incorruptible. The body was first left unprotected in the open courtyard, but no traces of damage were found seven days later when it was moved to Cihuisi 慈慧寺 for burial. Unfortunately, the grave, built hurriedly, was repeatedly flooded with water. But seven months later, when Lu Jizhong 陸基忠 (1549–1616), Lu Guangzu's son, excavated the body to bring it back to Jiangnan, once again the body was found intact.

Taken as somatic evidence of supreme spiritual achievement, Zhenke's voluntary death and his body's incorruptibility greatly enhanced his prestige as an eminent monk.[97] Perceived as evidence of liberation from the bondage of life and death, a death at one's discretion has been most cherished by Chinese Buddhists, especially Chan practitioners. Robert Sharf has pointed out that "the continued integrity of the body after death is thus associated with holiness and spiritual purity—the purity of mind simultaneously effects the purity of the physical body and the elimination of the defilements that lead to decomposition after death. The bodies of Buddhist masters who resisted decay after death were accordingly worshiped as reservoirs of meritorious karma and spiritual power."[98] Unsurprisingly, therefore, after witnessing Zhenke's death, those prisoners present were moved to such a degree that they started chanting the Buddha's name aloud. Also, people from everywhere—in the capital, along the Grand Canal, and in Jiangnan—rushed to worship the body as the news of its incorruptibility spread. Deqing noticed how effectively these somatic miracles had affected people's reception of Zhenke, saying that "[people] may not entirely trust the master's life and experiences. But after learning how quick and convenient his last act was, everybody, whether upper or lower, admire him. Alas! At the moment of life and death, the master discarded the great Four Elements [as easily as] taking off a broken shoe. How could he accomplish that?" (師生平行履, 疑信相半. 即此末後快便一著, 上下聞之無不嘆服. 于戲! 師于死生, 視四大如脫敝屣, 何法所致哉?).[99] In particular, Lu Jizhong explained why Zhenke's death was so attractive and convincing for scholar-officials like him.

I heard that the sages in the past were free in coming and leaving [i.e., life and death], that relics formed because of the strength of their meditation and wisdom, and that their physical bodies were imperishable, whether in water or in fire. Unexpectedly I witnessed the miracles [from Master Zhenke]. . . . How could he accomplish that if not the embodiment of the Buddha?

聞古賢聖, 去來如意. 定慧力故, 結成舍利. 入火入水, 色身不壞. 不圖愚蒙, 睹此奇异 . . . 非肉身佛, 豈能若是?[100]

The death caused by politics hence encouraged scholar-officials to reevaluate Zhenke, and their resulting moving closer paradoxically neutralized the negative effect politics imposed on Buddhism. As discussed in chapter 5, for example, the Putao Association was in tension with Zhenke. Among other factors their stress on practicality and authenticity, as represented by Yuan Hongdao's 袁宏道 (1568–1610, *jinshi* 1592) criticism of "wild Chan," spurred a growing suspicion of Zhenke's spiritual achievements. But Zhenke's death triggered a process of reevaluation. Tao Wangling 陶望齡 (1562–1609, *jinshi* 1589), a major figure of the Putao Association, exemplifies such a shift. Once planning to visit Zhenke in Tanzhesi, Tao finally abandoned the plan because of criticism by his friends in the Putao Association. "Afterward," Tao confessed with regret, "I read the master's last words and investigated his deeds in life, finding that [he] was truly awakened. With his deep kindness and high level of moral integrity, few monks who presided over the teaching seat in the *saṃgha* was comparable to him" (後讀其遺言, 審其生平, 真證密行, 深慈高節, 一時叢林踞師席者, 誠罕其比).[101] In this sense, death was not an end but a new start that further enhanced Zhenke's reputation and influence. Zhenke was later glorified as one of the three greatest Buddhist masters of the time, and this status helped legitimize the religious enterprises he advocated. After his death, the Jiaxing canon project was thus carried over by scholar-officials in Jiangnan under the rubric of fulfilling "Zibo's entrustment" (*Zibo zhutuo* 紫柏囑托).[102] Politics had limits in affecting Buddhism, and late-Ming Buddhism evolved with a certain degree of independence.

MIAOFENG FUDENG: INVOLVED BUT NOT ENTANGLED WITH POLITICS

Born and active in northern China, Miaofeng Fudeng, a close friend of both Deqing's and Zhenke's, played a similarly significant part in late-Ming Buddhist society. But Fudeng distinguished himself from his friends in some decisive ways, representing a type of eminent monk seldom seen in Jiangnan. Fudeng was held in high esteem by his contemporaries. Even Deqing, who was well known for his pride, confessed that "I deeply appreciate him [i.e., Fudeng] for what I have learned from our discussions. Although in name we are friends sharing the same Way, at heart [I] deem him as a master" (予深感切磋之力, 名雖道友, 其實心師之也).[103] Despite this, Fudeng was seriously underestimated in life and quickly sank into oblivion after death.[104]

Building Three Copper Halls

In Fudeng's biography, Deqing said that "at the start, he obtained assistance from unimportant princes, but finally he had both the emperor and the Holy Mother [i.e., Cisheng] as *dānapati* [patrons]. Whatever he intended to build, the alms-giving for the Buddha truth would surge up immediately after [he] caught the idea. Wherever [his] feet stepped, the place would naturally become a precious abode [i.e., a temple]" (始以小王助道, 終至聖天子聖母諸王為檀越. 凡所營建, 法施應念雲湧; 投足所至, 遂成寶坊).[105] What is highlighted here is that Fudeng was capable of garnering enormous resources with ease and that his patrons came from across the full spectrum of society. This success constituted a sharp contrast with Deqing's and Zhenke's failed struggle in following through with their plans.

A case in point was Fudeng's fulfilling a vow to cast three copper halls, a money-consuming project. In 1589, on Cisheng's orders, Fudeng escorted a copy of the Buddhist canon to Mount Jizu, Yunnan. Two years later, on his return, he visited Mount Emei, where he was deeply impressed by the severity of the weather at the peak. Thus he vowed to build a copper hall for each of the three Buddhist sacred sites, intending to make them shelter against the severe environment. In 1599, Fudeng started the planned project after waiting eight years. The first hall was sponsored exclusively by Zhu Liyao 朱理堯 (dates unknown), the Prince of Shen 瀋 in Shanxi, who donated ten thousand taels of silver. When casting the hall, Fudeng obtained support from Wang Xiangqian 王象乾 (1546–1630, *jinshi* 1571), the grand coordinator of Sichuan, and had the project completed quickly in Jingzhou 荊州 (present-day Jingzhou), Hubei. It was a gold-ornamented (*shen-jin* 滲金) hall, twenty-six feet high and more than thirteen feet wide and deep, with a statue of Puxian (Skt. Samantabhadra) inside surrounded by ten thousand smaller Buddha statues. Once the hall had been erected at Mount Emei, patrons for the second, intended for Putuo Island, appeared immediately. This time it was Wang Xiangqian and a eunuch called Qiu Shengyun 邱嵊雲 (dates unknown). With Wang's assistance, copper was shipped from Sichuan to Jingzhou and the hall was soon completed. But when the hall was shipped down the Yangtze River and arrived in Nanjing, it was declined by the monks from Putuo for fear that it would attract Japanese pirates. In 1605, the hall was instead sent to Longchangsi 隆昌寺 at nearby Mount Baohua 寶華, to which site Cisheng and Wanli each bestowed a copy of the Buddhist canon. One year later, the third hall was finished. "Dedicated to Manjushri,. . . [the hall] is an exquisite integration of architecture, sculpture, and pictorial art."[106] When Fudeng sent the hall to Xiantongsi at

Mount Wutai in 1608, once again Wanli and Cisheng came to his assistance, with the former bestowing on him three hundred taels of silver and one hundred fifty thousand in cash (*qian* 錢), and the latter several times those amounts. Eunuchs also made donations toward the project.[107] The expenditures of casting the three halls, estimated at more than forty thousand taels of silver, amounted to less than those for restoring Baoensi but more than for carving the Jiaxing canon.[108] Nonetheless, Fudeng had little difficulty in completing them within ten years' time.

Compared with Deqing's sole dependence on Cisheng and Zhenke's heavy reliance on scholar-officials, these casting projects were characterized by a large-scale convergence of resources that came from both the inner court and local societies. Why was this possible? The answer may lie in Fudeng's wholehearted service to people, especially those in local society, with his talents in construction. The year 1581 marked a drastic change in Fudeng's life. Before that, he concentrated on gaining spiritual achievements in isolation; after that, he became very active in both the sacred and secular worlds. In particular, Fudeng engaged in a variety of construction projects, especially bridges and monastery buildings, and proved to be one of the best architects in Chinese history. In order to better understand how his engagement in such projects related to the copper-hall projects, let us examine a few cases with stress on the nature of his patrons and the character of the projects.

In 1591 Fudeng was invited to reconstruct Wangusi 萬固寺 in Puzhou, where he had spent five years as a novice monk, and the result strengthened his relationship with local society. Originally built in 522, Wangusi rose to be the biggest Chan monastery in southern Shanxi in the early Ming. Unfortunately, during the Jiajing era this monastery was destroyed in a deadly earthquake, which encouraged the Wang 王 and Zhang 張 families in Puzhou to restore it.[109] At the time, these two families were both well known for producing high-ranking officials and successful salt merchants, and their star members included Wang Chonggu 王崇古 (1515–1588, *jinshi* 1541), who became the minster of war in 1577, and Zhang Siwei 張四維 (1525–1586, *jinshi* 1553), Wang's nephew, who served as the senior grand secretary in 1582.[110] The support of these families for Wangusi had started earlier. Notably, in their attempt to rebuild a pagoda there around the year 1585, a complex network had already surfaced linking the monastery with elites in the region, including local princes, officials, and powerful lineages. Fudeng had been trained by the Prince of Shanyin, a core figure of the network, for more than ten years, and he was by no means unfamiliar with these elites.[111] While restoring the monastery, therefore, he was actually working with the network consisting of powerful and wealthy figures. As the project progressed, he planted roots even deeper in southern Shanxi.

FIGURE 6.2 The bronze hall at Mount Wutai 五臺山 by Miaofeng Fudeng 妙峰福登

Photo by Dewei Zhang

Also, Fudeng engaged in non-Buddhist projects on the same, if not larger, scale. A case in point was his building of the Dragon Bridge 龍橋 in Sanyuan 三原, Shaanxi. This bridge, 360 feet long, 36 feet wide, and 82 feet high, is still extant. Fudeng's engagement came about at the request of Gao Jinxiao 高進孝 (*jinshi* 1589), the magistrate, and Wen Chun 溫純 (1539–1607, *jinshi* 1565), a Shanyuan native and minister of work at the time. The seat of Sanyuan county was split by the Qing River 清河, which was wide and deep. An estimated cost of the project was no less than thirty thousand taels of silver.[112] Although highly unaffordable for a county, Gao nonetheless obtained the full support of Wen Chun. The project started in 1591, the same year of Fudeng's rebuilding Wangusi, but Gao was finally dismissed from office on the charge of wasting government funds. Fortunately for the locals, the project was continued by the succeeding three magistrates and completed twelve years later. Starting in the middle of the Ming, Sanyuan rose to be a significant nexus in the economic map of Shaanxi in particular and of northwestern China in general, largely because of the *kaizhong* 開中 policy designed to support the armies stationed at the northwestern frontier.[113]

Seen from this perspective, what the Qing River divided was not only the city but also the social and economic life across the vast whole of northwestern China. Building a stone bridge would fix the problem. Shaanxi produced a number of powerful salt merchants at the time, with the majority living in eastern Shaanxi, including Sanyuan.[114] Thus Gao Jinxiao's appeal for donations received a positive response from officials and locals. The role that Fudeng played in the project was not well documented, but one account tells that he designed and coordinated the project. He also supported it financially by collecting donations.[115]

Aside from civilian projects, Fudeng took charge of those with military significance as well. Beginning in the fifth month of 1599, for example, Fudeng constructed the Guanghui 廣惠 Bridge across the Yang River 洋河 in Xuanhua 宣化. The Yang River, about three thousand feet wide, was difficult to cross because of the river's soft, sandy bottom and strong eddies. As Xuanhua became a crucial site for the defense against the Mongolian cavalry during the Ming, guaranteeing that armies could cross the river in a safe, quick, and reliable way became militarily significant. In one military action, the previously mentioned Wang Xiangqian, the grand coordinator (*xunfu* 巡撫) of Xuanhua prefecture 宣化府, became stranded in the river. Wang thus decided to build a bridge but found that the difficulty appeared to be insurmountable. Fortunately, Fudeng, who happened to be visiting, took up the task.[116] A vast number of human and material resources were mobilized:

> [It made use of] three hundred thousand laborers, seven hundred thousand soldiers, one hundred thousand trees, and three hundred thousand *zhang* (about 330,000 feet) of stone. [Also] eleven thousand taels of silver [were spent], among which two-tenths came from the government while eight-tenths were donated by the local gentry and common people.

> 匠之工三十萬, 卒之工七十萬, 椿之株十萬, 石之丈三萬. 金之兩萬有一千, 常平子錢十之二, 士民捐助十之八.[117]

Given that the bed was wide and the sand deep, Fudeng even jumped into the river to obtain first-hand data before designing the bridge. Only seventeen months later, an arched stone bridge had been completed. It was a beautiful bridge of twenty-three spans, with all its stone knitted tightly by iron chains. It would be used until the mid-Kangxi period, when the region lost its military significance.

In addition, Fudeng collaborated closely with the royal family, with Cisheng frequently involved, and took charge of construction projects on their behalf. For example, by Wanli's order, Fudeng built Ciyou yuanmingsi 慈佑圓明寺 in Fuping 阜平 on Cisheng's behalf in 1604. Four years later, he rebuilt Yongzuosi 永祚寺 in Taiyuan 太原, Shanxi, a project cosponsored by Cisheng and Zhu

Minchun 朱敏淳 (d. 1610), the Prince of Jin 晉. Compared with the locally backed projects, these royally commissioned undertakings were more religious in nature. Of note, in most of these cases it was the result of an invitation from royal members that Fudeng agreed to coordinate the projects, and only three projects, including the copper halls, were initiated by Fudeng and then attracted cooperation from Cisheng and other royal members.

Regarding the copper-hall project, a close look at its patrons and supporters discloses a mechanism through which Fudeng's service to the world was translated into support for his religious enterprises in a practical and tangible way. As revealed earlier, the spectrum of supporters was surprisingly wide, including all the court and local elites—the emperor, the empress dowager, eunuchs, local princes, local gentry, high-ranking civil and military officials, (salt) merchants, and common people. It is noteworthy that many of them invited Fudeng to take charge of projects or at least had certain links with him. For example, although Wang Xiangqian was not a devout Buddhist, the kind of generosity with which he backed the hall projects was rarely seen among Ming officials. Retrospectively, without Fudeng's great contribution to the Guanghui Bridge project in the first place, it is hard to believe that Wang would have done this. In particular, it may not be a coincidence that all three hall projects were associated with Shanxi and Shaanxi, the vast region where Fudeng's projects were most concentrated. In the case of the third hall, for example, most of its patrons lived in areas along the Sanggan 桑乾 River, the Fen 汾 River, and the Grand Canal.[118] Besides, given that this hall was cast in Jingyin 涇陰, a place close to Sanyuan, rather than in Jingzhou as were the first two, it is tempting to speculate that the choice was related to Fudeng's leading role in the Dragon Bridge project.

Genuine Son of the Buddha

The smoothness in completing the copper halls was typical of Fudeng's religious enterprises, but behind it was not a simple exchange of interest between the master and his patrons and supporters. On a deeper level, there remain more questions to explore. Why were the organizers of these projects willing to invite Fudeng, a Buddhist monk, to manage them? Why did Fudeng allow himself to get involved in affairs that were seemingly irrelevant to his spiritual cultivation and religious undertaking? How was he able to carry them through in the politico-religious milieu that failed both Deqing and Zhenke in fulfilling their vows? These questions concern Fudeng's unspoken motivations and signature strategies in mobilizing various forces with which he was associated.

The activism as expressed in Fudeng's engagement in the construction projects was closely related to his religious cultivation, especially his practice of the bodhisattva path. Fudeng's service was widely believed to be selfless, which won him respect and confidence from within the *saṃgha* and beyond. An author once confirmed this as follows:

> Fudeng traveled around the country, and the [number of] projects he completed was not a few. [He] spent millions in cash [on them] but did not take even a single coin [for himself]. People respected and trusted him, and thus donations were made like [a concentration of] clouds. Having known about him very well, the emperor and the Holy Mother [i.e., Cisheng] permitted their donated money to be used at his discretion without checking how it was spent.

> 福登周行天下, 所繕造工非一, 費數百萬, 錙銖無染, 人尊信之, 檀施雲集. 上與母后稔知其人, 捐金恣所使, 不問出入.[119]

Clearly, at the core of Fudeng's relationship with his supporters was the trust and respect they held for him, making them willing to entrust Fudeng with huge amounts of resources. Fudeng did not disappoint them as he proved to be both a technical specialist in building and a specialist in the art of soliciting funds. Significantly, for Fudeng's part, the activism was a display of his religious cultivation. According to Deqing, Fudeng "entered the Way in his early years from the contemplation of the Dharma realm. Thus, what he did throughout his life was entirely from a mind that cultivated the practice of [the bodhisattva] Puxian" (早從法界觀入道, 故生平建立, 皆從普賢行願法界心中流出).[120] As for the practice of Puxian, the *Huayan jing* explains,

> If a bodhisattva is in harmony with living beings, then that bodhisattva is in harmony with and makes offerings to all Buddhas. If he can honor and serve living beings, then he can honor and serve Tathāgata. When he brings joy to living beings, he brings joy to all Tathāgatas. Why is this? It is because all Tathāgatas sustain themselves on the mind of great compassion. Because of living beings, they develop great compassion. From great compassion the Bodhi Mind is born; and because of Bodhi Mind, they attain Supreme, Perfect Enlightenment.... Therefore, Bodhi belongs to living beings. Without living beings, no bodhisattva could achieve Supreme, Perfect Enlightenment.

> 菩薩若能隨順眾生, 則為隨順供養諸佛. 若於眾生尊重承事, 則為尊重承事如來. 若令眾生生歡喜者, 則令一切如來歡喜. 何以故? 諸佛如來以大悲心而為體故. 因

於眾生, 而起大悲; 因於大悲, 生菩提心; 因菩提心, 成等正覺. . . . 是故菩提屬於
眾生. 若無眾生, 一切菩薩終不能成無上正覺.[121]

The bodhisattva path, as revealed here, is always directed to sentient beings and the secular world and thus serves as a strong link between the earthly and the spiritual worlds.[122] Fudeng's unusual devotion to civilian and military projects, from which he pocketed nothing for himself, embodied the Mahayana spirit.

More specifically, in engaging in these projects Fudeng was responding to desperate needs caused by a catastrophic earthquake and the increasingly felt military pressure deriving from northwestern China as a frontier area. On the twelfth day of the twelfth month of Jiajing 34 (January 23, 1556), the catastrophic Jiajing earthquake (*Jiajing da dizhen* 嘉靖大地震) occurred in the intersecting parts of Shaanxi and Shanxi. This earthquake, to this day, remains the deadliest on record in the world, killing approximately eight hundred thousand thirty people.[123] More than ninety-seven counties in the provinces of Shaanxi, Shanxi, Henan, Gansu, Hebei, Shandong, Hubei, Hunan, Jiangsu, and Anhui were affected, and 60 percent of the population in some counties were wiped out.[124] Puzhou was among the places suffering the greatest loss, with an estimated eighty thousand people dying.[125] Huge numbers of bridges, buildings, and roads were seriously damaged in the earthquake, and there was an urgent need for construction projects. Another reason, similarly important but long ignored, was that after the earthquake the course of the Yellow River, the largest river and crossing through the entirety of northern China, frequently changed and caused much flooding in Shanxi and Shaanxi. This created still greater need for bridges and river management.[126] Fudeng's projects, all located at critical sites, were clearly intended to meet those needs.

Although in these projects Fudeng was very likely driven by his religious passion rather than by utilitarian purposes, his active engagement indeed improved his relationship as a Buddhist monk with other social groups. In studying bridge building in imperial China, Kieschnick has rightly pointed out that "in China, the bridge was a symbol of charity, compassion, and good governance, ideas that weighed heavily on the minds of various figures on the local scene, including monks, officials, and prominent members of the community, when the need for a bridge became apparent."[127] In Fudeng's case, those inviting him to undertake projects were not necessarily devout Buddhists but were important figures in power and with good reputations. As their collaborations went smoothly, positive changes occurred in their relationships. Let us look back to two cases. Wen Chun could not help but express in a poem how pleased he was to see the completion of the Dragon Bridge,[128] in which we can detect a subtle and meaningful shift in his attitude toward Buddhism. Previously, in the essay he wrote appealing for donations, Wen Chun compared Buddhism and Confucianism in terms of their philanthropic philosophy and practices. He first pointed out that building roads and bridges was a long-valued tradition, and then went on to say,

> For people seeking blessings from the unseen and unknown realm, even if they build Buddhist temples and Daoist abbeys, what [benefits] are they expecting [to gain]? Only if they contribute to the road that is visible and present will they have good reward even if they donate little wealth and make the least effort.

彼希福利於冥冥無知之域, 即建梵宇、築玄宮, 亦奚以為? 惟積功行於昭昭見在之途, 雖蠲一財, 出一力, 終有善報.[129]

Here Wen Chun represented a staunch group in defense of Confucianism, seeing Buddhist projects as a competitor with Confucian ones for resources. As the bridge was completed, however, Wen gave great credit to Fudeng and softened his discrimination against the latter as a monk.

In the Guanghui Bridge case, a letter that Bi Ziyan 畢自嚴 (1569–1638, *jinshi* 1592) wrote to Wang Xiangqian reveals the respect Fudeng received from high-ranking officials:

> Master Miaofeng has excelled in Buddhist teachings and spread compassion widely. As for [building] a bridge across the Fen River, for several hundred years [its difficulties] have made people tremble with fear and not dare to discuss it. Now the master has generously taken up the responsibility and is expected to finish it with perseverance. Such unwavering judgments and acts are rarely seen even among Confucians. Every time I meet and talk to him, [I] feel my desires quenched and calm down. The two successive provincial governors both wanted to make use of the advantageous conditions he provided to do good for local society. Thus, the master requests nothing from the world, while the world has to rely on the master. In order to protect [his projects], how can I spare my strength? I have received your instruction, which I will follow mindfully and respectfully.

上人妙峯精通法乘, 廣布慈航. 惟是汾河之橋, 數百年來, 寒心咋舌而不敢議. 今上人慨然任之, 總而期之於有恆. 此等定見定力, 雖儒者猶或難焉. 每一晤對, 不覺令人欲心平而躁心釋矣. 緣先後兩撫臺咸欲借重上人福緣, 為地方永賴計. 是上人無求於世, 而世不能無求於上人也. 諸所護持, 寧顧問哉? 伏承鼎命, 敬鏤心膂.[130]

Bi Ziyan met Fudeng personally and held Fudeng in high esteem for his selfless devotion to the world. It is interesting that he compared Fudeng as a Buddhist monk with Confucians. Obviously, for a sixty-year-old monk who could jump into the turbulent river just for the benefit of other people, everybody, regardless of their background and agendas, must have found him admirable and heroic.

In particular, Fudeng maintained good terms with Wanli while serving Cisheng, thereby demonstrating an alternative possibility for eminent monks to tackle the reigning emperor. Like Deqing, Fudeng established a tie with Cisheng through the Wutai Dharma assembly around 1582. But two years later, when receiving Cisheng's summoning, unlike Deqing, who deliberately shunned it, Fudeng visited Beijing in response and thereafter maintained a close link with the inner court. Of importance, unlike Deqing, who was judgmental of Wanli and thus completely sided with Cisheng, Fudeng managed to treat the morally flawed emperor equally. This is not to say that Fudeng lacked political sensitivity. On the contrary, very likely he had a better understanding of the political reality than Deqing and Zhenke and thus, consciously or not, kept independent from both Cisheng and Wanli by taking local society as his base. For example, Deqing did not visit Beijing regularly until 1589, when the mother-son tension had increased alarmingly, and Deqing had subsequently sided with Cisheng unambiguously. This made it only a matter of time for him to infuriate the emperor. In sharp contrast, during the period Fudeng kept himself far away from Beijing and was instead overwhelmed with civilian and military projects in Shanxi and Shaanxi. Also, Fudeng was clearly more careful than Zhenke, who lingered in Beijing amid increased political tensions: only after 1602 when the mother-son relationship grew warm again did he reappear in Beijing. Thanks to his flexibility combined with caution, Fudeng hence became a magnet for imperial largesse, from both Cisheng and Wanli. In 1584 when he proposed building Huayansi 華嚴寺 at Mount Luya 蘆芽 in northern Shanxi, for example, he received support from Cisheng.[131] "From that moment [i.e., the smooth completion of the temple], the imperial treasury was open to any temple building that [Fudeng] might propose."[132] Around the year 1607 when he sent the third hall to Mount Wutai, he received thirteen thousand taels of silver to renovate Xiantongsi.[133] At the same time, he was simultaneously assigned by Wanli to be the abbot of three imperially sponsored monasteries on Mounts Wutai, Emei, and Baohua. After Fudeng's death, both Wanli and Cisheng bestowed money for his funeral.

Behind the strikingly effective convergence in Fudeng's projects of resources from so many different or even conflicting sources was a unique mechanism through which every act obtained additional significance owing to its relation with others. First, through his well-qualified services on a variety of occasions, Fudeng had established networks that linked him with numerous people, many of whom were in power and had good reputations. Second, there was a positive link between the strong support he secured from local society and that from the inner court. On the one hand, local support helped Fudeng to maintain independence by freeing him from excessive reliance on the inner court for resources. On the other, the emperor and other royal members viewed Fudeng increasingly favorably since Fudeng provided them with good service but did not necessarily require repayment from them. And such a close relationship enhanced Fudeng's profile and influence significantly in local society, where royal patronage of any form could be easily turned into rare political, religious, and cultural capital. Third, the balanced stance that Fudeng assumed between Cisheng and Wanli mattered, because it both reduced the risk seen in Deqing's and Zhenke's cases and maximized support from potential patrons. These factors worked together to encourage a ready response to Fudeng's appeals. In the case of the copper halls, therefore, Fudeng was able not only to have them constructed with ease but also to start the project in 1599 when the mother-son relationship had fallen to its lowest point.

With all these advantages, Fudeng indeed made great contributions to the ongoing Buddhist renewal. Deqing pointed out that "over the two hundred years plus in our Ming dynasty, Master [Fudeng] was the only one [deserving to be mentioned] in terms of the achievements and virtue established for the Dharma gate" (我明二百餘年，其在法門建立之功行，亦唯師一人而已).[134] Thanks to Fudeng's efforts, more than ten monasteries were (re)built at sacred Buddhist sites. Much more than that, his other achievements meriting further exploration include (1) reshaping the landscape of Chinese Buddhism by greatly facilitating the distribution of the Buddhist canon; (2) providing great impetus for such Buddhist sacred sites as Putuo Island, Mount Jizu, Mount Baohua, and Mount Luya; (3) initiating the revival of Longchangsi on Mount Baohua, which would later become the foremost Vinaya temple in China.

Despite all this, however, Fudeng was probably the Buddhist master in late-Ming China who was most misunderstood and underestimated. An advanced Chan master with superior enlightenment though he was, frequently he was viewed merely as a monk cultivating merit.[135] The notion of merit, well established in the Buddhist tradition, surely helps to make sense of Fudeng's activism, especially his engagement in monastery and bridge construction in local society,[136] but it had little to do with Fudeng himself and was basically an expediency that he used to lead people to the Buddhist Way. What's more, probably to Fudeng's chagrin, his life and religious practice were rarely appreciated even within the *saṃgha*. Deqing, for example, commented on his friend with regret:

If he could use the resources he obtained to build a monastery like Nālandā Vihāra,[137] in which the Dharma-Nature school and that of Characteristics [i.e., the Faxiang school] are studied and Chan and Pure Land Buddhism are both practiced, and if for the forty years plus his feet remained within the shadow [of his shape] [i.e., staying in the monastery without traveling around], the contribution he could make to the *saṃgha* would be comparable with that of Donglin [i.e., Huiyuan 慧遠 (334–416)] and of Qingliang [i.e., Chengguan]. [In this way,] everywhere his eyes looked would be the pure land of the lotus world, which is better than the building of the ten monasteries at three mountains.

建剎如那蘭陀, 性相並樹, 禪淨雙修, 則四十餘年, 足不離影, 而於法門之功, 當與清涼東林比靈斯矣! 觸目華藏淨土莊嚴, 又不止三山十剎而已也!

Deqing would have liked Fudeng to spend more time preaching on Buddhist sutras, composing texts, and instructing people in cultivation. This way, he believed, would transform his influence into something more solid and more sustainable.

What Fudeng did and what Deqing expected of him represented two distinct paths within the *saṃgha*, and there was a clash between their views about the ideal state of eminent monks and Buddhism in general. Mahayana Buddhism stresses "both perpetuating the Dharma and saving sentient beings." Fudeng fulfilled these missions only in a seemingly paradoxical but perfect way: perpetuating the Dharma through forgetting it but serving sentient beings. Would it have been possible for Fudeng to receive such massive support had he not first served the world so intensively and devotedly? Probably not: although not always a direct and equal exchange of interest, the mechanism indeed worked behind the scenes to various degrees. In fact, Deqing and Zhenke attested the point with their experiences related to Shanxi. Although he lived at Mount Wutai as long as eight years, Deqing finally had to turn to Cisheng for his Baoensi project. That he could not rely on local Shanxi people had much to with his indifference to local interests.[138] Similarly, although Zhenke and Daokai attempted to mobilize resources from Shanxi for the Jiaxing canon project, their failure was predetermined considering their lack of strong connection with local society, let alone exchange of interest.

But eventually Fudeng lost the fight and quickly disappeared from history after his death, falling victim to the dominant discourse advocating political activism, especially fighting against the reigning emperor. By granting Fudeng the title *zhenzheng fozi* 真正佛子 (genuine son of the Buddha), Wanli gestured his support as the secular ruler to the master. But this recognition meant virtually nothing in the mainstream narrative of late-Ming Buddhism. Created primarily and supported by Jiangnan scholar-officials before they prevailed within the *saṃgha* and beyond, these narratives cherish intellectual achievements that Fudeng could hardly provide. More important, while recounting the history of contemporary Buddhism, these Jiangnan scholar-officials tended to laud political activism and encourage defiance of the ruling emperor mostly because they had fostered a growing sense of solidarity with Cisheng and monks in the fight against Wanli. Thus, they shaped both Deqing and Zhenke as victims for the public interest, whether it be monastic or political, and invented heroic stories to enshrine their loss and to elevate them to such heights of adulation. But Fudeng represented a type of eminent monk who maintained a balanced stance between active participation in the secular world and keeping out of the political fray. Although with his totally different stories and experiences he could have been a corrective to this intensely Jiangnan-based narrative template, as a politically inactive monk Fudeng sparked little interest from those in control of how to recount his life and actions. Before long, he was further sacrificed to the dominant narrative that had its own agenda. Fudeng's standard biography, written by Deqing, offers an example. The received version of the biography is actually a redacted one, about a thousand characters shorter than the original (or earlier) version. Some important sentences and paragraphs were deliberately deleted, and, most strikingly, in the parts describing how Fudeng helped Deqing with Chan practice, this relationship is reversed.[139] Most of the changes were made by Qian Qianyi, the figure who created the dominant framework for late-Ming Buddhism characterized by glorifying Deqing and Zhenke. With the widespread circulation of this adapted version, the real image of Fudeng was suppressed in favor of Deqing. His being ignored in history was thereafter fixed, as was the type of eminent monk he embodied.

The rise of Deqing, Zhenke, and Fudeng to become leading masters reinforced their efforts to fulfill their vows, while their vows, likewise, reinforced their rise to eminence. This synergy not only reveals part of the logic behind their becoming eminent monks but also displays some of the initiative and vitality within the *saṃgha* that was a key factor in the late-Ming Buddhist renewal. Their growth, their unceasing self-cultivation, and the support they received from the *saṃgha* and society are all impressive. Their vows, unprecedented in scale in the dynasty, illustrated a rekindled enthusiasm and courage within the *saṃgha* to advance its own interests. The end results, however, were essentially decided by the effectiveness of their dialectical interactions with the world, especially with politics, and not merely by the power of their religious commitments.

Without downplaying the importance of the charisma of these leading monks, strategies mattered. To a large extent, they chose their fates and determined the trajectories of their enterprises through their decisions on where and how to mobilize resources. Deqing's sole reliance on Cisheng, Zhenke's prioritizing of Jiangnan scholar-officials over eunuchs, and Fudeng's mobilization of all walks of society decided to what degree they could fulfill their vows from the very beginning. In particular, in the volatile politico-religious environment, to what extent these monks could carry through with their aims was basically decided by how reliably they could turn a region other than Beijing into the base from which to draw resources. Deeply rooted in Shanxi and Shaanxi, Fudeng's extraordinary success demonstrated how beneficial it could be when local support was strong enough to give a monk the flexibility of giving up on imperial patronage, which was often unreliable and involved danger.

Essentially but implicitly, they all suffered under structural restrictions on Buddhism that can be traced back to the early Ming. None of them had sufficient resources at their command, which resulted from the greatly weakened monastic economy. There were no orchestrated actions on a higher level when they engaged in these large-scale projects. The chance of success was significantly reduced, but this lack of collaboration had less to do with their personal choices than with the lost institutional autonomy of the *saṃgha*. Politically and ideologically, as shown by the attacks on Deqing and Zhenke, although Buddhism at times appeared promising, its weak and marginal position within the power structure was little improved. In this context, these ambitious monks had to depend heavily on the secular world, which rendered them vulnerable to contemporary politics.

Politics not only considerably affected eminent monks while they were alive but also essentially shaped their images after death. During the first two decades of the Wanli era, their ties with Cisheng significantly facilitated their rise as star monks. But in the following decade when the succession issue divided the inner court and factionalism was rife at court, Deqing was exiled for staking his success on engaging in court strife and Zhenke died in prison after being caught up in factionalism. Since this was the period when confronting the emperor could boost one's reputation, the moral superiority deriving from siding with Cisheng enshrined their tragic ends and glorified their images. Interestingly, political suppression could be beneficially educational, winning the affected monk additional respect by facilitating his spiritual achievements. An example of this was Deqing's "entering the Dharma of the Buddha because of the king's law" in his fifties.

In sharp contrast with Deqing and Zhenke, Fudeng represented a significant but oft-overlooked type of eminent monk. His smooth career and great success in life reveal that although politics governed everybody, there was still room left for monks to choose not to play with it. His being unjustifiably ignored reveals how the dominating narrative template, with its infatuation with politics, could twist an understanding of late-Ming Buddhism. In a broader context, Fudeng's clash with Deqing represented two paths in developing Buddhism. Given that the state had taken the upper hand in its relationship with Buddhism at least since the Song, Fudeng's experiences, in life and after death alike, not only encourage us to reevaluate how the tendency to stress confrontation affected the late-Ming Buddhist revival but also are revealing when we consider the future of Buddhism even now.

7

Temples

Evolving Under Influence

That Buddhist temples were constructed or refurbished on a large scale in late-Ming China was a most visually prominent expression of contemporary enthusiasm for Buddhism. Temples are not only religious places where people gather to study Buddhist doctrines and conduct religious practice but also sites of sociocultural significance where diverse forces meet and contend. Thus, the history of a temple is a set of shifting heterogeneous conversations involving a variety of elements,[1] resulting from both the inner dynamics of the *saṃgha* and its interaction with the secular world. We can expect to see different stories in different temples, varying with areas and times.

The focus of this chapter is the vicissitude in temple building, which reflected and resulted from the interaction of participating forces with one another in a material, straightforward, and most visible way. In discussing the common practice of erecting a stone stela to publicize the generosity of those sponsoring a temple building, Timothy Brook has aptly pointed out that "the stele is not a simple financial record. It documents not wealth alone, but status and power as well. By recording who gives, a stele announces who is capable of giving, who wishes to be known as having given, and who seeks to be known as having given in whose company. As such, it testifies to the structure of the social world of patrons and non-patrons alike."[2] Following the same logic, this chapter examines five temples in the mid- and late-Ming context to see how the participating forces, most of which have been examined in the preceding chapters, interplayed dynamically to affect the development of the temples involved. Not a full-spectrum examination, it has a special interest in revealing the geographical and temporal features of the relationships that have been so far overlooked. I examine some cases beyond the period under discussion on the assumption that over a longer duration we can better understand fluctuations they experienced than over a shorter time.

TEMPLES IN BEIJING

Beijing was a significant but confusing place in the history of Ming Buddhism. In medieval China when Buddhism enjoyed its glory in cosmopolitan cities like Chang'an, Luoyang, Nanjing, and Hangzhou, Buddhism in Beijing had little to boast of except for the stone canon at Fangshan 房山. Things began to change after it was made the Middle Capital 中都 of the Jin dynasty (1115–1234) and, under imperial sponsorship, some major Buddhist temples were built in the area in the Yuan dynasty (1271–1368). This upward trend halted temporarily in the early Ming when Beijing was replaced by Nanjing as the imperial capital and resumed only after 1418 following the restoration of its status as China's political center. Subsequently, Beijing saw a growing concentration of Buddhist temples. Unlike Buddhist institutions in Jiangnan, few Beijing temples have detailed accounts of their history. And this point remains true on a broader scale in Beizhili and Shanxi.[3] This paucity of evidence reflects a low level of involvement of scholar-officials in monastic affairs at the time. Fortunately, for Chongfusi 崇福寺 and Tanzhesi 潭柘寺, the former in the city of Beijing and the latter in mountains nearby, we have some information, especially epigraphic material, to know what happened to them.[4]

Chongfusi

Located in the southern part of the city of Beijing, Chongfusi remained a leading Buddhist temple in North China that kept close links with the imperial house. It was originally Minzhongsi 憫忠寺 built by Emperor Taizong of the Tang (r. 627–649) for his soldiers killed in the unsuccessful venture of conquering Koryo in 645. Under the reign of Emperor Shengzong (r. 972–1031) of the Liao dynasty, a great religious and cultural project—carving the Khitan canon 契丹藏, the second edition of the Chinese Buddhist canon—was carried out and completed there. Minzhongsi was destroyed in an earthquake in 1057 but rebuilt thirteen years later under imperial sponsorship. The monastery was renamed Chongfusi in 1437 and has since remained an important temple in Beijing.

In 1435, Chongfusi had its first major renovation project of the Ming, which would have not been possible without strong support from the eunuchs. In the autumn of that year, Song Wenyi 宋文毅 (dates unknown),[5] a eunuch in the Directorate of Ceremonial, met the abbot of the monastery while distributing

Buddhist scriptures in Beijing temples.[6] After learning that Chongfusi had a splendid history but that the abbot had no money to renovate it, Song decided to team up with his fellow eunuchs to take up the task. The project was commenced in the second month of 1437 and finished in the next fifth month. It was not a simple renovation but a complete restoration. One hundred and forty rooms were built or repaired, including the mountain gate (*shanmen* 山門) flanked by the drum and bell towers on both sides, three main halls and several small halls, the Dharma hall, kitchen, and the like. Also, new Buddhist statues were erected and necessary Dharma vessels were prepared. Song Wenyi requested the name tablet from the emperor for the monastery, which was part of the standard process for eunuchs' sponsoring Buddhist temples. Eight years later when the Northern Buddhist Canon came out for the first time, he had a copy bestowed on the monastery and constructed a building to store it. This was a money-consuming undertaking, led by six eunuchs, including Song. The participating patrons consisted of 134 eunuchs, 27 devout officials (*xinguan* 信官), and 27 ordinary laymen (*xinshi* 信士).[7] Obviously, the eunuchs not only made up the major proportion of sponsors but also showed an ability and willingness to mobilize resources from other social groups for Buddhist cause.[8] Song Wenyi claimed that his engagement in the Buddhist project was primarily to pray for the emperor's longevity.[9] Even if it was not totally a rhetorical claim given that he had benefited greatly from serving the imperial family for forty years, choosing to restore a Buddhist temple as a way of expressing gratitude nevertheless reflected the initial trend among eunuchs to build Buddhist temples. By the 1470s, as Beijing grew prosperous, it was said that "Buddhist and Daoist temples had come to thrive day after day. And it was taken as merit by all influential officials at the inner and outer courts to exhaust their wealth to construct [temples]" (是以佛老之宮日益崇盛，而凡中外貴臣，必各竭其資力有所建造以爲功德).[10] A social fashion based on religious ideology formally took shape.

One and half centuries later, a new renovation project was conducted in the second half of the Wanli period, from which we can see an ongoing change in the social status and origins of the patrons, especially the retreat of the eunuchs. In 1601, Zhuoshan Mingyu 琢山明玉 (dates unknown), an abbot well known for his hospitality, appealed for renovation funds for the monastery and received a ready response. This project had its images, halls, and walls refurbished and its bell and drum tower rebuilt. Notably, it was a Beijing native, a registrar (*jingli* 經歷) of the imperial guards, who donated several hundred taels of silver and led the project. A stone stela listing the patrons exists but is only partly readable. The remaining part lists 132 sponsors, including 26 low-ranking imperial guards, 22 devout officials, and 84 ordinary laymen. In addition, 5 villagers and 5 Shanxi people were listed separately.[11] No civil examination degree holders were involved as patrons. Only 1 eunuch appeared. Although the stela has one part missing, this fact nonetheless shows that the eunuchs as a group had significantly shrunk from their dominant role in the 1435 project. Given that the Cisheng-Wanli relationship had reached its lowest point by the time, this self-restraint can be seen as a clever response to the situation.[12]

The last major renovation project during the Ming came in 1634; it further attested these changes in the composition of patrons, especially the shift of major patrons from the eunuchs to local elites, which would later prove irreversible. Twenty-two people were listed as major patrons (*da gongde zhu* 大功德主), 17 of whom clearly came from six families. In addition, there were 127 devout officials, 59 ordinary laymen, and 25 monks. The composition of this list deserves attention. Once again the role of the eunuchs was negligible as we see only 1 eunuch. In sharp contrast, for the first time in the history of Chongfusi, educated local residents—including 8 county graduates, 4 tribute students (*gongsheng* 貢生), 1 student of the Imperial College (*jiansheng* 監生), and 2 low-level officials with the *jinshi* degree who appeared to play only a supplementary role—became the most prominent as the leaders of the renovation project.[13] Furthermore, the fact that 19 of the ordinary laymen came from Shanxi while 15 of the monks were from other temples suggests the existence of certain networks that could help the monastery to draw resources across regional boundaries. Such an unseen diversity in the composition of its patrons, especially the continued shift of major patrons from inner-court elites to local elites, can be understood only in connection with the broader context: as the dynasty was approaching its end, on the one hand the royal house and the eunuchs could no longer afford to support Buddhism even on a medium scale, and on the other local elites in the capital region obtained an opportunity to engage in Buddhist affairs relatively freely because the government had more urgent things to do than suppress them as before.

An essay written one year after the completion of the project showcases the general situation of Beijing Buddhism at the time:

> This monastery is a wonderful place whose buildings [are so high] it seems they could touch the sky. Day by day, [however], the number of monks in its two corridors is decreasing and its main halls are falling in decline. [Although] some people say that this is destiny, fortunately a native monk . . . bravely came out asking almsgivers [for help]. He made donations, and so did I. . . . In the *jiaxu* year [1634], [he] repaired the main Buddha hall and the Heavenly King hall. . . . I am not good at writing, but it was the place where my late father, a former vice–censor in chief, once stayed and where I joined in an association to discuss literature. I thus know its history very well.

乃今梵宇摩空, 頗稱勝地, 而兩廊僧眾日益削弱, 大殿日就傾圮. 或者曰氣數使然. 幸有鄉僧 … 慨然發心告諸檀那, 更自捐資, 余亦隨意佈施 … 歲在甲戌, 重修大佛寶殿, 天王殿 … 余 … 不能文, 但念先中丞居停之所, 不俟且結社論文於斯, 頗悉顛末.[14]

Chongfusi was still in good shape, but its resident monks kept decreasing. Such a crisis of brain drain facing it actually reflected the Beijing *saṃgha* slipping into decline as the dynasty approached its end, an issue I return to in the last chapter.

Chongfusi thrived again in the early Qing partly through restructuring the network of its patrons, especially relinking with the imperial house. New imperial patronage began with two princes who came to donate a big copper bell and a copy of the Buddhist canon. Then the early- and mid-Qing emperors all lent support to Chongfusi. They handwrote the name tablet for the monastery, granted it two copies of the Buddhist canon, had the monastery renovated with government money at least three times, and built one ordination platform there.[15] Intense patronage enabled the Manchu imperial house to claim the credit for protecting Chongfusi, and such a close connection with this significant monastery can be perceived as instrumental to its rule. On the part of the monastery, the royal patronage considerably promoted its publicity and helped to attract more patrons, especially from the ruling elites. The eunuchs vanished but, most strikingly, scholar-officials rushed to the monastery and kept active throughout the dynasty. They used it as a place to meet friends and patronized it with paintings and poems in great numbers.[16] In particular, for the first time they found strong interest in its history traceable to the Tang dynasty. Their freedom in Chongfusi constituted a sharp contrast with the restraint characteristic of their predecessors in the Ming, implying that Buddhism was no longer viewed as a significant threat to neo-Confucianism as an ideology. In this way, Chongfusi, which had been renamed Fayuansi 法源寺 in 1734, had itself embedded even more deeply in the everyday life of local people and thus broadened its foundation for sustainability.

Tanzhesi

Unlike Chongfusi, Tanzhesi, located seventy *li* west of Beijing, was connected to the city by only a rough road.[17] Originally built as Jiafusi 嘉福寺 during the Western Jin (265–316), this temple boasted a Huayan master in the early Tang as its first patriarch.[18] It was renamed the Great Qingshou monastery 大慶壽寺 in the Jin dynasty, during which Guanghui Tongli 廣慧通理 (1104–1175), backed by government funds, took ten years to rebuild it on a vast scale. After this landmark event in its history, Tanzhesi grew into a great monastery during the Yuan dynasty that housed more than one thousand monks.

Tanzhesi continued to expand in the early and middle Ming thanks to generous support from rich benefactors, especially the imperial family and the eunuchs. Having suffered grave losses in the late-Yuan wars, Tanzhesi had its first major renovation in the Ming around the year 1412 when Chan master Wuchu Deshi 無初德始 (d. 1429), on Yao Guangxiao's recommendation, took charge of the project with donations from a local prince.[19] One decade later, in 1427, the monastery was expanded owing to the donation from the empress dowager and princes, which helped to build new halls and pagodas. Seventy years later, Dai Yi 戴義 (dates unknown), a eunuch in the Directorate of Ceremonial, came up with a new renovation plan. He promised to pay the laborers' salaries with his own money but requested the emperor defray the expenses for the construction material. The project started in 1507 and finished one and half years later. Like the one led by Song Wenyi for Chongfusi, it not only refurbished all the buildings but also further expanded the monastery by adding more than fifty new buildings.

The first half of the Wanli era saw a new development at Tanzhesi as a significant stage where key Buddhist figures met. In his first visit to the monastery in 1586, Zibo Zhenke 紫柏真可 (1543–1604) found that "the yin [negative] force had built up within Tanzhesi for a long time and the wheel of the Dharma ceased to turn" (潭柘陰氣久積, 法輪弗轉).[20] But later this monastery became Zhenke's favorite, and his disciples, such as Yu Yuli 于玉立 (jinshi 1583), came to see him. In 1592, Zhenke sent a legendary brick from Tanzhesi to the inner court. The brick had been dented from the countless prostrations of the princess of Miaoyan 妙嚴 (dates unknown), a daughter of Kublai Khan (1215–1294) who became a nun there. Thus Zhenke clearly sought to encourage Cisheng 慈聖 (1545–1614) to practice Buddhism diligently. Shortly after, probably in response to Lu Guangzu's 陸光祖 (1521–1597, jinshi 1547) suggestion,[21] Cisheng ordered Xu Zhengguang 徐正光 (b. 1550) to renovate Tanzhesi. Although no details are available, this was a major project that, according to an epigraphic record written by Li Shida 李世達 (jinshi 1556) in 1594, added more than eighty rooms (八十餘楹) to the monastery.[22] Most important, Tanzhesi witnessed a major event that would punctuate the late-Ming Buddhist renewal—Zhenke's arrest. Zhenke bade farewell to Tanzhesi with a poem and, two weeks later, died in prison.

Similar to Chongfusi, Tanzhesi enjoyed a renewal in the early Qing with imperial patronage and support, and over the course of time the eunuchs as its main patrons gave way to organized laypeople. In 1686, the Kangxi emperor (r. 1661–1722) visited the monastery and bestowed it with gifts, including Buddhist sutras and statues. Six years later, the emperor granted the monastery ten thousand taels of silver, with which at least twenty-eight buildings were constructed. After that, the emperor returned to Tanzhesi twice and renamed it Xiuyun Chansi 岫雲禪寺. His mother and princes joined as benefactors of the temple as well.[23] The imperial patronage brought new waves of support to the monastery.

> Since then, companions of learning have come together like clouds, and the wealth of the Dharma has been donated like rain. New buildings have kept emerging daily, making the splendor of its statues in green and gold rank first among all monasteries on the western mountain.

自是學侶雲集, 法財兩施, 建造日新, 金碧像飾, 擅西山諸剎之勝.[24]

Among others we should pay particular attention to the incense associations (*xianghui* 香會) that appeared in various forms to organize ordinary Buddhist followers.[25] As Naquin has noted, shortly after the physical revival of the monastery in the 1690s, lay pilgrims begin to make their mark on the monastery. Although most of the bequests by these pilgrims were relatively modest, once organized they could be remarkable. For example, in 1714 the Dabei Society 大悲會 not only undertook building repairs themselves but also presented the temple with eight hundred fifty *mu* of land and fifty rooms, so that their rental income could fund rituals.[26] Tanzhesi had already amassed vast tracts of monastic lands over a period of centuries.[27] With the contributions made by these laypeople, especially their significant addition to its land, the shock caused by the departure of the eunuchs was effectively cushioned and Tanzhesi continued to operate smoothly. In time, notably, the image of Tanzhesi was actually reshaped by scholar-officials. Susan Naquin has noted that "in all these works, information about the monastic community was usually excluded, and the temple cast as a site for history, for imperial and literati visits, for the individual but not the group, for the marvelous and the poetic experience but not the devotional one."[28] Tanzhesi had multiple characteristics, but some were suppressed in favor of others, and it seemed to become less religious than before as a consequence.

TEMPLES IN JIANGNAN

Compared with the temples in Beijing, Buddhist institutions in Jiangnan had distinctive stories. Certain significant aspects of these stories, especially those related to their relationships with scholar-officials in the Wanli period, whether positive or negative, have been discussed in chapter 5 or by scholars like Timothy Brook. I therefore focus here instead on the transition period from mid-Jiajing to the early Wanli eras, during which some temples in Beijing started to receive support from the eunuchs in one way or another. But the situation seemed much worse for Buddhist institutions in Jiangnan, where they could fall prey to the secular world for various reasons. Shixingsi 實性寺 in Shaoxing prefecture and Fuyuan Puhui Chansi 福源普慧禪寺 in Jiaxing prefecture, both locally based and of medium scale, were typical of the Jiangnan region. They experienced a U-turn from dismantling to restoration during this short period. A close reading of their histories reveals how elite participants, especially local authorities and scholar-officials, adjusted their handling of Buddhist institutions in compliance with their own interests and the rapidly changing politico-religious environment.

Shixingsi

Shixingsi was a regionally famous temple close to the seat of Sheng county 嵊縣, Zhejiang. Originally Taiqing chapel 泰清院 founded in the Tang dynasty, this monastery owned a large number of imperially bestowed landholdings and was the place where local authorities held official ceremonies, such as praying for the health of the emperor and stability for the state. Its history was punctuated by some major events, including being destroyed in the middle of the ninth century, rebuilt in 935, and then repaired in 1490. What is most relevant for the present discussion is that Shixingsi was abolished in the Jiajing era but reinstalled in the early Wanli era.

Shixingsi was totally ruined in the Jiajing era under the joint pressure of local authorities and the local gentry. In 1537, Lü Zhang 呂章 (d. 1532 or later), magistrate of Sheng county, destroyed Shixingsi, converted its main hall into a shrine for Confucius, and moved its Buddha statues to a branch chapel. After that, the monks were ordered to lodge in a borrowed place to pay taxes on the monastic assets. As for the reason, Peng Fu 彭富 (*jinshi* 1562) said in an account that it was out of "personal hatred" (*shihui* 私恚),[29] while a local gazetteer claims that it was because the monks in the temple were found to be performing unlawful activities.[30] Historically, what happened to Shixingsi was not an exception among Buddhist institutions in Jiangnan during the Jiajing era. As discussed in chapters 2 and 5, Buddhism had a hard time during this period, frequently falling prey to diverse forms of encroachment and injustice by the state and scholar-officials. In this case, like many contemporary officials, Lü did not hesitate to act once discovering what he perceived as misdeeds by monks.

In the same move, a piece of the grounds belonging to Shixingsi was rented to the provincial graduate Zhou Zhen 周震 (d. 1575), who then built a private villa on the grounds and purchased nearby fields to extend the property.[31] After having occupied the monastic land for three decades, however, Zhou Zhen suddenly felt uneasy to such a degree that he eagerly wanted to have the problem fixed. Peng Fu described the change in vivid detail.

> Mr. Zhou had already lived there for thirty years. He later became an assistant department magistrate [biejia 別駕] in Hengzhou. After returning home from the post, he suddenly felt regretful and unhappy. He told his son [Zhou] Mengxiu [周夢秀, dates unknown], who was a county graduate,[32] "People in the past would not do a single unrighteous thing even if it could bring them everything under Heaven. Virtuous people in the Jin and Tang dynasties, like Chamberlain for the Capital [neishi 內史] Wang and Duke Xuan of Lu,[33] all donated their houses for Buddhist temples. On the contrary, I rented a temple as my house and thus gained a reputation of unrighteousness. I would rather die in a ravine than continue to live here. You must restore the temple."

> 居三十年矣. 周君後為衡州別駕, 歸, 忽悔恨不樂, 謂其子庠生夢秀曰: 古人行一不義, 雖得天下而不為也. 且晉唐名賢, 如王內史、陸宣公, 皆舍宅為寺, 予乃佃寺為宅, 負不義之名. 吾寧填死溝壑, 弗忍居於是矣. 汝必復之[34]

Compared with aristocrats in medieval China, scholar-officials in late-imperial China appeared less generous in handling Buddhist institutions, which reflected not only the shrinking of resources under their command but also their changed attitudes toward Buddhism. It is worth noting that it was around the year 1567 that Zhou Zhen felt guilt for having occupied the grounds. In other words, it was two years after Jiajing's death, when the politico-religious environment began to change in some significant aspects.

Only in the early Wanli era was the temple rebuilt, which was supported by both local elites and local officials. Peng Fu continued to recount what happened at the time:

> Mr. Zhou caught a serious illness in the winter of Wanli 2 [1574]. He summoned his close relatives and enjoined them, "I would like to see the restoration of the temple. I am waiting for it so that I can die without regret." His son immediately submitted a request for permission to restore the temple with the house and

nearby field they had bought. I approved it with happiness. Magistrate Zhu Yibai [dates unknown] summoned the monk Fazhang [dates unknown] and others, and returned the temple to them. Some people had antagonistic opinions, but they were all dismissed by the prefect and provincial governor. After having given away the house, Zhou [Mengxiu] moved to a place that was simple and shabby. Other people would not have been able to bear the change, but Zhou only felt happy because he had fulfilled his father's good deed.

萬曆二年冬, 周君寢疾, 會其族父兄子弟而囑之曰: "吾願及見寺之復也. 吾待而瞑矣." 於是周生立以其宅並益買旁近地請復為寺. 以狀來上, 余懼然嘉歎, 判而復之 邑令朱君一栢即召寺僧法彰等, 還寺如故. 有異議者, 守巡諸上官皆绌之 周生既舍宅, 乃徙居他舍. 他舍敝陋, 人所不堪, 周生惟以克成父善為樂.

Zhou Mengxiu did not act alone. Alongside the return of the monastic grounds, Lu Gao 陸杲 (1503–1575), Zhou Zhen's friend, and his son Lu Guangzu also helped Shixingsi to redeem its land with thirty taels of silver. Highly influential in local society, the Lu family's call for the return of the occupied land to Shixingsi received a positive response, in some cases even without a demand for a repayment of the money they had paid. The monks did nothing but wait, and only after that did they start running the temple again.

Nonetheless, it is important to know that there were still antagonistic opinions, showing that criticism against Buddhism lingered in Jiangnan even in the early Wanli era. It happened that Lu Guangzu cast light on the criticism in another letter.

Recently, I have clandestinely heard of controversies over [the project]. It could be found everywhere in the Tang and Song dynasties that virtuous people donated their houses [and converted them into] monasteries. My ancient ancestor Duke Xuan donated his house to become Nengrensi, and the ancestor of the fifteenth generation, the military affairs commissioner [shumi 樞密], donated his house to become Farensi. The offspring of our lineages have persisted in protecting and supporting [these two temples] without interruption.[35] Shixingsi is a temple with a history of thousands of years. What Ruiquan did is nothing more than returning what he had rented previously and restoring the temple. His cause is justifiable, and his act is suitable. That is different from building a new [temple]. Are there people who disapprove of it? Jishi and I both have to take on the task because it was the desire of our late fathers. Formerly, Su Shi [1037–1101] donated to a temple four statues of the Heavenly king, which had been cherished by his father. He wrote a record saying that "I donated it for my father. Who has no father?" His words are sorrowful and moving.

頃微聞有異同者, 夫唐宋名賢舍宅為寺, 班班可攷, 而我遠祖宣公亦舍宅為能仁寺, 十五世祖樞密公舍宅為法忍寺, 我陸氏子孫至今護持, 無敢廢墜. 況實性寺系千年古剎, 瑞泉不過以己之所佃還而復之, 其義甚正, 其名甚順, 又與創施者不同, 他復何說乎. 孤與繼實並以先人之意, 不敢不任. 昔蘇子瞻以老泉所寶四天王像施之佛寺而作記曰: "吾為父而施. 人孰無父哉?" 此言悲惻而感人.[36]

"Ruiquan" refers to Zhou Zhen and "Jishi" to his son Mengxiu.[37] The "military affairs commissioner" refers to Lu Xuanji 陸旋吉 (fl. 1074). In Wanli 3 (1575), when this letter was written, Lu Guangzu was still criticized for restoring Shixingsi. Both Lu Guangzu's and Zhou Mengxiu's fathers had died by this time, so in response Lu had recourse to filial piety, a cardinal Confucian value, as a discursive strategy to justify their conduct as sons.[38] Finally, Lu Guangzu rebuilt Shixingsi on a new foundation, since the government still occupied the old buildings. His efforts obtained support from Zhang Yuanbian 張元忭 (1538–1588, *jinshi* 1571), a new *jinshi* who became a compiler at the Hanlin Academy (*Hanlin xiuzhuan* 翰林修撰). In addition to restoring Shixingsi proper, they also built a chapel for it.[39]

Fuyuan Puhui Chansi

The ups and downs of Shixingsi was not an exception among Jiangnan temples during the period, and there was a similar case in which the Lu family was directly involved. After the restoration of Shixingsi, Lu Guangzu received a letter from Zhou Mengxiu, who reminded him that one of his houses had originally been a Buddhist temple. The temple involved was Fuyuan Puhui Chansi, a large temple founded in the Yuan dynasty and rebuilt in the Yongle era. In 1554, a large number of soldiers were stationed in Pinghu 平湖 county to defend against Japanese pirates. Required to immediately prepare a new headquarters for high-ranking officials, the magistrate thus destroyed Fuyuansi and transformed it expediently into the Military Defense Circuit (*bingbei si* 兵備司).[40] On the surface, this was a story about how the fate of a Jiangnan temple was affected by Japanese pirates, which was not uncommon at the time. Lu Guangzu's reply in 1576, however, discloses more layers beneath the story. In the letter, Lu appreciated the reminder and then explained to Zhou Mengxiu about things related to the house.

> When the temple was destroyed, I was serving in office. All its assets were rented by scholars-officials and commoners, with the exception of a [patch of land] in the southwestern corner and several small rooms. The magistrate reserved them

as he had other plans. When I returned home, Zhenchuan, the keeper of the land and rooms and who was my acquaintance, requested, out of fear that they would be robbed by others, me to purchase them. I declined several times, but [he] even cried in making his appeal. Finally, I had to buy them but deemed them as useless. Later, my late father bought a patch of field at the back of the rooms from Assistant Prefect [*tongpan* 通判] Pan and finally turned it into the grounds of the house.

I did not return home until more than one year after the temple had been destroyed, and the monks and the Pans did not sell the land until more than one year after I had returned. Therefore, I was the last one among dozens of officials and commoners who rented the monastic land. In addition, I bought it through a private transaction, without sending a single word [about it] to local officials. The year and month [of the transaction] and the contract are clear, and the monk selling the houses remains alive. I am always conscious of karma, knowing that even a blade of grass belonging to the *saṃgha* cannot be used, let alone its landholding and rooms.

When Magistrate Liu destroyed the temple, it happened all too suddenly. If I had been at home, although my rank was still low, probably I could have prevented him from doing so. Nowadays it has been changed as a government office, which looks magnificent. [This conversion] is a curse left to our county, and I really hate it. I do not enjoy the house outside the southern gate, but I am so old that I am hesitant to start another construction project. Besides, this matter is so significant that I fear it would frighten others and cause many troubles. Hence, I have done nothing about it. Also, it is because I am not guilty, for it is not my intention to rent the temple. If I felt guilty, I would replace the mat even before my imminent death—how could I have peaceful ease even only for a single day? Now you, Jishi, hope that I can sacrifice myself to frustrate the secret hope of evil persons of appropriating the temple, which really has aroused my interest.

當寺廢之時, 僕在官中, 士民告佃都盡, 惟西南一隅與小屋數間, 縣官始欲他用, 故未授人. 及僕歸, 而地屋主僧真傳者, 乃僕故人, 恐為他人所奪, 求售於僕. 僕堅辭數次, 至涕泣哀懇, 不得已而買之, 亦視為無用之物耳. 後先君於小屋之後又轉買潘通判之地, 遂成宅基. 蓋寺廢歲餘而僕始歸, 歸復歲餘而僧與潘家賣地, 故告佃而分寺地者, 官民凡數十家, 惟僕最後. 又買之於人, 絕無一字到官, 其年月與契券甚明, 賣屋僧尚在也. 僕素明因果, 凡僧伽藍之物, 雖一草不可用, 況地與屋耶? 當時邑令劉君廢寺, 起於倉卒. 使僕在家, 官雖尚小, 或能力阻之 今改為官署宏壯, 至遺吾邑之害, 甚可恨也. 然南門之宅非僕樂居於此, 但老年憚于他營, 又事體重大, 恐徒駭俗而多梗, 故遂因循. 亦以實非佃寺心, 無愧怍耳. 苟有愧怍, 雖臨死猶當易簀, 可苟一日安耶. 今繼實欲望僕損己以絕小人借寺之患, 僕不覺惻然動心.[41]

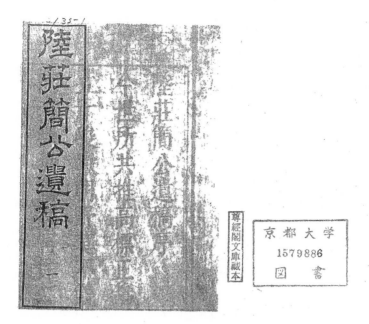

FIGURE 7.1 *Lu Zhuangjian gong yigao* 陸莊簡公遺稿 by Lu Guangzu 陸光祖

Courtesy of the Kyoto University Library

Not only were the buildings of Fuyuansi destroyed for military use but also, as in the case of Shixingsi, its landholdings had been grabbed by powerful local families in the name of selling or renting. That Zhenchuan cried while asking Lu to purchase the land and rooms from the temple reveals how desperate the *saṃgha* was in Jiangnan at the time. Fortunately for Fuyuansi, at the end of the letter Lu Guangzu invited Zhou Mengxiu to discuss the restoration plan face-to-face. Eventually, he donated the house and founded Nanchansi 南禪寺.[42]

The eventful fates of the two temples that were totally out of their control reflect drastic changes in the role that local officials and scholar-officials played with regard to Buddhist institutions in Jiangnan, behind which were similarly drastic changes in the politico-religious environment. Peng Fu once commented that "there were no scholar-officials to destroy Buddhist temples as their assets prior to the Hongzhi and Zhengde eras. This is because they maintained respect for the law and strictly abided by Confucian regulations. Only in recent ages have there been those who seek for their own interests on the pretext of driving the heterodox away" (余惟弘、德以前, 士大夫無毀寺為業者, 畏國憲而謹儒行也. 近世始有藉口異端之辟以姿其利便之私).[43] Insightfully, Peng first identifies a sharp change in scholar-officials' stance regarding Buddhism before and after the Zhengde era and then exposes the selfish purpose behind their encroachment on monastic institutions that took place under an ideological disguise. During the Jiajing era, it is not accidental that Shixingsi and Fuyuansi, exposed to diverse forms of encroachment but deprived of institutional, legal, and ideological protection, both fell into the hands of powerful local families. Their fates exemplify the fragility of the Jiangnan *saṃgha*.[44] In the early Wanli period, Zhou Mengxiu's action is not that surprising given that he was well known for contending that studying Buddhism was instrumental in understanding Confucianism.[45] But Lu Guangzu deserves particular attention. In addition to his pro-Buddhist family tradition, it seems to have been important to him to give up the material benefits associated with the large amount of land that the Lu family owned.[46] Already in the financially privileged class, it would be easy for Lu to instead gather social and cultural capital by backing Buddhism. Together, Zhou and Lu were harbingers of the turn to Buddhism among scholar-officials in Jiangnan, who as a whole would need more time to change their course. Thus, although a public reaccommodation of Buddhism started in Jiangnan at the time, the necessity was still there to justify their pro-Buddhism activities, as evidenced by what Lu Guangzu did.

CIGUANGSI AT MOUNT HUANG

Located in the vicinity of Jiangnan, Ciguangsi 慈光寺 at Mount Huang was not a temple with any social or cultural significance until the latter half of the Wanli era. The prominent rise of this rural temple in subsequent years took place in a particular context, and the process involved court and local elite groups, such as royal members, eunuchs, scholar-officials, and Huizhou 徽州 merchants.

The history of Ciguangsi started with Pumen Weian's 普門惟安 (1546–1625) converting, with support from a Huizhou merchant, a Daoist chapel into a Buddhist temple. Weian, a Shaanxi native, was a disciple of Kongyin Zhencheng 空印鎮澄 (1547–1617), a leading northern master based on Mount Wutai who maintained close links with figures like Cisheng and Hanshan Deqing 憨山德清 (1546–1623). He had spent most of his life in North China before setting out southward in 1604. Two years later, he arrived at Mount Huang and decided to stay as he recalled with surprise having seen the mountain thirteen years earlier while in meditation.[47] The Mount Huang area was three hundred miles in circumference, with its central part in the three counties of Xiuning 休寧, She 歙, and Taiping 太平. These counties belonged to She 歙 and Xuan 宣 subprefectures, respectively. At the time, Buddhism had little influence in the area, and only a few Buddhist temples were scattered there. Ciguangsi was originally a Daoist

Zhusha chapel 朱砂庵 built in the Jiajing era under the patronage of Wu Yangchun 吳養春 (d. 1626). Typical of Huizhou merchants, the Wu family amassed huge amounts of wealth through selling goods like salt, silk, and timber, and running *qianzhuang* 錢莊 (an old-style Chinese private bank).[48] Wu Yangchun had more than two thousand *mu* of forest in the area of Mount Huang. Convinced that Weian was the person he was looking for, Wu constructed a Chan hall for him on the site of the Zhusha chapel.[49]

Weian soon won a big following, but to sustain the community he had to visit Beijing to elicit resources, during which time he received much support from local sons. Weian renamed the chapel Fahai chanyuan 法海禪院. Modeling on the practice at Mount Wutai, Weian created the Pumen Association (*Pumenshe* 普門社) to practice meditation and a Huayan hall for laymen to recite the sutras. Nearly one hundred followers were attracted around him, but the growing attractiveness paradoxically caused a crisis during which Weian reportedly had no food to eat for nine months.[50] This comes as no surprise. In her study of Tanzhesi, Susan Naquin has aptly pointed out that "having rich and generous patrons in the vicinity was surely even more essential to the monastery's long-term survival. Not all mountain temples could count on these advantages."[51] In the autumn of 1610, Weian thus decided to visit the imperial capital to secure support. Although unusual for a temple in southern China, this idea made sense given Weian's background as a northern monk. During the visit, Weian obtained much assistance from local sons. With a landscape painting of the Tiandu peak rendered by a local painter, Weian made a deep impression on Wanli and the crown prince.[52] Bao Ying'ao 鮑應鰲 (*jinshi* 1595), a native of She county who was serving in the Ministry of Rites, not only composed a tribute essay (*shu* 疏) himself but also elicited another from his fellow officeholder.[53] Tang Binyin 湯賓尹 (1569–1628?, *jinshi* 1595), a native of Xuan subprefecture who led the notorious Xuan Faction (宣黨), wrote a short eulogy to publicize Fahaisi in the capital.

As expected, the inner-court elites, especially the eunuchs, brought a turning point to the temple. Ma Jin 馬進 (dates unknown), a eunuch in charge of Cimingsi 慈明寺, claimed that while in meditation he had previously met Weian, and thus Weian accepted his invitation to lodge in the temple. Cimingsi was Cisheng's private temple. Through Ma's network, especially the Buddhist association organized by the eunuchs, Weian caught the attention of some of the eunuchs. Later, when Weian visited Mount Pan 盤山 in Ji 薊 county (present-day Tianjin) with Ma Jin, an old man he came across decided to donate three hundred taels of silver to support his temple.[54] Things changed after this. With the money Weian first managed to purchase a copy of the Buddhist canon from the inner court and then, through the eunuch Yan Luan, mentioned in chapter 5, sent a memorial to Cisheng requesting a name for the temple and a protective edict for the canon.[55] In response, Wanli renamed Fahai Chanyuan Ciguang—literally, "the light of my mother [i.e., Cisheng]." Cisheng awarded Weian one purple robe, one walking staff (*zhang* 仗), and three hundred taels of silver. In addition, thanks to the eunuch Cai Qin's 蔡欽 (dates unknown) efforts, Cisheng bestowed on Ciguangsi a seven-tier gold-ornamented statue of the four-faced Vairocana (*simian qiceng piluzhena* 四面七層毗盧遮那).[56] Weian visited Beijing in a time when the succession issue was no longer a source of tension for Cisheng and Wanli, which made it possible for him to receive patronage simultaneously from them both.

Weian's success in the capital turned into a rapid mobilization of support in the Mount Huang region,[57] and those involved included local sons and others associated with them through certain networks. Notice of this imperial favor was urgently sent back by a local then in Beijing. Thrilled, local elites like Pan Zhiheng 潘之恒 (1556–1621), a native of She county, decided to build a pavilion for the temporary storage of the canon. Tang Binyin accepted the invitation to coordinate the project and wrote two essays soliciting support.[58] For Weian's part, in the sixth month of 1612 he embarked on a trip of taking back the statue and the canon, comprising seven thousand volumes, but the journey was more challenging and eventful than expected. Only two months later did he arrive in Linqing 臨清, Shandong. After that, with the assistance of Mi Wanzhong 米萬鍾 (1570–1628, *jinshi* 1595), who admired him, the trip became much easier as they arranged to take grain-transporting ships to travel southward on the Grand Canal. But when they arrived in Hangzhou, they found that many people had gathered and called for the destruction of the statue—Hangzhou was suffering a flood, and a rumor had spread that it was the Buddha statue they carried that had caused the flooding. Local violence seemed imminent. Yue Yuansheng 岳元聲 (1557–1628, *jinshi* 1583) wrote an urgent letter on Weian's behalf, and in response local officials immediately arranged for four hundred laborers to ship the cargo to She county on the same day.[59]

The wide support that Ciguangsi received from local society coincided with the growing popularity of Mount Huang, and it was the highlight of a campaign aimed at promoting local pride. The core of the region was then home to two influential groups: wealthy Huizhou merchants and huge numbers of *jinshi* with literary talents.[60] Prior to the Jiajing era local people had had little interest in the mountain. As local wealth increased and the social status of local sons grew, they increasingly felt dissatisfied with the obscurity of their hometown. Efforts to reshape and promote its image started. As an important step, they chose Mount Huang, which had gorgeous scenery, with the aim of promoting it to a status comparable to that of Mount Tai, Wutai, and Song in significance.

To that end, they compiled in a very short time at least three books dedicated exclusively to this mountain.[61] Thanks to the extraordinary success in the civil examination of a number of its degree holders and commerce and to its convenient location in the vicinity of Jiangnan's core region, this promotion campaign attracted the active participation of many leading literati from Jiangnan and other regions. Some wrote laudatory pieces after visiting the mountain, including Feng Mengzhen 馮夢楨 (1543–1608, *jinshi* 1577), Yuan Huang 袁黃 (1533–1606, *jinshi* 1586), Ge Yinliang 葛寅亮 (1570–1646, *jinshi* 1601), Qian Qianyi 錢謙益 (1582–1664, *jinshi* 1610), and Xu Xiake 徐霞客 (1857–1641). Dong Qichang 董其昌 (1555–1536, *jinshi* 1589) was even bolder: he ranked Mount Huang sixth in importance among China's mountains but without ever having set foot in the region.[62] Their writings effectively facilitated the expansion of publicity and influence of the mountain.[63] In this process, Pan Zhiheng, as a local son, served as a kind of coordinator through his extensive networks that linked with leading literati like Yuan Hongdao 袁宏道 (1568–1610, *jinshi* 1592), Li Zhi 李贄 (1527–1602), Tang Xianzu 湯顯祖 (1550–1616, *jinshi* 1583), and Tu Long 屠隆 (1543–1605, *jinshi* 1577). For example, in compiling the voluminous *Huanghai* 黃海 (The sea of [Mount] Huang), he received wide support from as many as fifty-five literati who helped to collate the draft.[64] Against this background, the royal patronage Weian received became the highlight of the campaign. Accordingly, Weian and the imperial gifts, along with the gorgeous scenery, were the subjects mentioned most frequently in the works related to the temple.[65] Bao Ying'ao distinguished Ciguangsi from other temples in the region by boasting about its bestowed statue.[66] In this sense, the support Pan Zhiheng and other local sons gave to Weian can be seen as part of the effort to promote local pride.

But securing imperial patronage was only half the battle; how the inner-court elites met local ones in the monastery was the other that proved much more unpredictable. The eunuchs became deeply involved in Weian's life after the latter's visit to Beijing. This involvement was not totally a voluntary or devotional act; the utilitarian logic behind the eunuchs' support of Buddhist temples in Beijing was still at work. In other words, it was a sort of trade between the two sides. In fact, in the second month of 1611, a monk who was clearly favored by the eunuchs had already been officially assigned as the abbot by the Ministry of Rites. Only after that, the eunuchs made the resources from the inner court available to Weian and Ciguangsi, including the name tablet, the protection edict, the gigantic statue, as well as other gifts given to Weian. The tie between the inner court and the southern temple continued even after the bestowal. For example, after learning that the temple had no place to house the canon and statue, Wanli collected several thousand taels of silver.[67] And as late as 1615, the eunuch Ma Jin was still seen at Ciguangsi.[68] But the problem was that in the Mount Huang region, not unlike other regions in China at the time, distrust or even hostility toward the eunuchs was clear, strong, and widespread. When the news arrived that three eunuchs would accompany Weian to Ciguangsi, for example, it caused panic in the region, such that Bao Ying'ao had to write a letter reassuring the locals that these eunuchs would not bother them.

On the part of local elites, however, the eunuchs' preinstalling the abbot of Ciguangsi constituted the biggest stumbling block for them in relation to the temple. As in the nearby Jiangnan region, enthusiasm for Buddhism was increasingly growing among the Mount Huang elites. Pan Zhiheng, for example, reestablished the Tiandu Association (*tiandu she* 天都社), in which members engaged in literary activities, practiced meditation, and recited the Buddha's name.[69] He also organized the Pumen Association, which was explicitly devoted to Buddhism. With some members overlapping, the Tiandu Association claimed itself as the outer protector of the former.[70] For literati members like Pan Zhiheng, with his ties to the inner court and Mount Wutai, a sacred Buddhist site,[71] Weian had special attraction. More important, the nature of Ciguangsi as a public monastery was particularly appealing to local elites. Aside from the conviction that this type of temple had a better chance of developing than hereditary temples, local literati found it possible as patrons to engage in, or even control when necessary, its operation. This was not a small matter. Two of three regulations that Pan Zhiheng set for the Pumen Association, for example, read as follows:

First, from its completion and beyond, the association should be permanently shared with people of the Way from ten directions. The head of the chapel is prohibited from accepting disciples without permission. In the case that his disciples or family members attempt to control the property, for the common benefit of the monastery [they] should be expelled from the temple on the charge of stealing the property of the monks of the ten directions. Second, this chapel shall not have a permanent head. A virtuous person should be selected as the leader at the start of a year. All things, whether big or small, should be carried out according to his direction. He steps down at the end of the year and can lead [the chapel] for another year if invited once again. If [a leader] is reluctant to resign because of craving for [benefits associated with] the position, he will be abandoned by all people.

一、是院既成, 永與十方爲道者共, 不許火主私度弟子. 如火主弟子、家人爭主其業者, 坐盜十方僧物, 以叢林大義共擯之 一、是院無常主, 每歲首推有德一人爲主事, 無大小悉聽施行, 至歲終告退. 如更請, 更主周歲. 貪位不退者, 共擯之[72]

At the core of the regulations is preventing the abbot from complete control over the chapel and allowing the association of local elites to join the decision-making process and the chapel's daily running. This may confirm Wu Jiang's argument that the involvement of literati with monastic administration was no longer a rarity but a reality in the late Ming and early Qing period.[73] But in the Ciguangsi case, since the monk, poorly accepted by locals—he was mentioned only once in the three volumes of mountain gazetteers[74]—was preinstalled as the abbot by the eunuchs, local elites lost a major chance to affect the monastery. Probably sensing an ambush by the eunuchs, they began avoiding the temple as the enthusiasm initially sparked by the bestowal waned.

Partly impacted by such a serious schism among its patrons, Ciguangsi failed to develop any self-sustaining ability, and Weian eventually died in regret. Ciguangsi did receive some support, but it was far from enough. A hall that Weian designed to house the statue, for example, was never constructed, and the statue was thus dismantled to place in several rooms. Without a suitable place to store it, the canon suffered insect damage. In fact, Ciguangsi never gained economic security during the Ming—one year, hundreds of its monks had only bamboo seeds to eat for several months. Weian left Ciguangsi to live separately. With local support, he built a hall where a Guanyin bodhisattva (Avalokiteśvara) with fourteen arms was erected in the middle, with the bodhisattvas Yaowang 藥王 (Bhaiṣajya-rāja) and Yaoshang 藥上 (Bhaiṣajya-rāja-samudgata) flanking it on two sides.[75] But it seemed that he was not in a better situation. In 1623, Weian suddenly left for Xiangfusi 祥符寺 in Wuxi 無錫, where he suffered starvation for seven days. Two years later he traveled northward allegedly to curb the eunuchs' misdeeds, but he died on the way in unappeased disappointment. His last words were, "I would come back to accomplish the enterprise" (再來了 此一局).[76]

New hope for Ciguangsi did not come until the early Qing, again with support from a network linking mercantile elites, eminent monks, and implicit royal patronage. In 1662, Yuling Tongxiu 玉林通琇 (1614–1675), a leading Linji Chan master, paid a visit to Ciguangsi and predicted its revival after having witnessed miracles there.[77] Four years later, Huang Zhuan 黃儁 (fl. 1670), a major Huizhou merchant who had engaged in the salt trade in Yangzhou for twenty years, came to the rescue. Huang Zhuan had met Weian before, but his decision to rebuild Ciguangsi after learning of its recent situation from Tongxiu's disciple may have more to do with Tongxiu's status as the master of the Shunzhi emperor (r. 1644–1661). From 1666 to 1670, with more than forty thousand taels of silver, he reconstructed Ciguangsi by modeling it after the Great Baoen monastery in Nanjing, Deqing's "home" monastery. With more than one hundred rooms, the monastery became the largest in the region.[78] In the broader view, this was a part of the seventeenth-century revitalization of Chan Buddhism. Afterward, a wave of patronage followed. By the late seventeenth century, Ciguangsi reportedly housed more than one thousand monks. Its abbot was held in high esteem for both his religious achievements and his artistic talents.[79] Unfortunately, the monastery caught fire in 1737, from which it never recovered.

Several types of growth of Buddhist institutions during the mid and late Ming have been examined here. The diversity of outcomes of different temples reflects how the availability of resources varied greatly with time and region, owing to the different interactions of contributing forces.

The composition of the affecting forces and their respective influence on Buddhist institutions differed significantly depending on time and region. In Jiangnan and nearby regions, scholar-officials and mercantile elites were allowed to and indeed served as a leading force in supporting Buddhist institutions, as shown in the Ciguangsi case, but in Beijing patronage from the imperial household and the eunuchs was favored while the involvement of scholar-officials was purposefully suppressed. In time, responding to the drastic changes that characterized the politics of the period, these forces could adjust their handling of temples swiftly. During the Jiajing period scholar-officials and local officials in Jiangnan were frequently predators of Buddhist institutions, but, following Cisheng's entrance into the political arena in the early Wanli era, some of them quickly emerged as protectors. In Beijing, although the eunuchs were the chief patrons, they gave way to laypeople and local elites in the second half of the Wanli period, when the Cisheng-Wanli relationship had reached its lowest point, and the shift continued irreversibly in the ensuing Qing as they dwindled considerably in scale.

The history of Buddhist institutions thus allows us to visualize materially the progress of the ongoing Buddhist revival along the three dimensions of time, region, and society. Contemporary politics left a clear mark on this history. Jiangnan temples like Shixingsi and Puhuisi easily fell prey to the government or local power during the Jiajing period but were revivified in a U-turn shift in the early Wanli period. The Ciguangsi case is more complicated. The royal patronage that was available only after Cisheng had reconciled with Wanli contributed greatly to its rise, but the conflicts arising from the competition between the inner-court elites and local elites for control halted its growth. And understanding the conflict itself requires us to consider the agenda of promoting local pride, which resulted partly from the "localist turn" among scholar-officials and the hostility toward the eunuchs felt among ordinary people. Consequently, although Susan

Naquin argues that "at Tanzhesi diversification seems to have been pursued as a strategy of survival, and even prized,"[80] once the eunuchs appeared with scholar-officials in Jiangnan, it often if not always meant a disaster for the temple involved.

From all these cases we see that Buddhist institutions at the time had the courage and initiative to fight an uphill battle to recover from stagnancy and to seek a brighter future, but it is also evident that they were basically in a worrisome situation. In radical cases like those of Shixingsi and Puhuisi, little was heard from the temples themselves when their fates were decided. In major projects like the 1592 one at Tanzhesi and the 1667 one at Ciguangsi, the external inputs were mostly uninvited, which implied that despite the efforts of the *saṃgha*, it had to wait passively without knowing if, when, and on what scale they would come. Against this background, the sustainability of Tanzhesi and the fragility of Ciguangsi (which once looked promising) are revealing: Tanzhesi remained steady over centuries because of strong support from the huge amounts of monastic lands it had amassed, while the fate of Ciguangsi seemed to have been doomed, since it never developed the self-sustaining ability to fulfill its own economic and social needs, as evidenced by the report that the monks there were starving to death, at least on three occasions.

8

Setbacks

Losing Beijing as a Growth Engine

The in-depth case studies in the preceding two chapters illustrate how eminent monks and Buddhist institutions could develop in a particularized context in a distinctive way. Given that case studies are inherently fragmentary in nature, this last chapter turns to quantitative analysis in an attempt to obtain a holistic picture that exceeds anecdotal descriptions and regional narratives. It begins with an experiment to make visible the unfolding of the Buddhist renewal by tracing changes of two indicators—the state of Buddhist institutions and the retention of eminent monks—in North China–Beijing and the Jiangnan region during the mid- and late-Ming period. Special attention is given not only to the development of Buddhism in the two regions but also to their interconnections at the national level. The examination then situates the renewal in the politico-religious context as examined in the preceding chapters to understand why it progressed as it did. The ups and downs of Beijing in its status in the Buddhist world are highlighted to see how politics, in connection with other factors, realized its influence on Buddhism by affecting the contributing groups. Finally, through the eyes of contemporary leading monks, it briefly examines what Buddhism looked like by the end of the Wanli period after having experienced such a string of crises.

"SEEING" THE UNFOLDING OF THE BUDDHIST REVIVAL

Based on a qualitative analysis of the two concrete indicators used throughout this study, it's possible to display the complex unfolding of the Buddhist renewal in a visible way. Fluid and with great initiative, the activities of eminent monks were more sensitive to fluctuations of Buddhism in a relatively short period, while temples, characterized by sustainability and immutability, had the advantage of reflecting the tendency in a longer duration. Research on them can thus be supplementary and enables us to see the evolution of the renewal more clearly, which would be hard to visualize if viewed through a different lens.

The Mobility of Eminent Monks

Eminent monks, who were highly mobile, represented the most dynamic element within the *saṃgha*, and a close look at their mobility pattern helps disclose how the state of Buddhism varied with time and space. A typical mobility pattern includes facts concerning the birthplace of a monk, the places he visited for Buddhist instruction, the master from whom he received the Dharma transmission,[1] and the area where he finally settled and trained novices.[2] These activities can be seen as a series of responses to opportunities and challenges that the monk perceived within the *saṃgha* and beyond. Once sufficient cases are examined, they will provide important information otherwise unavailable, such as the regional diversity in terms of the interest in Buddhism, regional differences in the ability of attracting monks, major Buddhist centers that not only concentrated resources but also extended influence to other regions, and the interconnection of Buddhism in different regions on a national level.

I first consider the temporal distribution of eminent monks during the mid- and late-Ming period. The relevant information derives from five collected *Biographies of Eminent Monks* (*Gaoseng zhuan* 高僧传),[3] a conventional genre that records their lives and thought[4] and that constitutes the most comprehensive source of information about this group.[5] A detailed explication of table 8.1 runs as follows: (1) In this table, "formal biography" refers to a detailed account contributed for a major figure, "appended biography" (*fuzhuan* 附傳 or *fujian* 附見) to biographical information mentioned only in passing when recounting other figures' stories, and "nominal biography" to that which offers nothing but a name. That they are categorized as such is because there are at least three kinds of biographies in the *Biographies of Eminent Monks*, depending both on the importance of the central character as perceived by the compiler and on the accessibility of information. Generally, the historical usefulness of a biography decreases as we move through the formal to the appended and finally to the nominal biography. (2) "T–S" represents the Tianqi–Southern Ming period from 1621 to 1662. Rather than discussing this in detail, this period is used here only for comparison, so as to better reveal trends. (3) The monks concerned are grouped according to the

TABLE 8.1 Temporal distribution of eminent monks, 1522–1662

Death year		Type			Total
		Formal biography	Appended biography	Nominal biography	
Jiajing period (1522–1566)	1–10	0	1	9	10
	11–20	0	0	0	0
	21–30	0	1	1	2
	31–40	3	0	0	3
	41–45	5	0	7	12
	Unclear	15	5	1	21
Subtotal	45	23	7	18	48
Longqing period (1567–1572)	1–6	4	0	1	5
Wanli period (1573–1620)	1–10	12	1	0	13
	11–20	18	4	0	22
	21–30	16	1	0	17
	31–40	8	3	1	12
	41–48	9	1	0	10
	Unclear	35	28	3	66
Subtotal	48	98	38	4	140
T–S period (1621–1662)	Tianqi 1–7	13	2	5	20
	Chongzhen 1–17	26	11	0	37
	Southern Ming 1–18	29	10	0	39
Subtotal	42	68	23	5	96
Unclear		5	10	3	18
Total	141	198	78	31	307

year of their death in a span from 1522 (Jiajing 1) to 1662, the final year of the Southern Ming.[6] The Southern Ming overlapped with the Qing dynasty for nearly twenty years. A monk is counted in the T–S group if he was vaguely reported in our sources to have lived in the late Ming and early Qing (*mingmo qingchu* 明末清初). (4) "Unclear" is used for monks who were ambiguously said to have died in a given reign period but for whom no precise year of death is available.

The three periods each cover a similar span of time—that is, more than forty years. If not considering the weight differences of the three kinds of biography, table 8.1 shows that the appearance of eminent monks fluctuated drastically during the three periods: forty-eight monks emerged in the Jiajing period, and the number nearly tripled in the Wanli period, which was followed by a one-third drop in the T–S period. More specifically, during the thirty years from 1531 (Jiajing 10) to 1561 (Jiajing 40) it is rare to see eminent monks, and when you do encounter them, very little information is given except their names. The last five years of the Jiajing period saw a soaring fourfold increase over the preceding ten years. This surge extended into the Longqing period (1567–1572) and finally reached its peak in the 1590s. Then a continuous drop came during the next thirty years, during which the lowest point appeared in the first years of the 1600s. Beginning with the 1620s, once again eminent monks became increasingly active, to a moderate degree, until 1662. Such a description of the ups and downs is applicable even when we consider only the formal biography, with the only exception that the figure during the Jiajing is still lower, less than one-fourth of the Wanli period. Both ways of analysis confirm the general impression that Buddhism was reinvigorated in the late Ming period from its declining state in the mid-Ming.

More complexities are revealed in the mobility of eminent monks if viewed from a spatial perspective. For the Jiajing era, during which only a small number of these monks appeared, the paucity of information prevents us from making any meaningful analysis. Nonetheless, there was a clear concentration of eminent monks in Beijing and Jiangnan,[7] which was confirmed by Hanshan Deqing's 憨山德清 (1546–1623) observation as follows:

> Since [the court was] moved northward [from Nanjing to Beijing], the Chan school has fallen into obscurity, while the doctrinal schools alone have concentrated in the capital. In the Jiangnan region, the way of Dharma fell into decay gradually so that it was no longer known to anybody. By the Zhengde and Jiajing transition, even in the [Buddhist] lecturing altars [i.e., Buddhist society] of northern China, there were only the two great masters Tong and Tai. They occupied the magnificent seat in the capital [to preach Buddhist teachings], and learners congregated there from all over the country.

自北遷之後, 而禪道不彰. 獨講演一宗, 集於大都. 而江南法道, 日漸靡無聞焉.
正、嘉之際, 北方講席, 亦唯通、泰二大老, 踞華座於京師, 海內學者畢集.[8]

In the Wanli period and after, when eminent monks surged, a regional concentration continued, but the modes of their mobility became increasingly complicated. Based on their biographies, I have created tables 8.2 and 8.3 to represent the mobility patterns of eminent monks, with those in North China and Jiangnan singled out for separate treatment given their relative importance—they amounted to 87 percent of the entire country during the Wanli era and 74 percent in the T–S period. These monks are first categorized according to their decisions to leave or to stay. And then those departing are split into two groups according to their destinations—to Beijing/Jiangnan or to other places,[9] while those staying are split into three groups according to their origins—natives, from Beijing/Jiangnan, or from other places. The last line of the two tables shows the number of eminent monks appearing in a given region and the percentage they occupied in the entire country.

Table 8.1 shows that during the Wanli period, with a share of 46 percent of all eminent monks appearing in the country, North China attracted more elite monks than any other region comparable by scale. In the T–S period, however, its percentage dropped dramatically to 17. This fall is applicable to Beijing, whose percentages plummeted to 8 in the T–S period from 34 in the Wanli period. According to table 8.2, the share of the Jiangnan region increased from 41 to 57 percent between these two periods, constituting a sharp contrast with North China–Beijing, which ran out of steam in the T–S period. Considering tables 8.1 and 8.2 together, it becomes evident that during the Wanli period the development of Buddhism was pushed forward by two engines—North China–Beijing and Jiangnan—with the former slightly more powerful than the latter, but in the following T–S period the former lost its function as an engine and the latter had to work alone.

Fluctuations in Temple Building

The fluctuation of temple-building activities is another sensitive indicator,[10] which reflects the state of Buddhism in a given region. Without suitable material covering temple building across regions, let alone the entire country, I concentrate on Beijing and the three prefectures of Suzhou, Songjiang, and Hangzhou, examining them as representative of North China and Jiangnan, the two chief engines for the growth of Buddhism at the time.

TABLE 8.2 Mobility patterns of eminent monks in Beijing–North China

Pattern	Place	Time			
		Wanli period		T–S period	
		Beijing	North China	Beijing	North China
Destinations of the monks who left	Jiangnan	9	14	2	6
	Other places	2	2	1	1
Origins of the monks who stayed	Natives	5	7	0	0
	Jiangnan	1	1	0	0
	Other places	18	23	3	5
Total counts and (percentage value) for the country		35 (34)	47 (46)	6 (8)	12 (17)

TABLE 8.3 Mobility patterns of eminent monks in Jiangnan

Pattern		Time	
		Wanli period	T–S period
Destinations of the monks who left	Beijing	1	1
	Elsewhere	2	3
Origins of the monks who stayed	Natives	26	19
	Beijing	1	2
	Elsewhere	12	16
Total counts and (percentage value) for the country		42 (41)	41 (57)

This analysis is based on the following parameters. (1) All construction projects taking place at a temple are counted, including building, restoration, repairing, and renovation. (2) If there was more than one project at a temple, each of them is counted separately. (3) The "unclear" category is used to group those projects that are ambiguously placed in a certain reign period. (4) The data for the Tianqi-Chongzhen period is used only for comparison. (5) I roughly categorize Buddhist institutions into temples and chapels, with the first including buildings called *si* 寺 (monastery), *miao* 廟 (temple), *chang* 廠 (workshop) and *lin* 林 (gathering, forest), and the second including *an* 菴/庵 (chapel), *yuan* 院 (yard), and *ta* 塔 (stupa). No strict distinctions existed between the two categories, but some major differences can still be listed. A temple in the Ming usually had a name tablet conferring legitimate status, whereas a chapel did not. A temple was bigger in scale and generally older in pedigree than a chapel. Moreover, a chapel had a higher chance of housing nuns than a temple, and many chapels in Jiangnan were built exclusively for meditation practice.[11] Distinguishing the two categories may help reduce the distortion inherent in the quantitative analysis: it treats all temples as an equal unit without considering their differences in scope and thus in terms of the investments required to maintain them.

Now, let us look first at temple-building activities in Beijing.

Some observations can be made on the basis of table 8.4:

1. If we consider temples and chapels together without distinction, temple building in the Beijing area became less active from the Jiajing through the Wanli periods and ended with a drastic fall in the Tianqi-Chongzhen period.
2. A different picture is painted once we split the building projects according to their categories. The percentage of chapels in the projects is as high as 47 percent during the Jiajing period, and then decreases to 32 percent in the Wanli period. For the category of temple, we can see a moderate increase of 19 percent from the Jiajing to the Wanli periods, which was followed by a drop of 81 percent in the T–S period.
3. These two pictures are not necessarily contradictory: the high share of chapels during the Jiajing period may well reflect the suppressed enthusiasm for Buddhism in Beijing, which was characteristic of the period.
4. More specifically, in the Jiajing era, building frequency decreased in the second decade, but the tendency was reversed in the third decade. The Longqing era continued the rising trend. In the first decade of the Wanli era, the yearly average of temple construction reached its highest point. This figure decreased a little in the second decade but dropped by half in the third decade. There was a slight increase in the fourth decade, which was followed by an

even greater drop. Finally, we see the lowest figure in the last twenty years of the dynasty.

5. Temple-building projects, exclusive of the "unclear" group, were most active in the area during the forty-two years from 1551 (Jiajing 30) to 1592 (Wanli 20), with a yearly average of 3.45, but least active in the forty-two years from 1603 (Wanli 31) to 1644 (Chongzhen 17), with a yearly average of 1.31.

TABLE 8.4   Temple-building activities in the Beijing area

Building year		Type			Yearly average
		Temples	Chapels	Total	
Jiajing period (1522–1566)	1–10	14	11	25	
	11–20	9	6	15	
	21–30	14	8	22	
	31–40	17	20	37	
	41–45	11	9	20	
	Unclear	14	15	29	
Subtotal	45	79	69	148	3.29
Longqing period (1567–1572)	1–6	12	6	18	3
Wanli period (1573–1620)	1–10	27	15	42	
	11–20	17	11	28	
	21–30	11	3	14	
	31–40	14	6	20	
	41–48	7	5	12	
	Unclear	18	4	22	
Subtotal	48	94	44	138	2.88
Tianqi-Chongzhen period (1621–1644)	Tianqi 1–7	5	0	5	
	Chongzhen 1–17	13	5	18	
Subtotal	24	18	5	23	0.92
Total	123	203	124	327	2.66

Sources: *Rixia jiuwen kao* 日下舊聞攷, *Wanshu zaji* 宛署雜記, *Changping zhouzhi* 昌平州志 (1886), *Changping waizhi* 昌平外志 (1892), *Wanping xianzhi* 宛平縣志 (1684), *Yanqing zhouzhi* 延慶州志 (1680), *Huairouxian xinzhi* 懷柔縣新志 (1721), and *Tongzhou zhi* 通州志 (1697).

Now, let us turn to the Jiangnan region by taking Hangzhou, Suzhou, and Songjiang prefectures as the sample. Apart from the same characteristics as in table 8.4, tables 8.5, 8.6, and 8.7 add a "destroyed" category to count temples that were once destroyed (*hui* 毀), occupied (*zhan* 占), or converted (*gai* 改). In the original sources, the "destroyed" temples were damaged either in wars or by fires,

TABLE 8.5 Temple-building activities in Hangzhou prefecture

Building year		Type			Total	Yearly average
		Temples	Chapels	Destroyed		
Jiajing period (1522–1566)	1–10	0	2			
	11–20	2	0			
	21–30	0	0			
	31–40	2	1			
	41–45	1	0			
	Unclear	7	3	–11		
Subtotal	45	12	6	–11	18 (–11)	0.16
Longqing period (1567–1572)	1–6	2	5	0	7	1.17
Wanli period (1573–1620)	1–10	0	0			
	11–20	0	1			
	21–30	5	5			
	31–40	6	3			
	41–48	4	3			
	Unclear	27	48			
Subtotal	48	42	60	0	102	2.13
Tianqi-Chongzhen period (1621–1644)	Tianqi 1–7	1	9	–1		
	Chongzhen 1–17	10	22	–6		
Subtotal	24	11	31	–7	42 (–7)	1.46
Total	123	67	102	–18	169 (–18)	1.23

Source: *Hangzhou fuzhi* 杭州府志 (1764; repr., Taipei: Dongfang wenhua gongyin she, 1970), fasc. 28–32.

TABLE 8.6 Temple-building activities in Suzhou prefecture

Building year		Temples	Chapels	Destroyed	Total	Yearly average
		Type				
Jiajing period (1522–1566)	1–10	2				
	11–20	0				
	21–30	1				
	31–40	3	1			
	41–45	1				
	Unclear	9	6	–13		
Subtotal	45	16	7	–13	23 (–13)	0.22
Longqing period (1567–1572)	1–6	5	2	0	7	1.17
Wanli period (1573–1620)	1–10	6	3			
	11–20	11	4			
	21–30	5	4			
	31–40	7	14			
	41–48	7	2			
	Unclear	14	24	–3		
Subtotal	48	50	51	–3	101 (–3)	2.04
Tianqi-Chongzhen period (1621–1644)	Tianqi 1–7	7	14	0		
	Chongzhen 1–17	23	32	1		
Subtotal	24	30	46	–1	76 (–1)	3.17
Total	123	101	106	–17	207 (–17)	1.54

Source: *Suzhou fuzhi* (1693; repr., Taipei: Dongfang wenhua gongying she, 1970), fasc. 38–40.

the "occupied" ones were taken over by powerful families or local officials, and the "converted" ones were changed by local authorities into public places like schools and headquarters for armies. In assessing how active temple building was in a given period, these "destroyed" buildings are detached from the overall building statistics.

TABLE 8.7 Temple-building activities in Songjiang prefecture

Building year		Temples	Chapels	Destroyed	Total	Yearly average
Jiajing period (1522–1566)	1–10					
	11–20	1	1			
	21–30					
	31–40					
	41–45	1	1			
	Unclear		3	–11		
Subtotal	45	2	5	–11	7 (–11)	0
Longqing period (1567–1572)	1–6	1	2		3	0.5
Wanli period (1573–1620)	1–10		6			
	11–20	1	3			
	21–30	1	2			
	31–40	3	3			
	41–48	1	4			
	Unclear	10	10	–1		
Subtotal	48	16	28	–1	44 (–1)	0.9
Tianqi-Chongzhen period (1621–1644)	Tianqi 1–7	0	11	0		
	Chongzhen 1–17	0	5	0		
Subtotal	24	0	16	0	16	0.67
Total	123	19	51	–12	70 (–12)	0.47

Source: Songjiang fuzhi (1631; repr., Beijing: Shumu wenxian chubanshe, 1991), fasc. 50–52.

Based on these three tables, some observations can be made about temple-building activities in Hangzhou, Suzhou, and Songjiang prefectures:

1. In Hangzhou, clearly there was an upward tendency from the Jiajing era to the Longqing and Wanli eras, which was followed by a drop in the Tianqi-Chongzhen period. In terms of the yearly average, the Longqing era showed

seven times the activity of that of the Jiajing era, and the figure was further doubled in the Wanli era. A drop of about 30 percent appeared in the Tianqi-Chongzhen period, however. Suzhou had a similar pattern, except that there was an increase of about 50 percent from the Wanli era to the Tianqi-Chongzhen period. The experience of Songjiang was more like that of Hangzhou.

2. In the Jiajing era, temple-building activities were almost negligible in Hangzhou, as well as in Suzhou. In Songjiang, owing to the great losses in the wars against Japanese pirates, destroyed temples outnumbered those that were newly built by four. In Hangzhou during the Wanli era, starting in the 1590s, there was a jump that was sustained until the end of the Chongzhen era. Suzhou and Songjiang display a similar pattern, except that the rise in Songjiang ceased earlier—by the end of the Tianqi era.

3. Taking these three prefectures into consideration together, we can see that temple building turned moderately active during the first three decades of the Wanli era. A sudden increase occurred in the fourth decade and the upward tendency continued until the end of this dynasty.

The preceding analyses reveal how vastly different were the building trends that Buddhist institutions experienced in Beijing and North China compared with those in Jiangnan. First, during the last twenty years of the Jiajing era when temple and especially chapel building was quite active in Beijing, very little was invested in Buddhist institutions in Jiangnan. Second, during the first two decades of the Wanli era, when building activities reached their highest point in Beijing, Jiangnan had only started to warm up. Third, after the early 1590s when temple building began to decrease in Beijing, the number increased in Jiangnan. Finally, as a result of these opposing trends, by the Chongzhen era temple-building activities became the least active in Beijing, whereas they were most active in Jiangnan. Apparently, Jiangnan was late in supporting temple-building projects on a scale comparable to Beijing, but the gap was closing, and Jiangnan eventually got the upper hand over Beijing around 1600 and then maintained dominance for the rest of the Ming.

The Buddhist Renewal and Politics

Based on analysis of these two indicators, we can now say that far from being homogenized, the development of Buddhist institutions was multilayered and full of regional variations. Within a region, these layers of Buddhism did not grow at the same pace. In North China–Beijing, for example, changes in the mobilization of material resources seemed to always take place earlier than that of human resources: although temple-building activities started escalating in the 1550s, we have to wait at least ten more years to see a clear rise in the appearance of eminent monks. Similarly, temple-building activities hit a low beginning in the early 1590s (after Wanli 20), but eminent monks kept active in the city until ten years later when Zhenke died in prison. Across regions, the trajectories varied so greatly that they could even go in opposite directions, as demonstrated by the temple building discussed in the preceding. These diversities within and across regions present a much richer and more complex picture. Generally, the evolution of Buddhism during the period can generally be outlined as follows: it hit a new low in the first half of the Jiajing era, and only in the early Wanli period was the downward tendency essentially reversed. This rising wave continued for two decades, and then slowed down. Clearly there was a building up of enthusiasm and momentum over this time and, despite the lack of a precise threshold, the renewal started in the early Wanli period after more than one hundred years of stagnation.

The complex unfolding of the late-Ming Buddhist renewal was structurally conditioned by politics in its direction and pace. In fact, the turning points in the process corresponded precisely with major political events, including Jiajing's enthronement as an emperor hostile to Buddhism, the reversal of the decades-long policy of repressing Buddhism following Jiajing's death, the timely entrance into the political arena of Cisheng as a successful coordinator on behalf of Buddhism, and the heightened tensions between Cisheng and Wanli that were exacerbated by court factionalism.

Far from in a straightforward manner, politics shaped the contours of Buddhism primarily through affecting people's acts and interactions in a subtle and complicated way. As examined in previous chapters, the makeup of the forces shaping Buddhism varied vastly over time and across regions, with the inner-court elites serving as major patrons in Beijing while scholar-officials played a similar role in Jiangnan. Considerable differences in their sensitiveness to politics and their way of responding to it made them distinguish from each other in their attitudes toward and actual influence on Buddhism. The fluctuations in temple-construction projects exemplify this point. Although the inner-court elite shunned Buddhism in the first half of the Jiajing era under escalating pressure from the emperor, these elites took advantage of the emperor's long-term absence from the court in the second half and started engaging in temple building cautiously, patronizing chapels over temples. Out of the same political shrewdness, they held back as the Wanli-Cisheng relationship deteriorated, and the drop in their patronage that occurred almost exactly post-1595, the year Deqing was exiled, resulted in a clear decrease in Beijing's temple-building activities. As for scholar-officials, determined by their dual identity, they were indifferent to or even preyed upon Buddhism throughout the Jiajing period. So in the early Wanli era when the eunuchs naturally expanded their support of Buddhism, it took time for scholar-officials to change their course and embrace Buddhism. But after 1600, when temple building dropped in Beijing, with their political enthusiasm dampened by the sinister situation, their increased patronage finally brought the peak time to the temple-building activities in Jiangnan.

THE COLLAPSE OF BEIJING AS A BUDDHIST CENTER: A GAME OF ITINERANT MONKS

The acquisition and rapid loss of Beijing in its leading role in the Buddhist world were the landmark events in the Buddhist renewal. Understanding them in connection with the features unique to the *saṃgha* of Beijing as the imperial capital helps to disclose how politics realized its impact on Buddhism in the local context and eventually obtained significance on the national level.

Buddhism thrived in Beijing in the first three decades of the Wanli period, to which favorable political conditions made a great contribution. As shown in table 8.2, the city attracted up to one-third of all the eminent monks during the Wanli era, and the numbers were even higher in the 1580s and 1590s. Contemporary observers confirmed such a leading status. Tao Wangling 陶望齡 (1562–1609, *jinshi* 1589), for example, pointed out that the imperial capital was "where the genuine Dharma existed" (道法所在) and where the Dharma seeker must visit. And Buddhist temples dotted inside and outside the capital everywhere.[12] Similarly, Wang Yuanhan 王元翰 (1565–1633, *jinshi* 1601) described Beijing as "a sea of monks" (僧海) where the number of temples was as high as one-third the number of civilian houses and the donations to temples were as great as three-tenths of the provisions to the frontier armies. In an oft-quoted paragraph, Wang recalled the prosperity of Buddhism in the 1580s and 1590s.

At that time, people seeking the Buddhist Way in the capital were as dense as a forest. The great friends included Daguan [i.e., Zibo Zhenke 紫柏真可 (1543–1604)], Langmu [Langmu Benzhi 朗目本智 (1555–1606)], Hanshan [Hanshan Deqing], Yuechuan [i.e., Kongyin Zhencheng 空印鎮澄 (1547–1617)], Xuelang [Xuelang Hong'en 雪浪洪恩 (1545–1608)], Yin'an [Yin'an Rujin 隱庵如進 (dates unknown)], Qingxu [dates unknown], Yu'an [dates unknown], and others. Officials included Huang Shenxuan [Huang Hui 黃輝 (1555–1612, *jinshi* 1589)], Li

Zhuowu [Li Zhi 李贄 (1527–1602)], Yuan Zhonglang [Yuan Hongdao 袁宏道 (1568–1610, *jinshi* 1591)], Yuan Xiaoxiu [Yuan Zhongdao 袁中道 (1570–1626, *jinshi* 1616)], Wang Xinghai [Wang Erkang 王爾康 (1564–1601, *jinshi* 1595)], Duan Huanran [dates unknown], Tao Shikui [Tao Wangling 陶望齡 (1562–1609, *jinshi* 1589)], Cai Wuyue [Cai Shanji 蔡善繼 (*jinshi* 1601)], Tao Butui [Tao Ting 陶 珽 (b. 1573, *jinshi* 1610)], and Cai Chengzhi [*jinshi* 1583]. They sought a common interest from one another and matched one another like a case and its cover.

其時京師學道人如林. 善知識有達觀、朗目、憨山、月川、雪浪、隱庵、清虛、愚庵 諸公. 宰官則有黃慎軒、李卓吾、袁中郎、袁小修、王性海、段幻然、陶石簣、蔡五 嶽、陶不退、蔡承植諸君. 聲氣相求, 函蓋相合.[13]

Although not precisely correct in its details, the prosperity was not exaggerated. In fact, Beijing–North China was a must-go place for Dharma seekers in the first half of the Wanli period. Almost all important monks who completed their apprenticeship before 1600, such as Deqing, Zhenke, Yunqi Zhuhong 雲棲袾宏 (1535–1615), Hong'en, and Daqian Changrun 大千常潤 (1514–1585), had something in common: a trip to Beijing.[14] The establishment of this status attributed a great deal to the patronage of the inner court coordinated by Cisheng, which appeared immediately after Wanli's enthronement, earlier than that by scholar-officials in Jiangnan. This seems to reveal that, unlike what has been suggested by scholars like Timothy Brook and Jiang Wu, a localist turn was not a necessary condition for Buddhism to thrive, at least in some regions.[15]

This prosperity was not only a regional event; it enabled North China–Beijing to occupy national leadership in the Buddhist world, which was later lost to the Jiangnan region.[16] Eminent monks were a rare asset for anyplace they lived. The more a region exported eminent monks to other regions, the greater its contribution to and thus impact on the growth of Buddhism on the national level. In light of that, the impact of a given region, based on the mobility of eminent monks, can be roughly distinguished as "national" and "regional."

Table 8.8 is based on tables 8.2 and 8.3. According to it, Beijing–North China exported about one-third of its eminent monks during the Wanli period and more than half during the T–S period. In sharp contrast, in Jiangnan the percentage was as low as 7 percent in the Wanli period and rose slightly to 10 percent in the T–S period. Since Beijing–North China had the highest percentage of eminent monks in the country during the Wanli period, this much higher degree of output than any other region meant North China–Beijing occupied the leading role in shaping the development of Buddhism nationwide. But as Beijing–North China lost traction in the T–S period, it lost its position of national leadership to Jiangnan as well.

TABLE 8.8 Impact indexes of Beijing and Jiangnan as revealed
by eminent monks

Pattern		Time	
		Wanli period	T–S period
Beijing–North China*	National significance	11 (31), 16 (34)	3 (50), 7 (58)
	Regional significance	24 (69), 31 (66)	3 (50), 5 (42)
Jiangnan*	National significance	3 (7)	4 (10)
	Regional significance	39 (93)	37 (90)

*Amounts consist of the count of a category and its percentage value.

That Beijing could quickly lose its national importance directs us to a feature unique to the *saṃgha* there: the majority of eminent monks appearing in the city were nonnative. The Beijing *saṃgha* was characterized by two features. First, for eminent monks it had a much lower retention degree when compared with Jiangnan. As shown in table 8.8, Beijing lost nearly one-third its the eminent monks during the Wanli period and then more than half in the T–S period. In sharp contrast, the rate in Jiangnan was as low as 7 percent and 10 percent in the two periods, respectively. Second, Beijing showed little success in producing eminent monks locally. As depicted in tables 8.2 and 8.3, among the eminent monks, the percentages of those who were locally produced were much lower in Beijing than in Jiangnan: in Beijing the figure was 14 in the Wanli era and 0 in the T–S period, while in Jiangnan it was 62 and 46, respectively. Evidently, Beijing failed to nurture natives as high-quality monks in a significant way, and the gap with Jiangnan kept widening rather than narrowing over time.[17]

Thus, the prosperity of Beijing Buddhism hinged on a significant and continuous input of monks from other regions, and its great impact on the Buddhist world was essentially because of the unique position it held in the brain circulation across the country. "Brain circulation" here can be defined as the circular movement of skilled monks across regions, which brings to the home region much intangible knowledge that proves invaluable for the region's development. In favorable situations, Buddhism in Beijing could enhance its attractiveness by mobilizing massive resources from the inner-court elites. Beijing first recruited established monks or nurtured those who went on to greatness elsewhere in the realm, linked themselves to a much bigger network, and honed their skills.[18] And then, after some time, with one-third to one-half of them leaving, their influence expanded in the Buddhist world. These departed monks, with their experience

FIGURE 8.1 Bronze statue of Zibo Zhenke 紫柏真可, whose death marked a major recession of late-Ming Buddhist renewal

Courtesy of Sun Xuhui

and social contacts, brought Beijing to the attention of novices, while those who stayed served as guides for new visitors. This circulation continued to guarantee that there were always quite a few monks active in the capital.

Such a dependence on a huge and continuous flow of empirewide input of eminent monks to maintain its status, however, left Beijing Buddhism highly vulnerable to political changes, with which the Wanli court was characterized. Understandably this influx of eminent monks was sensitive to the regional environment, requiring a safe, reliable, predictable, and high chance of success. In the early Wanli era these features were the source of Beijing's attraction. By the turn of the seventeenth century, however, as court strife and factional conflicts among officials intensified sharply and, to compound things further, eminent monks were actively getting involved in politics, the Beijing area became increasingly unpredictable and dangerous for monks. Deqing was the first victim of significance. The inner-court elites were quick to receive the warning and backed off from their support of Buddhism, as evidenced by the drop in their patronage of temple-building projects in Beijing almost immediately after 1595. But the *saṃgha* failed to realize the gravity of the situation; eminent monks continued heading to the capital. Some of them, like Zhenke, held the illusion that they could prevail and rise above the difficulties, although in reality they were probably the group least likely to control the situation. Trouble came as expected, including the disbanding of the Putao Association and the suicide of Li Zhi in 1602. Zhenke's death in 1603 delivered the most serious warning to the *saṃgha*, both because of his enormous influence and because it revealed how the situational unpredictability could evolve into an affair of life or death. All taking place around the turn of the seventeenth century, these occurrences of death, exile, and arrests caused panic to prevail in Beijing's Buddhist circles and declared that Beijing was no longer a place suitable for monks.

Beijing suffered a rapid loss of eminent monks as a consequence. Deqing recalled that "since the disaster [i.e., Zhenke's death] befell to the Dharma, the Beijing *saṃgha* was shocked and all monks felt that they were in an all-around perilous situation. Even those who have been respected as masters all escaped like frightened fish and birds" (自法門一變, 京師叢林震驚, 人人自危. 即素稱師匠者, 皆鳥驚魚散).[19] My data also show that the percentage of eminent monks who chose to leave Beijing increased from 24 to 42 percent starting in the fourth decade of the Wanli period and finally jumped to 64 percent in the T–S period,[20] demonstrating that these monks were more likely to scurry away rather than fight.

Worse, the Beijing *saṃgha* no longer attracted new blood from other regions as easily as before. Not confined to Beijing, the alarm signals at this time found their way to major Buddhist sites across the country. In Hangzhou, central to

Jiangnan, for instance, Jieshan Furu 戒山傅如 (dates unknown) was implicated in Zhenke's case and taken to the capital for interrogation. Mount Emei, located in Sichuan, saw the mysterious death of Master Wuqiong Zhenfa 無窮真法 (1537–1603) after being invited by Cisheng to Beijing.[21] In Shaolinsi, the abbot Wuyan Zhengdao 無言正道 (d. 1609) was also invited by Cisheng to the capital, but the trip ended with his spending several months behind bars.[22] Jiangnan and Sichuan were strategic regions from which a major flow of eminent monks was channeled to Beijing, while Shaolinsi had long been a highly influential monastery in the realm. In an unmistakable way, these events reminded monks what risk they took in visiting the capital under these circumstances. Thus, the mass exodus of eminent monks to Beijing from other regions ceased.

As the input of eminent monks dropped sharply while the brain drain accelerated, Buddhism in the capital saw a quickly progressive meltdown, a change that was not only a regional affair but also of national significance. When Yuan Hongdao came back to Beijing in 1606, he compared what he saw with the thriving situation in 1590, lamenting that "I return to the capital only to find that the ash in the teaching altar of Buddhism was cold."[23] The influence of Buddhism waned in the region, leaving a religious vacuum that was quickly occupied by popular religion, which, with its promise of imminent salvation from the miserable age, became irresistible to most people, including the inner-court elites.[24] But not only a regional affair, Beijing's loss of its unique position in the Buddhist world reverberated also across the empire and indicated a crucial moment of the failure of one of the two growth engines. Not strictly compartmentalized, the Wanli-era world of Buddhism abounded in interregional relations and influence, which made it possible for major changes in a place to extend nationally. Concerning eminent monks, the most mobile and valuable factor in the renewal, Beijing's loss of influence became, at least partly, Jiangnan's gain. Just after the turn of the seventeenth century, the eminent monks who would have headed for the capital now redirected their steps to the Jiangnan region. This was not a small matter as the majority of the monks leaving Beijing–North China finally settled in Jiangnan—my data show that the percentages were, respectively, 82 and 88 percent in the Wanli period and 67 and 86 percent in the T–S period. It happened that this time saw more scholar-officials, frustrated by the political reality, returned to or went to Jiangnan. With the confluence of monks and scholar-officials in Jiangnan, more and more temples and chapels were built or repaired in the region. In this sense, the decline of Buddhism in Beijing–North China contributed to the rise of Buddhism in Jiangnan. A sharp change occurred in the contours of Buddhism starting around the turn of the seventeenth century.

WAS THE BUDDHIST BOOM CLOSE TO ITS END?

The series of attacks against Buddhism unsettled its prospects for success. Beijing Buddhism would never recover in the remaining years of this dynasty, although the mother-son relationship that triggered the crisis turned warmer almost immediately after Zhenke's death. All this took place within Cisheng's direct reach, and very likely the results were even beyond Wanli's expectation. But once things get started, they evolve following their own logic and cannot easily be changed in their course by anyone. In the shaky and volatile status quo, actual or perceived changes could trigger violence or panic. Roughly marked by Zhenke's death, a clear shift in preference from Chan to Pure Land Buddhism occurred. This change happened among not only scholar-officials like the Yuan brothers but also among monks:

> At the time, Master Zibo had died, Master Han(shan) was still confined in exile, and Master [Mi]zang had hidden his traces [i.e., disappeared]. Nobody in the realm dared to talk about Chan Buddhism. Only Pure Land Buddhism was advocated and practiced by the clergy and the laity as if it was the established standard. . . . The term *wu* [awakening] was most tabooed as it was viewed as an evil cave. The master lowered his head to promote Pure Land Buddhism as well. He changed his name to Hanhui [Cold Ashes], hinting that his mind to spread the Dharma had become utterly cold. His former conduct all vanished with a sigh of remorse.

> 時紫柏罹難既寂, 憨師遭竄猶縈, 藏公絕影, 天下無敢言禪者, 惟以淨土獨唱, 緇素翕然若定於一間. . . . 而最忌者唯悟之一字, 號為魔窟焉. 師亦俛首說淨土, 更號寒灰叟. 弘法之心, 徹底灰冷. 昔時行履, 泯然著于諸嗟之外矣.[25]

With this change in Buddhist practices came Hanhui's retreat from the world, revealing a clear uncertainty and disappointment that was widely felt by leading monks about the future. Similarly, in a letter addressed to Zhencheng in the 1610s, Deqing revealed his loneliness and disappointment after a long and illustrious career:

> Ashamed of a lack in me, I previously followed the dragon and elephant of the Dharma gate in hopes of making a modest contribution [to Buddhism]. I wished to pluck a blade of grass [i.e., a small contribution] and offer it to the ten

directions. How could I know that I would not escape my predestined karma and remain degraded into old age? My heart has broken since Master Da[guan]'s [i.e., Zhenke's] death, and I no longer pay attention to this world.

自愧下劣, 向從法門龍象之後, 志期稍有建立, 拈一莖艸供養十方. 豈知定業難逃, 沈淪至老. 自達師化後, 此心已殞, 無復人間.[26]

This was simply not the Deqing with whom we have become familiar. During his 1595 exile, Deqing challenged adversity by turning it into a chance to advance his spirituality. But twenty years later when his reputation and influence had reached their peak, he appeared disillusioned and disappointed. Nothing could cheer him up. In the final years of his life, we are told that Deqing lost interest in Buddhist affairs and retreated into personal cultivation in silence. This formed a sharp contrast to the strong drive in his early life.[27] On another occasion, he lamented,

I have spent my life in vain, without accomplishing anything important. . . . As for [my vow to restore] Caoxi [i.e., Nanhuasi 南華寺], the original residence of the sixth Chan patriarch [i.e., Huineng], I have failed to fulfill it owing to my negative karma, which is too great. . . . This time I come to Caoxi only in response to others' hope, daring not to take any action recklessly. I am old, and the right timing has been lost. Even if I hold on to this long-cherished wish, it will have to await until the next life.

不慧 . . . 泛泛一生, 無所建立. 至於曹谿為六祖道場, 又以障重, 不能卒業. . . . 今來曹谿, 但了人情, 非敢妄意有為. 況年已衰, 時已過, 縱有夙願, 亦待來生耳.[28]

Given that little progress had been made in restoring the Great Baoen monastery and reforming Nanhuasi though he was already old, Deqing's despondence is understandable.

Significantly, his low spirits had a familiar ring. Before his death in the sixth month of 1615, Zhuhong wrote a short piece titled the *Shi ketan* 十可嘆 (The ten things lamentable): "My life is now like a lamp in the wind, with anything likely taking place at any time. [But] nobody believes in me, and nobody takes pity on me. How can I continue living in a world like this?" (我今命若風燈, 朝不保暮. 無信我者, 無憐我者, 此間如何住得?). In a most emotional and forthright way, Zhuhong disclosed his frustration with the world around him. At first glance this feeling is hard to understand since Zhuhong was enjoying great popularity in Jiangnan. In reality, this was strongly reminiscent of the grief Zhenke expressed a decade earlier: "What's the point [for me] to live longer in a world like this?" (世事如此, 久住何爲?). Deqing was deeply moved after reading the *Shi ketan*, asserting that

> each of its characters is a drop of tears. How sad it is! Even [people of] steel and stone would shed tears. If viewing the piece as normal, people are highly ungrateful for [the master's] kindness and favor.

一字一泪, 可勝悲悼哉? . . . 即鐵石亦當墜泪. 若視爲尋常, 是爲大負恩德也.[29]

Deqing, Zhenke, and Zhuhong have been the three masters most frequently singled out as representative of the late-Ming Buddhist revival, but unambiguously they shared a strong sense of hopelessness when their lives approached the end. They had a deeper understanding of the tragic events when compared with ordinary monks and detected, with more pain, that the future of Buddhism was not promising.

These masters active in the Wanli era had good reason to believe that the best time belonging to them had passed, but Buddhism itself did not cease to evolve and, beyond their view, a second wave of resurrection was on the way in Jiangnan. Before long, as Jiang Wu has noted, a "new style" Chan would appear but rely "on the literati for intellectual, even spiritual guidance because as experts in handling China's rich literary tradition, [including] Chan literature . . . the literati had the necessary textual authority over Chan's textualized past."[30] Deqing and Zhenke would be depreciated as "Chan masters without a clear Dharma lineage" (法嗣未詳) by this reinvented Chan, which bore the strong flavor of scholar-officials. A second and new phase of renewal, the so-called Chan revitalization, had begun, but that is a story beyond the purview of this study.[31]

The quantitative analysis used in this study of history, despite its weakness as a method, indeed helps to paint a holistic picture of the unfolding of the late-Ming Buddhist revival. As demonstrated by the fluctuations of the two indicators, far from being homogeneous, Buddhism evolved unequally in the three dimensions of time, region, and society in late-Ming China. In particular, Beijing–North China and the Jiangnan region functioned as the two major engines driving Buddhism forward. The trajectories along which Buddhism evolved are distinctly different depending on the region: N-shaped in Beijing–North China but rising steadily in Jiangnan. After sharing a decline with Jiangnan during the first three decades of the Jiajing era, Buddhism in Beijing picked up steam about twenty years earlier than occurred in Jiangnan. When Beijing ran out of steam in the first decade of the seventeenth century, the Jiangnan region picked up the slack and stood out as the realm's Buddhist center in the remaining years of the dynasty.

Behind this picture, characterized by multiple layers and regional variations, was the strong but complex and subtle working of politics on the forces related to Buddhism. Essentially because of their distinctively different composition depending on time and region, the monks and the patronal forces responded to the volatile political climate in vastly different ways. Contingent on a continuous and large-scale inflow of eminent monks from other regions, the booming of Buddhism in Beijing–North China was much more sensitive to political changes than was Jiangnan, where Buddhism was more successful in engaging local elites and could thus produce most of its eminent monks locally. As far as the main patrons are concerned, in Beijing–North China, the eunuchs and imperial family, who had extraordinary political sensitiveness, changed course swiftly, and they always took action related to Buddhism earlier than other social groups. In contrast, in Jiangnan, local elites could be more resistant to political changes. These elites were damaging to the *saṃgha* during the Jiajing era. Also, it took more time for them to rekindle enthusiasm for Buddhism during the Wanli era, but once they did, their support was more stable and consistent than that of their counterparts in the North.

Although full of regional variations, the late-Ming Buddhist world can nevertheless be understood as a loose unity on the national level, and the interrelation of its different parts manifests itself in at least two crucial moments. First, following Cisheng's appearance as the most generous patron, established or promising monks were increasingly attracted into Beijing–North China from all over the country, especially Jiangnan. Before long, Beijing, as the center of education, spread its influence across the realm, thereby kicking off the Buddhist renewal. Second, when eminent monks were scared away from Beijing–North China at the turn of the seventeenth century, most of them took Jiangnan as their destination. This exodus cost Beijing its status as the chief engine in the Buddhist world but benefited Jiangnan with additional elite monks.

The fall of Beijing–North China as the Buddhist center at the turn of the seventeenth century was a landmark event in the late-Ming Buddhist renewal. The prior period had since become a memory of splendor for celebrity monks like Deqing and Zhuhong. Moreover, the meeting of the scared eminent masters with the scholar-officials, who were increasingly turning to local society in Jiangnan, would help to prepare a second wave of Buddhist revival, the Chan revitalization starting in the 1630s.

Conclusion

The late-Ming Buddhist renewal, as defined in this study, was a dynamic movement engaging huge numbers of elites that, instead of a singular all-encompassing and steady development, was marked by apparent disjunctures and by a pattern of advances and retrenchment. Over its course, the weight that different regions occupied in China's entire Buddhist world fluctuated vastly. Among other fluctuations, the drastic changes of Beijing–North China relative to Jiangnan are particularly significant. The rapid rise of the northern region in the early Wanli era provided the initial traction pushing Buddhist institutions out of their long-term stagnation, while the region's abrupt fall in the first years of the seventeenth century marked a new stage of the renewal by stalling one of its two main growth engines.

This renewal was driven jointly by religious and nonreligious dynamics, internal and external to the *saṃgha*. Of the secular elites, I have examined emperors, court women (especially the empress dowager), eunuchs, and scholar-officials. Within the *saṃgha*, Buddhist masters who were strongly driven by commitment to their religion made impressive efforts to reform the *saṃgha*, as is well illustrated by the great initiative and courage of Hanshan Deqing 憨山德清 (1546–1623), Zibo Zhenke 紫柏真可 (1543–1604), and Miaofeng Fudeng 妙峰福登 (1540–1612) in engaging in large-scale projects, which greatly improved the situation of Buddhist institutions. Although dealt with separately in different chapters, these forces were all indispensable for the revival to emerge and develop. It is important to note, too, that whether the handling of Buddhism by any particular actors was supportive or damaging could not be completely controlled by any individual. The cumulative outcomes of their activities were specific to their times and regions, sometimes reinforcing one another and others canceling one another out.

To better understand the vastly different roles that each of these figures played requires a deeper look into the decision-making processes and a better appreciation of the mechanisms by which the inner workings of the *saṃgha* and the external dynamics of society interacted in a dialectical way. The components of this study, taken together, constitute an effort to lay bare these social processes and improve our understanding of how individual and collective actions established the necessary conditions for the late-Ming Buddhist renewal.

What makes Buddhism a religion, although not emphasized in this study, is nonetheless significant to the emergence and evolution of the renewal. This significance should therefore not be underestimated. In late-Ming China, when individuals found nowhere to escape from existentialist anxiety and social vulnerability, the features of Buddhism that make it a religion were always at work in the engagement of its practitioners. Eminent monks, with their spiritual achievements and creative practices, attracted huge followings and powerful patrons, as exemplified by Deqing's relationship with Empress Dowager Cisheng 慈聖 (1545–1614) and that of Yunqi Zhuhong 雲棲袾宏 (1535–1615) with Yuang Hongdao 袁宏道 (1568–1610, *jinshi* 1592). Such teacher-disciple relationships, which were informed by religious piety, undergirded the mission to reinvigorate Buddhism. As for the followers, continual deaths, such as those encountered by Yuan Hongdao and Feng Mengzhen 馮夢禎 (1548–1608, *jinshi* 1577), sparked a strong appreciation of impermanence. The increasing uncertainty endured by court women and eunuchs in the Wanli era stimulated their need for soteriological deliverance, pushing them to Buddhism. Even Jiajing's enthrallment with the longevity techniques of Daoism benefited Buddhism by paradoxically loosening the suffocating restrictions that had been placed on it.

But in the context of mid- and late-Ming China when Buddhism had suffered serious weakening in its autonomy and political centralism was already strengthened to an unprecedented degree, it was court politics that ultimately decided the direction and pace of the late-Ming Buddhist renewal. A variety of factors and elements, such as social disintegration, intellectual redirection, an economic boom in Jiangnan, and even contingencies—Jiajing's surviving the assassination attempt and Lady Zheng's failing to produce Wanli's first son, for example—left their marks on the development of monastic Buddhism. Nonetheless, it was politics that proved an overarching key variable, operating both on the structural level of policy and on the level of real-life, context-dependent interactions. At the structural level, the renewal was inherently political from the very start. "Constitutionally," Ming Buddhist policies were an ideological and political solution that the early-Ming emperors provided out of concern for the status of Buddhism. Following their enforcement, these policies—infused with the utilitarian spirit of supporting in order to control—seriously harmed Buddhism in such strategic fields as its institutional, economic, and intellectual health. The autonomy of Buddhism was neutered, thereby creating a structural reliance on external support. Jiajing's persecution of Buddhism further deepened the crisis. The political disruption of Buddhism and the many crises facing late-Ming China laid the groundwork for Buddhism to change course in the Wanli era through the relaxing of restrictions and a readjusted relationship with the greater society.

At the level of context-dependent interactions in real life, normal politics shaped the renewal in a more tangible way by motivating people to adjust not only their stance toward Buddhist ideas and institutions but also their interaction with one another. In Beijing, for example, the eunuchs who had entered Cisheng's orbit in the first half of the Wanli era left in the second. In Jiangnan (and probably other regions beyond Beijing), by contrast, although scholar-officials exacerbated the harm caused by the emperor to Buddhism during the Jiajing era, this group increasingly showed solidarity with Cisheng and Buddhist monks, thereby neutralizing the impact from the court. Behind these changes was the complicated response of various figures to contemporary politics. Notably, constitutional politics may lurk behind events that were caused by normal politics and thus at first glance seem accidental. Illustrative cases include the charge levied against Deqing for building Haiyinsi 海印寺 without official permission and that against Zhenke for conniving with scholar-officials. Also, that Wanli could tighten the restrictions on Cisheng's spending on Buddhism was predetermined by their roles as an emperor and court woman, respectively.

Crucially, given that the Buddhist renewal as defined in this study was a major socioreligious movement in nature, the key to the influence of politics on its evolution may lie less in individual figures or events than in its impact, positively or negatively, on networks that functioned to engage the elites for the cause of Buddhism. Multilayered, these networks tended to expand but could be greatly strengthened or weakened by politics, and the extent to which they mobilized people essentially decided the scale and visibility of the renewal. On the one hand, connecting with one another through networks enabled participants to coordinate their otherwise isolated resources and, in many if not most cases, provided them with a better chance of distributing resources in more effective and meaningful ways. During the early Wanli era, for instance, a large-scale cooperation of this kind, centered on Cisheng but tying together emperors, court women, eunuchs, scholar-officials, and eminent monks in loose ways, provided the traction necessary for the shift from the mid-Ming *saṃgha*, whose institutional autonomy was seriously compromised and short of support. On the other hand, also of importance, the networks were fragile and paradoxically subject particularly to the pressure of politics they might have triggered. In the very early years of the seventeenth century, the networks, originally encompassing the entire realm and crossing all social groups, disintegrated, costing the renewal Beijing as a major growth engine and inner-court elites as a key supporting force. Afterward, the remaining parts kept alive would later lead to the so-called Chan revitalization in Jiangnan. Nonetheless, things had since changed forever. The scale of the Buddhist renewal greatly dwindled, and its vitality was also compromised in some significant aspects.

Despite a high degree of correspondence, a simple causal relationship cannot be established between politics as an influencing factor and the renewal as a resulting phenomenon. For one thing, political participants differed vastly from one another in important ways, such as the resources under their command, effectiveness in organizing their strengths, patterns of response to influential figures, and their regional, socioeconomic, and educational backgrounds. Furthermore, politics rarely worked in isolation; on most if not all occasions it also functioned as a catalyst triggering changes in other variables, enriching or limiting its intended effects by shaping people's interactions with characteristics born of social stratification and regional diversity. Consequently, the causality between politics and the Buddhist renewal resists any simplistic reductionism. Although the renewal would never have occurred without the political crisis, the crisis alone could not entail the renewal or determine its complexities.

Nonetheless, the renewal indeed empowered Buddhist institutions in multiple ways, but it is hard to say that the renewal successfully established the *saṃgha* on a foundation solid enough for a more independent and sustained development. Discussing the achievements in detail is beyond the scope of this study, but mentioning a few is helpful: Buddhism increased its public presence on some significant occasions; the number of followers increased greatly; some masters emerged who were able to command a vast influence; Buddhist temples were (re)built; the Buddhist canon was widely circulated and a new version was in preparation; traditional Buddhist sacred sites like Putuo Island and Mount Emei gained popularity and new sacred sites like Mount Jizu were on the rise; Buddhist schools, including Chan, Pure Land Buddhism, the Tiantai school, and the Vinaya school all gained new momentum. But on a deeper level, not enough progress had been made in all the strategically critical fields taken up in this study. Thus, the tortuous development of Buddhism, especially the quick collapse of Beijing Buddhism in the first decade of the seventeenth century, reflects a fragility deriving from inherent weaknesses. It is no accident that pessimism dominated the final years of top monks like Deqing, Zhenke, and Zhuhong. The real problem facing them was how to maintain a vibrant Buddhism over subsequent generations, but the

Buddhist community seemed to have not created a long-term development strategy.

Viewed from a *longue durée* perspective, the late-Ming renewal emerged not so much from something intrinsic to Buddhism that was destined to happen as from an event-driven exception in the overall current of disfavor toward Buddhism, and it eventually failed to restore the seriously compromised autonomy of Buddhist institutions to a healthy level. In light of that, the Baoensi story with which I began this book exemplifies the entire course of the renewal. The monastery enjoyed its best times in the early Ming when the Yongle emperor had a personal interest in backing it. Then a decline followed in the wake of policy enforcement and the relocation of the imperial capital. The darkest time came following Jiajing's discrimination against Buddhism, which left Baoensi struggling to survive. It was against this background that Deqing left for North China looking for a chance to restore the glory of the monastery. In retrospect, this decision made in the Longqing-Wanli transition was right, because at that time nowhere in Jiangnan could Deqing have secured enough resources for his ambitious project. In the following two decades Deqing grew from a young monk to a leading master. But his full reliance on imperial patronage from the inner court, which was owing in part to a lack of institutional support, eventually got him entangled in court strife. Finally, Baoensi was restored, though only in part and not because of Deqing. This half success was symbolic of the late-Ming Buddhist renewal, illustrating that the newly obtained momentum did help the *saṃgha* to improve its situation but did not reverse the general state of decline.

Since this study started by asking why the renewal took place after Jiajing's long-term persecution, let me conclude by asking the similar question of why the Buddhist renewal came to an end in the early Qing dynasty and remained thereafter at a low ebb.

Despite the renewal, there were worrying signals regarding the long-term economic health of the *saṃgha*, let alone economic self-sufficiency and independence. In Beijing, where more than one thousand temples were built in the Ming, for example, only thirty-one temples were built throughout the Qing dynasty.[1] The small scale of growth in the Qing showcases the relative impotence of the *saṃgha* to develop on its own after the drastic dwindling of the eunuchs' power. The situation in Jiangnan was more intricate and delicate. Evidence shows that core areas of Jiangnan indeed saw a wave of patronage and contributions starting in the early seventeenth century, but the scale was still limited. Also of importance was the likelihood that resources were not allocated to the highest-impact activities. Michael Walsh has stressed the significance of landholdings in maintaining a healthy monastic economy by aptly pointing out that "the idea of merit and the idea of protecting the sangha had to be made more material, more tangible from a socioeconomic perspective, otherwise the survival of the Chinese sangha would have been threatened. Some kind of material exchange process had to take place. The most important such process in which monasteries were engaged was the exchange of merit for land."[2] A close look at the resources channeled to the *saṃgha* in Suzhou, Hangzhou, and Nanjing, all core regions and cities of Jiangnan, however, discloses that the majority of them were directed not to monastic lands but to such construction projects as (re)building temples, renovating their halls, casting bells, and erecting statues.[3] This way of allocating resources impeded the *saṃgha* from improving its economic health.

Also, there was little progress in the Buddhist society obtaining institutional autonomy because of the subordinate status of the *saṃgha* in its relationship with the state. Never an independent institution like Christianity in medieval Europe, institutional Chinese Buddhism was characterized by expanding influence but without a substantial increase in its strength.[4] This seemingly contradictory feature explains both its success and its fragility. Alert to possible threats from any large-scale organized forces, imperial governments in China made consistent efforts to keep all religions, including Buddhism, under strict supervision. Thus, a strategy used by Buddhist apologists to justify institutional Buddhism was to distinguish it from popular religion,[5] which was often labeled as rebellious but whose boundaries were actually fluid over time. More important, Buddhism was forced to structurally and institutionally dismantle itself and remained in a disunited and fragmented state of existence in imperial China. This does not mean a general lack of organization. Instead, the system of monastic officials was established as early as the fourth century and had since been standardized as a persisting institutional structure. Determined by its official nature, however, this system was aimed less at management on behalf of the *saṃgha* than at supervision on behalf of the state and would suppress any voluntary organizations within the *saṃgha* lest they become a threat to political authority. Such a loss of institutional autonomy had profound and far-reaching consequences, depriving Buddhism of the chance to translate its influence into strength—it had spread everywhere in China and infiltrated deep into society, but a lack of subordinate administrative relationships between its disjointed parts made it impossible for the religion to be coordinated into a unified and independent force. Consequently, Buddhist institutions grew weaker compared with the increasingly organized state and society, although not necessarily in an absolute sense. This was even truer in the late-imperial period when political centralism reached its peak and a variety of social organizations, such as family lineages and other voluntary networks, took shape. The situation not only encouraged patrons to step up their influence (or what might be viewed as intervention) on monastic affairs ranging from doctrinal discussions to the inner management of temples but also implied that the state and local society shared an interest in further weakening the independence of the *saṃgha*. The Ciguangsi case revealed external intervention in monastic affairs. Later in the seventeenth century when Chan communities sought to form an organized force through reconstructing Dharma lineages, as Jiang Wu has potently argued, the pressure from both the state and local society would also frustrate the effort.

Intellectually, Buddhism faced multifaceted challenges, including a major intellectual reorientation and growing difficulties in controlling social discourse.[6] Amid the ever-deepening social and political crisis, the Wang Yangming school, which had helped to enable a widespread acceptance of Buddhism, was criticized as "abstract learning" in the early years of the seventeenth century.[7] This marked an intellectual shift to the so-called practical learning (*shixue* 實學), which called for a reassessment of Buddhism. Li Zhi's 李贄 (1527–1602) suicide, Zhenke's death in prison, and the dissolution of the Putao Association 葡萄社 all took place in this context. And as the other side of the coin, Yuan Hongdao's shift from Chan to Pure Land Buddhism and his rediscovery of the value of fulfilling Confucian responsibilities also occurred at this time. Another oft-overlooked but more profound challenge was that, by the late-Ming period, as demonstrated by Feng Mengzhen and Yuan Hongdao, scholar-officials as a group had developed a certain degree of capability to lead Buddhist discussions. This tendency would become clearer in the post-1630 Chan revitalization, which, according to Jiang Wu, was textually constructed. Skillful in textual matters, scholar-officials proved to be the key to the Chan revitalization. For the *saṃgha*, the impact of losing the monopoly of interpretation was far-reaching and cost it a loss in the competition to shape discourse on the narrative of Buddhism and history. Fudeng, for example, was totally overlooked, despite the high esteem he commanded in the contemporary world, but Deqing and Zhenke were enshrined by highlighting their confrontation with the reigning emperor. These outcomes resulted from dominant narratives of the time, which, initially proposed and backed primarily by Jiangnan scholar-officials, tended to politicize Buddhist affairs and polarize the *saṃgha*-state relationship. Adopting this narrative strategy left Buddhism in a place of distrust and sparked suspicion on the part of the state.[8]

As the Qing government recovered the sociopolitical order from late-Ming chaos, it also brought into play factors like growing state activism, early-Qing rulers' interventions in Buddhist affairs, the intellectual shift leading to the "investigation" school of thought, and the easing of anxiety available when people returned to normal life. All these destroyed the outside conditions favorable to the religious movement and finally brought an end to it around the 1680s. After that, Buddhism was still ubiquitously present in the elites' life and culture, but its spirit had been sapped. Keenly noticing the departure of Buddhist influence, Emperor Qianlong (r. 1736–1795) could thus claim with confidence that "presently the Buddhists and the Daoists are no more than poor countrymen who have nothing to rely on. They enter the order only to make a living. How can they compare with heterodoxies in ancient times and be harmful to the orthodox teaching [i.e., Confucianism]?" (今之僧道, 不過鄉里無依之貧民, 竄入空門以爲糊口計, 豈古昔异端之可比、而能爲正教之害耶?).[9]

The emperor was correct. Buddhism remained socially active, but it was backed mainly by the less-educated masses. The elites had departed from Buddhism, in sharp contrast to their active involvement during the late-Ming renewal. This dramatic shift signified a new decline in Buddhism.[10] A complete circle, from decline to renewal and back to decline, formed. What lessons and inspiration can we draw from this circle? This question carries both theoretical and practical significance, especially for present-day Chinese Buddhism, which has been seeking a renewal in recent decades, but I leave that to other scholars and stop here.

Notes

INTRODUCTION

1. Joachim Wach, *Sociology of Religion* (London: Kegan Paul, Trench, Trubner, 1947), 17–34. The term "practical" used by Wach is from the Greek word *praxis*, referring to things that religion always involves to get in touch with the sacred, such as prayer, group and individual worship, meditation, pilgrimage, holy war, ritual sacrifice, etc.

2. For the emergence of this centrism as part of Japanese scholars' efforts to promote the autonomy of Japanese Buddhism and its superiority over Chinese Buddhism, see, for example, Helen Josephine Baroni, *Ōbaku Zen: The Emergence of the Third Sect of Zen in Tokugawa Japan* (Honolulu: University of Hawai`i Press, 2000); Theodore Griffith Foulk, "Ritual in Japanese Zen Buddhism," in *Zen Ritual: Studies of Zen Buddhist Theory in Practice*, ed. Steven Heine and Dale Stuart Wright (Oxford: Oxford University Press, 2008), 27–31; Erik Schicketanz, *Daraku to fukkō no kindai Chūgoku bukkyō: Nihon bukkyō to no kaikō to sono rekishizō no kōchiku* 堕落と復興の近代中国仏教: 日本仏教との邂逅とその歴史像の構築 (Kyoto: Hōzōkan, 2016).

3. Protestant Buddhism first emerged in Sri Lanka in the late nineteenth century and received the name because it resembles many of the key features of Protestant Christianity. Claims it makes about Buddhism include ritual is not necessary, Buddhism does not believe in gods or spirits or demons, and Buddhist institutions can be useful but are not necessary. This romantic notion has influenced much of modern Western understanding of Buddhism.

4. This tendency can be clearly seen in studies of the history of Chinese Buddhism that were published at the time. See, for example, Kenneth K. S. Ch'en, *Buddhism in China: A Historical Survey* (Princeton, N.J.: Princeton University Press, 1964), and Arthur F. Wright, *Buddhism in Chinese History* (Stanford, Calif.: Stanford University Press, 1959). In the chapter titled "Recession and Decline: Ming and Ch'ing Dynasties," Ch'en even claims that "events during the last five hundred years of decline do not warrant devoting one chapter to each dynasty" (434n1).

5. Chen Yuan 陳垣, *Mingji Dian Qian fojiao kao* 明季滇黔佛教攷 (Beijing: Furen daxue, 1940; repr., Beijing: Kexue chubanshe, 1959).

6. For reflections on this paradigm in the study of Chinese Buddhism, see, for example, James Robson, "Formation and Fabrication in the History and Historiography of Chan Buddhism," *HJAS* 71, no. 2 (2011): 311–49, and Peter N. Gregory, "The Vitality of Buddhism in the Sung," in *Buddhism*

in the Sung, ed. Peter N. Gregory and Daniel A. Getz Jr. (Honolulu: University of Hawai`i Press, 1999), 1–20.

7. For a survey of the lingering influence, see Schicketanz, *Daraku to fukkō*, 6–9.

8. For criticism of Protestant Buddhism, see Gregory Schopen, "Archaeology and Protestant Presuppositions in the Study of Indian Buddhism," *History of Religions* 31, no. 1 (1991): 1–23; Donald S. Lopez, *Curators of the Buddha: The Study of Buddhism under Colonialism* (Chicago: University of Chicago Press, 1995); and Robert H. Sharf, "On the Allure of Buddhist Relics," *Representations*, no. 66 (1999): 93n7.

9. For this new view of Ming Buddhism, see Chün-fang Yü, *The Renewal of Buddhism in China: Chu-hung and the Late Ming Synthesis* (New York: Columbia University Press, 1981), 4–6, 65–66; Timothy Brook, *Praying for Power: Buddhism and the Formation of Gentry Society in Late-Ming China* (Cambridge, Mass.: Harvard University Press, 1993), 31; Timothy Brook, "Rethinking Syncretism: The Unity of the Three Teachings and Their Joint Worship in Late-Imperial China," *Journal of Chinese Religions* 21, no. 1 (1993): 13–44; and William Chu, "Syncretism Reconsidered: The Four Eminent Monks and Their Syncretistic Styles," *Journal of the International Association of Buddhist Studies* 29, no. 1 (2006): 43–86.

10. My thanks to Professor Daniel Stevenson for encouraging me to trace how the concepts of "renewal" and "decline" have been used in the history of Chinese Buddhism. Given the importance of his comment, I cite it here: "Clearly 'decline' and 'revival' have become routine academic tropes, but one suspects that they also saw normative use among monastic and lay Buddhists at various points as well. 'Revival,' as a case in point, has a well-established normative Chinese Buddhist equivalent in '中興,' as we see in Northern Song Tiantai circles, where we find in situ Buddhist (esp. Tiantai) documents concurrent in time with Zhili and Zunshi referring to an activist Tiantai '中興.' That idea, once attached to the person of Zhili himself, becomes an entrenched historical trope by Southern Song, particularly with massive lineage histories/chronicles such as Zhipan's *Fozu tongji* (where Zhili becomes the seventeenth trunk line patriarch, and all Tiantai history of Song is writ around his line)." The mention of Zhili here is to Siming Zhili 四明知禮 (960–1028); Zunshi refers to Ciyun Zunshi 慈雲遵式 (964–1032); and Zhipan's *Fozu tongji* is a reference to Zhipan's 志盤 (fl. 1253) *Fozu tongji* 佛祖統紀.

11. This observation is made primarily through a keyword search of CBETA Chinese Electronic Tripiṭaka Collection. Ideally other types of materials like local gazetteers and literary collections should also be included for investigation, but I believe that we will achieve a similar result in any event.

12. Taixu 太虛, "Zhendan fojiao shuailuo zhi yuanyin lun" 震旦佛教衰落之原因論, *Haichaoyin* 海潮音 2, no. 3 (1921): 1–9. Notably, other leading monks at the time, like Yinguang 印光 (1862–1940) and Xuyun 虛雲 (1840?–1959), held similar admiration for late-Ming Buddhism. See, for example, Yinguang, "Yu foxue baoguan shu" 與佛學報館書, in *Yinguang fashi wenchao* 印光法師文鈔 (Beijing: Zongjiao wenhua chubanshe, 2000), 1:17, and Xuyun, *Xuyun laoheshang fahui, shige* 虛雲老和尚法匯·詩歌, in *Xuyun laoheshang nianpu fahui zengding ben* 虛雲老和尚譜法匯增訂本, ed. Cen Xuelü 岑學呂 (Taipei: Dasheng jingshe, 1982), 378.

13. Araki Kengo, "Confucianism and Buddhism in the Late Ming," in *The Unfolding of Neo-Confucianism*, ed. Wm. Theodore de Bary (New York: Columbia University Press, 1975), 54–55.

14. Shengyan 聖嚴 [Chang Sheng-yen 張聖嚴], *Mingmo fojiao yanjiu* 明末佛教研究 (Taipei: Dongchu chubanshe, 1987), 2. For a good review of this book, see Jennifer Eichman, "Humanizing the Study of Late Ming Buddhism," *Chung-Hwa Buddhist Journal* 26 (2013): 153–85.

15. For Master Taixu's criticism of "funerary Buddhism," see, for example, Yinshun 印順, ed., *Taixu dashi quanshu* 太虛大師全書 (Taipei: Shandaosi fojing liutongchu, 1980), 18:604–5. For Master Taixu's use of the dispirited image of contemporary Buddhism as a discourse strategy, see Holmes Welch, *The Buddhist Revival in China* (Cambridge, Mass.: Harvard University Press, 1968), chap.

3. In Japan, the so-called New Buddhism similarly blamed Edo-period Buddhism as moral and spiritual bankruptcy for the latter's alleged overemphasis on funeral rituals. See Orion Klautau, "Against the Ghosts of Recent Past: Meiji Scholarship and the Discourse on Edo-Period Buddhist Decadence," *Japanese Journal of Religious Studies* 35, no. 2 (2008): 263–303.

16. Jiang Wu, *Enlightenment in Dispute: The Reinvention of Chan Buddhism in Seventeenth-Century China* (New York: Oxford University Press, 2008), 280.

17. For the early twentieth-century *saṃgha* despised by Buddhist reformists as degenerated for its major concern with routine practices, Holmes Welch found nothing wrong with it. Not viewing it in a state of decline, he instead argues that what it needed was not a restoration to the level of early stages but "a series of innovations" or "a redirection from the religious to the secular" (*Buddhist Revival in China*, 264).

18. Wu, *Enlightenment in Dispute*, 265–85.

19. Brook, *Praying for Power*, 311–34.

20. Instead of a fixed and clear-cut boundary, more likely we find multilayered and floating regulations whose interpretations and enforcement varied considerably with region and social class. This situation made it hard to say if and when those regulations were broken through. Furthermore, in late-imperial China when the economic, institutional, and intellectual autonomy of Buddhism was seriously compromised, breaking through the boundary appeared to be more a result of than a precondition for the emergence of the Buddhist renewal.

21. The elites in late-imperial China have been extensively conceptualized and discussed since the 1980s, mostly owing to a redefinition of them in connection with local society. See, for example, Robert Hymes, *Statesmen and Gentlemen: The Elite of Fu-Chou, Chiang-Hsi, in Northern and Southern Sung* (New York: Cambridge University Press, 1986); Joseph W. Esherick and Mary Backus Rankin, eds., *Chinese Local Elites and Patterns of Dominance* (Berkeley: University of California Press, 1990); Brook, *Praying for Power*; and Peter K. Bol, "The Rise of Local History: History, Geography, and Culture in Southern Song and Yuan Wuzhou," *HJAS* 61, no. 1 (2001): 37–76.

22. For example, ordinary people in the Ming preferred *jiao* Buddhism, which was characterized by lavish rituals, while a major portion of the elites tended to criticize *jiao* Buddhism as empty and formulistic and instead favored Chan and doctrinal Buddhism.

23. A similarly important reason for this maintenance was that ordinary adherents, the major audience targeted by routine practices, were also a major force supporting those practices, regardless of the opinions of their elite counterparts.

24. For institutional and diffused religions, see Ching Kun Yang, *Religion in Chinese Society: A Study of Contemporary Social Functions of Religion and Some of Their Historical Factors* (Berkeley: University of California Press, 1961). "Basic to Yang's distinction between the two forms," Stephen Teiser has pointed out, "is the judgment that in traditional Chinese society, diffused religion was everywhere and always primary. Yang thus inverts the traditional model for discussing Chinese religion, which looked first at the precepts of the organized religions and only secondarily, if at all, at other forms of religion" ("Popular Religion," *JAS* 54, no. 2 [1995]: 379).

25. "Folk Religion: Folk Buddhism," in *Encyclopedia of Religion*, ed. Lindsay Jones, 2nd ed., 15 vols. (Detroit: Thomson Gale, 2005), http://www.encyclopedia.com/environment/encyclopedias -almanacs-transcripts-and-maps/folk-religion-folk-buddhism. We may better understand folk Buddhism by borrowing insights from other religious traditions. For example, R. Daniel Shaw has argued that "folk religion is the religion of the 'folk'—real people struggling with the realities of life. Folk Christianity emphasizes the experiences of Christian folk as they seek to connect their religious experience, as expressed in the Bible and the church, to the reality of their lives. In the process, people tend to rely on their understanding of who God is and what God can do for them. This produces an appreciation of the practical effects of what Christianity claims to be on the one hand (formal/institutional religion), and personal experience on the other (informal/personalized

religion). . . . Folk Christianity should reflect beliefs and values expressed in actual behavior" ("Folk Christianity," in *The Encyclopedia of Christian Civilization*, ed. G. T. Kurian [Chichester, West Sussex, U.K.; Malden, Mass.: Wiley-Blackwell, 2011], doi:10.1002/9780470670606.wbecc0549).

26.   Folk Buddhism, especially that in the sectarian form in Ming-Qing China, has sparked a growing interest since the 1970s among scholars seeking to understand how Buddhism was accepted and practiced in real life. See, for example, Daniel L. Overmyer, "Folk-Buddhist Religion: Creation and Eschatology in Medieval China," *History of Religions* 12, no. 1 (1972): 42–70; Daniel L. Overmyer, *Folk Buddhist Religion: Dissenting Sects in Late Traditional China* (Cambridge, Mass.: Harvard University Press, 1976); B. J. ter Haar, *Practicing Scripture: A Lay Buddhist Movement in Late Imperial China* (Honolulu: University of Hawai`i Press, 2014); Stephen F. Teiser, *The Ghost Festival in Medieval China* (Princeton, N.J.: Princeton University Press, 1988); Michibata Ryōshū 道端良秀, *Chūgoku bukkyō shisō shi no kenkyū: Chūgoku minshū no bukkyō juyō* 中国仏教思想史の研究:中国民衆の仏教受容 (Kyoto: Heirakuji shoten, 1979); Li Tiangang 李天剛, *Jinze: Jiangnan minjian jisi tanyuan* 金泽: 江南民间祭祀探源 (Beijing: Sanlian shudian, 2017).

27.   Daniel Overmyer, a pioneering and arguably the most important scholar of Chinese folk Buddhism, has pointed out that "to reach a more comprehensive understanding of these groups we must do our best to free ourselves from the prevailing bias of the Chinese sources, and from our own tendency to concentrate on political and social change. We are dealing here for the most part with obscure local congregations of peasants, laborers, and artisans who needed support, assurance, and a renewed sense of their own worth and continuity. A method tuned to macro-history can grasp these people only when they formed into large lumps; the surrounding earth which supported these lumps slips through its fingers. What is needed is an approach which sees these groups not from the top down, but from eye-level" ("Alternatives: Popular Religious Sects in Chinese Society," *Modern China* 7, no. 2 [1981]: 155–56).

28.   Recent studies of Tibetan Buddhism in the Ming have revealed that it infiltrated into the society of China proper in a degree much deeper than has been recognized. Although the focus of this study is Chinese Buddhism (*hanchuan fojiao* 漢傳佛教), it may be worth noting that Tibetan Buddhism experienced a trajectory similar to its Chinese counterpart while extending its influence to China proper during the Ming, and that it obtained a fresh momentum in the early Wanli era. See, for example, Shen Weirong 沈衞榮, "Lun Mengyuan wangchao yu Mingdai Zhongguo de zhengzhi he zongjiao yichan: Zangchuan fojiao yu Xixia, Yuan, Ming sandai zhengzhi he zongjiao tizhi xingcheng zhongde jueshe yanjiu" 論蒙元王朝於明代中國的政治和宗教遺產: 藏傳佛教於西夏、元、明三代政治和宗教體制形成中的角色研究, in *8–15 shiji zhongxibu Xizang de lishi, wenhua yu yishu* 8–15 世紀中西部西藏的歷史、文化和藝術, ed. Erika Forte (Beijing: Zhongguo zangxue chubanshe, 2015); Shen Weirong, "Wenben duikan yu lishi jiangou: Zangchuan fojiao yu Xiyu he Zhongyuan chuanbo lishi yanjiu daolun" 文本對勘與歷史建構: 藏傳佛教于西域和中原傳播歷史研究導論, in *Wenben yu lishi: Zangchuan fojiao lishi xushi de xingcheng he Han-Zang foxue yanjiu de jiangou* 文本與歷史: 藏傳佛教歷史敘事的形成和漢藏佛學研究的建構, by Shen Weirong and Hou Haoran 侯浩然, (Beijing: Zhongguo zangxue chubanshe, 2016), 241–324; and Shen Weirong, "*Dasheng yaodao miji* yu Xixia, Yuan, Ming sandai zangchuan mijaoshi yanjiu" 《大乘要道密集》與西夏、元、明三代藏傳密教史研究, in Shen and Hou, *Wenben yu lishi*, 325–415.

29.   Pippa Norris and Ronald Inglehart, *Sacred and Secular: Religion and Politics Worldwide*, 2nd ed. (Cambridge: Cambridge University Press, 2011), 4.

30.   See, for example, Araki Kengo 荒木見悟, *Bukkyō to jukyō: Chūgoku shisō o keiseisuru mono* 佛教と儒教: 中国思想を形成するもの (Tokyo: Kenbun shuppan, 1963); Araki Kengo, *Yōmeigaku no tenkai to bukkyō* 陽明學の開展と仏教 (Tokyo: Kenbun shuppan, 1984), and Araki Kengo, *Yōmeigaku to bukkyō shingaku* 陽明學と仏教心學 (Tokyo: Kenbun shuppan, 2008).

31.   The sociological approach to Chinese religions can be traced back to at least J. J. M. de Groot, *The Religious System of China: Its Ancient Forms, Evolution, History and Present Aspect, I–VI* (Leiden:

Brill, 1892–1910). Other important research includes Erik Zürcher, *The Buddhist Conquest of China: The Spread and Adaptation of Buddhism in Early Medieval China* (1959; repr., Leiden: Brill, 2007), and Chikusa Masaaki 竺沙雅章, *Chūgoku bukkyō shakaishi kenkyū* 中國佛教社會史研究 (Kyoto: Dōhōsha shuppan, 1982).

32. Timothy Brook's stance on this dichotomy between society and the state, as Jennifer Eichman has noted, became softened when he later published *The Chinese State in Ming Society* (London: RoutledgeCurzon, 2005); see Jennifer Eichman, *A Late Sixteenth-Century Chinese Buddhist Fellowship: Spiritual Ambitions, Intellectual Debates, and Epistolary Connections* (Leiden: Brill, 2016), 16n37.

33. Susan Naquin and Chün-fang Yü, eds., *Pilgrims and Sacred Sites in China* (Berkeley: University of California Press, 1992); Beverley Foulks McGuire, *Living Karma: The Religious Practices of Ouyi Zhixu* (New York: Columbia University Press, 2014); Jimmy Yu, *Sanctity and Self-Inflicted Violence in Chinese Religions, 1500–1700* (Oxford: Oxford University Press, 2012); Eichman, *Late Sixteenth-Century*.

34. For important studies in this field, see, for example, Stanley Weinstein, *Buddhism under the T'ang* (Cambridge: Cambridge University Press, 1987); Antonino Forte, *Political Propaganda and Ideology in China at the End of the Seventh Century: Inquiry into the Nature, Authors and Function of the Tunhuang Document S.6502, Followed by an Annotated Translation* (Kyoto: Italian School of East Asian Studies, 2005); and Jinhua Chen, "Śarīra and Scepter: Empress Wu's Political Use of Buddhist Relics," *Journal of the International Association of Buddhist Studies* 25, no. 1-2 (2002): 33–150.

35. That the question of whether a monk should bow (i.e., pay homage) to a secular ruler, a once hotly debated issue in medieval China, became silent in favor of the emperor during this period exemplifies the change.

36. In an extreme instance, Emperor Yongzheng (r. 1723–1735) expanded his powers from politics into Buddhist communities, and even took up the role of judge of religious affairs; see Wu, *Enlightenment in Dispute*, chap. 6.

37. "The localist turn" refers to an apparent current, most prominently in the Jiangnan region, in which scholar-officials turned their attention away from the state to local society and used resources according to local agendas under their control. By contrast, "state activism" refers to the state's effort to infiltrate in local society to maximize its influence, which curbed the centrifugal tendency caused by the localist turn. See Peter K. Bol, "The 'Localist Turn' and 'Local Identity' in Later Imperial China," *Late Imperial China* 24, no. 2 (2003): 1–50.

38. Wu, *Enlightenment in Dispute*, 285, says that "it is arguable that most Buddhist revivals happened in the periods when state control was weakened and local society flourished."

39. See, for example, Chen Yunü 陳玉女, "Mindai bukkyō shakai no chiiki teki kenkyū—Kasei Manreki nenkan (1522–1620) o chūshin toshite" 明代仏教社会の地域的の研究—嘉靖・萬曆年間 (1522–1620) を中心として (Ph.D. diss., Kyushu University, 1995); Du Changshun 杜常順, *Mingdai gongting yu fojiao guanxi yanjiu* 明代宮廷與佛教關系研究 (Beijing: Zhongguo shehui kexue chubanshe, 2013); Jiang Canteng 江燦騰, *Wanming fojiao gaige shi* 晚明佛教改革史 (Guilin: Guangxi shifan daxue chubanshe, 2006), 39–190.

40. Wolfram Eberhard, for example, took fifty years as the unit of time to count temple buildings, but the unit is too big for the Jiajing-Wanli period, when drastic changes could occur within a few years. See Wolfram Eberhard, "Temple-Building Activities in Medieval and Modern China: An Experimental Study," *Monumenta Serica* 23 (1964): 264–318.

41. For the development of the French Annales school and the challenge facing it, see Peter Burke, *The French Historical Revolution: The "Annales" School, 1929–2014* (Stanford, Calif.: Stanford University Press, 2015), and Lynn Hunt, "French History in the Last Twenty Years: The Rise and Fall of the Annales Paradigm," *Journal of Contemporary History* 21, no. 2 (1986): 209–24.

42. On opinion leaders, see Elihu Katz and Paul Felix Lazarsfeld, *Personal Influence: The Part Played by People in the Flow of Mass Communications* (New Brunswick, N.J.: Transaction Publishers, 2005). For agenda setting, see Walter Lippmann, *Public Opinion* (New York: Routledge, 2017).

43. The climate, for example, has often been overlooked in historical studies. But Timothy Brook has cogently argued how significantly the climate impacted the history of Yuan and Ming China; *The Troubled Empire: China in the Yuan and Ming Dynasties* (Cambridge, Mass.: Belknap Press, 2010). For a similar exception, see Timothy Barrett, "Climate Change and Religious Response: The Case of Early Medieval China," *Journal of the Royal Asiatic Society*, 3rd ser., 17, no. 2 (2007): 139–56.

1. SETTING THE STAGE

1. The use of the terms "structure" and "structural" in this study is strongly influenced by the French Annales school, especially by Fernand Braudel's conception of plural temporality. Braudel conceives of history as operating on three levels of time—the geographical (the *longue durée*), the social (the medium time of economies, societies, and cultures), and the individual (the short time of discrete events). Among the three, the medium time is characterized by trends or cycles and can be measured by periods of decades, generations, or even centuries. In his works Braudel stresses this level of historical time as a means of reconstructing "structural temporalities," from which this study has drawn a lot of inspiration. See Fernand Braudel, *Civilization and Capitalism, 15th–18th Century*, 3 vols. (New York: Harper and Row, 1981–84); Fernand Braudel, *The Mediterranean and the Mediterranean World in the Age of Philip II*, 2 vols., 2nd rev. ed., trans. Sian Reynolds (Berkeley: University of California Press, 1972–1973).

2. Zhu Yuanzhang 朱元璋, *Ming Taizu ji* 明太祖集 (Hefei: Huangshan shushe, 1991), 10:215; Ge Yinliang 葛寅亮, *Jinling fancha zhi* 金陵梵剎志 (Taipei: Mingwen shuju, 1980), 1:77, 81, 99, 102 (hereafter cited as *FCZ*).

3. *FCZ*, 2:232.

4. Huanlun 幻輪, *Shijian jigulüe xuji* 釋鑑稽古略續集 2, in *T*, vol. 49, no. 2038, 932a7–18. For the early history of *jiao* Buddhism and its specialization in the Ming, see Chen Yunü 陳玉女, "Mingdai yuqie jiaoseng de zhuanzhi hua jiqi jingchan huodong" 明代瑜伽教僧的專職化及其經懺活動, in *Mingdai de fojiao yu shehui* 明代的佛教與社會 (Beijing: Beijing daxue chubanshe, 2011), 248–82, and Li Mingyang 李明陽, "Ming Hongwuchao yuqie jiaoseng guifanhua licheng jiqi yuanyin tanjiu" 明洪武朝瑜伽教僧規範化歷程及其原因探究, *Wutaishan yanjiu* 五臺山研究 no. 2 (2017): 19–25. See also Zhou Qi 周齊, *Mingdai fojiao yu zhengzhi wenhua* 明代佛教與政治文化 (Beijing: Renmin chubanshe, 2005), 114–20.

5. My thanks to Professor James Benn for reminding me of this implication.

6. *Daozang* 道藏, ed. Daozang yanjiu suo 道藏研究所, 36 vols. (repr., Shanghai: Shanghai shudian, 1988), 9:1.

7. For the use of Buddhism for "subtly transforming the deeply villainous who could not be moved otherwise," see John Dardess, *Confucianism and Autocracy: Professional Elites in the Founding of the Ming Dynasty* (Berkeley: University of California Press, 1983), 227–28.

8. The term *zhenji* refers to the boundaries of a piece of land in its four directions. There was a kind of record in the Ming that registered such boundaries in detail to legitimatize land ownership.

9. About half the clergy were *jiao* monks in the Ming, and the proportion increased to about 80 percent in modern China. See Shengkai 聖凱, *Zhongguo fojiao chanfa yanjiu* 中國佛教懺法研究 (Beijing: Zongjiao wenhua chubanshe, 2004), 368–75, 403–5.

10. Zhu, *Ming Taizu ji*, 14:272.

11. For the Bureau of Buddhist Patriarchs, see Chen, "Mindai bukkyō shakai," 21–27; He Xiaorong 何孝榮, "Ming chu Shanshiyuan kao" 明初善世院攷, *Xinan daxue xuebao* 西南大學學報 35, no. 2 (2009): 46–50. For the ranking system of officials in imperial China, see the first section of Charles O. Hucker, *A Dictionary of Official Titles in Imperial China* (Stanford, Calif.: Stanford University Press, 1985).

12. For the Hongwu canon, see Li Fuhua 李富華 and He Mei 何梅, *Hanwen fojiao dazangjing yanjiu* 漢文佛教大藏經研究 (Beijing: Zongjiao wenhua chubanshe, 2003), 375–406.

13. *FCZ*, 2:210. For changes in the management bureau of Buddhism in the early Ming, see Nogami Shunjō 野上俊靜, "Minsho no sōdō gamon" 明初の僧道衙門, *Ōtani gakuhō* 大谷學報, no. 98 (1946): 8–15; Ryūchi Kiyoshi 龍池清, "Mindai no sōkan" 明代の僧官, *Shina bukkyō shigaku* 支那仏教史學 4, no. 3 (1945): 35–46; Xie Chongguang 謝重光 and Bai Wengu 白文固, *Zhongguo sengguan zhidu shi* 中國僧官制度史 (Xining: Qinghai renmin chubanshe, 1990), 231–49.

14. *Ming Taizu shilu* 明太祖實錄, 144:2262–63.

15. *Ming Taizu shilu*, 167:2563.

16. For the event, see He Xiaorong 何孝榮, "Yuanmo Mingchu mingseng Zongle shiji kao" 元末明初名僧宗泐事迹考, *Jiangxi shehui kexue* 江西社會科學, no. 12 (2012): 99–105. See also Kageki Motohiro 蔭木原洋, "Kobutei no bukkyō seisaku—Sō Ren to Kitan Sōroku ni shōten o atete—jō, ge" 洪武帝の仏教政策—宋濂と季潭宗泐に焦點を當てて— (上下), *Tōyō shihō* 東洋史訪 5 (1999): 13–24; 6 (2000): 1–16.

17. *Ming Taizu shilu*, 209:3109.

18. The distinction between the public monastery and the hereditary temple started in the Song. See Theodore Griffith Foulk, "Myth, Ritual, and Monastic Practice in Sung Ch'an Buddhism," in *Religion and Society in T'ang and Sung China*, ed. Patricia Buckley Ebrey and Peter N. Gregory (Honolulu: University of Hawai'i Press, 1993), 163–64.

19. *FCZ*, 2:240.

20. Huanlun, *Shijian jigulüe xueji* 2, in *T*, vol. 49, no. 2038, 934c1–2; *FCZ*, 2:223. For the *zhenji daoren*, see Noguchi Tetsurō 野口鐵郎, "Mindai jiden no zeieki to chinki dōjin" 明代寺田の税役と砧基道人, *Bukkyō shigaku* 仏教史學 14, no. 2 (1968): 17–33.

21. *FCZ*, 2:232.

22. *FCZ*, 2:251–54.

23. *FCZ*, 16:768–71. *Qing* 頃 was a unit of land equal to 100 *mu*, or 16.47 acres.

24. Huanlun, *Shijian jigulüe xuji* 2, in *T*, vol. 49, no. 2038, 931c14–16.

25. *FCZ*, 2:251–52.

26. Yonglin Jiang, trans., *The Great Ming Code / Da Ming lü* (Seattle: University of Washington Press, 2005), p. 71, art. 83, p. 87, art. 120. See also Anne Gerritsen, "The Hongwu Legacy: Fifteenth-Century Views on Zhu Yuzhang's Monastic Policies," in *Long Live the Emperor! Uses of the Ming Founder across Six Centuries of East Asian History*, ed. Sarah Schneewind (Minneapolis: Center for Early Modern History, 2008), 55–72.

27. *Ming Taizong shilu* 明太宗實錄, 14:249. Yongle exempted the temples that had been founded prior to 1382 and had the imperially bestowed name tablet. Thus, some amalgamated temples retrieved independence. For examples, see *Jiaxing fuzhi* (1600), fasc. 4.

28. *Ming Taizong shilu*, 189:2008.

29. *Ming Taizong shilu*, 205:2109. See also Xu Xueju 徐學聚, *Guochao dianhui* 國朝典彙 (Beijing: Beijing daxue chubanshe, 1993), 205:1615.

30. *Ming Taizong shilu*, 223:2203, 225:2211–12. For the rebellion, see Gu Yingtai 谷應泰, *Mingshi jishi benmo* 明史紀事本末 (Beijing: Zhonghua shuju, 1958), 23:371–74.

31. For early studies of Ming Buddhist policies, see Ryūchi Kiyoshi 龍池清, "Min no Taiso no bukkyō seisaku" 明の太祖の仏教政策, *Bukkyō shisō kōza* 仏教思想講座 8 (1939): 83–112; Shimizu Taiji 清水泰次, "Mindai ni okeru butsudō no torishimari" 明代における佛道の取締, *Shigaku zasshi* 史學雜誌

40, no. 3 (1929): 263–310; and Shimizu Taiji, "Mindai butsudō tōsei kō" 明代佛道統制考, *Tōyō shikai kiyo* 東洋史會紀要, no. 2 (1937): 1–19.

32. Timothy Brook, "State Censorship and the Book Trade," in *The Chinese State in Ming Society* (London: RoutledgeCurzon, 2005), 133–34, 137–38; Timothy Brook, "At the Margin of Public Authority: The Ming State and Buddhism," in *The Chinese State*, 139–57.

33. Brook, "At the Margin," 150.

34. The enforcement of these policies at the local level still requires more study.

35. *Gusu zhi* 姑蘇志 (1542), fasc. 29–30.

36. *Songjiang fuzhi* 松江府志 (1631), fasc. 50–52. Nevertheless, thirty-two temples there remained independent without being incorporated.

37. *Hangzhou fuzhi* 杭州府志 (1579), fasc. 97–100.

38. *Daming fuzhi* 大名府志 (1506), 4:704a.

39. See *Zhengding fuzhi* 正定府志 (1752), fasc. 9; *Baoding fuzhi* 保定府志 (1680), fasc. 29; and *Taiyuan fuzhi* 太原府志 (1612), fasc. 24.

40. Chün-fang Yü, *The Renewal of Buddhism in China: Chu-hung and the Late Ming Synthesis* (New York: Columbia University Press, 1981), 146, states that Hongwu's limits on the number of temples was imposed in prefectures close to the capital and lasted only a few years, but this evaluation is open to question, and evidence shows that the amalgamation of most temples was irreversible. However, exceptions indeed existed. In Shaoxing 紹興 prefecture, for example, although it was not far from Nanjing, it seems that no temples there were amalgamated; see *Shaoxing fuzhi* 紹興府志 (1683), fasc. 23.

41. For example, *Hangzhou fuzhi* (1764), fasc. 28–32, reports that only twelve temples were absorbed but forty-two monasteries remained, which constitutes a contrast with what was recorded in *Hangzhou fuzhi* (1579). Another example is Xuanmiaosi 宣妙寺 in Shaoxing. *Shengxian zhi* 嵊縣志 (1671), 6:27b, reveals that the temple was amalgamated in the Hongwu era, but nothing about the event is mentioned in the *Hangzhou fuzhi* (1764).

42. For example, by 1685 eighty-nine Buddhist temples had stelae showing that they were imperially built, and many of them were preserved from the Ming dynasty; see *Kangxi Shuntian fuzhi* 康熙順天府志, 3:114–17.

43. See *Huzhou fuzhi* 湖州府志 (1758), fasc. 9–10, *Suzhou fuzhi* 蘇州府志 (1693), fasc. 38–40, and *Hangzhou fuzhi* (1764), fasc. 28–32. The temple-building projects in Suzhou during the Hongwu era were much fewer than those of Hangzhou and of Huzhou. So, this relatively higher number in the area during the Yongle era can be taken as a supplement to the deficiency.

44. He Xiaorong 何孝榮, "Lun mingdai de duseng" 論明代的度僧, *Shijie zongjiao yanjiu* 世界宗教研究, no. 1 (2004): 31n14.

45. *Ming Yingzong shilu* 明英宗實錄, 206:4422.

46. For instance, on one occasion in the Chenghua era, seventy thousand ordination certificates were issued to collect urgently needed money. The practice of selling the certificate can be traced back to the mid–Tang dynasty (618–907). For the practice in the Song and Jin dynasties, see Chikusa Masaaki 竺沙雅章, *Chūgoku bukkyō shakaishi kenkyū* 中國仏教社會史研究 (Tokyo: Dōhōsha shuppan, 1982), chap. 1; Wang Zhongyao 王仲堯, *Nansong fojiao zhidu wenhua yanjiu* 南宋佛教制度文化研究 (Beijing: Shangwu yinshuguan, 2012), 108–32. For the changing prices of the ordination certificate, see He Xiaorong, "Lun Mingdai de duseng," 33–34; He Xiaorong, "Lun Mingdai zhonghouqi de yudie duseng" 論明代中後期的鬻牒度僧, *Nankai xuebao* 南開學報, no. 5 (2005): 61–67.

47. Free ordination certificates were canceled in 1539, and thereafter every monk intending to receive the certificate had to pay.

48. The controversy surrounds the impact of selling certificates on the *saṃgha*. Yü, *The Renewal of Buddhism*, 162, claims that the practice was conducive to the retrieval of autonomy in the *saṃgha*. In

contrast, Timothy Brook, *Praying for Power: Buddhism and the Formation of Gentry Society in Late-Ming China* (Cambridge, Mass.: Harvard University Press, 1993), 32, criticizes it as "a sharp depreciation in the status of monk," arguing that it "did more to weaken the *saṃgha* than all the conscious attempts by the post-Tang state to limit the power of Buddhism." Jiang Canteng 江燦騰, *Wan-ming fojiao gaige shi* 晚明佛教改革史 (Guilin: Guangxi shifan daxue chubanshe, 2006), 22–28, agrees with this judgment. But Brook modified his ideas later. In *The Chinese State*, 151, he says that "the assumption behind this judgment—that the men who bought the certificates went on to become incompetent monks—I regard as mistaken. The polite fiction surrounding the sale of certificates was that the purchaser was a monk. In fact, most if not all purchasers were simply paying the government a flat fee for a permanent tax exemption. . . . Few, if any, who bought a monk's certificate as a lump-sum prepayment on future service levies were interested in becoming a monk. Who would want to buy his way into such a non-lucrative profession?"

49.   Zhao Yi 趙翼, *Gaiyu congkao* 陔餘叢攷 (Shijiazhuang: Hebei renmin chubanshe, 1990), 18:288.

50.   For the recovery of lost land assets and illegal occupation of others' land, see Bai Wengu 白文固, "Yuandai de siyuan jingji" 元代的寺院經濟, *Qinghai shehui kexue* 青海社會科學, no. 6 (1987): 76.

51.   Bai, "Yuandai de siyuan jingji," 77.

52.   Liang Fangzhong 梁方仲, *Zhongguo lidai hukou, tiandi, tianfu tongji* 中國歷代戶口、田地、田賦統計 (Beijing: Zhonghua shuju, 2008), 442. For the two bestowals of lands that Great Chengtian Husheng monastery received in 1330 and 1347, each 162,000 *qing*, Liang believes that they refer to the same event. Li Gan 李幹 and Zhou Zhizheng 周祉征, "Yuandai siyuan jingji chutan" 元代寺院經濟初探, *Sixiang zhanxian* 思想戰線, no. 5 (1986): 85, disagrees. For the two bestowals, see Song Lian 宋濂, ed., *Yuanshi* 元史 (Beijing: Zhonghua shuju, 1976), 34:756, 41:879.

53.   This was the general governmental attitude, but of course exceptions existed. For a telling example in which lost monastic land was recovered with government assistance, see *FCZ*, 2:216.

54.   This patch of land was bestowed by the Xuande emperor (r. 1426–1435) to Tianquan Zuyuan 天泉祖淵 (1389–1449). See Minghe 明河, *Buxu gaoseng zhuan* 補續高僧傳 18, in *X*, vol. 77, no. 1524, 496c14–16.

55.   *FCZ*, 2:206. See also Ouyang Nan 歐陽楠, "Wanming Nanjing diqu de siyuan dengji yu siyuan jingji: Yi *Jinling fancha zhi* wei zhongxin de kaocha" 晚明南京地區的寺院等級與寺院經濟: 以《金陵梵剎志》爲中心的考察, *Shijie zongjiao yanjiu* 世界宗教研究, no. 3 (2012): 39–50.

56.   *FCZ* 2:250–51. Evidence shows that the privilege of imperially bestowed lands had been partly lost by the Wanli period. See *FCZ*, 50:1601–20.

57.   For a canonical warning against state intervention in Buddhist affairs, see, for example, *Foshuo ren-wang boreboluomi jing* 佛說仁王般若波羅蜜經 2, in *T*, vol. 8, no. 245, 833b17–25.

58.   Jacques Gernet, *Buddhism in Chinese Society: An Economic History from the Fifth to the Tenth Centuries* (New York: Columbia University Press, 1995), 231–47.

59.   Michael J. Walsh, *Sacred Economies: Buddhist Monasticism and Territoriality in Medieval China* (New York: Columbia University Press, 2009), 21. For the point that land was the mainstay of Buddhist monastic economic practices, see chaps. 3–6.

60.   Xie Chongguang 謝重光, *Zhongguo fojiao sengguan zhidu he shehui shenghuo* 中國佛教僧官制度和社會生活 (Beijing: Shangwu yinshuguan, 2009), 160–253, 400–413.

61.   For lands bestowed to temples in the Song, see Huang Minzhi 黃敏枝, *Songdai fojiao jingji shehui shi lunji* 宋代佛教社會經濟史論集 (Taipei: Taiwan xuesheng shuju, 1989), 23–27, 52–60.

62.   For the tension between the monk population and the weakened monastic economy, see Jiang, *Wanming fojiao gaige shi*, 20–38.

63.   This mechanism is called Gresham's law in economics. According to the theory, if coins containing metal of different value legally have the same value, the coins composed of the cheaper metal will be used for payment, while those made of more expensive metal tend to disappear from circulation because they will be hoarded. The applicability of this principle to society lies in the fact that

forms of human behavior have a competitive edge against other behaviors. Self-interested groups tend toward what works, so bad (in a moral sense) drives out good if it causes superior practical effects.

64. For these intense waves of purging, see Denis C. Twitchett and Frederick W. Mote, eds., *The Cambridge History of China, Volume 7: The Ming Dynasty, 1368–1644, Part 1* (Cambridge: Cambridge University Press, 1988), 149–81. The purging eventually led to the execution, in 1380, of Hu Weiyong 胡惟庸, the left (senior) chief minister. See Edward L. Farmer, *Early Ming Government: The Evolution of Dual Capitals* (Cambridge, Mass.: Harvard University Press, 1976), 79–86.

65. For the early-Ming political structure, see Edward L. Dreyer, *Early Ming China: A Political History, 1355–1435* (Stanford, Calif.: Stanford University Press, 1982); Charles O. Hucker, *The Ming Dynasty: Its Origins and Evolving Institutions* (Ann Arbor: Center for Chinese Studies, University of Michigan, 1978).

66. Zhu Yuanzhang 朱元璋, *Huang Ming zuxun* 皇明祖訓, in *Zhongguo zhenxi falü dianji xubian* 中國珍稀法律典籍續編 (Harbin: Heilongjiang renmin chubanshe, 2002), 483. For more studies on the *Huang Ming zuxun*, see Denis Twitchett and Frederick W. Mote, eds., *The Cambridge History of China, Volume 8: The Ming Dynasty, 1368–1644, Part 2* (Cambridge: Cambridge University Press, 1998), 16n4; Edward L. Farmer, *Zhu Yuanzhang and Early Ming Legislation: The Reordering of Chinese Society Following the Era of Mongol Rule* (Leiden: Brill, 1995), 66–69.

67. For the increased influence of the grand secretary during this period, see Twitchett and Mote, *The Cambridge History of China, Volume 7*, 286–88.

68. Long Wenbin 龍文彬, *Ming huiyao* 明會要 (Beijing: Zhonghua shuju, 1956), 39:699.

69. According to the procedure, the grand secretaries first reviewed memorials submitted to the emperor and then suggested appropriate responses by posting on each a draft comment for imperial approval. The emperor usually adopted their advice and then asked the eunuchs to transcribe the responses in vermilion ink in his name so that these rescripts could be sent to the respective ministry for implementation. As for how the eunuchs manipulated the procedure for their own interests, see Liu Ruoyu 劉若愚, *Zhuozhong zhi* 酌中志, in vol. 431 of *Xuxiu Siku quanshu* 續修四庫全書, ed. Gu Tinglong 顧廷龍 et al. (Shanghai: Shanghai guji chubanshe, 1995–2001), 13:481–83, and Zhao Yifeng 趙軼峰, "Piaoni zhidu yu Mingdai zhengzhi" 票擬制度與明代政治, *Dongbei shifan daxue xuebao* 東北師範大學學報, no. 2 (1989): 35–41.

70. *Mingshi* 明史 (1736; repr., Beijing: Zhonghua shuju, 1974), 109:3306.

71. For the constitutional weakness of the Ming regime, see Twitchett and Mote, *The Cambridge History of China, Volume 7*, 358–70.

72. For the Great Rites Controversy, see Carney T. Fisher, *The Chosen One: Succession and Adoption in the Court of Ming Shizong* (Sydney: Allen and Unwin, 1990), and Zhang Xianqing 張顯清, *Zhang Xianqing wenji* 張顯清文集 (Shanghai: Shanghai cishu chubanshe, 2005), 253–70.

73. For changes in the ethics of officialdom, see Hu Jixun 胡吉勳, *"Dali yi" yu Mingting renshi bianju* "大禮議"與明廷人事變局 (Beijing: Shehui kexue wenxian chubanshe, 2007), 538–53.

74. For an apt comment on the poisoned relationship, see Wan Sitong 萬斯同, *Shiyuan wenji* 石園文集, in *jibu* 集部, vol. 1415, of *Xuxiu Siku quanshu*, 5:485.

75. For the power struggle during this phase, see Twitchett and Mote, *The Cambridge History of China, Volume 7*, 518–22, and Ray Huang, *1587, A Year of No Significance: The Ming Dynasty in Decline* (New Haven, Conn.: Yale University Press, 1981), 32–43.

76. The reason for this assassination attempt is unclear. Some sources locate the provocation in the emperor's harsh treatment of palace girls and their use in his pursuit of attaining longevity. For a discussion of sexual techniques aimed at obtaining health and longevity in China, see N. H. van Straten, *Concepts of Health, Disease and Vitality in Traditional Chinese Society: A Psychological Interpretation* (Wiesbaden: Steiner, 1983), 89–107, 132–45. See also Robert Hans van Gulik, *Sexual Life*

in Ancient China: A Preliminary Survey of Chinese Sex and Society from ca. 1500 B.C. till 1644 A.D. (Leiden: Brill, 2003).

77. On West Park, see Maggie C. K. Wan, "Building an Immortal Land: The Ming Jiajing Emperor's West Park," *Asia Major*, 3rd ser., 22, no. 2 (2009): 65–99.

78. On the succession issue, see Gu, *Mingshi jishi benmo*, 67:1061–76, and Mark C. Carnes and Daniel K. Gardner, *Confucianism and the Succession Crisis of the Wanli Emperor* (New York: Pearson Longman, 2005).

79. For the rules concerning the crown prince, see Zhu, *Huang Ming zuxun*, 496.

80. For example, starting in 1588, Wanli cut off regular contact with court officials by canceling imperial audiences. Shen Yiguan 沈一貫 (1531–1615, *jinshi* 1568) saw the emperor only twice during the twelve years he served as the grand secretary, while Zhu Geng 朱賡 (1535–1608, *jinshi* 1568) never obtained a chance to meet the emperor in the six years of his service in the office of grand secretary.

81. For an extreme story illustrating how weak the grand secretary position was in relation to the emperor, see Shen Defu 沈德符, *Wanli yehuo bian* 萬曆野獲編 (repr., Beijing: Zhonghua shuju, 1959), 1:25 (hereafter cited as *WLYH*).

82. For the increase in censors' influence, see *Mingshi*, 236:6161. This was partly because once impeached by the censors, officials tended to leave office. Furthermore, since Wanli refused to assign enough censors, the incumbent ones became rare resources eagerly courted by other officials.

83. For the Donglin faction and the bitter factionalism at the Wanli court, see Frederic Wakeman Jr., "Romantics, Stoics, and Martyrs in Seventeenth-Century China," *JAS* 43, no. 4 (1984): 631–65; John W. Dardess, *Blood and History in China: The Donglin Faction and Its Repression, 1620–1627* (Honolulu: University of Hawai'i Press, 2002); Jie Zhao, "A Decade of Considerable Significance: Late-Ming Factionalism in the Making, 1583–1593," *T'oung Pao*, 2nd ser., 88, no. 1 (2002): 112–50; and Ono Kazuko 小野和子, *Minki tōsha kō: Tōrintō to Fukusha* 明季黨社考: 東林黨と復社 (Kyoto: Dōhōsha shuppan, 1996).

84. For instance, Wanli was so cruel to the eunuchs that he frequently beat them to death and then confiscated their wealth. See *Mingshi*, 236:6157; Wen Bing 文秉, *Dingling zhulüe* 定陵注略 (repr., Taipei: Weiwen tushu chubanshe, 1976), 1:17; and Liang Shaojie 梁紹傑, ed., *Mingdai huanguan beizhuan lu* 明代宦官碑傳錄 (Hong Kong: Xianggang daxue zhongwenxi, 1997), 196, 199, 202.

85. Zhang Juzheng, for example, relied heavily on Feng Bao. See *Mingshi*, 305:7802; *WLYH*, 9:232–33; and Fan Shuzhi 樊樹志, "Zhang Juzheng he Feng Bao: Lishi de ling yimian" 張居正和馮保: 歷史的另一面, *Fudan xuebao* 復旦學報, no. 1 (1999): 80–87.

86. Fan Zhongyan 范仲淹, *Fan Zhongyan quanji* 范仲淹全集 (Chengdu: Sichuan daxue chubanshe, 2007), 8:195.

87. See, for example, Zhang Han 張瀚, *Songchuang mengyu* 松窗夢語 (Beijing: Zhonghua shuju, 1985), 8:149.

88. Ye Xianggao 葉向高, *Cangjia xucao* 蒼葭續草, in *jibu* 集部, vols. 124–25, of *Siku jinhui shu congkan* 四庫禁毀書叢刊, ed. Siku jinhui shu congkan bianzuan weiyuanhui 四庫禁毀書叢刊編纂委員會 (Beijing: Beijing chubanshe, 2000), 22:362a–b.

89. For Li Tingji, see *Mingshi*, 217:5739–41. Shortly after entering the Grand Secretariat, Li decided to resign from office because of a fierce attack by the censors. But the emperor turned a deaf ear to his requests, and, finally, after having submitted 123 memorials asking for retirement, Li left office without permission.

90. Araki Kengo, "Confucianism and Buddhism in the Late Ming," in *The Unfolding of Neo-Confucianism*, ed. Wm. Theodore de Bary (New York: Columbia University Press, 1975), 39.

91. Brook, "At the Margin," 150, points out that "fifteenth-century emperors allowed most of the late-Hongwu legislation against Buddhism to become a dead letter. They occasionally even went back to reviving the early-Hongwu patronal pose, comfortable with the assumption that Buddhist beliefs

could still be invoked to buttress public authority." It is worth noting that, apart from Buddhism, other alternatives were also available for late-Ming scholar-officials, like mathematics, medicine, and geography. See Timothy Brook, *The Confusions of Pleasure: Commerce and Culture in Ming China* (Berkeley: University of California Press, 1998), 218–39, and Luo Zongqiang 羅宗強, *Mingdai houqi shiren xintai yanjiu* 明代後期士人心態研究 (Tianjin: Nankai daxue chubanshe, 2006), chap. 3.

2. EMPEROR JIAJING (R. 1522–1566)

1. For a brief survey of Buddhism during the Jiajing period, see Jiang Wu, *Enlightenment in Dispute: The Reinvention of Chan Buddhism in Seventeenth-Century China* (Oxford: Oxford University Press, 2008), 21–45.

2. For Jiajing's infatuation with Daoism, see Miyagawa Hisayuki 宮川尚志, "Min no Kasei jidai no dōkyō" 明の嘉靖時代の道教, in *Dōkyō kenkyū ronshū: Dōkyō no shisō to bunka; Yoshioka hakushi kanreki kinen* 道教研究論集: 道教の思想と文化: 吉岡博士還暦記念, ed. Yoshioka Yoshitoyo Hakushi kanreki kinen ronshū kankōkai 吉岡義豊博士還暦記念論集刊行会 (Tokyo: Kokusho kankōkai, 1977); and He Xiaorong 何孝榮, "Ming Shizong jinfo" 明世宗禁佛, *Mingshi yanjiu* 明史研究, no. 7 (2001): 164–76.

3. For example, it is still controversial regarding Jiajing's influence on the development of Buddhism. Both Kubota Ryōen and Jiang Canteng believe that the influence was significant, while Du Changshun argues that it was superficial. See Kubota Ryōen 久保田量遠, *Chūgoku ju dō butsu sangyōshi ron* 中國儒道佛三教史論 (Kyoto: Kokusho kankōkai, 1986), 608–9; Jiang Canteng 江燦騰, *Wanming fojiao conglin gaige yu foxue zhengbian zhi yanjiu: Yi Hanshan Deqing de gaige shengya wei zhongxin* 晚明佛教叢林改革與佛學諍辯之研究: 以憨山德清的改革生涯為中心 (Taipei: Xin wenfeng chuban gongsi, 1990); Du Changshun 杜常順, *Mingdai gongting yu fojiao guanxi yanjiu* 明代宮廷與佛教關系研究 (Beijing: Zhongguo shehui kexue chubanshe, 2013), 125–26.

4. *Ming Shizong shilu* 明世宗實錄, 3:151.

5. Li Dongyang 李東陽 and Shen Shixing 申時行, eds., *Da Ming huidian* 大明會典 (Taipei: Wenhai chubanshe, 1985), 104:1578a. As for the dismantlement of illegitimate temples (*yinci* 淫祠) in the capital area, see Huanlun 幻輪, *Shijian jigulüe xuji* 釋鑑稽古略續集 2, in *T*, vol. 49, no. 2038, 949a3–5.

6. Since ancient times, people in the Huguang region appear to have been more superstitious than those in other regions in China. Jiajing's persistent devotion to religious Daoism, particularly his search for immortality, derived from the influence of the milieu of his childhood. See Chen Yunü 陳玉女, "Mindai bukkyō shakai no chiiki teki kenkyū—Kasei Manreki nenkan (1522–1620) o chūshin toshite" 明代仏教社會の地域的研究—嘉靖・萬曆年間 (1522–1620) を中心として" (Ph.D. diss., Kyushu University, 1995), 70–80. For the faith of Ming local princes in Daoism, see Richard G. Wang, "Ming Princes and Daoist Ritual," *T'oung Pao* 95, no. 1-3 (2009): 51–119.

7. Deng Shilong 鄧士龍, *Guochao diangu* 國朝典故 (Beijing: Beijing daxue chubanshe, 1993), 35:614–15.

8. Yang Tinghe 楊廷和, *Yang Shizhai ji* 楊實齋集, in *Huang Ming jingshi wenbian* 皇明經世文編 (Beijing: Zhonghua shuju, 1962), 121:1164.

9. Deng, *Guochao diangu*, 35:615.

10. Jiajing had little interest in the Quanzhen school, which had become prominent in northern China beginning in the Yuan dynasty.

11. For Shao Yuanjie, see Luther Carrington Goodrich and Chaoying Fang, eds., *Dictionary of Ming Biography, 1368–1644* (New York: Columbia University Press, 1976), 1169–70, and Ishida Kenji

石田憲司, "Kasei-chō dōkyōkai no konran ni tsuite: Shō Gensetsu, Tō Chūbun, to Chō Tenshi" 嘉靖朝道教界の混乱について: 邵元節、陶仲文と張天師, in *Mindai Chūgoku no rekishiteki isō: Yamane Yukio kyōju tsuitō kinen ronsō* 明代中国の歴史的位相: 山根幸夫教授追悼記念論叢 (Tokyo: Kyūko shoin, 2007), 267–86.

12. Shen Defu 沈德符, *Wanli yehuo bian buyi* 萬曆野獲編補遺 (repr., Beijing: Zhonghua shuju, 1959), 1:795.

13. Liu Ruoyu 劉若愚, *Zhuozhong zhi* 酌中志, in vol. 431 of *Xuxiu Siku quanshu* 續修四庫全書, ed. Gu Tinglong 顧廷龍 et al. (Shanghai: Shanghai guji chubanshe, 1995–2001), 16:520. For the scripture workshop, see Scarlett Jang, "The Eunuch Agency Directorate of Ceremonial and the Ming Imperial Publishing Enterprise," in *Culture, Courtiers, and Competition: The Ming Court (1368–1644)*, ed. David M. Robinson (Cambridge, Mass.: Harvard University Press, 2008), and Wei Zuhui 韋祖輝, "Ming silijian dazang jingchang de shengshuai" 明司禮監大藏經廠的盛衰, *Beijing shiyuan* 北京史苑, no. 3 (1985): 364–68.

14. Lu Rong 陸容, *Shuyuan zaji* 菽園雜記 (Beijing: Zhonghua shuju, 1985), 5:59.

15. For the Chaotian abbey, see Liu Dong 劉侗, *Dijing jingwu lüe* 帝京景物略 (Beijing: Beijing guji chubanshe, 1980), 4:184–87.

16. Deng, *Guochao diangu*, 35:636.

17. Tan Qian 談遷, *Guoque* 國榷 (Beijing: Zhonghua shuju, 1958), 53:3369.

18. The part from "僧道盛者" to "今天下" is missing in the *Da Ming Shizong su huangdi baoxun* 大明世宗肅皇帝寶訓 (Taipei: Zhongyang yanjiuyuan lishi yuyan yanjiusuo, 1967).

19. The character 無 is missing in the *Guochao dianhui*, 134:1626–27.

20. Both the *Mingshi* and the *Ming Shizong shilu* say that Jiajing ordered officials to check and abrogate Buddhist and Daoist monks lacking an ordination certificate, but the *Mingshi* has no reference concerning the prohibition of ordination and founding of privately sponsored temples. Instead, it says that the emperor approved Huo Tao's suggestion of destroying privately founded temples; *Mingshi* 明史 (1736; repr., Beijing: Zhonghua shuju, 1974), 196:5189.

21. Tan, *Guoque*, 53:3369. Other evidence substantiates this point. For example, see Zhang Xuan 張萱, *Xiyuan wenjian lu* 西園聞見錄, in *Xuxiu Siku quanshu*, 105:400, and *Nanhai xianzhi* 南海縣志 (1687), fasc. 11.

22. Xu Xueju 徐學聚, *Guochao dianhui* 國朝典彙 (Beijing: Beijing daxue chubanshe, 1993), 134:1628a.

23. For Yao Guangxiao, see *Mingshi*, 145:4079–82; Goodrich and Fang, *Dictionary of Ming Biography*, 1561–65; Makita Tairyō 牧田諦亮, "Dōen den shōkō—Yō Kōkō no shōgai" 道衍伝小稿—姚広孝の生涯, *Tōyōshi kenkyū* 東洋史研究 18, no. 2 (1959): 57–79; and Zheng Yonghua 鄭永華, *Yao Guangxiao shishi yanjiu* 姚廣孝史事研究 (Beijing: Renmin chubanshe, 2011).

24. *Ming Shizong shilu*, 116:2759–60.

25. "Dezu" was the posthumous title for Zhu Yuanzhang's great-great-grandfather.

26. *Ming Shizong shilu*, 116:2759.

27. Deng, *Guochao diangu*, 35:653.

28. *Ming Shizong shilu*, 132:3134–35.

29. Xu, *Guochao dianhui*, 134:1627.

30. Gu Yingtai 谷應泰, *Mingshi jishi benmo* 明史紀事本末 (Beijing: Zhonghua shuju, 1958), fasc. 52; *Ming Shizong shilu*, 174:3787.

31. Li and Shen, *Da Ming huidian*, 104:1578.

32. A case in point was Jiajing's unprecedented promotion of the Daoist Tao Zhongwen in 1541 and 1544; see *Mingshi*, 307:7896–97. For studies on Tao, see Goodrich and Fang, *Dictionary of Ming Biography*, 1266–68, and Barend ter Haar, "Tao Zhongwen 陶仲文: ca. 1481–1560; original *ming*: Tao Dianzhen," in *The Encyclopedia of Taoism*, ed. Fabrizio Pregadio (London: Routledge, 2008), 971–72.

33. Gu, *Mingshi jishi benmo*, 52:789.

34. *Ming Shizong shilu*, 313:5859–60.

35. *Ming Shizong shilu*, 562:10722.

36. Li and Shen, *Da Ming huidian*, 104:1578.

37. Tan, *Guoque*, 64:4030. This charge may be unfounded.

38. *Ming Shizong shilu*, 562:10722.

39. Barend J. ter Haar, *The White Lotus Teachings in Chinese Religious History* (Leiden: Brill, 1992), chap. 6. See also Daniel L. Overmyer, "Attitudes Toward the Ruler and State in Chinese Popular Religious Literature: Sixteenth and Seventeenth Century Pao-chüan," *HJAS* 44, no. 2 (1984): 347–79.

40. Zhang, *Xiyuan wenjian lu*, 105:395.

41. Yuan Hongdao 袁宏道, *Yuan Hongdao ji jianjiao* 袁宏道集箋校, ed. Qian Bocheng 錢伯城 (Shanghai: Shanghai guji chubanshe, 1981), 54:1556–57 (hereafter cited as *YHD*).

42. Hanyue Fazang 漢月法藏, *Hong jiefa yi* 弘戒法儀 2, in *X*, vol. 60, no. 11266, 12b1–12.

43. For efforts to reform the *saṃgha* in late-Ming China, see, for example, Chün-fang Yü, *The Renewal of Buddhism in China: Chu-hung and the Late Ming Synthesis* (New York: Columbia University Press, 1981), 192–231, and Jiang Canteng 江燦騰, *Wanming fojiao gaige shi* 晚明佛教改革史 (Guilin: Guangxi shifan daxue chubanshe, 2006), 119–90.

44. This paragraph is cited in He Xiaorong 何孝榮, *Mingdai Nanjing siyuan yanjiu* 明代南京寺院研究 (Beijing: Zhongguo shehui kexue chubanshe, 2000), 123–25.

45. Zhan Ruoshui 湛若水, *Quanweng daquan ji* 泉翁大全集 (Zhuming shuyuan, 1593), 82:1–21.

46. For more discussion about Zhan Ruoshui's efforts to prohibit the practice of cremating the dead, see Zhu Honglin 朱鴻林, "Mingdai Jiajing nianjian de Zengcheng *Shadi xiangyue* 明代嘉靖年間的增城沙堤鄉約, in *Kongmiao congsi yu xiangyue* 孔廟從祀與鄉約 (Beijing: Sanlian shudian, 2015), 292–360.

47. For this movement among Confucian scholars, see, for example, Chen Xiyuan 陳熙遠, "Zai guojia quanli yu minjian xinyang jiaojie de bianyuan: Yi Mingru Zhan Ruoshui jinhui Nanjing yinci wei lizheng" 在國家權力與民間信仰交界的邊緣: 以明儒湛若水禁毀南京淫祠為例證, in *Ming Qing falü yunzuo zhongde quanli yu wenhua* 明清法律運作中的權力與文化, ed. Qiu Pengsheng 邱澎生 and Chen Xiyuan (Taipei: Lianjing chuban shiye youxian gongsi, 2009), 87–143; Wang Jian 王健, "Lixue jianxing ji difang xiangying: Mingdai zhongye Jiangnan hui yinci shijian tanxi" 理學踐行及地方響應: 明代中葉江南毀淫祠事件探析, in *Zhongguo jinshi difang shehui zhongde zongjiao yu guojia* 中國近世地方社會中的宗教與國家, ed. Wang Gang 王崗 and Li Tiangang 李天剛 (Shanghai: Fudan daxue chubanshe, 2014), 54–68; and Zhu Honglin 朱鴻林, "Mingdai zhongqi difang shequ zhian chongjian lixiang zhi zhanxian: Shanxi Henan diqu suoxing xiangyue zhili" 明代中期地方社區治安重建理想之展現: 山西河南地區所行鄉約之例, in *Kongmiao congsi yu xiangyue*, 270–91.

48. *Wulin Da Zhaoqing lüsi zhi* 武林大昭慶律寺志, 2:40.

49. Zhenhua 震華, *Xu Biqiuni zhuan* 續比丘尼傳 (Taipei: Fojiao chubanshe, 1988), 3:53.

50. For the support the Wang Yangming school lent to Jiajing in the Great Rites Controversy, see Luo Zongqiang 羅宗強, *Mingdai houqi shiren xintai yanjiu* 明代後期士人心態研究, (Tianjin: Nankai daxue chubanshe, 2006), 113–48.

51. *WLYH*, 27:685.

52. Chen Yunü 陳玉女, *Mingdai de fojiao yu shehui* 明代的佛教與社會 (Beijing: Beijing daxue chubanshe, 2011), 60–95; Thomas Shiyu Li and Susan Naquin, "The Baoming Temple: Religion and the Throne in Ming and Qing China," *HJAS* 48, no. 1 (1988): 131–88. Unlike scholars who tend to use Jiajing's failure to argue how strong the protection of Buddhism was in the inner court, Chen shifts the focus to the emperor's motivation behind the campaign, aptly pointing out that it was part of his attacks against the privileged interest group left from previous ages.

53. John Dardess notes that "[Empress Dowager Zhangsheng] shared and surely reinforced her son's deep concern for ritual and etiquette, and that she and Jiajing were, at the same time, deeply devoted to one another, as a matter of sentiment. Jiajing's filial piety was not feigned" (*Four Seasons: A Ming*

Emperor and His Grand Secretaries in Sixteenth-Century China [Lanham, Md.: Rowman and Littlefield, 2016], 55).

54. The genre *baojuan* in Ming and Qing China has two major types, with one resembling folk literature and novels that recount stories and the other serving as a kind of "scripture" for popular sects that thrived at the time. Believed to have been divinely revealed to sect leaders, the second type of *baojuan* contains teachings and ritual instructions that help us better understand a lively, widespread, but oft-ignored religious tradition outside the mainstream "three teachings." For the most comprehensive study of *baojuan* so far, see Daniel L. Overmyer, *Precious Volumes: An Introduction to Chinese Sectarian Scriptures from the Sixteenth and Seventeenth Centuries* (Cambridge, Mass.: Harvard University Asia Center, 1999).

55. Liu, *Dijing jingwu lüe*, 5:215. Notably, Daoist nuns (女道尼) resided in the nunnery as well. See Jiang Yikui 蔣一葵, *Chang'an kehua* 長安客話 (Beijing: Beijing guji chubanshe, 1982), 3:60.

56. For the name list, see Yu Tao 于㯟, "Baomingsi zhong kao" 保明寺鍾攷, *Wenwu chunqiu* 文物春秋, no. 5 (2009): 71.

57. Zhang, *Xiyuan wenjian lu*, 105:400. There is, however, a lack of evidence of this large-scale destruction; Chen, "Mindai," 152, identifies only one instance in all of Beizhili.

58. *Ming Shizong shilu*, 83:1867.

59. For persecutions of Buddhism prior to the Ming, see, for example, Kenneth K. S. Ch'en, *Buddhism in China: A Historical Survey* (Princeton, N.J.: Princeton University Press, 1964), chap. 7; Kenneth K. S. Ch'en, "The Economic Background of the Hui-ch'ang Suppression of Buddhism," *HJAS* 19, no. 1/2 (1956): 67–105; and Makita Tairyō 牧田諦亮, "Goshū Sesō no bukkyō seisaku" 後周世宗の佛教政策, *Tōyōshi kenkyū* 東洋史研究 11, no. 3 (1951): 10–20.

60. For a survey of the economic crisis, see Denis Twitchett and Frederick W. Mote, eds., *The Cambridge History of China, Volume 7: The Ming Dynasty, 1368–1644, Part 1* (Cambridge: Cambridge University Press, 1988), 485–88.

61. *Mingshi*, 317:7896–98.

3. EMPRESS DOWAGER CISHENG (1545–1614)

1. Li Dongyang 李東陽 and Shen Shixing 申時行, eds., *Da Ming huidian* 大明會典 (Taipei: Wenhai chubanshe, 1985), 104:1578–79. See also Chen Yunü 陳玉女, "Ming Huayan zongpai Bianrong heshang ruyu kao—jianshu Long, Wan nianjian fojiao yu jingshi quangui de wanglai" 明華嚴宗派遍融和尚入獄攷—兼述隆、萬年間佛教與京師權貴的往來, in *Mingdai de fojiao yu shehui* 明代的佛教與社會 (Beijing: Beijing daxue chubanshe, 2011), 215–58.

2. For Cisheng's life, see *Mingshi* 明史 (1736; repr., Beijing: Zhonghua shuju, 1974), 114:3534–36, and Luther Carrington Goodrich and Chaoying Fang, eds., *Dictionary of Ming Biography, 1368–1644* (New York: Columbia University Press, 1976), 856–59. For Cisheng's political role, see, for example, Chen Yinque 陳寅恪, *Liu Rushi biezhuan* 柳如是別傳 (Beijing: Sanlian shudian, 2001), chap. 5. For Cisheng's relationship with Buddhism, see Susan Naquin, *Peking: Temples and City Life, 1400–1900* (Berkeley: University of California Press, 2000), 156–61, and Chen Yunü 陳玉女, "Ming Wanli shiqi Cisheng huang taihou de chongfo—jianlun fo, dao liang shili de duizhi" (明萬曆時期慈聖皇太后的崇佛—兼論佛、道兩勢力的對峙), in *Mingdai de fojiao yu shehui*, 96–146. For a general discussion of women's role in imperial Chinese politics, see Lien-sheng Yang, "Female Rulers in Imperial China," in *Excursions in Sinology*, Harvard-Yenching Institute Studies 24 (Cambridge, Mass.: Harvard University Press, 1969), 27–42.

3. For example, Cisheng was said to have read the Confucian classics, historical books, and the *Lengyan jing*. See *Ming chaoben Wanli qiju zhu* 明抄本萬曆起居注 (Beijing: Zhonghua quanguo

tushuguan wenxian suowei fuzhi zhongxin, 2001), 1:414, and Feng Mengzhen 馮夢槙, *Kuaixuetang ji* 快雪堂集, in *jibu* 集部, vols. 164–65, of *Siku Quanshu cunmu congshu* 四庫全書存目叢書, comp. Siku quanshu cunmu congshu bianzuan weiyuanhui 四庫全書存目叢書編纂委員會 (Jinan: Qilu shushe, 1994–1997), 56:769 (hereafter cited as *KXT*). It would be interesting to know how and to what degree education contributed to Cisheng's success in the inner court. After the sixteenth century, it was not uncommon for women from gentry families in southern China to receive an education, but Cisheng's case was unusual as she was brought up in a lower-class family in northern China.

4. *Mingshi*, 114:3535.

5. Wen Bing 文秉, *Dingling zhulüe* 定陵注略 (Taipei: Weiwen tushu chubanshe, 1976), 1:18.

6. *Ming chaoben*, 1:253–54, 261–67.

7. *Mingshi*, 113:3505.

8. *Ming Taizu shilu* 明太祖實錄, 52:1017–18. For the same reason, when the Hongwu emperor became seriously ill in the twelfth month of 1397, he ordered the suicide of a consort in hopes of precluding usurpers like Empress Wu (r. 690–705).

9. *Ming Taizu shilu*, 52:1017.

10. Denis Twitchett and Frederick W. Mote, eds., *The Cambridge History of China, Volume 8: The Ming Dynasty, 1368–1644, Part 2* (Cambridge: Cambridge University Press, 1998), 18, confirms that "the court was probably less troubled by palace women in Ming times than was the case in any other major dynasty."

11. A carved image of this bodhisattva can be found in Chün-fang Yü, *Kuan-yin: The Chinese Transformation of Avalokiteśvara* (New York: Columbia University Press, 2000), 147. For the mysterious origins of this image and its circulation, see *Ming chaoben*, 4:380–82, 469–70, and Hanshan Deqing 憨山德清, *Hanshan laoren mengyou ji* 憨山老人夢遊集 33, in *X*, vol. 73, no. 1456, 705c14–16 (hereafter cited as *HSMY*). Given that devotion to Guanyin was also popular in tantric Buddhism and in folk religion and that the so-called Nine-Lotus Bodhisattva had a strong flavor of folk religion, it is hard to tell to what extent this bodhisattva reflected Cisheng's belief in Pure Land Buddhism. Yü, *Kuan-yin*, 490–93, discusses problems related to Guanyin, gender, and Chinese belief in individuals perceived as incarnations of Guanyin.

12. Yü, *Kuan-yin*, 380.

13. *Mingshi*, 114:3536. It turned out that Empress Wang produced only a girl, in the twelfth month of 1581.

14. Zhu Quan 朱權 et al., *Ming gong ci* 明宮詞 (Beijing: Beijing guji chubanshe, 1987), 149.

15. Little information about Lady Wang is available, and some of it is misleading. For example, it has long been said that she was much older than the emperor, but the unearthing of her epitaph in 1958 reveals that she was three years younger. Moreover, her relationship with the emperor, at least in the first few years, was not as bad as people believed, for she had the chance to give birth to a daughter for the emperor in the seventh month of 1584.

16. *Beijing tushuguan cang zhongguo lidai shike taben huibian* 北京圖書館藏中國歷代石刻拓本彙編 (Zhengzhou: Zhongzhou guji chubanshe, 1989), vol. 59, 38 (hereafter cited as *SKHB*). As for Wanli's children and their mothers, including his fourth daughter, born to Lady Wang, see Liu Ruoyu 劉若愚, *Zhuozhong zhi* 酌中志, in vol. 431 of *Xuxiu Siku quanshu* 續修四庫全書, ed. Gu Tinglong 顧廷龍 et al. (Shanghai: Shanghai guji chubanshe, 1995–2001), 22:575.

17. It is unclear when Lady Zheng entered the inner court. In the eighth month of 1581 an edict was issued to select "nine consorts" (*jiupin* 九嬪), and, six months later when the results were announced, Lady Zheng was one of the winners. See *Ming Shenzong shilu* 明神宗實錄, 120:2245–46, 121:2276. However, Cheng Sizhang 程嗣章 says that Lady Zheng entered the inner court in 1578 when Wanli got married; see Zhu, *Ming gong ci*, 149.

18. According to Liu, *Zhuozhong zhi*, 22:575, Lady Zheng gave birth to Wanli's second, third (i.e., Zhu Changxun), and fourth sons and second and seventh daughters.

19. Wen Bing 文秉, *Xianbo zhishi* 先撥志始, in *shibu* 史部, vol. 437, of *Xuxiu Siku quanshu*, 1:588; Huang Jingfang 黃景昉, *Guoshi weiyi* 國史唯疑 (Taipei: Zhengzhong shuju, 1969), 11:697. See also *Mingshi*, 231:6040, 233:6089.

20. See, for example, *Mingshi*, 218:5753, 233:6072.

21. *SKHB*, vol. 58, 23–24.

22. Lin Qiaowei 林巧薇, "Beijng Dongyuemiao yu Ming Qing guojia jisi guanxi tanyan" 北京東嶽廟與明清國家祭祀關係探研, *Shijie zongjiao yanjiu* 世界宗教研究, no. 5 (2014): 61–71.

23. During the Ming, there were more than forty official sacrifices held at Mount Tai to pray for rain, the heir, or to declare the establishment of the crown prince and the enthronement of the emperor.

24. For the Sanyang abbey, see Nie Wen 聶鈫, *Taishan daoli ji* 泰山道里記, in *shibu* 史部, vol. 242, of *Siku Quanshu cunmu congshu*, 106.

25. These three stelae are cited in Wang Chuanming 王傳明 and Zhou Ying 周穎, "Mingdai gongting douzheng yu Taishan zhi guanxi" 明代宮廷鬥爭與泰山之關係, *Taishan yanjiu luncong* 泰山研究論叢, no. 5 (1992): 64–65.

26. Luo Zhufeng 羅竹風, ed., *Hanyu da cidian* 漢語大詞典 (Shanghai: Hanyu da cidian chubanshe, 1997), vol. 5, 601.

27. *Mingshi*, 235:6133; Huang, *Guoshi weiyi*, 10:638–39.

28. The *Guanyin lingke* instructs people to make divination by using copper coins. Various versions of it are still extant. See http://openarmed.blogspot.com/2009/08/blog-post_19.html.

29. Quotation from Xin Deyong 辛德勇, "Shu shiyin Ming Wanli keben *Guanshiyin ganying lingke*" 述石印明萬曆刻本《觀世音感應靈課》, *Zhongguo dianji yu wenhua* 中國典籍與文化, no. 3 (2004): 106–11.

30. Lady Zheng came to hate Cisheng to such a degree that in 1613 a eunuch serving Lady Zheng used black magic (*wugu* 巫蠱) to curse Zhu Changluo, Wanli, and Cisheng. See Gu Yingtai 谷應泰, *Mingshi jishi benmo* 明史紀事本末 (Beijing: Zhonghua shuju, 1958), 67:1073.

31. *SKHB*, vol. 58, 131–32.

32. *SKHB*, vol. 58, 61–62.

33. *SKHB*, vol. 57, 177–78.

34. *Ming Shenzong shilu*, 270:5248.

35. *Mingshi*, 305:7804; *WLYH*, 6:171.

36. Given that the princess was Wanli's first daughter by Empress Wang, building the temple may have been partly out of her gratitude to Cisheng for protecting her mother; see Yu Minzhong 于敏中 and Zhu Yizun 朱彝尊, *Rixia jiuwen kao* 日下舊聞攷 (Beijing: Beijing guji chubanshe, 1983), 60:955 (hereafter cited as *RXJW*).

37. Huang, *Guoshi weiyi*, 10:643, comments on this event.

38. Wen, *Dingling zhulüe*, 245.

39. See, for example, *RXJW*, 59:959, 110:1840.

40. *Mingshi*, 120:6233.

41. Wen, *Dingling zhulüe*, 417–20; *Mingshi*, 120:3650, 240:6232–33.

42. For the rise of Putuo Island in the Wanli period, see Ishino Kazuharu 石野一晴, "Mindai Banreki nenkan ni okeru Fudasan no fukkō—Chūgoku junreishi kenkyū josetsu" 明代萬曆年間における普陀山の復興—中國巡禮史研究序説, *Tōyōshi kenkyū* 東洋史研究 64, no. 1 (2005): 1–36. See also Marcus Bingenheimer, *Island of Guanyin: Mount Putuo and Its Gazetteers* (New York: Oxford University Press, 2016).

43. For Cisheng's interest in the *Lengyan jing*, see *KXT*, 56:769, and *HSMY* 30, in *X*, vol. 73, no. 1456, 680a6–8.5.

44. For the religious beliefs of Ming women, see Chen, *Mingdai de fojiao yu shehui*, 322–80.

45. For this sect, see Thomas Shiyu Li and Susan Naquin, "The Baoming Temple: Religion and the Throne in Ming and Qing China," *HJAS* 48, no. 1 (1988): 131–88.

46. Beginning in the mid-Ming, a high percentage of court elites, including eunuchs and court women, came from places close to Beijing where popular religion was widespread.

47. See, for example, *RXJW*, 59:959, and *SKHB*, vol. 58, 186–87.

48. The Beijing area and Shanxi had much in common because of their geographical proximity and shared history after the Tang when they fell into the hands of non-Chinese regimes. I chose these three prefectures as a unit of analysis for two reasons: First, Buddhism had been rooted deeply there since the medieval era. Second, they must have become even closer in religious beliefs after hundreds of thousands of people were moved to the Beijing area from Shanxi, especially Taiyuan prefecture, in the early Ming. See Yamazaki Hiroshi 山崎宏, *Shina chūsei bukkyō no tenkai* 支那中世仏教の展開 (Tokyo: Shimizu shoten, 1942), 241. For the large-scale relocation of Shanxi people, see *Ming Taizu shilu*, 62:1199, and *Ming Taizong shilu* 明太宗實錄, 12b:217. For a summary of relocation schemes imposed by the Ming court between 1364 and 1405, see Timothy Brook, *The Confusions of Pleasure: Commerce and Culture in Ming China* (Berkeley: University of California Press, 1998), 28–29, 268n23.

49. Jiangnan, both a geographic and a cultural concept, is hard to define precisely. Geographically, this region typically consists of eight prefectures and one subprefecture as designated in the Ming—Suzhou, Songjiang, Changzhou, Zhenjiang, Yingtian, Hangzhou, Jiaxing, Huzhou, and Taichang 太倉. But in a broader sense, it includes Shaoxing 紹興 and Ningbo 寧波 on the south, a definition that I follow in this study, or even Yangzhou 揚州 north of the Yangtze River. See, for example, Li Bozhong 李伯重, "Jianlun 'Jiangnan diqu' de jieding" 簡論"江南地區"的界定, *Zhongguo shehui jingji shi yanjiu* 中國社會經濟史研究, no. 1 (1991): 100–107, and Antonia Finnane, *Speaking of Yangzhou: A Chinese City, 1550–1850* (Cambridge, Mass.: Harvard University Press, 2004), 29–30, 339n55.

    Also, it is worth noting that Jiangnan is one of the nine physiographic macroregions that William Skinner, on the basis of what he called regional systems analysis (RSA), defined and delimited for agrarian China in the late Qing. This macroregion concept, later further developed by Shiba Yoshinobu 斯波义信, was praised by Paul Cohen as "a new conceptual vocabulary that enables us to look at old problems in new ways and to see connectedness where previously we had been blind to it" (G. William Skinner, ed., *The City in Late Imperial China* [Stanford, Calif.: Stanford University Press, 1977]; Paul A. Cohen, *Discovering History in China: American Historical Writing on the Recent Chinese Past* [New York: Columbia University Press, 1984], 165; Shiba Yoshinobu, *Sōdai Kōnan keizai shi no kenkyū* 宋代江南経済史の研究 [Tokyo: Tokyo daigaku shuppankai, 1988], 30–45).

50. Fewer than ten names appear on the stelae erected after 1594 commemorating Cisheng's contribution.

51. See, for example, *RXJW*, 59:959.

52. For studies on the Buddhist canons produced in the Ming, see Li Fuhua 李富華 and He Mei 何梅, *Hanwen fojiao dazangjing yanjiu* 漢文佛教大藏經研究 (Beijing: Zongjiao wenhua chubanshe, 2003), chaps. 9–10. See also Nozawa Yoshimi 野沢佳美, *Mindai daizōkyō shi no kenkyū: Nanzō no rekishigakuteki kiso kenkyū* 明代大藏經史の研究: 南藏の歷史學的基礎研究 (Tokyo: Kyūko shoin, 1998), and Hasebe Yūkei 長谷部幽蹊, "Mindai ikō ni okeru zōkyō no kaichō" 明代以降における藏経の開雕, *Aichigakuin daigaku ronsō, ippan kyōiku kenkyū* 愛知學院大學論叢, 一般教育研究 30, no. 3 (1983): 793–813; 31, no. 1 (1983–1984): 3–28; 31, no. 2 (1984): 185–211.

53. *HSMY* 29, in *X*, vol. 73, no. 1456, 668b14–15.

54. For recent studies on the bestowal of the Ming northern canon, see He Xiaorong 何孝榮, *Mingdai Beijing fojiao siyuan xiujian yanjiu* 明代北京佛教寺院修建研究 (Tianjin: Nankai daxue chubanshe,

2007), 317–22; Nozawa Yoshimi 野沢佳美, "Mindai hokuzō kō 1: Kashi jōkyō o chūshin ni" 明代北藏考(一): 下賜状況を中心に, *Risshō daigaku bungakubu ronsō* 立正大学文学部論叢 117 (2003): 81–106; and Dewei Zhang, "Where the Two Worlds Met: Spreading the Ming Beizang 明北藏 in Wanli (1573–1620) China," *Journal of the Royal Asiatic Society*, 3rd ser., 26, no. 3 (2016): 487–508.

55. *Jizu shanzhi* 雞足山志, 8:474.

56. *Jizu shanzhi*, 8:475.

57. *Qingliang shanzhi* 清涼山志, 7:221.

58. *Jizu shanzhi*, 8:474.

59. *Jizu shanzhi*, 8:475.

60. *Qingliang shanzhi*, 7:222.

61. During the wars against Japan, the Ming government sent more than 166,700 soldiers to Korea and spent more than 17 million taels of silver in total, or 2.4 million taels a year—more than two-fifths its annual income. See Li Guangtao 李光濤, "*Chaoxian renchen wohuo shiliao* xuwen" 《朝鮮王辰倭禍史料》序文, *Zhongyang yanjiu yuan lishi yuyan yanjiusuo shiliao jikan* 中央研究院歷史語言研究所史料集刊 37a (1967): 167.

62. Yunqi Zhuhong, *Yunqi fahui* 雲棲法彙, in *JXZ*, vol. 33, no. B277, 195b19–20. (Note: the *Jiaxing* canon consists of four sections, and in order to distinguish the continued section [*xuzang* 續藏] from the formal section [*zhengzang* 正藏], the locator numbers in the former are prefixed with the letter B.)

63. For a discussion of Cisheng's expenditures on Buddhism, see Chen, "Ming Wanli shiqi Cisheng," 209–20. Naquin, *Peking*, 169n145, says that "Ray Huang has noted that Empress Dowager Li had an annual income from palace estates of nearly fifty thousand ounces of silver. If the preceding estimates are roughly correct, this sum could have accommodated even her energetic religious activities." For the figures she mentions, see Ray Huang, *Taxation and Governmental Finance in Sixteenth-Century Ming China* (London: Cambridge University Press, 1974), 303, 325. However, Naquin did not notice that this figure included Empress Dowager Rensheng's income as well.

64. For other cases in which Cisheng prayed for the benefit of her oldest grandson, see, for example, Mizang Daokai 密藏道開, *Mizang Kai chanshi yigao* 密藏開禪師遺稿 1, in *JXZ*, vol. 23, no. B118, 11b21–24 (hereafter cited as *MKCY*).

65. Yu Tao 于㧟, "Baomingsi zhong kao" 保明寺鍾玫, *Wenwu chunqiu* 文物春秋, no. 5 (2009): 73–74.

66. *HSMY* 29, in *X*, vol. 73, no. 1456, 668b8–11.

67. *SKHB*, vol. 56, 109. As discussed in chapter 4, the low profile of these powerful people was characteristic of the eunuchs' patronage of Buddhism in the final years of the Jiajing era.

68. *HSMY* 29, in *X*, vol. 73, no. 1456, 668a22–b2

69. *HSMY* 29, in *X*, vol. 73, no. 1456, 670c4–5. A "substitute monk" was one who, as a substitute for a newborn prince, resided in a temple to educated according to the Buddhist teachings. This practice was popular in the Ming but elicited criticism. See Kong Lingbin 孔令彬, "Fojiao zhong 'tiseng' xianxiang kaolüe" 佛教中"替僧"現象考略, *Zongjiao xue yanjiu* 宗教學研究, no.2 (2011): 76–79.

70. *HSMY* 21, in *X*, vol. 73, no. 1456, 617a18–22.

71. They were Yanshousi 延壽寺, Haihuisi 海會寺, Cheng'ensi 承恩寺, Puansi 普安寺, Xiyushuanglinsi 西域雙林寺, Cishousi 慈壽寺, Cishansi 慈善寺, and Wanshousi 萬壽寺.

72. One *li* in the Ming dynasty was about one-third mile.

73. The *Luoyang qielan ji* by Yang Xuanzhi 楊衒之 (fl. 547) is well known for its detailed description of the prosperity of Buddhism in Luoyang during the Northern Wei dynasty (386–534). For an English translation of the book, see Yang Hsüan-chih, *A Record of Buddhist Monasteries in Lo-Yang*, trans. Yi-t'ung Wang (Princeton, N.J.: Princeton University Press, 2014).

74. *WLYH* 27:686–87.

75. *HSMY* 22, in *X*, vol. 73, no. 1456, 621b6–15.

76. *Qingliang shanzhi*, 2:77.

77. For another example regarding the relationship between Cisheng and Mount Wutai, see James A. Benn, *Burning for the Buddha: Self-Immolation in Chinese Buddhism* (Honolulu: University of Hawai`i Press, 2007), 233–34.

78. An edict was issued in 1581 announcing a land-tax exemption for the entire Wutai Buddhist community, which was very likely aimed to help Cisheng initiate her connection with the sacred mountain.

79. They were the Prince of Shen and the Prince of Dai, whose patronage of Buddhism are mentioned again in chapter 5.

80. *HSMY* 29, in *X*, vol. 73, no. 1456, 669c13–20.

81. Longquansi was founded in the Jiajing era by Master Wuzhuding 無住定 (dates unknown), who once studied at Shaolinsi 少林寺. Later, Wuzhu's disciple Yunya 雲崖 (d. 1582), a native of Baoding and versed in the precepts, went to Beijing and rebuilt Sanshengsi 三聖寺. Five years after Yunya's death in 1585, his Dharma grandson Yongqing inherited Sanshengsi, and then Cisheng stepped in, sponsoring the temple's renovation and renaming the temple Mingyinsi. See *RXJW*, 58:947, and *HSMY* 22, in *X*, vol. 73, no. 1456, 620b21–c6.

82. On Yongqing, see Zibo Zhenke 紫柏真可, *Zibo zunzhe bieji* 紫柏尊者別集 1, in *X*, vol. 73, no. 1453, 408c21.

83. Apart from monks, eunuchs were included in the escort as well. For those canons granted by Wanli, however, monks were excluded in most cases. It seems that this difference derived from the fact that Cisheng's bestowal was organized, to a large part, by eminent monks themselves. For example, see Zhenke, *Zibo zunzhe bieji* 3, in *X*, vol. 73, no. 1453, 424c9–16.

84. *KXT*, 47:667–68, 671.

85. *Jizu shanzhi*, 4:262, 6:401–2.

86. *HSMY* 22, in *X*, vol. 73, no. 1456, 619a12–b7.

87. *Ming Shenzong shilu*, 24:618.

88. *Mingshi*, 227:5958. See also Zhang Xuan 張萱, *Xiyuan wenjian lu* 西園聞見錄, in vols. 1168–70 of *Xuxiu Siku quanshu*, 105:396.

89. *Ming Shenzong shilu*, 2:22.

90. *Ming Shenzong shilu*, 84:1794; Tan Qian 談遷, *Guoque* 國榷 (Beijing: Zhonghua shuju, 1958), 70:4341.

91. The ordination platform that Jiajing closed would not reopen until 1617. See *Qingliang shanzhi*, 3:146–48. Before the formal reopening, thanks to its relationship with Cisheng, the Wanshou ordination platform at Zhaoqingsi had at least one opportunity to confer the precepts in 1588. See Yu Meian 喻昧庵, *Xinxu gaosengzhuan siji* 新續高僧傳四集 (Taipei: Liuli jingfang, 1967), 43:908.

4. THE EUNUCHS

1. Susan Naquin has pointed out that even in Beijing, for example, "although the presence of the emperor was a distinguishing characteristic of the capital, outside the imperial domain the throne had direct involvement in only 10 percent of the city's temples" (*Peking: Temples and City Life, 1400–1900* [Berkeley: University of California Press, 2000], 58–59).

2. The Jianzhang palace, built by Emperor Wu (r. 141–87 BCE) of the Western Han in 104 BCE, was one of the three major palaces in the Han dynasty.

3. *Ming Xianzong shilu* 明憲宗實錄, 260:5229. See also *Tanzheshan Xiuyun sizhi* 潭柘山岫雲寺志, 13–14, and *RXJW*, 60:986–87.

4. Lu Rong 陸容, *Shuyuan zaji* 菽園雜記 (Beijing: Zhonghua shuju, 1985), 5:59.

5.   Liu Ruoyu 劉若愚. *Zhuozhong zhi* 酌中志, in vol. 431 of *Xuxiu Siku quanshu* 續修四庫全書, ed. Gu Tinglong 顧廷龍 et al. (Shanghai: Shanghai guji chubanshe, 1995–2001), 22:575.

6.   For the relations of the eunuchs and the Beijing *saṃgha*, Chen Yunü's studies deserve particular attention as they have uncovered the economic nature behind the cooperation between the eunuchs and monks; see in particular Chen Yunü 陳玉女, *Mingdai ershi si yamen huanguan yu beijing fojiao* 明代二十四衙門宦官與北京佛教 (Taipei: Ruwen chubanshe, 2001).

7.   See He Xiaorong 何孝榮, *Mingdai Beijing fojiao siyuan xiujian yanjiu* 明代北京佛教寺院修建研究 (Tianjin: Nankai daxue chubanshe, 2007), 757–68. He defines the Beijing area as consisting of Wanping 宛平 and Daxing 大興 counties. According to him, 144 temples and chapels were built, rebuilt, or renovated in Beijing in the Jiajing era, 18 in the Longqing era, and 136 in the Wanli era. It is worth noting that when he discusses these temples in his chap. 5 (564–93), these figures become 104, 14, and 85, respectively. No explanation is offered for the discrepancies.

8.   For the assessed contribution of different social groups to Beijing temples during the Ming and Qing periods, see Naquin, *Peking*, 58–59.

9.   Susan Naquin, "Sites, Saints, and Sights at the Tanzhe Monastery," *Cahiers d'Extrême-Asie*, no. 10 (1998): 188.

10.   Naquin, *Peking*, 180.

11.   Chen, *Mingdai ershi si yamen*, 195–240. On pages 70–82 Chen lists 144 Beijing temples that were (re)built or renovated under the sponsorship of Ming eunuchs, but the list is still incomplete.

12.   Chen, *Mingdai ershi si yamen*, 114.

13.   He Xiaorong 何孝榮, *Mingdai Nanjing siyuan yanjiu* 明代南京寺院研究 (Beijing: Zhongguo she-hui kexue chubanshe, 2000), 107.

14.   Timothy Brook, "The Politics of Religion: Late-Imperial Origins of the Regulatory State," in *Making Religion, Making the State: The Politics of Religion in Modern China*, ed. Yoshiko Ashiwa and David L. Wank (Stanford, Calif.: Stanford University Press, 2009), 30–31.

15.   Naquin, *Peking*, 175. Naquin also has an excellent discussion about Beijing's double identity and its significance for the development of this city (171–79).

16.   For the relationship between Beijing temples and nonresidents, see Naquin, *Peking*, 177, 193.

17.   Lu Guangzu 陸光祖 (1521–1597, *jinshi* 1547) alone contributed to two projects, one in the late Jiajing era and the other in the early Wanli era. See *Tanzheshan Xiuyun sizhi*, 14–15, and Yu Meian 喻昧庵, *Xinxu gaosengzhuan siji* 新續高僧傳四集 (Taipei: Liuli jingfang, 1967), 7:328, 20:679, 691.

18.   *Foshuo zuiye yingbao jiaohua diyu jing* 佛說罪業應報教化地獄經 1, in *T*, vol. 17, no. 724, 451c21–22.

19.   Eugene Wang, "Of the True Body: The Buddha's Relics and Corporeal Transformation in Tang Imperial Culture," in *Body and Face in Chinese Visual Culture*, ed. Wu Hung and Katherine T. Mino (Cambridge, Mass.: Harvard University Press, 2004), 117–18.

20.   Jinhua Chen, "The Tang Buddhist Palace Chapels," *Journal of Chinese Religions* 32, no.1 (2004): 155.

21.   *Huayan jing zhuanji* 華嚴經傳記 1, in *T*, vol. 51, no. 2073, 156c18–27. Fazang said that the event happened in the Dahe (大和) era, but no such reign title existed in Northern Qi. It might refer to Taihe 太和 (477–500) in Northern Wei. For a detailed study of the story, see Liu Shufen 劉淑芬, *Zhonggu de fojiao yu shehui* 中古的佛教與社會 (Shanghai: Shanghai guji chubanshe, 2008), 47–53.

22.   *HSMY* 31, in *X*, vol. 73, no. 1456, 685a20.

23.   *Guang Qingliang zhuan* 廣清涼傳 2, in *T*, vol. 51, no. 2099, 1112c12–13.

24.   As for the three scripture workshops, see Liu, *Zhuozhong zhi*, 16:520.

25.   Liu, *Zhuozhong zhi*, 16:525.

26.   So far Chen Yunü has made the most important contribution to this field, from which I have drawn much inspiration.

27.   *Ming Xiaozong shilu* 明孝宗實錄, 174:3184–85. For the notion of "field of merit," see, in the present volume, chap. 6, n. 135.

28. *Ren* was a Chinese unit of measure whose length varied. It was about six feet in the Zhou dynasty (ca. 1046–256 BCE). The term *jiuren* is usually used to describe a place extremely high or deep.

29. Shen Bang 沈榜, *Wanshu zaji* 宛署雜記 (Beijing: Beijing guji chubanshe, 1980), 20:256.

30. Eunuchs' sponsorship could move in the opposite direction, however. The cases are not few in which a eunuch first met a Buddhist master whom he believed deserved to have a temple. Then, the eunuch petitioned the emperor to grant the temple a name tablet and to appoint the monk as a monastic official residing there. Once the request was sanctioned, a "protection edict" and other official documents were then issued by the Ministry of Rites.

31. *Ming Shizong shilu*, 118:2815.

32. *Shuntian fuzhi* 順天府志 (1886), 17:548.

33. Xin Xiuming 信修明, *Lao taijian de huiyi* 老太監的回憶 (Beijing: Yanshan chubanshe, 1987), 93–94.

34. Some large cemeteries were thus formed. For example, by the early twentieth century, the Enji estate (*Enji zhuang* 恩濟莊) had more than five thousand stone stelae and twenty-six hundred tombs for eunuchs; Xin, *Lao taijian de huiyi*, 90–91.

35. *SKHB*, vol. 55, 145–46.

36. For the administrative system of eunuchs, see Shen Defu 沈德符, *Wanli yehuo bian buyi* 萬曆野獲編補遺 (1616; repr., Beijing: Zhonghua shuju, 1959), 1:814–15.

37. Chen Yunü 陳玉女, "Mingdai ershi si yamen de fojiao xingyang" 明代二十四衙門的佛教信仰, *Chenggong daxue lishi xuebao* 25 (1999): 190–91.

38. *Mingshi* 明史 (1736; repr., Beijing: Zhonghua shuju, 1974), 305:7804.

39. Liu, *Zhuozhong zhi*, 14:483.

40. For the way in which a *nianfo hui* was organized, see Chen, *Mingdai ershi si yamen*, 211–13.

41. *SKHB*, vol. 58, 101–2.

42. David Robinson, "Notes on Eunuchs in Hebei During the Mid-Ming Period," *Ming Studies* 34, no. 1 (1995): 1–16. Notably, this understanding of Ming eunuchs derives from a major shift in the understanding of local elites in late-imperial China. From the 1950s to the 1970s, local elites were considered a homogeneous group of scholar-officials who, with power coming directly from the imperial state, were believed to have worked for the state as government officials and local leaders. Starting in the mid-1980s, however, a broader understanding of local elites has emerged, taking them as a diverse group of degree holders who did not necessarily work for the imperial government. This expansion of the meaning of local elites has not only led to research on various forms of local organization, such as market towns, charity, lineages, and religions, but has also called attention to regional variation in elite types, whose power came from a variety of sources, including commerce, landownership, local militia, philanthropy, and rituals. For these newer studies, see, for example, Robert Hymes, *Statesmen and Gentlemen: The Elite of Fu-Chou, Chiang-Hsi, in Northern and Southern Sung* (New York: Cambridge University Press, 1986); Beverly J. Bossler, *Powerful Relations: Kinship, Status, and the State in Sung China (960–1279)* (Cambridge, Mass.: Council on East Asian Studies, 1998); Peter K. Bol, "The Rise of Local History: History, Geography, and Culture in Southern Song and Yuan Wuzhou," *HJAS* 61, no. 1 (2001): 37–76"; and Chang Woei Ong, *Men of Letters within the Passes: Guanzhong Literati in Chinese History, 907–1911* (Cambridge, Mass.: Harvard University Asia Center, 2008).

43. Even before the Jingtai era, there were cases in which officials or eunuchs castrated children from ordinary families, with some finally taken into the inner court; see Shen, *Wanli yehuo bian buyi*, 1:820.

44. Shen, *Wanli yehuo bian buyi*, 1:815–17; Gu Yanwu 顧炎武, *Rizhilu jishi: Wai qizhong* 日知錄集釋: 外七種, annot. Huang Rucheng 黃汝成 (Shanghai: Shanghai guji chubanshe, 1985), 9:771–75.

45. *Mingshi*, 183:4856.

46. *WLYH*, 24:613. Yu Jin 余金 claimed that there were a hundred thousand eunuchs by the fall of the dynasty, but this figure has recently been denied as exaggeration by Hu Dan 胡丹, who argues that the number of Ming eunuchs usually fluctuated between ten thousand and fifteen thousand and was never more than thirty thousand; Yu Jin, *Xichao xinyu* 熙朝新語 (Taipei: Wenhai chubanshe, 1985), 4:143–44; Hu Dan, *Mingdai huanguan zhidu yanjiu* 明代宦官制度研究 (Hangzhou: Zhejiang daxue chubanshe, 2018), 354–57.

47. *SKHB*, vol. 53, 37.

48. *SKHB*, vol. 58, 7–8.

49. *SKHB*, vol. 53, 5.

50. *SKHB*, vol. 53, 105.

51. *SKHB*, vol. 54, 144.

52. Chen, "Mingdai ershi si yamen," 236.

53. *Qing Shengzu shilu* 清聖祖實錄 (Taipei: Huawen chubanshe, 1964), 240:10a; Chen Yuanlong 陳元龍, *Airi tang shiji* 愛日堂詩集, in *jibu* 集部, vol. 254, of *Siku quanshu cunmu congshu* 四庫全書存目叢書, comp. Siku quanshu cunmu congshu bianzuan weiyuanhui 四庫全書存目叢書編纂委員會 (Jinan: Qilu shushe, 1994–1997), 20:14.

54. Tian Qi 田奇, *Beijing de fojiao simiao* 北京的佛教寺廟 (Beijing: Shumu wenxian chubanshe, 1993), 2–3.

55. For example, see *SKHB*, vol. 71, 115; vol. 73, 92; vol. 82, 58; vol. 83, 81; vol. 85, 8.

56. These eunuchs coming from Hubei would maintain a tight hold on almost all key positions in the twenty-four yamens related to eunuchs throughout the Jiajing era, and this kind of replacement was not without precedents. See Liang Shaojie 梁紹傑, ed., *Mingdai huanguan beizhuan lu* 明代宦官碑傳錄 (Hong Kong: Xianggang daxue zhongwenxi, 1997), 154, 156.

57. For the danger facing patrons, there is the case related to Tianningsi 天寧寺 in Beijing. A censor suggested in 1546 that both its leading monks and major patrons be arrested. See *Ming Shizong shilu*, 313:5859–60.

58. It seems that Wang Zhen composed the inscription commemorating the completion of this project. Interestingly, his personal name 振 was gouged out and replaced with 鎮, a character with a similar pronunciation, which may have happened after 1449 and as a result of his being blamed for the Tumubao debacle.

59. Zhenwu allegedly helped both Hongwu and Yongle to establish their reigns. Thus he was worshipped as an imperial guardian god at the Qin'an 欽安 hall in the Forbidden City throughout the Ming. The cult of Zhenwu also took shape by taking Mount Wudang in Hubei as its base. See Willem A. Grootaers, "The Hagiography of the Chinese God Chen-wu," *Folklore Studies* 11, no. 2 (1952): 139–81.

60. This was not the only Buddhist temple that included a Daoist image or structure within its walls as a way of protecting itself. For another instance, see Dahuisi 大慧寺 in *Shuntian fuzhi* (1886), 17:548–49.

61. For the two stelae, see *SKHB*, vol. 56, 12, 114.

62. One example can be seen in *Songshu* 嵩書, ed. Zhengzhou shi tushuguan 郑州市圖書館 (Zhengzhou: Zhongzhou guji chubanshe, 2003), 538, and another in *Putuo Luojiashan xinzhi* 普陀洛迦山新志, 4:212–14.

63. *SKHB*, vol. 58, 104.

64. Cisheng once ordered a eunuch surnamed Jiang to build a temple on Mount Funiu 伏牛, a critical site for Chan Buddhism in the Ming, especially the mid-Ming. Very likely this eunuch was Jiang Dayin. See *HSMY* 22, in *X*, vol. 73, no. 1456, 621c14–18.

65. *HSMY* 29, in *X*, vol. 73, no. 1456, 671a11–13.

66. *SKHB*, vol. 59, 125.

67. *WLYH*, 27:686–87.

68. Chen Yunü 陳玉女, *Mingdai de fojiao yu shehui* 明代的佛教與社會 (Beijing: Beijing daxue chubanshe, 2011), 101–22.

69. *Ziyi* was also called *zifu* 紫服 and *zijiasa* 紫袈裟. The bestowal of the purple robe was popular in Tang China and Japan. For discussion of the history and function of the robe, see Nakamura Hajime 中村元, *Bukkyōgo daijiten* 佛教語大辭典 (Tokyo: Tōkyō shoseki, 1975), 546a.

70. For this story, see Huanlun, *Shijian jigulüe xuji* 釋鑑稽古略續集 3, in *T*, vol. 49, no. 2038, 951b5–9. The eunuch involved was Zhang Ben; see *FCZ*, 4:521.

71. *Wulin Lingyin sizhi* 武林靈隱寺志, 5:246.

72. For an example, see *KXT*, 42:603–4, 58:41.

73. *Qingliang shanzhi* 清涼山志, 7:220, says that this event occurred in the first month of 1582.

74. Huang Zongxi 黃宗羲, *Ming wenhai* 明文海 (Beijing: Zhonghua shuju, 1987), 73:685.

75. See *FCZ*, 4:521; *Emei shanzhi* 峨嵋山志, 6:233; *Mingzhou Ayuwang shanzhi* 明州阿育王山志, 8a:374; and *Putuo luojia xinzhi*, 4:209.

76. *WLYH*, 27:692.

77. It is still unclear if Zhang Ben was executed, because it seems that, as late as 1602, Zhenke was still trying to save the eunuch. See Zibo Zhenke 紫柏真可, *Zibo zunzhe bieji* 紫柏尊者別集, in *X*, vol. 73, no. 1453431c22–24.

78. As for Ming eunuchs' belief in Daoism, see Chen, *Mingdai de fojiao*, 125n2.

79. *RXJW*, 41:639.

80. Even in 1607 Wanli had Zhang Guoxiang 張國祥 (d. 1611) compile and carve the continuation of the Daoist canon (*Xu daozang* 續道藏). Chen Yunü discusses Wanli's belief in Daoism in *Mingdai de fojiao*, 123–26, and in "Mindai bukkyō shakai no chiiki teki kenkyū—Kasei Manreki nenkan (1522–1620) o chūshin toshite" 明代仏教社會の地域的研究—嘉靖・萬曆年間 (1522–1620) を中心として (Ph.D. diss., Kyushu University, 1995), 130–39. Her reliance on Deqing's autobiography annotated by Fuzheng, however, has left her discussion open to question.

81. *SKHB*, vol. 56, 168–69.

82. *SKHB*, vol. 57, 40–41.

83. *SKHB*, vol. 57, 134–35.

84. *SKHB*, vol. 57, 177–78, 188–89. Notably, a stela was also established in another Dongyue temple in Beijing in the same year (187).

85. In an extreme instance, for example, the patrons were all palace ladies without a single eunuch involved, and the palace ladies' patronage was all by Cisheng's order. See *SKHB*, vol. 57, 141–42.

86. Partly because of this, by the final year of the Wanli era, there were still around eight hundred names carved on a stela at this temple; see *SKHB*, vol. 59, 155. As time passed, the contribution of common people was on the rise, which would ensure that the Dongyue cult continued to thrive throughout the Qing dynasty.

87. Liu, *Zhuozhong zhi*, 22:577.

88. Liang, *Mingdai huanguan beizhuan lu*, 68, 302. Wang Yan repaired and (re)built at least twelve Buddhist temples in his later years. See Wang Chunyu 王春瑜 and Du Wanyan 杜婉言, *Mingchao huanguan* 明朝宦官 (Xi'an: Shanxi renmin chubanshe, 2007), 244.

89. Zhao Shiyu 趙世瑜 has traced changes in Gangtie's image during the Ming dynasty; *Kuanghuan yu richang: Ming Qing yilai de miaohui yu minjian shehui* 狂歡與日常: 明清以來的廟會與民間社會 (Beijing: Sanlian shudian, 2002), 325–31.

90. *SKHB*, vol. 53, 35.

91. *SKHB*, vol. 54, 191.

92. For a brief biography of Gao Zhong, see *Mingshi*, 304:7795. For Mai Fu, see Qi Chang 齊暢, *Gongnei, chaoting yu bianjiang: Shehuishi shiye xiade Mingdai huanguan yanjiu* 宮內、朝廷與邊疆: 社會史視野下的明代宦官研究 (Beijing: Zhongguo shehui kexue chubanshe, 2014), 101–40.

93. *SKHB*, vol. 55, 155.

94. *Mingshi*, 304:7795.

95. *Shuntian fuzhi* (1886), 17:548–49.

96. Some believe that the term *heishan hui* 黑山會 refers to the place where Gangtie was buried, while others claim that it means gathering at Heishan 黑山, where Gangtie's grave was. See Zhao, *Kuanghuan yu richang*, 332.

97. *SKHB*, vol. 55, 155.

98. It continued to be used by eunuchs as a cemetery in the Qing; see, for example, *SKHB*, vol. 87, 87.

99. *SKHB*, vol. 58, 195.

100. Zhao, *Kuanghuan yu richang*, 346–47, points out that during the Qing eunuchs would no longer express such feelings, and Gangtie was seen only as an ancestral god. This change had much to do with their forced retreat from the political arena.

101. Wang Shizhen 王世貞, *Yanshantang bieji* 弇山堂別集 (Beijing: Zhonghua shuju, 1985), 90:1728.

102. *Mingshi*, 304:7795.

103. *Mingshi*, 305:7831.

104. *SKHB*, vol. 65, 182.

105. *SKHB*, vol. 90, 208.

5. SCHOLAR-OFFICIALS

1. Benjamin A. Elman, *A Cultural History of Civil Examinations in Late Imperial China* (Berkeley: University of California Press, 2000).

2. Peter K. Bol, *Neo-Confucianism in History* (Cambridge, Mass.: Harvard University Press, 2008). Notably, Bol thus defines neo-Confucians as "people who identified themselves as participants in the intellectual streams that emerged from the philosophical teachings of the eleventh-century brothers Cheng Yi [程頤] and Cheng Hao [程顥]; to the doctrines on human morality, human nature, and the cosmos developed from that foundation; and to the social activities that linked adherents of these views together and allowed them to put their ideas into practice" (78).

3. Confucians based their claim of the right on the so-called succession to the Way (*daotong* 道統), which was reported to have been passed down from ancient sages. See Benjamin A. Elman, "The Formation of 'Dao Learning' as Imperial Ideology During the Early Ming Dynasty," in *Culture and State in Chinese History: Conventions, Accommodations, and Critiques*, ed. Theodore Huters, Roy Bin Wong, and Pauline Yu (Stanford, Calif.: Stanford University Press, 1997), 58–82, and Thomas A. Wilson, *Genealogy of the Way: The Construction and Uses of the Confucian Tradition in Late Imperial China* (Stanford, Calif.: Stanford University Press, 1995).

4. Based on Fuzhou materials, Robert Hymes has argued that elite society underwent a sea change during the Northern–Southern Song transition, from a capital-centered elite characterized by long-distance marriage alliances, to local elites that were focused on their own localities and largely alienated from the government. This shift of localization has been widely debated by scholars like Beverly Bossler, Peter K. Bol, Patricia Ebrey, and Kondō Kazunari. See Robert Hymes, *Statesmen and Gentlemen: The Elite of Fu-Chou, Chiang-Hsi, in Northern and Southern Sung* (New York: Cambridge University Press, 1986), and Robert Hymes, "Sung Society and Social Change," in *The Cambridge History of China, Volume 5, Part Two: Sung China, 960–1279*, ed. John W. Chaffee and Denis Twitchett (Cambridge: Cambridge University Press, 2015), 627–50; see also n. 42 in chap. 4.

5. Ping-Ti Ho, *The Ladder of Success in Imperial China: Aspects of Social Mobility, 1368–1911* (New York: Columbia University Press, 1962).

6.   Lü Miaofen 呂妙芬, "Ru Shi jiaorong de shengren guan: Cong Wanming rujia shengren yu pusa xingxiang xiangsichu ji dui shengsi yiti de guanzhu tanqi" 儒釋交融的聖人觀: 從晚明儒家聖人與菩薩形象相似處及對生死議題的關注談起, *Zhongyang yanjiuyuan jindaishi yanjiusuo jikan* 中央研究院近代史研究所集刊 32 (1999): 165–208.

7.   For the interaction between the elites and local government, see, for example, Sukhee Lee, *Negotiated Power: The State, Elites, and Local Governance in Twelfth- to Fourteenth-Century China* (Cambridge, Mass.: Harvard University Asia Center, 2014).

8.   Jinhua Jia, *The Hongzhou School of Chan Buddhism in Eighth- through Tenth-Century China* (Albany: State University of New York Press, 2006); Mario Poceski, *Ordinary Mind as the Way: The Hongzhou School and the Growth of Chan Buddhism* (New York: Oxford University Press, 2007).

9.   Jia Jinhua 賈晉華, *Tangdai jihui zongji yu shiren qun yanjiu* 唐代集會總集與詩人群研究, 2nd ed. (Beijing: Beijing daxue chubanshe, 2015), chap. 5.

10. For example, Luo Hongxian 羅洪先 (1504–1564, *jinshi* 1529), a famous scholar of the Yangming school, once claimed that "[I] would not be reluctant to stay in the secular world if [I] could save thousands lives in this life" (此生若活得千人命, 便甘心不向世外走). Echoing this, Lu Shanji 鹿善繼 (1575–1636, *jinshi* 1613) declared that "there is no need for action if things in the world remain well, and little can be accomplished if they become only a little bad. Only when [things] have become worse can [we] accomplish [our mission]" (天下事未壞不必為, 小壞不可為, 可為者獨大壞耳) (*Renzhen chao* 認真草, in *Congshu jicheng chubian* 叢書集成初編, comp. Wang Yunwu 王雲五 [Taipei: Xin wenfeng chuban gongsi, 1985], 8:107–8).

11. Qian Gu 錢穀, *Wudu wencui xuji* 吳都文粹續集, in vols. 1385–86 of *Wenyuange yingyin Siku quanshu* 文淵閣影印四庫全書 (Taipei: Shangwu yinshuguan, 1983), 30:4b–5a.

12. See, for example, *Suzhou fuzhi* 蘇州府志 (1693), fasc. 38, and *Pinghu xianzhi* 平湖縣志 (1627), 3:163.

13. *Mingshi* 明史 (1736; repr., Beijing: Zhonghua shuju, 1974), 197:5214.

14. Zhang Xianqing 張顯清, *Zhang Xianqing wenji* 張顯清文集 (Shanghai: Shanghai cishu chubanshe, 2005), 30–49, 83–104.

15. For the rapid development of local lineages in southern China after the sixteenth century, see Michael Szonyi, *Practicing Kinship: Clan and Descent in Late Imperial China* (Stanford, Calif.: Stanford University Press, 2002); Timothy Brook, "Funerary Ritual and the Building of Clans in Late Imperial China," *HJAS* 49, no. 2 (1989): 465–99; and Patricia Buckley Ebrey, *Kinship Organization in Late Imperial China, 1000–1940* (Berkeley: University of California Press, 1986).

16. *Ming Shizong shilu* 明世宗實錄, 82:1845.

17. This kind of practice had already appeared before the Jiajing period. For instance, an order was issued in 1482 prohibiting monastic assets from being presented to local princes. See Dai Jin 戴金, *Kōmin jōhō jiruisan* 皇明條法事類纂 (Tokyo: Koten kenkyūkai, 1966), 1:316–17.

18. For instance, see Yu Meian 喻昧庵, *Xinxu gaosengzhuan siji* 新續高僧傳四集 (Taipei: Liuli jingfang, 1967), 927, 1569, 1571, and *KXT*, 35:496.

19. Susanna Thornton, "Buddhist Monasteries in Hangzhou in the Ming and Early Qing" (Ph.D. diss., London University, 1996), 183.

20. For the sale of monastic lands in the Jiajing era, see *Mingshi*, 78:1901, and *Mingyin sizhi* 明因寺志, in *Congshu jicheng xubian* 叢書集成續編 (Taipei: Xin wenfeng chuban gongsi, 1989), 23:1b.

21. For Jiajing's expenditures on Daoist affairs, see *Mingshi*, 78:1907.

22. *Fujian tongzhi* 福建通志 (1872; repr., Taipei: Huawen shuju, 1968), 55:1137. Emperors of the Wuyue kingdom contributed greatly to this situation with their generous bestowals. Moreover, since Fujian was a peripheral and late-coming region in medieval China, monks obtained a unique opportunity to claim huge tracts of uncultivated land after their large-scale entry into the province in the Song.

23. In 1542, among the province's registered fields, which amounted to 13,577,500 *mu*, it is estimated that only 1.64 percent of it, or about 230,000 *mu*, belonged to the Buddhist temples. Lin Feng 林楓, "Fujian sitian chongxiang qianxi" 福建寺田充餉淺析, *Xiamen daxue xuebao* 廈門大學學報, no. 4 (1998): 49. See also T'ien Ju-K'ang, "The Decadence of Buddhist Temples in Fu-chien in Late Ming and Early Ch'ing," in *Development and Decline of Fukien Province in the 17th and 18th Centuries*, ed. E. B. Vermeer (Leiden: Brill, 1990), 83–100.

24. *Quanzhou Kaiyuan sizhi* 泉州開元寺志, 180–81.

25. *Dengwei Sheng'en sizhi* 鄧尉聖恩寺志, 7:217; Qian, *Wudu wencui xuji*, fasc. 30.

26. For the dilapidation of this temple during the Jiajing and early Wanli periods, see *Weimo sizhi* 維摩寺志, 1:13.

27. *KXT*, 46:657. *Weimo sizhi*, 1:14–15, also recounts this event briefly.

28. *KXT*, 41:595.

29. *Jinshan Longyou chansi zhilüe* 金山龍遊禪寺志略, 251, 252–54.

30. *KXT*, 49:706; 53:741; 57:8, 11, 13.

31. For the participation of Jiangnan scholar-officials in the Jiaxing canon, see Kawakatsu Kenryō 川勝賢亮, "Mindai Kōnan shitaifu bukkyōgaku ryūkō to daizōkyō kaihan" 明代江南士大夫仏教學流行と大藏経開版, *Odai shigaku* 鴨台史學, no. 5 (2005): 1–25.

32. Zhanran Yuancheng 湛然圓澄, *Kaigu lu* 慨古錄1, in *X*, vol. 65, no. 1285, 375a8–9.

33. *FCZ*, 16:763.

34. Feng Mengzhen said that after 1587 "[I] always take notes at night of what I have experienced during the day. These notes are numerous and disorderly. I have deleted three-tenths of them and turned [the remaining] into a diary" (日所曆, 夜必記之 甚龐雜不次, 今芟其什三, 為日記) (*KXT*, 47:666). When publishing his diary, Feng deleted some politically sensitive parts.

35. *WLYH*, 10:251–52, 259–60.

36. Qian Qianyi 錢謙益, *Chuxue ji* 初學集 (Shanghai: Shanghai guji chubanshe, 1985), 51:1300. For Feng's close relationship with Daokai, see *KXT*, 34:485, 40:580.

37. Feng Mengzhen was afflicted with illness throughout his life; for example, see *KXT*, 44:640, 53:731, 55:759.

38. See, for example, *KXT*, 42:610; 43:613, 615, 620, 625; 44:640.

39. *KXT*, 42:607. For the parable of the burning house, see *The Lotus Sutra*, in *T*, vol. 262, no. 9, 12b21.

40. *KXT*, 40:75. Another example can be seen in *KXT*, 43:618.

41. For the practice of self-examination, see Pei-Yi Wu, "Self-Examination and Confession of Sins in Traditional China," *HJAS* 39, no. 1 (1979): 5–38.

42. Their correspondence is preserved in *MKCY* 1, in *JXZ*, vol. 23, no. B118, 13b28–c12, 15c21–b12, and 18c01–20a16. See also *KXT*, 38:549, 40:580, 47:667.

43. See *KXT*, 37:522–23, 530–33. It could be a problem as to how Lu Guangzu took part in the arrangement as he had already resigned the preceding year.

44. *Mingshi*, 224:5891; *MKCY* 1, in *JXZ*, vol. 23, no. B118, 8c29–9a29, and 9c06–10a19. For studies on Lu Guangzu, see Araki Kengo 荒木見悟, "Bukkyō koji tosite no Riku Kōso" 仏教居士としての陸光祖, *Nagoya daigaku Chūgoku tetsugaku ronshū* 名古屋大學中國哲學論集, no. 3 (2004): 1–26.

45. *MKCY* 1, in *JXZ*, vol. 23, no. B118, 20a01–16.

46. See *KXT*, 37:533; 40:574, 581.

47. *KXT*, 37:536.

48. For Feng's lack of political ambition, see *KXT*, 42:607, 43:613. For his reluctance to solve problems by himself, see *KXT*, 43:613, 44:635. For his discussion of the contemporary political and social situation, see *KXT*, 42:596. For his concern about the impending rebellion, see *KXT*, 32:456; 39:561; 43:615, 620. For his lamentation regarding the emperor's activities, see *KXT*, 35:506, 42:605, 43:615.

49. See, for example, *KXT*, 36:533, 536; 40:574.

50. *KXT*, 25:372; 42:607, 609.This memorial is intriguing. It begins with a short summary of his contributions to the state, implying that he was a qualified official. Then, Feng asks to be permitted to retire, applying rather awkward logic: since the censor who impeached him had had no grudge against him in the past, his being impeached proved that he must have made mistakes somewhere, hence he should quit his office.

51. *KXT*, 38:549.

52. *KXT*, 42:605, 43:616, 50:708, 47:669.

53. *KXT*, 42:610.

54. *KXT*, 35:504.

55. For this famous Daoist hermit, see Yusa Noboru 遊佐昇, "Gen Kunpei no densetsu to shinkō" 嚴君平の伝説と信仰, *Meikai daigaku gaikokugo gakubu ronshū* 明海大学外国語学部論集, no. 17 (2005): 131–45.

56. *KXT*, 63:104–5.

57. *KXT*, 63:105.

58. Feng Mengzhen's financial situation improved a bit in the latter part of his life, but it was still fairly unstable. For Feng's incomes, see Ding Xiaoming 丁小明, "Zhenshi jushi de zhenshiyan: Feng Mengzhen *Kuaixuetang riji* duhou" 真實居士的真實言: 馮夢禎《快雪堂日記》讀後, preface to *Kuaixuetang riji* 快雪堂日記 (Nanjing: Fenghuang chubanshe, 2010).

59. Ouyi Zhixu 蕅益智旭, *Lingfeng Ouyi dashi zonglun* 靈峰蕅益大師宗論 6, in *JXZ*, vol. 36, no. B348, 354b28–30.

60. See, for example, *KXT*, 38:544; 43:625, 638.

61. For Huang, see *KXT*, 43:617; for Dong, see *KXT*, 32:453–54.

62. *KXT*, 42:608, 610.

63. *KXT*, 57:18.

64. For example, Feng once defended Xuelang Hong'en's dissipated life; see *WLYH*, 27:693.

65. Feng did not mention anything about Daokai's disappearance in his diary and letters, which is simply impossible given their close relationship. The only reasonable explanation for me is that he deleted some paragraphs to cover up something sensitive when printing the diaries.

66. Zibo Zhenke 紫柏真可, *Zibo zunzhe bieji* 紫柏尊者別集 3, in *X*, vol. 73, no. 1453, 419c22–420a4.

67. Feng mentioned Zhenke's tragedy in his diary at least eight times, including his inquiries for more details of three monks who had just returned from Beijing; see *KXT*, 60:75; 61:79, 84; 62:87; 64:113.

68. Zhenke, *Zibo zunzhe bieji* 3, in *X*, vol. 73, no. 1453, 419a15–19.

69. For the literati association of this kind, see Joanna F. Handlin Smith, "Liberating Animals in Ming-Qing China: Buddhist Inspiration and Elite Imagination," *JAS* 58, no. 1 (1999): 51–84.

70. Tea was an important part of literati culture in the Ming; see James A. Benn, *Tea in China: A Religious and Cultural History* (Honolulu: University of Hawai'i Press, 2015), chap. 8; for his discussion on Yuan Hongdao, see 187–88, 195–96.

71. *YHD*, 5:201. For studies on Yuan, see Chih-P'ing Chou, *Yüan Hung-tao and the Kung-an School* (New York: Cambridge University Press, 2006); Ming-shui Hung, *The Romantic Vision of Yuan Hung-tao, Late Ming Poet and Critic* (Taipei: Bookman Books, 1997).

72. *YHD*, 5:242. This translation is quoted from Hung-tao Yuan, *Pilgrim of the Clouds: Poems and Essays from Ming Dynasty China*, trans. Jonathan Chaves (Buffalo, N.Y.: White Pine Press, 2005), 21. For Yuan Hongdao's similar complaint, see *YHD*, 5:208, 213, 219–20; 6:272, 310.

73. Yuan Zhongdao 袁中道, *Kexuezhai ji* 珂雪齋集 (Shanghai: Shanghai guji chubanshe, 1989), 17:726; 18:756–57.

74. *YHD*, app. 2, 1652.

75. These two citations are from *YHD*, 5:224, 239, respectively.

76. *YHD*, 5:205–6. Yuan Hongdao's idea in this regard was shared by his younger brother Yuan Zhongdao; see Yuan, *Kexuezhai ji*, 5:192.

77. Yuan cites Pang Yun sixteen times in his work, claiming that "White-haired Mr. Pang was my master" (白首龐公是我師). For Pang Yun, see his entry in Robert E. Buswell and Donald S. Lopez, eds., *The Princeton Dictionary of Buddhism* (Princeton, N.J.: Princeton University Press, 2014), http://www.oxfordreference.com/view/10.1093/acref/9780190681159.001.0001/acref-97801906 81159-e-3103.

78. For studies on Li Zhi, see Rivi Handler-Spitz, *Symptoms of an Unruly Age: Li Zhi and Cultures of Early Modernity* (Seattle: University of Washington Press, 2017); Wm. Theodore de Bary, "Individualism and Humanitarianism in Late Ming Thought," in *Self and Society in Ming Thought*, ed. Wm. Theodore de Bary (New York: Columbia University Press, 1970), 145–248; Jiang Canteng 江燦騰, *Wanming fojiao gaige shi* 晚明佛教改革史 (Guilin: Guangxi shifan daxue chubanshe, 2006), 235–95; Mizoguchi Yūzō 溝口雄三, *Chūgoku zen kindai shisō no kussetsu to tenkai* 中国前近代思想の屈折と展開 (Tokyo: Tōkyō daigaku shuppankai, 1980); and Timothy Brook, *The Troubled Empire: China in the Yuan and Ming Dynasties* (Cambridge, Mass.: Belknap Press, 2010), 179–82.

79. *YHD*, 5:222.

80. The term *jinchang* 金閶 originally referred to Suzhou's two gates, the Jin gate (金門) and Chang gate (閶門). It was borrowed here to refer to Suzhou.

81. Quotations in this paragraph are from *YHD*, 5:211; 2:99; 6:297, 309.

82. For his request letters, see *YHD*, 7:313–23. For his claim that it was a matter of life or death, see *YHD*, 6:275.

83. For the relationship between the organization of society (*jieshe* 結社) and the loathing of being officials, see He Zongmei 何宗美, "Gong'an pai jieshe de xingshuai yanbian jiqi yingxiang" 公安派結社的興衰演變及其影響, *Xinan shifan daxue xuebao* 西南師範大學學報 32, no. 4 (2006): 173. Yuan's resignation was also connected to his conflict with local society, particularly with Wang Baigu 王百穀 (1535–1613) and Zhang Xianyi 張獻翼 (1534–1604), who were both famous literati of the time. Yuan managed to survive the crisis, but the event became the last straw that pushed him to leave.

84. *YHD*, 21:742. For Yuan's life in Beijing, see *YHD*, 21:741, 744, 748.

85. For Yuan's Buddhist thought and the change taking place around Wanli 27, see Zhou Qun 周群, "Lun Yuan Hongdao de foxue sixiang" 論袁宏道的佛學思想, *Zhonghua foxue yanjiu* 中華佛學研究 6 (2002): 383–417.

86. Yuan, *Kexuezhai ji*, 17:707–8.

87. Yuan, *Kexuezhai ji*, 18:758.

88. *YHD*, 22:792. As shown in a letter in 22:778, this change took place one year before.

89. Yuan Hongdao 袁宏道, *Xifang helun* 西方合論 10, in *T*, vol. 47, no. 1976, 417a22–24.

90. *YHD*, 10:437.

91. *YHD*, 14:606.

92. In addition, before 1598 Yuan had lost his grandfather and one of his good friends, Wang Yiming 王一鳴 (*jinshi* 1586). In 1600, his daughter Chan'na 禪那 (b. 1587) died from an acute illness, which was followed by the death of his friend Pan Shizao 潘士藻 (1537–1600, *jinshi* 1583) and of his nephew.

93. *YHD*, 21:758.

94. *YHD*, 43:1254. Yuan returned to his hometown after the death of his older brother, but he continued to lose family members and friends. In the third month of 1602, Li Zhi committed suicide in prison. In the tenth month, his grandmother died. Two months later, his uncle Gong Zhongqing 龔仲慶 (1550–1602), with whom Yuan had maintained a close relationship like that of a brother, died. In 1605, Yuan's other grandmother, Madame Shu 舒氏, died. In the autumn, one of his best friends, Jiang Jinzhi 江進之 (1553–1605), passed away.

95. For example, see *YHD*, 27:881, 885, 899; 30:991.

96. Zhixu's preface to the *Xifang helun*, 748a. For more about this work, see Charles B. Jones, "Transmission: Yuan Hongdao and the *Xifang helun*; Pure Land Theology in the Late Ming Dynasty," in

Path of No Path: Contemporary Studies in Pure Land Buddhism Honouring Roger Corless, ed. Richard Karl Payne and Roger Corless (Berkeley, Calif.: Numata Center for Buddhist Translation and Research, 2009), 89–126.

97.   Zhixu, *Lingfeng Ouyi dashi zonglun* 6, in *JXZ*, vol. 36, no. B348, 365c12–20.

98.   *YHD*, 53:1503–6; *Mingshi*, 288:7398.

99.   *YHD*, app. 2, 1655.

100. The four quotations in this paragraph are from, respectively. *YHD*, 11:506, 15:622, 55:1611, and 55:1595.

101. *YHD*, 22:775.

102. Master Shengyan has observed that although chanting the Buddha's name was the dominant practice in late-Ming Buddhism, Chan remained the pillar of its spirit. See Shengyan 聖嚴, *Wanming fojiao yanjiu* 晚明佛教研究 (Beijing: Zongjiao wenhua chubanshe, 2006), 204, 228.

103. *YHD*, 22:788, 43:1262–63.

104. Timothy Brook, *Praying for Power: Buddhism and the Formation of Gentry Society in Late-Ming China* (Cambridge, Mass.: Harvard University Press, 1993), 73.

105. *YHD*, 55:1597.

106. Dong Qichang 董其昌, *Huachan shi suibi* 畫禪室隨筆, in vol. 12 of *Biji xiaoshuo daguan* 筆記小說大觀, comp. Qian Yong 錢泳 et al. (Yangzhou: Guangling guji keyinshe, 1983), 4:131.

107. For the eight major members, see Yuan, *Kexuezhai ji*, 17:709–10. These members were influenced mostly by the Wang Yangming school and had a strong interest in Chan Buddhism. See He Zongmei 何宗美, *Mingmo Qingchu wenren jieshe yanjiu* 明末清初文人結社研究 (Tianjin: Nankai daxue chubanshe, 2003), 117–18.

108. Yuan, *Kexuezhai ji*, 17:729.

109. Yuan Zongdao 袁宗道, *Yuan Zongdao ji jianjiao* 袁宗道集箋校, ed. Meng Xiangrong 孟祥榮 (Wuhan: Hubei renmin chubanshe, 2003), 2:23–24.

110. *YHD*, 15:643. For their activities in the Putao Association, see 26:872.

111. The designation Taiqiu 太丘 referred to Chen Shi 陳寔 (104–187), who made friends with many people but did not choose them carefully. See Fan Ye 范曄, *Hou Hanshu* 後漢書 (Beijing: Zhonghua shuju, 1965), 62:2065–69.

112. *WLYH*, 27:691.

113. For Zhang Wenda's memorial, see *Ming Shenzong shilu* 明神宗實錄, 369:6917–19.

114. For Feng Qi's memorial, see Gu Yanwu 顧炎武, *Rizhilu jishi: Wai qizhong* 日知錄集釋: 外七種, annot. Huang Rucheng 黃汝成 (Shanghai: Shanghai guji chubanshe, 1985), 18:1409–11.

115. Tao Wangling 陶望齡, *Xiean ji* 歇庵集, in *jibu* 集部, vol. 1365, of *Xuxiu Siku quanshu* 續修四庫全書, ed. Gu Tinglong 顧廷龍 et al. (Shanghai: Shanghai guji chubanshe, 1995–2001), 16:436a–b.

116. On Huang's Buddhist beliefs, see Jennifer Lynn Eichman, "Intertextual Alliances: Huang Hui's Synthesis of Confucian and Buddhist Paths to Liberation," *T'oung Pao* 100, no. 1-3 (2014): 120–63.

117. Tao, *Xiean ji*, 15:405.

118. *WLYH*, 10:271.

119. Feng Qi 馮琦, "Su guanchang shu" 肃官常疏, http://www.sinoat.net/weifangwenshi/test097.htm.

120. The so-called Donglin faction may not have been an actual political group but so labeled by rivals as a convenient target for attack. See Fan Shuzhi 樊树志, "Donglin shuyuan de shitai fenxi: 'Donglindang' zhiyi" 東林書院的實態分析: "東林黨" 質疑, *Zhongguo shehui kexue* 中國社會科學, no. 2 (2001): 188–204.

121. On He Xinyin, see Ronald Dimberg, *The Sage and Society: The Life and Thought of Ho Hsin-Yin* (Honolulu: University Press of Hawaii, 1974).

122. The inclusion of Wang's spirit tablet in a Confucian temple at the time exemplified the change. See Tan Qian 談遷. *Guoque* 國榷 (Beijing: Zhonghua shuju, 1958), 72:4492–94. For implications behind the event, see Zhu Honglin 朱鴻林, "Ruzhe congsi Kongmiao de xueshu yu zhengzhi wenti"

儒者從祀孔廟的學術與政治問題, in *Qinghua lishi jiangtang xubian* 清華歷史講堂續編 (Beijing: Sanlian shudian, 2008), 336–55; Hung-lam Chu, "The Debate over Recognition of Wang Yang-ming," *HJAS* 48, no. 1 (1988): 47–70.

123. He, *Mingmo Qingchu wenren*, 118.

124. The short-lived Shoushan Academy 首善書院 was such a case. See Liu Dong 劉侗, *Dijing jingwu lüe* 帝京景物略 (Beijing: Beijing guji chubanshe, 1980), 4:149–52. See also John Meskill, *Academies in Ming China: A Historical Essay* (Tucson: University of Arizona Press, 1982), 153.

125. For the religious cause in the Huang Hui case, see Yuan, *Kexuezhai ji*, 23:979, and *Mingshi*, 288:7394. Notably, after the "evil pamphlet" event, there was a tendency to use violence to resolve differing opinions. See Fang Zhiyuan 方志遠, "'Shangren' yu Wanming zhengju" "山人"與晚明政局, *Zhong-guo shehui kexue* 中國社會科學, no. 1 (2010): 199–220, and Kin Bunkyō 金文京, "Mindai Banreki nenkan no sanjin no katsudō" 明代萬曆年間の山人の活動, *Tōyōshi kenkyū* 東洋史研究 61, no. 2 (2002): 237–77.

126. The five instructors were Yuan Zongdao, Huang Hui, Dong Qichang, Xiao Yunju 蕭雲舉 (1554–1627, *jinshi* 1586), and Jiao Hong. For their official biographies, see *Mingshi*, 288:7392, 7394–97; 216:5706–7, 5716; 226:5944–46; 240:6243–49.

127. Yuan, *Kexuezhai ji*, 17:710.

128. *Mingshi*, 288:7394; 235:6133.

129. Qian Qianyi 錢謙益, *Liechao shiji xiaozhuan* 列朝詩集小傳 (Shanghai: Shanghai guji chubanshe, 1959), 622; *WLYH*, 10:270–71.

130. Timothy Brook, "At the Margin of Public Authority: The Ming State and Buddhism," in *The Chinese State in Ming Society* (London: RoutledgeCurzon, 2005), 154.

131. *YHD*, 15:648.

132. After returning to the capital from exile, Liu Yuxi 劉禹錫 (772–842) used the term 劉郎 to refer to himself in a poem recording his revisit to an old place.

133. *YHD*, 55:1608. For a similar situation, see 45:1318–19.

134. See, for example, *YHD*, 55:1600, 1603, 1611.

135. *YHD*, 21:740.

6. EMINENT MONKS

1. This autobiography was dictated by Deqing and recorded by his disciple Fushan 福善 (1587?–1623?), with the last year added after his death. It is now usually printed together with an annotation by another of Deqing's disciples, Fuzheng 福徵 (i.e., Tan Zhenmo 譚貞默 [1550–1665, *jinshi* 1628]), under the title *Hanshan dashi nianpu shuzhu* 憨山大師年譜疏註 (hereafter cited as *Nianpu shu-zhu*). The *Nianpu shuzhu* used here is collected in vols. 52–53 of *Beijing tushuguan cang zhenben nianpu congkan* 北京圖書館藏珍本年譜叢刊 (Beijing: Beijing chubanshe, 1999). Upasaka Lu K'uan Yü has translated this biography and its annotation into English but missed some important parts; *Practical Buddhism* (Wheaton, Ill.: Theosophical Publication House, 1973), 57–162.

2. See, for example, the first part of Sung-peng Hsu, *A Buddhist Leader in Ming China: The Life and Thought of Han-shan Te-ch'ing, 1546–1623* (University Park: Pennsylvania State University Press, 1978); Araki Kengo 荒木見悟, *Yōmeigaku no tenkai to bukkyō* 陽明學の開展と仏教 (Tokyo: Ken-bun shuppan, 1984), chap. 6; Jiang Canteng 江燦騰, *Wanming fojiao gaige shi* 晚明佛教改革史 (Gui-lin: Guangxi shifan daxue chubanshe, 2006), 69–190; and Chen Yunü 陳玉女, *Mingdai de fojiao yu shehui* 明代的佛教與社會 (Beijing: Beijing daxue chubanshe, 2011), 123–36.

3. For blood writing in Chinese Buddhism, see John Kieschnick, "Blood Writing in Chinese Bud-dhism," *Journal of the International Association of Buddhist Studies* 23, no. 2 (2000): 177–94, and

Jimmy Yu, *Sanctity and Self-Inflicted Violence in Chinese Religions, 1500–1700* (Oxford: Oxford University Press, 2012), chap. 2.

4. The *wuzhe fahui* is an important Buddhist service held for various purposes. See Daniel B. Stevenson, "Text, Image, and Transformation in the History of the *Shuilu fahui*, the Buddhist Rite for Deliverance of Creatures of Water and Land," in *Cultural Intersections in Later Chinese Buddhism*, ed. Marsh Weidner (Honolulu: University of Hawai`i Press, 2001), 30–70.

5. Much of the information given by Deqing and Fuzheng about this event is misleading. See Dewei Zhang, "Challenging the Reigning Emperor for Success: Hanshan Deqing 憨山德清 (1546–1623) and Late Ming Court Politics," *Journal of the American Oriental Society* 134, no. 2 (2014): 263–85.

6. *Nianpu shuzhu*, 1:693.

7. For Deqing's training by Xilin Yongning and his efforts to save the monastery, see *Nianpu shuzhu*, 1:630–32, 635–37.

8. *Nianpu shuzhu*, 1:631.

9. After Xuelang rebuilt the pagoda thirty years later, for example, Deqing mentioned it several times with pleasure and relief.

10. *HSMY* 29, in *X*, vol. 73, no. 1456, 472a19–20.

11. *Nianpu shuzhu*, 1:695.

12. For details of the confiscation, see Chen Shilong 陳時龍, "Wanli Zhangfu chaojia shi shuwei: Yi Qiu Shun *Wangjinglou yigao* wei zhuyao shiliao" 萬曆張府抄家事述微—以丘橓《望京樓遺稿》爲主要史料, *Zhongguo wenhua yanjiusuo xuebao* 中國文化研究所學報, no. 53 (2011): 110–36.

13. It has been a part of traditional Chinese wisdom that "gentlemen should hone their talents and wait for the right time to act" (君子藏器於身, 待時而動). Besides, Deqing's pride might also have disallowed him ready access to the court. See, for example, *HSMY* 2, in *X*, vol. 73, no. 1456, 471c17–472a3.

14. *HSMY* 2, in *X*, vol. 73, no. 1456, 472b1–4.

15. *HSMY* 13, in *X*, vol. 73, no. 1456, 547b1–11.

16. For Fudeng's role in the distribution, see *HSMY* 13, in *X*, vol. 73, no. 1456, 547b4–6.

17. For the relief Deqing then felt, see *Nianpu shuzhu*, 1:701.

18. *Nianpu shuzhu*, 1:720–21.

19. Chen, *Mingdai de fojiao yu shehui*, 129–32, discusses the expenses that the Cining palace, where Cisheng lived, incurred for food and the possible results if Deqing's plan had been carried out.

20. *HSMY* 2, in *X*, vol. 73, no. 1456, 471a23–b1.

21. *HSMY* 55, in *X*, vol. 73, no. 1456, 848c9–11.

22. *HSMY* 55, in *X*, vol. 73, no. 1456, 851b7–10.

23. *Nianpu shuzhu*, 1:726–28.

24. For the plaint, see http://lib.sdsqw.cn/bin/mse.exe?seachword=&K=b2&A=65&rec=72&run=13.

25. Chen Guofu 陳國符, *Daozang yuanliu kao* 道藏源流攷 (Beijing: Zhonghua shuju, 1963), 685.

26. Zibo Zhenke 紫柏真可, *Zibo zunzhe quanji* 紫柏尊者全集 1, in *X*, vol. 73, no. 1452, 143a5–6.

27. For the meeting, see *HSMY* 27, in *X*, vol. 73, no. 1456, 654a7–8.

28. *Nianpu shuzhu*, 1:719.

29. *HSMY* 15, in *X*, vol. 73, no. 1456, 565a21–b2.

30. *HSMY* 13, in *X*, vol. 73, no. 1456, 547b17–c10.

31. *HSMY* 14, in *X*, vol. 73, no. 1456, 554a14. Deqing repeatedly stressed how beneficial this disaster was for his religious achievements. For example, see his two letters at 14:554a5.

32. *HSMY* 14, in *X*, vol. 73, no. 1456, 560a20–23.

33. For the canonical basis of this practice, see, for example, *Zhongguan lunshu* 中觀論疏 1, in *T*, vol. 42, no. 1824, 5c17–19.

34. *HSMY* 13, in *X*, vol. 73, no. 1456, 551b20–21.

35. *HSMY* 14, in *X*, vol. 73, no. 1456, 554b13–16.

36. Pei-Yi Wu has noted that "Te-ch'ing's [i.e., Deqing's] punishment seems to have solidified his alliance with the leading Neo-Confucians of his day, and the journey south looked more like a triumphant march" ("The Spiritual Autobiography of Te-ch'ing," in *The Unfolding of Neo-Confucianism*, ed. Wm. Theodore de Bary [New York: Columbia University Press, 1970], 81).

37. *HSMY* 13, in *X*, vol. 73, no. 1456, 545c6–7.

38. *HSMY* 46, in *X*, vol. 73, no. 1456, 777c15–22.

39. Qian Qianyi is such an example. Although meeting Deqing only once, in 1617, Qian claimed himself as "the disciple of Haiyin" (海印弟子). He not only wrote a biography for Deqing but also coordinated the compilation and publication of Deqing's collected writings.

40. *WLYH*, 27:693.

41. For a detailed study of Deqing's reforms at Nanhuasi, see Jiang, *Wanming fojiao gaige shi*, 129–90, and Hasebe Yūkei 長谷部幽蹊, "Minmatsu sōrin ni okeru shūgyō seikatsu no ichikeitai: Tokushin ni yoru Sōkei no fukkō o megutte" 明末叢林における修行生活の一形態: 徳清による曹渓の復興をめぐって, *Zen kenkyūjo kiyō* 禅研究所紀要, no. 8 (1979): 21–52.

42. *HSMY* 54, in *X*, vol. 73, no. 1456, 844b3–5.

43. Honda Michitaka 本多道隆, "Kakō daizōkyō no kankoku jigyō to Shihaku Shinka—butsugo no denpa to jishin no senmei" 嘉興大蔵経の刊刻事業と紫柏真可—仏語の伝播と自心の闡明, *Shūkan tōyō gaku* 集刊東洋學 95 (2006): 81–100; Nakajima Ryūzō 中嶋隆藏, "Kakōzō nyūzō butten to Mitsuzō Dōkai no tachiba" 嘉興蔵入蔵佛典と密藏道開の立場, *Tōhō gakuhō* 東方學報 113, no. 1 (2007): 34–50.

44. The main body of the canon was completed by the end years of the Kangxi period (1662–1722), but new texts were still taken in until the Jiaqing period (1796–1820). See Wang Lei 王蕾 and Han Xiduo 韓錫鐸, "Cong Liaotu cangben renshi Jiaxingzang" 從遼圖藏本認識嘉興藏, *Zhongguo dianji yu wenhua* 中國典籍與文化, no. 1 (2009): 67.

45. For recent studies on the Jiaxing canon, see Lan Jifu 藍吉富, "Jiaxing dazangjing de tese jiqi shiliao jiazhi" 嘉興大藏經的特色及其史料價值, in *Fojiao de sixiang yu wenhua: Yinshun daoshi bazhi jinliu shouqing lunwenji* 佛教的思想與文化: 印順導師八秩晉六壽慶論文集, ed. Shengyan 聖嚴 et al. (Taipei: Faguang chubanshe, 1991), 255–66; Chen Yunü, *Mingdai fomen neiwai sengsu jiaoshe de changyu* 明代佛門內外僧俗交涉的場域 (Taipei: Daoxiang chubanshe, 2010), chaps. 4 and 5; and Shi Fachuang 釋法幢, ed., *Dazangjing de bianxiu, liutong, chuancheng: Jingshan zang guoji xueshu yanjiuhui lunwenji* 大藏經的編修、流通、傳承: 徑山藏國際學術研討會論文集 (Hangzhou: Zhejiang guji chubanshe, 2017).

46. *MKCY* 1, in *JXZ*, vol. 23, no. B118, 5c12.

47. It comes as no surprise that it was Yuan Huang who suggested this change given his clear utilitarian tendency in the religious field, as evidenced by the *gongguo ge* 功過格 (the ledgers of merit and demerit) he forcefully advocated. For Yuan's promotion of the *gongguo ge*, see Cynthia Brokaw, *The Ledgers of Merit and Demerit: Social Change and Moral Order in Late Imperial China* (Princeton, N.J.: Princeton University Press, 1991), and Sakai Tadao 酒井忠夫, *Zōho Chūgoku zensho no kenkyū* 增補中国善書の研究 (Tokyo: Kokusho kankōkai, 1999–2000).

48. The concertina binding models how Buddhist scriptures were first bound in India, while the thread-binding form was usually used in China to print non-Buddhist books. Thus some Buddhists, including Daokai in his early years, took the concertina binding as a sacred format and resisted any changes to it. See Zhenke, *Zibo zunzhe quanji* 13, in *X*, vol. 73, no. 1452, 253b2–3.

49. Zhenke, *Zibo zunzhe quanji* 13, in *X*, vol. 73, no. 1452, 253b5–13.

50. Zhenke, *Zibo zunzhe quanji* 13, in *X*, vol. 73, no. 1452, 253b19–21.

51. *MKCY* 1, in *JXZ*, vol. 23, no. B118, 2a23–26.

52. *MKCY* 1, in *JXZ*, vol. 23, no. B118, 3a30–3b02.

53. *MKCY* 1, in *JXZ*, vol. 23, no. B118, 17b05–06.

54. *MKCY* 2, in *JXZ*, vol. 23, no. B118, 24b18–22.

55. Nakajima Ryūzō 中嶋隆蔵, *Min Banreki Kakōzō no shuppan to sono eikyō* 明萬曆嘉興蔵の出版とその影響 (Sendai: Tōhoku daigaku daigakuin bungaku kenkyūka, 2005), 29.

56. *MKCY* 1, in *JXZ*, vol. 23, no. B118, 18a13–22.

57. For activities of Quanzhen Daoism and the Luo teachings in this region, see Chen, *Mingdai fomen*, chaps. 4 and 5.

58. Zhenke left virtually nothing meaningful at Lingyansi, except a poem describing its dilapidation. See Zhenke, *Zibo zunzhe quanji* 28, in *X*, vol. 73, no. 1452, 389c21–390a5.

59. In 1589 when the project was about to start, Shen Zibin 沈自邠 (1554–1589, *jinshi* 1577) already noticed the close relationship between Mount Wutai as the carving site and the symbolic meaning of the bodhisattva Mañjuśrī. See Nakajima, *Min Banreki*, 22.

60. A memorial to Cisheng, for example, was written by Daokai in a tone used between friends. See *MKCY* 1, in *JXZ*, vol. 23, no. B118, 7b05–16.

61. *MKCY* 1, in *JXZ*, vol. 23, no. B118, 17b04–05.

62. *MKCY* 1, in *JXZ*, vol. 23, no. B118, 18c18–19a1.

63. It is impossible for us to know exactly how many texts were carved during the period, considering that some of them were later recarved or simply disappeared in history. The existing colophons show that forty-six texts in 579 fascicles were produced at Miaode chapel, but Daokai once mentioned that they had completed 20 percent of the canon, which was a remarkable accomplishment. See *MKCY* 1, in *JXZ*, vol. 23, no. B118, 29b2–29.

64. *MKCY* 1, in *JXZ*, vol. 23, no. B118, 17a14–18.

65. Only two short letters that Daokai wrote to local Shanxi figures other than Fudeng exist: one to a General called Ji 稽將軍 (dates unknown) and the other to a squad leader (*bazong* 把總) called Feng 馮 (dates unknown).

66. *MKCY* 1, in *JXZ*, vol. 23, no. B118, 18a27–18b03.

67. Daokai warned Feng Mengzhen of the impossibility of obtaining a correct Buddhist canon without his assistance, which implied Daokai's influence in the inner court. See *MKCY* 1, in *JXZ*, vol. 23, no. B118, 13a06–09.

68. *MKCY* 1, in *JXZ*, vol. 23, no. B118, 18b28.

69. *MKCY* 1, in *JXZ*, vol. 23, no. B118, 17b15–21. None of the eunuchs appears in the existing colophons, suggesting that they may have left the project.

70. For other cases, see *MKCY* 1, in *JXZ*, vol. 23, no. B118, 18b7–9.

71. *MKCY* 1, in *JXZ*, vol. 23, no. B118, 18c18–19a1.

72. *MKCY* 2, in *JXZ*, vol. 23, no. B118, 31a1–12.

73. *MKCY* 1, in *JXZ*, vol. 23, no. B118, 6c16–23.

74. *MKCY* 2, in *JXZ*, vol. 23, no. B118, 29b28–29.

75. For the Wutai case, see *MKCY* 2, in *JXZ*, vol. 23, no. B118, 29b30–c19. For the destruction of forests at Mount Wutai, see Chen Yunü, "Ming Wutaishan zhu fosi jianzhu cailiao zhi qude yu yunshu—yi mucai, tong, tie deng jiancai weizu" 明五臺山諸佛寺建築材料之取得與運輸—以木材、銅、鐵等建材為主," in Chen, *Mingdai de fojiao yu shehui*, 216–47.

76. For Lu's visit to Mount Wutai, see *Qingliang shanzhi* 清涼山志, 6:264.

77. For Daokai's efforts to secure an official permit (*zafu* 箚付) for recarving the canon from the Ministry of Rites, see *MKCY* 2, in *JXZ*, vol. 23, no. B118, 25c24–30, 23c13–21. It is unclear if the project got the permit.

78. When Zhenke was arrested in 1603, one charge against him was that he had collected thirty thousand taels of silver in the name of making a new canon. See *Ming Shenzong shilu* 明神宗實錄, 370:6926.

79. *MKCY* 1, in *JXZ*, vol. 23, no. B118, 20a02.

80. *MKCY* 2, in *JXZ*, vol. 23, no. B118, 20b14–20.

81. For the record of Zhenke's arrest and investigation, see Zibo Zhenke 紫柏真可, *Zibo zunzhe bieji* 紫柏尊者別集 4, in *X*, vol. 73, no. 1453, 150b.

82. *HSMY* 27, in *X*, vol. 73, no. 1456, 654b17–18.

83. In a memorial, for example, Kang Piyang pointed out that "although [Zhenke] has continued traveling in the Wu and Yue regions in recent years, his primary attention has always been on the imperial capital" (況數年以來, 遍曆吳越, 究其主念, 總在京師). See *Ming Shenzong shilu*, 370:8689.

84. *HSMY* 27, in *X*, vol. 73, no. 1456, 654b10.

85. Zhenke, *Zibo zunzhe bieji* 3, in *X*, vol. 73, no. 1453, 419b6–c3.

86. Zhenke, *Zibo zunzhe bieji* 3, in *X*, vol. 73, no. 1453, 419a5–8.

87. It is not clear why Zhenke lingered in Beijing. While being investigated, Zhenke confessed that he was trying to save Deqing, complete the continuation of the *Records of the Transmission of the Lamp* (*Xu chuandeng lu* 續傳燈錄), compile the *Biographies of Eminent Monks*, enlist support for the Jiaxing canon project, and send the Buddha's tooth relic to the inner court. In Zhenke's biography by Deqing, Deqing adds as a major task stopping the mineral taxes (*kuangshui* 礦稅). Shen Defu instead claimed that it was because of Zhenke's intention to reinvigorate Buddhism and Cisheng's plan to build a monastery in the capital for him. See Zhenke, *Zibo zunzhe bieji* 4, in *X*, vol. 73, no. 1453, 431c19–20; *HSMY* 27, in *X*, vol. 73, no. 1456, 654a14–15; and *WLYH*, 27:690–91.

88. *KXT*, 60:75. For a similar letter to Tang Xianzu 湯顯祖, see Zhenke, *Zibo zunzhe quanji* 23, in *X*, vol. 73, no. 1452, 347a21–b8.

89. On the evil-pamphlet event, see *Mingshi* 明史 (1736; repr., Beijing: Zhonghua shuju, 1974), 226:5546–47; Yang Xiangyan 楊向豔, *Shen Yiguan zhizheng yu Wanli dangzheng: Yi Chuzong, Yaoshu, Jingcha sanshi wei zhongxin de kaocha* 沈一貫執政與萬曆黨爭: 以楚宗、妖書、京察三事為中心的考察 (Beijing: Shangwu yinshuguan, 2018), chap. 2; and Guo Zhengyu 郭正域, *Wanli sanshiyinian guimao "chushi" "yaoshu" shimo* 萬曆三十一年癸卯"楚事""妖書"始末, in *Zhongguo yeshi jicheng xubian* 中國野史集成續編, vol. 20 (Chengdu: Bashu shushe, 2000).

90. For Wanli's suspicion of Zhenke for lobbyism, see *WLYH*, 27:690. For Zhenke's criticism of Wanli, see Zhenke, *Zibo zunzhe bieji* 4, in *X*, vol. 73, no. 1453, 430b1–3. See also Matteo Ricci and Nicolas Trigault, *Li Madou Zhongguo zhaji* 利瑪竇中國札記, trans. He Gaoji 何高濟, Wang Zhunzhong 王遵仲, et al. (Beijing: Zhonghua shuju, 1983), 439; Xiao Daheng 蕭大亨, *Xingbu zouyi* 刑部奏議, 5:44; and Fang Zhiyuan 方志遠, "'Shanren' yu Wanming zhengju" "山人"與晚明政局, *Zhongguo shehui kexue* 中國社會科學, no. 1 (2010): 199–220.

91. For the role that politics played in the deaths of Li Zhi and Zhenke, see Satō Rentarō 佐藤鍊太郎, "Ri Takugo to Shihaku Takkan no shi o megutte" 李卓吾と紫柏達觀の死をめぐって, in *Yamane Yukio kyōju taikyū kinen Mindaishi ronsō* 山根幸夫教授退休記念明代史論叢, ed. Yamane Yukio 山根幸夫 and Okuzaki Hiroshi 奧崎裕 (Tokyo: Kyūko shoin, 1990), 189–207.

92. *Mingshi*, 305:7814, 226:5947.

93. Zhenke, *Zibo zunzhe quanji* 1, in *X*, vol. 73, no. 1453, 147c17–19.

94. Wen Bing 文秉, *Xianbo zhishi* 先撥志始, in *shibu* 史部, vol. 437, of *Xuxiu Siku quanshu* 續修四庫全書, ed. Gu Tinglong 顧廷龍 et al. (Shanghai: Shanghai guji chubanshe, 1995-2001), 1:593. Wang Qiyuan suspects that the monk evicted by Guo Zhengyu was Xuelang Hong'en rather than Zhenke; "Zibo dashi wanjie yu Wanli jian fojiao de shengchun kongjian" 紫柏大師晚節與萬曆間佛教的生存空間," *Shijie zongjiao yanjiu* 世界宗教研究, no. 1 (2015): 228-41.

95. Zhenke, *Zibo zunzhe bieji* 4, in *X*, vol. 73, no. 1453, 432a3–5. According to the Vinaya, killing an arhat is one of the "five heinous crimes" that lead to immediate rebirth in one of the hells. See, for example, *Foshuo si nili jing* 佛說四泥犁經1, in *T*, vol. 2, no. 139, 861c15–19.

96. It is interesting to compare this description of Zhenke's death with a secular and dull one; see *Xingbu zouyi*, 5:43: "[Zhenke] suffered an acute illness during the period from 11 p.m. to 1 a.m. He coughed up phlegm, sat up, and died of the illness by the period from 9 to 11 a.m." (子時得患急症, 吐痰起坐, 至本日巳時病故).

97. For a discussion of somatic evidence of supreme spiritual achievements, see James A. Benn, *Burning for the Buddha: Self-Immolation in Chinese Buddhism* (Honolulu: University of Hawai'i Press, 2007), chaps. 2, 6.

98. Robert H. Sharf, "The Idolization of Enlightenment: On the Mummification of Ch'an Masters in Medieval China," *History of Religions* 32, no. 1 (1992): 9.

99. Zhenke, *Zibo zunzhe quanji* 1, in *X*, vol. 73, no. 1453, 141c3–6.

100. Zhenke, *Zibo zunzhe quanji* 1, in *X*, vol. 73, no. 1453, 138c2–9.

101. Zhenke, *Zibo zunzhe quanji* 1, in *X*, vol. 73, no. 1453, 138a16–19.

102. Qian Qianyi 錢謙益, *Muzhai chuxue ji* 牧齋初學集 (Shanghai: Shanghai guji chubanshe, 2003), 1721.

103. *HSMY* 30, in *X*, vol. 73, no. 1456, 676b22–24.

104. For studies on Fudeng, see Puay-peng Ho, "Building for Glitter and Eternity: The Works of the Late Ming Master Builder Miaofeng on Wutai Shan," *Orientations* (Hong Kong) 27, no. 5 (1996): 67–73; Hibino Takeo 日比野丈夫, "Myōhō Fukutō no jiseki ni tsuite" 妙峰福登の事蹟について, in *Bukkyō shigaku ronshū: Tsukamoto Hakushi shōju kinen* 佛教史學論集: 塚本博士頌壽記念 (Kyoto: Tsukamoto Hakushi shōju kinenkai, 1961), 583–95; and Dewei Zhang, "Engaged but Not Entangled: Miaofeng Fudeng 妙峰福登 (1540–1612) and the Late Ming Court," in *The Middle Kingdom and the Dharma Wheel: Aspects of the Relationship between the Buddhist Saṃgha and the State in Chinese History*, ed. Thomas Jülch (Leiden: Brill, 2016), 322–78.

105. *HSMY* 30, in *X*, vol. 73, no. 1456, 676b12–14.

106. Marsha Weidner, "Imperial Engagements with Buddhist Art and Architecture: Ming Variations on an Old Theme," in *Cultural Intersections in Later Chinese Buddhism*, ed. Marsha Weidner (Honolulu: University of Hawai'i Press, 2001), 130–32, offers a detailed description of the copper hall.

107. *HSMY* 30, in *X*, vol. 73, no. 1456, 675c20–676a14. For the acquisition and transportation of materials used for temple buildings at Mount Wutai, see Chen, *Mingdai de fojiao yu shehui*, 216–47.

108. Qin Peiheng 秦佩珩 claims that a million *jin* of copper was used for this hall and its accompanying Buddha statues (並共用一百萬斤). Based on this figure, Chen, *Mingdai de fojiao yu shehui*, 239, estimates that it cost one hundred forty thousand taels of silver. However, Cui Zhengshen 崔正森 says that only a hundred thousand *jin* of copper was used. If so, the cost was about fourteen thousand taels of silver. This result seems to me more acceptable as the figure is close to the expenditures for the first two copper halls. See Qin Peiheng, "Qingliang tongdian zakao" 清涼銅殿雜考, *Zhengzhou daxue xuebao* 鄭州大學學報, no. 3 (1984): 79; Cui Zhengshen, "Wutaishan yu Putuoshan fojiao wenhua jiaoliu" 五台山與普陀山佛教文化交流, *Wutaishan yanjiu* 五台山研究, no. 3 (1998): 38–45.

109. These families first made a fortune from the lucrative salt trade and then invested it in education. Consequently, Pucheng saw an unusual success of its sons in the civil service examination. See *Puzhou fuzhi* 蒲州府志 (1754; repr., Nanjing: Fenghuang chubanshe, 2005), 24.85.

110. For Wang Chonggu, see *Mingshi*, 222:5838–44; for Zhang Siwei, see *Mingshi*, 220:5769–71.

111. In his early life, Fudeng exchanged poems with members of the two families. See Li Ronghe 李榮河 et al., eds., *Yongji xianzhi* 永濟縣誌 (1886) (repr., Beijing: Beijing tushuguan chubanshe, 2002), 15:17a. When Fudeng visited Beijing in pursuit of the Buddhist canon, his success was owed partly to Wang Chonggu, who introduced him to the eunuch in charge of the canon. See *Baohua shanzhi* 寶華山志, 12:485.

112. According to another source, the cost was fifty thousand to seventy thousand taels of silver (五、七萬金); see Jiao Yunlong 焦雲龍 and He Ruilin 賀瑞麟, eds., *Sanyuan xian xinzhi* 三原縣新志 (repr., Taipei: Chenwen chubanshe, 1968), 2:89.

113. For the *kaizhong* policy, see *Mingshi*, 80:1935. According to the policy, anybody transferring certain amounts of grain to armies there would be given a government license (*yanyin* 鹽引), allowing them to purchase the so-called Huai salt (淮鹽) in Jiangsu and then sell it elsewhere.

114. Regarding Shaanxi merchants in the Ming, see Fu Yiling 傅衣淩, *Ming Qing shidai shangren ji shangye ziben* 明清時代商人及商業資本 (Beijing: Renmin chubanshe, 1956), 161–75. On the prosperity of Sanyuan, see Li Weizhen 李維楨, "Sanyuan xian Longqiao ji" 三原縣龍橋記, which is quoted in part in Yang Guozhen 楊國楨, Fu Yiling 傅衣淩, and Chen Zhiping 陳支平, eds., *Mingshi xinbian* 明史新編 (Taipei: Yunlong chuban, 2002), 378.

115. Wen Chun 溫純, *Wen Gongyi ji* 溫恭毅集, in *jibu* 集部, vol. 96, of *Wenyuange yingyin Siku quanshu* 文淵閣影印四庫全書 (Taipei: Shangwu yinshuguan, 1983), 22:22.

116. Guo Zhengyu 郭正域, "Yanghe jian Guanghui qiao beiji" 洋河建廣惠橋碑記, in *Xuanhua xian xinzhi* 宣化縣新志, ed. Chen Jizeng 陳繼曾 and Guo Weicheng 郭維城 (repr., Taipei: Chenwen shuju, 1968), 16:45a.

117. Guo, "Yanghe jian," 16:45b.

118. On the composition of those contributing, see Jianwei Zhang, "A Study of the Three Buddhist Copper Hall Projects, 1602–1607," *Frontiers of History in China* 10, no. 2 (2015): 289–322.

119. Huang Zongxi 黃宗羲, *Ming wenhai* 明文海 (Beijing: Zhonghua shuju, 1987), 373:3852.

120. *HSMY* 32, in *X*, vol. 73, no. 1456, 698c17–18.

121. *Dafangguangfo Huayan jing* 大方廣佛華嚴經 40, in *T*, vol. 10, no. 293, 846a10–28.

122. In this sense, Hirakawa Akira is correct in concluding that Mahayana is a kind of Buddhism characterized by both self-benefit and altruism, one in which a continuity exists between the laity and renunciants; Hirakawa Akira 平川彰, "Daijō bukkyō no kyōri to kyōdan" 大乘佛教の教理と教團, in *Hirakawa Akira chosakushū* 平川彰著作集 (Tokyo: Shunjūsha, 1997), vol. 5, 3–5.

123. This number consists of those reported to the court as having died in the earthquake. Any additional deaths were unknown or unreported. See *Ming Shizong shilu* 明世宗實錄, 430:3.

124. A collection of original records related to this earthquake can be found in Xie Yushou 謝毓壽 and Cai Meibiao 蔡美彪, eds., *Zhongguo dizhen lishi ziliao huibian* 中國地震歷史資料匯編 (Beijing: Kexue chubanshe, 1985), vol. 2, 402–68.

125. This earthquake was traditionally called the Huaxian earthquake 華縣地震, implying that Huaxian in Shaanxi was its center. Modern research, however, reveals that the center was in the area of Puzhou 蒲州, Chaoyi 朝邑, Tongguan 潼關, and Huayin 華陰.

126. Wang Yuanlin 王元林, "Mingdai Huanghe xiao beiganliou hedao bianqian" 明代黃河小北幹流河道變遷, *Zhongguo lishi dili luncong* 中國歷史地理論叢, no. 3 (1999): 188–200.

127. John Kieschnick, *The Impact of Buddhism on Chinese Material Culture* (Princeton, N.J.: Princeton University Press, 2002), 203.

128. For the poem, see Wen, *Wen Gongyi ji*, 22:22.

129. Wen, *Wen Gongyi ji*, 15:1–2.

130. Bi Ziyan 畢自嚴, *Shiyin yuan canggao* 石隱園藏稿, in *jibu* 集部, vol. 1293, of *Wenyuange yingyin Siku quanshu*, 8:8a.

131. Huang, *Ming wenhai*, 73:685.

132. See Fudeng's modern biography by Else Glahn in *Dictionary of Ming Biography, 1368–1644*, ed. Luther Carrington Goodrich and Chaoying Fang (New York: Columbia University Press, 1976).

133. In most cases, the bestowal consisted of several hundred taels of silver plus honorary gifts, such as the Buddhist canon, the imperial purple robe, or Buddha statues. For this big money bestowed to renovate Xiantongsi, see Zang Maoxun 臧懋循, *Fubaotang wenxuan* 負苞堂文選, in vol. 1361 of *Xuxiu Siku quanshu*, 4:116b.

134. *HSMY* 30, in *X*, vol. 73, no. 1456, 676c2–4.

135. *HSMY* 30, in *X*, vol. 73, no. 1456, 676c1–2. From very early on, the notion of merit appeared in mainstream Buddhist scriptures. See *Foshuo zhude futian jing* 佛說諸德福田經 1, in *T*, vol. 16, no. 683, 777b2–8. For studies on cultivating merit, see Tokiwa Daijō 常盤大定, *Zoku Shina bukkyō no kenkyū* 續支那仏教の研究 (Tokyo: Shunjūsha shōhakukan, 1941), 473–98, and Michibata Ryōshū, *Chūgoku bukkyō to shakai fukushi jigyō* 中国仏教と社会福祉事業 (Kyoto: Hōzōkan, 1967), 6–9.

136. Over time, that merit could be gained through the construction of bridges and monasteries became well entrenched in the public psyche. See Kieschnick, *Impact of Buddhism*, 200–202. For earlier monks who devoted themselves to bridge building, see, for example, Huang Minzhi 黃敏枝, *Song-dai fojiao shehui jingjishi lunji* 宋代佛教社會經濟史論集 (Taipei: Taiwan xuesheng shuju, 1989), 135.

137. Nālandā Vihāra was a renowned Indian center of Buddhist learning, where famous Chinese monks, including Xuanzang 玄奘 (602–664) and Yijing 義淨 (635–713), studied. It was built by King Śakrāditya of the Gupta dynasty and destroyed in the fourteenth century.

138. In his voluminous writings, for example, Deqing never mentioned the sufferings the catastrophic earthquake caused to the people of Shanxi, which constitutes a sharp contrast with his enthusiasm for the inner court.

139. Deqing composed a standard biography of Fudeng, which, with some modifications, is included in *Buxu gaoseng zhuan* 補續高僧傳 and monastic gazetteers such as the *Qingliang shanzhi* and *Emei shanzhi* 峨嵋山志. What is included in the *Baohua shanzhi* 寶華山志 (repr., Taipei: Mingwen shuju, 1980), 12:475–501, however, is an earlier version of the received text. The current *Mengyou ji* 夢遊集 was compiled by Qian Qianyi, who admitted that he had deleted details he perceived as wordy and even rewritten some sentences. So it seems safe to attribute the unjust change in Fudeng's biography to Qian Qianyi. For the compilation of the *Mengyou ji*, see Luo Shaofeng 雒少鋒, "Sishi juan *Hanshan laoren mengyou quanji* bianzuan xushuo" 四十卷《憨山老人夢游全集》編纂敘說, https://wenku.baidu.com/view/9a2cf6bd2af90242a895e5b7.html (accessed June 18, 2018).

7. TEMPLES

1. For elements shaping the history of a temple, for example, see James A. Benn, Lori Rachelle Meeks, and James Robson, eds., *Buddhist Monasticism in East Asia: Places of Practice* (London: Routledge, 2010).

2. Timothy Brook, *Praying for Power: Buddhism and the Formation of Gentry Society in Late-Ming China* (Cambridge, Mass.: Harvard University Press, 1993), xiv.

3. Among the more than two hundred kinds of monastic gazetteers that have been reprinted in recent years, those about Beijing temples are fewer than ten. Susan Naquin points out that "of the three thousand temples that had existed in the greater Peking area in the course of the Ming and Qing periods, only two [i.e., Guangjisi 廣濟寺 and Tanzhesi] produced such institutional histories" ("Sites, Saints, and Sights at the Tanzhe Monastery," *Cahiers d'Extrême-Asie*, no. 10 [1998]: 192). For more information on monastic gazetteers in Beizhili and Shanxi, see Timothy Brook, *Geographical Sources of Ming-Qing History* (Ann Arbor: University of Michigan, 1988), 43–48, 98–103. For general information about monastic gazetteers, see Marcus Bingenheimer [馬德偉], "Zhongguo fosi zhi chutan ji shumu yanjiu" 中國佛寺志初探及書目研究, *Hanyu foxue pinglun* 漢語佛學評論, no. 2 (2010): 377–408, and Cao Ganghua 曹剛華, *Mingdai fojiao fangzhi yanjiu* 明代佛教方志研究 (Beijing: Renmin daxue chubanshe, 2011).

4. For recent studies on Buddhist temples in Ming Beijing, see Susan Naquin, *Peking: Temples and City Life, 1400–1900* (Berkeley: University of California Press, 2000); He Xiaorong 何孝榮, *Ming-dai Beijing fojiao siyuan xiujian yanjiu* 明代北京佛教寺院修建研究 (Tianjin: Nankai daxue

chubanshe, 2007); Timothy Brook, *The Chinese State in Ming Society* (London: RoutledgeCurzon, 2005), chaps. 7, 8; Dong Xiaoping 董曉平 and Lü Min [Marianne Bujard], eds., *Beijing neicheng simiao beike zhi* 北京内城寺廟碑刻志, 4 vols. (Beijing: Guojia tushuguan chubanshe, 2011–2017); and Chen Yunü 陳玉女, "Kinsei Kahoku chiiki ni okeru bukkyō no shakaiteki shintō no patān—Mindai Hokuchokurei o sokutei no waku toshite " 近世華北地域における仏教の社會的浸透のパターン—明代北直隸を測定の枠として, in *Higashi Ajia ni okeru seisan to ryūtsū no rekishi shakaigakuteki kenkyū* 東アジアにおける生産と流通の歴史社会学的研究, ed. Kawakatsu Mamoru 川勝守 (Fukuoka: Chūgoku shoten), 303–405.

5. This eunuch was brought to the inner court from Vietnam and had served four emperors by the time in question. See Zhao Qichang 趙其昌, *Jinghua ji* 京華集 (Beijing: Wenwu chubanshe, 2008), 209.

6. *Fayuan sizhi gao* 法源寺志稿, 4:100–101.

7. *Fayuan sizhi gao*, 4:95. The rest of the paragraph is unreadable.

8. Both Song's seniority and his post in the Directorate of Ceremonial helped him to enlist support from other eunuchs.

9. *Fayuan sizhi gao*, 4:99–100.

10. *Fayuan sizhi gao*, 4:97–98.

11. *Fayuan sizhi gao*, 4:107–9, 112–15.

12. Susan Naquin has pointed out that "in Ming Peking, although we can identify some families whose influence rested on landownership and literary accomplishment (e.g. that of Mi Wanzhong, official and painter of the Wanli period), their influence was not comparable to that of contemporaries in central China. Local families seem to have been overshadowed by the much richer and more powerful society associated with the imperial court: the women of the imperial family, the high-ranking members of the imperial bodyguard (the Jinyiwei), and the managerial eunuchs who ran the imperial household, and their often closely interconnected families. Given the resources that such people could command and their power to elicit imperial involvement, they became the most influential patrons of monasteries in the capital area" ("Sites, Saints, and Sights at the Tanzhe Monastery," *Cahiers d'Extrême-Asie*, no. 10 [1998]: 188).

13. Wang Xunwen 王巽文, Xu Ziqiang 徐自强, and Ji Yaping 冀亚平, eds., "Fayuansi zhenshi lu" 法源寺貞石錄, in *Fayuan si* 法源寺 (Beijing: Zhongguo fojiao tushuguan, 1981). See also *Fayuan sizhi gao*, 4:115.

14. *Fayuan sizhi gao*, 4:112–15.

15. *Fayuan sizhi gao*, 5:197–240.

16. By the time the gazetteer was finished, for example, the art collection of this temple had twenty-seven couplets, all but one composed by Qing artists. As for paintings related to Buddhist stories, nine were done prior to the Ming, two in the Ming, and twelve in the Qing. This unbalance reached an extreme in the area of landscape paintings: except for one produced in the Ming, all thirty-five were composed in the Qing. See *Fayuan sizhi gao*, 5:224–62.

17. For the best study to date on Tanzhesi, see Naquin, "Sites, Saints, and Sights."

18. *Tanzheshan Xiuyun sizhi* 潭柘山岫雲寺志, 53–55.

19. Wuchu Deshi was a native of Higashi Shinshū 東信州 in Japan. He first studied with a Chan master at Lingyinsi in Hangzhou and then moved to Tanzhesi, at the time called Qingshousi 慶壽寺, where he established a close relationship with Yao Guangxiao 姚廣孝 (1335–1418). In 1412, the Yongle emperor ordered him to take charge of this monastery.

20. Zibo Zhenke 紫柏真可, *Zibo zunzhe quanji* 紫柏尊者全集 27, in *X*, vol. 73, no. 1452, 376b8.

21. *Tanzheshan Xiuyun sizhi*, 14–15.

22. Zhang Yuntao 張雲濤, *Tanzhesi beiji* 潭柘寺碑記 (Beijing: Zhongguo wenshi chubanshe, 2010), 278.

23. *Tanzheshan Xiuyun sizhi*, 79–86.

24. *Tanzheshan Xiuyun sizhi*, 71.

25. For the thirty existing stelae that record seventeen incense associations, see Zhang, *Tanzhesi beiji*, 96–106, 283–437.

26. Zhang, *Tanzhesi beiji*, 287–91.

27. According to Naquin, "Sites, Saints, and Sights," 199–200, these laypeople together represented the equivalent of about six thousand *mu* of land and five thousand taels of silver, exclusive of the sums Emperor Kangxi spent for the restoration. As for its landholdings, a recent source has stated that Tanzhesi, together with its several branch temples, amassed thirty-four thousand *mu* of land throughout the capital area.

28. Naquin, "Sites, Saints, and Sights," 202.

29. *Shaoxing fuzhi* 紹興府志 (1673), 23:50a–51a.

30. Lü was praised in local society as a diligent, astute, and capable official; see *Shengxian zhi* 嵊縣志 (1870), 9:8a.

31. *Shengxian zhi* (1870), 8:2a.

32. For Zhou Mengxiu, see *Shengxian zhi* (1870), 13:1209–10, and Hayasaka Toshihiro 早阪俊廣, Shen Xulu 申緒路, and Liu Xinyi 劉心奕, "Chenmo de Zhou Mengxiu: Wang Ji yu Shengxian Zhoushi 沉默的周夢秀: 王畿與嵊縣周氏," *Guiyang xueyuan xuebao* 貴陽學院學報, no. 6 (2017): 18–25. Jennifer Lynn Eichman, *A Late Sixteenth-Century Chinese Buddhist Fellowship: Spiritual Ambitions, Intellectual Debates, and Epistolary Connections* (Leiden: Brill, 2016), 74–75, also mentions Zhou Mengxiu briefly.

33. "Chamberlain for the Capital Wang" refers to Wang Xizhi 王羲之 (303–361) and "Duke Xuan of Lu" is a reference to Lu Zhi 陸贄 (754–805), whose biography is included in Liu Xu 劉昫, *Jiu Tangshu* 舊唐書 (Beijing Zhonghua shuju, 1975), 139:3791–3819. The monastery converted from Wang Xizhi's old house was Puzhaosi 普照寺 in Linyi 臨沂, Shandong province, while the one Lu Zhi donated his house to build was Nengrensi 能仁寺 (originally named Fuye chapel 福業院) in Jiaxing, Zhejiang province.

34. *Shaoxing fuzhi* (1673), 23:50a–51a.

35. For the relationship between the Lu lineage, Buddhism, and local society, see Fang Fuxiang 方復祥 and Yao Lijun 姚立軍, "Ming Qing Pinghu Lushi yu difang shehui" 明清平湖陸氏與地方社會, *Wenshizhi* 文史哲, no. 1 (2006): 54–59.

36. Lu Guangzu 陸光祖, *Lu Zhuangjian gong yigao* 陸莊簡公遺稿 (1629), 6:9a–10b. Feng Mengzhen narrated a mysterious story about how the temple was lost to Zhou's hands and how it was restored in the Jiajing-Wanli period; see *KXT*, 46:654–55.

37. This recovery from a residential house to a temple even attracted Zhuhong's attention. Zhuhong praised Zhou Mengxiu for his unselfishness but insisted that Zhou be repaid with a good price given that he was poor and innocent; see Yunqi Zhuhong 雲棲袾宏, *Yunqi fahui* 雲棲法彙 16, in *JXZ*, vol. 33, no. B277, 85a29–b07.

38. Lu, *Lu Zhuangjian gong yigao*, 6:9a–10b.

39. *Shengxian zhi* (1684), 6:22b.

40. *Pinghu xianzhi* 平湖縣志 (1627), 3:165–66.

41. Lu, *Lu Zhuangjian gong yigao*, 6:19a–20a.

42. *Pinghu xianzhi* (1627), 3:175.

43. *Shaoxing fuzhi* (1673), 23:50a–51a.

44. In another case, Jingcisi 淨慈寺 in Hangzhou lost three hundred *mu* of land, one-sixth of its landholding in the twelve years before 1573; see *Jingcisi zhi* 净慈寺志, 6:395.

45. For Zhou's understanding of the relationship between Confucianism and Buddhism, see his preface to the *Zhiru bian* 知儒編, http://tripitaka.cbeta.org/D60n9021_001.

46. My thanks to Professor Chen Yunü, who, in a conversion July 15, 2018, reminded me of the importance of the financial situation of the Lu family.

47.   *Huangshan zhi dingben* 黄山志定本 (hereafter cited as *HZD*), in vols. 9–10 of *Zhongguo mingshan zhi* 中國名山志, ed. Jiang Yasa 姜亞沙, Jing Li 經莉, and Chen Zhanqi 陳湛綺 (Beijing: Quanguo tushuguan wenxian suowei fuzhi zhongxin, 2005), 2:375; 3:498; 5:132–33, 170.

48.   Wu Yangchun's father, for example, was so rich that, in 1597, he contributed as much as three hundred thousand taels of silver to the court. Paradoxically, their wealth brought a disaster to the Wu family in the Tianqi era. See Gu Yingtai 谷應泰, *Mingshi jishi benmo* 明史紀事本末 (Beijing: Zhonghua shuju, 1958), 71:1155.

49.   *HZD*, 2:342–43, 390. For a mysterious version of this switch from a Daoist temple to a Buddhist one, see 2:212–13, 365–66.

50.   For Weian's attraction, see *HZD*, 3:474; 4:703, 716. For the famine, see 4:767, 5:136.

51.   Naquin, "Sites, Saints, and Sights," 206.

52.   The painter was Zheng Zhong 鄭重 (d. 1638 or later), who observed the Tiandu peak where Fahaisi was for one year before starting painting; see *HZD*, 3:576. It is no accident that Pumen took the painter Zheng Zhong as his companion on the trip. In studying temples on the Southern Marchmount (i.e., Mount Heng), James Robson points out that "it is clear that the natural setting of a monastery was clearly more than just a backdrop, but could actually help to constitute its numinous qualities. Indeed, it was precisely that type of information about a site's special qualities that traveled widely and made emperors, writers, and potential patrons take note and encourage practitioners and pilgrims to travel there" ("Monastic Spaces and Sacred Traces: Facets of Chinese Buddhist Monastic Records," in Benn, Meeks, and Robson, *Buddhist Monasticism in East Asia*, 55). In her study of Tanzhesi, Susan Naquin makes a similar argument about the significance of scenery.

53.   See *HZD*, 3:562, 610.

54.   For the invitation, see *HZD*, 2:330–31. For the travel, see 5:126, 137, 144.

55.   For Weian's acquisition of the canon, see *HZD*, 3:562–63, 5:136–37. For his memorial requesting the name tablet, see 3:455–56.

56.   In tantric Buddhism, the four-faced Vairocana refers to the Dharma body as wisdom (*zhi fashen* 智法身) in the Diamond Realm (*jingang jie* 金剛界, Skt. *Vajradhātu*). See the *Jingangding yuqie zhong lüechu niansong jing* 金剛頂瑜伽中略出念誦經 1, in *T*, vol. 18, no. 866, 227b25–28, 229c22–29. That the four-faced Vairocana sits on a pedestal comprising the lotus of one thousand petals has a canonical basis in the *Fanwang jing* 梵網經 2, in *T*, vol. 24, no. 1484, 1003b16. The statue at Ciguangsi no longer exists, but similar statues can be found at Shaolinsi in Henan and Fayuansi in Beijing; see http://tupian.hudong.com/a3_54_67_01300000044935121040677395402_jpg.html.

57.   This was not a phenomenon unique to the Ming. Scholars have noted that in the Song, once receiving royal patronage the chance for a temple to develop a national influence greatly increased and thus attracted more support from local society. See Koichi Shinohara, "From Local History to Universal History: The Construction of the Sung T'ien-t'ai Lineage," in *Buddhism in the Sung*, ed. Peter N. Gregory and Daniel A. Getz Jr., (Honolulu: University of Hawai`i Press, 1999), 527–76.

58.   *HZD*, 3:492–94, 565; 4:743–62.

59.   The rumor had it that the Buddha statue was the daughter of the water mother (*shuimu* 水母), who could not stand three straight days without rain. For the general situation, see *HZD*, 2:330; 3:451, 503. For Bao's letter, see 5:126–28. For Mi Wanzhong's meeting with Pumen, see 3:639–60. For the trouble in Hangzhou, see 2:342, 5:129–30. Nevertheless, the statue did not arrive in Ciguangsi until 1605; see *Huanghai* 黄海, in *shibu* 史部, vols. 229–30, of *Siku quanshu cunmu congshu* 四庫全書存目叢書, comp. Siku quanshu cunmu congshu bianzuan weiyuanhui 四庫全書存目叢書編纂委員會 (Jinan: Qilu shushe, 1994–1997), 67–68.

60.   Huizhou merchants and the family lineages there have sparked strong scholarly interest. For recent studies, see Harriet T. Zurndorfer, "Learning, Lineages, and Locality in Late Imperial China: A Comparative Study of Education in Huichow (Anhwei) and Foochow (Fukien) 1600–1800. Part I,"

Journal of the Economic and Social History of the Orient 35, no. 2 (1992): 109–44; "Part II," 209–38; Qitao Guo, *Ritual Opera and Mercantile Lineage: The Confucian Transformation of Popular Culture in Late Imperial Huizhou* (Stanford, Calif.: Stanford University Press, 2005).

61. For their ambitions, see Pan, *Huanghai*, 49–50.

62. Pan, *Huanghai*, 50.

63. *Huangshan zhi xuji* 黄山志續集, in vols. 9–10 of *Zhongguo mingshan zhi*, ed. Jiang Yasa 姜亞沙, Jing Li 經莉, and Chen Zhanqi 陳湛綺 (Beijing: Quanguo tushuguan wenxian suowei fuzhi zhongxin, 2005), 7.

64. For this kind of network, see Tobie Meyer-Fong, "Packaging the Men of Our Times: Literary Anthologies, Friendship Networks, and Political Accommodation in the Early Qing," *HJAS* 64, no. 1 (2004): 5–56, and Timothy Brook, "Family Continuity and Cultural Hegemony: The Gentry of Ningbo, 1368–1911," in *Chinese Local Elites and Patterns of Dominance*, ed. Joseph W. Esherick and Mary Backus Rankin (Berkeley: University of California Press, 1990), 27–50.

65. See, for example, Pan, *Huanghai*, 164b, 173b.

66. *HZD*, 3:568.

67. *HZD*, 3:499.

68. Pan, *Huanghai*, 179a.

69. Tiandu is the major peak of Mount Huang. For the Tiandu Association, which first appeared seventy years previously, see *HZD*, 2:324–26, 5:211–12.

70. *HZD*, 3:487–88, 565; Pan, *Huanghai*, 35.

71. As a disciple of Zhencheng, a leading monk favored by both Cisheng and Wanli, Weian's activities at Mount Huang, including the Pumen Association, had clear parallels with Wutai; see *HZD*, 3:486–88, and Pan, *Huanghai*, 37. Weian requested his master to write an essay for the Dabei chapel and got a positive response. See *HZD*, 3:472–73.

72. Pan, *Huanghai*, 37a–b.

73. Jiang Wu, *Enlightenment in Dispute: The Reinvention of Chan Buddhism in Seventeenth-Century China* (Oxford: Oxford University Press, 2008), 258–63.

74. For the invitation letters and official document assigning Ruxiao as the abbot, see *HZD*, 3:451–53; 5:134–37, 141–44.

75. *HZD*, 2:212–13, 331; 3:472–74. This Dabei Buddha was very likely a tantric form of Guanyin (my thanks to Professor Chün-fang Yü for this association), with its fourteen arms representing her fourteen merits of fearlessness (*shisi wuwei de* 十四無畏德). The textual source for this sort of icon can be found in the *Lengyan jing helun* 楞嚴經合論 6, in *X*, vol. 12, no. 272, 515a–b11. The Yaowang bodhisattva and Yaoshang bodhisattva had medicinal attributes and applications, and their inclusion in this hall might be because Cisheng suffered from eye disease and other illnesses in her final years.

 Professor Yü also pointed out that placing this bodhisattva in the center flanked by Yaowang and Yaoshang was a most unusual iconic arrangement. I suspect that this arrangement had something to do with the *Qianshou qianyan guanshiyin pusa guangda yuanman wuai dabeixin tuoluoni jing* 千手千眼觀世音菩薩廣大圓滿無礙大悲心陀羅尼經, which has seven extant Chinese translations and which has been popular among laypeople and monks in China. This dharani, although devoted to Avalokiteśvara, includes Yaowang and Yaoshang. More important, it promises to cure human eye disease (*T*, vol. 20, no. 1060, 110b02–09) and protect the state from domestic troubles and foreign invasion (*T*, vol. 20, no. 1060, 109c12–26), two things about which Cisheng and Wanli worried most at the time. For the images and the confessional ritual related to this dharani, see Pu Wenqi 濮文起, Xia Jingshan 夏荊山, and Lou Yutian 婁玉田, eds., *Zhongguo lidai guanyin wenxian jicheng* 中國歷代觀音文獻集成 (Beijing: Zhonghua quanguo tushuguan wenxian suowei fuzhi zhongxin, 1998), 2:173–685.

76. *HZD*, 5:166–72.

77. *HZD*, 3:413–14.
78. *HZD*, 2:404, 5:111; *Huangshan zhi xuji*, 3:159–64.
79. See *Huangshan zhi xuji*, 7:617, 628; 1:15–17, 75–80, 83–87.
80. Naquin, "Sites, Saints, and Sights," 207.

8. SETBACKS

1. It can be controversial as to when and where a monk received his dharma transmission because the judgment involves not only the completion of his apprenticeship but also the choice to align himself with a specific line of Buddhism. Jiang Wu points out that it was not unusual to fabricate such a clan because "by means of dharma transmission, Dharma heirs gain legitimacy to succeed to the patriarchal position in an imagined family" (*Enlightenment in Dispute: The Reinvention of Chan Buddhism in Seventeenth-Century China* [Oxford: Oxford University Press, 2008], 34). When controversy arises, I follow the conventional opinion as much as possible.

2. A typical biography of a monk includes such details as his name, native place, reasons for leaving home, masters and monasteries he visited or was affiliated with, his activities after becoming a senior monk, and a description of his death. Sometimes his age, the death year, and even birth year are also given. However, this genre rarely offers information about when these events happened.

3. The five collections comprise the following: *Da Ming gaoseng zhuan* 大明高僧傳 (6 vols.), compiled by Ruxing 如惺; *Buxu gaoseng zhuan* (26 vols.), by Minghe 明河; and *Shijian jigulüe xuji* (2 vols.), by Huanlun 幻輪. They were all compiled in the Ming. By contrast, the *Gaoseng zhaiyao* 高僧摘要 (4 vols.) was collected by Xu Changzhi 徐昌治 in the early Qing and the *Xinxu gaosengzhuan siji* 新續高僧傳四集 by Yu Meian 喻昧庵 in the early twentieth century. Together, they cover the biographical information for 307 eminent monks who lived in the period under discussion.

4. For studies based on these biographies, see, for example, Yamazaki Hiroshi 山崎宏, *Shina chūsei bukkyō no tenkai* 支那中世仏教の展開 (Tokyo: Shimizu shoten, 1942); Shigenoi Shizuka 滋野井恬, "Jūisseiki igo Chūgoku no bukkyō kyōsen no gaikyō" 11世紀以後中國の仏教教線の概況, *Ōtani daigaku kenkyū nenpō* 大谷大學研究年報, no. 19 (1967): 255–312; Chen Yunü 陳玉女, "Mindai bukkyō shakai no chiiki teki kenkyū—Kasei Manreki nenkan (1522–1620) o chūshin toshite" 明代仏教社會の地域的研究—嘉靖・萬曆年間 (1522–1620) を中心として (Ph.D. diss., Kyushu University, 1995), 162–95; Zhang Weiran 張偉然, "Zhongguo fojiao dili yanjiu shiji shuping" 中國佛教地理研究史籍述評, *Dili xuebao* 地理學報 51, no. 4 (1996): 369–73.

5. Comprehensive though it is, the *Biographies of Eminent Monks* contains some problems, owing partly to the nature of the genre. For one thing, the information accessible to the compilers was always limited, a situation that could be exacerbated by sociopolitical disorders. Second, sectarian concerns sometimes became so evident that their standards of inclusion and exclusion are open to question. For discussion of this genre, see Koichi Shinohara, "Two Sources of Chinese Buddhist Biographies: Stupa Inscriptions and Miracle Stories," in *Monks and Magicians: Religious Biographies in Asia*, ed. Phyllis Granoff and Koichi Shinohara (Oakville, Ont.: Mosaic Press, 1988), 94–128; Koichi Shinohara, "Biographies of Eminent Monks in a Comparative Perspective: The Function of the Holy in Medieval Chinese Buddhism," *Zhonghua foxue xuebao* 中華佛學學報 7 (1994): 477–500; and Erik Zürcher, "Perspectives in the Study of Chinese Buddhism," *Journal of the Royal Asiatic Society of Great Britain and Ireland*, no. 1 (1982): 164–65.

6. The *Shijian jigulüe xuji* is compiled chronologically and is of comparatively poor quality. Given that it assembles under a single year the biographies of monks who had died in the preceding interval of time, this year is used as the death year of those monks for analysis unless other information is available.

7. Six of them sought Buddhist instruction in Beijing and seven in Jiangnan. Notably, three of the seven monks in Jiangnan were recorded not because of their spiritual or intellectual achievements but because of their efforts to protect monasteries from being appropriated by the local powerful or plundered by Japanese pirates.

8. *HSMY* 30, in *X*, vol. 73, no. 1456, 677a10–13.

9. For the definitions of North China and Jiangnan used in this book, see footnote 49 in chapter 3. Despite its geographical proximity, Datong 大同 prefecture in Shanxi is excluded from North China in favor of Taiyuan prefecture. This is because Mount Wutai, the most important Buddhist site in East Asia, was in Datong prefecture. If included, the huge numbers of pilgrims attracted by Mount Wutai, many of whom were monks who visited the sacred site only for a few days, may well distort the whole picture of monks' mobility.

10. For an important study in the field, see Wolfram Eberhard, "Temple-Building Activities in Medieval and Modern China: An Experimental Study," *Monumenta Serica* 23 (1964): 264–318.

11. For the distinctions of these terms, see *Jiuhua shanzhi* 九華山志, 32, and Timothy Brook, *Praying for Power: Buddhism and the Formation of Gentry Society in Late-Ming China* (Cambridge, Mass.: Harvard University Press, 1993), 4.

12. *SKHB*, vol. 58, 136.

13. Wang Yuanhan 王元翰, *Ningcui ji* 凝翠集, in vol. 117 of *Congshu jicheng xubian* 叢書集成續編 (Taipei: Xin wenfeng chuban gongsi, 1989), 201. Some of the monks did not appear in the capital at the same time. For example, Deqing had been exiled to Guangdong before Li Zhi arrived in Beijing.

14. There were several key monks who attracted Dharma seekers to Beijing during this period. In connection with the doctrinal tradition, Dharma masters Song 松 and Xiu 秀 magnetized many young people. For the Chan tradition, it was Bianrong Zhenyuan 遍融真圓 (1506–1584) and Xiaoyan Debao 笑岩德寶 (1512–1581). In fact, almost all these monks mentioned here once sought instruction from Bianrong Zhenyuan and Xiaoyan Debao.

15. For Wu's argument, see, for example, Wu, *Enlightenment in Dispute*, 285.

16. Part of this section appears in Dewei Zhang, "The Collapse of Beijing as a Buddhist Centre: Viewed from the Activities of Eminent Monks, 1522 to 1620," *Journal of Asian History* 43, no. 2 (2009): 137–63.

17. This result may not be that surprising considering how reluctant local people were to pursue a religious career. In the 1590s, for example, there were more than 570 Buddhist and Daoist temples in Wanping 宛平 county of Beijing. According to Shen Bang 沈榜 (1540–1597), the magistrate of the county, however, only fewer than 10 were indigenous among the thousands of Buddhist and Daoist monks housed in those temples; *Wanshu zaji* 宛署雜記 (Beijing: Beijing guji chubanshe, 1980), 19:237.

18. Of course, not all monks came to Beijing for the Dharma. For example, Tao Wangling revealed that "[monks] inherited the Dharma in the past but now what they inherit is wealth" (古嗣法，今嗣貨). Similarly, Wang Yuanhan pointed out that there were three purposes for monks' visiting Beijing: the best for the Dharma of the masters, the worst for the money of high-ranking officials, and the middle for the essays of famous literati. See Tao Wangling 陶望齡, *Xiean ji* 歇庵集, in *jibu* 集部, vol. 1365, of *Xuxiu Siku quanshu* 續修四庫全書, ed. Gu Tinglong 顧廷龍 et al. (Shanghai: Shanghai guji chubanshe, 1995–2001), 31a–33a; Wang, *Ningcui ji*, 244–45.

19. *HSMY* 30, in *X*, vol. 73, no. 1456, 680a3–4.

20. See Zhang, "Collapse of Beijing."

21. Long Xianzhao 龍顯昭, ed., *Bashu fojiao beiwen jicheng* 巴蜀佛教碑文集成 (Chengdu: Bashu shushe, 2004), 459–60.

22. *Songshu* 嵩書, in *Songyue wenxian congkan* 嵩嶽文獻叢刊, ed. Zhengzhou shi tushuguan 鄭州市圖書館 (Zhengzhou: Zhongzhou guji chubanshe, 2003), 555–57.

23. *YHD*, 54:1561. Brook, *Praying for Power*, 76, notes a shift that took place in Beijing's intellectual circle from tolerating or even appreciating Buddhism to criticizing it at the turn of the seventeenth century.

24. See Hubert Michael Seiwert, with Ma Xisha 馬西沙, *Popular Religious Movements and Heterodox Sects in Chinese History* (Leiden: Brill, 2003), chaps. 5–7.

25. Hanyue Fazang 漢月法藏, *Sanfeng Zang heshang yulu* 三峰藏和尚語錄 16, in *JXZ*, vol. 34, no. B299, 202a2–8.

26. *HSMY* 13, in *X*, vol. 73, no. 1456, 549b23–c1.

27. Ouyi Zhixu 蕅益智旭, *Lingfeng Ouyi dashi zonglun* 靈峰蕅益大師宗論 4, in *JXZ*, vol. 36, no. B348, 319c06–08.

28. *HSMY* 14, in *X*, vol. 73, no. 1456, 555c2–7.

29. Yunqi Zhuhong 雲棲袾宏, *Yunqi fahui* 雲棲法彙 21, in *JXZ*, vol. 33, no. B277, 153.

30. Wu, *Enlightenment in Dispute*, 48.

31. Wu, *Enlightenment in Dispute*, 5.

CONCLUSION

1. Tian Qi 田奇, *Beijing de fojiao simiao* 北京的佛教寺廟 (Beijing: Shumu wenxian chubanshe, 1993), 2–3. In 1745 when Li Zongwan 勵宗萬 (1705–1759, *jinshi* 1721) undertook some fieldwork, he already witnessed the decline: "The Western Mountains are where Buddhist and Daoist temples are most flourishing. But when I asked the monks, [I] found that there are only twenty or thirty left" (若夫梵宮仙宇, 西山最盛, 乃詢之僧侶, 僅存二三十處.) (*Jingcheng guji kao* 京城古蹟攷 [Beijing: Beijing chubanshe, 1964], 4).

2. Michael J. Walsh, *Sacred Economies: Buddhist Monasticism and Territoriality in Medieval China* (New York: Columbia University Press, 2009), 21.

3. This assessment is based on *Wulin fanzhi* 武林梵志 by Wu Zhijing 吳之鯨 (*juren* 1609), *Jinling fancha zhi* by Ge Yinliang 葛寅亮 (1570–1646, *jinshi* 1601), and *Wudu facheng* 吳都法乘 by Zhou Yongnian 周永年 (1582–1647). The current edition of *Wudu facheng* includes some texts written as late as 1775.

4. For a brief discussion of problems related to cultural conflict, see Stephen F. Teiser, "Social History and the Confrontation of Cultures: Foreword to the Third Edition," in *The Buddhist Conquest of China: The Spread and Adaptation of Buddhism in Early Medieval China*, ed. Erik Zürcher (Leiden: Brill, 2007), xxiv–xxvii.

5. Hubert Michael Seiwert and Ma Xisha 馬西沙, *Popular Religious Movements and Heterodox Sects in Chinese History* (Leiden: Brill, 2003), 103–57, 458–65.

6. For the intellectual reorientation in the late Ming and early Qing period, see, for example, On-cho Ng, "An Early Qing Critique of the Philosophy of Mind-Heart (*Xin*): The Confucian Quest for Doctrinal Purity and the 'Doxic' Role of Chan Buddhism," *Journal of Chinese Philosophy* 26, no. 1 (March 1999): 89–120; Ying-shih Yu, "Some Preliminary Observations on the Rise of Ch'ing Confucian Intellectualism," *Tsing Hua Journal of Chinese Studies* 11, no. 1-2 (1975): 105–36; Wang Fansen 王汎森, "Qingchu sixiang zhong xing'ershang xuanyuan zhi xue de moluo" 清初思想中形而上玄遠之學的沒落, *Lishi yuyan yanjiusuo jikan* 歷史語言研究所集刊 69, no. 3 (1998): 557–83; and Benjamin A. Elman, *From Philosophy to Philology: Intellectual and Social Aspects of Change in Late Imperial China* (Cambridge, Mass.: Harvard University Press, 1984).

7. This criticism may not totally be fair. *Shixue* was an essential component of Wang Yangming's thought, and the Wang Yangming school did not deny conventional Confucian responsibilities

but attempted to provide an alternative other than the Cheng-Zhu school to better fulfill it. See Joanna F. Handlin, *Action in Late Ming Thought: The Reorientation of Lü Kun and Other Scholar-Officials* (Berkeley: University of California Press, 1983); Lü Miaofen 呂妙芬, *Yangming xue shiren shequn: Lishi, sixiang yu shijian* 陽明學士人社群: 歷史、思想與實踐 (Taipei: Zhongyang yanjiuyuan jindaishi yanjiusuo, 2003), 293–94; and Chung-ying Cheng, "Practical Learning in Yen Yuan, Chu Hsi, and Wang Yang-ming," in *Principle and Practicality: Essays in Neo-Confucianism and Practical Learning*, ed. Wm. Theodore de Bary and Irene Bloom (New York: Columbia University Press, 1979), 39–45.

8. Jennifer Lynn Eichman, *A Late Sixteenth-Century Chinese Buddhist Fellowship: Spiritual Ambitions, Intellectual Debates, and Epistolary Connections* (Leiden: Brill, 2016), 75–76, notes that by the mid-seventeenth century growing Confucian criticism had dampened enthusiasm for the use of Buddhist doctrine to illuminate Confucian ideas.

9. *Qing Gaozong Chun huangdi shilu* 清高宗純皇帝實錄 (Beijing: Zhonghua shuju, 1986) 242:13207.

10. Marcus Bingenheimer has observed that "after the spectacular rise between circa 1570 and 1670 . . . the figures I have for temple construction, gazetteer production point only to a light decrease. The statistics in our person authority database, however, show indeed a strong drop in known Buddhist persons after 1700" (personal communication, July 16, 2011); see https://authority.dila.edu.tw /person/.

References

Akiyama Motohide 秋山元秀. "Gozan: Taizan—gensei to meikai o musubu 'Tōgaku'" 五山：泰山—現世と冥界を結ぶ「東嶽」(The five Sacred Mountains: Mount Tai—the Eastern Marchmount linking the secular world and the nether one). *Gekkan shinika* 月刊しにか 11, no. 8 (2000): 16–19.

Araki Kengo 荒木見悟. "Bukkyō koji toshite no Riku Kōso" 仏教居士としての陸光祖 (Lu Guangzu as a lay Buddhist). *Nagoya daigaku Chūgoku tetsugaku ronshū* 名古屋大學中國哲學論集, no. 3 (2004): 1–26.

——. *Bukkyō to jukyō: Chūgoku shisō o keiseisuru mono* 佛教と儒教：中国思想を形成するもの (Buddhism and Confucianism: The formation of Chinese thought). Tokyo: Kenbun shuppan, 1963.

——. "Confucianism and Buddhism in the Late Ming." In *The Unfolding of Neo-Confucianism*, ed. Wm. Theodore de Bary, 39–66. New York: Columbia University Press, 1975.

——. *Mindai shisō kenkyū: Mindai ni okeru jukyō to bukkyō no kōryū* 明代思想研究：明代における儒教と佛教の交流 (Studies on Ming thought: The exchange between Confucianism and Buddhism in the Ming). Tokyo: Sōbunsha, 1972.

——. "Minmatsu ni okeru ju butsu chōwaron no seikaku" 明末に於ける儒仏調和論の性格 (The compatibility of Confucianism and Buddhism in the late Ming). *Nihon Chūgoku gakkaihō* 日本中國學會報, no. 15 (1966): 210–24.

——. *Unsei Shukō no kenkyū* 雲棲袾宏の研究 (A study on Yunqi Zhuhong). Tokyo: Daizō shuppan, 1985.

——. *Yōmeigaku no tenkai to bukkyō* 陽明學の開展と仏教 (The unfolding of the Yangming school and Buddhism). Tokyo: Kenbun shuppan, 1984.

——. *Yōmeigaku to bukkyō shingaku* 陽明學と仏教心學 (The Yangming school and the "mind" learning of Buddhism). Tokyo: Kenbun shuppan, 2008.

——. "Zenso Munen Shin'yō to Ri Takugo" 禪僧無念深有と李卓吾 (Chan master Wunian Shenyou and Li Zuowu). In *Yōmeigaku to bukkyō shingaku* 陽明學と仏教心學, 174–96. Tokyo: Kenbun shuppan, 2008.

Asai Motoi 淺井紀. *Min Shin jidai minkan shūkyō kessha no kenkyū* 明清時代民間宗教結社の研究 (A study of folk religious associations in Ming and Qing China). Tokyo: Kenbun shuppan, 1990.

——. "Mindai Saidaijōkyō no kyōgi keisei" 明代西大乘教の教義形成 (The formation of the religious teachings of the Xidacheng sect in the Ming). *Tōkai daigaku kiyō, bungakubu* 東海大學紀要.文學部, 81 (2004): 1–18.

Bai Wengu 白文固. "Yuandai de siyuan jingji" 元代的寺院經濟 (The monastic economy in the Yuan dynasty). *Qinghai shehui kexue* 青海社會科學, no. 6 (1987): 74–79, 88.

Baroni, Helen Josephine. *Ōbaku Zen: The Emergence of the Third Sect of Zen in Tokugawa Japan*. Honolulu: University of Hawai'i Press, 2000.

Barrett, Timothy. "Chinese Religion in English Guise: The History of an Illusion." *Modern Asian Studies* 39, no. 3 (2005): 509–33.

——. "Climate Change and Religious Response: The Case of Early Medieval China." *Journal of the Royal Asiatic Society*, 3rd ser., 17, no. 2 (2007): 139–56.

Bartlett, Thomas. "Phonology as Statecraft in Gu Yanwu's Thought." In *The Scholar's Mind: Essays in Honor of Frederick W. Mote*, ed. Perry Link, 181–206. Hong Kong: Chinese University Press, 2009.

Beijing tushuguan cang Zhongguo lidai shike taben huibian 北京圖書館藏中國歷代石刻拓本彙編 (Collected Chinese stone rubbings of all generations, preserved by the Beijing Library). Zhengzhou: Zhongzhou guji chubanshe, 1989.

Benn, James A. *Burning for the Buddha: Self-Immolation in Chinese Buddhism*. Honolulu: University of Hawai`i Press, 2007.

——. *Tea in China: A Religious and Cultural History*. Honolulu: University of Hawai`i Press, 2015.

Benn, James A., Lori Rachelle Meeks, and James Robson, eds. *Buddhist Monasticism in East Asia: Places of Practice*. London: Routledge, 2010.

Berling, Judith A. *The Syncretic Religion of Lin Chao-en*. New York: Columbia University Press, 1980.

Bi Ziyan 畢自嚴. *Shiyin yuan canggao* 石隱園藏稿 (A manuscript hidden in the Shiyin garden). In *jibu* 集部, vol. 1293, of *Wenyuange yingyin Siku quanshu* 文淵閣影印四庫全書. Taipei: Shangwu yinshuguan, 1983.

Bingenheimer, Marcus. *Island of Guanyin: Mount Putuo and Its Gazetteers*. New York: Oxford University Press, 2016.

—— [馬德偉]. "Zhongguo fosi zhi chutan ji shumu yanjiu" 中國佛寺志初探及書目研究 (A preliminary study of Chinese Buddhist gazetteers and their bibliographies). *Hanyu foxue pinglun* 漢語佛學評論, no. 2 (2011): 377–408.

Bol, Peter. K. "The 'Localist Turn' and 'Local Identity' in Later Imperial China." *Late Imperial China* 24, no. 2 (2003): 1–50.

——. "Neo-Confucianism and Local Society, Twelfth to Sixteenth Century: A Case Study." In *The Song-Yuan-Ming Transition in Chinese History*, ed. Paul Jakov Smith and Richard von Glahn, 241–83: Cambridge, Mass.: Harvard University Asia Center, 2003.

——. *Neo-Confucianism in History*. Cambridge, Mass.: Harvard University Press, 2008.

——. "The Rise of Local History: History, Geography, and Culture in Southern Song and Yuan Wuzhou." *HJAS* 61, no. 1 (2001): 37–76.

Bossler, Beverly J. *Powerful Relations: Kinship, Status, and the State in Sung China (960–1279)*. Cambridge, Mass.: Council on East Asian Studies, 1998.

Braudel, Fernand. *Civilization and Capitalism, 15th–18th Century*. 3 vols. New York: Harper and Row, 1981–1984.

——. *The Mediterranean and the Mediterranean World in the Age of Philip II*. 2 vols. 2nd rev. ed. Trans. Sian Reynolds. Berkeley: University of California Press, 1972–1973.

——. *On History*. Trans. Sarah Matthews. Chicago: University of Chicago Press, 1982.

Brokaw, Cynthia. *The Ledgers of Merit and Demerit: Social Change and Moral Order in Late Imperial China*. Princeton, N.J.: Princeton University Press, 1991.

——. "Yuan Huang (1533–1606) and the Ledgers of Merit and Demerit." *HJAS* 47, no. 1 (1987): 137–95.

Brook, Timothy. "At the Margin of Public Authority: The Ming State and Buddhism." In *The Chinese State in Ming Society*, 139–57. London: RoutledgeCurzon, 2005.

——. "Buddhism in the Chinese Constitution: Recording Monasteries in North Zhili." In *The Chinese State in Ming Society*, 158–81. London: RoutledgeCurzon, 2005.

——. *The Chinese State in Ming Society*. London: RoutledgeCurzon, 2005.

——. *The Confusions of Pleasure: Commerce and Culture in Ming China*. Berkeley: University of California Press, 1998.

——. "Family Continuity and Cultural Hegemony: The Gentry of Ningbo, 1368–1911." In *Chinese Local Elites and Patterns of Dominance*, ed. Joseph W. Esherick and Mary Backus Rankin, 27–50. Berkeley: University of California Press, 1990.

——. "Funerary Ritual and the Building of Lineages in Late Imperial China." *HJAS* 49, no. 2 (1989): 465–99.

——. *Geographical Sources of Ming-Qing History*. Ann Arbor: University of Michigan, 1988.

——. "The Politics of Religion: Late-Imperial Origins of the Regulatory State." In *Making Religion, Making the State: The Politics of Religion in Modern China*, ed. Yoshiko Ashiwa and David L. Wank, 22–42. Stanford, Calif.: Stanford University Press, 2009.

——. *Praying for Power: Buddhism and the Formation of Gentry Society in Late-Ming China*. Cambridge, Mass.: Harvard University Press, 1993.

——. "Rethinking Syncretism: The Unity of the Three Teachings and Their Joint Worship in Late-Imperial China." *Journal of Chinese Religions* 21, no. 1 (1993): 13–44.

——. "State Censorship and the Book Trade." In *The Chinese State in Ming Society*, 118–36. London: RoutledgeCurzon, 2005.

——. *The Troubled Empire: China in the Yuan and Ming Dynasties*. Cambridge, Mass.: Belknap Press, 2010.

Burke, Peter. *The French Historical Revolution: The "Annales" School, 1929–2014*. Stanford, Calif.: Stanford University Press, 2015.

Buswell, Robert E., and Donald S. Lopez, eds. *The Princeton Dictionary of Buddhism*. Princeton, N.J.: Princeton University Press, 2014.

Cao Ganghua 曹剛華. *Mingdai fojiao fangzhi yanjiu* 明代佛教方志研究 (Studies on Buddhist monastic gazetteers in the Ming). Beijing: Renmin daxue chubanshe, 2011.

Carnes, Mark C., and Daniel K. Gardner. *Confucianism and the Succession Crisis of the Wanli Emperor*. New York: Pearson Longman, 2005.

Cen Xuelü 岑學呂, ed. *Xuyun laoheshang nianpu fahui zengding ben* 虛雲老和尚年譜法彙增訂本 (An extended edition of the chronicle and collected writings of Master Xuyun). Taipei: Dasheng jingshe, 1982.

Chen Guofu 陳國符. *Daozang yuanliu kao* 道藏源流攷 (A study of the history of the Daoist canon). Beijing: Zhonghua shuju, 1963.

Chen, Jinhua. "Śarīra and Scepter: Empress Wu's Political Use of Buddhist Relics." *Journal of the International Association of Buddhist Studies* 25, no. 1-2 (2002): 33–150.

——. "The Tang Buddhist Palace Chapels." *Journal of Chinese Religions* 32, no. 1 (2004): 101–73.

Ch'en, Kenneth K. S. *Buddhism in China: A Historical Survey*. Princeton, N.J.: Princeton University Press, 1964.

——. "The Economic Background of the Hui-ch'ang Suppression of Buddhism." *HJAS* 19, no. 1/2 (1956): 67–105.

Chen Lai 陳來. *You Wu zhi jing: Wang Yangming zhexue de jingshen* 有無之境—王陽明哲學的精神 (The state of being and nonbeing: The spirit of Wang Yangming's philosophy). Beijing: Renmin chubanshe, 1991.

Chen Shilong 陳時龍. "Wanli Zhangfu chaojia shi shuwei: Yi Qiu Shun *Wangjinglou yigao* wei zhuyao shiliao" 萬曆張府抄家事述微—以丘橓《望京樓遺稿》爲主要史料 (A detailed account of the confiscation of Zhang Juzheng's family estates in the Wanli period, based mainly on Qiu Shun's *Wangjinglou yigao*). *Zhongguo wenhua yanjiusuo xuebao* 中國文化研究所學報, no. 53 (2011): 110–36.

Chen Xiyuan 陳熙遠. "Zai guojia quanli yu minjian xinyang jiaojie de bianyuan: Yi Mingru Zhan Ruoshui jinhui Nanjing yinci wei lizheng" 在國家權力與民間信仰交界的邊緣：以明儒湛若水禁毀南京淫祠為例證 (On the boundaries between state power and folk beliefs: Taking as example Zhan Ruoshui's ban on the illegal temples in Nanjing). In *Ming Qing falü yunzuo zhongde quanli yu wenhua* 明清法律運作中的權力與文化 (Power and culture in the operation of law during the Ming-Qing period), ed. Qiu Pengsheng 邱澎生 and Chen Xiyuan, 87–143. Taipei: Lianjing chuban shiye youxian gongsi, 2009.

Chen Yinque 陳寅恪. *Liu Rushi biezhuan* 柳如是別傳 (A special biography of Liu Rushi). Beijing: Sanlian shudian, 2001.

Chen Yuan 陳垣. *Mingji Dian Qian fojiao kao* 明季滇黔佛教攷 (Studies on Buddhism in the Dian-Qian region in the ending years of the Ming). Beijing: Furen daxue, 1940. Reprint, Beijing: Kexue chuban-she, 1959.

——. *Qingchu sengzheng ji* 清初僧諍記 (Debates among monks in the early Qing). Beijing: Zhonghua shuju, 1962.

Chen Yuanlong 陳元龍. *Airi tang shiji* 愛日堂詩集 (Collected poems of the Airi hall). In *jibu* 集部, vol. 254, of *Siku quanshu cunmu congshu* 四庫全書存目叢書, comp. Siku quanshu cunmu congshu bianzuan weiyuanhui 四庫全書存目叢書編纂委員會. Jinan: Qilu shushe, 1994–1997.

Chen Yunü 陳玉女. "Kinsei Kahoku chiiki ni okeru bukkyō no shakaiteki shintō no patān— Mindai Hoku-chokurei o sokutei no waku toshite" 近世華北地域における仏教の社會的浸透のパターン―明代北直隷 を測定の枠として (The pattern of the infiltration of Buddhism in society in North China in modern times: Taking Beizhili in the Ming dynasty as the frame of evaluation). In *Higashi Ajia ni okeru seisan to ryūtsū no rekishi shakaigakuteki kenkyū* 東アジアにおける生産と流通の歴史社會學的研究, ed. Kawakatsu Mamoru 川勝守, 303–405. Fukuoka: Chūgoku shoten, 1993.

——. "Min Kasei shoki ni okeru Gireiha seiken to bukkyō shukusei—'Kokoji jiken' o kōsatsu no chūshin ni shite" 明嘉靖初期における議礼派政権と仏教粛正―「皇姑寺事件」を考察の中心にして (The power of the Ritual-Debate faction and the purging of Buddhism in the early Jiajing period, centered on the Huanggu temple event). *Kyūshū daigaku tōyōshi ronshū* 九州大学東洋史論集, no. 23 (1995): 1–37.

——. "Mindai bukkyō shakai no chiiki teki kenkyū—Kasei Manreki nenkan (1522–1620) o chūshin toshite" 明代仏教社會の地域的研究―嘉靖・萬暦年間 (1522–1620) を中心として (Regional studies of Buddhist societies in the Ming, with a focus on the Jiajing-Wanli [1522–1620] period). Ph.D. diss., Kyushu University, 1995.

——. "Ming Huayan zongpai Bianrong hesang ruyu kao—jianshu Long, Wan nianjian fojiao yu jingshi quangui de wanglai" 明華嚴宗派遍融和尚入獄攷―兼述隆、萬年間佛教與京師權貴的往來 (An inves-tigation of imprisonment of Bianrong, a Huayan monk in the Ming—concurrently discussing the con-nection of Buddhism with the powerful and noble in the capital during the Long[qing]-Wan[li] period). In *Mingdai de fojiao yu shehui* 明代的佛教與社會 (Buddhism and society in Ming China), 215–58. Beijing: Beijing daxue chubanshe, 2011.

——. "Ming Wanli shiqi Cisheng huang taihou de chongfo—jianlun fo, dao liang shili de duizhi" 明萬暦 時期慈聖皇太后的崇佛―兼論佛、道兩勢力的對峙 (The enthrallment with Buddhism of Empress Dowager Cisheng in the Wanli period: Concurrently discussing the confrontation between Bud-dhism and Daoism). In *Mingdai de fojiao yu shehui* 明代的佛教與社會 (Buddhism and society in Ming China), 96–146. Beijing: Beijing daxue chubanshe, 2011.

——. "Ming Wutaishan zhu foshi jianzhu cailiao zhi qude yu yunshu—yi mucai, tong, tie deng jiancai weizhu" 明五臺山諸佛寺建築材料之取得與運輸―以木材、銅、鐵等建材為主 (The acquirement and transport of construction materials of monasteries on Mount Wutai: Focusing on wood, copper, and iron). In *Mingdai de fojiao yu shehui* 明代的佛教與社會 (Buddhism and society in Ming China), 216–47. Beijing: Beijing daxue chubanshe, 2011.

——. *Mingdai de fojiao yu shehui* 明代的佛教與社會 (Buddhism and society in the Ming). Beijing: Beijing daxue chubanshe, 2011.

——. "Mingdai ershi si yamen de fojiao xinyang" 明代二十四衙門的佛教信仰 (Buddhist belief in the twenty-four yamens of the Ming). *Chenggong daxue lishi xuebao* 25 (1999): 174–236.

——. *Mingdai ershi si yamen huanguan yu Beijing fojiao* 明代二十四衙門宦官與北京佛教 (The Ming eunuchs of the twenty-four yamens and Beijing Buddhism). Taipei: Ruwen chubanshe, 2001.

——. *Mingdai fomen neiwai sengsu jiaoshe de changyu* 明代佛門內外僧俗交涉的場域 (The sacred and secu-lar contexts where Buddhist monks and laypeople interacted in the Ming). Taipei: Daoxiang chuban-she, 2010.

——. "Mingdai yuqie jiaoseng de zhuanzhi hua jiqi jingchan huodong" 明代瑜伽教僧的專職化及其經懺活 動 (Specialization of Ming esoteric monks and their ritual activities). In *Mingdai de fojiao yu shehui* 明

代的佛教與社會 (Buddhism and society in Ming China), 248–82. Beijing: Beijing daxue chubanshe, 2011.

Chen Zilong 陳子龍. *Huang Ming jingshi wenbian* 皇明經世文編 (Collected writings of actionism in the Great Ming). Beijing: Zhonghua shuju, 1962.

Cheng, Chung-ying. "Practical Learning in Yen Yuan, Chu Hsi, and Wang Yang-ming." In *Principle and Practicality: Essays in Neo-Confucianism and Practical Learning*, ed. Wm. Theodore de Bary and Irene Bloom, 39–45. New York: Columbia University Press, 1979.

Chikusa Masaaki 竺沙雅章. *Chūgoku bukkyō shakaishi kenkyū* 中國仏教社會史研究 (A study on the social history of Chinese Buddhism). Tokyo: Dōhōsha shuppan, 1982.

——. "Mindai jiden no fueki" 明代寺田の賦役 (Labor taxes on monastic lands in the Ming). In *Min Shin jidai no seiji to shakai* 明清時代の政治と社會, ed. Ono Kazuko 小野和子, 487–512. Kyoto: Kyōto daigaku jinbun kagaku kenkyūjo, 1983.

Chou, Chih-P'ing. *Yüan Hung-tao and the Kung-an School*. New York: Cambridge University Press, 2006.

Chu, Hung-lam. "The Debate over Recognition of Wang Yang-ming." *HJAS* 48, no. 1 (1988): 47–70.

Chu, William. "Syncretism Reconsidered: The Four Eminent Monks and Their Syncretistic Styles." *Journal of the International Association of Buddhist Studies* 29, no. 1 (2006): 43–86.

Cleary, Jonathan Christopher. "Zibo Zhenke: A Buddhist Leader in Late Ming China." Ph.D. diss., Harvard University, 1985.

Cohen, Paul A. *Discovering History in China: American Historical Writing on the Recent Chinese Past*. New York: Columbia University Press, 1984.

Cui Zhengsen 崔正森. "Wutaishan yu Putuoshan fojiao wenhua jiaoliu" 五台山與普陀山佛教文化交流 (The exchange of Buddhist culture between Mount Wutai and Putuo Island). *Wutaishan yanjiu* 五台山研究, no. 3 (1998): 38–45.

Da Ming Shizong su huangdi baoxun 大明世宗肅皇帝寶訓 (The precious instructions of Emperor Shizong of the Great Ming). Taipei: Zhongyang yanjiuyuan lishi yuyan yanjiusuo, 1967.

Dafangguangfo Huayan jing 大方廣佛華嚴經. In *T*, vol. 10, no. 293.

Dai Jin 戴金. *Kōmin jōhō jiruisan* 皇明條法事類纂 (A categorized collection of statutory precedents of the Great Ming). Tokyo: Koten kenkyūkai, 1966.

Dai, Lianbin. "The Economics of the Jiaxing Edition of the Buddhist Tripitaka." *T'oung Pao* 94, no. 5 (2008): 306–59.

Daozang 道藏 (The Daoist canon). Ed. Daozang yanjiu suo 道藏研究所. 36 vols. Reprint, Shanghai: Shanghai shudian, 1988.

Dardess, John W. *Blood and History in China: The Donglin Faction and Its Repression, 1620–1627*. Honolulu: University of Hawai`i Press, 2002.

——. *Confucianism and Autocracy: Professional Elites in the Founding of the Ming Dynasty*. Berkeley: University of California Press, 1983.

——. *Four Seasons: A Ming Emperor and His Grand Secretaries in Sixteenth-Century China*. Lanham, Md.: Rowman and Littlefield, 2016.

de Bary, Wm. Theodore. "Individualism and Humanitarianism in Late Ming Thought." In *Self and Society in Ming Thought*, ed. Wm. Theodore de Bary, 145–248. New York: Columbia University Press, 1970.

de Bary, Wm. Theodore, and Irene Bloom, eds. *Principle and Practicality: Essays in Neo-Confucianism and Practical Learning*. New York: Columbia University Press, 1979.

de Bruyn, Pierre-Henry. "Wudang Shan: The Origins of a Major Center of Modern Taoism." In *Religion and Chinese Society: Taoism and Local Religion in Modern China*, ed. John Lagerwey, 553–90. Hong Kong: Chinese University Press; Paris: École française d'Extrême-Orient, 2004.

Deng Shilong 鄧士龍. *Guochao diangu* 國朝典故 (Statutory precedents of our dynasty). Beijing: Beijing daxue chubanshe, 1993.

Dimberg, Ronald. *The Sage and Society: The Life and Thought of Ho Hsin-Yin*. Honolulu: University Press of Hawaii, 1974.

Ding Xiaoming 丁小明. "Zhenshi jushi de zhenshi yan: Feng Mengzhen *Kuaixuetang riji* duhou" 真實居士的真實言: 馮夢禎《快雪堂日記》讀後 (The real words of Layman Zhenshi: Some comments on Feng Mengzhen's *Diary of Kuaixue Hall*). Preface to Feng Mengzhen 馮夢楨, *Kuaixuetang riji* 快雪堂日記. Nanjing: Fenghuang chubanshe, 2010.

Ditmanson, Peter Brian. "Contesting Authority: Intellectual Lineages and the Chinese Imperial Court from the Twelfth to the Fifteenth Centuries." Ph.D. diss., Harvard University, 1999.

Dong Qichang 董其昌. *Huachan shi suibi* 畫禪室隨筆 (Jottings from the Huachan house). In *Biji xiaoshuo daguan* 筆記小說大觀, comp. Qian Yong 錢泳 et al., vol. 12. Yangzhou: Guangling guji keyinshe, 1983.

Dong Xiaoping 董曉平 and Lü Min [Marianne Bujard], eds. *Beijing neicheng simiao beike zhi* 北京內城寺廟碑刻志 (Collection of the temple epigraphs in the inner city of Beijing). 4 vols. Beijing: Guojia tushuguan chubanshe, 2011–2017.

Dreyer, Edward L. *Early Ming China: A Political History, 1355–1435.* Stanford, Calif.: Stanford University Press, 1982.

Du Changshun 杜常順. *Mingdai gongting yu fojiao guanxi yanjiu* 明代宮廷與佛教關系研究 (A study of the relationship between the Ming court and Buddhism). Beijing: Zhongguo shehui kexue chubanshe, 2013.

Eberhard, Wolfram. "Temple-Building Activities in Medieval and Modern China: An Experimental Study." *Monumenta Serica* 23 (1964): 264–318.

Ebrey, Patricia Buckley. *Kinship Organization in Late Imperial China, 1000–1940.* Berkeley: University of California Press, 1986.

Eichman, Jennifer Lynn. "Intertextual Alliances: Huang Hui's Synthesis of Confucian and Buddhist Paths to Liberation." *T'oung Pao* 100, no. 1-3 (2014): 120–63.

——. *A Late Sixteenth-Century Chinese Buddhist Fellowship: Spiritual Ambitions, Intellectual Debates, and Epistolary Connections.* Leiden: Brill, 2016.

Elman, Benjamin A. *A Cultural History of Civil Examinations in Late Imperial China.* Berkeley: University of California Press, 2000.

——. *Education and Society in Late Imperial China, 1600–1900.* Berkeley: University of California Press, 1997.

——. "The Formation of 'Dao Learning' as Imperial Ideology During the Early Ming Dynasty." In *Culture and State in Chinese History: Conventions, Accommodations, and Critiques*, ed. Theodore Huters, Roy Bin Wong, and Pauline Yu, 58–82. Stanford, Calif.: Stanford University Press, 1997.

——. *From Philosophy to Philology: Intellectual and Social Aspects of Change in Late Imperial China.* Cambridge, Mass.: Harvard University Press, 1984.

——. "Imperial Politics and Confucian Societies in Late Imperial China: The Hanlin and Donglin Academies." *Modern China* 15, no. 4 (1989): 379–418.

——. "Political, Social, and Cultural Reproduction via Civil Service Examinations in Late Imperial China." *JAS* 50, no. 1 (1991): 7–28.

Fan Shuzhi 樊樹志. "Donglin shuyuan de shitai fenxi: 'Donglindang' zhiyi" 東林書院的實態分析:"東林黨"質疑 (An analysis of the reality of the Donglin Academy: Questioning the "Donglin" faction). *Zhongguo shehui kexue* 中國社會科學, no. 2 (2001): 188–204.

——. "Zhang Juzheng he Feng Bao: Lishi de ling yimian" 張居正和馮保: 歷史的另一面 (Zhang Juzheng and Feng Bao: Another face of history). *Fudan xuebao* 復旦學報, no. 1 (1999): 80–87.

Fan Ye 范曄. *Hou Hanshu* 後漢書 (Book of the Later Han dynasty). Beijing: Zhonghua shuju, 1965.

Fan Zhongyan 范仲淹. *Fan Zhongyan quanji* 范仲淹全集 (The complete collection Fan Zhongyan). Chengdu: Sichuan daxue chubanshe, 2007.

Fang Fuxiang 方復祥 and Yao Lijun 姚立軍. "Ming Qing Pinghu Lushi yu difang shehui" 明清平湖陸氏與地方社會 (The Lu clan and local society in the Ming-Qing period). *Wenshizhi* 文史哲, no. 1 (2006): 54–59.

Fang Zhiyuan 方志遠. "'Shanren' yu Wanming zhengju" "山人"與晚明政局 ("Mountain men" and late-Ming politics). *Zhongguo shehui kexue* 中國社會科學, no. 1 (2010): 199–220.

Fanwang jing 梵網經 (*Brahmajāla sūtra*). In *T*, vol. 24, no. 1484.

Farmer, Edward L. *Early Ming Government: The Evolution of Dual Capitals*. Cambridge, Mass.: Harvard University Press, 1976.

——. *Zhu Yuanzhang and Early Ming Legislation: The Reordering of Chinese Society Following the Era of Mongol Rule*. Leiden: Brill, 1995.

Faure, Bernard. 1992. "Relics and Flesh Bodies: The Creation of Ch'an Pilgrimage Sites." In *Pilgrims and Sacred Sites in China*, ed. Susan Naquin and Chün-fang Yü, 158–89. Berkeley: University of California Press.

Fazang 法藏. *Huayan jingzhuan ji* 華嚴經傳記 (Biographies related to the *Huayan jing*). In *T*, vol. 51, no. 2073.

Feng Mengzhen 馮夢禎. *Kuaixuetang ji* 快雪堂集 (Collected writings of the Kuaixue hall). 1616. In *jibu* 集部, vols. 164–65, of *Siku quanshu cunmu congshu* 四庫全書存目叢書, comp. Siku quanshu cunmu congshu bianzuan weiyuanhui 四庫全書存目叢書編纂委員會. Jinan: Qilu shushe, 1994–1997.

Feng Qi 馮琦. "Su guanchang shu" 肅官常疏 (A memorial requesting the cleansing of officials' behavior). http://www.sinoat.net/weifangwenshi/test097.htm.

Finnane, Antonia. *Speaking of Yangzhou: A Chinese City, 1550–1850*. Cambridge, Mass.: Harvard University Press, 2004.

Fisher, Carney T. *The Chosen One: Succession and Adoption in the Court of Ming Shizong*. Sydney: Allen and Unwin, 1990.

"Folk Religion: Folk Buddhism." In *Encyclopedia of Religion*, ed. Lindsay Jones. 2nd ed. 15 vols. Detroit: Thomson Gale, 2005. http://www.encyclopedia.com/environment/encyclopedias-almanacs-transcripts-and-maps/folk-religion-folk-buddhism.

Forte, Antonino. *Political Propaganda and Ideology in China at the End of the Seventh Century: Inquiry into the Nature, Authors and Function of the Tunhuang Document S.6502, Followed by an Annotated Translation*. Kyoto: Italian School of East Asian Studies, 2005.

Foshuo renwang boreboluomi jing 佛説仁王般若波羅蜜經 (The *Prajñāpāramitā* sutra preached by the Buddha on the humane king). In *T*, vol. 8, no. 245.

Foshuo si nili jing 佛説四泥犁經 (The sutra preached by the Buddha on the four hells). In *T*, vol. 2, no. 139.

Foshuo zhude futian jing 佛説諸德福田經 (The sutra preached by the Buddha on various fields of merit). In *T*, vol. 16, no. 683.

Foulk, Theodore Griffith. "Myth, Ritual, and Monastic Practice in Sung Ch'an Buddhism." In *Religion and Society in T'ang and Sung China*, ed. Patricia Buckley Ebrey and Peter N. Gregory, 147–208. Honolulu: University of Hawaii Press, 1993.

——. "Ritual in Japanese Zen Buddhism." In *Zen Ritual: Studies of Zen Buddhist Theory in Practice*, ed. Steven Heine and Dale Stuart Wright. Oxford: Oxford University Press, 2008.

Fu Yiling 傅衣凌. *Ming Qing shidai shangren ji shangye ziben* 明清時代商人及商業資本 (Merchants and commercial capital in the Ming and Qing periods). Beijing: Renmin chubanshe, 1956.

Gernet, Jacques. *Buddhism in Chinese Society: An Economic History from the Fifth to the Tenth Centuries*. New York: Columbia University Press, 1995.

Gerritsen, Anne. "The Hongwu Legacy: Fifteenth-Century Views on Zhu Yuzhang's Monastic Policies." In *Long Live the Emperor! Uses of the Ming Founder across Six Centuries of East Asian History*, ed. Sarah Schneewind, 55–72. Minneapolis: Center for Early Modern History, 2008.

Goodrich, Luther Carrington, and Chaoying Fang, eds. *Dictionary of Ming Biography, 1368–1644*. New York: Columbia University Press, 1976.

Gregory, Peter N. "The Vitality of Buddhism in the Sung." In *Buddhism in the Sung*, ed. Peter N. Gregory and Daniel A. Getz Jr., 1–20. Honolulu: University of Hawai`i Press, 1999.

Gregory, Peter N., and Daniel A. Getz Jr., eds. *Buddhism in the Sung*. Honolulu: University of Hawai`i Press, 1999.

Groot, J. J. M. de. *The Religious System of China: Its Ancient Forms, Evolution, History and Present Aspect, I–VI*. Leiden: Brill, 1892–1910.

Grootaers, Willem A. "The Hagiography of the Chinese God Chen-wu." *Folklore Studies* 11, no. 2 (1952): 139–81.

Gu Tinglong 顧廷龍 et al., eds. *Xuxiu Siku quanshu* 續修四庫全書 (A continuation to the *Siku quanshu*). Shanghai: Shanghai guji chubanshe, 1995-2001.

Gu Yanwu 顧炎武. *Rizhilu jishi: Wai qizhong* 日知錄集釋: 外七種 (A collective annotation to the *Rizhilu*, with seven supplements). Annotated by Huang Rucheng 黃汝成. Shanghai: Shanghai guji chubanshe, 1985.

Gu Yingtai 谷應泰. *Mingshi jishi benmo* 明史紀事本末 (The beginning and end of events in Ming history). Beijing: Zhonghua shuju, 1958.

Guo Peng 郭朋. *Ming Qing fojiao* 明清佛教 (Buddhism in Ming and Qing China). Fuzhou: Fujian renmin chubanshe, 1982.

Guo, Qitao. *Ritual Opera and Mercantile Lineage: The Confucian Transformation of Popular Culture in Late Imperial Huizhou*. Stanford, Calif.: Stanford University Press, 2005.

Guo Zhengyu 郭正域. *Wanli sanshiyinian guimao "Chushi" "Yaoshu" shimo* 萬曆三十一年癸卯 "楚事" "妖書"始末 (The origin and development of "the event of Chu" and "the evil pamphlet" in the thirty-first year, *guimao*, of the Wanli period). In *Zhongguo yeshi jicheng xubian* 中國野史集成續編, vol. 20. Chengdu: Bashu shushe, 2000.

Guoxiang 果祥. *Zibo dashi yanjiu* 紫柏大師研究 (Studies on Master Zibo). Taipei: Dongchu chubanshe, 1987.

Haar, B. J. ter. *Practicing Scripture: A Lay Buddhist Movement in Late Imperial China*. Honolulu: University of Hawai`i Press, 2014.

——. "Shao Yuanjie 邵元節: 1459–1539; *zi*: Zhongkang 仲康; *hao*: Xueya 雪崖 (Snowy Cliff)." In *The Encyclopedia of Taoism*, ed. Fabrizio Pregadio, 878–89. London: Routledge, 2008.

——. "Tao Zhongwen 陶仲文: ca. 1481–1560; original *ming*: Tao Dianzhen." In *The Encyclopedia of Taoism*, ed. Fabrizio Pregadio, 971–72. London: Routledge, 2008.

——. *The White Lotus Teachings in Chinese Religious History*. Leiden: Brill, 1992.

Handler-Spitz, Rivi. *Symptoms of an Unruly Age: Li Zhi and Cultures of Early Modernity*. Seattle: University of Washington Press, 2017.

Handlin, Joanna F. *Action in Late Ming Thought: The Reorientation of Lü Kun and Other Scholar-Officials*. Berkeley: University of California Press, 1983.

Hanshan Deqing 憨山德清. *Hanshan laoren mengyou ji* 憨山老人夢遊集 (Collected writings of the dream-like journey of the venerable Hanshan). In *X*, vol. 73, no. 1456.

Hanshan Deqing 憨山德清 and Fuzheng 福徵. *Hanshan dashi nianpu shuzhu* 憨山大師年譜疏註 (Annotated chronicle of Master Hanshan). In *Beijing tushuguan cang zhenben nianpu congkan* 北京圖書館藏珍本年譜叢刊, vols. 52–53. Beijing: Beijing chubanshe, 1999.

Hanyue Fazang 漢月法藏. *Hong jiefa yi* 弘戒法儀 (Dharma rituals for promoting the precepts). In *X*, vol. 60, no. 1126.

——. *Sanfeng Zang heshang yulu* 三峰藏和尚語錄 (Recorded sayings of Master Sanfeng [Fa]zang). In *JXZ*, vol. 34, no. B299.

Hasebe Yūkei 長谷部幽蹊. *Min Shin bukkyō kenkyū shiryō: Bunken no bu* 明清仏教研究資料: 文獻之部 (Materials for the study of Ming and Qing Buddhism: Primary documents). Nagoya: Komada insatsu, 1987.

——. *Min Shin bukkyō kyōdanshi kenkyū* 明清佛教教団史研究 (Studies on the history of Buddhist societies in Ming and Qing China). Kyoto: Dōhōsha shuppan, 1993.

——. *Min Shin bukkyōshi kenkyū josetsu* 明清仏教史研究序説 (A preliminary study of the history of Ming and Qing Buddhism). Taipei: Xin wenfeng chuban gongsi, 1979.

——. "Mindai ikō ni okeru zōkyō no kaichō" 明代以降における藏経の開雕 (The carvings of the Buddhist canon since the Ming). *Aichi gakuin daigaku ronsō, ippan kyōiku kenkyū* 愛知學院大學論叢, 一般教育研究 30, no. 3 (1983): 793–813; 31, no. 1 (1983–1984): 3–28; 31, no. 2 (1984): 185–211.

——. "Minmatsu sōrin ni okeru shūgyō seikatsu no ichikeitai: Tokushin ni yoru Sōkei no fukkō o megutte" 明末叢林における修行生活の一形態: 德清による曹渓の復興をめぐって (A type of cultivating life in the late-Ming *saṃgha*: With respect to Deqing's revival of Caoxi). *Zen kenkyūjo kiyō* 禅研究所紀要, no. 8 (1979): 21–52.

——. "Min-Shin jidai bukkyōkai no tenbō—jisatsu no fukkō o megutte" 明清時代佛教界の展望—寺刹の復興をめぐって (The future of Buddhism in Ming and Qing China: With respect to the renovation of temples). *Zen kenkyūjo kiyō* 禅研究所紀要 6 (1976): 189–225.

Hayasaka Toshihiro 早阪俊廣, Shen Xulu 申緒璐, and Liu Xinyi 劉心奕. "Chenmo de Zhou Mengxiu: Wang Ji yu Shengxian Zhoushi" 沉默的周夢秀: 王畿與嵊縣周氏 (The silent Zhou Mengxiu: Wang Ji and the Zhou family in Sheng county). *Guiyang xueyuan xuebao* 貴陽學院學報, no. 6 (2017): 18–25.

He Xiaorong 何孝榮. "Lun Mingdai de duseng" 論明代的度僧 (Studies on the ordination of monks in the Ming dynasty). *Shijie zongjiao yanjiu* 世界宗教研究, no. 1 (2004): 26–37.

——. "Lun Mingdai zhonghouqi de yu die duseng" 論明代中後期的鬻牒度僧 (Studies on the ordination of monks and the selling of ordination certificates in the mid and late Ming dynasty). *Nankai xuebao* 南開學報, no. 5 (2005): 61–67.

——. "Ming chu Shanshiyuan kao" 明初善世院攷 (Research on the Buddhist World-Improving Bureau in the early Ming). *Xinan daxue xuebao* 西南大學學報 35, no. 2 (2009): 46–50.

——. "Ming Shizong jinfo" 明世宗禁佛 (The ban by Emperor Shizong of the Ming on Buddhism). *Mingshi yanjiu* 明史研究, no. 7 (2001): 164–76.

——. *Mingdai Beijing fojiao siyuan xiujian yanjiu* 明代北京佛教寺院修建研究 (Studies on the building of Buddhist temples in Ming Beijing). Tianjin: Nankai daxue chubanshe, 2007.

——. *Mingdai Nanjing siyuan yanjiu* 明代南京寺院研究 (Studies on Buddhist temples in Ming Nanjing). Beijing: Zhongguo shehui kexue chubanshe, 2000.

——. "Yuanmo Mingchu mingseng Zongle shiji kao" 元末明初名僧宗泐事迹考 (Studies on Zongle, an eminent Monk in the late Yuan and early Ming dynasties). *Jiangxi shehui kexue* 江西社會科學, no. 12 (2012): 99–105.

He Zongmei 何宗美. "Gong'an pai jieshe de xingshuai yanbian jiqi yingxiang" 公安派結社的興衰演變及其影響 (The rise and fall of the Gong'an school and its influence). *Xinan shifan daxue xuebao* 西南師範大學學報 32, no. 4 (2006): 169–75.

——. *Mingmo Qingchu wenren jieshe yanjiu* 明末清初文人結社研究 (Studies on literati gatherings in the late-Ming and early-Qing period). Tianjin: Nankai daxue chubanshe, 2003.

Hibino Takeo 日比野丈夫. "Myōhō Fukutō no jiseki ni tsuite" 妙峰福登の事蹟について (About the deeds of Miaofeng Fudeng). In *Bukkyō shigaku ronshū: Tsukamoto Hakushi shōju kinen* 佛教史學論集: 塚本博士頌壽記念, 583–95. Kyoto: Tsukamoto Hakushi shōju kinenkai, 1961.

Hikita Keisuke 疋田啓佑. "En shi sankyōdai to Ri Takugo" 袁氏三兄弟と李卓吾 (The three brothers of the Yuan family and Li Zhuowu). *Bungei to shisō* 文芸と思想 59 (1995): 1–14.

Hirakawa Akira 平川彰. *Hirakawa Akira chosakushū* 平川彰著作集 (Collected works of Hirakawa Akira). Tokyo: Shunjūsha, 1997.

Ho, Ping-Ti. *The Ladder of Success in Imperial China: Aspects of Social Mobility, 1368–1911*. New York: Columbia University Press, 1962.

Ho, Puay-peng. "Building for Glitter and Eternity: The Works of the Late Ming Master Builder Miaofeng on Wutai Shan." *Orientations* (Hong Kong) 27, no. 5 (1996): 67–73.

Honda Michitaka 本多道隆. "Kakō daizōkyō no kankoku jigyō to Shihaku Shinka—butsugo no denpa to jishin no senmei" 嘉興大蔵経の刊刻事業と紫柏真可-仏語の伝播と自心の闡明 (The enterprise of carving the Jiaxing canon and Zibo Zhenke: The spread of Buddha's words and the illumination of one's own mind). *Shūkan tōyōgaku* 集刊東洋學 95 (2006): 81–100.

——. "Minmatsu bukkyō no kenkyū: Shihaku Shinka o chūshin toshite" 明末仏教の研究: 紫柏真可を中心として (A study on late-Ming Buddhism, with special reference to Zibo Zhenke). Ph.D. diss., Hiroshima Daigaku, 2007.

Hsiao, Kung-chüan. *A History of Chinese Political Thought*. Trans. F. W. Mote. Princeton, N.J.: Princeton University Press, 1979.

Hsieh, B. H. "From Charwoman to Empress Dowager: Serving-Women in the Ming Palace." *Ming Studies* 42, no. 1 (1999): 26–80.

Hsu, Sung-peng. *A Buddhist Leader in Ming China: The Life and Thought of Han-shan Te-ch'ing*. University Park: Pennsylvania State University Press, 1978.

Hu Dan 胡丹. *Mingdai huanguan zhidu yanjiu* 明代宦官制度研究 (Studies on the institution of eunuchs in the Ming). Hangzhou: Zhejiang daxue chubanshe, 2018.

Hu Jixun 胡吉勳. *"Dali yi" yu Ming ting renshi bianju* "大禮議"與明廷人事變局 (The Great Rites Controversy and personnel changes in the Ming court). Beijing: Shehui kexue wenxian chubanshe, 2007.

Huang Hui 黃輝. *Huang taishi Yichun tang canggao* 黃太史怡春堂藏稿 (Preserved drafts from the Yichun hall of Junior Compiler Huang). 1625.

Huang Jingfang 黃景昉. *Guoshi weiyi* 國史唯疑 (Queries on our national history). Taipei: Zhengzhong shuju, 1969.

Huang Minzhi 黃敏枝. *Songdai fojiao shehui jingji shi lunji* 宋代佛教社會經濟史論集 (Collected studies on the socioeconomic history of Buddhism in the Song). Taipei: Taiwan xuesheng shuju, 1989.

Huang, Ray. *1587, A Year of No Significance: The Ming Dynasty in Decline*. New Haven, Conn.: Yale University Press, 1981.

——. *Taxation and Governmental Finance in Sixteenth-Century Ming China*. London: Cambridge University Press, 1974.

Huang Zongxi 黃宗羲. *Ming wenhai* 明文海 (The sea of Ming literature). Beijing: Zhonghua shuju, 1987.

Huanlun 幻輪. *Shijian jigulüe xuji* 釋鑑稽古略續集 (Continuum to the *Shijian jigulüe*). In *T*, vol. 49, no. 2038.

Hucker, Charles O. *A Dictionary of Official Titles in Imperial China*. Stanford, Calif.: Stanford University Press, 1985.

——. *The Ming Dynasty: Its Origins and Evolving Institutions*. Ann Arbor: Center for Chinese Studies, University of Michigan, 1978.

Hucker, Charles O., and Tilemann Grimm. *Chinese Government in Ming Times: Seven Studies*. New York: Columbia University Press, 1969.

Hung, Ming-shui. *The Romantic Vision of Yuan Hung-tao, Late Ming Poet and Critic*. Taipei: Bookman Books, 1997.

Hunt, Lynn. "French History in the Last Twenty Years: The Rise and Fall of the Annales Paradigm." *Journal of Contemporary History* 21, no. 2 (1986): 209–24.

Hymes, Robert. *Statesmen and Gentlemen: The Elite of Fu-Chou, Chiang-Hsi, in Northern and Southern Sung*. New York: Cambridge University Press, 1986.

——. "Sung Society and Social Change." In *The Cambridge History of China, Volume 5, Part Two: Sung China, 960–1279*, ed. John W. Chaffee and Denis Twitchett, 627–50. Cambridge: Cambridge University Press, 2015.

Ishida Kenji 石田憲司. "Kasei-chō dōkyōkai no konran ni tsuite: Shō Gensetsu, Tō Chūbun, to Chō Tenshi" 嘉靖朝道教界の混亂について: 邵元節・陶仲文と張天師 (About the chaos in the Daoist world in the Jiajing era: Shao Yuanjie, Tao Zhongwen, and Heavenly Master Zhang). In *Mindai Chūgoku no rekishiteki isō: Yamane Yukio kyōju tsuitō kinen ronsō* 明代中国の歴史的位相: 山根幸夫教授追悼記念論叢, ed. Yamane Yukio kyōju tsuitō kinen ronsō henshū iinkai 山根幸夫教授追悼記念論叢編集委員会, 267–86. Tokyo: Kyūko shoin, 2007.

Ishida Noriyuki 石田德行. "Mindai Nankin no jishō ni tsuite—toku ni jishō no zeieki futan o chūshin toshite" 明代南京の寺莊について—特に寺莊の税役負擔を中心として (About monastic assets in Ming Nanjing, with special reference to the burden of tax of monastic assets). *Zengaku kenkyū* 禪學研究, no. 2 (1966): 79–97.

Ishino Kazuharu 石野一晴. "Mindai Banreki nenkan ni okeru Fudasan no fukkō—Chūgoku junreishi kenkyū josetsu" 明代萬曆年間における普陀山の復興—中國巡禮史研究序説 (The revival of Putuo

Island in the Wanli period of the Ming: A preliminary study of the history of pilgrimage in China). *Tōyōshi kenkyū* 東洋史研究 64, no. 1 (2005): 1–36.

Jang, Scarlett. "The Eunuch Agency Directorate of Ceremonial and the Ming Imperial Publishing Enterprise." In *Culture, Courtiers, and Competition: The Ming Court (1368–1644)*, ed. David M. Robinson, 116–85. Cambridge, Mass.: Harvard University Press, 2008.

Jia, Jinhua 賈晉華. *The Hongzhou School of Chan Buddhism in Eighth- through Tenth-Century China*. Albany: State University of New York Press, 2006.

——. *Tangdai jihui zongji yu shiren qun yanjiu* 唐代集會總集與詩人群研究 (Studies on the collected writings composed in literary assemblies and groups of poets in Tang China). 2nd ed. Beijing: Beijing daxue chubanshe, 2015.

Jiang Canteng 江燦騰. *Wanming fojiao conglin gaige yu foxue zhengbian zhi yanjiu: Yi Hanshan Deqing de gaige shengya wei zhongxin* 晚明佛教叢林改革與佛學諍辯之研究：以憨山德清的改革生涯為中心 (Studies on the reform of the *saṃgha* and debates on Buddhist teachings in the late Ming, with special reference to Hanshan Deqing's reform). Taipei: Xin wenfeng chuban gongsi, 1990.

——. *Wanming fojiao gaige shi* 晚明佛教改革史 (A history of the reform of Buddhism in the late Ming). Guilin: Guangxi shifan daxue chubanshe, 2006.

Jiang, Yonglin, trans. *The Great Ming Code / Da Ming lü*. Seattle: University of Washington Press, 2005.

Jin Shen 金申. *Fojiao meishu congkao* 佛教美術叢考 (Studies on Buddhist arts). Beijing: Kexue chubanshe, 2004.

Jingangding yuqie zhong lüechu niansong jing 金剛頂瑜伽中略出念誦經 (Sutra for recitation abridged from the Vajraśekhara Yoga). In *T*, vol. 18, no. 866.

Johnson, David G., Andrew J. Nathan, and Evelyn S. Rawski, eds. *Popular Culture in Late Imperial China*. Berkeley: University of California Press, 1985.

Jones, Charles B. "Transmission: Yuan Hongdao and the *Xifang Helun*; Pure Land Theology in the Late Ming Dynasty." In *Path of No Path: Contemporary Studies in Pure Land Buddhism Honouring Roger Corless*, ed. Richard Karl Payne and Roger Corless, 89–126. Berkeley, Calif.: Numata Center for Buddhist Translation and Research, 2009.

Kageki Motohiro 蔭木原洋. "Kobutei no bukkyō seisaku—Sō Ren to Kitan Sōroku ni shōten o atete—jō, ge" 洪武帝の仏教政策—宋濂と季潭宗泐に焦點を當てて—(上下) (Buddhist policies of Emperor Hongwu, with special reference to Song Lian and Jitan Zongle, 1 and 2). *Tōyō shihō* 東洋史訪 5 (1999): 13–24, 6 (2000): 1–16.

Katz, Elihu, and Paul Felix Lazarsfeld. *Personal Influence: The Part Played by People in the Flow of Mass Communications*. New Brunswick, N.J.: Transaction Publishers, 2005.

Kawakatsu Kenryō 川勝賢亮. "Min Taiso no sōrin seido ni kansuru ichi kōsatsu: Min Shin bukkyō no kihonteki seikaku o megutte" 明太祖の叢林制度に関する一考察：明清仏教の基本的性格をめぐって (A study of the *saṃgha* system designed by Emperor Taizu of the Ming, with special reference to the basic feature of Ming-Qing Buddhism). In *Satō Seijun hakushi koki kinen ronbunshū: Tōyō no rekishi to bunka* 佐藤成順博士古稀記念論文集：東洋の歴史と文化, ed. Satō Seijun Hakushi koki kinen ronbunshū kankōkai 佐藤成順博士古稀記念論文集刊行会, 53–70. Kyoto: Sankibō busshorin, 2004.

——. "Mindai Kōnan shitaifu bukkyōgaku ryūkō to daizōkyō kaihan" 明代江南士大夫仏教學流行と大蔵経開版 (The spread of Buddhism among Jiangnan scholar-officials and the carving of the Buddhist canon in the Ming). *Odai shigaku* 鴨台史學, no. 5 (2005): 1–25.

Keika Atsuyoshi 桂華淳祥. "Chihōshi ni kisai sareru iori no kiroku yori mita Min Shin bukkyō—Sekkō chihō o chūshin ni" 地方誌に記載される庵の記録よりみた明清仏教—浙江地方を中心に (Ming and Qing Buddhism in chapels recorded in local gazetteers, with special reference to the Zhejiang area). *Ōtani gakuhō* 大谷學報 75, no. 1 (1995): 13–25.

Kieschnick, John. "Blood Writing in Chinese Buddhism." *Journal of the International Association of Buddhist Studies* 23, no. 2 (2000): 177–94.

——. *The Impact of Buddhism on Chinese Material Culture*. Princeton, N.J.: Princeton University Press, 2002.

Kin Bunkyō 金文京. "Mindai Banreki nenkan no sanjin no katsudō" 明代萬曆年間の山人の活動 (The activity of "mountain-men" in the Wanli era of the Ming). *Tōyōshi kenkyū* 東洋史研究 61, no. 2 (2002): 237–77.

Klautau, Orion. "Against the Ghosts of Recent Past: Meiji Scholarship and the Discourse on Edo-Period Buddhist Decadence." *Japanese Journal of Religious Studies* 35, no. 2 (2008): 263–303.

Kong Lingbin 孔令彬. "Fojiao zhong 'tiseng' xianxiang kaolüe" 佛教中 "替僧" 現象考略 (A brief study of the "substitution monks" in Buddhism). *Zongjiao xue yanjiu* 宗教學研究, no. 2 (2011): 76–79.

Kubota Ryōon 久保田量遠. *Chūgoku ju dō butsu sangyōshi ron* 中國儒道佛三教史論 (Studies on the history of the Chinese three teachings of Confucianism, Daoism, and Buddhism). Kyoto: Kokusho kankōkai, 1986.

Lan Jifu 藍吉富. "Jiaxing dazangjing de tese jiqi shiliao jiazhi" 嘉興大藏經的特色及其史料價值 (Features of the Jiaxing canon and its values as historical material). In *Fojiao de sixiang yu wenhua: Yinshun daoshi bazhi jinliu shouqing lunwenji* 佛教的思想與文化: 印順導師八秩晉六壽慶論文集, ed. Shengyan 聖嚴 et al., 255–66. Taipei: Faguang chubanshe, 1991.

Lee, Sukhee. *Negotiated Power: The State, Elites, and Local Governance in Twelfth- to Fourteenth-Century China*. Cambridge, Mass.: Harvard University Asia Center, 2014.

Lengyan jing helun 楞嚴經合論 (Combined explanations of the *Śūraṅgama sūtra*). In *X*, vol. 12, no. 272.

Lewis, James Bryant. *The East Asian War, 1592–1598: International Relations, Violence, and Memory*. Abingdon, Oxon: Routledge, 2015.

Li Bozhong 李伯重. "Jianlun 'Jiangnan diqu' de jieding" 簡論 "江南地區" 的界定 (A brief discussion of the definition of the Jiangnan region). *Zhongguo shehui jingji shi yanjiu* 中國社會經濟史研究, no. 1 (1991): 100–107.

Li Dongyang 李東陽 and Shen Shixing 申時行, eds. *Da Ming huidian* 大明會典 (Collected official regulations of the Great Ming). Taipei: Wenhai chubanshe, 1985.

Li Fuhua 李富華 and He Mei 何梅. *Hanwen fojiao dazangjing yanjiu* 漢文佛教大藏經研究 (Studies on the Chinese Buddhist canons). Beijing: Zongjiao wenhua chubanshe, 2003.

Li Gan 李幹 and Zhou Zhizheng 周祉征. "Yuandai siyuan jingji chutan" 元代寺院經濟初探 (A tentative study on the monastic economy in the Yuan). *Sixiang zhanxian* 思想戰線, no. 5 (1986): 87–92.

Li Guangtao 李光濤. "*Chaoxian Renchen wohuo shiliao* xuwen"《朝鮮王辰倭禍史料》序文 (Preface to the *Chaoxian Renchen wohuo shiliao*). *Zhongyang yanjiu yuan lishi yuyan yanjiusuo shiliao jikan* 中央研究院歷史語言研究所史料集刊 37a (1967): 167–84.

Li Mingyang 李明陽. "Ming Hongwuchao yuqie jiaoseng guifanhua licheng jiqi yuanyin tanjiu" 明洪武朝瑜伽教僧規範化歷程及其原因探究 (An exploration into the process of and reasons for the standardization of esoteric *jiao* monks during the Hongwu era of the Ming). *Wutaishan yanjiu* 五臺山研究, no. 2 (2017): 19–25.

Li, Thomas Shiyu, and Susan Naquin. "The Baoming Temple: Religion and the Throne in Ming and Qing China." *HJAS* 48, no. 1 (1988): 131–88.

Li Tiangang 李天剛. *Jinze: Jiangnan minjian jisi tanyuan* 金泽: 江南民间祭祀探源 (Jinze: Tracing the origins of folk sacrifice in the Jiangnan region). Beijing: Sanlian shudian, 2017.

Li Zongwan 勵宗萬. *Jingcheng guji kao* 京城古跡攷 (An examination of ancient sites in the capital). Beijing: Beijing chubanshe, 1964.

Lian Ruizhi 連瑞枝. "Qian Qianyi de fojiao shengya yu linian" 錢謙益的佛教生涯與理念 (Qian Qianyi's life and Buddhism-related thoughts). *Zhonghua foxue xuebao* 中華佛學學報 7 (1994): 317–70.

Liang Fangzhong 梁方仲. *Zhongguo lidai hukou, tiandi, tianfu tongji* 中國歷代戶口、田地、田賦統計 (Statistics on households, lands, and land taxes in past dynasties of China). Beijing: Zhonghua shuju, 2008.

Liang Shaojie 梁紹傑. "Heishanhui Huguosi: Ming Qing liangdai huanguan de zumiao jiqi bianqian" 黑山會護國寺: 明清兩代宦官的祖廟及其變遷 (Huguosi at Heishanhui: The ancestral temple of eunuchs in the Ming-Qing period and its evolution). *Bulletin of Ming-Qing Studies* 明清史集刊 7 (2002): 195–271.

——, ed. *Mingdai huanguan beizhuan lu* 明代宦官碑傳錄 (A collection of epitaphs related to Ming eunuchs). Hong Kong: Xianggang daxue zhongwenxi, 1997.

Liao Zhaoheng 廖肇亨. "Wanming wenren chanhui shuxie yiyun shixi: Yi Yuan Zhongdao *Xinlü* wei zhongxin de kaocha" 晚明文人懺悔書寫義蘊試析：以袁中道《心律》爲中心的考察 (A tentative analysis of the repentance written by late-Ming literati: An examination centered on the *Xinlü* by Yuan Zhongdao). In *Zhongyi puti: Wanming Qingchu kongmen yimin jiqi jiyi lunshu tanxi* 忠義菩提：晚明清初空門遺民及其節義論述探析, 141–78. Taipei: Zhongyang yanjiuyuan Zhongguo wenzhe yanjiusuo, 2013.

Lin Feng 林楓. "Fujian sitian chongxiang qianxi" 福建寺田充餉淺析 (A preliminary analysis of the defraying of military expenditures with monastic lands in Fujian). *Xiamen daxue xuebao* 廈門大學學報, no. 4 (1998): 48–53.

Lin Qiaowei 林巧薇. "Beijng Dongyuemiao yu Ming Qing guojia jisi guanxi tanyan" 北京東嶽廟與明清國家祭祀關係探研 (A study on the relationship between the Dongyue temples in Beijing and the state sacrifice in Ming and Qing China). *Shijie zongjiao yanjiu* 世界宗教研究, no. 5 (2014): 61–71.

Lippmann, Walter. *Public Opinion*. New York: Routledge, 2017.

Liu Dong 劉侗. *Dijing jingwu lüe* 帝京景物略 (A brief record of scenery in the imperial capital). Beijing: Beijing guji chubanshe, 1980.

Liu Ruoyu 劉若愚. *Zhuozhong zhi* 酌中志 (A record of compromise). In vol. 431 of *Xuxiu Siku quanshu* 續修四庫全書, ed. Gu Tinglong 顧廷龍 et al. Shanghai: Shanghai guji chubanshe, 1995–2001.

Liu Shufen 劉淑芬. "Cibei xishe: Zhonggu shiqi fojiaotu de shehui fuli shiye" 慈悲喜捨：中古時期佛教徒的社會福利事業 (Compassion and charity with pleasure: The social-welfare enterprise of medieval Buddhists). *Beixian wenhua* 北縣文化, no. 40 (1994): 17–20.

Liu Xu 劉昫. *Jiu Tangshu* 舊唐書 (Old history of the Tang dynasty). Beijing: Zhonghua shuju, 1975.

Long Wenbin 龍文彬. *Ming huiyao* 明會要 (Collection of core official regulations of the Ming). Beijing: Zhonghua shuju, 1956.

Long Xianzhao 龍顯昭, ed. *Bashu fojiao beiwen jicheng* 巴蜀佛教碑文集成 (A comprehensive collection of epitaphs related to Buddhism in the Ba-Shu region). Chengdu: Bashu shushe, 2004.

Lopez, Donald S. *Curators of the Buddha: The Study of Buddhism under Colonialism*. Chicago: University of Chicago Press, 1995.

Lu Guangzu 陸光祖. *Lu Zhuangjian gong ji* 陸莊簡公集 (Collected works by Duke Zhuangjian of Lu). In *Huang Ming jingshi wenbian* 皇明經世文編, ed. Chen Zilong 陳子龍, vol. 23. Taipei: Guolian tushu chuban youxian gongsi, 1964.

——. *Lu Zhuangjian gong yigao* 陸莊簡公遺稿 (The bequeathed draft of Duke Zhuangjian of Lu). 1629.

Lu Rong 陸容. *Shuyuan zaji* 菽園雜記 (Miscellaneous records of Shu Garden). Beijing: Zhonghua shuju, 1985.

Lu Shanji 鹿善繼. *Renzhen chao* 認真草 (A draft in earnest). In *Congshu jicheng chubian* 叢書集成初編, comp. Wang Yunwu 王雲五, vol. 76. Taipei: Xin wenfeng chuban gongsi, 1985.

Lü Miaofen 呂妙芬. "Ru Shi jiaorong de shengren guan: Cong Wanming rujia shengren yu pusa xingxiang xiangsichu ji dui shengsi yiti de guanzhu tanqi" 儒釋交融的聖人觀：從晚明儒家聖人與菩薩形象相似處及對生死議題的關注談起 (Views of the sage that mixes Confucianism with Buddhism, based on similarities between the images of Confucian sages and those of Buddhist bodhisattvas as well as their concern with the life-or-death issue in late-Ming China). *Zhongyang yanjiuyuan jindaishi yanjiusuo jikan* 中央研究院近代史研究所集刊 32 (1999): 165–208.

——. *Yangming xue shiren shequn: Lishi, sixiang yu shijian* 陽明學士人社群：歷史、思想與實踐 (Associations of Yangming scholars: History, thoughts, and practice). Taipei: Zhongyang yanjiuyuan jindaishi yanjiusuo, 2003.

Luo Zhufeng 羅竹風, ed. *Hanyu da cidian* 漢語大詞典 (Comprehensive dictionary of Chinese). Shanghai: Hanyu da cidian chubanshe, 1997.

Luo Zongqiang 羅宗強. *Mingdai houqi shiren xintai yanjiu* 明代後期士人心態研究 (Studies on the psychological state of late-Ming scholar-officials). Tianjin: Nankai daxue chubanshe, 2006.

Makita Tairyō 牧田諦亮. "Dōen den shōkō—Yō Kōkō no shōgai" 道衍伝小稿—姚広孝の生涯 (A small biography of Daoyan: The life of Yao Guangxiao). *Tōyōshi kenkyū* 東洋史研究 18, no. 2 (1959): 57–79.

——. "Goshū Sesō no bukkyō seisaku" 後周世宗の佛教政策 (The Buddhist policy of Emperor Shizong of the Later Zhou). *Tōyōshi kenkyū* 東洋史研究 11, no. 3 (1951): 10–20.

——. "Mindai no shomin bukkyō" 明代の庶民仏教 (Folk Buddhism of the Ming). *Rekishi kyōiku* 歴史教育 17, no. 3 (1969): 43–49.

Mano Senryū 間野潛龍. "Chūgoku Mindai no sōkan ni tsuite" 中國明代の僧官について (On monastic officials in the Ming). *Ōtani gakuhō* 大谷學報 36, no. 3 (1957): 52–62.

McCombs, M. E., and D. L. Shaw. "The Agenda-Setting Function of Mass Media." *Public Opinion Quarterly* 36, no. 2 (1972): 176–87.

McGuire, Beverley Foulks. *Living Karma: The Religious Practices of Ouyi Zhixu.* New York: Columbia University Press, 2014.

McRae, John R. *The Northern School and the Formation of Early Ch'an Buddhism.* Honolulu: University of Hawai'i Press, 1986.

Meskill, John. *Academies in Ming China: A Historical Essay.* Tucson: University of Arizona Press, 1982.

Meyer-Fong, Tobie. "Packaging the Men of Our Times: Literary Anthologies, Friendship Networks, and Political Accommodation in the Early Qing." *HJAS* 64, no. 1 (2004): 5–56.

Michibata Ryōshū 道端良秀. *Chūgoku bukkyō shisō shi no kenkyū: Chūgoku minshū no bukkyō juyō* 中国仏教思想史の研究: 中国民衆の仏教受容 (Studies on Chinese Buddhist thought: The acceptance of Buddhism by Chinese people). Kyoto: Heirakuji shoten, 1979.·

——. *Chūgoku bukkyō to shakai fukushi jigyō* 中国仏教と社会福祉事業 (Chinese Buddhism and social charity enterprise). Kyoto: Hōzōkan, 1967.

Ming chaoben Wanli qiju zhu 明抄本萬曆起居注 ("Record of Emperor Wanli's daily life," transcribed in the Ming). Beijing: Zhonghua quanguo tushuguan wenxian suowei fuzhi zhongxin, 2001.

Ming shilu 明實錄 (Veritable records of the Ming). 2,911 vols. Reprint, Taipei: Zhongyang yanjiuyuan lishi yuyan yanjiusuo, 1962–1968. Those cited in this study include *Ming Taizu shilu* 明太祖實錄, *Ming Taizong shilu* 明太宗實錄, *Ming Xuanzong shilu* 明宣宗實錄, *Ming Yingzong shilu* 明英宗實錄, *Ming Xianzong shilu* 明憲宗實錄, *Ming Xiaozong shilu* 明孝宗實錄, *Ming Wuzong shilu* 明武宗實錄, *Ming Shizong shilu* 明世宗實錄, and *Ming Shenzong shilu* 明神宗實錄.

Mingban Jiaxing da zangjing 明版嘉興大藏經 (The Jiaxing Buddhist canon, Ming version). Reprint, Taipei: Xing wenfeng chuban gongsi, 1986–1987.

Minghe 明河. *Buxu gaoseng zhuan* 補續高僧傳 (Supplement to the continued *Biographies of Eminent Monks*). In *X*, vol. 77, no. 1524.

Mingshi 明史 (History of the Ming). 1736. Reprint, Beijing: Zhonghua shuju, 1974.

Miyagawa Hisayuki 宮川尚志. "Min no Kasei jidai no dōkyō" 明の嘉靖時代の道教 (Daoism in the Jiajing era of the Ming). In *Dōkyō kenkyū ronshū: Dōkyō no shisō to bunka; Yoshioka hakushi kanreki kinen* 道教研究論集: 道教の思想と文化吉岡博士還暦記念, ed. Yoshioka Yoshitoyo Hakushi kanreki kinen ronshū kankōkai 吉岡義豊博士還暦記念論集刊行会, 639–44. Tokyo: Kokusho kankōkai, 1977.

Mizang Daokai 密藏道開. *Mizang Kai chanshi yigao* 密藏開禪師遺稿 (The bequeathed draft by Chan master Mizang [Dao]kai). In *JXZ*, vol. 23, no. B118.

Mizoguchi Yūzō 溝口雄三. *Chūgoku zen kindai shisō no kussetsu to tenkai* 中国前近代思想の屈折と展開 (The unfolding of Chinese thought in the premodern period). Tokyo: Tōkyō daigaku shuppankai, 1980.

Nakajima Ryūzō 中嶋隆藏. "Kakōzō nyūzō butten to Mitsuzō Dōkai no tachiba" 嘉興藏入藏佛典と密藏道開の立場 (Buddhist texts collected in the Jiaxing canon and Mizang Daokai's stance). *Tōhō gakuhō* 東方學報 113, no. 1 (2007): 34–50.

——. *Min Banreki Kakōzō no shuppan to sono eikyō* 明萬曆嘉興藏の出版とその影響 (The publication of the Jiaxing canon in the Wanli era of the Ming and its influence). Sendai: Tōhoku daigaku daigakuin bungaku kenkyūka, 2005.

Nakamura Hajime 中村元. *Bukkyōgo daijiten* 佛教語大辭典 (A comprehensive dictionary of Buddhist terms). Tokyo: Tōkyō shoseki, 1975.

Naquin, Susan. *Peking: Temples and City Life, 1400–1900*. Berkeley: University of California Press, 2000.

——. "Sites, Saints, and Sights at the Tanzhe Monastery." *Cahiers d'Extrême-Asie*, no. 10 (1998): 183–211.

Naquin, Susan, and Chün-fang Yü, eds. *Pilgrims and Sacred Sites in China*. Berkeley: University of California Press, 1992.

Ng, On-cho. "An Early Qing Critique of the Philosophy of Mind-Heart (*Xin*): The Confucian Quest for Doctrinal Purity and the 'Doxic' Role of Chan Buddhism." *Journal of Chinese Philosophy* 26, no. 1 (March 1999): 89–120.

Nie Wen 聶鈫. *Taishan daoli ji* 泰山道里記 (Records of the distance and paths on Mount Tai). In *shibu* 史部, vol. 242, of *Siku Quanshu cunmu congshu* 四庫全書存目叢書, comp. Siku quanshu cunmu congshu bianzuan weiyuanhui 四庫全書存目叢書編纂委員會. Jinan: Qilu shushe, 1994–1997.

Nishi Giyū 西義雄, Tamaki Kōshirō 玉城康四郎, and Kawamura Kōshō 河村孝照, eds. *Manji shinsan dai Nihon zoku zōkyō* 卍新纂大日本續藏經 (The great continued Japanese Buddhist canon, newly compiled). Tokyo: Kokusho kankōkai, 1975–1989.

Nogami Shunjō 野上俊靜. "Minsho no sōdō gamon" 明初の僧道衙門 (The yamen in charge of Buddhism and Daoism in the early Ming). *Ōtani gakuhō* 大谷學報, no. 98 (1946): 8–15.

Noguchi Tetsurō 野口鉄郎. "Mindai jiden no zeieki to chinki dōjin" 明代寺田の税役と砧基道人 (Land tax and corvée of monastic land and the *zhenji daoren* in the Ming). *Bukkyō shigaku* 仏教史學 14, no. 2 (1968): 17–33.

Norris, Pippa, and Ronald Inglehart. *Sacred and Secular: Religion and Politics Worldwide*. 2nd ed. Cambridge: Cambridge University Press, 2011.

Nozawa Yoshimi 野沢佳美. "Kobu nanzō kara Eiraku nanzō e" 洪武南蔵から永楽南蔵へ (From the Hongwu Southern Canon to the Yongle Southern Canon). *Komazawa shigaku* 駒澤史學 52 (1998): 218–39.

——. *Mindai daizōkyō shi no kenkyū: Nanzō no rekishigaku teki kiso kenkyū* 明代大藏經史の研究: 南蔵の歴史學的基礎研究 (Studies on the history of the Buddhist canons produced in the Ming: A basic study on the history of the Southern Canon). Tokyo: Kyūko shoin, 1998.

——. "Mindai hokuzō kō 1: Kashi jōkyō o chūshin ni" 明代北蔵攷 (一): 下賜狀況を中心に (A study of the Northern Canon of the Ming [1], with special reference to its bestowal). *Risshō daigaku bungakubu ronsō* 立正大學文學部論叢 117 (2003): 81–106.

——. "Minsho ni okeru 'futatsu no nanzō': 'Kobu nanzō kara Eiraku nanzō e' sairon" 明初における「二つの南蔵」:「洪武南蔵から永楽南蔵へ」再論 ("Two Southern versions of the Buddhist canon" in the early Ming: A revisit of "from the Hongwu Southern Canon to the Yongle Southern Canon"). *Risshō daigaku jinbunkagaku kenkyūjo nenpō* 立正大學人文科學研究所年報 45 (2007): 15–23.

Okamoto Tensei 岡本天晴. "Soden ni mieru rinjū no zengo" 僧伝にみえる臨終の前後 (Before and after death as discussed in biographies of monks). *Nihon bukkyō gakkai nenpō* 日本仏教學會年報 46 (1980): 443–58.

Ong, Chang Woei. *Men of Letters within the Passes: Guanzhong Literati in Chinese History, 907–1911*. Cambridge, Mass.: Harvard University Asia Center, 2008.

Ono Kazuko 小野和子. *Minki tōsha kō: Tōrintō to Fukusha* 明季黨社考: 東林黨と復社 (Studies of political factions and associations in the final years of the Ming: The Donglin faction and the Fu association). Kyoto: Dōhōsha shuppan, 1996.

Ouyang Nan 歐陽楠. "Wanming Nanjing diqu de siyuan dengji yu siyuan jingji: Yi *Jinling fancha zhi* wei zhongxin de kaocha" 晚明南京地區的寺院等級與寺院經濟: 以《金陵梵剎志》爲中心的考察 (Hierarchy of Buddhist temples and monastic economy in the late-Ming Nanjing area: A study centered on the *Jinling fancha zhi*). *Shijie zongjiao yanjiu* 世界宗教研究, no. 3 (2012): 39–50.

Ouyang Xiu 歐陽修. *Xin Tangshu* 新唐書 (New history of the Tang). Beijing: Zhonghua shuju, 1975.

Ouyi Zhixu 蕅益智旭. *Lingfeng Ouyi dashi zonglun* 靈峰蕅益大師宗論 (The principal treatise of the great master Lingfeng Ouyi). In *JXZ*, vol. 36, no. B348.

Overmyer, Daniel L. "Alternatives: Popular Religious Sects in Chinese Society." *Modern China* 7, no. 2 (1981): 153–90.

——. "Attitudes Toward the Ruler and State in Chinese Popular Religious Literature: Sixteenth and Seventeenth Century Pao-chüan." *HJAS* 44, no. 2 (1984): 347–79.

——. "Folk-Buddhist Religion: Creation and Eschatology in Medieval China." *History of Religions* 12, no. 1 (1972): 42–70.

——. *Folk Buddhist Religion: Dissenting Sects in Late Traditional China*. Cambridge, Mass.: Harvard University Press, 1976.

——. *Precious Volumes: An Introduction to Chinese Sectarian Scriptures from the Sixteenth and Seventeenth Centuries*. Cambridge, Mass.: Harvard University Asia Center, 1999.

Ping-ti, Ho. *The Ladder of Success in Imperial China*. New York: Columbia University Press, 1962.

Poceski, Mario. *Ordinary Mind as the Way: The Hongzhou School and the Growth of Chan Buddhism*. New York: Oxford University Press, 2007.

Pu Wenqi 濮文起, Xia Jingshan 夏荆山, and Lou Yutian 婁玉田, eds. *Zhongguo lidai guanyin wenxian jicheng* 中國歷代觀音文獻集成 (A collection of Guanyin-related literature in China's past dynasties). Beijing: Zhonghua quanguo tushuguan wenxian suowei fuzhi zhongxin, 1998.

Qi Chang 齊暢. *Gongnei, chaoting yu bianjiang: Shehuishi shiye xia de Mingdai huanguan yanjiu* 宮内、朝廷與邊疆: 社會史視野下的明代宦官研究 (The inner court, the outer court, and the frontiers: Studies on Ming eunuchs from the sociological view). Beijing: Zhongguo shehui kexue chubanshe, 2014.

Qian Gu 錢穀. *Wudu wencui xuji* 吳都文粹續集 (A continued anthology of writings [produced] in the Suzhou area). In *jibu* 集部, vols. 1385–86, of *Wenyuange yingyin Siku quanshu*, 文淵閣影印四庫全書. Taipei: Shangwu yinshuguan, 1983.

Qian Qianyi 錢謙益. *Chuxue ji* 初學集 (Collected works of a learning beginner). Shanghai: Shanghai guji chubanshe, 1985.

——. *Liechao shiji xiaozhuan* 列朝詩集小傳 (Brief biographies of poets of past dynasties). Shanghai: Shanghai guji chubanshe, 1959.

Qianshou qianyan guanshiyin pusa guangda yuanman wuai dabeixin tuoluoni jing 千手千眼觀世音菩薩廣大圓滿無礙大悲心陀羅尼經 (Dharani of the thousand-eyed, thousand-handed Avalokiteśvara who observes the world with vast, complete, and unimpeded great compassion). In *T*, vol. 20, no. 1060.

Qianshou qianyan guanshiyin pusa zhibing heyao jing 千手千眼觀世音菩薩治病合藥經 (Sutra on the use of medicinal herbs for healing by the thousand-eyed, thousand-handed Avalokiteśvara). In *T*, vol. 20, no. 1059.

Qing Gaozong Chun huangdi shilu 清高宗純皇帝實錄 (The veritable record of Emperor Gaozong of the Qing). Beijing: Zhonghua shuju, 1986.

Qing Shengzu shilu 清聖祖實錄 (The veritable record of Emperor Shengzu of the Qing). Taipei: Huawen chubanshe, 1964.

Qin Peiheng 秦佩珩. "Qingliang tongdian zakao" 清涼銅殿雜考 (A study on the copper hall at Mount Wutai). *Zhengzhou daxue xuebao* 鄭州大學學報, no. 3 (1984): 79–84.

Ricci, Matteo, and Nicolas Trigault. *Li Madou Zhongguo zhaji* 利瑪竇中國札記 (China in the sixteenth century: The journals of Mathew Ricci). Trans. He Gaoji 何高濟, Wang Zhunzhong 王遵仲, et al. Beijing: Zhonghua shuju, 1983.

Robinson, David. *Bandits, Eunuchs, and the Son of Heaven: Rebellion and the Economy of Violence in Mid-Ming China*. Honolulu: University of Hawai'i Press, 2001.

——. "Notes on Eunuchs in Hebei During the Mid-Ming Period." *Ming Studies* 34, no. 1 (1995): 1–16.

Robson, James. "Formation and Fabrication in the History and Historiography of Chan Buddhism." *HJAS* 71, no. 2 (2011): 311–49.

——. "Monastic Spaces and Sacred Traces: Facets of Chinese Buddhist Monastic Records." In *Buddhist Monasticism in East Asia: Places of Practice*, ed. James A. Benn, Lori Rachelle Meeks, and James Robson, 43–64. London: Routledge, 2010.

Ruxing 如惺. *Da Ming gaoseng zhuan* 大明高僧傳 (Biographies of eminent monks, composed in the Great Ming). In *T*, vol. 50, no. 2062.

Ryūchi Kiyoshi 龍池清. "Min no Taiso no bukkyō seisaku" 明の太祖の仏教政策 (The Buddhist policies of Emperor Taizu of the Ming). *Bukkyō shisō kōza* 仏教思想講座 8 (1939): 83–112.

——. "Mindai no sōkan" 明代の僧官 (Monastic officials in the Ming). *Shina bukkyō shigaku* 支那仏教史 學 4, no. 3 (1945): 35–46.

——. "Mindai no yūga kyōsō" 明代の瑜伽教僧 (Yoga monks in the Ming). *Tōhō gakuhō* 東方學報 11, no. 1 (1940): 405–13.

——. "Minsho no jiin" 明初の寺院 (Buddhist temples in the early Ming). *Shina bukkyō shigaku* 支那仏教 史學 2, no. 4 (1938): 9–29.

Sakai Shiro 酒井紫朗. "Kahoku Godaisan no daizōkyō" 華北五臺山の大藏經 (The Buddhist canons at Mount Wutai, North China). *Mikkyō kenkyū* 密教研究 87 (1944): 70–79.

Sakai Tadao 酒井忠夫. *Zōho Chūgoku zensho no kenkyū* 增補中國善書の研究 (Studies on Chinese morality books, enlarged and supplemented). Tokyo: Kokusho kankōkai, 1999–2000.

Satō Rentarō 佐藤錬太郎. "Ri Takugo to Shihaku Takkan no shi o megutte" 李卓吾と紫柏達觀の死をめぐ って (About the deaths of Li Zhuowu and Zibo Daguan). In *Yamane Yukio kyōju taikyū kinen Mindai-shi ronsō* 山根幸夫教授退休記念明代史論叢, ed. Yamane Yukio 山根幸夫 and Okuzaki Hiroshi 奧崎裕, 189–207. Tokyo: Kyūko shoin, 1990.

Schicketanz, Erik. *Daraku to fukkō no kindai Chūgoku bukkyō: Nihon bukkyō to no kaikō to sono rekishizō no kōchiku* 墮落と復興の近代中國仏教: 日本仏教との邂逅とその歴史像の構築 (The decline and renewal of modern Chinese Buddhism: Its encounter with Japanese Buddhism and the formation of its historical image). Kyoto: Hōzōkan, 2016.

Schopen, Gregory. "Archaeology and Protestant Presuppositions in the Study of Indian Buddhism." *History of Religions* 31, no. 1 (1991): 1–23.

——. *Bones, Stones, and Buddhist Monks: Collected Papers on the Archaeology, Epigraphy, and Texts of Monastic Buddhism in India.* Honolulu: University of Hawaiʻi Press, 1997.

Seiwert, Hubert Michael, with Ma Xisha 馬西沙. *Popular Religious Movements and Heterodox Sects in Chinese History.* Leiden: Brill, 2003.

Sharf, Robert H. "The Idolization of Enlightenment: On the Mummification of Chʼan Masters in Medieval China." *History of Religions* 32, no. 1 (1992): 1–31.

——. "On the Allure of Buddhist Relics." *Representations*, no. 66 (1999): 75–99.

Shaw, R. Daniel. "Folk Christianity." In *The Encyclopedia of Christian Civilization*, ed. G. T. Kurian. Chichester, West Sussex, U.K.; Malden, Mass.: Wiley-Blackwell, 2011. https://onlinelibrary.wiley.com/doi /abs/10.1002/9780470670606.wbecc0549.

Shen Bang 沈榜. *Wanshu zaji* 宛署雜記 (Miscellaneous records from the Wanping county office). Beijing: Beijing guji chubanshe, 1980.

Shen Defu 沈德符. *Wanli yehuo bian* 宛曆野獲編 (Unofficial gleanings from the Wanli reign). 1616. Reprint, Beijing: Zhonghua shuju, 1959.

——. *Wanli yehuo bian buyi* 萬曆野獲編補遺 (Supplement to the *Wanli yehuo bian*). 1616. Reprint, together with *Wanli yehuo bian*, Beijing: Zhonghua shuju, 1959.

Shen Weirong 沈衛榮. "*Dasheng yaodao miji* yu Xixia, Yuan, Ming sandai zangchuan mijaoshi yanjiu" 《大乘要道密集》與西夏、元、明三代藏傳密教史研究 (The *Dasheng yaodao miji* and the history of Tibetan tantric Buddhism in the Tangut Xia, Mongol Yuan, and Han Chinese Ming periods). In *Wenben yu lishi: Zangchuan fojiao lishi xushi de xingcheng he Han-Zang foxue yanjiu de jiangou* 文本與歷史: 藏傳佛教歷史敘事的形成和漢藏佛學研究的建構, by Shen Weirong and Hou Haoran 侯浩然, 325–415. Beijing: Zhongguo zangxue chubanshe, 2016.

——. "Lun Mengyuan wangchao yu Mingdai Zhongguo de zhengzhi he zongjiao yichan: Zangchuan fojiao yu Xixia, Yuan, Ming sandai zhengzhi he zongjiao tizhi xingcheng zhongde jueshe yanjiu" 論蒙元王朝於明代中國的政治和宗教遺產: 藏傳佛教於西夏、元、明三代政治和宗教體制形成中的角色研究

(Studies on the political and religious legacy left by the Mongolian Yuan dynasty to Ming China: The role Tibetan Buddhism played in the formation of the political and religious institutions in Tangut Xia, Yuan, and Ming China). In *8–15 shiji zhongxibu Xizang de lishi, wenhua he yishu* 8–15世紀中西部西藏的歷史·文化和藝術, ed. Erika Forte. Beijing: Zhongguo zangxue chubanshe, 2015.

——. "Wenben duikan yu lishi jiangou: Zangchuan fojiao yu Xiyu he Zhongyuan chuanbo lishi yanjiu daolun" 文本對勘與歷史建構: 藏傳佛教于西域和中原傳播歷史研究導論 (History through textual criticism: The spread of Tibetan Buddhism in China proper and the western regions). In *Wenben yu lishi: Zangchuan fojiao lishi xushi de xingcheng he Han-Zang foxue yanjiu de jiangou* 文本與歷史: 藏傳佛教歷史敘事的形成和漢藏佛學研究的建構, by Shen Weirong and Hou Haoran 侯浩然, 241–324. Beijing: Zhongguo zangxue chubanshe, 2016.

Shengkai 聖凱. *Zhongguo fojiao chanfa yanjiu* 中國佛教懺法研究 (Studies on the repentance ceremonies of Chinese Buddhism). Beijing: Zongjiao wenhua chubanshe, 2004.

Shengyan 聖嚴 [Chang Sheng-yen 張聖嚴]. *Mingmo fojiao yanjiu* 明末佛教研究 (Studies on Buddhism in the late Ming). Taipei: Dongchu chubanshe, 1987.

——. *Minmatsu Chūgoku bukkyō no kenkyū: Tokuni Chigyoku o chūshin toshite* 明末中國佛教の研究: 特に智旭を中心として (Studies on late-Ming Buddhism, with special reference to Zhixu). Tokyo: Sankibō busshōrin, 1975.

——. *Wanming fojiao yanjiu* 晚明佛教研究 (Studies on late-Ming Buddhism). Beijing: Zongjiao wenhua chubanshe, 2006.

Shi Fachuang 釋法幢, ed. *Dazangjing de bianxiu, liutong, chuancheng: Jingshan zang guoji xueshu yanjiuhui lunwenji* 大藏經的編修·流通·傳承: 徑山藏國際學術研討會論文集 (Compilation, circulation, and inheritance: The proceedings of the international conference on the Jingshan Canon). Hangzhou: Zhejiang guji chubanshe, 2017.

——. "Jingshan kezang kaoshu" 徑山刻藏考述 (An investigation of the carving of the Jingshan Canon). *Zhonghua foxue xuebao* 中華佛學學報 13 (2012): 53–89.

Shi Yanfeng 石衍豐. "Ming Shizong chongxin de daoshi Shao Yuanjie yu Tao Zhongwen" 明世宗寵信的道士邵元節與陶仲文 (Shao Yuanjie and Tao Zhongwen, the Daoists favored by Emperor Shizong of the Ming). *Shijie zongjiao yanjiu* 世界宗教研究, no. 2 (1989): 89–94.

Shiba Yoshinobu 斯波義信. *Sōdai Kōnan keizai shi no kenkyū* 宋代江南経済史の研究 (Studies on the economic history of Jiangnan in the Song). Tokyo: Tōkyō daigaku shuppankai, 1988.

Shiga Takayoshi 滋賀高義. "Minsho no hōe to bukkyō seisaku" 明初の法會と佛教政策 (The Dharma assembly and Buddhist policies in the early Ming). *Ōtani daigaku kenkyū nenpō* 大谷大學研究年報 21 (1969): 197–237.

Shigenoi Shizuka 滋野井恬. "Jūisseiki igo Chūgoku no bukkyō kyōsen no gaikyō" 11世紀以後中國の仏教教線の概況 (A survey of the territorial line of Buddhism in post-11th-century China). *Ōtani daigaku kenkyū nenpō* 大谷大學研究年報, no. 19 (1967): 255–312.

Shimizu Hiroko 清水浩子. "Suirikue" 水陸會 (The water-and-land ceremony). *Taishō daigaku sōgō bukkyō kenkyūjo nenpō* 大正大學綜合佛教研究所年報 28 (2006): 97–101.

Shimizu Taiji 清水泰次. "Mindai butsudō tōsei kō" 明代佛道統制考 (On the Ming system of administering Buddhism and Daoism). *Tōyōshikai kiyō* 東洋史會紀要, no. 2 (1937): 1–19.

——. "Mindai ni okeru butsudō no torishimari" 明代における佛道の取締 (Bans on Buddhism and Daoism in the Ming). *Shigaku zasshi* 史學雜誌 40, no. 3 (1929): 263–310.

Shinohara Kōichi 篠原亨一. "Biographies of Eminent Monks in a Comparative Perspective: The Function of the Holy in Medieval Chinese Buddhism." *Zhonghua foxue xuebao* 中華佛學學報 7 (1994): 477–500.

——. "From Local History to Universal History: The Construction of the Sung T'ien-t'ai Lineage." In *Buddhism in the Sung*, ed. Peter N. Gregory and Daniel A. Getz Jr., 527–76. Honolulu: University of Hawai'i Press, 1999.

——. "Two Sources of Chinese Buddhist Biographies: Stupa Inscriptions and Miracle Stories." In *Monks and Magicians: Religious Biographies in Asia*, ed. Phyllis Granoff and Koichi Shinohara, 94–128. Oakville, Ont.: Mosaic Press, 1988.

Skinner, G. William, ed. *The City in Late Imperial China*. Stanford, Calif.: Stanford University Press, 1977.

Smith, Joanna F. Handlin. "Benevolent Societies: The Reshaping of Charity During the Late Ming and Early Ch'ing." *JAS* 46, no. 2 (1987): 309–37.

——. "Liberating Animals in Ming-Qing China: Buddhist Inspiration and Elite Imagination." *JAS* 58, no. 1 (1999): 51–84.

Song Lian 宋濂, ed. *Yuanshi* 元史 (History of the Yuan dynasty). Beijing: Zhonghua shuju, 1976.

Stevenson, Daniel B. "Text, Image, and Transformation in the History of the *Shuilu fahui*, the Buddhist Rite for Deliverance of Creatures of Water and Land." In *Cultural Intersections in Later Chinese Buddhism*, ed. Marsh Weidner, 30–70. Honolulu: University of Hawai`i Press, 2001.

Straten, N. H. van. *Concepts of Health, Disease and Vitality in Traditional Chinese Society: A Psychological Interpretation*. Wiesbaden: Steiner, 1983.

Szonyi, Michael. *Practicing Kinship: Clan and Descent in Late Imperial China*. Stanford, Calif.: Stanford University Press, 2002.

——. "Secularization Theories and the Study of Chinese Religions." *Social Compass* 56, no. 3 (2009): 312–27.

Taixu 太虛. "Zhendan fojiao shuailuo zhi yuanyin lun" 震旦佛教衰落之原因論 (On the reasons for the decline of Chinese Buddhism [1914]). *Haichaoyin* 海潮音 2, no. 3 (1921): 1–9.

Takakusu Junjirō 高楠順次郎 and Watanabe Kaigyoku 渡邊海旭 et al., eds. *Taishō shinshū daizōkyō* 大正新修大藏經 (Great [Buddhist] canon, newly compiled in the Taishō era). Tokyo: Taishō Issaikyō kankōkai 大正一切經刊刻會, 1924–1932.

Tan Qian 談遷. *Guoque* 國榷 (An evaluation of events of our dynasty). Beijing: Zhonghua shuju, 1958.

Tan Weilun 譚偉倫. "Jianli minjian fojiao yanjiu lingyu chuyi" 建立民間佛教研究領域芻議 (Suggestions regarding establishing the field of folk-Buddhism studies). In *Minjian fojiao yanjiu* 民間佛教研究, ed. Tan Weilun, 3–12. Beijing: Zhonghua shuju, 2007.

Tao Wangling 陶望齡. *Xie an ji* 歇庵集 (Collected writings of the Xie hall). In *jibu* 集部, vol. 1365, of *Xuxiu Siku quanshu* 續修四庫全書, ed. Gu Tinglong 顧廷龍 et al. Shanghai: Shanghai guji chubanshe, 1995–2001.

Teiser, Stephen F. *The Ghost Festival in Medieval China*. Princeton, N.J.: Princeton University Press, 1988.

——. "Popular Religion." *JAS* 54, no. 2 (1995): 378–95.

——. "Social History and the Confrontation of Cultures: Foreword to the Third Edition." In *The Buddhist Conquest of China: The Spread and Adaptation of Buddhism in Early Medieval China*, ed. Erik Zürcher, xiii–xxviii. Leiden: Brill, 2007.

Thornton, Susanna. "Buddhist Monasteries in Hangzhou in the Ming and early Qing." Ph.D. diss., London University, 1996.

Tian Qi 田奇. *Beijing de fojiao simiao* 北京的佛教寺廟 (Buddhist temples in Beijing). Beijing: Shumu wenxian chubanshe, 1993.

T'ien Ju-K'ang. "The Decadence of Buddhist Temples in Fu-chien in Late Ming and Early Ch'ing." In *Development and Decline of Fukien Province in the 17th and 18th Centuries*, ed. E. B. Vermeer, 83–100. Leiden: Brill, 1990.

Tsai, Shih-shan Henry. *The Eunuchs in the Ming Dynasty*. New York: State University of New York Press, 1996.

Tuotuo 托托 et. al., eds. *Song shi* 宋史 (History of the Song dynasty). Beijing: Zhonghua shuju, 1977.

Twitchett, Denis, and Frederick W. Mote, eds. *The Cambridge History of China, Volume 7: The Ming Dynasty, 1368–1644, Part 1*. Cambridge: Cambridge University Press, 1988.

——, eds. *The Cambridge History of China, Volume 8: The Ming Dynasty, 1368–1644, Part 2*. Cambridge: Cambridge University Press, 1998.

van Gulik, Robert Hans. *Sexual Life in Ancient China: A Preliminary Survey of Chinese Sex and Society from ca. 1500 B.C. till 1644 A.D.* Leiden: Brill, 2003.

Wach, Joachim. *Sociology of Religion*. London: Kegan Paul, Trench, Trubner, 1947.

Wakeman, Frederic, Jr. "Romantics, Stoics, and Martyrs in Seventeenth-Century China." *JAS* 43, no. 4 (1984): 631–65.

Walsh, Michael J. *Sacred Economies: Buddhist Monasticism and Territoriality in Medieval China*. New York: Columbia University Press, 2009.

Wan, Maggie C. K. "Building an Immortal Land: The Ming Jiajing Emperor's West Park." *Asia Major*, 3rd ser., 22, no. 2 (2009): 65–99.

Wan Sitong 萬斯同. *Shiyuan wenji* 石園文集 (Collected writings by Shiyuan). In *jibu* 集部, vol. 1415, of *Xuxiu Siku quanshu* 續修四庫全書, ed. Gu Tinglong 顧廷龍 et al. Shanghai: Shanghai guji chubanshe, 1995–2001.

Wang Chuanming 王傳明 and Zhou Ying 周穎. "Mingdai gongting douzheng yu Taishan zhi guanxi" 明代宮廷鬥爭與泰山之關係 (The relationship between court strife and Mount Tai in the Ming). *Taishan yanjiu luncong* 泰山研究論叢, no. 5 (1992): 52–69.

Wang Chunyu 王春瑜 and Du Wanyan 杜婉言. *Mingchao huanguan* 明朝宦官 (Eunuchs in the Ming). Xi'an: Shanxi renmin chubanshe, 2007.

Wang, Eugene. "Of the True Body: The Buddha's Relics and Corporeal Transformation in Tang Imperial Culture." In *Body and Face in Chinese Visual Culture*, ed. Wu Hung and Katherine T. Mino, 79–118. Cambridge, Mass.: Harvard University Press, 2004.

Wang Fansen 王汎森. "Qingchu sixiang zhong xing'ershang xuanyuan zhi xue de moluo" 清初思想中形而上玄遠之學的沒落 (The decline of metaphysics in the thought of the early Qing). *Lishi yuyan yanjiusuo jikan* 歷史語言研究所集刊 69, no. 3 (1998): 557–83.

Wang Jian 王健. "Lixue jianxing ji difang xiangying: Mingdai zhongye Jiangnan hui yinci shijian tanxi" 理學踐行及地方響應: 明代中葉江南毀淫祠事件探析 (The practice of neo-Confucianism and feedback from local society: An investigation into the destruction of heterodox shrines in mid-Ming Jiangnan). In *Zhongguo jinshi difang shehui zhongde zongjiao yu guojia* 中國近世地方社會中的宗教與國家, ed. Wang Gang 王崗 and Li Tiangang 李天剛, 54–68. Shanghai: Fudan daxue chubanshe, 2014.

Wang Lei 王蕾 and Han Xiduo 韓錫鐸. "Cong Liaotu cangben renshi Jiaxingzang" 從遼圖藏本認識嘉興藏 (Understanding the Jiaxing canon based on the copy held in the Liaoning library). *Zhongguo dianji yu wenhua* 中國典籍與文化, no. 1 (2009): 67–70.

Wang Qi 王錡. *Yupu zaji* 寓圃雜記 (Miscellaneous records of Yupu). Beijing: Zhonghua shuju, 1984.

Wang Qiyuan 王啓元. "Zibo dashi wanjie yu Wanli jian fojiao de shengchun kongjian" 紫柏大師晚節與萬曆間佛教的生存空間 (The integrity of Master Zibo's later years and the space for the survival of Buddhism during the Wanli period). *Shijie zongjiao yanjiu* 世界宗教研究, no. 1 (2015): 228–41.

Wang, Richard G. "Ming Princes and Daoist Ritual." *T'oung Pao* 95, no. 1-3 (2009): 51–119.

Wang Shizhen 王世貞. *Yanshantang bieji* 弇山堂別集 (A supplementary collection of the Yanshan hall). Beijing: Zhonghua shuju, 1985.

Wang Yuanhan 王元翰. *Ningcui ji* 凝翠集 (Collected writings of thick green). In vol. 117 of *Congshu jicheng xubian* 叢書集成續編. Taipei: Xin wenfeng chuban gongsi, 1989.

Wang Yuanlin 王元林. "Mingdai Huanghe xiaobei ganliu hedao bianqian" 明代黃河小北幹流河道變遷 (Changes in the course of the Yellow River in the Xiaobeigan area during the Ming). *Zhongguo lishi dili luncong* 中國歷史地理論叢, no. 3 (1999): 188–200.

Wei Daoru 魏道儒. *Zhongguo huayan zong tongshi* 中國華嚴宗通史 (A general history of the Huayan school in China). Nanjing: Jiangsu guji chubanshe, 2001.

Wei Zuhui 韋祖輝. "Min silijian dazang jingchang de shengshuai" 明司禮監大藏經廠的盛衰 (The rise and fall of the scripture workshop of the Directorate of Ceremonial in the Ming). *Beijing shiyuan* 北京史苑, no. 3 (1985): 364–68.

Weidner, Marsha. "Imperial Engagements with Buddhist Art and Architecture: Ming Variations on an Old Theme." In *Cultural Intersections in Later Chinese Buddhism*, 117–44. Honolulu: University of Hawai'i Press, 2001.

——, ed. *Latter Days of the Law: Images of Chinese Buddhism, 850–1850*. Honolulu: University of Hawai'i Press, 1994.

Weinstein, Stanley. *Buddhism under the T'ang*. Cambridge: Cambridge University Press, 1987.

Welch, Holmes. *The Buddhist Revival in China*. Cambridge, Mass.: Harvard University Press, 1968.

Welter, Albert. Review of *Cultural Intersections in Later Chinese Buddhism*, by Marsha Weidner. *China Review International* 11, no. 1 (2004): 193–98.

Wen Bing 文秉. *Dingling zhulüe* 定陵注略 (A brief note on the Ding mausoleum [i.e., the Wanli emperor]). Taipei: Weiwen tushu chubanshe, 1976.

——. *Xianbo zhishi* 先撥志始 (Tracing things in their early stage). In *shibu* 史部, vol. 437, of *Xuxiu Siku quanshu* 續修四庫全書, ed. Gu Tinglong 顧廷龍 et al. Shanghai: Shanghai guji chubanshe, 1995–2001.

Wen Chun 溫純. *Wen Gongyi ji* 溫恭毅集 (Collected writings of Wen Gongyi). In *jibu* 集部, vol. 96, of *Wenyuange yingyin Siku quanshu* 文淵閣影印四庫全書. Taipei: Shangwu yinshuguan, 1983.

Wilson, Thomas A., ed. *Genealogy of the Way: The Construction and Uses of the Confucian Tradition in Late Imperial China*. Stanford, Calif.: Stanford University Press, 1995.

Wright, Arthur F. "Biography and Hagiography: Hui-chiao's Lives of Eminent Monks." 1954. Reprinted in *Studies in Chinese Buddhism*, ed. Robert M. Somers, 73–111. New Haven, Conn.: Yale University Press, 1990.

——. *Buddhism in Chinese History*. Stanford, Calif.: Stanford University Press, 1959.

Wu, Jiang. *Enlightenment in Dispute: The Reinvention of Chan Buddhism in Seventeenth-Century China*. Oxford: Oxford University Press, 2008.

——. *Leaving for the Rising Sun: Chinese Zen Master Yinyuan and the Authenticity Crisis in Early Modern East Asia*. Oxford: Oxford University Press, 2015.

Wu, Pei-Yi. "Self-Examination and Confession of Sins in Traditional China." *HJAS* 39, no. 1 (1979): 5–38.

——. "The Spiritual Autobiography of Te-ch'ing." In *The Unfolding of Neo-Confucianism*, ed. Wm. Theodore de Bary, 67–91. New York: Columbia University Press, 1970.

Wu Shushan 武樹善. *Shanxi jinshi zhi* 陝西金石志 (Collected epigraphs of Shaanxi province). Nanjing: Jiangsu guji chubanshe, 1998.

Xiao Daheng 蕭大亨. *Xingbu zouyi* 刑部奏議 (Memorials presented by the Ministry of Justice). Wanli ed. preserved as rare book in Hōsa bunko, Nagoya.

Xie Chongguang 謝重光. *Zhongguo fojiao sengguan zhidu he shehui shenghuo* 中國佛教僧官制度和社會生活 (The monastic official system and social life in China). Beijing: Shangwu yinshuguan, 2009.

Xie Chongguang 謝重光 and Bai Wengu 白文固. *Zhongguo sengguan zhidu shi* 中國僧官制度史 (History of the system of monastic officials in China). Xining: Qinghai renmin chubanshe, 1990.

Xie Yushou 謝毓壽 and Cai Meibiao 蔡美彪, eds. *Zhongguo dizhen lishi ziliao huibian* 中國地震歷史資料匯編 (Collected materials on the history of China's earthquakes). Beijing: Kexue chubanshe, 1985.

Xin Deyong 辛德勇. "Shu shiyin Ming Wanli keben *Guanshiyin ganying lingke*" 述石印明萬曆刻本《觀世音感應靈課》 (An introduction to the lithographically printed *Guanshiyin ganying lingke*, originally carved in the Wanli period of the Ming). *Zhongguo dianji yu wenhua* 中國典籍與文化 3 (2004): 106–11.

Xin Xiuming 信修明. *Lao taijian de huiyi* 老太監的回憶 (A memoir of an old eunuch). Beijing: Yanshan chubanshe, 1987.

Xingtong 性統. *Xudeng zhengtong* 續燈正統 (Orthodox transmissions of the lamp). In *X*, vol. 84, no. 1583.

Xu Changzhi 徐昌治. *Gaoseng zhaiyao* 高僧摘要 (Extracted *Biographies of Eminent Monks*). In *X*, vol. 87, no. 1626.

Xu Hongzu 徐弘祖. *Xu Xiake youji* 徐霞客遊記 (Travel diaries of Xu Xiake). Shanghai: Shanghai guji chubanshe, 1980.

Xu Xueju 徐學聚. *Guochao dianhui* 國朝典彙 (Compendium of statutes of the dynasty). Beijing: Beijing daxue chubanshe, 1993.

Yamazaki Hiroshi 山崎宏. *Shina chūsei bukkyō no tenkai* 支那中世仏教の展開 (The unfolding of Buddhism in medieval China). Tokyo: Shimizu shoten, 1942.

Yang, Ching Kun. *Religion in Chinese Society: A Study of Contemporary Social Functions of Religion and Some of Their Historical Factors*. Berkeley: University of California Press, 1961.

Yang Guozhen 楊國楨, Fu Yiling 傅衣淩, and Chen Zhiping 陳支平, eds. *Mingshi xinbian* 明史新編 (A new history of the Ming dynasty). Taipei: Yunlong chuban, 2002.

Yang, Lien-sheng. "Female Rulers in Imperial China." In *Excursions in Sinology*, Harvard-Yenching Institute Studies 24, 27–42. Cambridge, Mass.: Harvard University Press, 1969.

Yang Xiangyan 楊向豔, *Shen Yiguan zhizheng yu Wanli dangzheng: Yi Chuzong, Yaoshu, Jingcha sanshi wei zhongxin de kaocha* 沈一貫執政與萬曆黨爭: 以楚宗、妖書、京察三事為中心的考察 (The Shen Yiguan government and factionalism at the Wanli court: An examination centered on three events, the fake Prince of Chu, "the evil pamphlet," and the personnel examination). Beijing: Shangwu yinshuguan, 2018.

Ye Xianggao 葉向高. *Cangjia xucao* 蒼葭續草 (A sequel to the *Cangjia cao*). In *jibu* 集部, vols. 124–25, of *Siku jinhui shu congkan* 四庫禁毀书叢刊, ed. Siku jinhui shu congkan bianzuan weiyuanhui 四庫禁毀书叢刊編纂委員會. Beijing: Beijing chubanshe, 2000.

Yinguang 印光. *Yinguang fashi wenchao* 印光法師文鈔 (Collected writings of Dharma master Yinguang). Beijing: Zongjiao wenhua chubanshe, 2000.

Yinshun 印順, ed. *Taixu dashi quanshu* 太虛大師全書 (The complete writings of Master Taixu). Taipei: Shandaosi fojing liutongchu, 1980.

Yongjue Yuanxian 永覺元賢. *Yongjue Yuanxian chanshi guanglu* 永覺元賢禪師廣錄 (A comprehensive record of sayings by Chan master Yongjue Yuanxian). In *X*, vol. 72, no. 1437.

Yü, Chün-fang. *Kuan-yin: The Chinese Transformation of Avalokiteśvara*. New York: Columbia University Press, 2000.

——. "Master Sheng Yen and Chinese Buddhism." In *Shengyan fashi yanjiu* 聖嚴法師研究, vol. 2, 125–38. Taipei: Fagu wenhua chuban gongsi, 2011.

——. "Ming Buddhism." In *The Cambridge History of China, Volume 8: The Ming Dynasty, 1368–1644, Part 2*, ed. Denis Twitchett and Frederick W. Mote, 893–952. Cambridge: Cambridge University Press, 1998.

——. *The Renewal of Buddhism in China: Chu-hung and the Late Ming Synthesis*. New York: Columbia University Press, 1981.

Yu, Jimmy. *Sanctity and Self-Inflicted Violence in Chinese Religions, 1500–1700*. Oxford: Oxford University Press, 2012.

Yu Jin 余金. *Xichao xinyu* 熙朝新語 (New words in a prosperous and peaceful reign). Taipei: Wenhai chubanshe, 1985.

Yü, Lu K'uan. *Practical Buddhism*. Wheaton, Ill.: Theosophical Publishing House, 1973.

Yu Meian 喻昧庵. *Xinxu gaosengzhuan siji* 新續高僧傳四集 (A fourth continuation of the *Biographies of Eminent Monks*, newly compiled). Taipei: Liuli jingfang, 1967.

Yu Minzhong 于敏中 and Zhu Yizun 朱彝尊. *Rixia jiuwen kao* 日下舊聞攷 (Old tales heard in the capital). Beijing: Beijing guji chubanshe, 1983.

Yu Shenxing 于慎行. *Gushan bizhu* 穀山筆麈 (Desultory notes at Mount Gushan). Beijing: Zhonghua shuju, 1997.

Yu Tao 于弢. "Baomingsi zhong kao" 保明寺鍾攷 (A study on the bells at Baomingsi). *Wenwu chunqiu* 文物春秋, no. 5 (2009): 71–74.

Yu, Ying-shih. "Some Preliminary Observations on the Rise of Ch'ing Confucian Intellectualism." *Tsing Hua Journal of Chinese Studies* 11, no. 1-2 (1975): 105–36.

Yuan Hongdao 袁宏道. *Pilgrim of the Clouds: Poems and Essays from Ming Dynasty China*. Trans. Jonathan Chaves. Buffalo, N.Y.: White Pine Press, 2005.

——. *Xifang helun* 西方合論 (A comprehensive discourse on [the Pure Land]). In *T*, vol. 47, no. 1976.

——. *Yuan Hongdao ji jianjiao* 袁宏道集箋校 (The collected works of Yuan Hongdao, collated and annotated). Ed. Qian Bocheng 錢伯城. Shanghai: Shanghai guji chubanshe, 1981.

Yuan Zhongdao 袁中道. *Kexuezhai ji* 珂雪齋集 (Collected works of the Kexue hall). Shanghai: Shanghai guji chubanshe, 1989.

Yuan Zongdao 袁宗道. *Yuan Zongdao ji jianjiao* 袁宗道集箋校 (The collected writings of Yuan Zongdao, annotated and collated). Ed. Meng Xiangrong 孟祥榮. Wuhan: Hubei renmin chubanshe, 2003.

Yunqi Zhuhong 雲棲袾宏. *Yunqi fahui* 雲棲法彙 (Collected teachings of Yunqi). In *JXZ*, vol. 33, no. B277.

Yusa Noboru 遊佐昇. "Gen Kunpei no densetsu to shinkō" 嚴君平の伝説と信仰 (The legend of and belief in Yan Junping). *Meikai daigaku gaikokugo gakubu ronshū* 明海大學外國語學部論集 17 (2005): 131–45.

Zang Maoxun 臧懋循. *Fubaotang wenxuan* 負苞堂文選 (Selected writings of the Fubao hall). In vol. 1360 of *Xuxiu Siku quanshu* 續修四庫全書, ed. Gu Tinglong 顧廷龍 et al. Shanghai: Shanghai guji chubanshe, 1995–2001.

Zhan Ruoshui 湛若水. *Quanweng daquan ji* 泉翁大全集 (A complete collection of Quanweng [Zhan Ruoshui]). Zhuming shuyuan, 1593.

Zhang, Dewei. "Challenging the Reigning Emperor for Success: Hanshan Deqing 憨山德清 (1546–1623) and Late Ming Court Politics." *Journal of the American Oriental Society* 134, no. 2 (2014): 263–85.

——. "The Collapse of Beijing as a Buddhist Centre: Viewed from the Activities of Eminent Monks, 1522 to 1620." *Journal of Asian History* 43, no. 2 (2009): 137–63.

——. "Engaged but Not Entangled: Miaofeng Fudeng 妙峰福登 (1540–1612) and the Late Ming Court." In *The Middle Kingdom and the Dharma Wheel: Aspects of the Relationship between the Buddhist Saṃgha and the State in Chinese History*, ed. Thomas Jülch, 322–78. Leiden: Brill, 2016.

——. "Where the Two Worlds Met: Spreading the Ming Beizang 明北藏 in Wanli (1573–1620) China." *Journal of the Royal Asiatic Society*, 3rd ser., 26, no. 3 (2016): 487–508.

Zhang Han 張瀚. *Songchuang mengyu* 松窗夢語 (Dreamlike speaking behind a pine window). Beijing: Zhonghua shuju, 1985.

Zhang Hongwei 章宏偉. "Mingdai Wanli nianjian Jiangnan minzhong de fojiao xinyang: Yi Wanli shiqinian zhi ershinian Wutaishan fangcezang shikewen wei zhongxin de kaocha" 明代萬曆年間江南民眾的佛教信仰: 以萬曆十七年至二十年五臺山方冊藏施刻文爲中心的考察 (Buddhist faith of the Jiangnan people in the Wanli period of the Ming: An investigation centered on the votive texts in the thread-binding canon carved on Mount Wutai from Wanli 17 to 20). *Qinghua daxue xuebao* (zhexue shehui kexue) 清華大學學報(哲學社會科學), no. 5 (2016): 111–26.

Zhang, Jianwei. "A Study of the Three Buddhist Copper Hall Projects, 1602–1607." *Frontiers of History in China* 10, no. 2 (2015): 289–322.

Zhang Weiran 張偉然. "Zhongguo fojiao dili yanjiu shiji shuping" 中國佛教地理研究史籍述評 (Review of studies on Chinese Buddhist geography). *Dili xuebao* 地理學報 51, no. 4 (1996): 369–73.

Zhang Xianqing 張顯清. *Zhang Xianqing wenji* 張顯清文集 (Collected writings of Zhang Xianqing). Shanghai: Shanghai cishu chubanshe, 2005.

Zhang Xuan 張萱. *Xiyuan wenjian lu* 西園聞見錄 (Records of that seen and heard in the western park). In vols. 1168–70 of *Xuxiu Siku quanshu* 續修四庫全書, ed. Gu Tinglong 顧廷龍 et al. Shanghai: Shanghai guji chubanshe, 1995–2001.

Zhang Xuesong 張雪松. "Zai shu shiyin Ming Wanli keben *Guanshiyin ganying lingke*" 再述石印明萬曆刻本《觀世音感應靈課》 (A revisit to the lithographically printed *Guanshiyin ganying lingke*, originally carved in the Wanli period of the Ming). *Zhongguo dianji yu wenhua* 中國典籍與文化 4 (2009): 29–35.

Zhang Yuntao 張雲濤. *Tanzhesi beiji* 潭柘寺碑記 (Epigraphic texts at Tanzhe temple). Beijing: Zhongguo wenshi chubanshe, 2010.

Zhanran Yuancheng 湛然圓澄. *Kaigu lu* 慨古錄 (Records of sighs of the past), in *X*, vol. 65, no. 1285.

Zhao, Jie. "A Decade of Considerable Significance: Late-Ming Factionalism in the Making, 1583–1593." *T'oung Pao*, 2nd ser., 88, no. 1 (2002): 112–50.

Zhao Qichang 趙其昌. *Jinghua ji* 京華集 (A collection related to the capital). Beijing: Wenwu chubanshe, 2008.

Zhao Shiyu 趙世瑜. *Kuanghuan yu richang: Ming Qing yilai de miaohui yu minjian shehui* 狂歡與日常: 明清以來的廟會與民間社會 (Revelry and ordinary life: Temple fairs and folk societies from the Ming and Qing periods onward). Beijing: Sanlian shudian, 2002.

Zhao Yi 趙翼. *Gaiyu congkao* 陔餘叢攷 (Miscellaneous investigations made in the time after having attended parents). Shijiazhuang: Hebei renmin chubanshe, 1990.

Zhao Yifeng 趙軼峰. *Mingdai guojia zongjiao guanli zhidu yu zhengce yanjiu* 明代國家宗教管理制度與政策研究 (Studies on the administration and policies of religions in Ming China). Beijing: Zhongguo shehui kexue chubanshe, 2008.

——. "Piaoni zhidu yu Mingdai zhengzhi" 票擬制度與明代政治 (The *piaoni* system and Ming politics). *Dongbei shifan daxue xuebao* 東北師範大學學報, no. 2 (1989): 35–41.

Zhao Yuan 趙園. *Ming Qing zhiji shidafu yanjiu* 明清之際士大夫研究 (Studies on scholar-officials in the Ming-Qing transition period). Beijing: Beijing daxue chubanshe, 1999.

——. *Zhidu, yanlun, xintai: "Ming Qing zhiji shidafu yanjiu" xubian* 制度、言論、心態：《明清之際士大夫研究》續編 (Institutions, discourses, and mentality: A sequel to *Ming Qing zhiji shidafu yanjiu*). Beijing: Beijing daxue chubanshe, 2006.

Zheng Yonghua 鄭永華. *Yao Guangxiao shishi yanjiu* 姚廣孝史事研究 (Studies on historical events related to Yao Guangxiao). Beijing: Renmin chubanshe, 2011.

Zhenhua 震華. *Xu Biquini zhuan* 續比丘尼傳 (A sequel to the *Biqiuni zhuan*). Taipei: Fojiao chubanshe, 1988.

Zhou Mengxiu 周夢秀. *Zhiru bian* 知儒編 (A collection on understanding Confucianism), http://tripitaka.cbeta.org/D60n9021_001.

Zhou Qi 周齊. *Mingdai fojiao yu zhengzhi wenhua* 明代佛教與政治文化 (Buddhism and the political culture in the Ming). Beijing: Renmin chubanshe, 2005.

Zhou Qun 周群. "Lun Yuan Hongdao de foxue sixiang" 論袁宏道的佛學思想 (Studies on Yuan Hongdao's Buddhist thought). *Zhonghua foxue yanjiu* 中華佛學研究 6 (2002): 383–417.

Zhou Shaoliang 周紹良. "Lüelun Ming Wanli nianjian wei jiulian pusa bianzhao de liangbu jing" 略論明萬曆年間爲九蓮菩薩編造的兩部經 (A brief discussion of two scriptures composed for the Nine-Lotus Bodhisattva during the Wali era of the Ming). *Gugong bowuyuan yuankan* 故宮博物院院刊 2 (1985): 37–40.

Zhou Yongchun 周永春. *Silun lu* 絲綸錄 (Record of silk ribbons). In *shibu* 史部, vol. 74, of *Siku jinhui shu congkan* 四庫禁毀書叢刊, ed. Siku jinhui shu congkan bianzuan weiyuanhui 四庫禁毀書叢刊編纂委員會. Beijing: Beijing chubanshe, 2000.

Zhu Honglin [Chu, Hung-lam] 朱鴻林. "Mingdai Jiajing nianjian de Zengcheng *Shadi xiangyue*" 明代嘉靖年間的增城沙堤鄉約 (The *Shadi xiangyue* during the Jiajing era of the Ming). In *Kongmiao congsi yu xiangyue* 孔廟從祀與鄉約, 292–360. Beijing: Sanlian shudian, 2015.

——. "Mingdai zhongqi difang shequ zhian chongjian lixiang zhi zhanxian: Shanxi Henan diqu suoxing xiangyue zhili" 明代中期地方社區治安重建理想之展現：山西河南地區所行鄉約之例 (Mid-Ming manifestation of the ideal of community safety: The case of community compacts in Shanxi and Henan localities). In *Kongmiao congsi yu xiangyue* 孔廟從祀與鄉約, 270–91. Beijing: Sanlian shudian, 2015.

——. "Ruzhe congsi Kongmiao de xueshu yu zhengzhi wenti" 儒者從祀孔廟的學術與政治問題 (Intellectual and political problems in canonizing Confucians in the Confucian temple). In *Qinghua lishi jiangtang xubian* 清華歷史講堂續編, 336–55. Beijing: Sanlian shudian, 2008.

——. "Yangming congsi dianli de zhengyi he cuozhe" 陽明從祀典禮的爭議和挫折 (The debate and the frustration of the bid to canonize Wang Yangming). *Zhongguo wenhua yanjiusuo xuebao* 中國文化研究所學報, new ser., no. 5 (1996): 167–81.

Zhu Quan 朱權 et al. *Ming gong ci* 明宮詞 (Lyrics related to the Ming court). Beijing: Beijing guji chubanshe, 1987.

Zhu Yuanzhang 朱元璋. *Huang Ming zuxun* 皇明祖訓 (The ancestral instructions of the Great Ming). In *Zhongguo zhenxi falü dianji xubian* 中國珍稀法律典籍續編, 481–506. Harbin: Heilongjiang renmin chubanshe, 2002.

——. *Ming Taizu ji* 明太祖集 (The collected writings of Emperor Taizu of the Ming). Hefei: Huangshan shushe, 1991.

——. *Ming Taizu yuzhi wenji* 明太祖御製文集 (Collected writings imperially composed by Emperor Taizu of the Ming). Taipei: Xuesheng shuju, 1965.

Zibo Zhenke 紫柏真可. *Zibo zunzhe bieji* 紫柏尊者別集 (Additional collection of works by the honored Zibo). In *X*, vol. 73, no. 1453.

——. *Zibo zunzhe quanji* 紫柏尊者全集 (A complete collection of writings by the honored Zibo). In *X*, vol. 73, no. 1452.

Zurndorfer, Harriet T. "Learning, Lineages, and Locality in Late Imperial China: A Comparative Study of Education in Huichow (Anhwei) and Foochow (Fukien) 1600–1800, Part I." *Journal of the Economic and Social History of the Orient* 35, no. 2 (1992): 109–44; "Part II," no. 3:209–38.

Zürcher, Erik. *The Buddhist Conquest of China: The Spread and Adaptation of Buddhism in Early Medieval China.* 1959. Reprint, Leiden: Brill, 2007.

——. "Perspectives in the Study of Chinese Buddhism." *Journal of the Royal Asiatic Society of Great Britain and Ireland*, no. 1 (1982): 161–76.

GAZETTEERS

Monastic and local gazetteers are listed by title. Bai Huawen 白化文 and Zhang Zhi 張智, eds., *Zhongguo fosi zhi congkan* 中國佛寺志叢刊 (Yangzhou: Guangling shushe, 2006), is abbreviated *FSZK*; Du Jiexiang 杜潔祥, ed., *Zhongguo fosi shizhi huikan* 中國佛寺史志彙刊 (Taipei: Mingwen shuju, 1980), is abbreviated *FSSZ*.

Baoding fuzhi 保定府志 (Gazetteer of Baoding prefecture). 1680.

Baohua shanzhi 寶華山志 (Gazetteer of Mount Baohua). In *FSSZ*.

Beijing shizhi gao 北京市志稿 (Draft gazetteer of the city of Beijing). Ed. Wu Tingxie 吳廷燮. Beijing: Beijing yanshan chubanshe, 1998.

Changzhou xianzhi 長洲縣志 (Gazetteer of Changzhou county). 1765. Reprint, Nanjing: Jiangsu guji chubanshe, 1991.

Chijian Hongciguangjisi xinzhi 敕建弘慈廣濟寺新志 (New gazetteer of imperially built Hongciguangji temple). In *FSZK*.

Chijian Longxing sizhi 敕建隆興寺誌 (Gazetteer of imperially built Longxing temple). In *Luoshi xuetang cangshu yizhen* 羅氏雪堂藏書遺珍. Reprint, Beijing: Beijing zhonghua quanguo tushuguan wenxian suowei fuzhi zhongxin, 2001.

Chongxiu Putuoshan zhi 重修普陀山志 (Newly edited gazetteer of Putuo Island). In *FSSZ*.

Daming fuzhi 大名府志 (Gazetteer of Daming prefecture). 1506. Reprint, Shanghai: Shanghai guji shudian, 1981.

Danyang xianzhi 丹陽縣志 (New gazetteer of Danyang county). 1885. Reprint, Nanjing: Jiangsu guji chubanshe, 1991.

Daxingshansi jilüe 大興善寺紀略 (A brief gazetteer of the Great Xingshan monastery). In *FSZK*.

Dayuetaihe shan jilüe 大嶽太和山記略 (A brief gazetteer of Mount Dayuetaihe). In *Zhongguo daoguan zhi congkan* 中國道觀志叢刊. Reprint, Yangzhou: Jiangshu guji chubanshe.

Dengwei Sheng'en sizhi 鄧尉聖恩寺志 (Gazetteer of Sheng'en temple on Mount Dengwei). In *FSZK*.

Emei shanzhi 峨嵋山志 (Gazetteer of the Mount Emei). In *FSSZ*.

Emei shanzhi bu 峨嵋山志補 (Supplement to *Gazetteer of the Mount Emei*). In *FSSZ*.

Fayuan sizhi gao 法源寺志稿 (A draft gazetteer of Fayuan temple). In *FSZK*.

Fujian tongzhi 福建通志 (Provincial gazetteer of Fujian). 1872. Reprint, Taipei: Huawen shuju, 1968.

Guang Qingliang zhuan 廣清涼傳 (An extended gazetteer of Mount Qingliang). In *T*, vol. 51, no. 2099.

Guanghua sizhi 廣化寺志 (Gazetteer of Guanghua temple). In *FSZK*.

Guangxi tongzhi 廣西通志 (Provincial gazetteer of Guangxi). 1733.

Guizhou tongzhi 貴州通志 (Provincial gazetteer of Guizhou). 1697.

Gushan zhi 鼓山志 (Gazetteer of Mount Gushan). In *FSSZ*.

Gusu zhi 姑蘇志 (Gazetteer of Gusu). In *Beijing tushuguan zhenben congkan* 北京圖書館珍本叢刊. Beijing: Shumu wenxian chubanshe, 1988.

Hangzhou fuzhi 杭州府志 (Gazetteer of Hangzhou prefecture). 1579. Reprint, Beijing: Zhonghua shuju, 2006.

Hangzhou fuzhi 杭州府志 (Gazetteer of Hangzhou prefecture). 1764. Reprint, Taipei: Dongfang wenhua gongyin she, 1970.

Hangzhou Shangtianzhu jiangsi zhi 杭州上天竺講寺志 (Gazetteer of Upper Tianzhu Doctrinal temple in Hangzhou). In *FSSZ*.

Hejian fuzhi 河間府志 (Gazetteer of Hejian prefecture). 1540. Reprint, Shanghai: Shanghai guji shudian, 1964.

Huang Ming siguan zhi 皇明寺觀志 (Gazetteer of Buddhist and Daoist temples in the Great Ming). In *FSZK*.

Huangbo shanzhi 黃檗山志 (Gazetteer of Mount Huangbo). In *FSZK*.

Huanghai 黃海 (The sea of [Mount] Huang). In *shibu* 史部, vols. 229–30, of *Siku quanshu cunmu congshu* 四庫全書存目叢書, comp. Siku quanshu cunmu congshu bianzuan weiyuanhui 四庫全書存目叢書編纂委員會. Jinan: Qilu shushe, 1994–1997.

Huangshan zhi dingben 黃山志定本 (Standard gazetteer of Mount Huang). In *Zhongguo mingshan zhi* 中國名山志, ed. Jiang Yasa 姜亞沙, Jing Li 經莉, and Chen Zhanqi 陳湛綺, vols. 9–10. Beijing: Quanguo tushuguan wenxian suowei fuzhi zhongxin, 2005.

Huangshan zhi xuji 黃山志續集 (Supplementary gazetteer of Mount Huang). In vols. 9–10 of *Zhongguo mingshan zhi* 中國名山志, ed. Jiang Yasa 姜亞沙, Jing Li 經莉, and Chen Zhanqi 陳湛綺. Beijing: Quanguo tushuguan wenxian suowei fuzhi zhongxin, 2005.

Huguang tongzhi 湖廣通志 (Provincial gazetteer of Huguan province). 1733. Reprint, Taipei: Taiwan shangwu yinshuguan, 1983.

Huqiu shanzhi 虎丘山志 (Gazetteer of Mount Huqiu). Reprint, Haikou: Hainan chubanshe, 2001.

Huzhou fuzhi 湖州府志 (Gazetteer of Huzhou prefecture). Ca. 1570. Reprint, Jinan: Qilu shushe, 1997.

Huzhou fuzhi 湖州府志 (Gazetteer of Huzhou prefecture). 1758. In *Zhongguo minsu zhi* 中國民俗志, ed. Lou Zikuang 婁子匡, vols. 8–9. Taipei: Dongfang wenhua gongyin she, 1970.

Jiangnan fancha zhi 江南梵剎志 (Gazetteer of monasteries in the Jiangnan region). In *FSSZ*.

Jiangnan tongzhi 江南通志 (Comprehensive gazetteer of Jiangnan). 1737. Reprint, Taipei: Taiwan shangwu yinshuguan, 1983.

Jiaxing fuzhi 嘉興府志 (Gazetteer of Jiaxing prefecture). 1600. Reprint, Taipei: Dongfang wenhua gongying she, 1970.

Jifu fancha zhi 畿輔梵剎志 (Gazetteer of monasteries in the capital). In *FSSZ*.

Jingci sizhi 淨慈寺志 (Gazetteer of Jingci temple). In *FSSZ*.

Jingkou sanshan zhi (Jiaoshan zhi) 京口三山志 (焦山志) (Gazetteer of the three mountains at Jingkou [Gazetteer of Mount Jiao]). In *FSSZ*.

Jingshan shizhi 徑山史志 (Historical record of Mount Jing). Zhejiang: Zhejiang daxue chubanshe, 1995.

Jinling Dabaoensi tazhi 金陵大報恩寺塔志 (Gazetteer of the pagoda at the Great Baoen monastery in Jinling). In *FSZK*.

Jinling fancha zhi 金陵梵剎志 (Gazetteer of monasteries in Jinling). In *FSSZ*.

Jinshan longyou chansi zhilüe 金山龍遊禪寺志略 (A brief gazetteer of Longyou Chan temple on Mount Jin). In *FSSZ*.

Jinshan zhi 金山志 (Gazetteer of Mount Jin). In *FSSZ*.

Jiuhua shanzhi 九華山志 (Gazetteer of Mount Jiuhua). In *FSSZ*.

Jizhou zhi 薊州志 (Gazetteer of Ji subprefecture). 1852. Reprint, Taipei: Taiwan xuesheng shuju, 1968.

Jizu shanzhi 雞足山志 (Gazetteer of Mount Jizu). In *FSSZ*.

Kangxi Shuntian fuzhi 康熙順天府志 (Gazetteer of Shuntian prefecture, produced in the Kangxi era). Ca. 1680. Ed. Zhang Jiwu 張吉午, annot. Yan Chongnian 閻崇年. Reprint, Beijing: Zhonghua shuju, 2009.

Laoshan zhi 崂山志 (Gazetteer of Mount Lao). Ca. 1630. Reprint, Taipei: Wenhai chubanshe, 1974.

Linggu chanlin zhi 靈穀禪林志 (Gazetteer of Linggu Chan temple). In *FSSZ*.

Lingyan zhi 靈岩志 (Gazetteer of Mount Lingyan). In *FSZK*.

Longhua sizhi 龍華寺志 (Gazetteer of Longhua temple). In *FSZK*.

Luoyang qielan ji jiaojian 洛陽伽藍記校箋 (A record of Buddhist monasteries in Luoyang, annotated and collated). Ed. Yang Xuanzhi 楊炫之 and Yang Yong 楊勇. Beijing: Zhonghua shuju, 2006.

Lushan zhi 廬山志 (Gazetteer of the Mount Lu). In *FSSZ*.

Mingyin sizhi 明因寺志 (Gazetteer of Mingyin temple). In *Congshu jicheng xubian* 叢書集成續編. Taipei: Xin wenfeng chuban gongsi, 1989.

Mingzhou Ayuwang shanzhi 明州阿育王山志 (Gazetteer of Mount King Aśoka in Ming prefecture). In *FSSZ*.

Nanhai Putuo shanzhi 南海普陀山志 (Gazetteer of Putuo Island in the South China Sea). Reprint, Haikou: Hainan chubanshe, 2001.

Nanhai xianzhi 南海縣志 (Gazetteer of Nanhai county). 1691. Reprint, Beijing: Shumu wenxian chubanshe, 1992.

Nanyue zhi 南嶽志 (Gazetteer of the southern mountain). 1753. In *Zhongguo daoguan zhi congkan xubian* 中國道觀志叢刊續編, ed. Zhang Zhi 張智 and Zhang Jian 張健, vols. 9–10. Nanjing: Jiangsu guji chubanshe, 2004.

Ningbo fuzhi 寧波府志 (Gazetteer of Ningbo). 1729. Reprint, Taipei: Zhonghua congshu, 1957.

Panshan zhi 盤山志 (Gazetteer of Mount Pan). In *FSZK*.

Pinghu xianzhi 平湖縣志 (Gazetteer of Pinghu county). 1627. In *Tianyige cang Mingdai fangzhi xuankan xubian* 天一閣藏明代方志選刊續編, vol. 27. Shanghai: Shanghai shudian, 1990.

Putuo Luojiashan xinzhi 普陀洛迦山新志 (New gazetteer of Mount Luojia on Putuo Island). In *FSSZ*.

Puzhou fuzhi 蒲州府志. (Gazetteer of Puzhou). 1754. Reprint, Nanjing: Fenghuang chubanshe, 2005.

Qingliang shanzhi 清涼山志 (Gazetteer of Mount Qingliang). In *FSSZ*.

Qingyuan zhilüe 青原志略 (A brief gazetteer of Qingyuan temple). In *FSSZ*.

Qixia shanzhi 棲霞山志 (Gazetteer of Mount Qixia). In *FSSZ*.

Quanzhou kaiyuan sizhi 泉州開元寺志 (Gazetteer of Kaiyuan temple, Quanzhou). In *FSSZ*.

Sanyuan xian xinzhi 三原縣新志 (New gazetteer of Sanyuan county). Ed. Jiao Yunlong 焦雲龍 and He Ruilin 賀瑞麟. Reprint, Taipei: Chenwen chubanshe, 1968.

Shangfang shanzhi 上方山志 (Gazetteer of Mount Shangfang). In *FSSZ*.

Shanxi tongzhi 山西通志 (Provincial gazetteer of Shanxi). 1734. Reprint, Beijing: Zhonghua shuju, 2006.

Shaoxing fuzhi 紹興府志 (Gazetteer of Shaoxing prefecture). 1586. Reprint, Taipei: Dongfang wenhua gongying she, 1970.

Shaoxing fuzhi 紹興府志 (Gazetteer of Shaoxing prefecture). 1683. Reprint, Beijing: Zhonghua shuju, 2006.

Shengxian zhi 嵊縣志 (Gazetteer of Sheng county). 1870.

Shengxian zhi 嵊縣志 (Gazetteer of Sheng county). 1671. Reprint, Shanghai: Shanghai shudian, 1993.

Shunde fuzhi 順德府志 (Gazetteer of Shunde prefecture). 1750. Reprint, Xingtai: Xingtai diqu difangzhi bianzuan weiyuanhui, 1985.

Shuntian fuzhi 順天府志 (Gazetteer of Shuntian prefecture). 1886. Reprint, Beijing: Beijing guji chubanshe, 1987.

Shuntian fuzhi 順天府志 (Gazetteer of Shuntian prefecture). 1593. Reprint, Jinan: Qilu shushe chubanshe, 1997.

Songjiang fuzhi 松江府志 (Gazetteer of Songjiang prefecture). 1631. Reprint, Beijing: Shumu wenxian chubanshe, 1991.

Songshan Shaolinsi jizhi 嵩山少林寺輯志 (Compiled gazetteer of Shaolin temple at Mount Song). In *FSSZ*.

Songshu 嵩書 (Book of Mount Song). In *Songyue wenxian congkan* 嵩嶽文獻叢刊, ed. Zhengzhou shi tushuguan 鄭州市圖書館. Zhengzhou: Zhongzhou guji chubanshe, 2003.

Suzhou fuzhi 蘇州府志 (Gazetteer of Suzhou prefecture). 1693. Reprint, Taipei: Dongfang wenhua gongying she, 1970.

Taiping xianzhi 太平縣志 (Gazetteer of Taiping county). 1820. Reprint, Shanghai: Shanghai shudian, 1993.

Taiyuan fuzhi 太原府志 (Gazetteer of Taiyuan prefecture). 1612.

Tanzheshan Xiuyun sizhi 潭柘山岫雲寺志 (Gazetteer of Xiuyun temple at Mount Tanzhe). In *FSZK*.

Tiantaishan fangwai zhi 天臺山方外志 (Gazetteer of Buddhism at Mount Tiantai). In *FSSZ*.

Tiantong sizhi 天童寺志 (Gazetteer of Tiantong temple). In *FSZK*.

Weimo sizhi 維摩寺志 (Gazetteer of Weimo temple). In *FSZK*.

Wu du fa cheng 吳都法乘 (Writings related to the Dharma in the Wu region). In *FSSZ*.

Wulian shanzhi 五蓮山志 (Gazetteer of Mount Wulian). 1757.

Wulin Da Zhaoqing lüsi zhi 武林大昭慶律寺志 (Gazetteer of the Great Zhaoqing Vinaya temple in Wulin). In *FSSZ*.

Wulin Lingyin sizhi 武林靈隱寺志 (Gazetteer of Lingyin temple in Wulin). In *FSSZ*.

Wuxi xianzhi 無錫縣志 (Gazetteer of Wuxi county). 1690.

Xuanhua xian xinzhi 宣化縣新志 (New gazetteer of Xuanhua county). Ed. Chen Jizeng 陳繼曾 and Guo Weicheng 郭維城. Reprint, Taipei: Chenwen shuju, 1968.

Yangshan cheng 仰山乘 (Gazetteer of Mount Yang). In *FSSZ*.

Yingtian fuzhi 應天府志 (Gazetteer of Yingtian prefecture). 1577. Reprint, Jinan: Qilu shushe chubanshe, 1997.

Yongji xianzhi 永濟縣誌 (Gazetteer of Yongji county). 1886. Ed. Li Ronghe 李榮河 et al. Reprint, Beijing: Beijing tushuguan chubanshe. 2002.

Yongping fuzhi 永平府志 (Gazetteer of Yongping prefecture). 1879. Reprint, Taipei: Taiwan xuesheng shuju, 1968.

Yunju shanzhi 雲居山志 (Gazetteer of Mount Yunju). In *FSZK*.

Yunju Shengshui sizhi 雲居聖水寺志 (Gazetteer of Shengshui temple on Mount Yunju). In *FSZK*.

Yuquan sizhi 玉泉寺志 (Gazetteer of Yuquan temple). In *FSSZ*.

Zhejiang tongzhi 浙江通志 (Provincial gazetteer of Zhejiang). 1736. Reprint, Taipei: Taiwan shangwu yinshuguan, 1983.

Zhending fuzhi 真定府志 (Gazetteer of Zhending prefecture). 1550. Reprint, Jinan: Qilu shushe, 1997.

Zhengding fuzhi 正定府志 (Gazetteer of Zhending prefecture). 1752. Reprint, Taipei: Taiwan xuesheng shuju, 1968.

Zhengding xianzhi 正定縣志 (Gazetteer of Zhengding county). 1875.

Zheyi fancha zhi 折疑梵剎志 (Solving puzzles in the *Fancha zhi*). In *FSZK*.

Zhiti sizhi 支提寺志 (Gazetteer of Zhiti temple). In *FSZK*.

Index